Mike McGrath

Windows 10

special edition

2nd Edition
Updated for the Windows 10 Creators Update

In easy steps is an imprint of In Easy Steps Limited
16 Hamilton Terrace · Holly Walk · Leamington Spa
Warwickshire · United Kingdom · CV32 4LY
www.ineasysteps.com

In Easy Steps Limited supports The Forest Stewardship Council (FSC), the leading international forest certification organization. All our titles that are printed on Greenpeace approved FSC certified paper carry the FSC logo.

MIX
Paper from
responsible sources
FSC® C020837

Printed and bound in the United Kingdom

ISBN 978-1-84078-755-9

Contents

1 Introducing Windows 10

This chapter introduces Microsoft's latest operating system, Windows 10. We see the new features, what editions are available, and take a look at some free Microsoft downloads.

Windows releases

There have been many versions of Microsoft Windows. The operating system was initially designed for IBM-compatible PCs, but was later extended to support larger computers such as servers and workstations. A derivative version, Windows CE, was also developed for smaller devices such as PDAs and cell phones.

The main versions of Windows that have been released include:

Date	Client PC	Server	Mobile
1985	Win 1.0		
1987	Win 2.0		
1990	Win 3.0		
1993		Win NT 3.1	
1995	Win 95		
1996		Win NT 4.0	Win CE 1.0
1998	Win 98		
2000	Win ME	Win 2000	Win CE 3.0, Pocket PC 2000
2001	Win XP		Pocket PC 2002
2003		Win Server 2003	Win Mobile 2003
2006	Win Vista		
2007		Win Home Server	Win Mobile 6
2009	Win 7	Win Server 2008	
2010			Win Phone 7
2012	Win 8	Win Server 2012	Win Phone 8
2015	Win 10		Win 10 Mobile

The first three versions of Windows listed above were designed for the 16-bit processor featured in the PCs of the day. Windows 95, 98 and ME added support for 32-bit processors. Windows NT was for 32-bit only, while XP and 2000 added 64-bit support. Windows Vista, Windows 7, Windows 8, Windows 10, and the newer server editions, support both 32-bit or 64-bit processors. Each version of Windows builds on the functions and features included in the previous versions, so that the knowledge and experience you have gained will still be valuable, even though the appearance and the specifics of the operations may have changed.

The original IBM PC was supported by PC-DOS and MS-DOS operating systems, developed for IBM-compatible PCs.

Windows 10 for PCs and larger tablets comes in four editions:

- Windows 10 Home
- Windows 10 Pro
- Windows 10 Enterprise
- Windows 10 Education

Windows 10 compatibility

With Windows 10, Microsoft has created an operating system designed to be compatible with a range of different devices. To make this possible, Windows 10 has a new feature called "Continuum" that helps the operating system work better with devices that support both a mouse and keyboard, and touch input. For example: Microsoft's Surface tablet or Lenovo's Yoga laptops. Continuum offers two operating modes for each type of device:

The New icon pictured above indicates a new or enhanced feature introduced with the latest version of Windows. The Continuum feature is new in Windows 10.

Tablet Mode

When a device is in Tablet Mode, the layout of the operating system is appropriate for touchscreen input. This means that the Start screen has tiles that you can tap to launch apps, the apps appear full-screen, and you can navigate using touch gestures. When you connect a mouse and keyboard, or flip your laptop around, you are prompted to change into Desktop Mode.

Desktop Mode

When a device is in Desktop Mode, the layout of the operating system is appropriate for mouse and keyboard input. This means that the Start menu has an A-Z list that you can click to launch apps, the apps appear in windows, and you can navigate using the mouse buttons or keyboard shortcuts. When you disconnect a mouse and keyboard, or flip your laptop around, you are prompted to change into Tablet Mode.

Tablet mode is less demanding of system resources, and its introduction in Windows 10 clearly indicates that Microsoft considers mobile devices to be where the future lies.

Windows 10 shares its styling and kernel code with multiple platforms including smartphones, tablets, PCs and even the Xbox games console. This move towards cross-compatibility is one which is intended to establish Microsoft in the mobile market.

OneDrive is the original SkyDrive facility. It was renamed for copyright reasons. Its features and functions remain unchanged.

A key element in this is the OneDrive app, which we'll look at later. OneDrive enables users to store all their data and apps online, and synchronize that data across all their devices. As a result, they will be able to log in to OneDrive on any Windows 10 device and immediately access their data, preference settings, etc. Whatever or whoever's device they are using, it will be as though they are using their own.

New features in Windows 10

Each new version of Windows adds new features and facilities. In Windows 10, these include:

Windows 10 provides free semi-annual "feature updates" that download automatically to add new features to the operating system when they become available. This book describes the Creators update of 2017.

The customizable Start menu is a new and welcome feature in Windows 10.

InstantGo is a hardware-dependent feature and Trusted Platform Module support requires TPM1.2.

Cortana is a new feature in Windows 10 and requires you to have a Microsoft account. Performance may vary by region and device.

Familiar and improved

- **Customizable Start menu** – a welcome return after the controversial removal of the Start menu in Windows 8.
- **Windows Defender & Windows Firewall** – integral anti-virus defense against malware and spyware.
- **Hiberboot and InstantGo** – fast startup and ready to instantly resume from Sleep mode.
- **Trusted Platform Module (TPM)** – secure device identification, authentication, and encryption.
- **Battery Saver** – limits background activity to make the most of your battery.
- **Windows Update** – automatically helps keep your device safer and running smoothly.

Cortana Personal Digital Assistant

- **Talk or type naturally** – lets you ask for assistance by typing into a text box or by speaking into a microphone.
- **Personal proactive suggestions** – provides intelligent recommendations based upon your personal information.
- **Reminders** – prompts you according to the time of day, your location, or the person you are in contact with.
- **Search the web, your device, and the Cloud** – find help, apps, files, settings, or anything, anywhere.
- **"Hey Cortana" hands-free activation** – passive voice activation recognizes your voice.

Windows Hello

- **Native fingerprint recognition** – the ability to log in to the operating system using a fingerprint reader.
- **Native facial and iris recognition** – the ability to log in to the operating system using a camera.
- **Enterprise level security** – the ability to log in to the operating system using a 4-digit PIN code or picture.

Windows Hello is new in Windows 10. Facial recognition requires a camera that has RGB, infrared, and 3D lenses.

Multi-doing

- **Virtual desktops** – multiple desktops to separate related tasks into their own workspaces.
- **Snap Assist** – easily position up to four apps on the screen.
- **Snap Across** – easily position apps across different monitors.

Continuum

- **Tablet Mode** – an interface appropriate for touch input and navigation using gestures.
- **Desktop Mode** – an interface appropriate for mouse and keyboard input, and navigation clicks and shortcuts.

Virtual desktops and Continuum are both new features in Windows 10.

Microsoft Edge

- **Web browser** – streamlined for compliance with the latest HTML5 web standards.
- **Reading view** – instantly remove formatting distractions from web pages to make reading easier.
- **Built-in ink support** – add Web Notes to existing web pages then save or share the edited page.
- **Cortana integration** – search the device, web, and Cloud to quickly find what you need.

Microsoft Edge is new in Windows 10. It lets you write Web Notes with your finger on touchscreen devices.

Editions of Windows 10

There are four editions of Windows 10 for PCs and tablets with a screen size of over 8 inches – Home, Pro, Enterprise, and Education.

Windows 10 also brings Xbox gaming to the PC.

Windows 10 Home edition is the consumer-focused desktop version that includes a broad range of Universal Windows Apps, such as Photos, Maps, Mail, Calendar, and Groove Music. Windows 10 Pro edition is the desktop version for small businesses, whereas Windows 10 Enterprise edition is the desktop version for large organizations. Windows 10 Education edition builds on the Enterprise edition to meet the needs of schools. The table below shows the features in Windows 10 and, as you can see, some of the features are specific to certain editions:

Features	Home	Pro	Enterprise	Education
Customizable Start menu	Y	Y	Y	Y
Windows Defender & Windows Firewall	Y	Y	Y	Y
Fast start with Hiberboot & InstantGo	Y	Y	Y	Y
TPM support	Y	Y	Y	Y
Battery Saver	Y	Y	Y	Y
Windows Update	Y	Y	Y	Y
Cortana Personal Digital Assistant	Y	Y	Y	Y
Windows Hello login	Y	Y	Y	Y
Virtual desktops	Y	Y	Y	Y
Snap Assist	Y	Y	Y	Y
Continuum Tablet & Desktop Modes	Y	Y	Y	Y
Microsoft Edge	Y	Y	Y	Y
Device Encryption	Y	Y	Y	Y
Domain Join	-	Y	Y	Y
Group Policy Management	-	Y	Y	Y
BitLocker	-	Y	Y	Y
Enterprise Mode Internet Explorer	-	Y	Y	Y
Assigned Access 8.1	-	Y	Y	Y
Remote Desktop	-	Y	Y	Y
Client Hyper-V	-	Y	Y	Y
Direct Access	-	Y	Y	Y
Windows To Go Creator	-	-	Y	Y

Features	Home	Pro	Enterprise	Education
AppLocker	-	-	Y	Y
Branch Cache	-	-	Y	Y
Start Screen Control with Group Policy	-	-	Y	Y
Side-loading Line of Business Apps	Y	Y	Y	Y
Mobile Device Management	Y	Y	Y	Y
Join Azure Active Directory	-	Y	Y	Y
Business Store for Windows 10	-	Y	Y	Y
Granular UX Control	-	-	Y	Y
Easy Upgrade Pro to Enterprise	-	Y	Y	-
Easy Upgrade Home to Education	Y	-	-	Y
Microsoft Passport	Y	Y	Y	Y
Enterprise Data Protection	-	Y	Y	Y
Credential Guard	-	-	Y	Y
Device Guard	-	-	Y	Y
Windows Update for Business	-	Y	Y	Y
Current Branch for Business	-	Y	Y	Y
Long Term Servicing Branch	-	-	Y	-

There are two editions of Windows 10 for smartphones and tablets with a screen size of under 8 inches – Windows 10 Mobile, and Windows 10 Mobile Enterprise.

Windows 10 Mobile edition is designed to deliver the best user experience on smaller touch-centric devices. It provides the same universal Windows Apps that are included in the versions for PCs and larger tablets. In addition, Windows 10 Mobile enables some new devices to take advantage of Continuum for Phone – so you can use your phone like a PC when connected to a larger screen. Windows 10 Mobile Enterprise edition is designed for businesses, so has extra security and mobile device management capabilities.

There are also special versions of Windows 10 Enterprise and Windows 10 Mobile Enterprise for industry devices, such as ATMs, retail point of sale, handheld terminals, and robotics, plus Windows 10 IoT Core for smaller devices, such as gateways.

Windows 10 is available in 111 languages!

Microsoft OneDrive

You need to have a Microsoft account to sign in to OneDrive.

By default, you get 5GB of free OneDrive storage space with Windows 10 (the free allowance was reduced from 15GB in January 2016). This is an excellent way to back up your important documents, since they are stored away from your computer. For up-to-date information on plan allowances and pricing visit **https://onedrive.live.com/about/plans/**

You can log in to access OneDrive with any web browser. Visit **onedrive.live.com**

A very important function built in to Windows 10 is its ability to utilize what is commonly known as "The Cloud". Essentially, cloud computing is a technology that uses the internet and centralized remote servers to maintain data and applications. It allows consumers and businesses to use applications they don't own, and to access their personal files on any computer that has internet access. The technology enables much more efficient computing by centralizing data storage, processing and bandwidth.

So how do you get into the Cloud? There are actually several ways: One is to open an account with a dedicated service such as Dropbox. You will be given a free amount of storage space; 2GB initially (which can be increased to 18GB by referring friends), in which you can store virtually anything you choose to. If you need more, you will be charged a fee depending on the amount required.

A second way is to buy a product from a major software manufacturer. A typical example is True Image from Acronis – a data backup program. Buy this, and you are given 250GB of online storage that enables you to create Cloud-based backups.

A third way is courtesy of Microsoft OneDrive, which can be accessed online. OneDrive is basically a portal that allows you to access 5GB of free online storage.

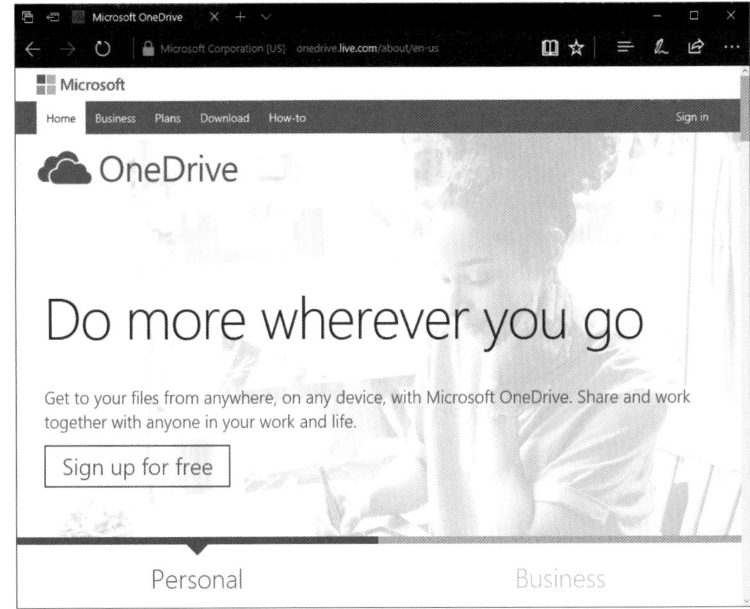

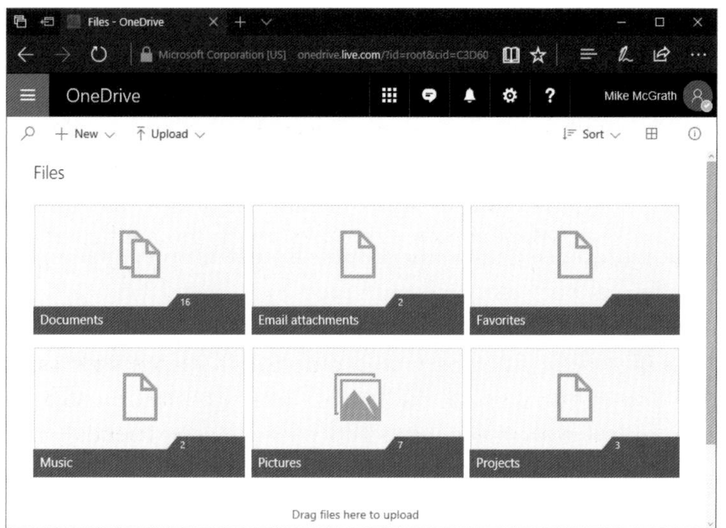

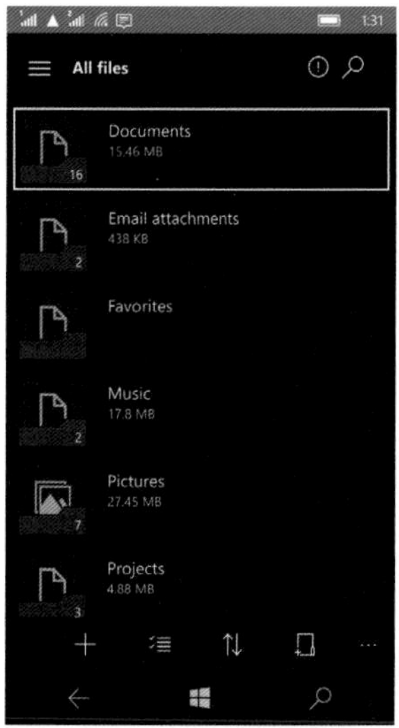

OneDrive on Windows 10 Home (above left) and on Windows 10 Mobile (above).

Once logged in, you will see that OneDrive has started you off with a number of pre-configured folders. Windows 10 is supplied configured to automatically synchronize these folders on OneDrive. You can delete these folders, rename them, create more folders, nest folders within folders, and upload/download files.

Once uploaded, your data can be accessed from any smartphone, tablet or PC, from anywhere in the world and at any time. You can also access and upload data from within programs in Microsoft's Essentials suite of applications, and Microsoft Office.

One of the coolest features of OneDrive is that it enables online sharing and collaboration. For example, you can share your holiday snaps with friends and family regardless of where they are, while business applications provide access to documents while on the move or sharing documents between offices.

A key aspect of OneDrive is that it enables data to be synchronized across a range of devices. For example, emails on your PC can be automatically loaded onto your smartphone or tablet, and vice versa. You can also synchronize various settings such as personalization, e.g. desktop background, theme, colors, passwords, app settings, and many more. This enables users to maintain the computing environment they are comfortable with across all their computing devices.

If you access OneDrive directly from a browser, you will have a "lite" version of Microsoft Office with which to create documents while online.

Windows 10 connectivity

Windows 10 is terrific at connecting all your devices – whether it's a 3-year-old printer or projecting to your brand new TV with Miracast. Windows 10 is built on a common core and includes Universal Windows Apps, so people using Windows 10 for both their PC and smartphone devices will get an optimal, seamless experience as they transition between devices throughout the day.

Miracast is a Wireless Display (WiDi) technology your PC can use to project its screen onto any TV that supports Miracast.

Microsoft recognizes that many people also use iPhone, iPad or Android devices but want to ensure their Windows 10 content remains available to them across all the devices they own, regardless of the operating system. So Microsoft has produced a number of apps for Android, iPad and iPhone devices to make them work great with a Windows 10 PC.

Cortana and the Groove Music app are new features in Windows 10.

So, whatever the operating system, this means that all your files and content can be magically available on your PC and phone:

- With the Cortana app on your phone you can have your Personal Digital Assistant always available.
- With the OneDrive app on your phone, every photo you take shows up automatically on your phone and Windows 10 PC.
- With the Groove Music app you can access and play your music from OneDrive on your phone or Windows 10 PC.
- With the OneNote app on your phone, any note you write on your Windows 10 PC will show up on your phone – and any note you write on your phone will show up on your PC.
- With the Skype app on your phone you can make video calls and messages – free over Wi-Fi.
- With Word, Excel, and PowerPoint apps on your phone you can work on Office documents without moving files around.
- With the Outlook app on your phone you can get your email messages and calendar reminders everywhere.

You must use the same Microsoft account on your PC, phone, and tablet to automatically synchronize your content across these devices.

To help people figure out how to make everything work together, the Microsoft Phone Companion app, which is available free from the Windows Store, will help you connect your Windows 10 PC to your phone or tablet.

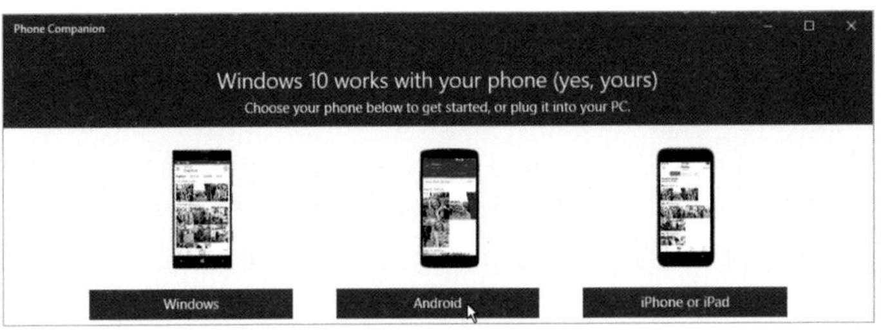

With a Windows phone nothing else is needed – the apps are already installed on that device.

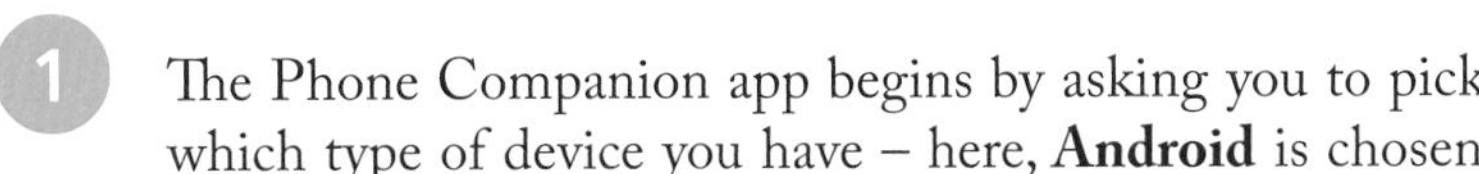

1. The Phone Companion app begins by asking you to pick which type of device you have – here, **Android** is chosen

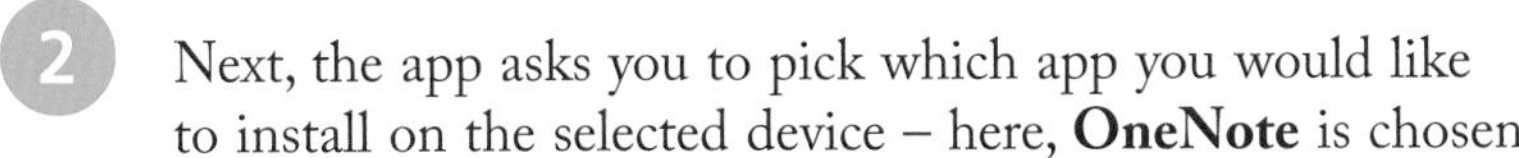

2. Next, the app asks you to pick which app you would like to install on the selected device – here, **OneNote** is chosen

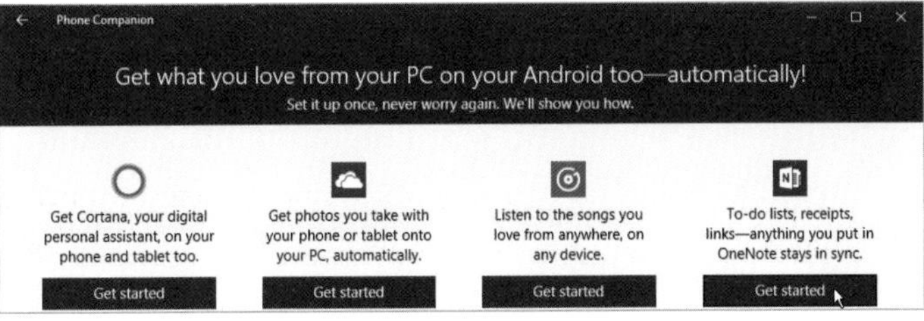

The Phone Companion app and support for other operating system connectivity is new for Windows 10.

3. Now, you are asked to sign in with a Microsoft account, if you are not already signed in to the PC with a Microsoft account

4. You are then given the opportunity to send an email containing a link to the chosen app

5. After opening the email on the chosen device the link will allow you to install the chosen app

You can, of course, search for the OneNote app on Google Play, but the Phone Companion app makes life simpler.

Microsoft Office Online

Microsoft Office is a very important application for many people, so here we will take a brief look at Microsoft Office Online and see how it fits in with Windows 10.

Office Online includes the core apps: Word, Excel, PowerPoint, Outlook and OneNote for both PC and touchscreen. Your completed documents, spreadsheets, and presentations can be saved online in your OneDrive for easy access or sharing. Alternatively, they can be downloaded to your computer and saved as a local file – just as you would with an installed app.

You will need a Microsoft account to sign in to Office Online apps.

1. Open the Microsoft Edge web browser and navigate to **office.live.com/start/default.aspx**

2. Click the **Sign in** button at the top-right of the page then type the email address for your Microsoft account

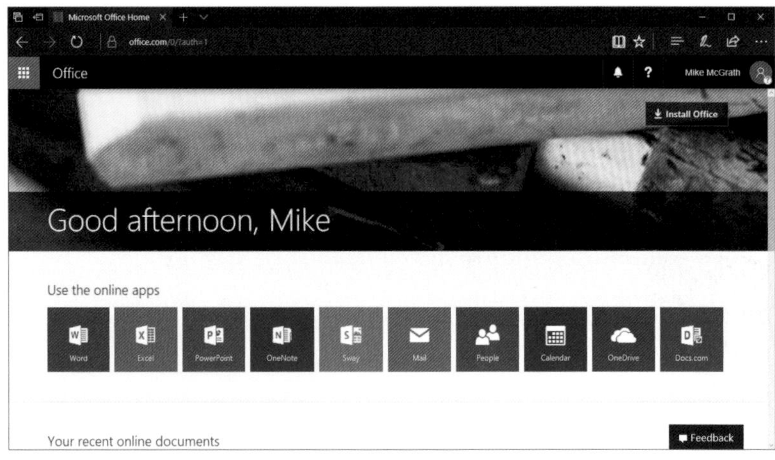

Other versions of Office can be compared at **products.office.com/en-us/compare-all-microsoft-office-products**

3. Choose the online app you wish to use. For example, choose the **Word** app to create a cover letter

4. When the Word app opens in the browser, you are presented with a number of ready-made templates. Choose the **Simple cover letter** template

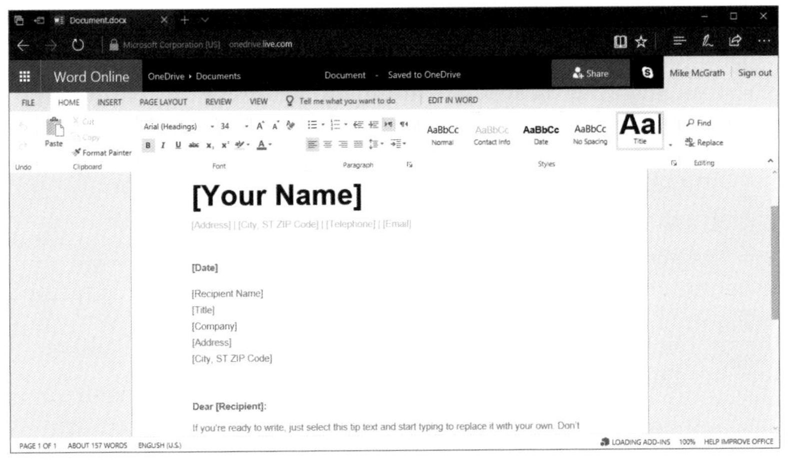

The Start menu in Windows 10 includes a **Get Office** item that makes it easy to start using Office apps.

5. Edit the template to suit your requirements by inserting your name and address details, etc.

6. When you are happy with the letter, click the **FILE** tab at the top-left of the window

7. Now, choose where you would like to save the letter and in what document format

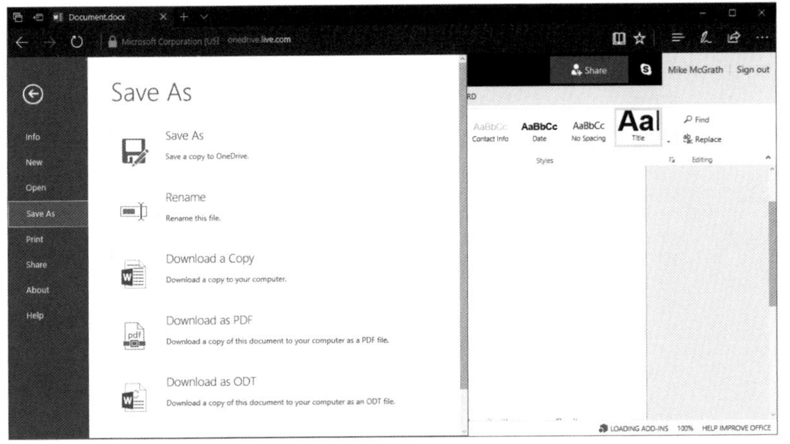

Use the **Rename** option before saving unless you are happy to use the automatically assigned default name.

Windows freebies

Microsoft knows we all like to get something for nothing so they offer free theme downloads with which to personalize your PC. These are available at **support.microsoft.com/en-us/help/17777/downloads-for-windows** and are divided into categories of interest, such as “Art (photographic)”. To grab a free theme:

Hot tip

Other free Microsoft downloads are available at this website, such as desktop wallpapers and language packs.

1. Select the **Themes** link then choose a category from the list on the left of the themes page

2. Scroll through the list to choose a theme, then click its **Download** link to get the “themepack” file

3. When the download completes you will find the themepack file in your **Downloads** folder

4. Right-click on the themepack file and choose **Open** to install that theme on your PC

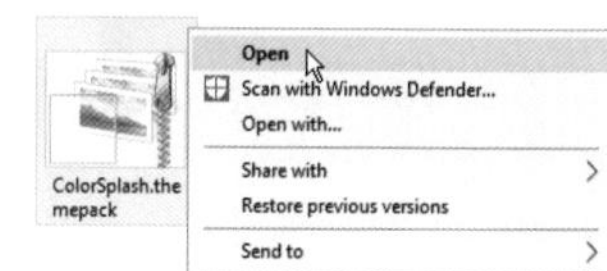

You can change or uninstall themes at any time from Settings, Personalization, Themes. See page 99-106 for more information on themes.

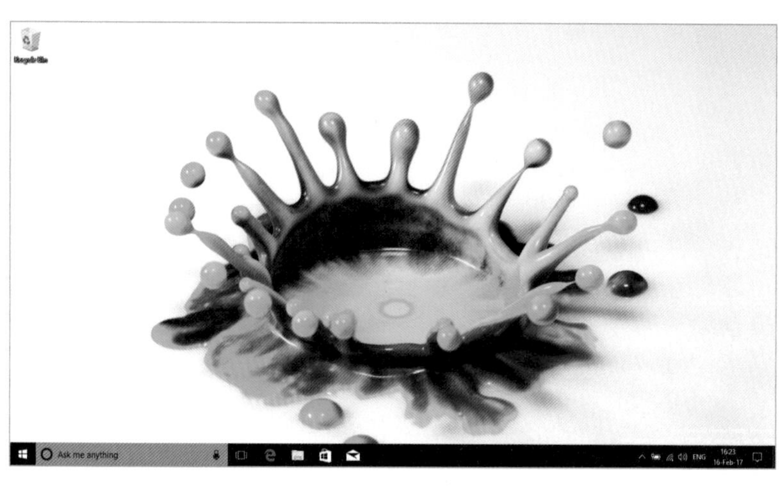

2 Choosing your computer

In this chapter we examine the hardware requirements of both Windows 10 and the computers on which it can be run. For example: CPUs, memory, touchscreens, sensors, and much more.

Windows 10 requirements

Traditionally, every edition of Windows has required more in the way of hardware resources than the editions that preceded it. This came to a stop with Windows 7, which ran quite satisfactorily on the same hardware that its predecessor, Windows Vista, did. This has continued with Windows 10, so users upgrading from either Windows 7 or Windows 8.1 do not have to also upgrade their computer hardware.

Don't forget

To get top performance from Windows 10 you need twice the recommended amount of memory.

The official system requirements of Windows 10 are as follows:

- **Processor** – 1GHz or faster, or SoC (System on a Chip)
- **Memory (RAM)** – 1GB (32-bit) or 2GB (64-bit)
- **Disk space** – 16GB (32-bit) or 20GB (64-bit)
- **Graphics** – Microsoft DirectX 9 with WDDM driver

Processor, disk space and video requirements on all modern computers are more than adequate in these respects.

Please note that the above is the absolute minimum required. While Windows 10 will run on this hardware, it may not do so particularly well. To be more specific, it will probably be on the slow side, and if you run resource-intensive software such as 3D games, Photoshop, etc., it may struggle to cope. If you wish to avoid this, our recommendation is to install twice the recommended amount of memory, i.e. 2GB on a 32-bit system and 4GB on a 64-bit system.

Cortana Personal Digital Assistant, Windows Hello login, and Continuum mode features are all new in Windows 10.

In addition, the following will be required to use some features:

- **Touch gestures** – tablet/monitor that supports multi-touch
- **Snap apps feature** – screen resolution of at least 1024 x 600 pixels
- **Internet access**
- **Microsoft account** – required for some features
- **Cortana support** – speech recognition requires a microphone
- **Windows Hello** – fingerprint reader or specialized camera
- **Continuum** – tablet or 2-in-1 PC, or manual mode selection
- **BitLocker To Go** – a USB drive
- **Hyper-V** – a 64-bit system with second level address translation (SLAT) plus an additional 2GB of memory

Processors

The Central Processing Unit (CPU), more than any other part, influences the speed at which the computer runs. It also determines how many things the PC can do concurrently, i.e. multi-task, before it starts to struggle.

Don't get fixated with CPU clock speed. You should also consider things like the number of cores and the size of the cache.

With regard to speed, a CPU is rated by its clock speed, for example 3.4GHz. We saw on the previous page that Windows 10 requires a 1GHz or faster CPU. As the slowest CPU currently on the market is 2GHz (twice as fast), the issue of CPU speed is not something the typical home user needs to be too concerned about. It's only important to users who require more power, such as hardcore gamers.

The CPU's, and hence the PC's, multi-tasking capabilities may well be a different story, though. Modern computers are frequently required to do a number of things at the same time. Each task requires a separate process or "thread" from the CPU, so anyone who is going to do a lot of multi-tasking will need a CPU that can handle numerous threads simultaneously.

This means buying a multi-core CPU. These devices are no faster than traditional single-core CPUs but because they have several cores, their multi-tasking capabilities are increased enormously. Currently, there are two-, four-, six- and even eight-core models on the market and, fairly obviously, the more your PC is going to have to do, the more cores you will need in your CPU.

For most users, anything over two cores is overkill. Don't waste your money on performance you will never use.

There is also the issue of the CPU manufacturer. Currently, the majority of computing devices are laptops and desktop PCs. These both use CPUs from Intel and AMD exclusively. While Intel CPUs are considered to be better than AMD's offerings, there really isn't much in it. In other words, whichever of them you buy from, you won't go wrong.

For those of you looking to buy a smartphone or tablet, the issue of the CPU is more complicated. This is because the CPU in these devices is usually part of a combination chipset that also houses the system's graphics, memory, interface controllers, voltage regulators and more. This combination chip is referred to as a System on a Chip (SoC), and its main benefit is that it reduces the space needed for these components. This, in turn, lowers power requirements and increases battery life.

Things are further confused by the fact that most SoC manufacturers, including Apple, Samsung, Texas Instruments, and NVIDEA, use a CPU architecture called ARM that is produced and licensed by a company called ARM Holdings. Therefore, this part of an SoC will be identical regardless of the manufacturer – the rest of the SoC, however, will not be. This makes it very difficult to compare SoCs on a like-for-like basis.

When you see the term ARM used in reference to a CPU, remember that the CPU is not manufactured by ARM but rather by a company licensed by ARM Holdings to use its CPU architecture.

Virtually all smartphones use SoCs, as do some tablets. There are some, though (usually the more capable ones), that use a specially designed low-power CPU of the same type found in desktop PCs. Intel's Atom CPU is a good example.

However, whatever the type of CPU, be it a full-size AMD FX, an Intel Atom, or an SoC, the basic premise of clock speed determining the speed of the CPU and the number of cores determining its multi-tasking capability, or power, is the same.

Hardware capabilities

If you are thinking about upgrading to Windows 10, there's a good chance you may also be considering upgrading your PC. If so, you need to give some thought to the hardware that will be in it. Alternatively, it may simply be time to give it a boost.

Whichever, to ensure your PC is capable of doing what you want it to, there are several components you need to consider. The CPU we've already looked at, but there is also the memory, video system and disk drive to consider.

If you wish to upgrade the memory on a PC that's more than two or three years old, it will almost certainly be using DDR2. You will not be able to replace it with the newer DDR3 – this requires a motherboard designed to use DDR3.

Random Access Memory (RAM)

As with the CPU, memory is a component that has a major impact on the performance of a computer. You can have the fastest CPU in the galaxy, but without an adequate amount of memory, all that processing power will do you no good at all.

This is a more straightforward issue than CPUs. While there are many different types of memory, as far as desktop PCs and laptops are concerned there is only really one choice – DDR3. This is currently the memory of choice and is installed on all new PCs. DDR2 will be found on many older PCs and is still a perfectly good type of memory.

The only issues for owners of modern PCs are how much memory do they need, and how much can they install? With regard to the former, this is a difficult question to answer – it depends mainly on what type of programs are going to be run on the PC. Applications that shift large amounts of data, such as 3D games, video and sound editing, or high-end desktop publishing, will require a much larger amount of memory – typically 6GB or more. Less intensive applications, such as web browsing, word-processing and games like FreeCell, will all run perfectly well on 2GB.

If you want to install more than 4GB of memory, you must be using a 64-bit PC.

The amount of memory that can be installed is determined by the motherboard. This is not going to be an issue for the average user as current motherboards can handle anything up to 64GB. However, the computer architecture being used may well be. 32-bit computers running a Windows operating system can utilize a maximum of 4GB of memory regardless of how much is installed. 64-bit PCs, on the other hand, can use an almost limitless amount.

Memory modules are rated in terms of speed, which is another consideration. Currently, speeds range from 1GHz to 2.8GHz. The faster the memory, the more expensive it will be.

Smartphones and tablets require much less memory than desktop PCs. High-end devices of these types currently come with about 1GHz of RAM. They also make more efficient use of the available memory by "suspending" apps that are not being used, thus releasing memory for other apps.

When considering a smartphone or tablet, it is also necessary to see what it has to offer in the way of built-in memory for storage purposes, and if it can be expanded by adding larger capacity memory cards.

Don't worry too much about memory speed. The real-world difference between the slowest and fastest modules is not significant. In any case, to get the best out of the high-speed modules, other parts such as the CPU also need to be top-end. Such a setup will be expensive.

You might think that devices such as smartphones, which do not generally come with much in the way of internal storage, would almost certainly offer a memory card slot. However, this is not always the case, as owners of iPhones will testify.

Video system

Video systems produce the pictures you see on the display. Two types are used in computers: integrated video that is built in to the motherboard or CPU, and stand-alone video cards.

Of the two, video cards produce by far the better quality video – for hardcore gamers, they are essential.

The problem with video cards is that they are not only expensive; they are also bulky, noisy, and power-hungry. Desktop computers and high-end laptops are large enough and powerful enough to accommodate these demands, but for smaller devices, such as Netbooks, tablets and smartphones, they are impractical.

If you want the best quality video on your PC, you will need a video card rather than integrated video.

Therefore, these all use an integrated video system. As we mentioned on page 28, in these devices the video will be just one part of a System on a Chip (SoC).

Solid-State Drives (SSDs)

Disk drives, or hard drives as they are more commonly known, are the devices used to store a user's data. They are electromechanical devices that provide huge amounts of storage space at a low price.

A relatively recent development in the hard drive market has seen the introduction of solid-state drives (SSDs). These devices employ solid-state memory and contain no moving parts which, apart from anything else, makes them extremely reliable.

Other advantages include instant startup, extremely fast data access speeds, completely silent operation, a much smaller footprint, weight (they are much lighter than mechanical drives), and low power requirements.

If you have a need for speed, make sure your devices use SSDs.

These qualities all make SSDs ideal for use in low-power devices such as tablets and smartphones. Apple, for example, uses them in its highly successful iPads, iPhones and iPods.

However, their use in desktop computers is somewhat limited by two factors: The first is the high cost of SSDs compared with mechanical drives. The second is that they provide much smaller storage capacities than mechanical drives. This has lead to low-capacity SSDs, typically around 60GB, being used for the boot drive (where the operating system is installed), with a high-capacity mechanical drive to provide data storage.

The result is a PC that typically boots up twice as quickly, is snappy and responsive to the user's commands, and also has loads of storage space.

Computer types

When it comes to buying a computer, buyers have quite a few different types to choose from, each having pros and cons that make them suitable for some purposes and less so for others.

Desktop PCs

Traditionally, the desktop PC, comprising a system case that houses the hardware, plus a monitor, keyboard and mouse, has been the most popular type of computer.

Their main advantage is that the addition of peripherals, such as printers and scanners, turns them into workhorses that enable almost any type of computational work to be done.

A big advantage of desktop PCs is that they are easy to expand and to upgrade.

Other advantages are that they are cheap to buy, easy to upgrade and repair, and easy to expand. Disadvantages are: size, noise, aesthetics, and lack of mobility.

All-in-ones

Increasingly popular due to their small footprint, all-in-one PCs are manufactured by a number of companies, including Apple, Lenovo and Samsung. Pictured below is the Lenovo IdeaCentre.

Other advantages include being lightweight, a minimal amount of messy wiring, many come with touchscreens, and a definite element of style – many of these devices look rather cool and not at all out of place in the living room.

All-in-ones are produced by a limited number of manufacturers and tend to be expensive.

The downside is that they are very difficult to repair/upgrade due to lack of accessibility. All-in-ones are also prone to heat issues due to the lack of air space in the case – this makes them unsuitable for high-end applications. Also, if one part goes wrong the whole unit has to go back – it's all or nothing.

...cont'd

Hybrid computers

Continuing the all-in-one's theme of style and elegance, we have the hybrid computer. It is comprised of nothing more than a very small and usually stylish case that contains the hardware.

Hybrid PCs are ideal where mobility is an issue. Don't expect to do any serious work or gaming on them, though.

The user simply places it where it is to be used and connects a monitor, keyboard and mouse.

These devices have only one real advantage – they are extremely portable. They have the same disadvantages as all-in-one PCs and, as such, are only suitable for lightweight applications.

Laptops

A laptop is basically a desktop PC condensed into a small, flat, portable case. It has the same components as a desktop, albeit on a smaller scale, and is capable of everything the desktop is.

Fairly obviously, their main advantage is portability – a laptop can be tucked under the arm and literally taken anywhere.

They also require little space and are easily secured, e.g. can be placed inside a safe.

If you buy a laptop with a view to portable computing, check out the battery capacity. Some models have low-capacity batteries that don't last long before needing to be recharged.

As ever though, there are downsides. Probably the main one is cost – laptops are considerably more expensive than desktops of equivalent capability.

These devices are also more difficult to use, due to smaller screens and the need for touchpads. There is a high risk of physical damage as they can be dropped, they are easily misplaced or lost, and are prone to theft.

Variations of the laptop theme include Ultrabooks and Netbooks. The former are an Intel invention and manufacturers of these devices must conform to standards set by Intel.

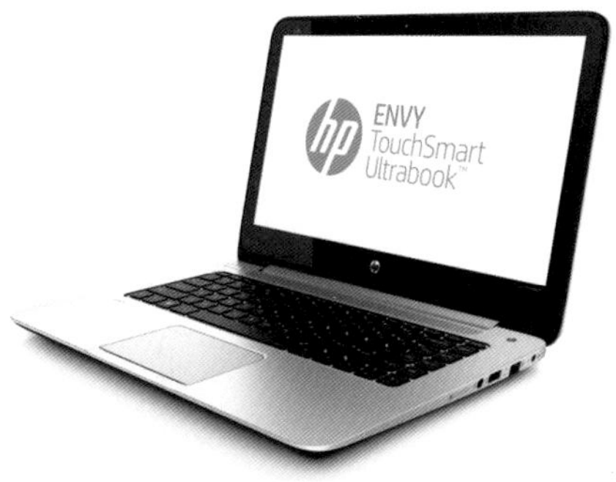

These state that Ultrabooks must use low-power Intel Core CPUs, solid-state drives and unibody chassis. This is to ensure that Ultrabooks are slim, high-end devices able to compete at the top-end of the laptop market against the likes of Apple's MacBook Air.

Basically, Ultrabooks are aimed at the top-end of the laptop market, while Netbooks are aimed at the bottom-end.

A Netbook is simply a miniature laptop. They usually have 10-inch screens, scaled-down keyboards and touchpads to match, and are extremely small and lightweight. As a result, they are inexpensive and easily transportable. These have become less popular recently, as their role is being taken over by Tablet PCs and Convertible Computers.

Tablet computers

Tablets are mobile computers that fit in between smartphones and Netbooks. The hardware is built in to a touchscreen, which is operated both by touch and by a keyboard (on screen or attached).

Unlike smartphones, the displays offered by tablets are large enough to enable serious work to be done. For example, with a suitable app you can easily write a properly punctuated letter, an email message, or even a novel.

Tablets are a good option if you need ultra-portability as well as computational functionality.

You'll need to choose a Tablet PC that can run Windows 10 with an Intel processor or equivalent, or simply buy a Tablet PC with Windows 10 already pre-installed.

Tablet PCs then offer the best of all worlds. The convenience and ultra-portability of smartphones, a camera, plus the ability to carry out serious computer work. Some even have a phone as well!

Convertible computers

A convertible computer is essentially a tablet computer that can be quickly transformed into a laptop by opening an integrated keyboard. Typically, this is achieved by means of a sliding or hinged mechanism. In all other respects they are just tablets but are popular as they provide a degree of flexibility.

Convertible computers offer a compromise in that you may consider the tablet too big, or the keyboard too small.

For example, by rotating the hinged keyboard, the Lenovo Yoga convertible computer, shown here, can be used in any one of its Tablet, Laptop, or Standing configurations.

Windows 10 supports connectivity with Android, iPhone, and iPad devices.

Smartphones

Windows 10 provides the opportunity to easily have all your files, music, photos, and videos available from anywhere. You can choose a cell phone running Windows 10 Mobile to carry your content in your pocket wherever you go.

Using a Windows 10 Mobile smartphone in conjunction with Windows 10 on your PC helps you to get the most from Windows 10.

There are a variety of Windows 10 Mobile smartphones for Enterprise and the individual, from budget to flagship. Each device, when connected to the internet, can share content via the magic of OneDrive. When you take a photo on your phone it gets added to the Camera Roll folder on your phone, and can be automatically copied to any of your other Windows 10 devices. Similarly, any reminders you save in the OneNote app on your PC can be automatically copied to your phone. You can choose to share any content across devices.

32-bit versus 64-bit

All modern CPUs support 64-bit architecture. But what is it and how does it benefit the user?

The term "64-bit" when used in reference to a CPU means that in one integer register the CPU can store 64 bits of data. Older CPUs, which could only support 32-bit architecture, could store only 32 bits of data in a register, i.e. half the amount. Therefore, 64-bit architecture provides better overall system performance, as it can handle twice as much data in one clock cycle.

Modern CPUs automatically detect whether an application or operating system is 32-bit or 64-bit, and operate accordingly.

However, the main advantage provided by 64-bit architecture is the huge amount of memory it can support. CPUs operating on a 32-bit Windows system can utilize a maximum of 4GB, whereas on a 64-bit system they can utilize up to 192GB.

The caveat is that a 64-bit system requires all the software to be 64-bit compatible, i.e. it must be 64-bit software. This includes the operating system and device drivers, and is the reason why more recent versions of Windows, including Windows 10, are supplied in both 32-bit (x86) and 64-bit (x64) versions. Note that most 32-bit software will run on a 64-bit system but the advantages provided by 64-bit architecture won't be available.

So who will benefit from a 64-bit system and who won't? The simple answer is that every PC user will benefit, as their system will be more efficient. Don't expect to see major speed gains over a 32-bit system when running day-to-day applications such as web browsers, word processing and 2D games, though – you probably won't notice any difference.

If you opt for a 64-bit system, all your software, including device drivers, will have to be 64-bit compatible. Even though 64-bit systems are now common, there is still software on the market that runs only on 32-bit systems.

However, when running CPU-intensive applications that require large amounts of data to be handled, e.g. video editing, 3D games, or CAD software, 64-bit systems will be faster. Also, if you need more memory than the current small limit of 4GB possible with a 32-bit system, 64-bit architecture allows you to install as much as you want (up to the limitations of the motherboard).

Users running Windows 10 Pro, Enterprise, or Education editions have access to a virtualization utility called Hyper-V. One of the requirements for building virtual PCs with Hyper-V is that the computer must be running on 64-bit architecture.

To get a 64-bit system, simply buy a modern CPU and install a 64-bit version of Windows.

Multi-touch

An important feature of Windows 10 is its support for touchscreen control. If you are considering buying a touchscreen monitor in order to take advantage of this feature, you should be aware of the following issues:

Beware

There are still touchscreens on the market that only support two touch points – don't buy one of these.

Bezel design

Some of the touch gestures required to control Windows 10 (opening menus, for example) are done by swiping a finger inwards from one edge of the screen towards the center.

However, it is a fact that many touchscreen monitors currently on the market have a raised bezel, which makes it more difficult than it need be to carry out this particular touch command. Our recommendation is that you choose a monitor in which the bezel is flush to the screen. Alternatively, look for a model that has at least a 20 mm border between the edge of the display and the start of the bezel.

Multi-touch

Multi-touch refers to a touchscreen's ability to recognize the presence of two or more points of contact with the surface. This plural-point awareness is necessary to implement functionality such as pinch to zoom-out, or the activation of predefined programs.

All modern touchscreens have this capability. However, to get the best out of Windows 10's touch feature, you need a touchscreen that supports at least five touch points – this allows you to use five fingers simultaneously.

The downside of capacitive touchscreens is that they cannot be operated with a gloved finger (not ideal on a freezing cold day, perhaps!).

Screen technology

There are various types of touchscreen technology, but when it comes to computer monitors and mobile devices there are just two: resistive and capacitive. Resistive screens can be operated with any pointed object, such as a stylus or a finger. Capacitive screens rely on the electrical properties of the human body, and thus only react to human touch (or a capacitive pen).

Of the two, the capacitive type is the one to go for – they are much more sensitive and accurate than resistive screens (these tend to be used more in business environments, e.g. shops and banks). Note that most current touchscreens are of the capacitive type, but do check it out just in case.

Sensors

One of the main differences between static desktop PCs and mobile computing devices is the range of sensors employed by the latter. Some of the sensors are important to the operation of these devices, while others add functionality. Sensors that you should look for include:

Increasingly, data from the various sensors in a device is being combined to produce more elaborate applications.

Ambient Light Sensor (ALS)

This sensor enables screen brightness to be automatically adjusted in accordance with the ambient light level. If it gets darker, then the screen brightness decreases; if it gets lighter, then the screen brightness increases. A useful side-effect of this is increased battery life.

Proximity sensor

The purpose of this device is to prevent accidental inputs – something that's easily done on a touchscreen. The most common scenario is the ear touching the screen during a call and triggering an event or action.

The proximity sensor is located next to the speaker and thus can detect when the ear (or another object) is close by. Any actions generated are assumed to be accidental, and thus ignored.

Accelerometer & Gyroscope

These two sensors are used to detect the orientation of a device so that the display can react accordingly. For example, if the device is moved from a vertical orientation to a horizontal one, the display will follow suit. Other uses include the camera – the sensors enable it to know if the picture is being taken in landscape or portrait mode.

New types of sensor are being developed for mobile devices. Examples are altimeters (which will detect which floor of a building you are on, for example), temperature & humidity sensors, and heart rate monitors.

Global Positioning System (GPS)

An embedded GPS sensor used in conjunction with a mapping service enables any mobile device to get real-time position tracking, text- and voice-guided directions, and points of interest.

Compass

Sensors that detect direction enable compass apps to be built. Sensors of this type do not sense magnetic fields as do traditional compasses, but rather the frequency and orientation of radio waves. In doing this, smartphone compass sensors are assisted by gyroscopes.

Other hardware features

Windows 10 includes several modern hardware features not seen in early Windows operating systems. We'll take a brief look at two of them here:

Near Field Communication (NFC)

Near Field Communication (NFC) is a set of standards for mobile devices to establish radio communication with each other by touch or bringing them into close proximity – usually no more than a few centimeters. The technology appears on many devices. Applications include:

Hot tip

NFC is similar in concept to Bluetooth but is somewhat slower in operation. It does, however, consume much less power.

Purchase Payment – used in conjunction with an electronic wallet, this effectively turns a smartphone into a credit card.

Setting Up Connections – connections such as Bluetooth can be quickly and easily established.

Smart Tagging – touching a smartphone to an NFC tag, e.g. tap-and-go at the gas pump.

Peer-to-Peer – sharing small snippets of information such as contacts, photos, and web pages is a typical use.

Unified Extensible Firmware Interface (UEFI)

A computer needs an interface between its operating system and hardware to make sure they can work together. Traditionally, this role has been carried out by a chip called the BIOS (this produces the black boot screens you see when starting your PC).

If your PC has UEFI, it can be accessed from Windows 10's Recovery, Advanced Options menu.

UEFI is a replacement for the now archaic BIOS. Windows 10 takes advantage of a security feature in UEFI known as Pre-boot Authentication. This prevents any software that doesn't have a recognized and valid security certificate from running and, as a result, rootkits, viruses and malware are unable to load themselves into the system's memory during the boot procedure, i.e. before the operating system. (A virus that manages to do this could circumvent any antivirus measures on the PC.)

Another feature of UEFI is its graphical display that allows navigation with a mouse and keyboard. However, before you go looking for it, be aware that your computer's motherboard must provide UEFI support. Only computers built in the last year or two are likely to have UEFI.

3 Installing Windows 10

Upgrading options for Windows 10 can be a confusing issue – this chapter explains exactly which editions of Windows can be upgraded to Windows 10. We compare installation options for upgrading and clean installing.

Upgrade paths

On this page we see the upgrade paths to Windows 10 from previous versions of Windows. It is not possible to upgrade from all earlier versions.

Windows 10 Home can be bought from the Microsoft Store for $119.99/£119.99, and Windows 10 Pro costs $199.99/£219.99. *(Prices correct at the time of printing.)*

Upgrade to Windows 10 Home

You can upgrade to Windows 10 Home and keep Windows settings, personal files, and applications from the following Windows operating system editions:

- Windows 7 Starter
- Windows 7 Home Basic
- Windows 7 Home Premium
- Windows 8.1
- Windows 8.1 with Bing

Upgrade to Windows 10 Pro

You can upgrade to Windows 10 Pro and keep Windows settings, personal files, and applications from the following Windows operating system editions:

- Windows 7 Professional
- Windows 7 Ultimate
- Windows 8.1 Pro

Windows Phone 8.1 users can also upgrade to Windows 10 Mobile.

Upgrades unavailable

You cannot upgrade to Windows 10 from the following operating system editions:

- Windows 7 Enterprise
- Windows 8 (must be upgraded to at least 8.1)
- Windows 8.1 Enterprise
- Windows RT
- Windows RT 8.1

Upgrade options

Upgrading an operating system can be done in three ways:

- An inplace upgrade
- A clean installation
- A migration

We'll start with the most common method:

Inplace upgrade

With this method, the operating system is simply installed over the top of the old one. While this is the easiest way to do the job, it will produce the worst results. This is because any problems on the original setup (file corruption, malware, etc.) will be carried over to the new installation. Issues of this type can also cause an upgrade to fail.

The only advantages of upgrading in this way are that the procedure is straightforward and that the user's data, files and programs are not affected – they will still be there at the end of it.

Clean installation

With a clean installation, all potential problems are eliminated right at the start due to the format procedure, which wipes the drive clean of all data. Therefore, nothing is carried over to the new setup from the old one.

The drawback with this method is that the formatting procedure also removes all the user's data – settings, files and programs. So when the new operating system has been installed, it will then be necessary to redo all the settings, reinstall all the programs and restore the data. Another issue is the time it will take to do all this – the best part of a day, in our experience.

For best results, we suggest you back up your personal data and perform a clean installation.

Migration

This is not a true upgrade option but we include it here as the procedure does transfer files and settings from one installation to another. It does not transfer programs, though.

To do a migration, you need a suitable application that copies the files and settings from the old setup to a medium such as a USB flash drive, then transfers them to the new setup.

Walkthrough clean install

Unlike an upgrade, which can be initiated from within Windows, a clean install has to be done from an installation disk. If your copy of Windows 10 has been supplied on a DVD or USB then you're all set. If not, it will be in the form of an ISO image file. However, before you can use this it will have to be burned to a DVD, a procedure that will require a DVD burning program.

If you are upgrading from Windows 7, you have a DVD burner built in. Just pop an empty DVD in the DVD drive and follow the prompts from the AutoPlay window that will open shortly afterwards.

If you don't have a built-in burner, you can find a free one on the internet. One that we recommend is ImgBurn from **imgburn.com** Use it as described below:

Microsoft provides a free **Windows 10 Media Creation Tool** that allows you to easily download the Windows 10 ISO image file, which must then be burnt to a DVD. You can also use this tool to download for USB media. Find details at **microsoft.com/en-us/software-download/windows10**

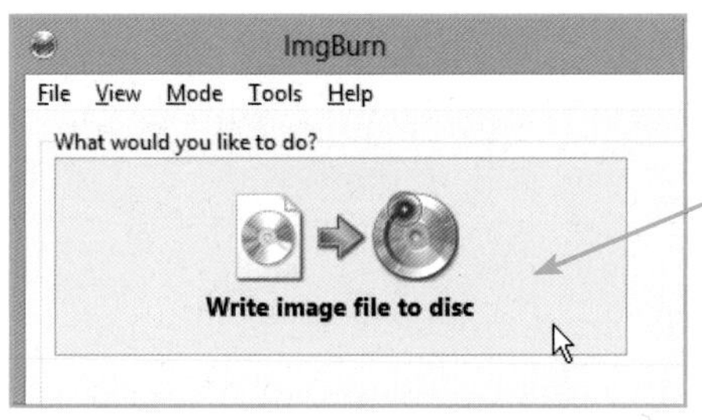

1. At the opening screen, click **Write image file to disc**
2. Under Source, click the browse link and select your ISO file

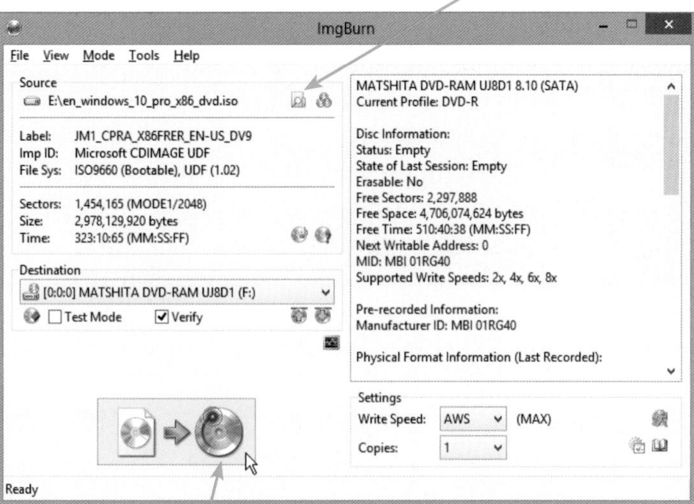

3. Click Write and wait while the DVD is burned

ImgBurn is just one of many free disk burners available on the internet.

Set the boot drive

Having created your installation disk, you now need to configure your computer to boot from it. This is done as follows:

1. Start the PC, and at the first boot screen press the key required to open the BIOS. This is usually the Delete or F2 key (it is often specified at the bottom of the screen)

2. On the main BIOS page, scroll to **Advanced BIOS Features** and hit the Enter key

3. On the next page, scroll down to **First Boot Device**. Using the Page Up/Page Down keys, cycle through the options and select the CD/DVD drive

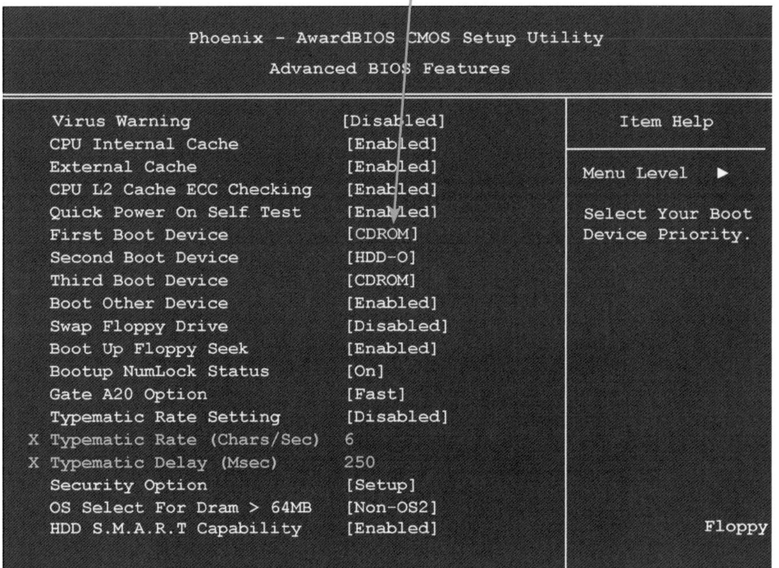

4. Press the **Esc** key to return to the main page

Note that you must save the change before exiting the BIOS, otherwise it will revert to the original setting. The BIOS option for this is to **Save & Exit Setup**, typically with the F10 key.

If you can't find the key to open the BIOS, check the motherboard manual.

The BIOS screens on your PC may differ from the example on the left – it depends on the age of your PC and the BIOS manufacturer.

All the tools needed to do a clean install of Windows 10 are on its installation disk. So, you must set the CD/DVD drive as the first boot device.

Windows setup

Don't forget

Before you start this procedure, make sure you have made a backup of any data that you want to keep, then configure the PC to boot from the CD/DVD drive.

On the following pages, we are going to show you a step-by-step procedure for doing a clean installation of Windows 10.

1. Place the Windows 10 installation disk in the CD/DVD drive and start the PC. When you see a **Press any key to boot from CD...** message, do so. Windows will now begin loading its installation files to the disk drive

2. The first screen you will see is the language, time and currency format, and input method preferences. Make your selections and press the **Next** button

3. On the second screen, click **Install now** to begin the installation procedure

Hot tip

Notice the option to **Repair your computer**, should you need to use the installer to rectify a serious system problem.

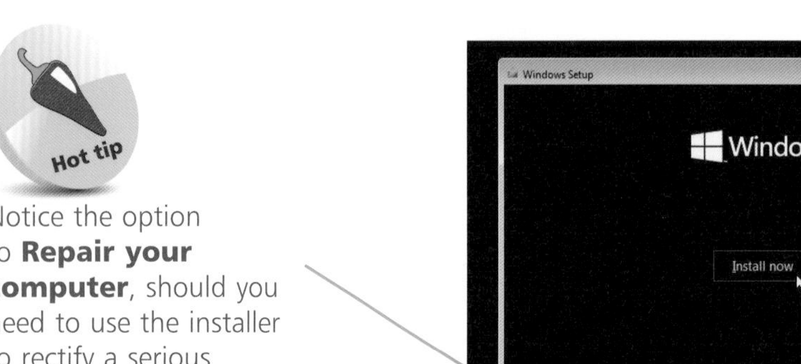

Enter product key

4. Next, enter your product key and click **Next**, or choose the **I don't have a product key** link to continue

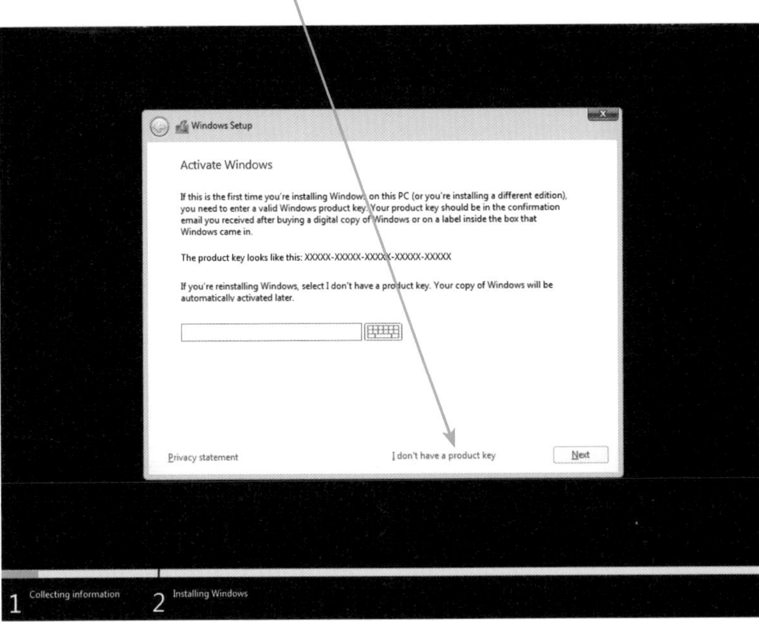

The product key will be found somewhere on the DVD packaging. If bought online, it will be in the email confirming the sale. If you are replacing Windows 7 or 8.1 the key may be on a sticker on the PC case or embedded in the BIOS. You can retrieve an embedded key using the Windows OEM Key Tool. For details, see **neosmart.net/OemKey**

5. Choose the version you wish to install, then click **Next**

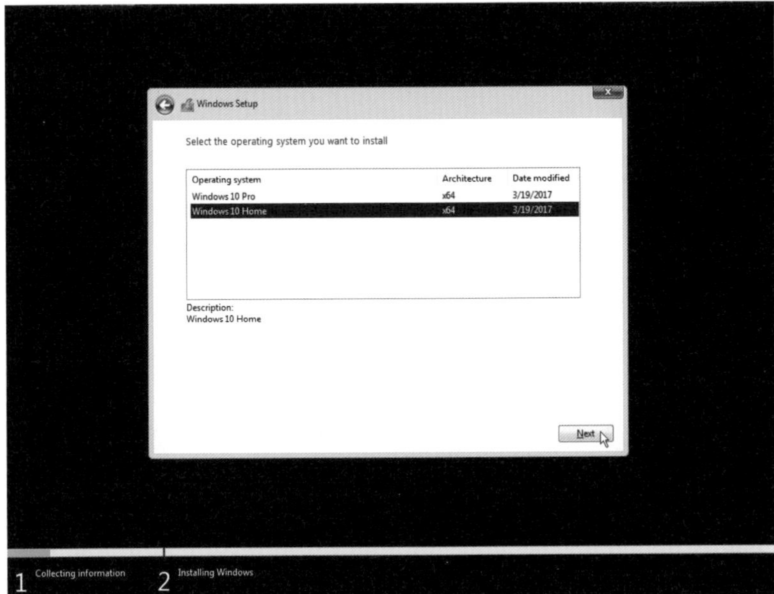

You will need a valid product key for the version you choose to install in order to complete activation of Windows 10.

Type of installation

6 Check the **I accept the license terms** box, then click **Next**

You can, of course, read the Windows 10 End User License Agreement (EULA) before consenting to accept its terms.

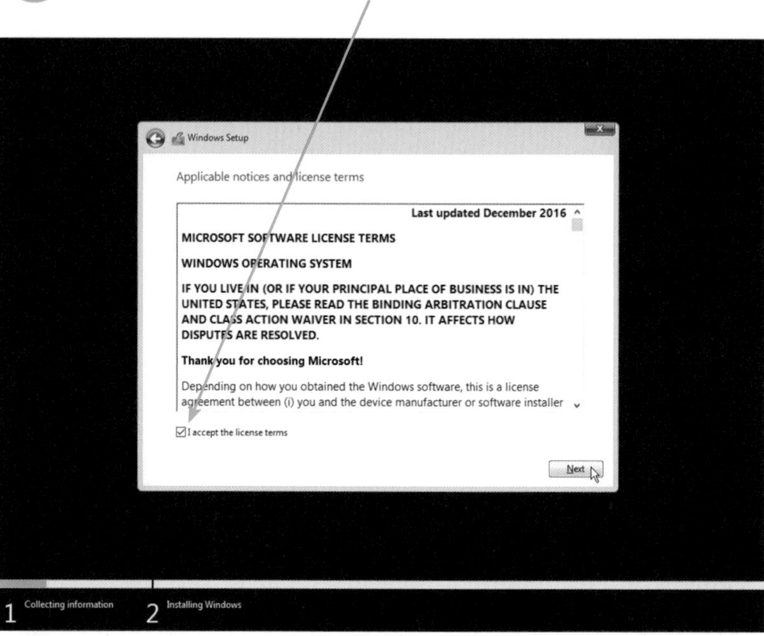

7 At the "Which type of installation do you want?" screen, select **Custom: Install Windows only (advanced)**

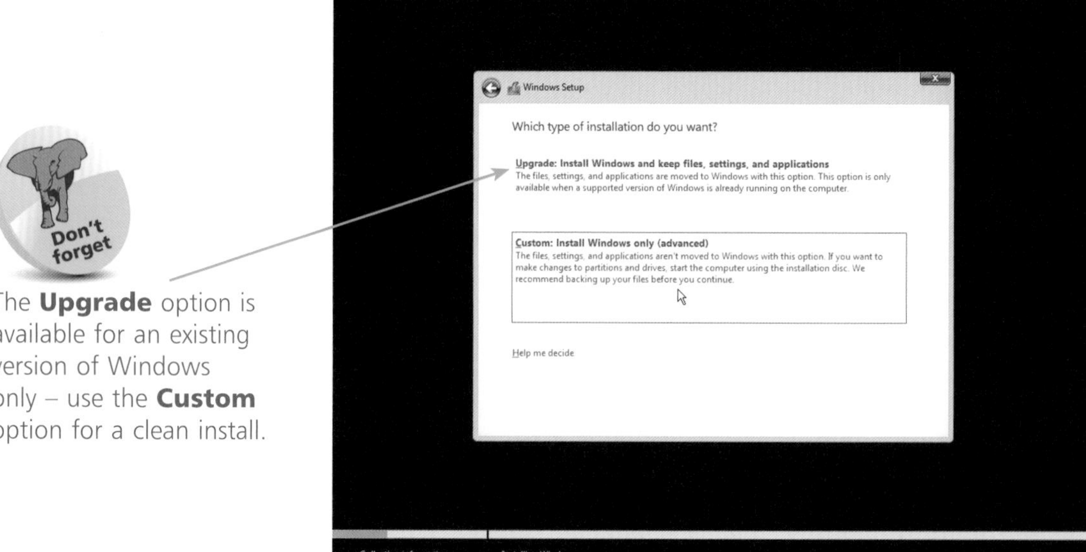

The **Upgrade** option is available for an existing version of Windows only – use the **Custom** option for a clean install.

8. In the "Where do you want to install Windows?" screen, select the required drive or partition, then click **Next**

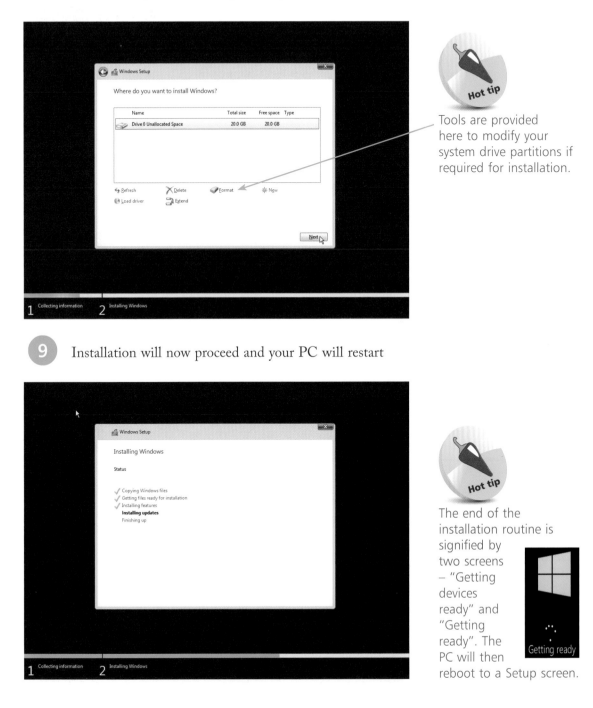

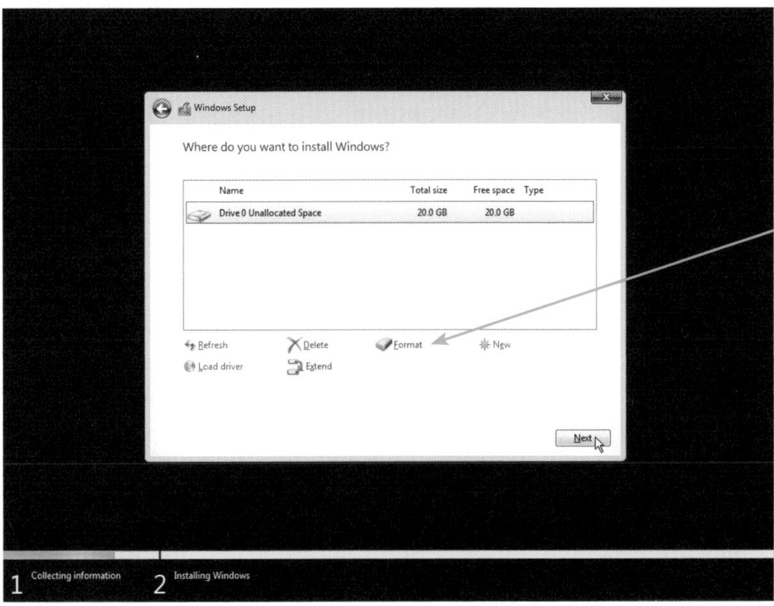

Tools are provided here to modify your system drive partitions if required for installation.

9. Installation will now proceed and your PC will restart

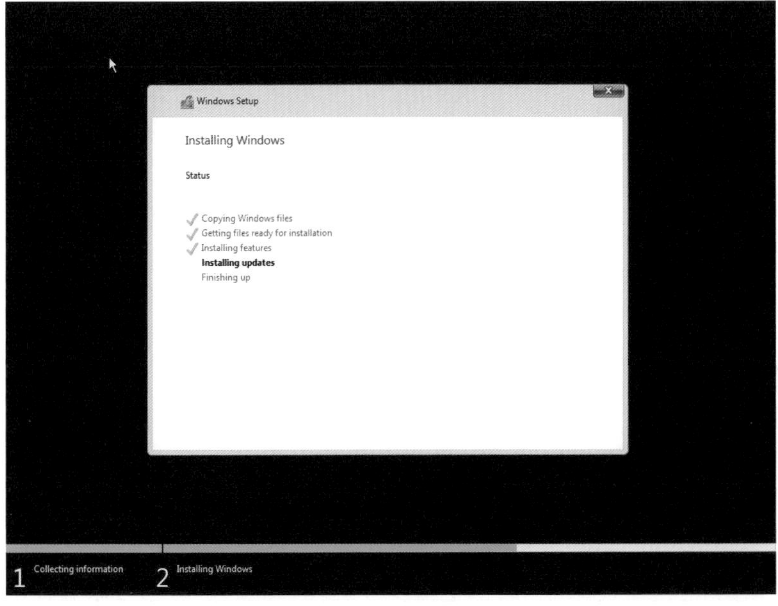

The end of the installation routine is signified by two screens – "Getting devices ready" and "Getting ready". The PC will then reboot to a Setup screen.

First start

Windows 10 starts up for the first time with a Setup screen:

The Windows 10 Creators Update added Cortana voice assistance to the setup procedure.

10 First choose your region, then click the **Yes** button

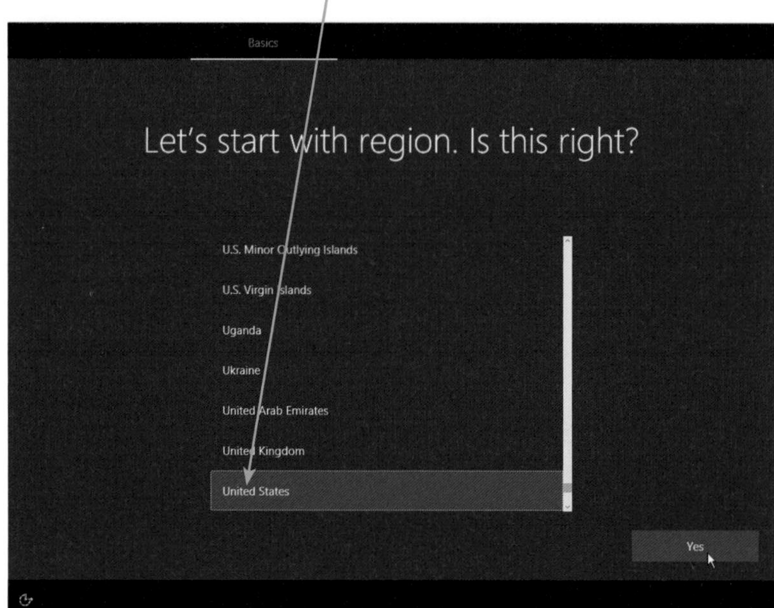

Drag the slider control on the Setup screen to see all the options.

11 Next, choose your keyboard, then click the **Yes** button

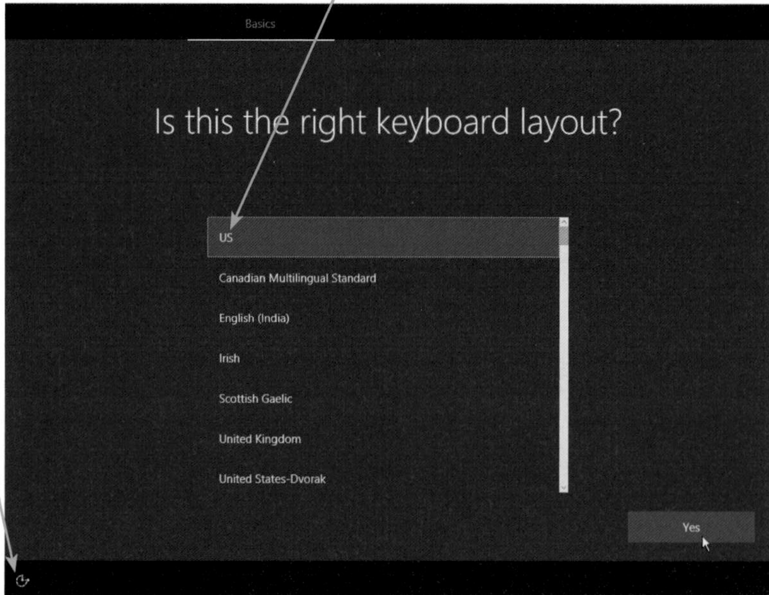

You can click the "Ease of access" icon to reveal aids for those users with physical impairments.

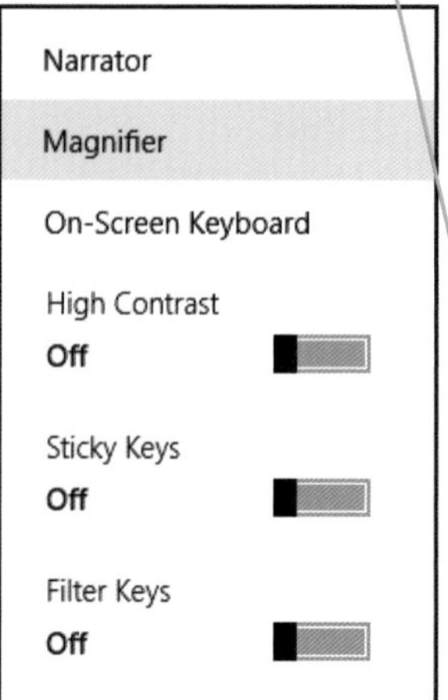

Sign in to your PC

12 Enter your Microsoft account details then click **Next**, or choose the **Offline account** link to continue

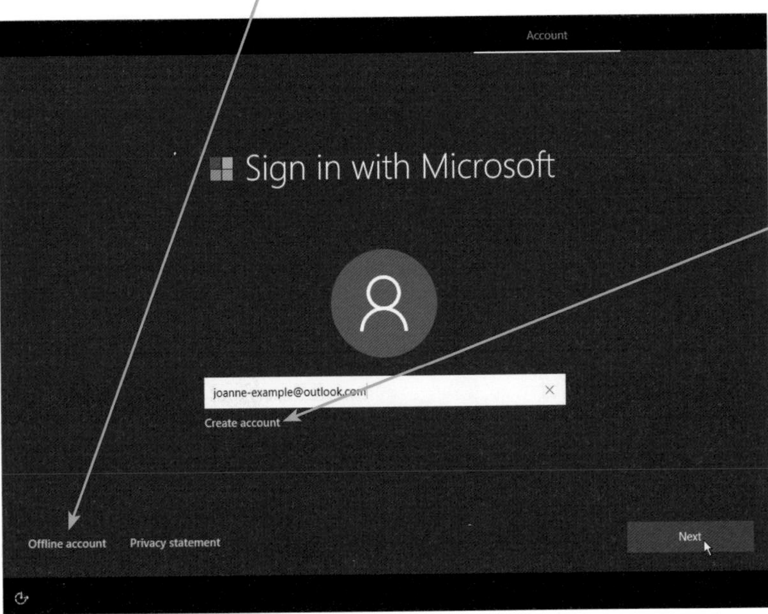

Use the **Create account** link if you don't already have a Microsoft account – avoid using an **Offline account** if you want to enjoy all the features and benefits of Windows 10 (see page 52).

13 Now, enter the password for your Microsoft account

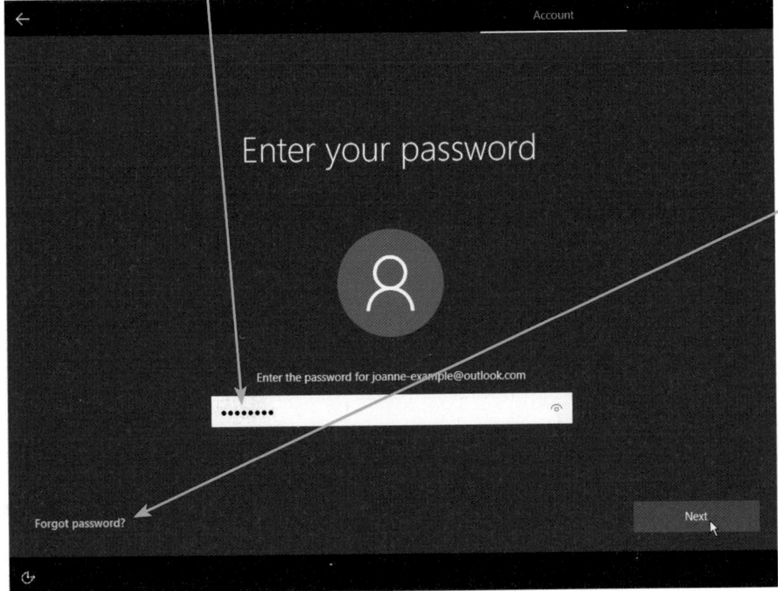

Use the **Forgot password?** link if you can't remember the password of your Microsoft account.

14 Next, click **Set a PIN** to log onto Windows with a 4-digit code

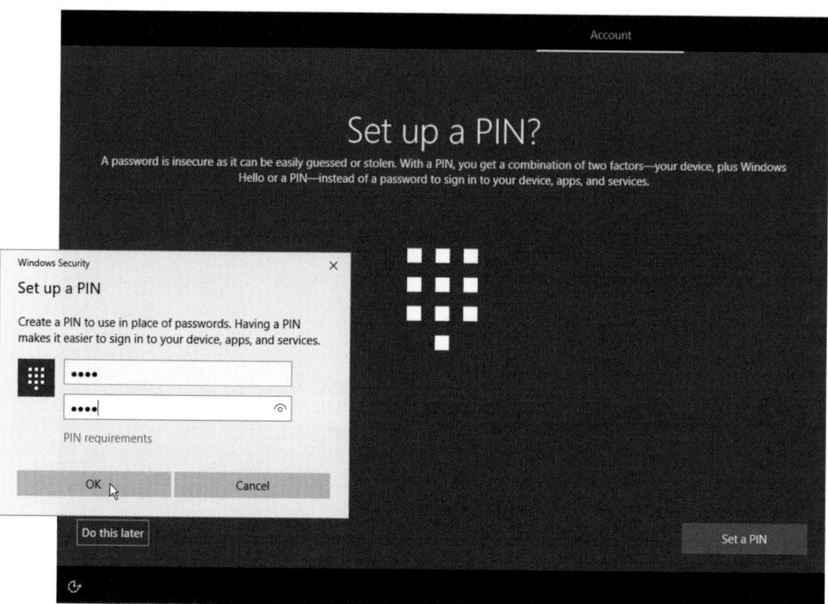

15 Now, click **Yes** to automatically synchronize files between your PC and your OneDrive cloud folder

You can click the **No** button here if you don't want to automatically sync your OneDrive folder with the Cloud. Whatever your choice, the PC will now restart.

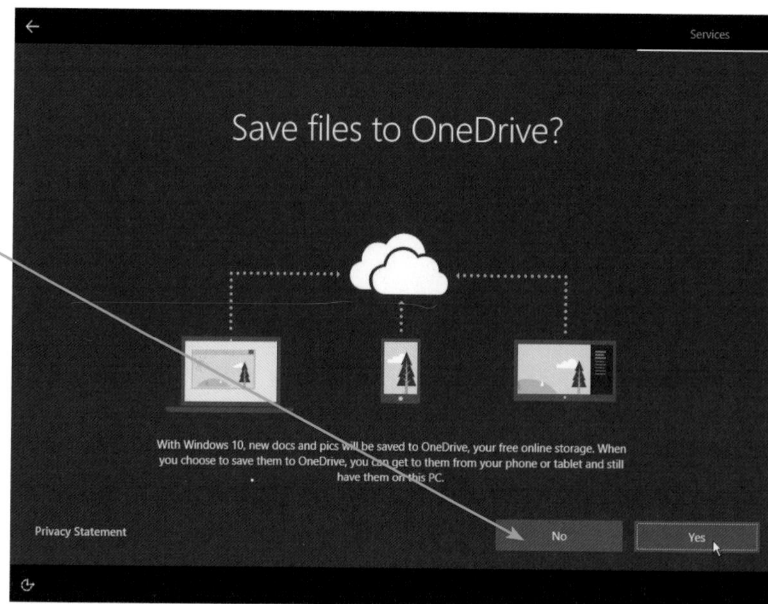

Finalizing settings

16 After the PC has restarted, click **Yes** to enable the **Cortana** Personal Digital Assistant

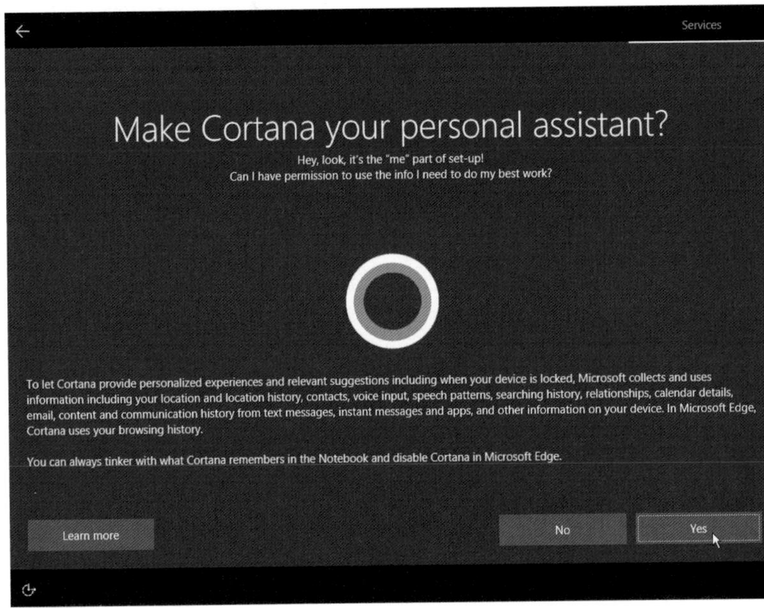

If you are concerned with privacy you can change Cortana settings later to restrict access.

17 Adjust **Privacy settings** as desired, then click **Accept**

After accepting privacy settings Windows will install apps – then your PC is ready to go.

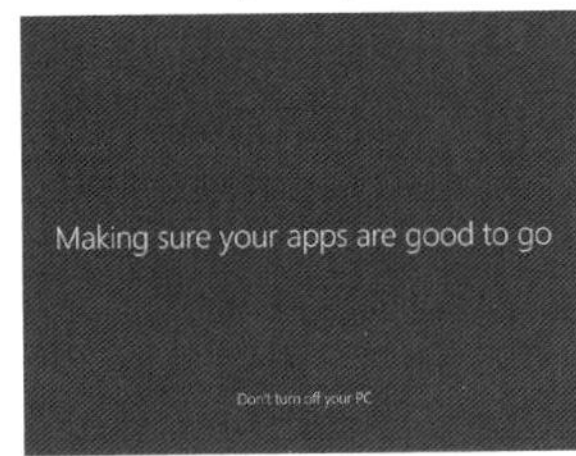

Restoring your data

You now have a brand new operating system. However, apart from the apps bundled with Windows 10, that's all you have.

The first thing you have to do now is install essential system drivers. The most important of these are the chipset drivers, and they will be found on the motherboard's installation disk. Pop this in the CD/DVD drive and wait for AutoPlay to open the disk's setup utility. Select the option that installs all the chipset drivers.

Don't forget

You may need to install the drivers for your chipset and other hardware. If you don't have them, they can be downloaded from the motherboard manufacturer's website.

When the driver installation is complete, the PC will reboot. When back in Windows, the next step is to install the drivers for any hardware connected to the computer. Typically, these include video cards, sound cards, printers, scanners, routers, monitors, mice and keyboards.

Finally, install your programs and any data backed up from your previous installation.

Local Offline accounts

As a final note, on page 49 we mentioned that it is not essential to have a Microsoft account to use Windows 10 and, indeed, it isn't. However, if you choose this option, you will find that some features of Windows 10 are denied to you.

The first is that you won't be able to synchronize your settings, email, passwords, etc. across your various devices. This means that one of the big attractions of Windows 10 – the ability to create and maintain a consistent computing environment regardless of which device you are using – will not be available. While this probably won't be a big deal for many users, for some it most definitely will be.

If you opt for an Offline account and don't specify a password, you will be able to automatically log on to Windows 10 without having to enter a password.

Also, you won't be able to get apps from the Windows Store. It will still be possible to browse the Store, but you won't be allowed to download any apps.

Furthermore, some Windows 10 apps won't work unless the user is signed in to a Microsoft account. Examples include the Mail, Calendar, People, and OneDrive apps.

4 The Windows 10 interface

This chapter describes the Windows 10 interface and introduces the Cortana Personal Digital Assistant. It also demonstrates how to change user settings for personalization and for access control.

Start Windows 10

When a Windows 10 PC is started, the first thing the user will see (once the boot screens have flashed past) is a black screen with the Windows logo, as shown below:

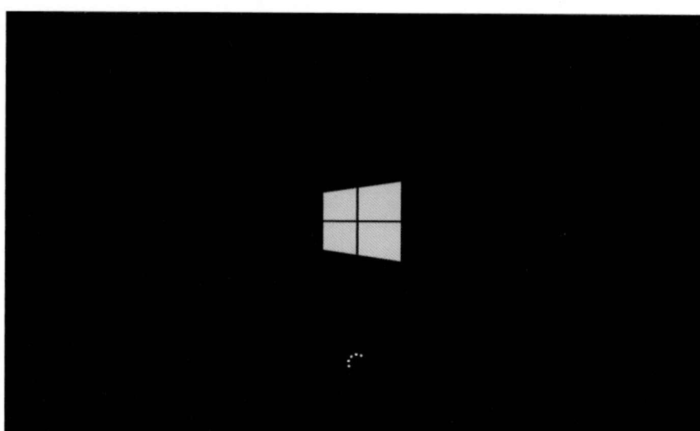

Hot tip

A Lock screen is not necessary when Windows 10 is used with a standard monitor. Many users will find it useful though, purely as a means of displaying information.

This is followed by the Lock screen. The basic purpose of this screen is to provide a protective barrier that prevents accidental inputs – this is necessary, as Windows 10 is a touch-supportive operating system.

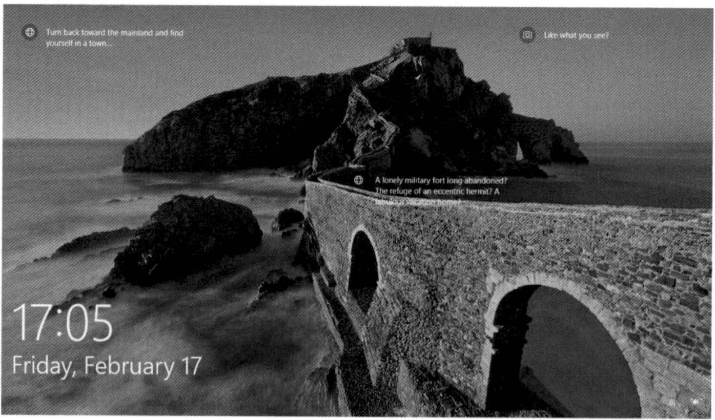

Don't forget

You can customize the Lock screen's background (see page 71).

Microsoft has evolved this basic function by enabling users to customize the screen by changing its background, and by specifying various notifications to be displayed.

By default, the Lock screen shows the current date and time, and has power status indicator icons, as in the image above.

Log on

Click or tap anywhere on the Lock screen and the log on screen will open. Above the log on box, you'll see the account picture. (This can be changed, as described on page 74.)

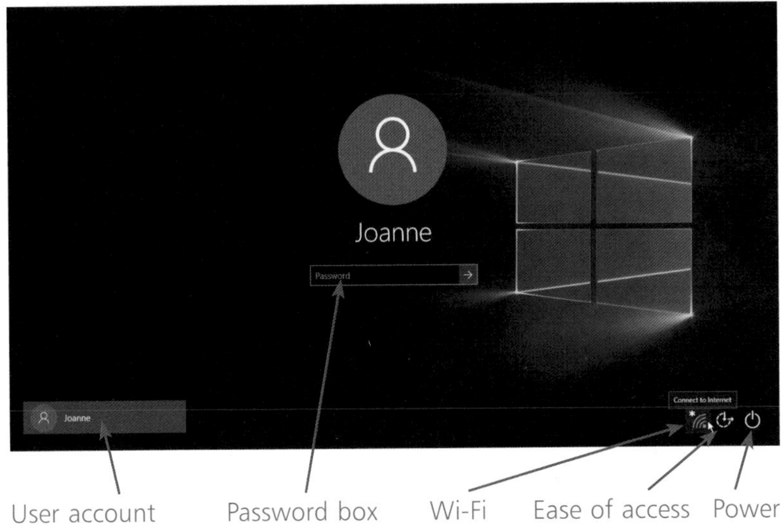

User account Password box Wi-Fi Ease of access Power

The log on screen will have a User account button for each account on the system – so you can choose which account to log on.

- **User account** – a button that selects the user to be logged onto the system.
- **Password box** – an input box to enter the password.
- **Wi-Fi** – an icon button that lets you connect to a network and indicates signal strength if already connected via Wi-Fi.
- **Ease of Access** – an icon button that provides the pop-up menu shown on the right, containing accessibility settings for users with impaired abilities. When this button is clicked, Windows reads and scans the menu as Narrator automatically provides audible guidance. Each item is explained and highlighted in turn. The user can select any item when it's highlighted by pressing the space bar.

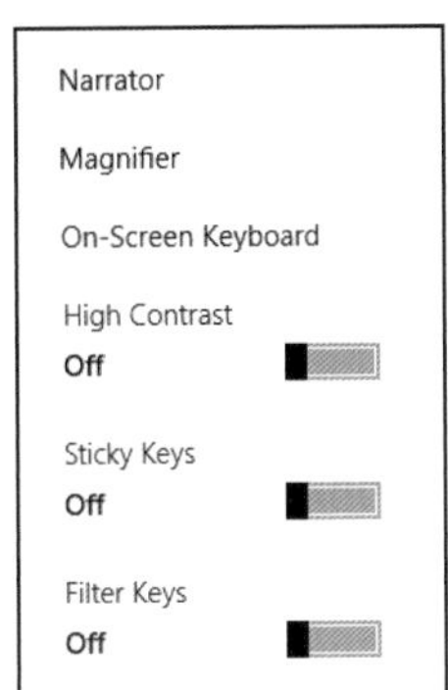

- **Power** – an icon button that provides a pop-up menu containing Sleep, Shut down, and Restart options.

The menus on the log on screen are easy to miss, as they are very small and placed right at the bottom of the screen.

Start screen

The customizable Start menu and Taskbar Search box are new features in Windows 10. You can modify many Start menu options in Settings, Start.

After logging on to a Windows 10 system you will see the Start screen in Desktop or Tablet Mode, appropriate for the device:

Desktop Mode

In Desktop Mode, open the Start menu by clicking the Start button to see the A-Z list of apps and pinned tiles.

Tablet Mode

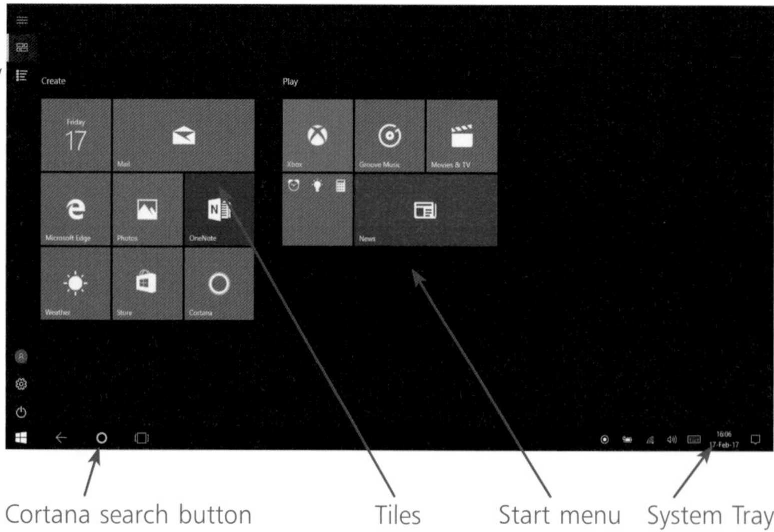

In Tablet Mode, tap the button to see the Start menu pinned tiles, then click the button to see an A-Z list of apps.

The Start menu tiles and A-Z list of all apps launch an app within a window in Desktop Mode or full-screen in Tablet Mode.

Any app can be added to the array of tiles by right-clicking on the listed app and choosing **Pin to Start** from the context menu. This allows you to populate the tiles with your favorite apps, so you can quickly launch them by clicking or tapping on a tile. Apps can also be pinned to the Taskbar in Desktop Mode.

Search box

The Search box lets you easily locate anything you need on your system or on the web. The icons down the side of the open Search box give access to:

- **Cortana** – Personal Digital Assistant (more on this later).
- **Home** – for latest news items.
- **Notebook** – for reminders, tips, events, recommendations, stock tracking, directions, and more.
- **Feedback** – for Microsoft.

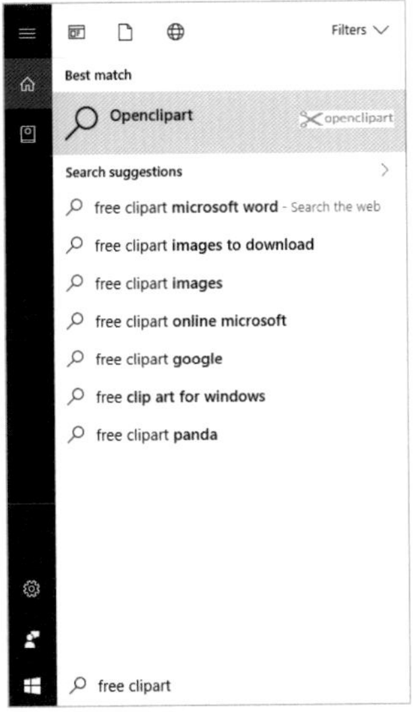

Icons of open or minimized apps appear on the Taskbar. Right-click on the Taskbar to see its options.

System Tray

The System Tray contains icons that typically give access to:

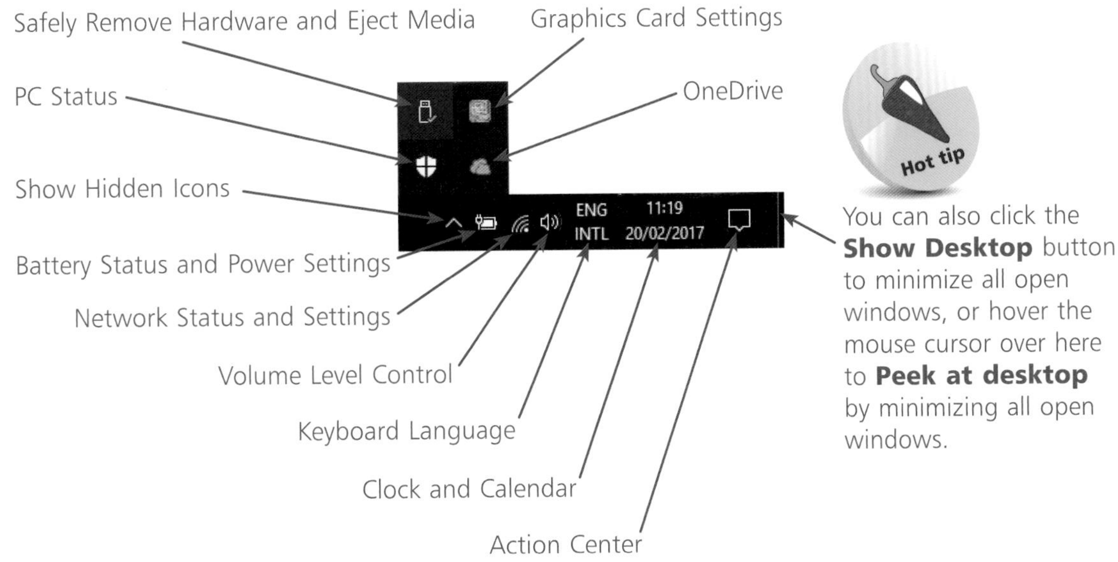

You can also click the **Show Desktop** button to minimize all open windows, or hover the mouse cursor over here to **Peek at desktop** by minimizing all open windows.

Navigation

In its drive for Windows 10 to be all-encompassing, Microsoft has made it possible to navigate the interface in three different ways: by touch, the mouse, and the keyboard.

Touch

Touch gestures include swiping, sliding, tapping, and pinching. The best way to get to grips with these is to experiment. The following, however, will get you off to a good start:

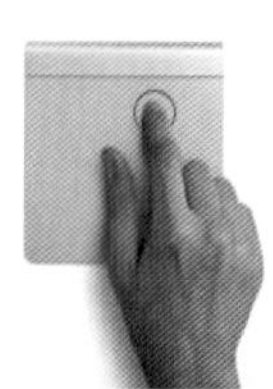

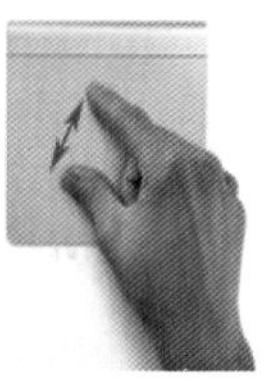

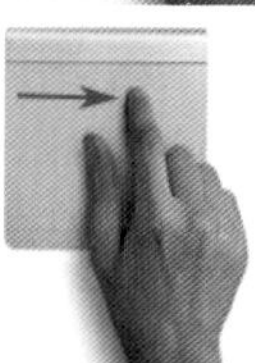

- **Tap** – opens, selects, or activates whatever you tap (similar to clicking with a mouse).
- **Tap and hold** – shows further info about the item, or opens a context menu (similar to right-clicking with a mouse).
- **Pinch or stretch** – visually zooms in or out, like with a map or picture. Pinch to zoom out and stretch to zoom in.
- **Rotate** – some items can be rotated by placing your fingers on them and turning your hand.
- **Slide to scroll** – dragging your finger across the screen scrolls through screen items (similar to scrolling a mouse wheel).
- **Slide to arrange** – dragging an item around the screen with your finger to position it (similar to dragging with a mouse).
- **Swipe to select** – a short, quick movement will select an item and often bring up app commands.
- **Swipe or slide from right edge** – opens the Action Center.
- **Swipe or slide from left edge** – opens the Task View feature.
- **Swipe or slide from top edge** – enables you to view the title bar in full-screen apps.
- **Swipe or slide from bottom edge** – enables you to view the Taskbar in full-screen apps.

In many cases, the touch commands available are dependent on the application in use. For example, various rotational commands can be used to manipulate objects in drawing and layout applications such as Microsoft PowerPoint.

Mouse

Using the mouse to get around in Windows 10 is no different from any other operating system, although you can spin the mouse wheel while on the Lock screen to open the password box.

Keyboard

Those of you who use the Windows 10 interface without the benefit of a touchscreen are well advised to get acquainted with the various keyboard commands relevant to it. In many cases, just as with keyboard commands and shortcuts in general, they are often quicker than using the mouse.

There is actually a whole bunch of these commands; the following being some of the more useful ones:

The key that will be used most is the Windows key (WinKey). Pressing this key opens and closes the Start menu. It can also be used in conjunction with other keys to perform other actions. For example, pressing **WinKey** + **X** opens the Power User Menu while **WinKey** + **C** opens the Cortana search feature.

The Home and End keys jump from one end of the "All apps" list on the Start menu to the other, while the arrow keys can be used to select a tile. The Enter key opens a selected app.

WinKey + **Tab** opens Task View, which allows the user to switch to a different app using the arrow keys to select an app. The Enter key can then be used to exit Task View and activate the app.

Alt + **Tab** opens a Switch list which allows the user to switch to a different app. Note that you must have at least two apps running for **WinKey** + **Tab** and **Alt** + **Tab** to work.

A rarely-used key known as the Context Menu key (usually located close to the space bar) brings up a menu of related options when pressed.

The Windows key is usually located at the bottom of the keyboard near to the space bar, and often has an image of a flying window on it.

Two of the most useful keyboard shortcuts are **WinKey** + **C** to open Cortana search, and **WinKey** + **X** to open the Power User Menu.

Action Center

The Action Center provides a notification area for messages and various Quick Action icons that enable you to quickly adjust some settings:

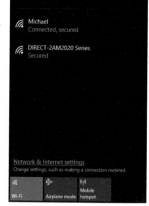

1. Click the Action Center button on the System Tray to open the Action Center

2. Click on **Expand** or **Collapse** to see all Quick Action icons or fewer Quick Action icons

3. Click the Action Center button on the System Tray once more to close the Action Center

Don't forget

Quick Actions that have been enabled appear in a different color. For example, the Location icon in the top picture.

When the Action Center is open you can click any Quick Action icon to adjust its current setting:

- **Tablet mode** – switch between Desktop Mode and Tablet Mode display configuration.

- **Network** – show current connection status and option icons.

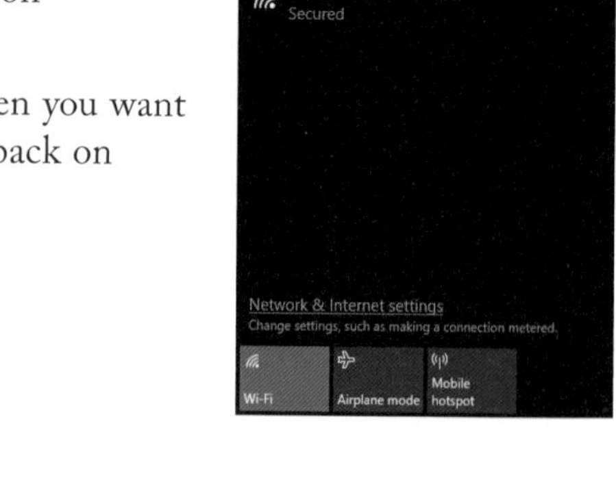

1. Click the Wi-Fi icon to turn off the Wi-Fi connection

2. Select how and when you want to turn the Wi-Fi back on

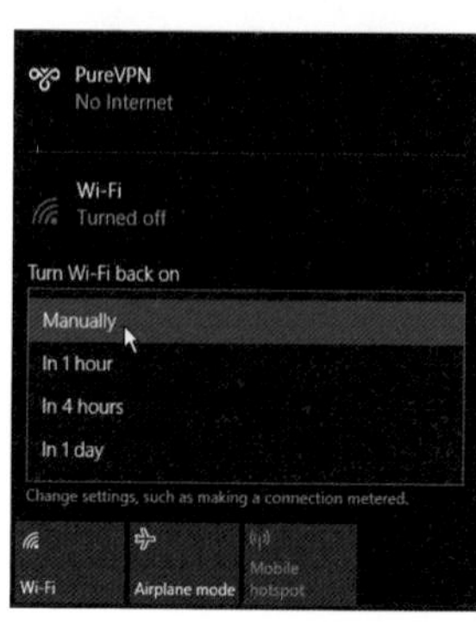

3. Click the Wi-Fi icon to turn on the Wi-Fi connection

Choosing to turn the Wi-Fi back on Manually means it will reconnect immediately when you click the Wi-Fi icon.

- **Note** – open the OneNote application to take a note.
- **All settings** – open the Windows Settings screen.
- **Airplane mode** – disable or enable all cellular, Wi-Fi, and Bluetooth wireless transmissions.
- **Location** – reveal or conceal the current global location of the device for GPS tracking.
- **Quiet hours** – deny or allow notifications from the system and external sources.
- **%** – adjust the screen brightness in successive steps through 0%-100%.
- **VPN** – connect or disconnect to the internet via a Virtual Private Network server for anonymity.
- **Battery saver** – enable or disable Battery Saver mode to control power consumption when running on battery only.
- **Project** – show current screen configuration for "PC screen only" and provide second screen options to Duplicate, Extend, or display on "Second screen only".
- **Connect** – connect wirelessly to another device via WiDi, such as to a smart TV that supports Miracast technology.
- **Mobile hotspot** – turn on or off the ability to share the internet connection with other devices over Wi-Fi.
- **Night light** – reduce blue light emissions from the screen to reduce eye strain at night.

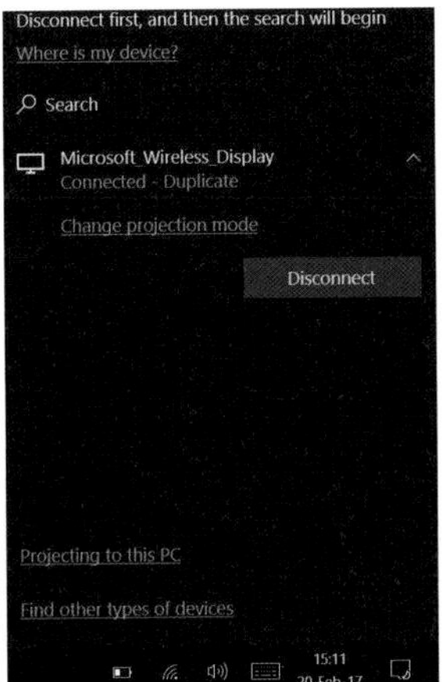

The Action Center was redesigned completely for Windows 10 and was further improved in the Creators Update.

You will need a subscription to a VPN service to connect to the internet via a VPN. Find out more online at **purevpn.com**

Ask Cortana

One of the great innovations in Windows 10 is the Personal Digital Assistant named "Cortana". This is an enhancement to the Search box feature that allows the user to search, and much more, by verbal communication once it has been enabled:

Cortana is new in Windows 10 but performance may vary by region. If Cortana is not working or enabled in your country, try setting your Region to "United States" in Settings, Time & language, Region & language. (Note: if you change your region, you might not be able to shop at the Store or use things you've purchased, like memberships and subscriptions, games, movies, TV, and music.)

1. Click in the Taskbar Search box then, when asked, enter your name and agree to give access to your location

2. Ensure your microphone is correctly configured, then click the microphone icon at the right of the Search box

3. Repeat the phrase that Cortana gives you, being sure to speak clearly without any background room noise, then click **Next** to close

4. Click the Search box, then click the Notebook icon and choose the **Settings** button

5. Slide the **Hey Cortana** toggle button to the **On** position

6. Upon completion of setup just say "Hey Cortana" to make Cortana listen

7. Now, ask Cortana anything you like. For example, try asking about the weather

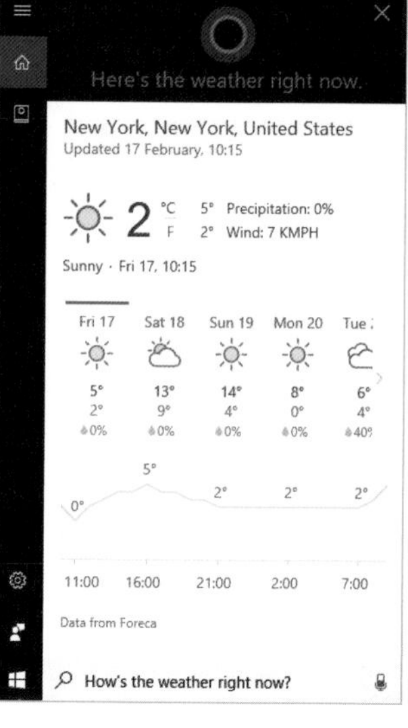

You can also click the microphone icon in the Search box to make Cortana begin listening.

The best way to learn Cortana commands is to simply try out different ways to phrase your question. Here are some Cortana commands that worked successfully when we tried them, and demonstrate some of the many things you can have Cortana do:

- **Cortana Search** – "Pink discography"
- **Cortana Calendar** – "Create a meeting with David"
- **Cortana Reminder** – "Remind me at 4pm"
- **Cortana Alarm** – "Wake me up in 2 hours"
- **Cortana Maps** – "Map of Washington DC"
- **Cortana Weather** – "What's the forecast this weekend?"
- **Cortana Music** – "Play music", "Pause music", "Resume music"
- **Cortana Pictures** – "Show me a picture of Cortana"
- **Cortana App Launch** – "Notepad"
- **Cortana News** – "Today's news"
- **Cortana Finance** – "Microsoft Stock today"
- **Cortana Sports** – "New York Jets' next game?"
- **Cortana Fun** – "Sing me a song"

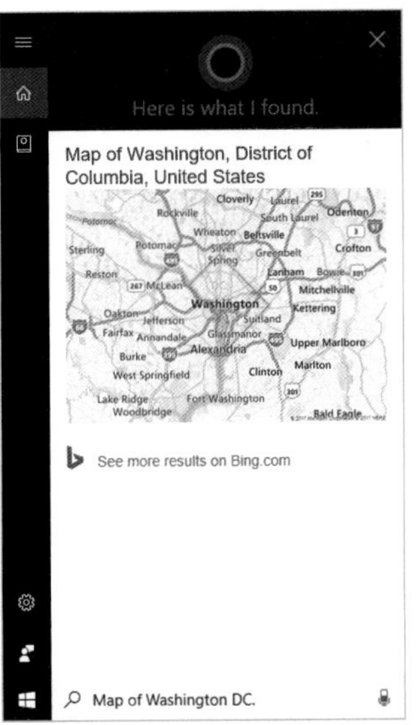

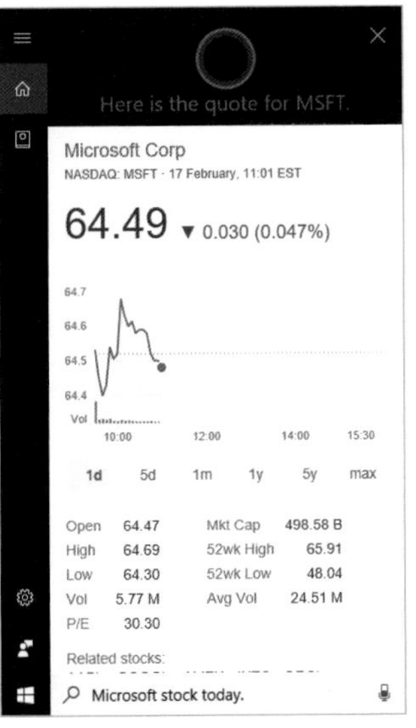

Cortana requires an internet connection, so will be unable to answer if you should lose your Wi-Fi connection.

Cortana collects users' personal data to further personalize results, and as such is subject to child-protection laws. Therefore, the user must be at least 13 years of age (checked against age data in user profiles) or Cortana will refuse to answer questions.

Cortana remote control

If your PC is idle and the **Hey Cortana** feature is enabled (see page 62), the Cortana interface will appear in full-screen mode. This allows you to read the screen from a distance to control Cortana remotely:

NEW

Cortana in full-screen mode and the ability to lock the screen remotely is a new feature introduced in the Windows 10 Creators Update.

1. Do not use your PC's mouse, screen, or keyboard for around 10 seconds, then say "Hey Cortana" – to see Cortana appear full screen

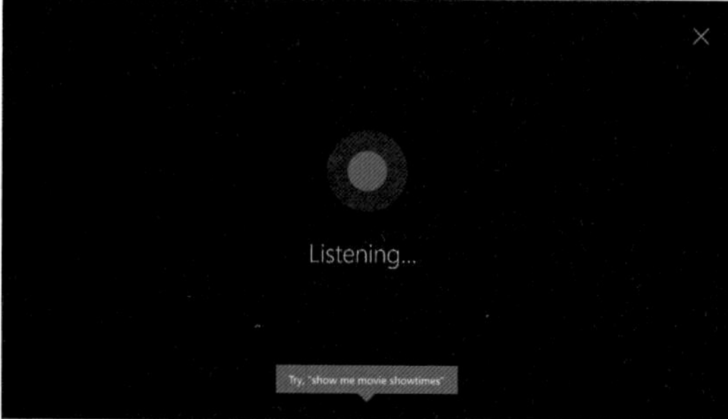

2. Next, walk away and say "Lock screen" – to remotely safeguard your PC

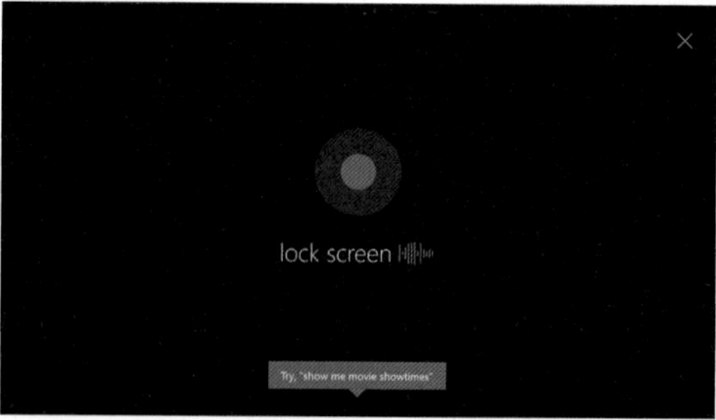

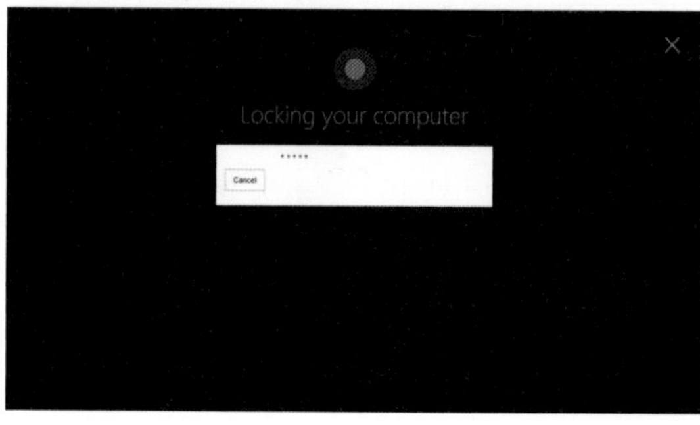

Some apps, such as TuneIn Radio (available free from the Store) provide voice playback controls. You can also ask Cortana "What song is playing?".

3. Now, say "Hey Cortana, play music" – to remotely playback your music on your PC

Notice that details of the track playing appear with playback controls on the Lock screen.

4. Say "Hey Cortana, volume up" or "Hey Cortana, volume down" – to remotely control the volume level

If you turn the volume level too high, Cortana may no longer hear your voice commands.

5. When you return to your PC, you will need to log in as normal to continue working

Cortana reminders

Cortana's Notebook lets you store information about your interests and favorite places. This allows Cortana to provide you with better personalized assistance. Most usefully, the Cortana Notebook also stores reminders you can set to appear only once or at recurring intervals:

Hot tip

Cortana's Notebook also contains categories with On/Off toggle buttons that determine what appears when you open Cortana. For example, the Cortana tips category will show tips when the **Tip cards** button is set to On.

1. Click the Search box to open Cortana, then select the **Notebook** icon in the left-hand pane and choose **Reminders**, then click the **+** button to add a reminder – or simply say "Hey Cortana, add a reminder"

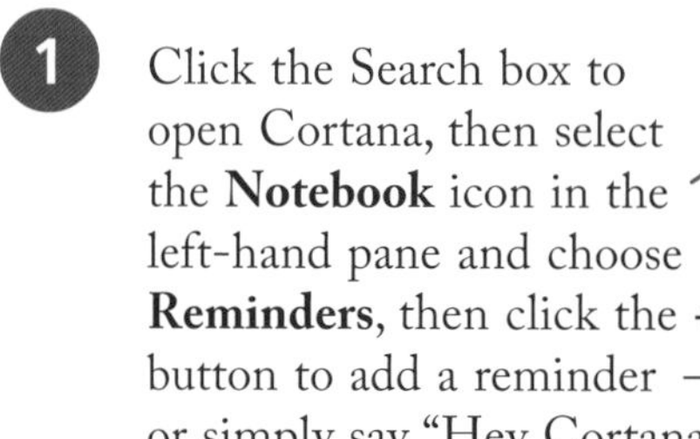

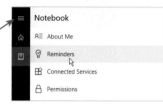

2. See that Cortana now prompts you to create a new reminder. You can Edit the "Remember to..." text by typing a reminder message in the box – or simply speak a reminder message, such as "Take a coffee break"

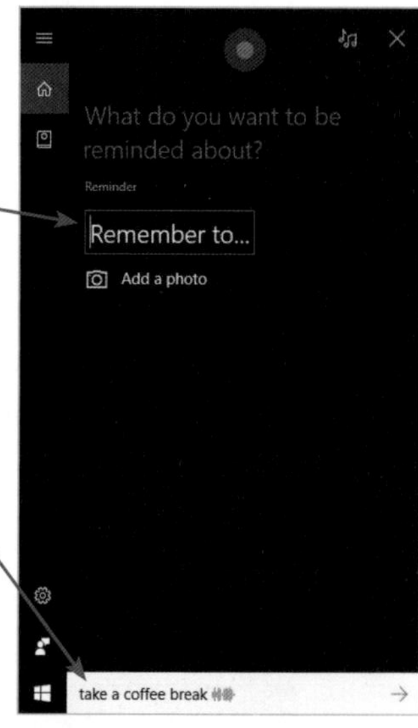

Don't forget

You can also click **Add a photo** to select a library image or camera photo to include in the Reminder.

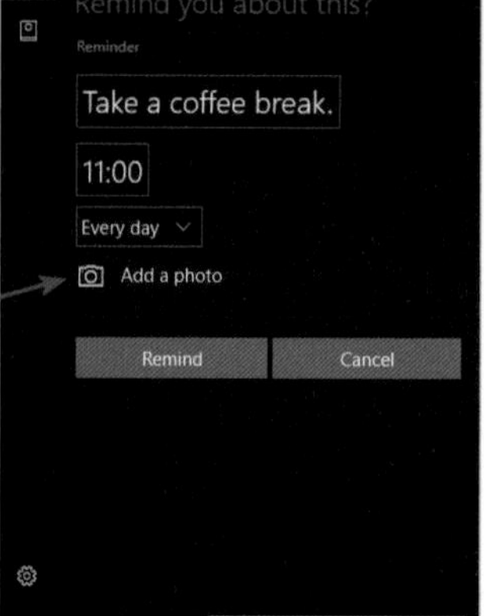

3. Select when to be reminded and choose to be reminded just once or at regular intervals by editing the boxes – or simply speak the time, such as "Eleven A.M. every day"

4. Click the **Remind** button, or simply say "Yes", to set the Reminder

5. To see the Reminders list, click the Search box, then the **Notebook** icon, and select **Reminders**

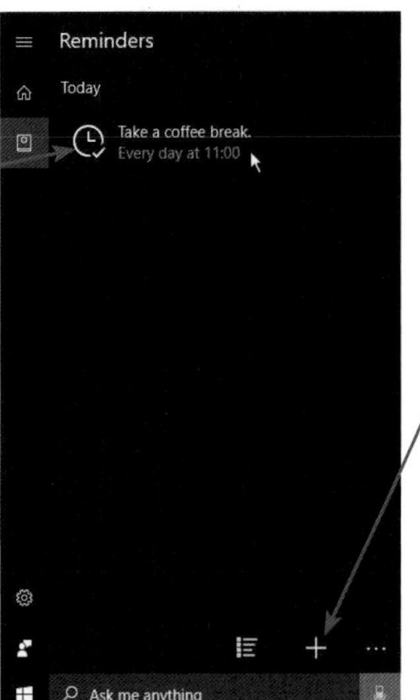

6. Select the reminder you want to edit or delete

7. Next change any detail in the boxes, for example change the reminder time to "12:30", then click the **Save** icon

8. See the reminder appear at the specified time

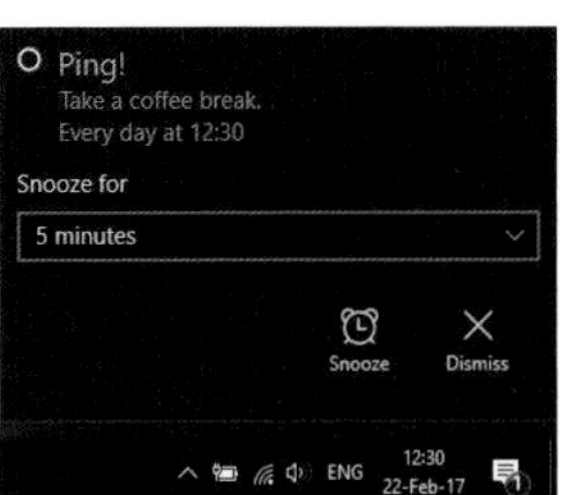

You can click the **+** button at the bottom of the Reminders list to add a new Reminder.

The **Dismiss** option will only close the Reminder box – it does not cancel the Reminder.

Notification sync

Windows 10 provides the ability to send information and notifications between multiple devices so your desktop PC, laptop, tablet, and smartphone, can be synchronized. This means that reminders can be created on any device to appear on all devices:

Cross-device notification syncing was improved in the Windows 10 Creators Update.

1. Click the Search box to open Cortana, then select the **Settings** icon in the left-hand pane

2. Scroll through the list to find **Send notifications and information between devices**
3. Slide the toggle button to the **On** position
4. Next, click the **Edit sync settings** button

In the **My devices** list "Windows Phone" only relates to devices running the Windows Phone operating system, whereas "Mobile device" relates to devices running Windows 10 or Windows 10 Mobile.

5. Select the first item in the **My devices** list

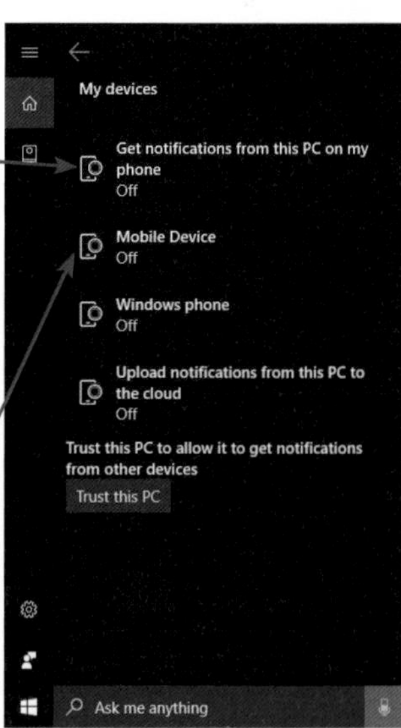

6. Slide the toggle button to the **On** position to get PC notifications on your phone

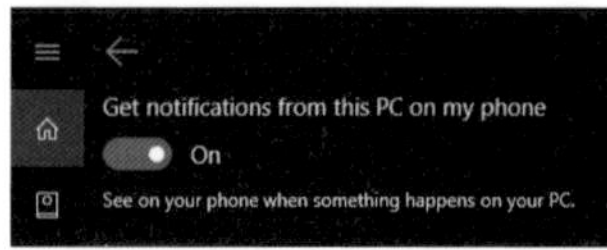

7. Click the back button then select the second list item
8. Slide the toggle buttons to the **On** position to get phone notifications on your PC

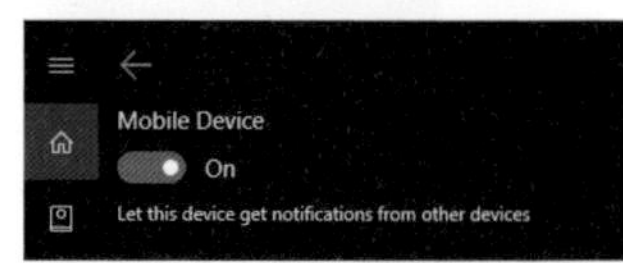

The option to **Upload notifications from this PC to the cloud** can be turned on to help prevent you receiving the same notification twice.

9. Click the back button, then click **Trust this PC** and complete the authorization to sync with other devices

10. Now, click the link below the **Edit sync settings** button if you also want to sync Android or Apple phones

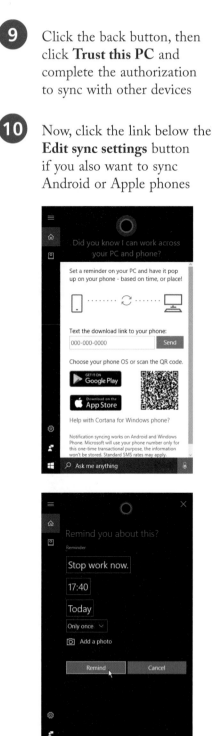

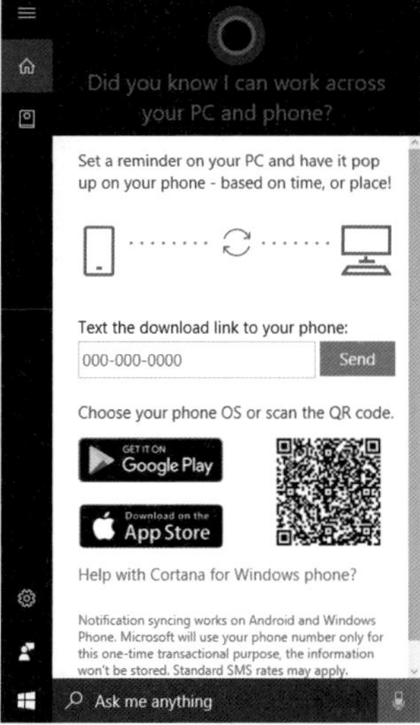

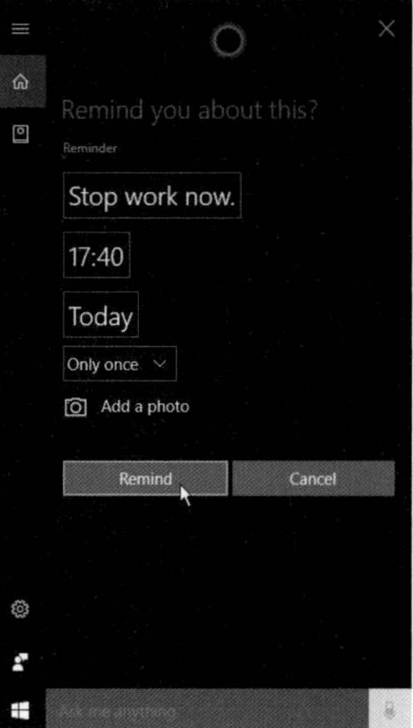

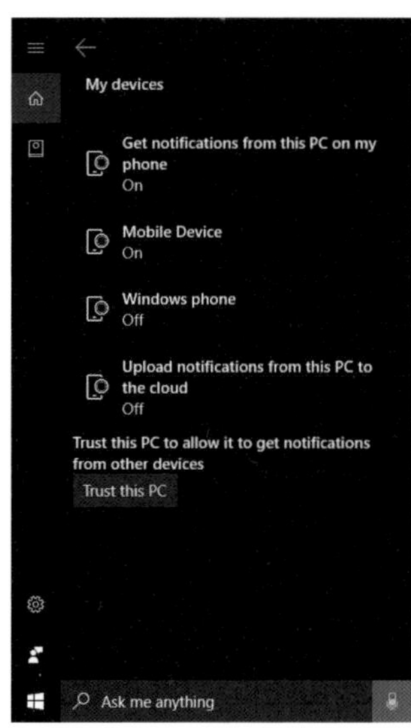

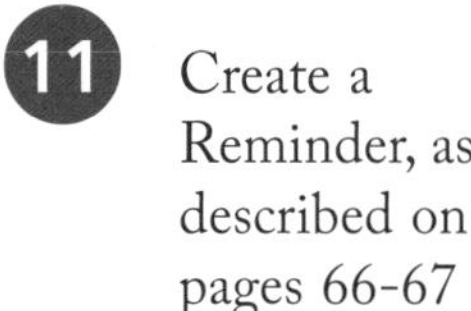

11. Create a Reminder, as described on pages 66-67

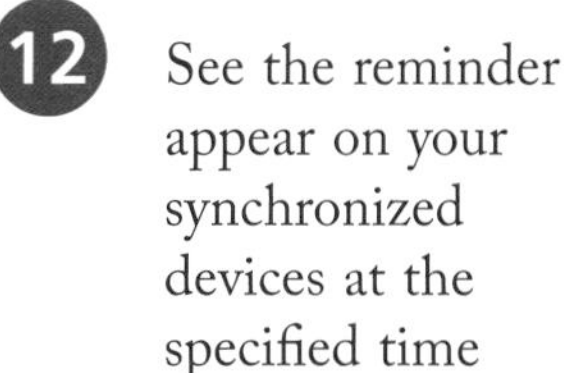

12. See the reminder appear on your synchronized devices at the specified time

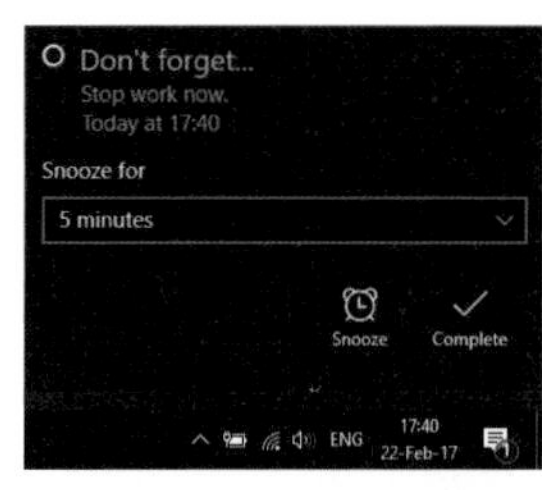

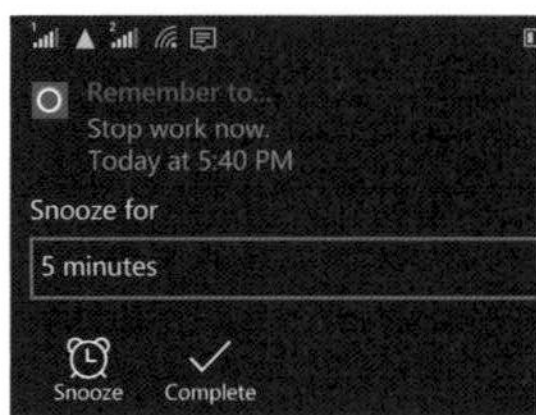

Trust authorization verifies your identity to ensure your information is not being synchronized maliciously.

To sync with Android or Apple phones you must install the Cortana app on that phone – available from Google Play and the Apple Store.

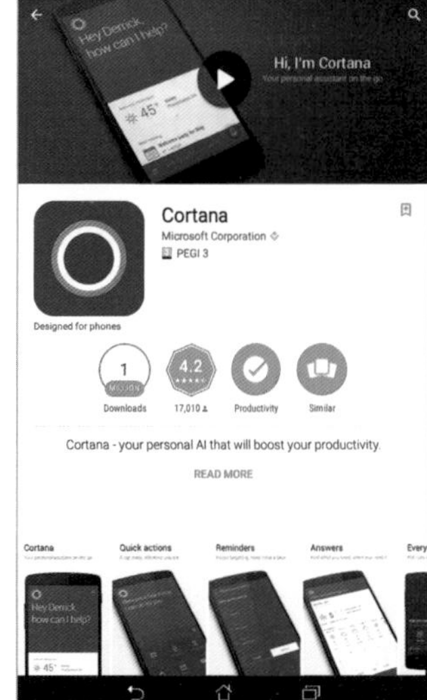

Personalization

You can easily customize your Desktop by replacing the default Windows 10 background with a picture of your choice or with a solid color by choosing from a swatch selection:

1. Click the Start button, then click the **Settings** icon

2. On the Settings screen, choose **Personalization**

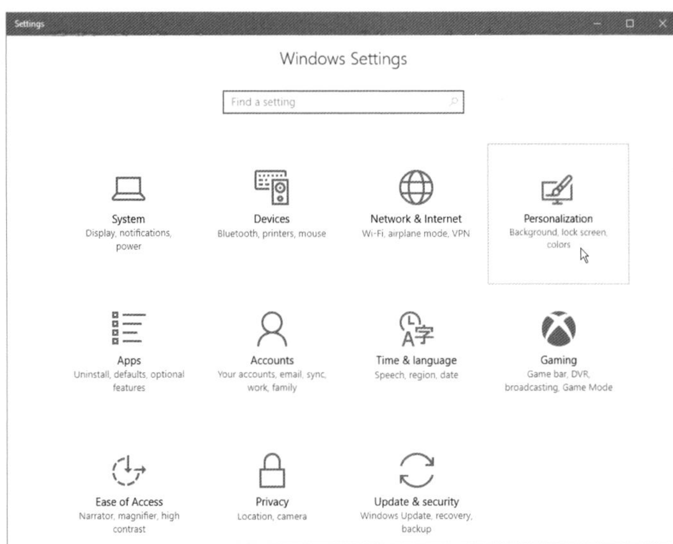

3. Click the **Background** drop-down menu and select **Picture**, then choose an image or select **Solid Color**, then choose a color from the swatch that appears

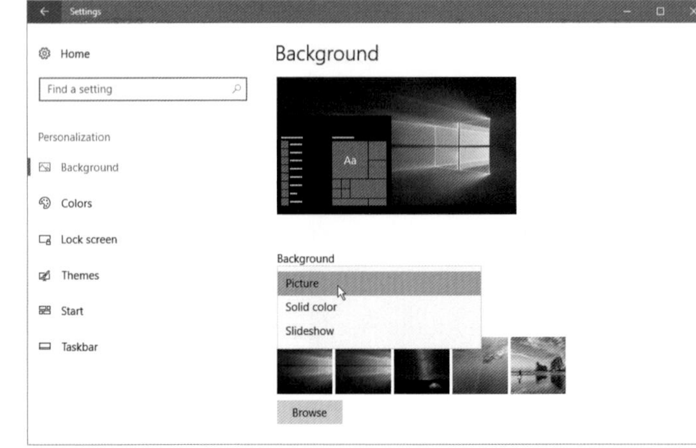

You can click Browse to choose an image from your Pictures folder. Search the web for background wallpapers to suit the resolution of your PC screen.

There is also a drop-down option to create a Slideshow that changes the background image at a frequency of your choice, and you can choose how to fit images on your screen.

The Lock screen, which appears when you boot your PC or when it's sleeping, can be customized in two ways:

Appearance

1. Go to Settings, Personalization then click the **Lock screen** option on the left-hand pane

2. Click the **Background** drop-down and select a picture

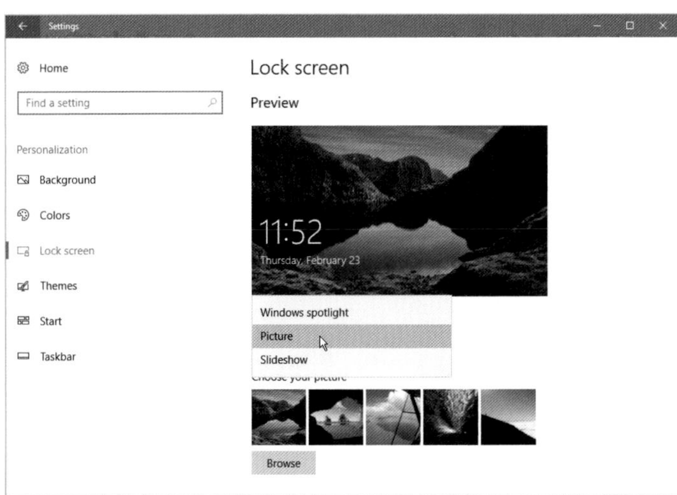

If you are leaving your PC and want to turn on the Windows 10 Lock screen, simply press **WinKey** + **L**.

Notifications

If you look below the default Background images you will see options to change the notifications displayed on the Lock screen.

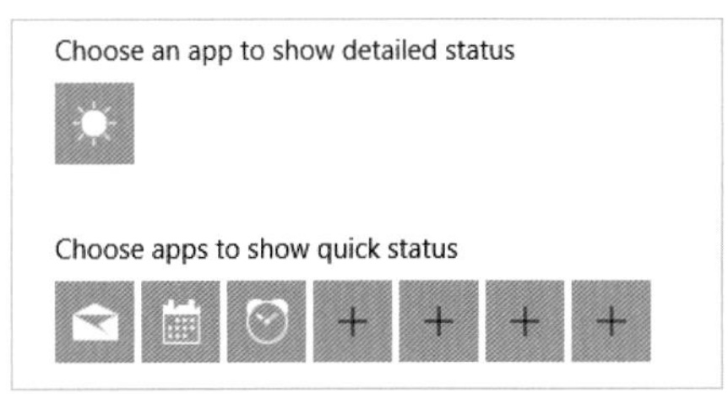

You can use the Lock screen to display useful information. For example, unread emails.

The only app showing a notification on the Lock screen in the picture above is the Weather app. You can add more simply by clicking one of the + add icons.

User settings

The Windows 10 interface provides a range of settings with regard to users. Amongst other things, these include switching accounts and changing account passwords.

Switch accounts

Windows 10 allows two types of account – a Microsoft account, which enables all of Windows 10's features to be used, and a Local account, which has restrictions. To switch from one to the other:

Two types of account can be used with the Windows 10 interface – a Microsoft account and a Local account.

1. On the Start menu, click **Settings** then choose **Accounts**
2. Click the link to **Sign in with a local account instead**

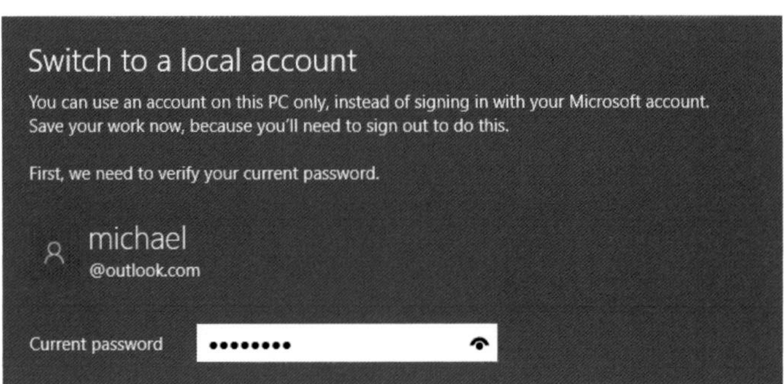

Switch to a local account
You can use an account on this PC only, instead of signing in with your Microsoft account.
Save your work now, because you'll need to sign out to do this.
First, we need to verify your current password.
michael
@outlook.com
Current password

3. In the screen that opens, enter your current password
4. In the next screen, enter a username, password and password hint for the account
5. Click **Sign out and finish** to be taken to the Lock screen, where you must log in with the new account's credentials

The "Switch to a local account" option effectively creates a new user account.

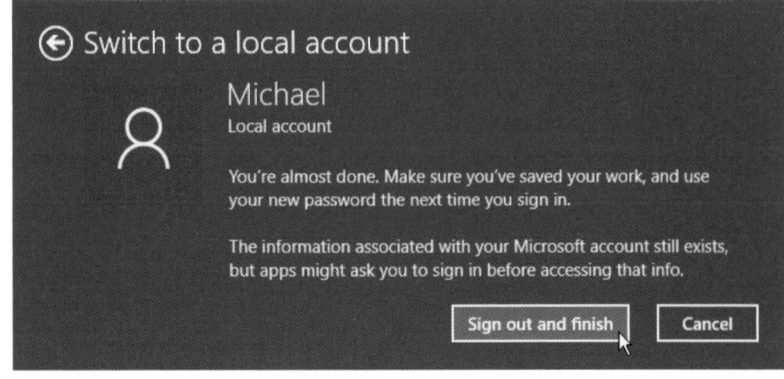

Switch to a local account
Michael
Local account
You're almost done. Make sure you've saved your work, and use your new password the next time you sign in.
The information associated with your Microsoft account still exists, but apps might ask you to sign in before accessing that info.
Sign out and finish
Cancel

Change account password

Should you ever wish to change your account's password, do it as described below:

1. On the Start menu, click **Settings** then choose **Accounts**

2. On the left-hand pane, click the **Sign-in options** item and you will see a **Change** button for your password

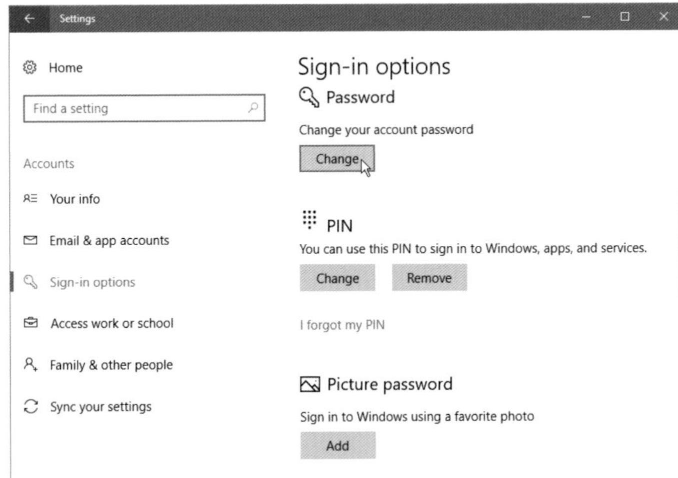

3. Click the button to open the "Change your Microsoft account password" window

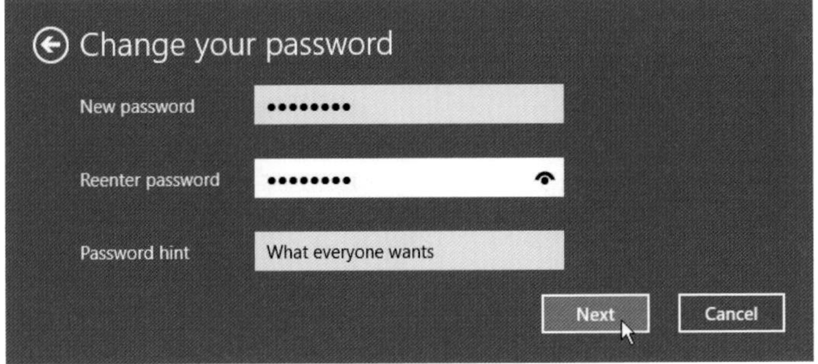

4. Enter your old password, then enter your new password twice and click **Next**

It is recommended that account passwords should have at least eight characters and include digits plus mixed-case letters.

The Windows 10 Creators Update added a **Dynamic lock** feature within Sign-in options, which can detect when you are away from the PC and automatically lock the screen.

Account picture

Should you wish to change your account picture you can choose any image to associate with your identity:

1. Go to Settings, Accounts then click the **Your info** option on the left-hand pane

2. Click the **Browse for one** button and select a picture

Hot tip

You can also click the Camera icon to have your webcam create a photo to use as your account picture if you like.

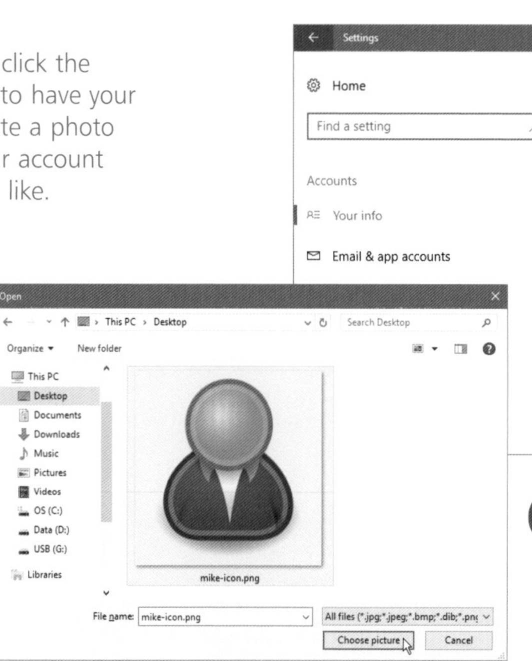

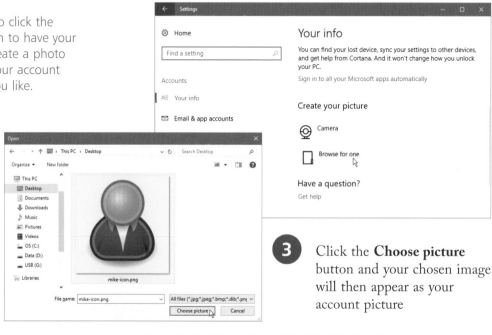

3. Click the **Choose picture** button and your chosen image will then appear as your account picture

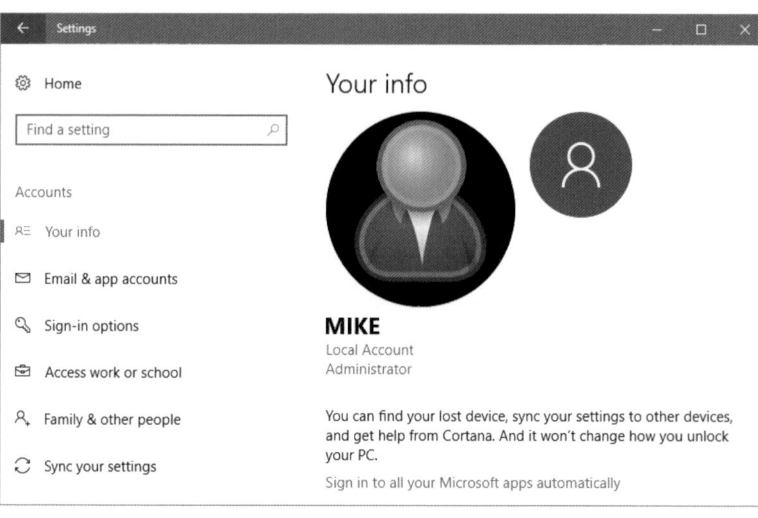

Picture password

Windows 10 allows users to present their login credentials in the form of a picture password rather than a text password. Set this up as follows:

1. On the Start menu, click **Settings** then choose **Accounts**
2. On the left-hand pane, click the **Sign-in options** item and you will see an **Add** button for your picture password
3. Click the button, then verify you are the account holder by entering the existing text password
4. At the next screen, click the **Choose picture** button to open File Explorer in your Pictures folder
5. Choose a suitable image and click the **Open** button
6. Now, click the **Use this picture** button to enter the "Set up your gestures" screen

7. Create three separate marks or gestures on the picture. Each gesture can be a straight line, a circle or a tap

The next time you log in to the PC, you will have the choice of using your text password or the picture password.

Because there are so many possible combinations of pictures and gestures, picture passwords can be more secure than text passwords.

If you make an error when confirming the gestures, hit **Start over**. Windows draws the gestures on the screen as guidelines.

PIN code

PIN (Personal Identification Number) codes are another security feature in Windows 10, and enable users to secure their computer with a four-digit code. You may question the need for this as there are already plenty of security options provided, not to mention the fact that a four-digit code isn't particularly secure anyway.

However, the feature is intended for use in tablets and smartphones, where the small keyboards provided make it difficult to enter a complex alpha-numeric password.

The PIN code feature is primarily intended for use on small touchscreen devices, but can make logging on quicker and simpler on any device.

1. On the Start menu, click **Settings** then choose **Accounts**

2. On the left-hand pane, click the **Sign-in options** item and you will see an **Add** button for your PIN

3. Click the button and enter a four-digit PIN – the PIN code option will now be available at the login screen

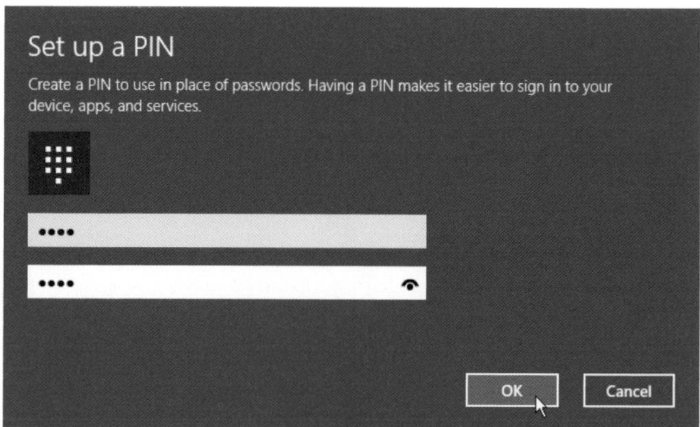

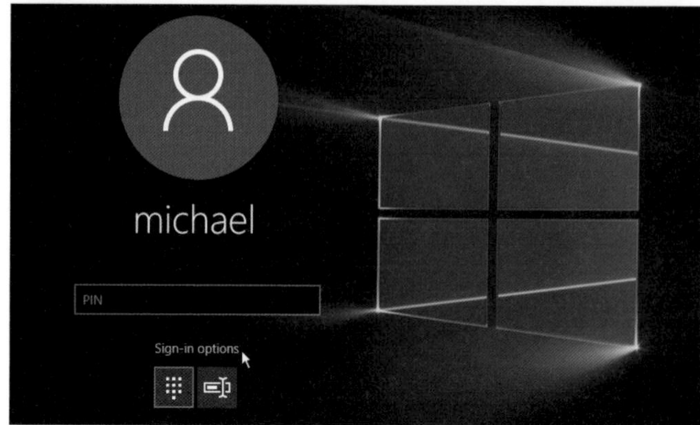

Add a user

An important feature in Windows 10 is the provision for setting up more than one user account. This allows a single PC to be shared by a number of people, each with their own computing environment. The procedure for adding a user is as follows:

When a user is added to a Windows 10 PC, the account type can be either a Local account or a Microsoft account.

1. On the Start menu, click **Settings** then choose **Accounts**

2. On the left-hand pane, click the **Family & other people** item and you will see an **Add someone else to this PC** button for "Other users"

3. Click the button, then enter user details of a Microsoft account, or click the link to enter user details without a Microsoft account then enter the user details

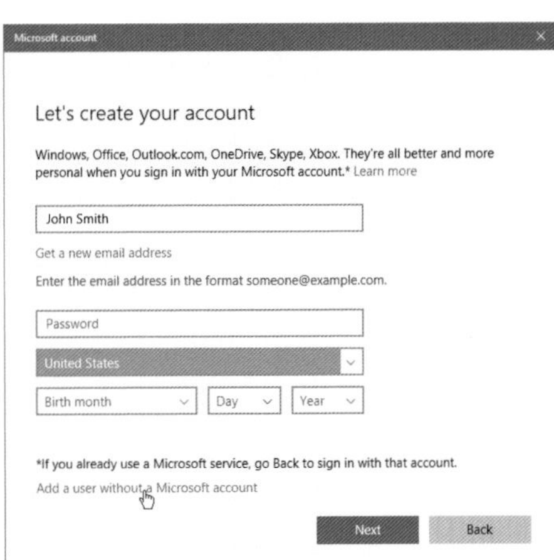

Microsoft account
Let's create your account
Windows, Office, Outlook.com, OneDrive, Skype, Xbox. They're all better and more personal when you sign in with your Microsoft account.* Learn more
John Smith
Get a new email address
Enter the email address in the format someone@example.com.
Password
United States
Birth month
Day
Year
*If you already use a Microsoft service, go Back to sign in with that account.
Add a user without a Microsoft account
Next
Back

4. The user will be added to the "Other people" list and will be able to log in the next time the PC is started

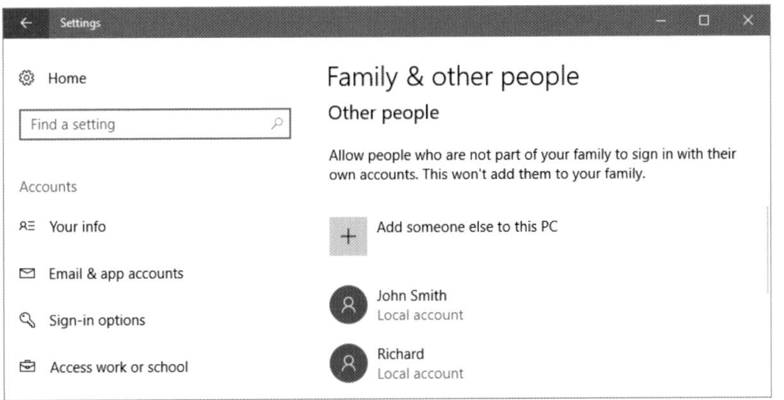

Close Windows 10

Windows 10 offers several ways of closing the system down:

Desktop Mode

Click the  **Start** button, then click the Power button, and choose to "Sleep", "Shut down", or "Restart" from the pop-up menu options.

You can also **Shut down** or **Sign out** from the Power User Menu (see page 110).

Tablet Mode

Click or tap the Power button icon and choose to "Sleep", "Shut down", or "Restart" from the pop-up menu options.

Keyboard

A keyboard command that has been around for a long time is still available in Windows 10. This is **Ctrl** + **Alt** + **Del**. Pressing these keys opens the options screen shown on the right – from where you can access the pop-up menu power options.

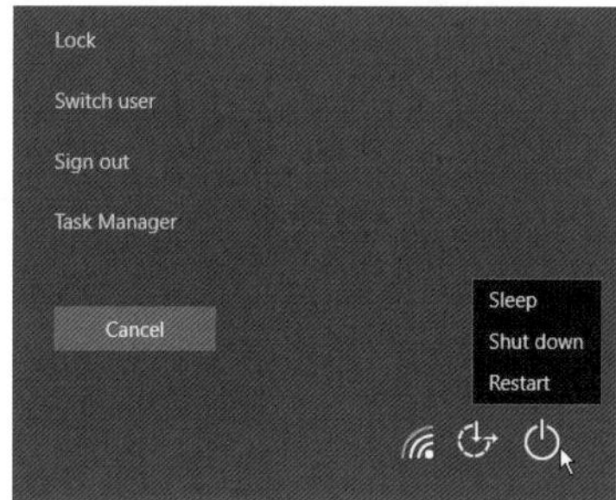

Shutdown/Restart shortcuts

1. Right-click on the Desktop, then select **New**, **Shortcut**
2. Enter **shutdown /s /t 0** as the location, then click **Next**
3. Enter "Shutdown" as the name, then click **Finish**
4. Repeat to create a shortcut named "Restart" with the location of **shutdown /r /t 0**

You will now see Shutdown and Restart tiles on the Start menu.

You can also create a "Sign out" tile using the value **shutdown /l**.

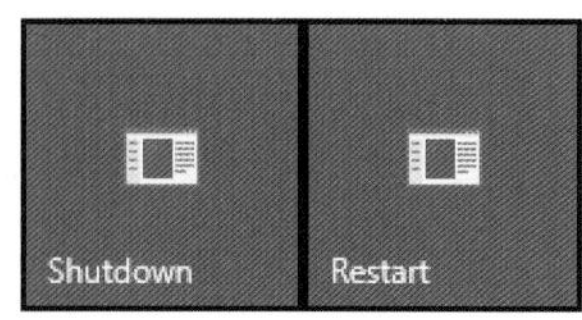

5 Windows 10 apps

Apps are an integral part of the Windows 10 interface. We explain how they work, how to access their options, and show some useful tips. We also review all the apps bundled with Windows 10.

Supplied with Windows 10

Windows 10 comes with lots of pre-installed applications ("apps"). There are familiar traditional programs, such as Notepad, but the A-Z list of apps on the Start menu contains many new "Universal Windows App" programs designed to run on PCs, tablets, and smartphones. The A-Z list of apps looks like this:

- **Alarms & Clock**
- **Calculator**
- **Calendar**
- **Camera**
- **Connect**
- **Cortana**
- **Facebook**
- **Feedback Hub**
- **Get Help**
- **Get Office**
- **Groove Music**
- **Mail**
- **Maps**
- **Messaging**
- **Microsoft Edge**
- **Microsoft Solitaire Collection**
- **Mixed Reality Portal**
- **Movies & TV**
- **OneDrive**
- **OneNote**
- **Paid Wi-Fi & Cellular**
- **Paint 3D**
- **People**
- **Phone**
- **Photos**
- **Settings**
- **Skype**
- **Sticky Notes**
- **Store**
- **Tips**
- **Twitter**
- **View 3D**
- **Voice Recorder**
- **Weather**
- **Windows Accessories** *
- **Windows Administrative Tools** *
- **Windows Defender Security Center**
- **Windows Ease of Access** *
- **Windows Media Player**
- **Windows PowerShell** *
- **Windows System** *
- **Xbox**

Items marked with an * asterisk are folders containing more apps. For example, **Windows Accessories** contains Notepad, Paint, WordPad, Internet Explorer, and many more.

Several of the bundled apps require the user to be logged in with a Microsoft account.

Universal Windows Apps are new in Windows 10 and are intended to provide a common experience across many devices.

If you need apps not supplied with Windows 10, you can find many more apps at the Windows Store.

Start apps

We will take a brief look at some of the pre-installed apps – the ones not covered here will be reviewed in later chapters.

People

Windows operating systems have always provided a contact manager, which provided a useful means of keeping phone numbers, addresses, etc. in one place. However, the advent of social media websites, such as Twitter, Facebook and LinkedIn, has seen this type of information stored and used in new ways.

The **People** app is Microsoft's attempt to update its old Contacts manager to make it relevant to today's needs. It stores the data from your contacts in a cloud-based location, which means they can be accessed from anywhere in the world, via any of your Windows 10 devices.

Furthermore, the app amalgamates data from all supported networks. Thus, people who use more than one social network will be recognized by the app as being the same person, and all their data, whatever the source, is presented as a single contact link.

The People app also integrates with other Universal Windows Apps. So from the People app, you can send emails via the Mail app, map addresses with the Maps app, and more.

Skype

This app replaces the Messaging app provided with Windows 8. It allows you to make audio and video calls to other **Skype** users on almost any device, pretty much anywhere in the world, for free.

It is also possible to share files, photos, and web page links with people you're chatting with. When you sign in to the app, all your contacts from the old Messaging app are automatically added to your existing list of contacts.

The **Skype** app is a new Universal Windows App introduced in the Windows 10 Creators Update.

Calendar

An updated version of a traditional Microsoft application, the **Calendar** app doesn't really offer anything new. It has been designed to be easy to read, and free of unnecessary distractions.

To this end, by default, the content displayed is kept to a minimum. Ease of navigation has been improved, there is a simple interface for adding events, many notification options, and some good advanced scheduling options.

Calendar syncs with Hotmail, Outlook, and Google accounts to bring all your events together for easy viewing.

The **Maps** app was improved in the Windows 10 Creators Update to allow you to organize your favorites and save places in collections.

Maps

Windows 10's **Maps** app is a particularly useful app. You can enter any address using its Search option and the app will attempt to produce a map showing that location and a street view photo if available. If the address is found by the app, you can get directions from a starting point of your choice to that address, and discover nearby hotels, coffee shops, restaurants, stores, and museums.

The Directions option lets you seek directions between any two points of your choice, and you can store your maps using the Favorites option.

There is also a 3D Cities option that provides aerial photographic views that you can zoom, tilt, and rotate.

Location must be enabled in **Settings** > **Privacy** > **Location**, for Directions to work.

Weather

The **Weather** app provides several menu options. The Home screen displays weather conditions for the current location. This includes an overview, an hourly breakdown, and a range of weather-related details.

The Maps option shows a temperature map of your location and the Historical Weather option displays a graph of past monthly temperature and rainfall at your location.

The Places option allows more locations to be selected to create a Favorite Places list so that multiple locations can be monitored in addition to those displayed on the Home screen.

A News option displays weather-related news items from around the world, describing typhoons, earthquakes, etc.

The **Get Help** app is new in the Windows 10 Creators Update and makes it easy to get help directly from a Microsoft Answer Tech.

Get Help

The **Get Help** app aims to provide direct assistance from Microsoft. Its **Accounts & Billing** category provides links to manage your Microsoft account, seek information for Xbox, Skype, or Windows Phone billing queries. It also provides access to get help via Online Chat or Scheduled Call to a Microsoft Answer Tech.

The **Technical support** and **Setting up** categories provide links to seek help on Windows installation, settings, activation, errors, performance, and security issues. There are links to seek answers from the Microsoft Community forum, and via Online Chat or Scheduled Call to a Microsoft Answer Tech.

These popular apps, which were previously bundled with Windows 10 by default, may now be absent from your A-Z apps list – but they can be easily installed using the Store app:

The new Universal Windows Apps of **Money**, **Weather**, **Sports**, and **News** provide the latest information on any device, wherever you are.

Sports

Updated content in real-time is provided by the MSN **Sports** app. It is dynamic, and provides an edition related to your location. For example, the US edition is devoted to popular American sports such as Football, Basketball, Baseball, Ice Hockey, Golf, and Soccer. The My Favorites option allows you to choose your Favorite Teams and Favorite Sports to follow more closely. Drilling down enables you to access detailed information such as the latest team news, results, fixture lists, and leading players.

News

Most people like to keep abreast of what's happening both in their locality and on the world stage. The MSN **News** app provides the conduit and, like the Sports app, provides an edition related to your location. For example, the US edition is devoted to American news items. The Home screen displays My News items with tabs for categories of news you can customize using the Interests menu option. The Local option allows you to receive items of local news from a location of your choice, and the Videos option shows a selection of recent news videos from the internet.

Money

The MSN **Money** app provides a wealth of finance-related information, with various menu options providing different types of data. You can drill down into items of interest to get detailed information.

When a news story is clicked in the **Money**, **Weather**, **Sports**, or **News** app it opens up the website that provides it in the app window.

The Markets option and World Markets option provide up-to-date stock, commodities, and bond market data. A Watchlist option provides a customizable list of companies you may want to follow closely. Information that can be monitored includes stock market performance (current and historic), revenue, profit, company profile, and more.

The Currencies option provides a handy Currency Converter and up-to-date exchange rates of world currencies. There is also a Mortgage Calculator option to calculate monthly payments.

App options

In addition to options provided on an app's toolbar, Windows 10 apps offer a range of options on a drop-down menu from a "hamburger button": ☰. Let's start by adding a favorite app to a custom Start group.

A good way to open the Start menu is to simply press the WinKey.

1. To add any app to a Start group, first click on the Start button, then find the app in the alphabetical list

2. Next, right-click on the app item to open a context menu, and choose the **Pin to Start** option

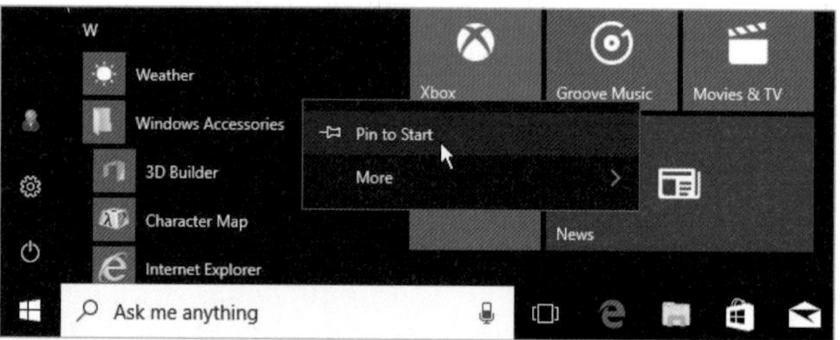

To arrange your Start menu groups, use the ═ icon at the right-hand side of a Start group title bar to drag that group.

3. Click the group title bar above the app icon that has been added to the Start group, and enter a custom group name

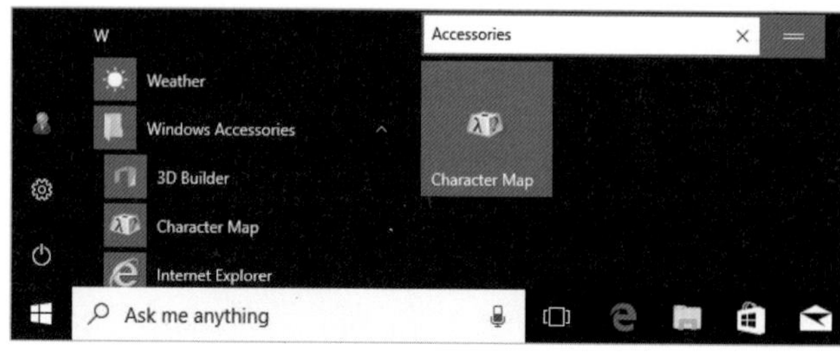

You can open a context menu of options by right-clicking on any app icon in a Start group. With an open app, clicking the app window's "hamburger button" reveals a list of options for that app. The app's Settings button can reveal settings options.

4. Launch an app (say, Weather) from the Start menu, then click the app's hamburger button to see the app's options

Windows can display apps in full-screen, or the window can be resized to display the app in a small floating window.

5. Click the Settings button to reveal the settings options

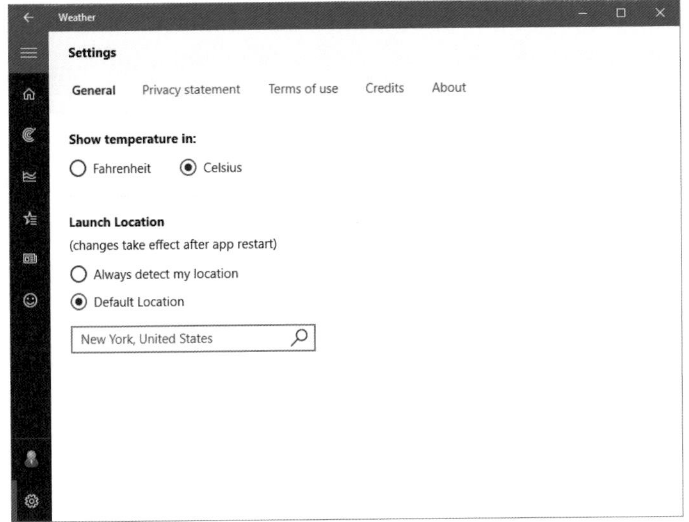

App options offered are related to each particular app in use.

App switcher & Task list

The Windows 10 App switcher can be used to quickly switch between running apps. It displays all running apps on the Desktop so you can easily select the one you want to work with. The App switcher is launched using a keyboard shortcut of **WinKey** + **Tab**.

"WinKey" refers to the Windows key. This is usually located close to the space bar (see page 59).

1. Open the App switcher by pressing **WinKey** + **Tab**

2. Tap or click to select the app you want to work with, or press **WinKey** + **Tab** again to close the App switcher

Alternatively, you can quickly select a running app to work with from a Task list. This, too, displays all running apps on the Desktop so you can easily select the one you want to work with. The Task list is launched using a keyboard shortcut with **Alt** and **Tab** keys.

3. Open the **Task list** by holding down the **Alt** key and pressing the **Tab** key once

When using the Task list, you can also select programs with the arrow keys.

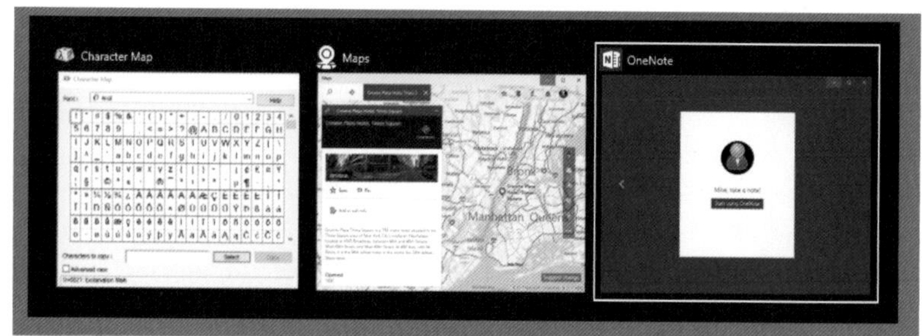

4. Keep the **Alt** key depressed and tap the **Tab** key to move through the list. When the focus is on the app you want to work with, release the **Alt** key to select that app

Snap apps

Windows 10 apps can run full-screen. With the large wide-screen monitors available today, many users will find it irritating to have their entire desktop real-estate taken up by just one program.

To address this issue, Windows 10 offers a feature called Snap, which enables users to run up to four apps side-by-side. The actual number depends on the monitor's resolution. Resolutions of 2,560 x 1,440 pixels can snap four apps. Resolutions of less than this will only be able to snap two or three apps.

For the Windows Snap feature to work, the device must have a screen width of at least 1,366 pixels. If you are having problems, check this out by going to Control Panel, Display, Adjust Resolution.

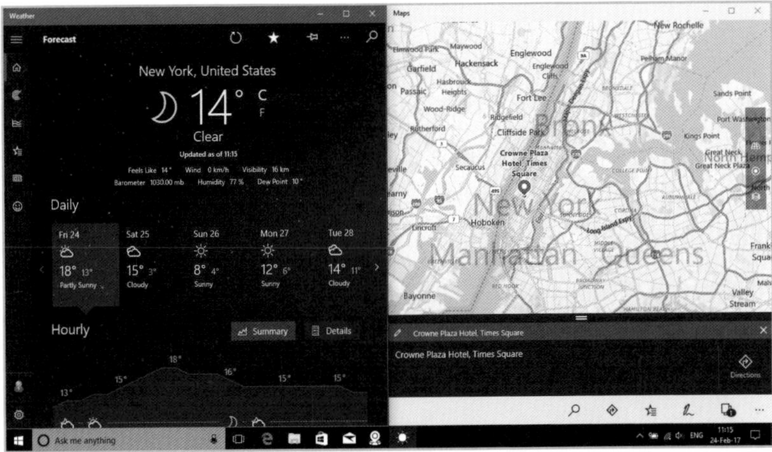

Here, two apps are snapped – the Weather app and the Maps app

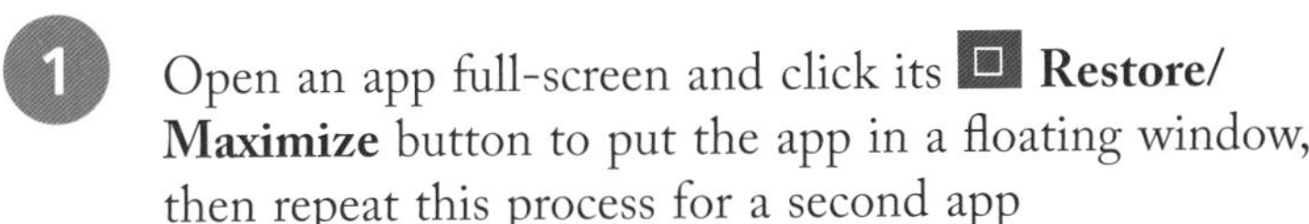
1. Open an app full-screen and click its ☐ **Restore/ Maximize** button to put the app in a floating window, then repeat this process for a second app

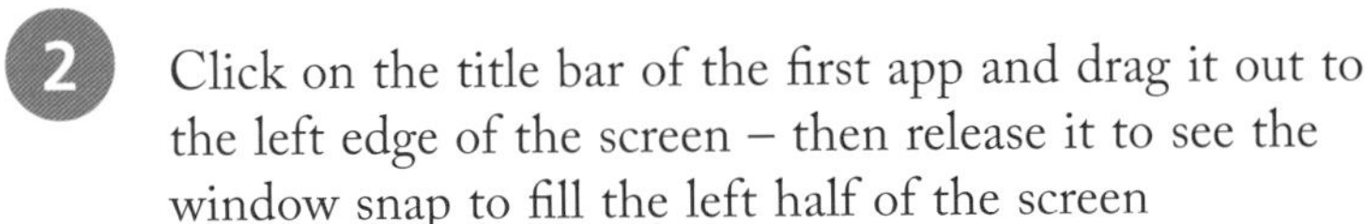
2. Click on the title bar of the first app and drag it out to the left edge of the screen – then release it to see the window snap to fill the left half of the screen

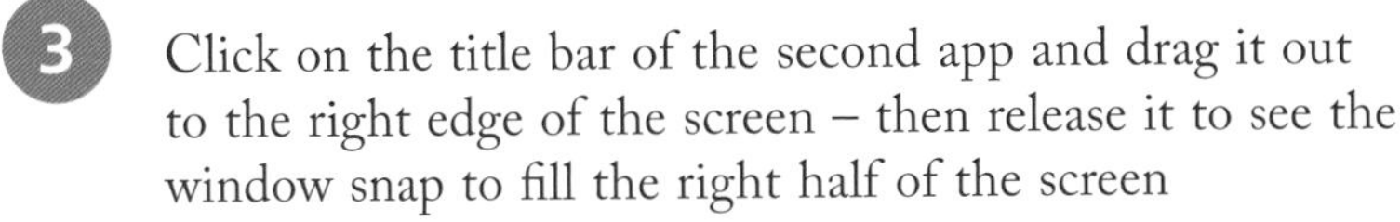
3. Click on the title bar of the second app and drag it out to the right edge of the screen – then release it to see the window snap to fill the right half of the screen

In addition to snapping apps to the left and right, Windows 10 lets you snap in a third and fourth app if the screen resolution allows it.

Close apps

Closing an app is very simple to do, but it must be pointed out that usually it is not actually necessary to close apps. This is because when a new app is opened, other running apps are switched to a state of suspension in which they use very little in the way of system resources.

However, there may be situations in which it is desirable or even necessary to close down an app. Here are five ways to do this:

Most of the time it is not necessary to shut an app down. Due to the way that Windows 10 minimizes the system resources required by apps that aren't being used, you can, in fact, have a whole bunch of apps running at the same time without any noticeable degradation of system performance.

- Simply press **Alt** + **F4** – this kills the app instantly.
- Click the Close button on the window bar.

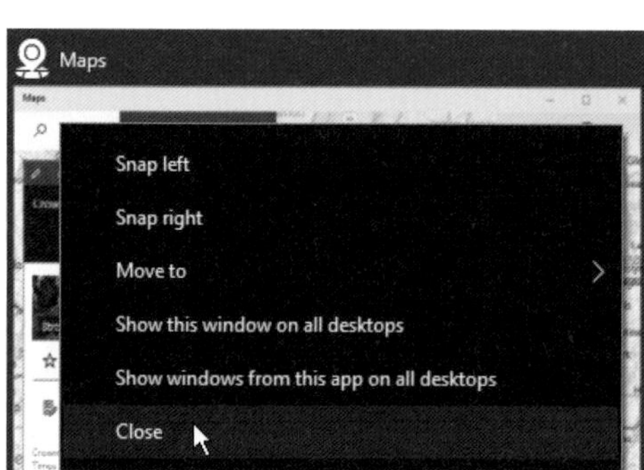

- Right-click the app in **App Switcher** and select **Close**.

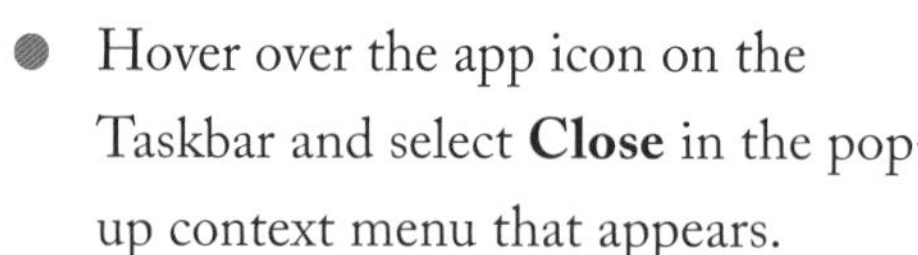

- Hover over the app icon on the Taskbar and select **Close** in the pop-up context menu that appears.

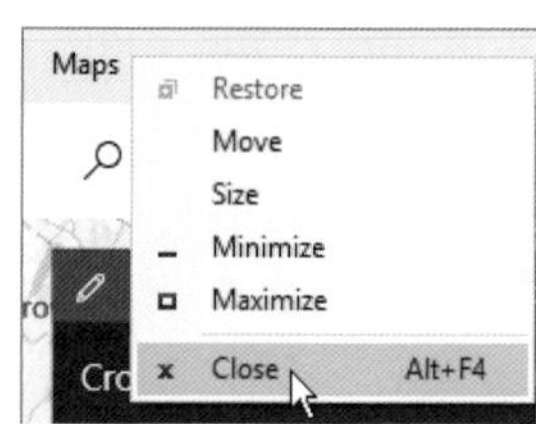

- Press **Ctrl** + **Shift** + **Esc** to open the Task Manager, then select the app on the Processes tab and click the **End task** button.

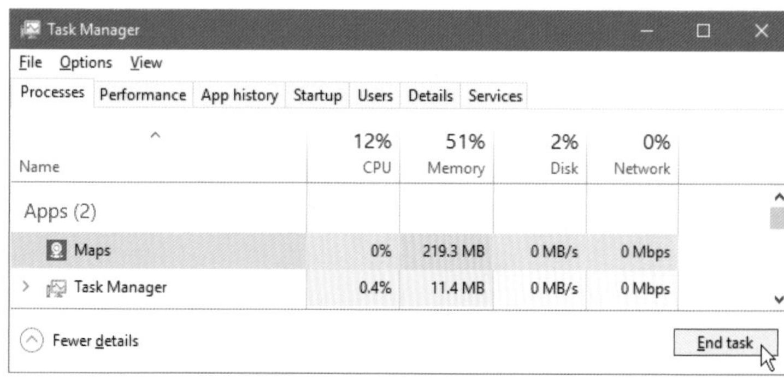

Get Office

The Get Office app lets you easily manage a Microsoft Office subscription. It is also a hub that provides buttons to easily install Office apps or to open Office apps you have already installed. Additionally, the hub provides a list of Office documents you've recently used, and other useful features:

The previous version of the **Get Office** app simply pointed to the Office 365 website, but the app was improved in the Windows 10 Creators Update to provide a much more useful hub.

1. Launch the Get Office app and select **Programs** in the left-hand pane

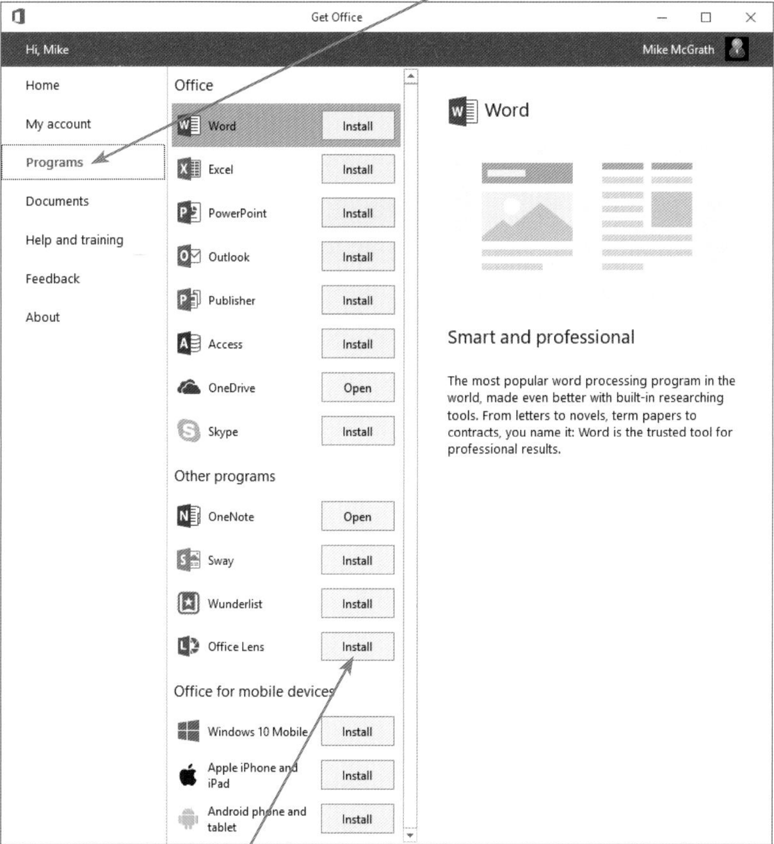

2. Click any button to install or open an app

3. In the left-hand pane, click **Documents** to see a list of Office documents you have recently used

4. Click **My account** to manage your Office subscription

You can also install Office for mobile devices via the Get Office hub.

Paint 3D

Paint 3D is a new app introduced in the Creators Update of Windows 10.

The **Paint 3D** app allows you to create and work with 3D objects and scenes. It also lets you share your 3D art with others via the online Remix 3D community. You can import and edit 3D objects created by fellow community members to build new models and scenes within the Paint 3D app.

The interface of the Paint 3D app comprises a toolbar, workspace, and right-hand pane that displays a collection of items according to the currently selected toolbar button:

The Time machine feature records every change you make to the object so you can rewind to start over from any previous point.

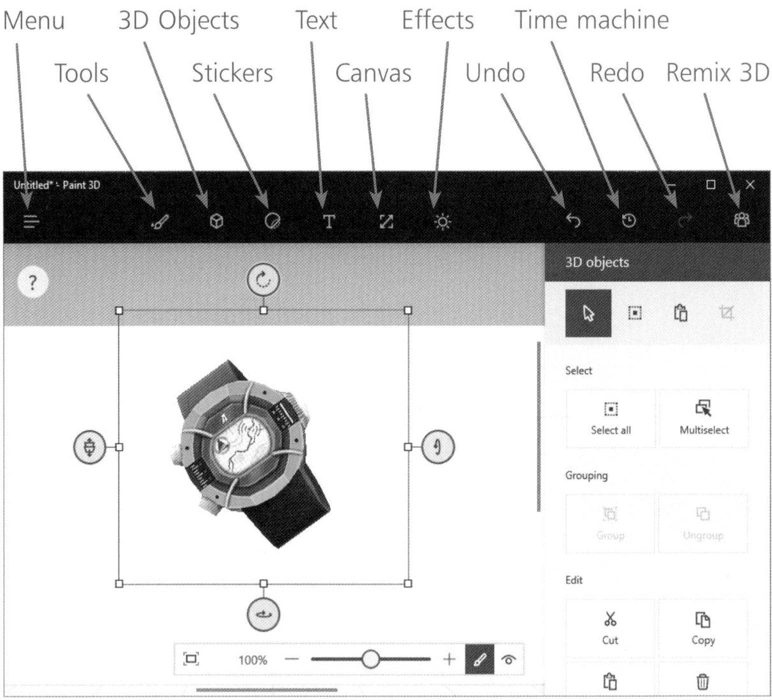

Select primary objects from the 3D Objects group, then decorate them using Tools, Text, or Stickers – a variety of textures that automatically map to the 3D surface.

An object selected on the canvas gets surrounded by a box with handles on each side. Three of the handles will rotate the object in space. The fourth handle, at the 9 o'clock position, will bring the object closer or further away from you. Multiple objects can be added to the canvas then grouped together to maintain their relative positions when the 3D model is rotated.

The hamburger menu button on the toolbar allows you to publish your 3D art in the Remix 3D community, export it as a 2D image in the popular file formats PNG, JPEG, BMP, GIF, and TIFF, or export it as a 3D image in the 3MF file format.

Windows 10 includes the **View 3D** app that is used to view 3D objects in the 3MF file format. This has a Turntable feature that automatically rotates the 3D model through 360 degrees:

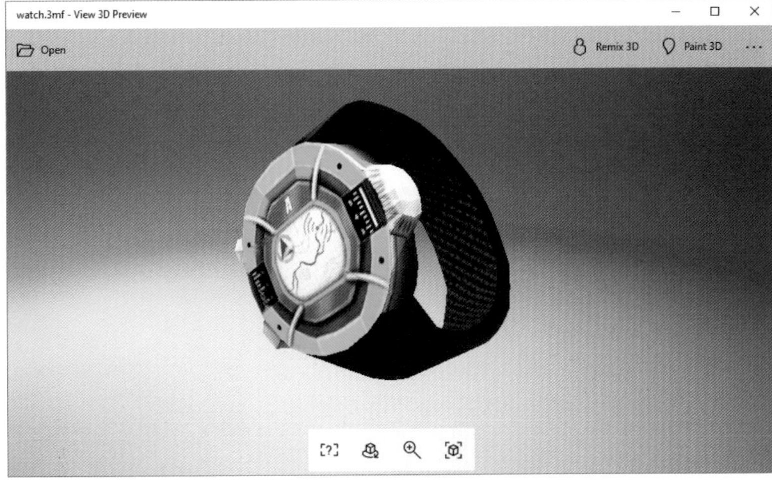

View 3D is a new app introduced in the Creators Update of Windows 10.

3D image files can be huge. Remix 3D has a publish limit of 64MB at the time of writing.

Windows 10 also includes the **3D Builder** app that can print 3D objects in the 3MF file format, using a 3D printer:

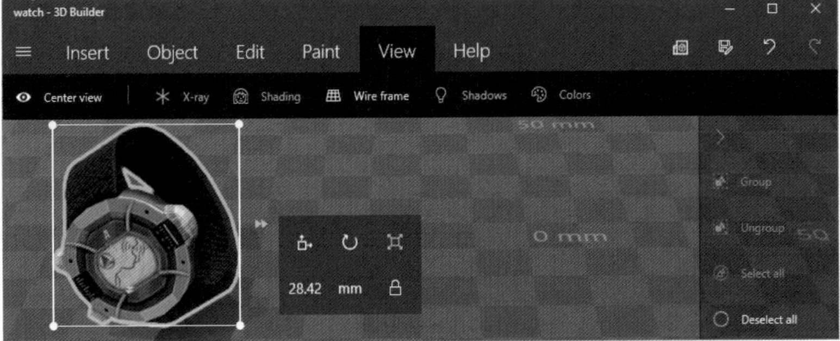

Dremel 3D printer.

Fans of mixed reality will be able to virtually place objects created in Paint 3D within the real world when viewed through a mixed reality headset, such as Microsoft's HoloLens headset.

Windows Ink Workspace

Windows 10 has a Windows Ink Workspace that is primarily intended for users of a digital pen on tablet devices. This feature provides Sticky Notes, Sketchpad, and Screen Sketch pen applications – but these can also be used without a digital pen. Sticky Notes simply allows you to jot down a quick note:

Don't forget

You can use the OneNote app for more extensive note-taking.

1. Right-click on the System Tray, then choose **Show Windows Ink Workspace button** to add this button to the tray

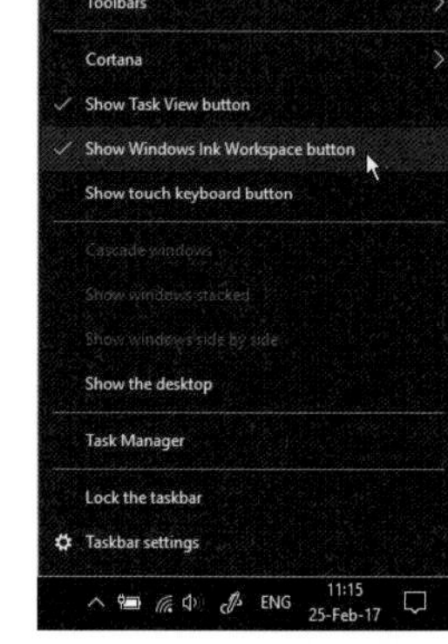

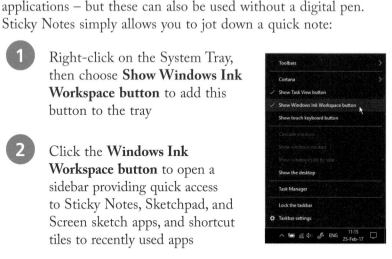

2. Click the **Windows Ink Workspace button** to open a sidebar providing quick access to Sticky Notes, Sketchpad, and Screen sketch apps, and shortcut tiles to recently used apps

3. Select **Sticky Notes** to open a new blank note on which you can jot down a note with a digital pen or your keyboard

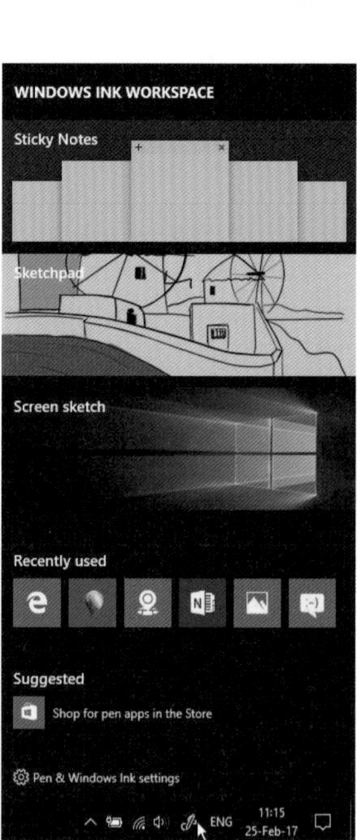

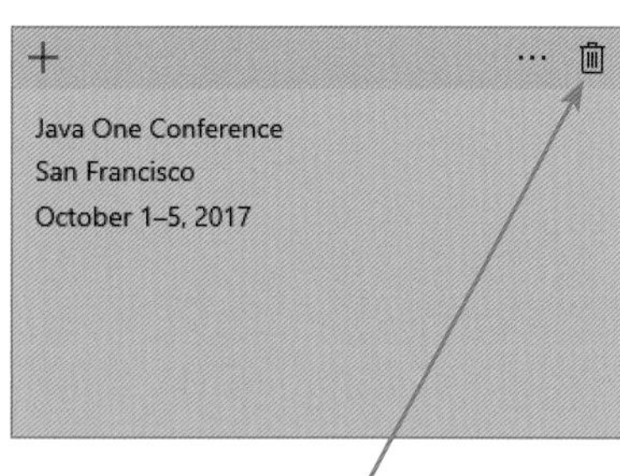

Hot tip

Discover much more on the Sticky Notes app on pages 125-127.

4. Click the trash can button to delete the note

Sketchpad

Sketchpad is a digital whiteboard that has options for different writing styles with thin pencils, colored pens, and highlighters. There are also nifty ruler and protractor tools to draw straight lines, arcs, and circles – just place the pen on the edge and draw:

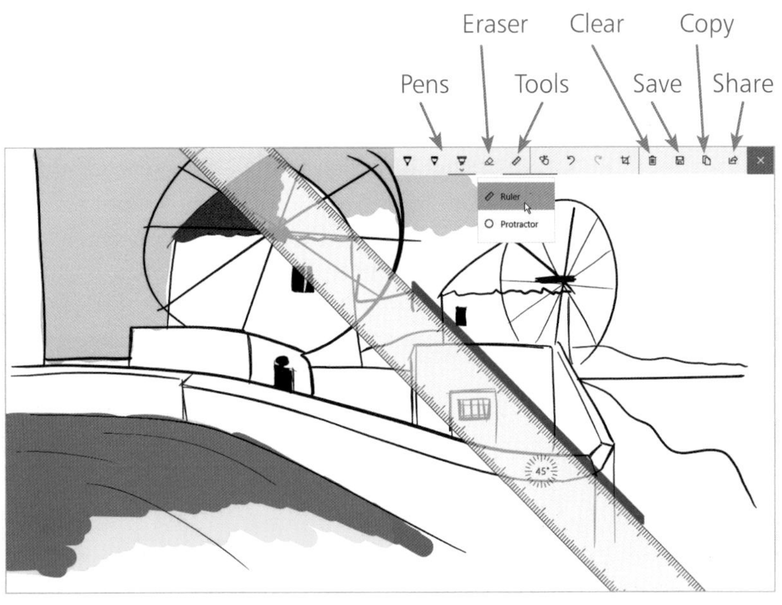

Sketchpad was improved in the Creators Update of Windows 10 with the introduction of the protractor tool.

Screen sketch

Screen sketch enables you to mark up your current screen, as it displays a screenshot and provides a selection of drawing tools similar to those in Sketchpad:

If you just want to capture your screen, simply use the **PrtScn** (Print Screen) key on your keyboard or use **Alt** + **PrtScn** to capture the current window.

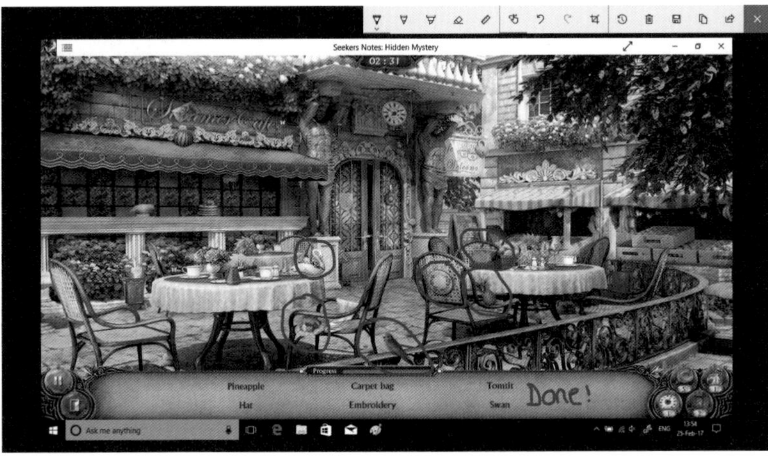

The Creators Update of Windows 10 added a new screenshot feature. Press **WinKey** + **Shift** + **S**, then drag the cursor to define a region of the screen to copy onto the clipboard.

Screenshots marked up in Screen sketch and Sketchpad whiteboards can be saved as an image file or sent to others using the Share button on their toolbars.

OneDrive

OneDrive

OneDrive is a Microsoft facility that allows users to store data in the Cloud via a Microsoft account. To get started, click the OneDrive item on the Start menu and log in with your Microsoft account (if you don't have an account you will need to create one). You will then be asked to choose which folders on your PC you wish to synchronize on OneDrive. Your selection now appears under the OneDrive category on your PC, marked with green check mark icons when they have been synchronized.

Hot tip

A OneDrive account can be accessed in two ways – directly from a web browser and via the OneDrive app. More options are available when it is accessed via a browser.

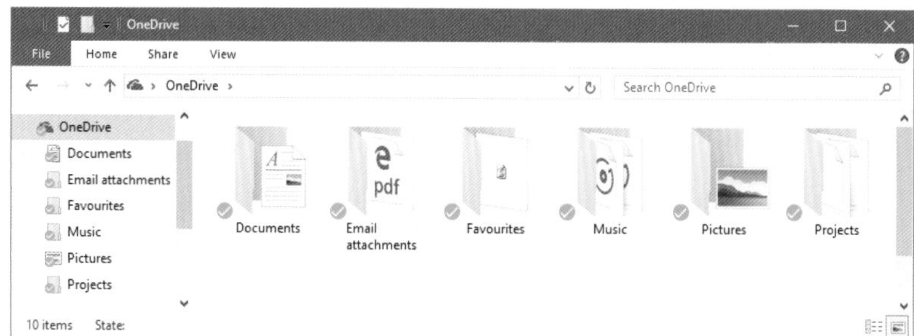

Copies of content added to these local folders are automatically uploaded to your online OneDrive folder to synchronize photos, documents, etc. across devices such as PCs, smartphones, and tablets. Your content can be accessed from anywhere using the OneDrive app on a device or by browsing to **onedrive.live.com** You can create **New** online folders and add files, or **Upload** folders and files to the online OneDrive folder from your device.

OneDrive is more important than ever in Windows 10, as it seeks convergence for all devices to make your data available to you wherever you may be.

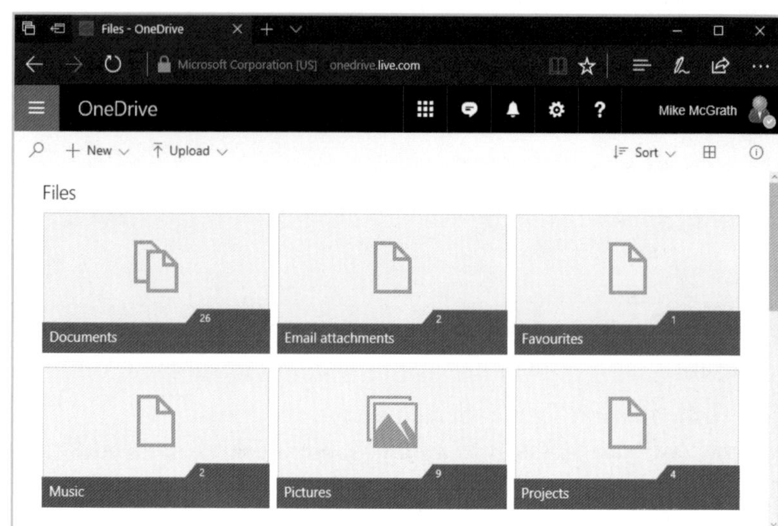

6 Desktop and Taskbar

You can control how Windows 10 displays text and graphics at the right size. You can also take advantage of multiple monitors and choose a Desktop theme with the style, appearance and features that most appeal to you.

Switching Desktops

Windows 10 has a virtual Desktop feature called "Task View". This allows you to have multiple Desktops so you can spread out various projects, so that each project is on a separate Desktop. When you need to jump from one project to another you can just switch Desktops and everything is right there waiting for you – no need to minimize and maximize windows to get back to work:

You can also access Task View by pressing **WinKey** + **Tab**.

1. Click the button on the Taskbar to access the Task View feature – thumbnail icons of all running apps and a **+ New Desktop** button appear on the screen

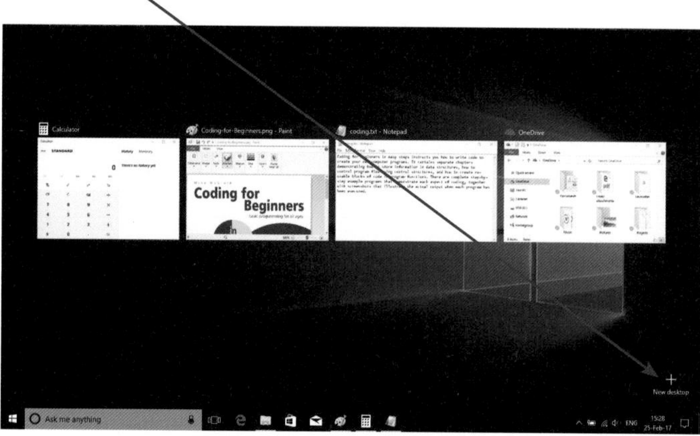

Virtual Desktops have been available in other operating systems for quite some time, but are new in Windows 10.

2. Next, click the **+ New Desktop** button – thumbnails of the original Desktop and one more Desktop appear in a bar across the bottom of the screen

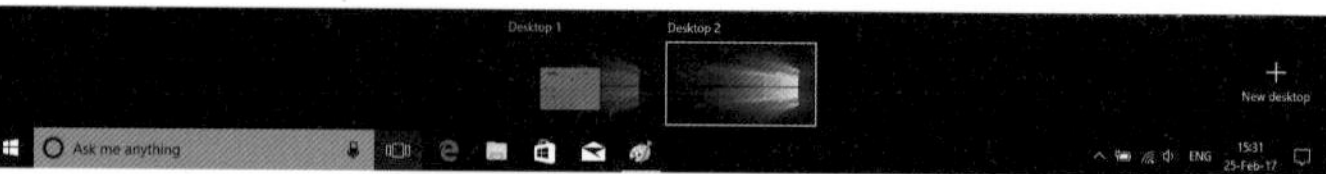

In Task View you can move between Desktops by holding down **Ctrl** + **WinKey** then pressing the left- or right-arrow keys.

3. Each Desktop thumbnail has a pop-up X button you can use to close that Desktop

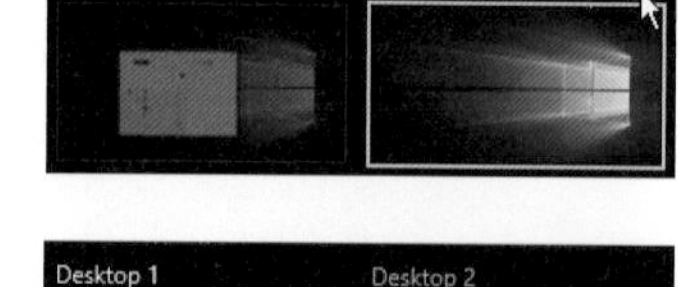

4. Select any Desktop thumbnail to switch to that Desktop, where you can open apps, or move open apps from one Desktop to another

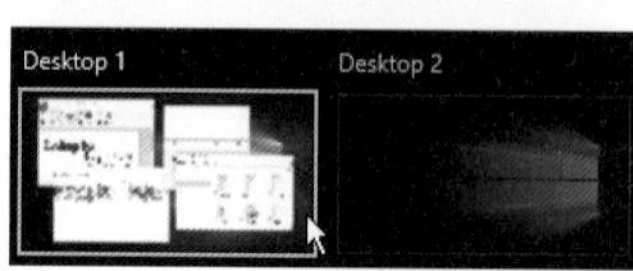

5. In Task View, right-click on the thumbnail icon of an open app you want to move, then select **Move to** and choose a Desktop from the context menu

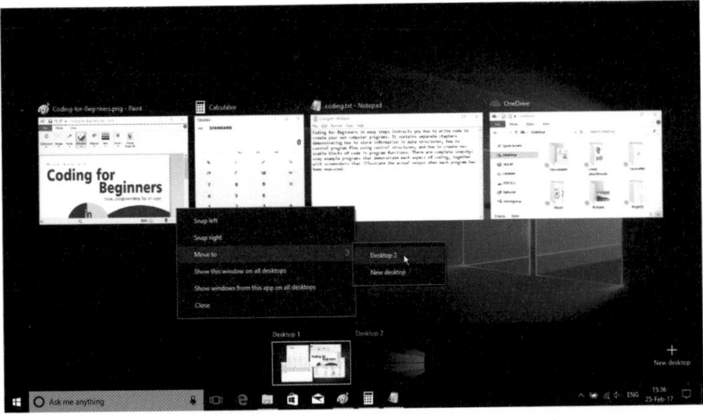

When you close a Desktop, all open apps on that Desktop automatically move to another existing Desktop.

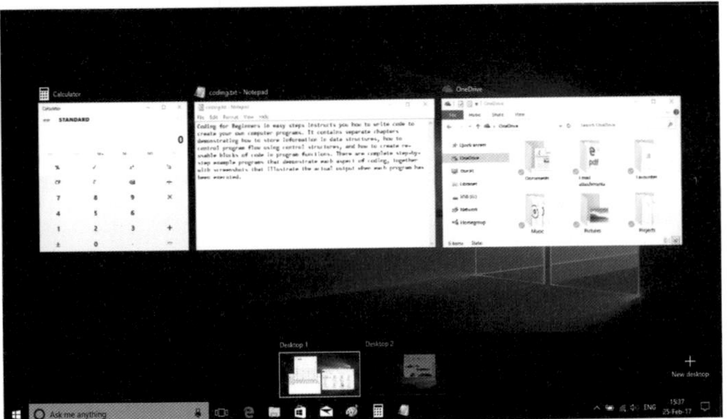

You can click an app thumbnail to switch to the Desktop in which it is open and activate the app, or click the Task View button once more to exit the feature.

Launching apps

There are various ways of launching an application:

Start menu/Desktop icons

Start menu items and Desktop icons are actually shortcuts that link to a program's executable file. So, to launch an app, just click on the menu item or Desktop icon – this activates the app, which then opens on the screen.

You can launch any program on the PC from the Search box.

Taskbar icons

Icons on the Taskbar are application shortcuts as well. Click one, and the associated application will open on the Desktop.

Search box

Applications that are located on the Start menu, Desktop, or Taskbar are easy to locate – they are literally right in front of your eyes. How about programs you can't see, though?

The Taskbar Search box is new in Windows 10.

Windows 10's Search box is the answer:

1. Enter the name of the app in the Search box
2. Choose the appropriate app from the search results

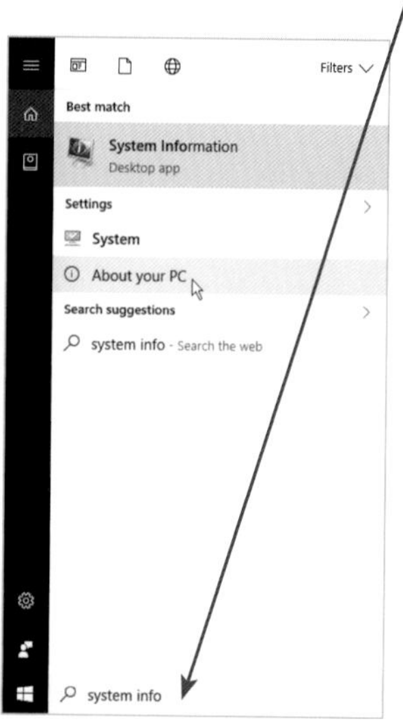

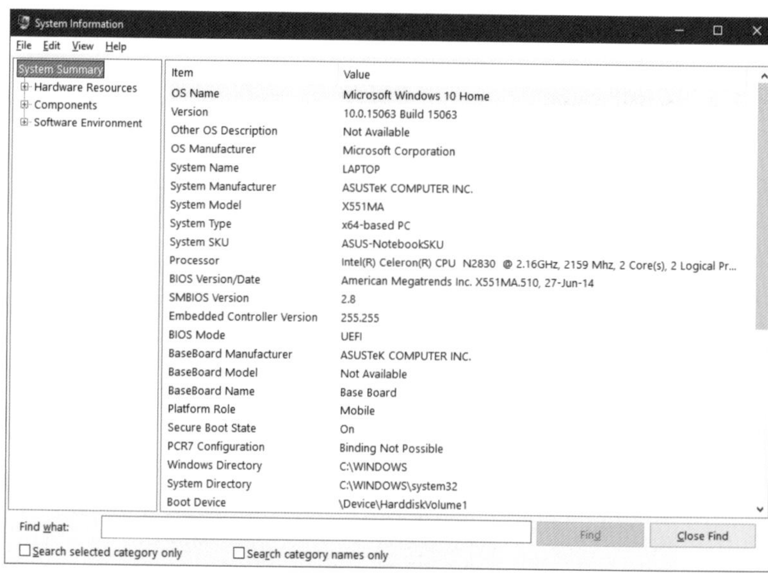

Personalize

You can give your computer a personal touch by changing the computer's window color, sounds, Desktop background, screen saver, and many other aspects. You can change the attributes individually, or select a pre-configured theme:

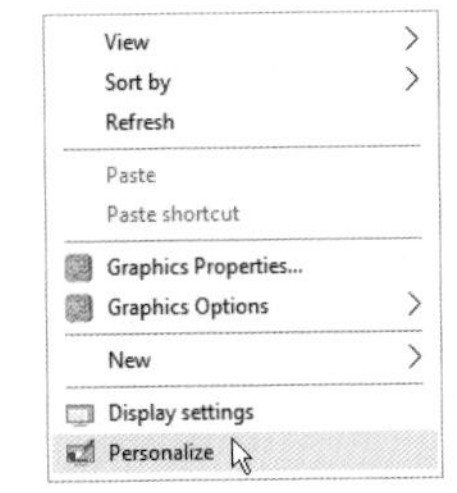

1. Right-click the Desktop and select **Personalize** to open a Settings screen

2. Choose **Themes** on the left-hand pane to see the currently selected theme

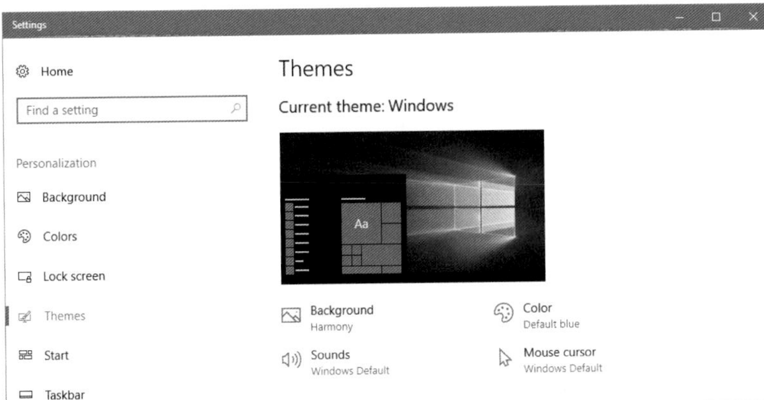

3. Scroll down to see other available themes and select one to see it get immediately applied to your PC

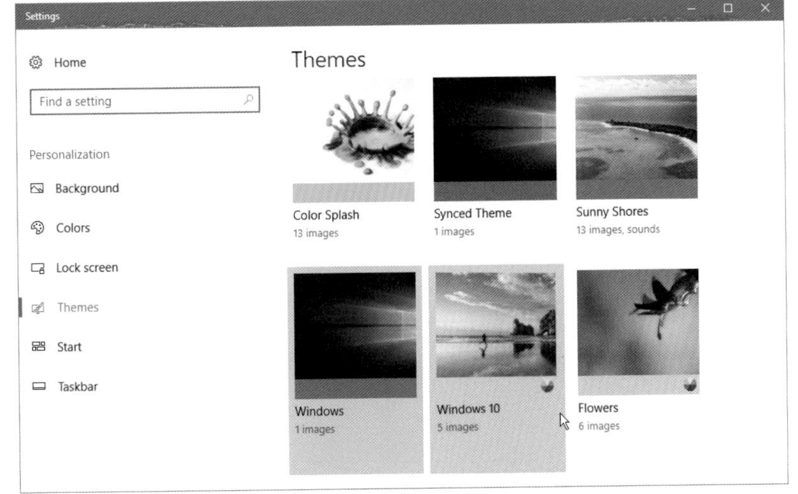

You can click the **Get more themes in the Store** link on the Personalization, Themes screen to add more great themes to your PC (see page 24).

There's no screen saver included in most themes since they already include a varying background. However, you can add a screen saver to any theme.

...cont'd

In the example below, one of the standard Windows 10 themes has been selected:

There will be a theme for the location appropriate to your installed version, for example, USA or UK.

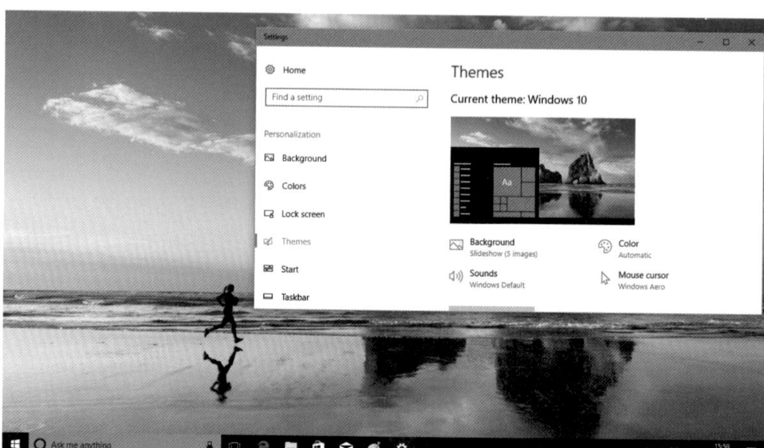

If you don't like the background image of a particular theme, right-click the Desktop, then select **Personalize** and click **Background** to choose another.

To retain the previous accent for icons and tiles, select **Colors** then turn off the option to "Automatically pick an accent color from my background". Below, we see the Windows 10 theme as above, but now with a different background and accent color.

If your selected theme has a slideshow background, by default the images will advance every 30 minutes – but you can adjust the timing and select random images.

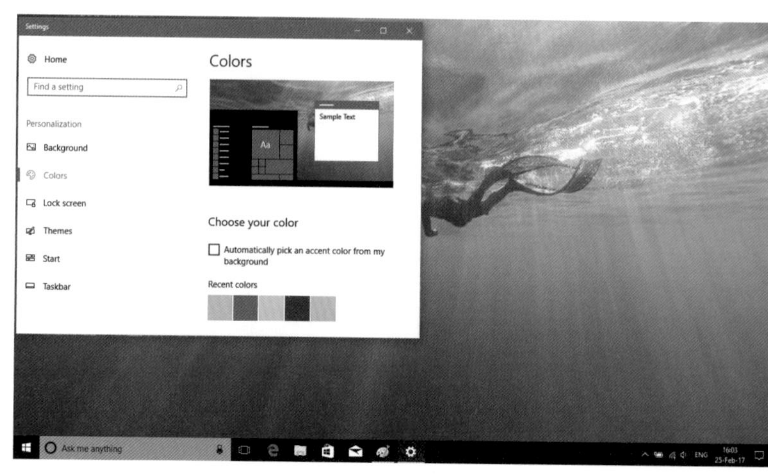

Create a theme

1. Right-click the Desktop and select **Background** on the Personalization screen

2. Next, click **Browse** and select the background image required, then click the **Choose picture** button

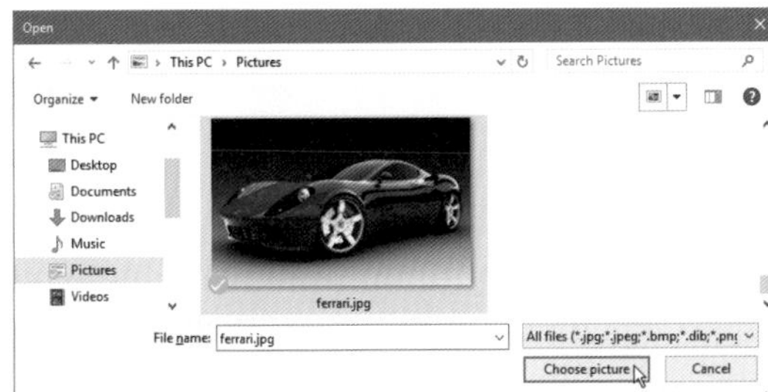

3. The selected image now appears in the Preview area

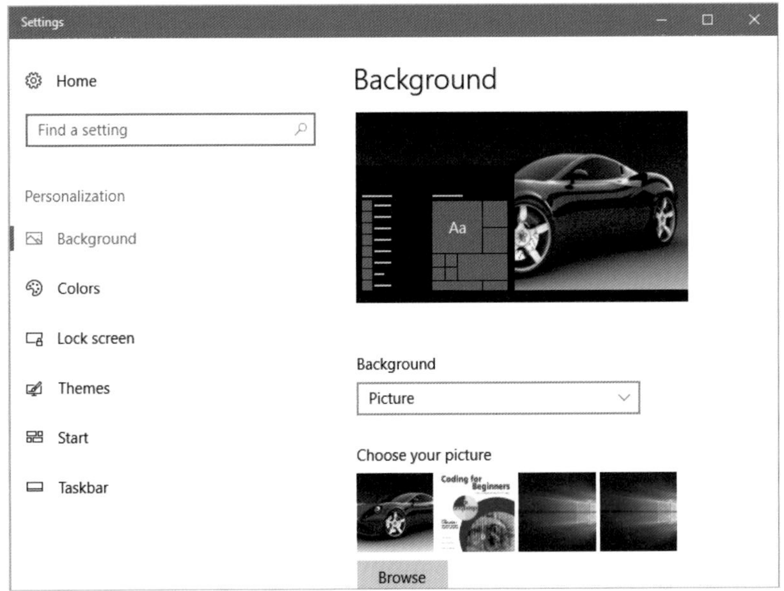

To create your own theme, start with an existing theme, the Windows 10 theme for example, and revise its components.

You can select **Slideshow** in the Background drop-down menu, then choose a selection of pictures and set the timing option to create a changing background for your theme.

...cont'd

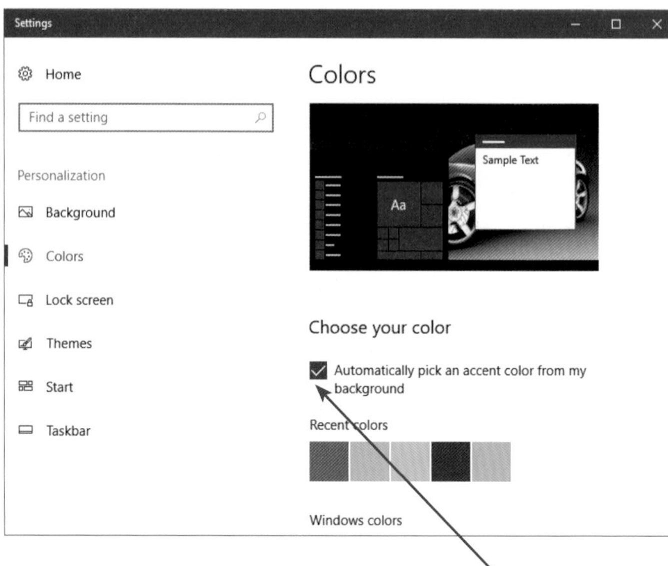

The modified theme is added to the My Themes section, as an unsaved theme.

4. Select **Colors** and turn **On** the option to "Automatically pick an accent color from my background" for color tiles

5. Adjust the other toggle buttons for color and transparency on the Start menu, Taskbar, and Action Center. Your changes appear in the Preview area and on your Desktop

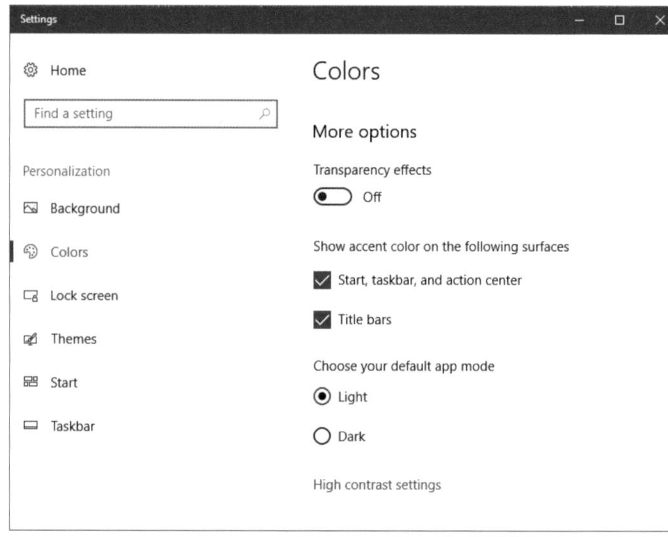

You can click the **High contrast settings** link to customize colors for high contrast themes.

Sound scheme

Next, choose a sound scheme:

1. Right-click the Desktop and select **Themes** on the Personalization screen, then choose the **Sounds** link

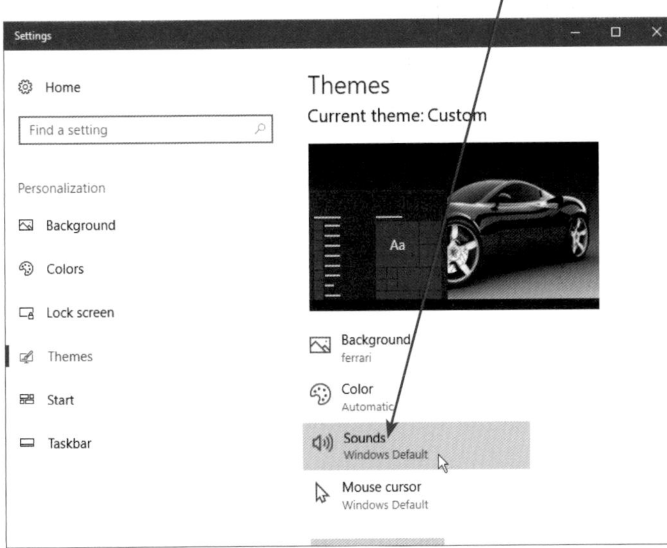

2. Select the **Sound Scheme** drop-down menu, and choose from the predefined sound schemes to find which you prefer

3. Select a Program Event such as "Windows Logon" and click **Test** to listen to the sound

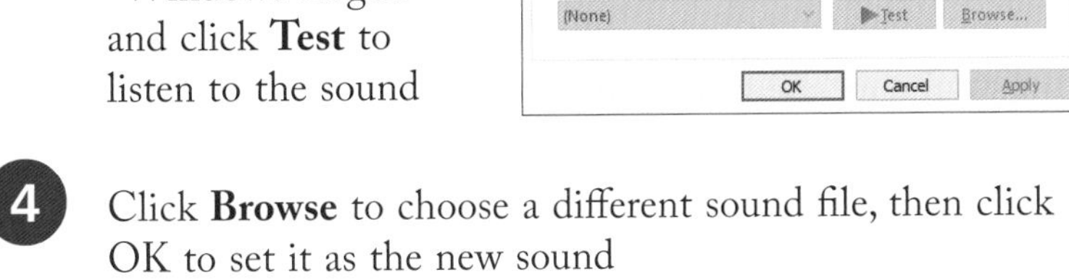

4. Click **Browse** to choose a different sound file, then click OK to set it as the new sound

5. Click **Save As...** to save the revised sound scheme

Most of the Windows themes provide their own sound scheme, so you can try these out to see which you prefer.

The default Windows 10 sound scheme has more mellow sounds than earlier versions.

Free additional sound schemes are available online from websites such as **winsounds.com**

Check the box **Play Windows Startup Sound** to hear sound when Windows starts up, or uncheck it to avoid the sound.

...cont'd

Desktop icons & Mouse pointer settings

Choose which icons to display on the Desktop:

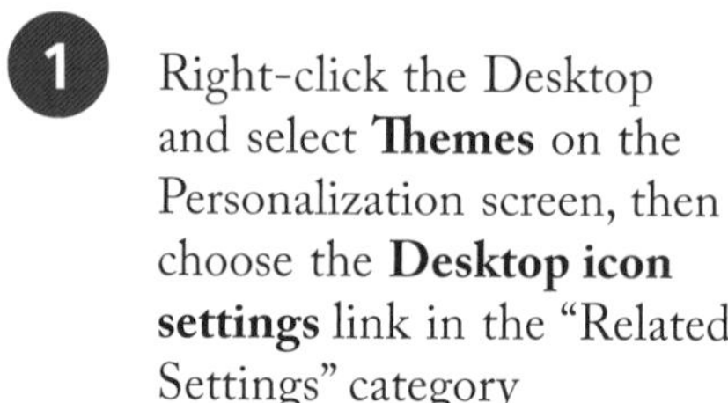

1. Right-click the Desktop and select **Themes** on the Personalization screen, then choose the **Desktop icon settings** link in the "Related Settings" category

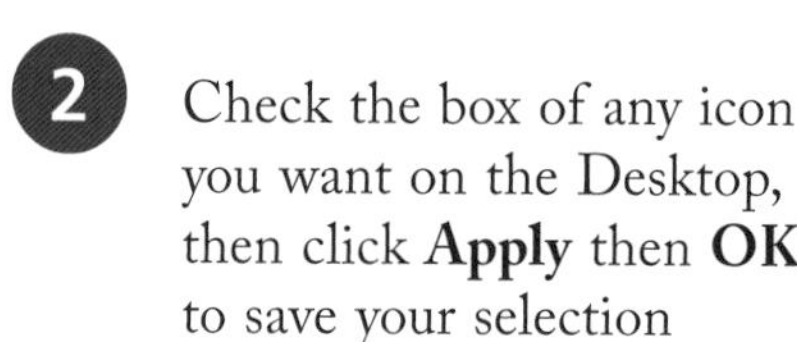

2. Check the box of any icon you want on the Desktop, then click **Apply** then **OK** to save your selection

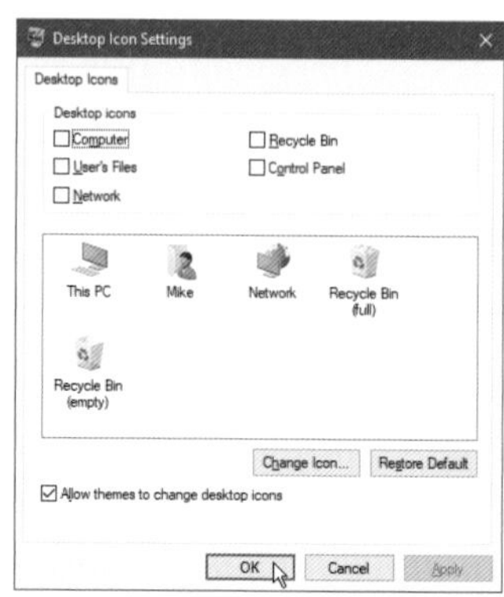

Don't forget

Check the box to "Allow themes to change desktop icons" if you want to use themes with their own custom icons.

3. Now, choose the **Mouse cursor** link on the Personalization screen

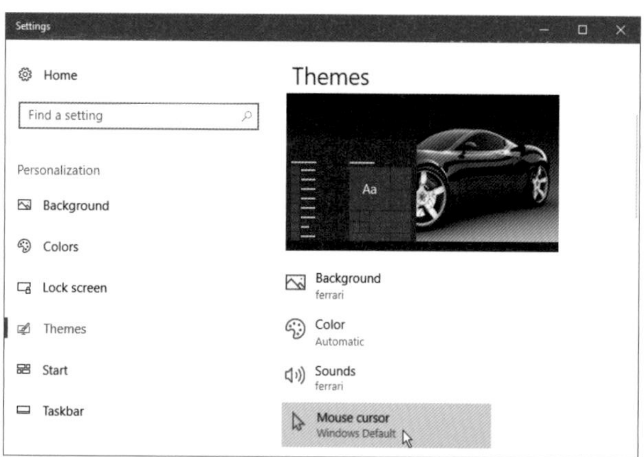

The Mouse Properties' Pointers tab lets you select from a variety of Windows pointer schemes.

4. Customize the performance of the mouse and the appearance of pointers using the tab options

5. Click **Apply** then **OK** to save the settings

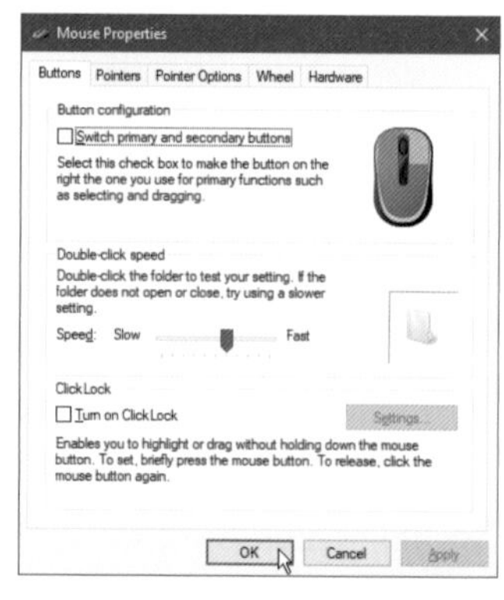

Save the theme

To save your theme:

1. Right-click the Desktop and select **Themes** on the Personalization screen, then click the **Save theme** link

2. Provide a name for your new theme and click **Save**

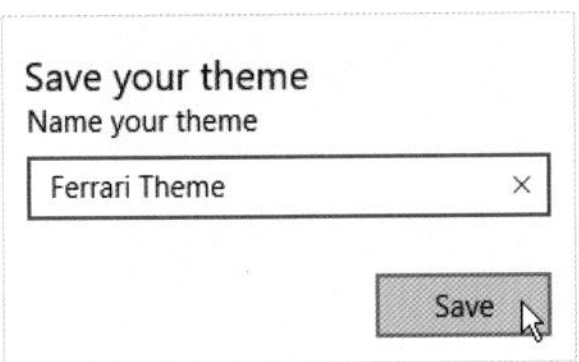

3. The theme remains in "Themes", under its new name

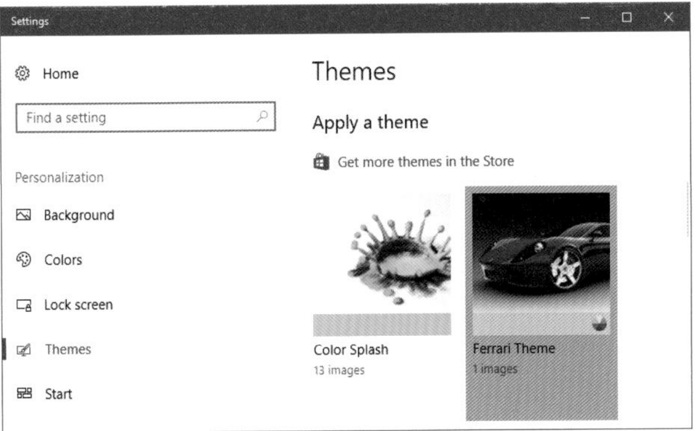

The theme file is stored in the user's applications data area, e.g. **C:\Users*name*\AppData\Local\Microsoft\Windows\Themes**, along with any Windows themes that have been downloaded.

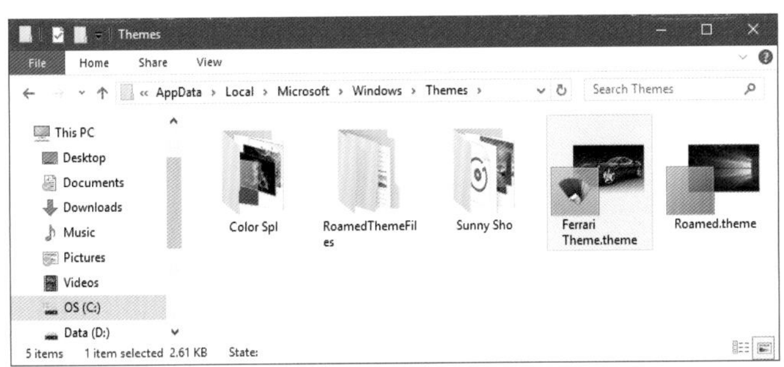

Your theme is stored as an Unsaved Theme until you choose to Save the theme.

If you cannot see the AppData folder in your User folder, you may need to check "Hidden items" on File Explorer's View menu.

...cont'd

If you have a number of photos as background images, the theme can be quite large.

By default, the themepack file will be saved in your Documents folder, but you can choose any location. For example, a HomeGroup folder.

To make the theme available to other users:

1. Right-click the theme and select **Save theme for sharing**

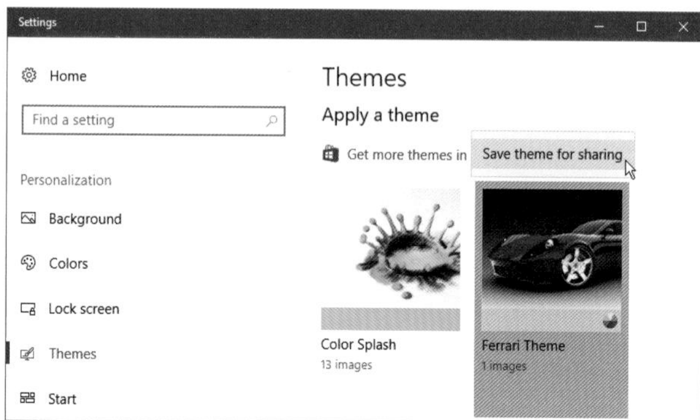

2. Specify the name and folder for the theme and click **Save**

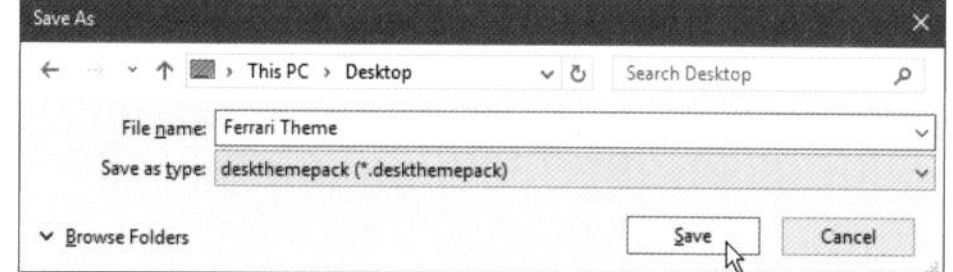

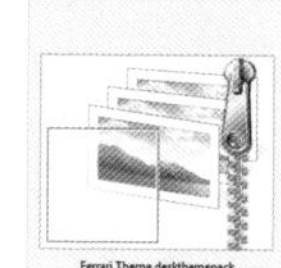

3. The background images, colors, sounds, and other theme settings are saved in a file of type **.deskthemepack**. Downloading this file or selecting it on a shared network drive will make the theme available to the other users

4. To remove a theme, first ensure it is not currently selected, then right-click and select **Delete**

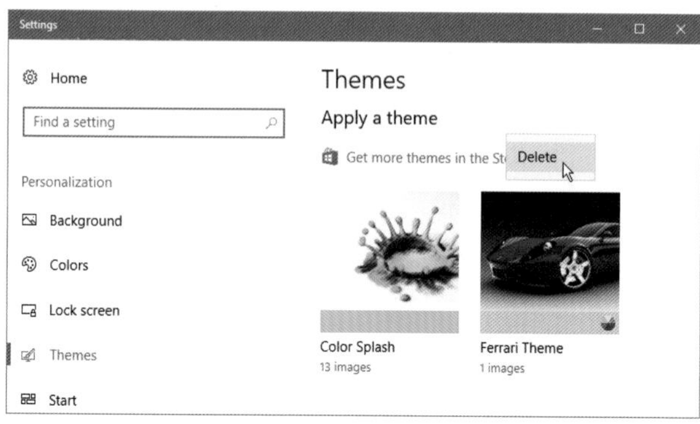

Screen resolution

To adjust the screen resolution:

1. Right-click the Desktop and select **Display settings** from the menu

2. Now, click the **Resolution** box and choose a setting from the drop-down menu

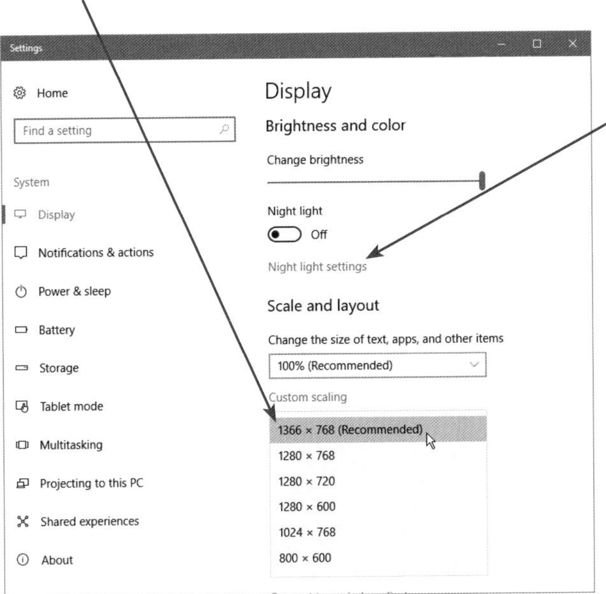

3. See the resolution change for 15 seconds

4. Click **Keep changes** during the change period to retain the new resolution you have selected

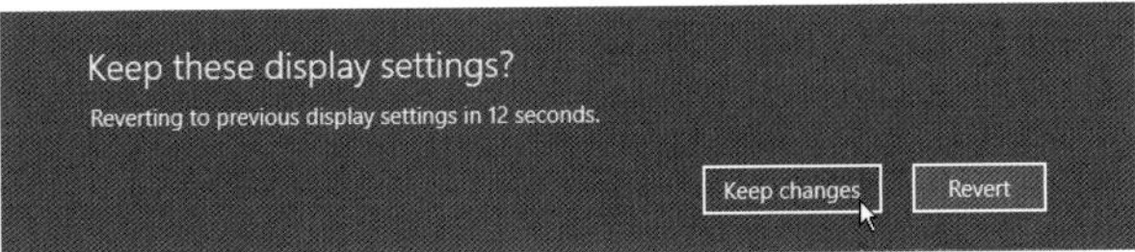

5. Drag the slider to adjust the brightness

6. Set the **Night light** to the "On" position to reduce blue light at night

Night light is a new feature introduced in the Windows 10 Creators Update. Use the **Night light settings** link to choose your preferred color temperature and schedule.

The screen resolution controls the size of the screen contents. Lower resolutions (e.g. 800 x 600) have larger items, so fewer can be displayed. Higher resolutions (e.g. 1920 x 1200) have smaller and sharper items, and more can be viewed on the screen.

You can also change the orientation from **Landscape** to **Portrait** – useful for tablet PCs and for a monitor that can be rotated.

Taskbar

The purpose of the Taskbar is to launch and monitor running applications. The version provided in Windows 10 has two specific regions – a small section at the right called the System Tray notification area, and the main body of the Taskbar on which program buttons and the Start button are displayed. To explore the Taskbar and see what it can do, it is necessary to go into its settings (right-click on the Taskbar and select Taskbar Settings).

Before you can move or resize the Taskbar, it must be unlocked.

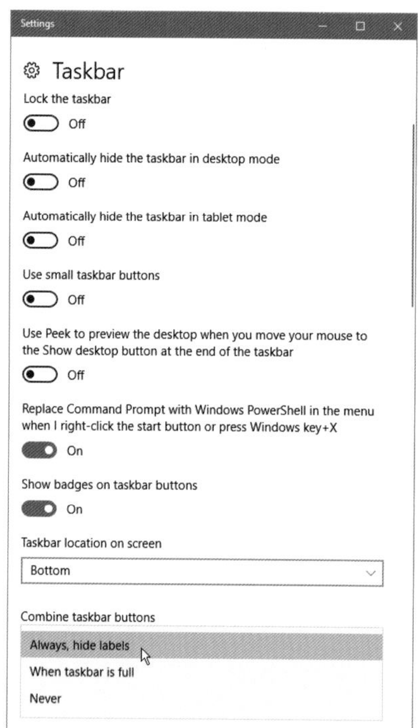

Taskbar Settings provides various options including:

- **Lock the taskbar** – when unlocked it can be moved and its depth can be increased.
- **Use small taskbar buttons** – enables the bar to hold more buttons.
- **Combine taskbar buttons, Always, hide labels** – each app appears as a single, unlabeled button, even if several windows for that app are currently open.
- **Combine taskbar buttons, When taskbar is full** – each window is shown as an individual button. When the Taskbar becomes crowded, apps with multiple open windows collapse into a single button.
- **Combine taskbar buttons, Never** – each window is shown as an individual, labeled button and are never combined, regardless of how many are open. As more apps and windows open, buttons get smaller, and will eventually scroll.
- **Notification area** – customize the area using **Select which icons appear on the taskbar** and **Turn system icons on or off.**

When the **Use Peek to preview the desktop...** option is enabled, hovering your mouse at the far-right of the Taskbar will temporarily hide all open windows.

You will also find options for configuring the Taskbar on multiple displays, as shown below – choose to have the Taskbar showing on all your displays, and how program buttons are displayed:

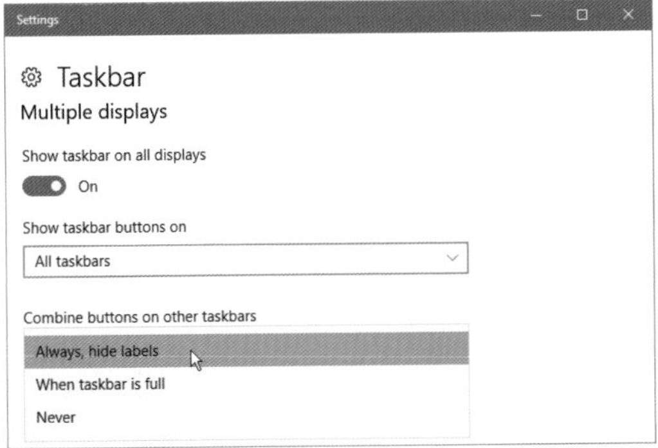

Folders and files cannot be added to the Taskbar. However, they can be dragged to the File Explorer icon on the Taskbar and accessed from its jump list. You can pin a folder to the Start menu tiles, then pin that tile to the Taskbar.

Right-click on the System Tray ^ arrow button, then select **Toolbars** to see a list of pre-configured toolbars that can be added to the Taskbar. For example, select **Address** to add an address toolbar to the Taskbar:

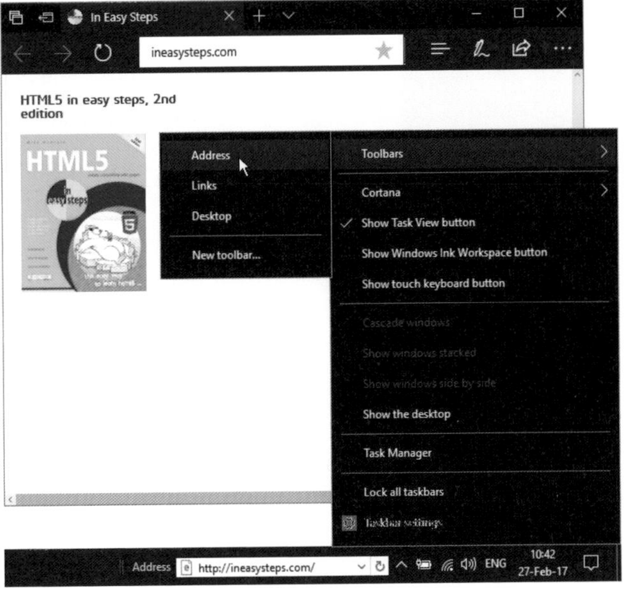

By right-clicking on the Taskbar ^ button and selecting **Toolbars**, **New toolbar...**, you can create your own Taskbar toolbars.

Any program can be "pinned" to the Taskbar – simply right-click on its icon in the Start menu, then select **More**, **Pin to taskbar** – or just drag-and-drop the icon onto the Taskbar.

Power User Menu

One of the major changes in Windows 8 was the omission of the Start button, which provided access to many different sections of the operating system in previous versions of Windows.

In Windows 10, however, the Start button is back. Instead of left-clicking on it to go to the Start menu, right-click. This will open the Power User Menu shown below:

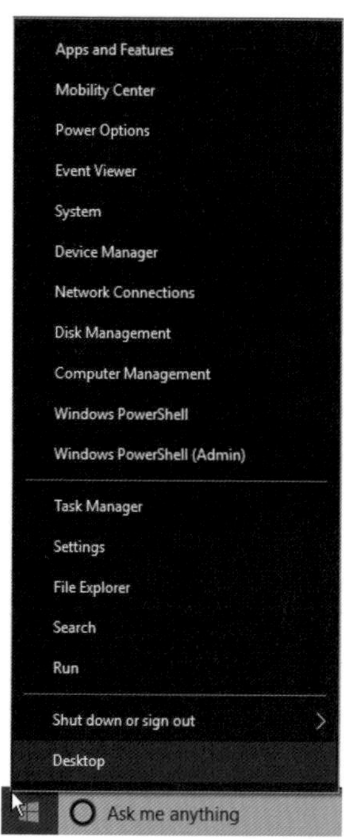

The more useful options include:

- **Apps and Features** – manage the programs installed on the PC, e.g. uninstall, repair.
- **Power Options** – this lets you configure a suitable power plan for the PC. Particularly useful for laptop and tablet users.
- **System** – provides details about your system, plus related links.
- **Device Manager** – enables all the PC's hardware to be viewed and configured.
- **Network Connections** – network management tools, e.g. Internet and HomeGroup.
- **Disk Management** – provides drive management tools, e.g. formatting and partitioning.
- **Computer Management** – tools for advanced system management. These are useful for system administrators.
- **Task Manager** – a program management tool that provides a range of options regarding the software running on the PC.
- **File Explorer** – a combined file manager application and navigation tool. Replaces Windows Explorer.
- **Search** – opens the Start screen's Search app. Enables users to locate data, programs, emails, etc.

Another method of opening the Power User Menu is to use the **WinKey** + **X** keyboard shortcut.

The **Control Panel** option was removed from the Power User Menu in the Windows 10 Creators Update, as emphasis was moved to the **Settings** feature.

Multiple displays

The graphics adapter on your computer is probably capable of handling more than one monitor, having for example both VGA (analogue) and HDMI (digital) connectors. You can also attach a second monitor to a laptop. To see how Windows handles this:

Your monitor may have both VGA and HDMI cables, but you should never attach the monitor to two connections on the same computer.

1. Right-click the Desktop and select **Display settings** from the menu

2. Now, attach a second monitor and see the monitors are duplicated

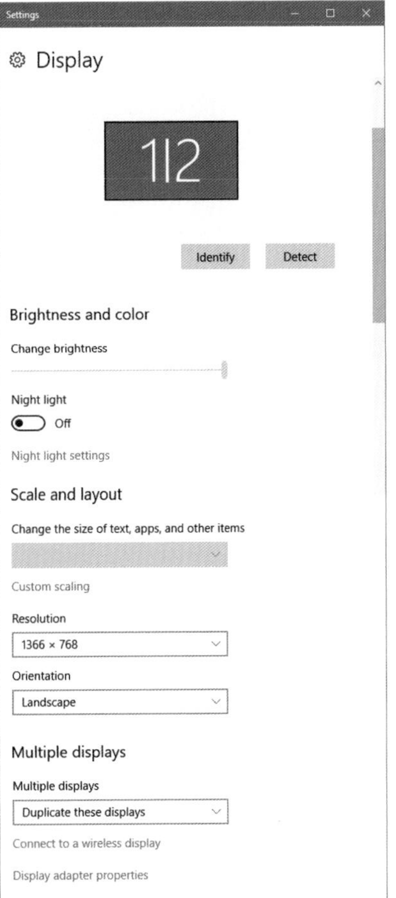

Windows resets both monitors to a resolution that both will be able to handle. If you want to continue duplicating the display, you can choose another more suitable resolution that both monitors can support.

To use the monitors for different information:

1. Select the **Multiple displays** box and choose **Extend these displays**

2. Click **Apply** to see the arrangement change for 15 seconds

3. Click **Keep changes** during the change period to retain the new arrangement you have selected

If you pick a resolution that is not supported by one of the monitors, you will get a warning message and the change will not be applied.

4. By default, the first monitor is the main display. To make the second monitor the main display, select the number two block then check the **Make this my main display** box

...cont'd

5. Click **Identify** to briefly display the numerals 1 and 2 on the monitor screens for identification

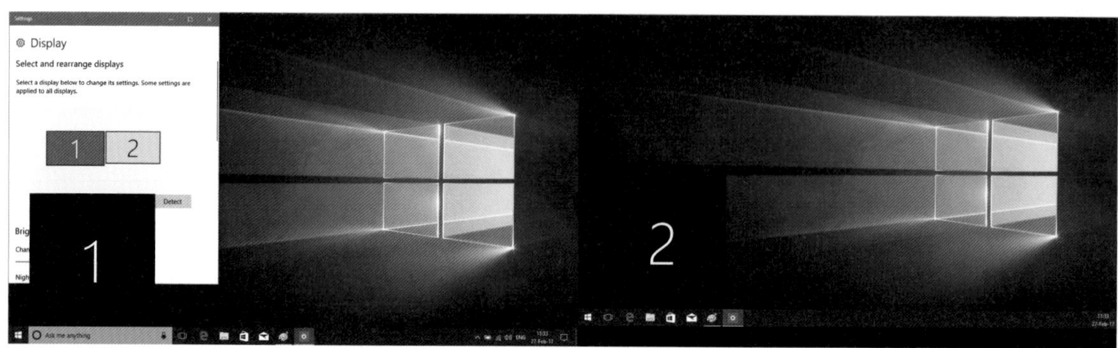

When you press **PrtScn** with dual monitors, you will capture an image of both monitors, in the positions as arranged.

6. By default, the monitors are arranged horizontally, so the mouse moves between them at the screen left and right. To arrange the monitors vertically, so the mouse moves between them at the screen top and bottom, drag one of the monitor blocks above the other, then click **Apply**

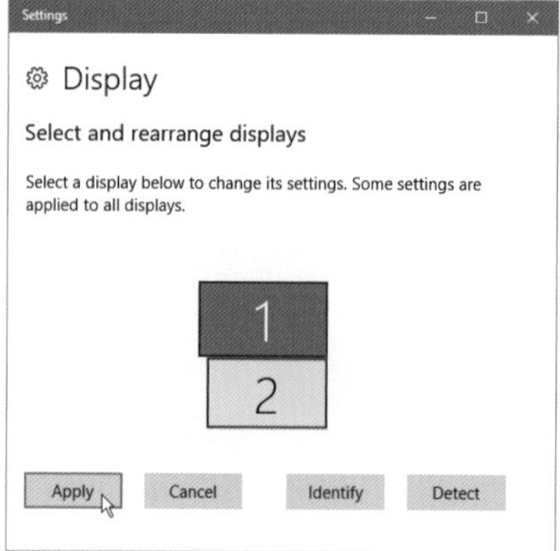

The Snap Across feature in Windows 10 allows you to drag an application window from one monitor to the other, or across both monitors.

7. To adjust the resolution of each monitor individually, select a monitor block then change its resolution setting

8. To connect to a wireless display, such as a smart TV with Miracast support, click **Connect to a wireless display**

Application windows

A very useful function in Windows is the ability to move and resize application windows. Apps in the Windows 10 interface can run in full-screen mode and can be resized.

1. To move a window, click the title bar area, hold down the mouse button and drag the window

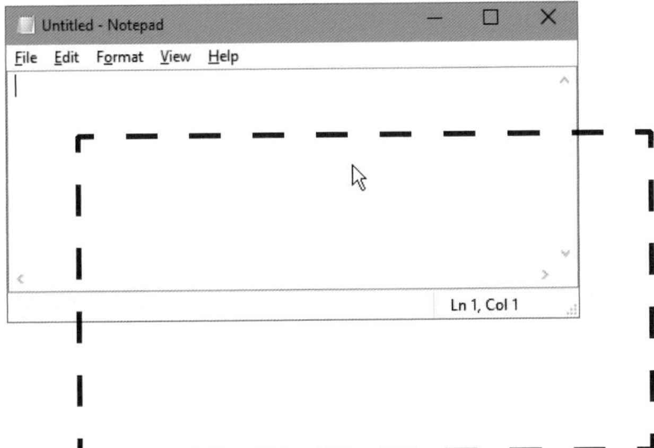

2. To resize a window, move the mouse pointer over any border or any corner until it becomes a double-headed arrow. Then click and drag until the window is the desired size

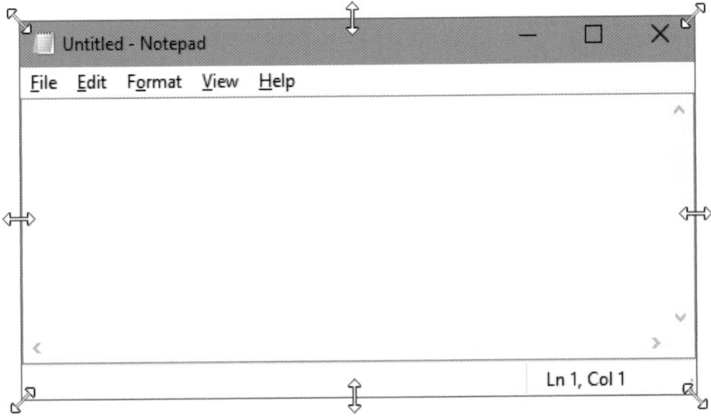

3. To make the window full-screen, click the Maximize button. The button will now change into the Restore button – click it again to return to the original size

When you drag a corner of the window, you can adjust the two adjacent borders simultaneously.

Double-clicking the title bar is an alternative to selecting the Maximize and Restore buttons.

By default, the window contents show as you drag. To display just the frame, select System Properties, Advanced system settings, and then Performance Settings.

Snap and Shake

Windows 10 includes two neat window manipulation features carried over from Windows 7. These are Snap and Shake.

Snap

Snap is a window docking feature that resizes two windows, each to half the size of the screen, and places them side-by-side. It is almost instant, requiring just two clicks to achieve what previously would need much dragging and resizing. Do it as follows:

1. Drag the title bar of a window to the left or right side of the screen until an outline of the expanded window appears
2. Release the window, which then expands to fill one half of the screen
3. Repeat with another window on the other side of the screen. You will now have two windows of equal size, side-by-side and filling the screen, as shown below:

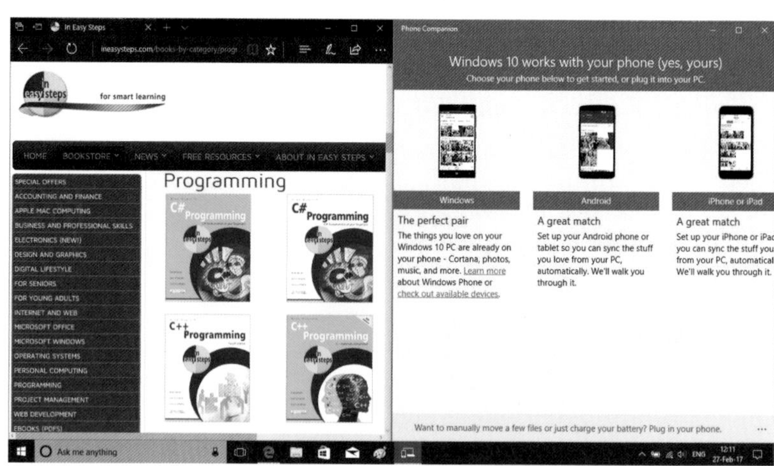

Shake

Ever need to cut through a cluttered Desktop and quickly focus on a single window? Just click the top of a pane and give your mouse a shake. Voilà! Every open window except that one instantly disappears. Shake it again – your windows are restored.

You can also use Snap to maximize a window to full-screen by dragging it to the top or bottom edges of the screen.

Snap is improved in Windows 10 with the new Snap Assist feature. This provides a thumbnail list of other open apps when you snap one app to a screen edge. Click any thumbnail to snap it to the other edge.

ClearType

ClearType font technology makes the text on your screen appear as sharp and clear as text that's printed on paper. It's on by default in Windows 10, but you can fine-tune the settings.

1. Enter "ClearType" in the **Search box**, then click to **Adjust ClearType text**

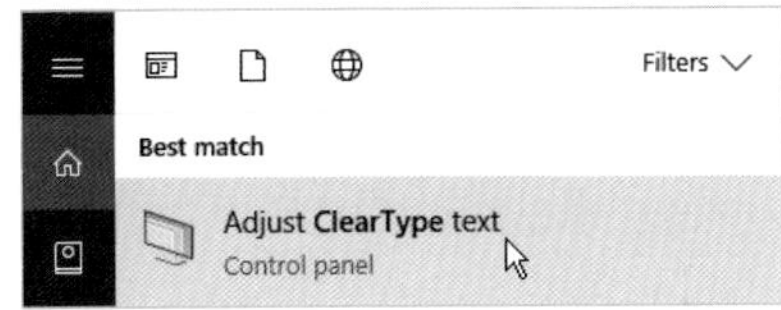

For the full benefit of ClearType, you need a high-quality, flat-panel monitor, such as LCD or plasma.

2. Check the **Turn on ClearType** text box (if unchecked)

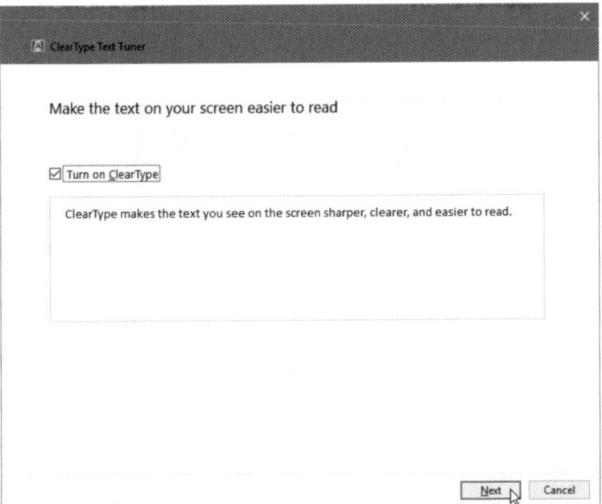

3. Click **Next** and Windows checks that you are using the native resolution for your monitor

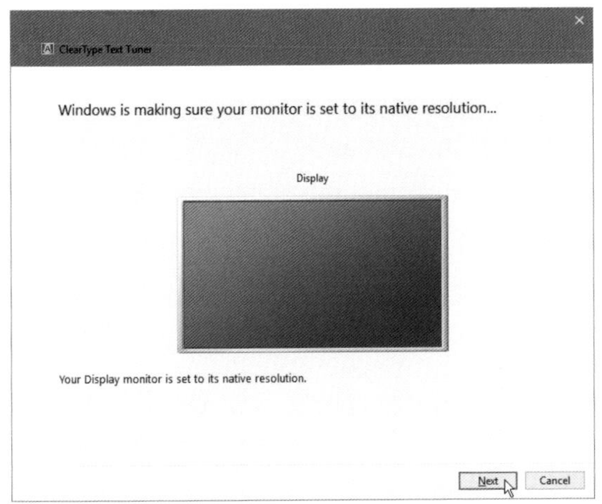

If the monitor is not set to the recommended resolution, you are given the opportunity to change it.

...cont'd

4. Click **Next** to run the "ClearType Text Tuner"

5. Click the text box that looks best to you, then click **Next**

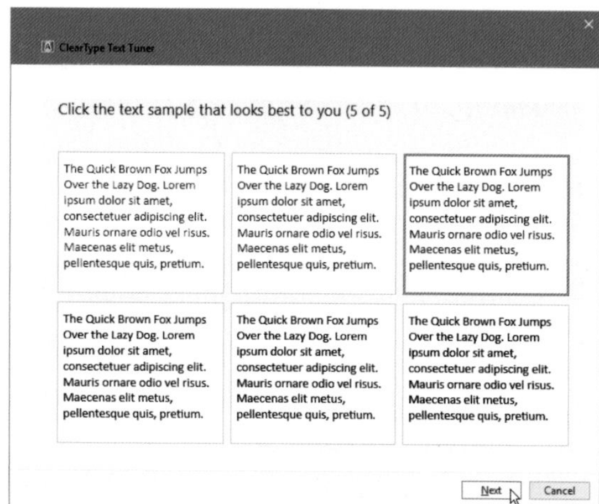

To review the settings on each of the five pages, click Next to accept the default selection.

6. Click **Finish** to close the "ClearType Text Tuner"

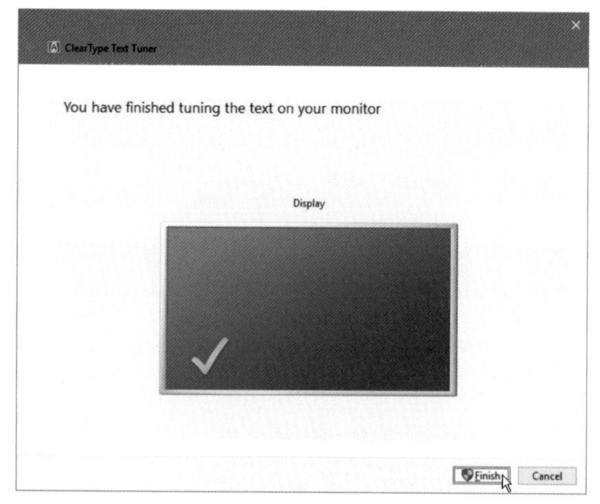

Any changes apply only to the current user. Each user account has its own ClearType settings recorded separately.

7 Built-in programs

There are programs built into Windows 10 to help you in many areas, including text processing, scanning, faxing, image management, and calculations. There are tools to record and process sound and images. There are also special tools available, such as Command Prompt and Windows PowerShell.

All apps

Windows 10 comes with a number of applications, services and functions, the presence of which many users will be completely unaware. Usually, these will be features and programs that they will never need to use. There will be times, though, when they miss out on something that would have been useful if only they had known it was there.

To make sure this doesn't happen to you, check to see exactly what is available in Windows 10:

1. Click the Start button

2. Scroll through the alphabetic listing of all available apps

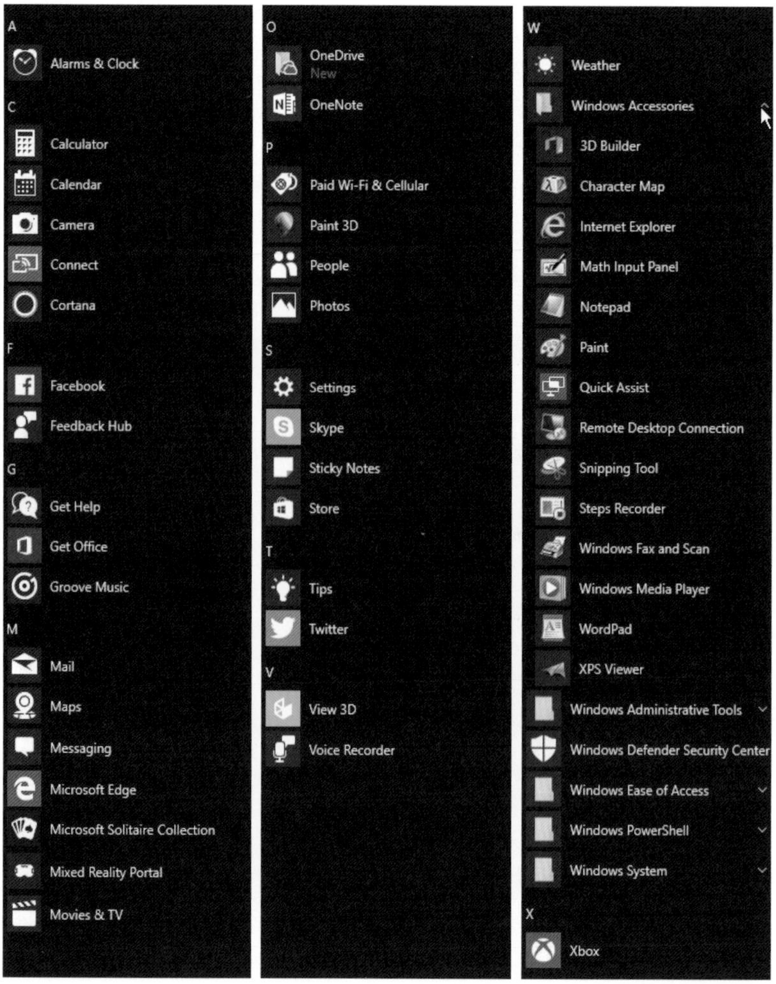

A
Alarms & Clock
C
Calculator
Calendar
Camera
Connect
Cortana
F
Facebook
Feedback Hub
G
Get Help
Get Office
Groove Music
M
Mail
Maps
Messaging
Microsoft Edge
Microsoft Solitaire Collection
Mixed Reality Portal
Movies & TV
O
OneDrive
New
OneNote
P
Paid Wi-Fi & Cellular
Paint 3D
People
Photos
S
Settings
Skype
Sticky Notes
Store
T
Tips
Twitter
V
View 3D
Voice Recorder
W
Weather
Windows Accessories
3D Builder
Character Map
Internet Explorer
Math Input Panel
Notepad
Paint
Quick Assist
Remote Desktop Connection
Snipping Tool
Steps Recorder
Windows Fax and Scan
Windows Media Player
WordPad
XPS Viewer
Windows Administrative Tools
Windows Defender Security Center
Windows Ease of Access
Windows PowerShell
Windows System
X
Xbox

In Windows 10, most items in the A-Z Start list are new Universal Windows Apps, whereas traditional programs are found in folders such as "Windows Accessories".

Traditional apps

Traditionally, Windows has provided a number of basic, but nevertheless useful, built-in applications such as those below:

- Calculator
- Character Map
- Command Prompt
- Magnifier
- Math Input Panel
- Notepad
- Paint
- Run
- Snipping Tool
- Sticky Notes
- Task Manager
- Voice Recorder
- WordPad
- Windows Fax & Scan
- Windows Media Player
- Windows PowerShell

The Calculator app has now been reborn as a Universal Windows App, but other traditional apps are still available in Windows 10 – within the Windows Accessories, Windows Ease of Access, or Windows System folders on the Start menu.

If you intend to use any traditional app often, it will be a good move to pin a shortcut to that app in a handy place. Locate the app in the Start menu, then right-click on the item and choose **Pin to Start** (if you want it on the Start group), or **More**, **Pin to taskbar**. This is demonstrated in the example below, where we are creating a handy shortcut to the Notepad app on the Start menu:

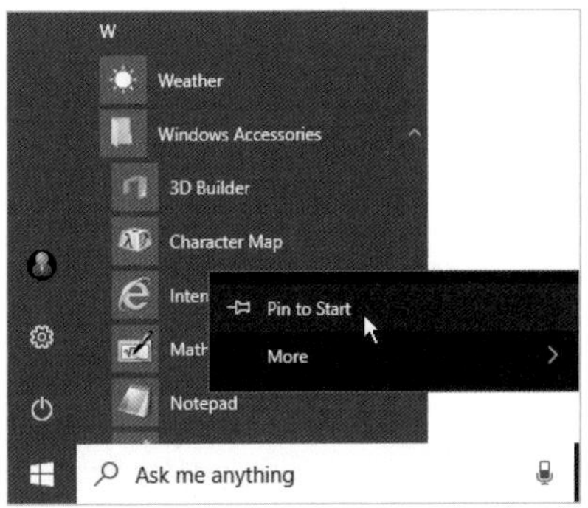

- Choose **More**, **Pin to taskbar** and the program will then be instantly accessible from the Taskbar on the Desktop.
- Choose **Pin to Start** and the program will then be instantly accessible from the Start group menu.

We'll take a look at the reborn Calculator program and some of the traditional Windows programs in the next few pages.

In the Windows 10 Creators Update, the Windows PowerShell app became the preferred default command-line app (rather than the previous Command Prompt app), the Snipping Tool app was further enhanced, and the Sound Recorder app was replaced by a new Voice Recorder app.

If you pin a lot of programs to the Taskbar, you may find yourself running out of room. Create more space by resizing the Taskbar. Right-click the Taskbar and uncheck **Lock the taskbar**, then simply drag its top edge upwards to make it taller.

Calculator

Whilst there's no spreadsheet capability built in to Windows 10, it does offer a handy calculator:

Open the Start menu, then find **Calculator** under "C"

Click calculator buttons or press equivalent keyboard keys, to enter numbers and operations such as Add, Subtract, Multiply, Divide, Square Root, Percent and Inverse.

To complete the calculation, click the **Equals** button, or press the **Enter** key

You can also store and recall numbers from memory, and the History capability keeps track of stages in the calculations.

This is just the Standard calculator. You can also choose to use the Scientific, or Programmer, version of the calculator.

Click the hamburger button and choose, for example, **Scientific**

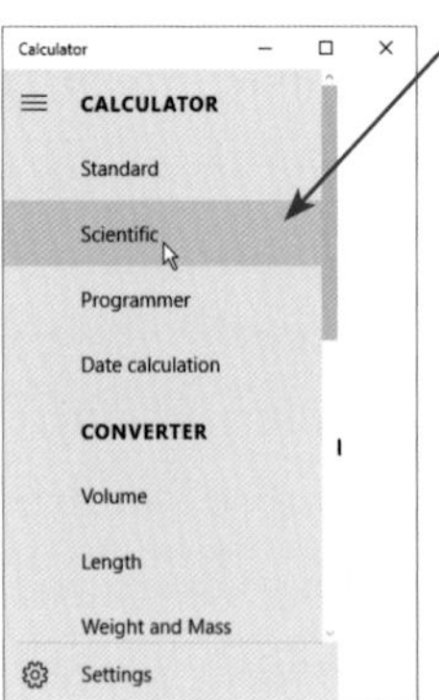

The Scientific calculator includes many functions and inverse functions, including logarithms and factorials. There is also a Programmer calculator view that can perform arithmetic on binary, octal, decimal and hexadecimal values. Converter options usefully convert between many different units of measure.

In Windows 10, **Calculator** is a Universal Windows App with more functionality than the old traditional program.

You can also use the numeric keypad to type numbers and operators. Press **Num Lock** if it is not already turned on.

Calculator clears the display when you switch views. You should use the memory buttons if you need to retain a number between mode switches.

Notepad

There are several applications that provide various levels of text management capabilities. One of these is Notepad.

The program is a basic text-editing application and it's most commonly used to view or edit text files, usually with the **.txt** file name extension, but any text file can be handled:

1. Open the Start menu, then find **Notepad** under "Windows Accessories". Type some text, pressing **Enter** to start a new line

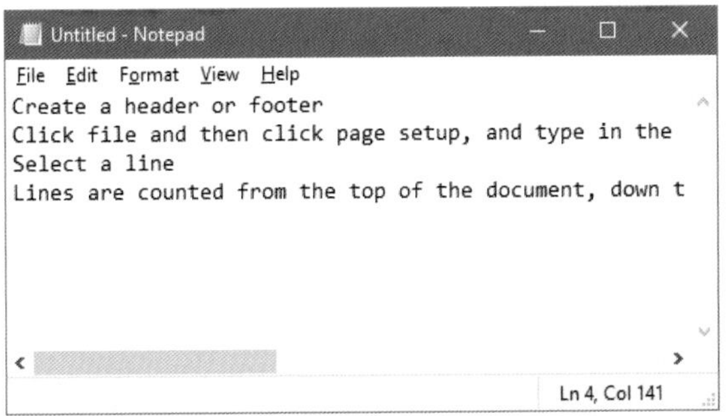

Select **Format**, **Font...** to choose the Font, Font Style and Size. This will apply to all the text in the whole document.

2. Parts of the lines may be hidden, if lines are longer than the width of the window

3. Select **Format**, **Word Wrap** to fit the text within the window width

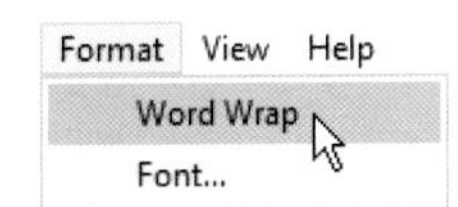

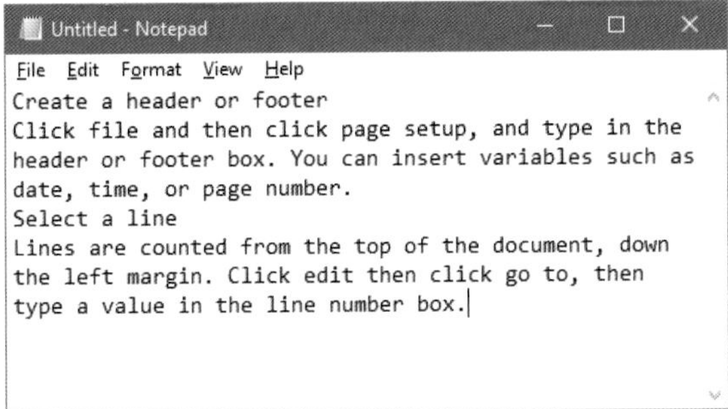

When you print a document the lines are wrapped between the margins, whatever the Word Wrap setting.

4. Select **Edit** to cut, copy and paste text, or to insert a Time/Date stamp into the document

5. Select **File** to save or print the document

WordPad

WordPad is a text-editing program you can use to create and edit documents that can include rich formatting and graphics. You can also link to or embed pictures and other documents:

Don't forget

The text automatically wraps as you type, and the Enter key starts a new paragraph.

1. Open the Start menu and find **WordPad** under "Windows Accessories". Then, type in some text

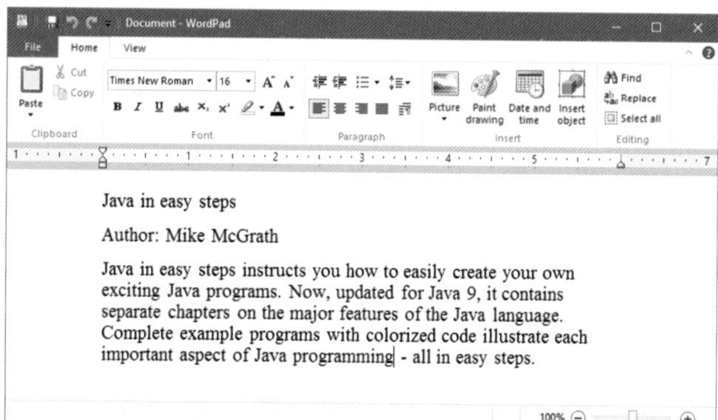

2. Select text and use the formatting bar to change font, etc.

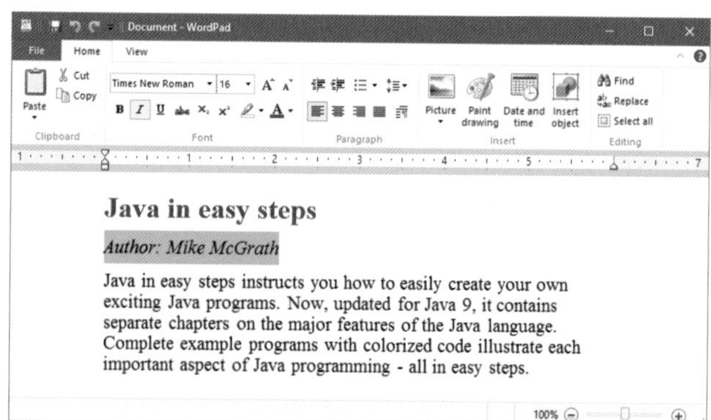

Saving as a Rich Text Document (**.rtf**), Open Office XML (**.docx**) or OpenDocument Text (**.odt**) will retain the text styling. However, the other formats save as plain text, and remove images or links.

3. Click the **Save** button on the Quick Access Toolbar, type the file name and confirm the file type, then click **Save**

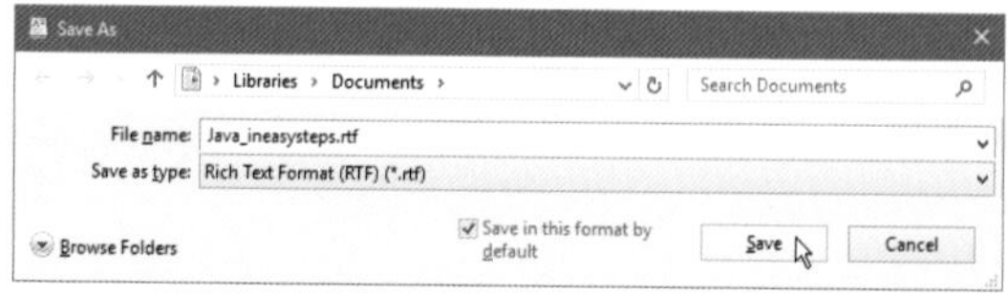

Paint

Paint allows you to create drawings on a blank drawing area or edit existing pictures, photographs, and web graphics. Open the program as described below:

1. Open the Start menu then find **Paint** under "Windows Accessories". The app launches a blank canvas:

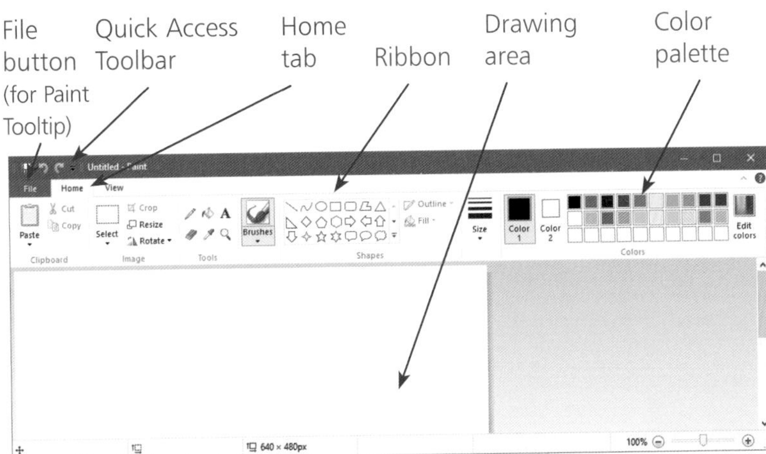

2. Or, right-click an image file and select **Open with, Paint**

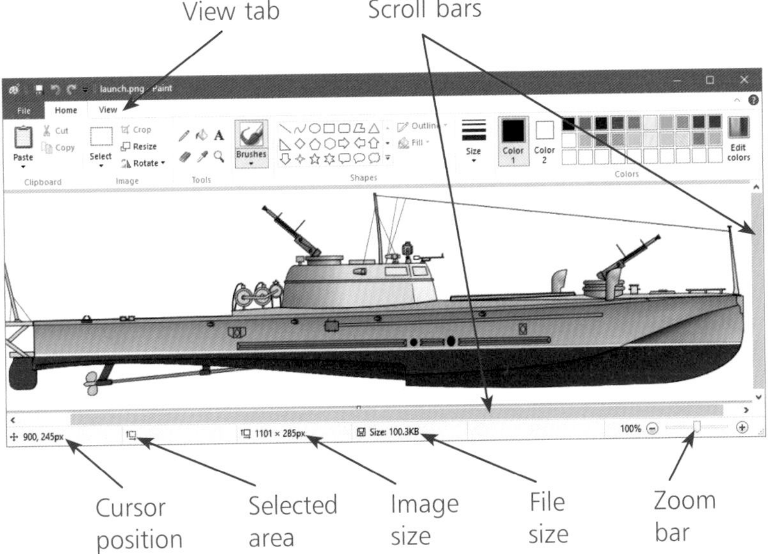

You can zoom in on a certain part of the picture or zoom out if the picture is too large, and show rulers and gridlines as you work.

In the Windows 10 Creators Update, a button was added to the Paint app giving you the option to open the image in the Paint 3D app (see page 90).

When you paste an image onto the **Paint** drawing area, it will be automatically resized if necessary to fit the whole image.

Paint can open and save as a number of image formats, including: **.bmp**, **.jpg**, **.gif**, **.tif** and **.png**.

Snipping tool

This will capture a screenshot, or Snip, of any object on your screen, and you can then annotate, save, or share the image. For example, if there's a window open with information to be copied:

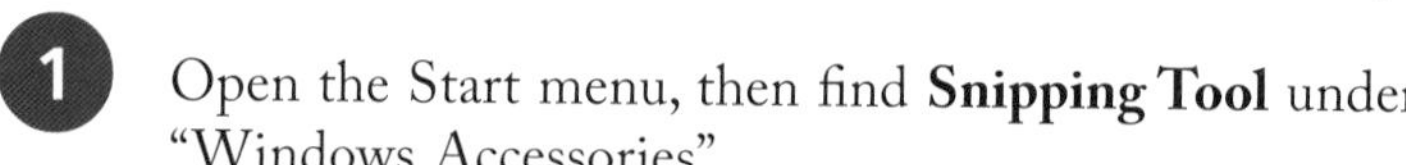

1. Open the Start menu, then find **Snipping Tool** under "Windows Accessories"

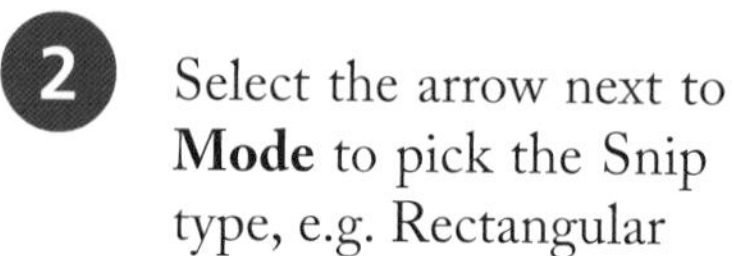

2. Select the arrow next to **Mode** to pick the Snip type, e.g. Rectangular

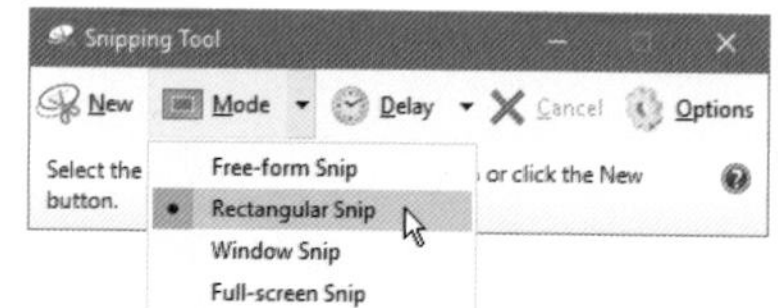

3. Click a corner and drag over the area you wish to capture

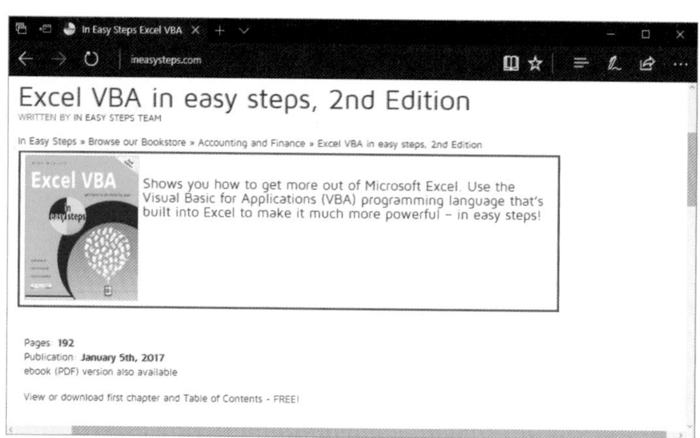

4. Release the mouse, and the Snip is copied to the Clipboard and the mark-up window

5. Use the tools to annotate the Snip if desired then click the **Save Snip** button, adjust the name and click **Save**

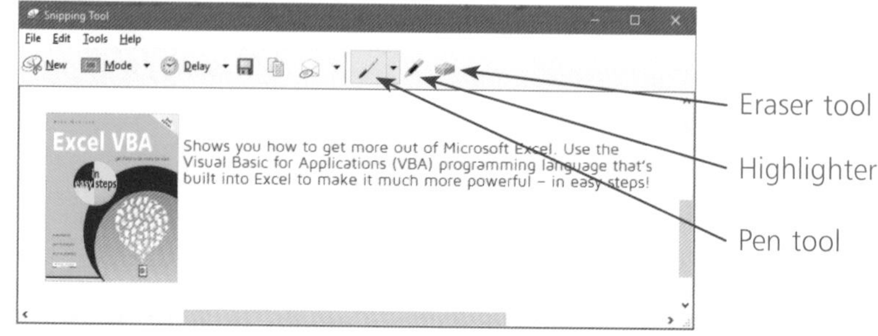

You can use the **Delay** options to give you time to select, and the **New** button to quickly capture a new Snip.

You can capture a free-form area, a rectangular area, a window or the full screen.

You can save the Snip as file type **.png**, **.gif**, **.jpg** or **.mht** (single file **.html**). You can then include the saved file in documents or email messages.

Sticky Notes

Sticky Notes

You can keep track of small pieces of information such as phone numbers, addresses or meeting schedules using Sticky Notes. You can use Sticky Notes with a tablet pen or a standard keyboard.

To create a new Sticky Note:

1. Open the Start menu, then find **Sticky Notes** under the "S" category

2. The new note appears on the Desktop with the typing cursor active

3. Type the text of the note or reminder that you want to record

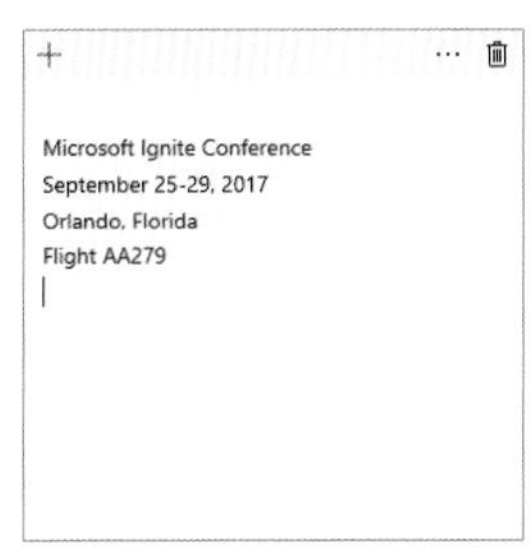

4. Text automatically wraps as you type, or you can press **Enter** to start a new line

5. To change the color of the note, first click the ... ellipsis button then choose a new color from the swatch that appears – see the note change color instantly

6. To provide simple formatting of the note text, first select the text that you want to change then use one of these keyboard shortcuts to format the text

Ctrl + B	Bold text
Ctrl + I	Italic text
Ctrl + U	Underlined text
Ctrl + T	Strikethrough

Microsoft Ignite Conference
September 25-29, 2017
Orlando, Florida
Flight AA279

The Sticky Notes app received various performance improvements in the Windows 10 Creators Update.

Sticky Notes automatically extend in length to accommodate text as you type. You can also drag a corner or edge to resize or reshape the note.

To create another note, click the + new note button. To remove a note, click the trash can icon.

Insights

Improved integration with Cortana Insights was introduced in the Windows 10 Creators Update.

The Sticky Notes application can be integrated with Cortana Insights to set reminders, send email messages, view web addresses, display stock prices, show flight details, and more:

To enable and use Insights in Sticky Notes:

1. Click the **...** ellipsis button to reveal the **Settings** button, then click the **Settings** button to display a Settings dialog

2. Slide the toggle button to the **On** position, then click the **X** button to close the Settings dialog – items recognized by Insights will now appear as links

If your Windows device has a pen or stylus, you can draw or write directly on a Sticky Note.

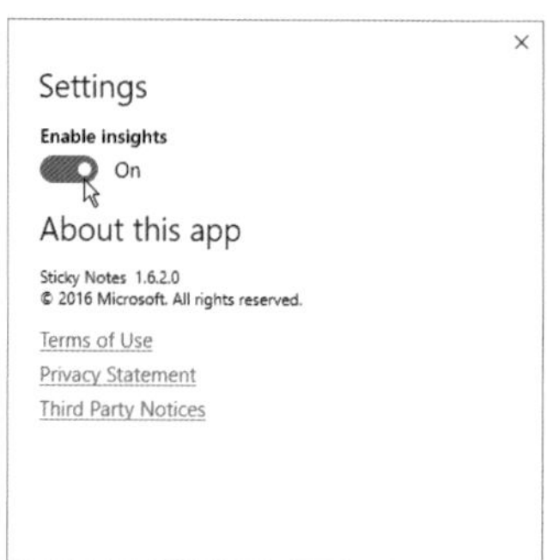

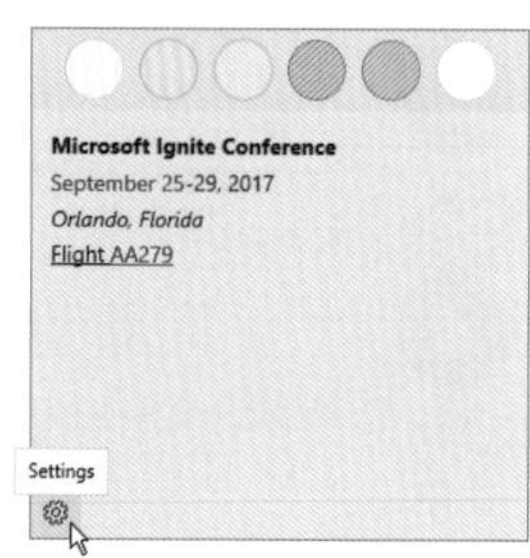

3. Select a date link and click the **Add Reminder** button that appears – Cortana will now ask if you want to set a reminder for this note on that selected date

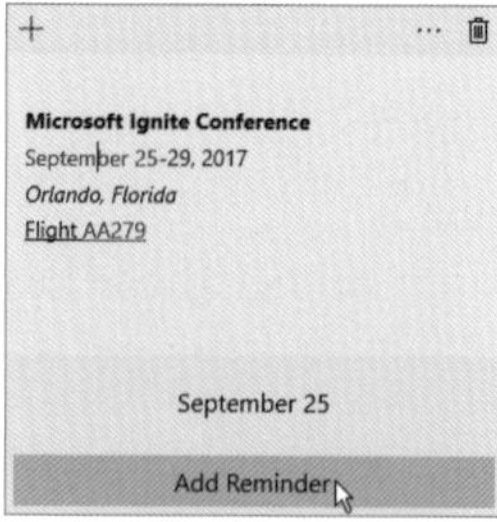

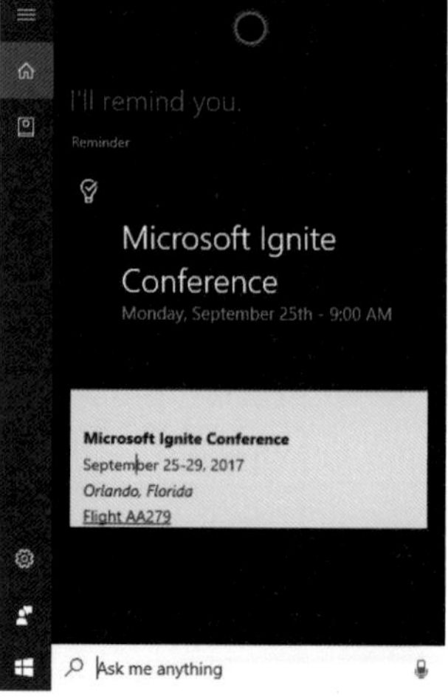

4. Click **Remind** to set the note for the selected date and see Cortana display a Reminder confirmation

5. Now, select the flight number link to see flight details – if it is an airline recognized by Cortana Insights

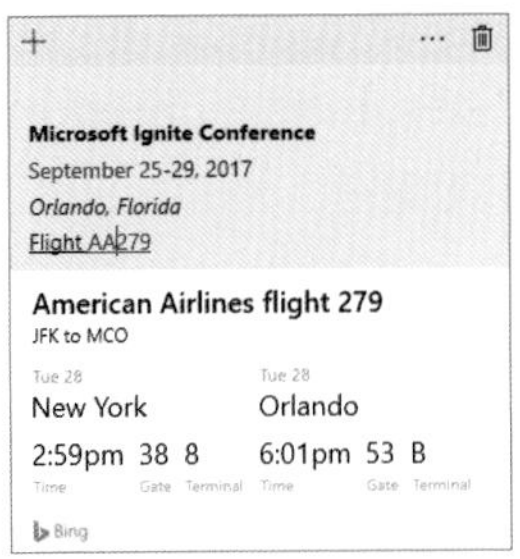

Support for other airlines in different regions will be added in the future.

Now, let's explore other useful Insights:

6. Click the **+** button to create a new note, and add a stock name such as **$MSFT**

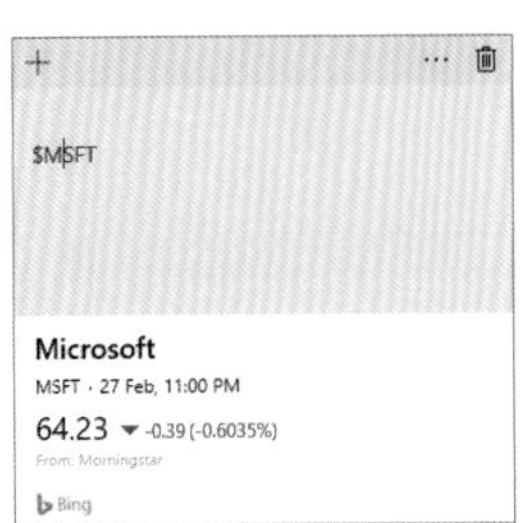

7. Select the stock link to see details of its current price

The Sticky Note buttons provided for Insights will use the program associated with that link. For example, **Send Email** may open the Mail app, **Open Link** may open the Edge browser, and **Call** may open the Skype app.

8. Create a new note and add a valid email address

9. Select the email address link to see a button appear that you can use to send a message

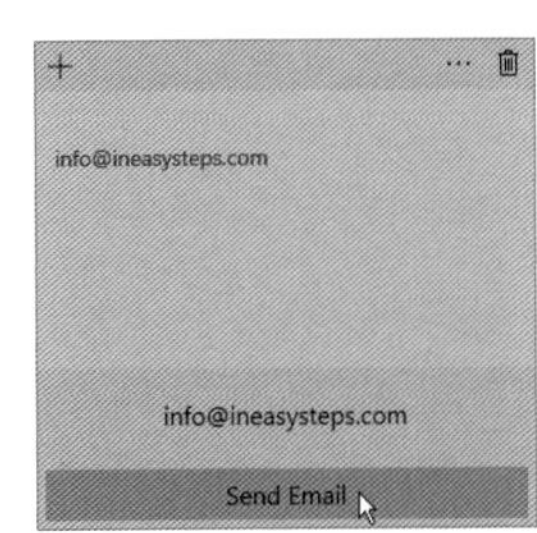

10. Click the **+** button to create a new note, and add a web address, such as **ineasysteps.com**

11. Select the web address link to see a button appear that you can use to open that address in a browser

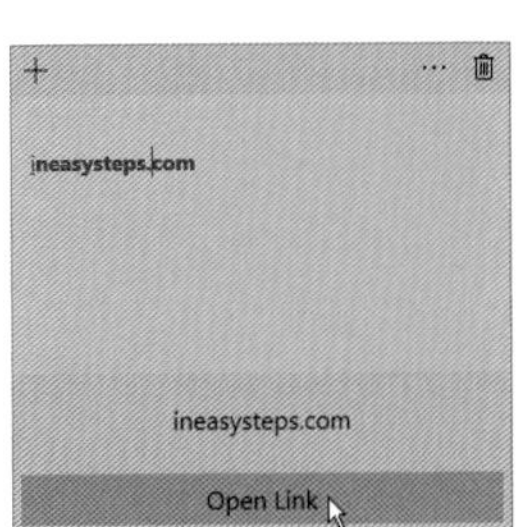

12. Click the **+** button to create a new note, and add a phone number

13. Select the phone number link to see a button appear that you can use to call that number

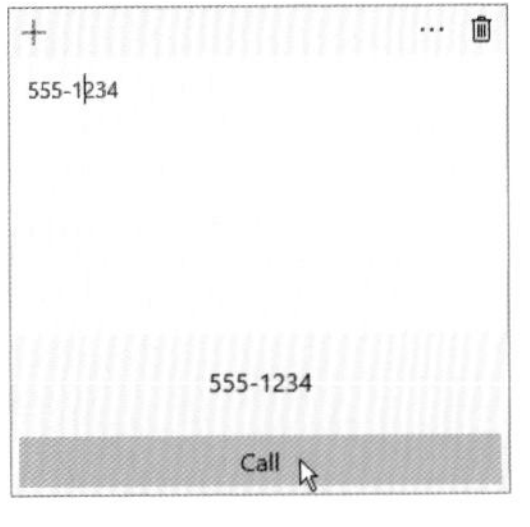

Insights also recognizes physical U.S. addresses and can display them on the Maps app. Microsoft will over time expand Insights to other languages and regions.

Fax and scan

Windows provides software to support sending and receiving faxes, but you need a fax modem installed or attached to your computer, plus a connection to a telephone line.

There's also support for scanning documents and pictures, but you need a scanner (or all-in-one printer) attached to your computer.

To start Windows Fax and Scan:

Open the Start menu, then find **Windows Fax and Scan** under "Windows Accessories"

Select **View**, then **Zoom** and you can choose a larger or smaller scale, or fit to page or fit to width, as desired.

2. An example document is displayed, and this provides guidance for getting started with faxes and scanning

3. To scan a document or photo, click the **Scan** button, then click **New Scan** on the toolbar, and follow the prompts

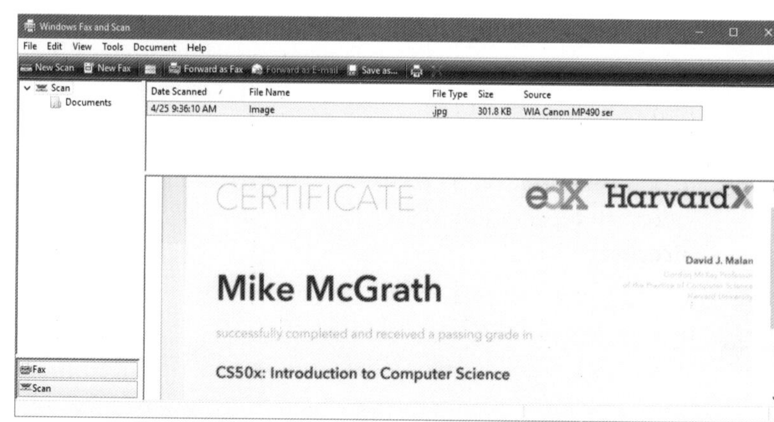

When you have scanned a document or picture, you can forward it as an email or a fax.

Command Prompt

All versions of Windows have included a command line feature for typing MS-DOS commands and other computer commands.

1. Open the Start menu, then find **Command Prompt** under "Windows System"

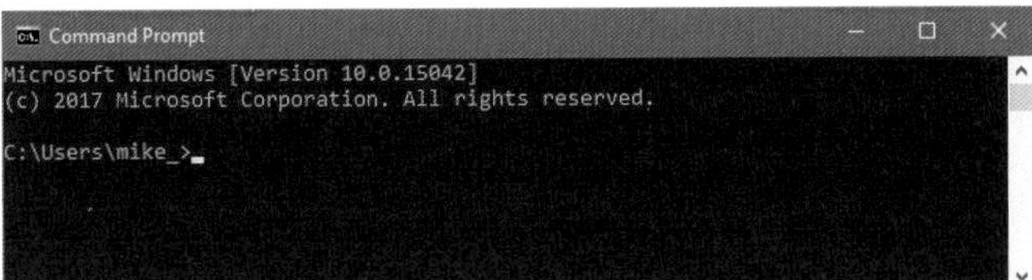

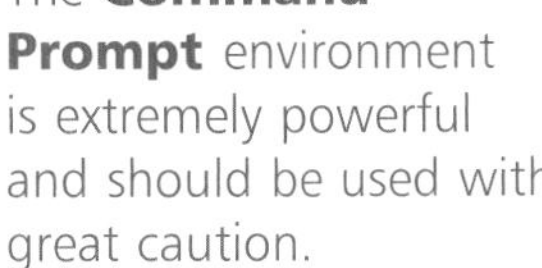

The **Command Prompt** environment is extremely powerful and should be used with great caution.

2. To display a list of commands with a brief description of each, type "Help" and press **Enter**

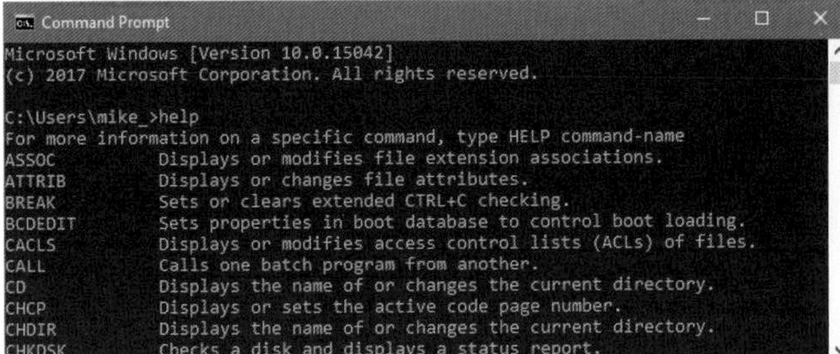

If the commands you use require authorization, right-click Command Prompt on the Start menu, and select **Run as administrator**.

3. For more details of a specific command, type **Help *Name*** then press **Enter**, e.g. **Help CHKDSK**

4. To adjust Command Prompt options, right-click the title bar and select **Defaults** or **Properties**

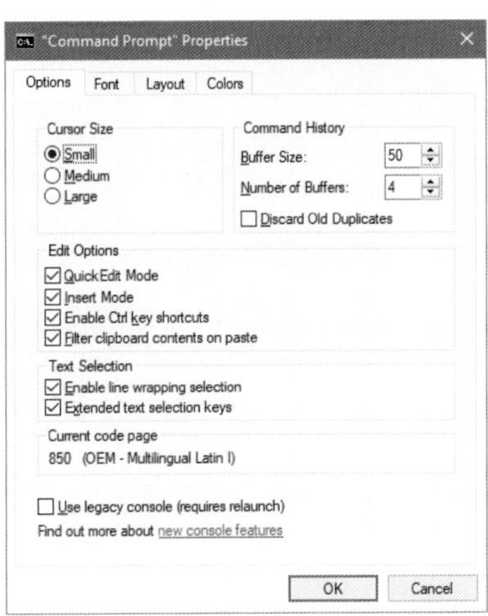

Select **Edit** from the right-click menu, and you can mark, copy and paste text onto the command line.

5. To close Command Prompt, type "Exit" then press **Enter**

Windows PowerShell

Windows PowerShell became the default command-line app in the Windows 10 Creators Update, rather than the earlier Command Prompt default shell app.

To support system administrators and advanced users, Windows provides a command-line and scripting environment, far more powerful than the old MS-DOS batch file system.

1. Open the Start menu, then find **Windows PowerShell** under "Windows PowerShell"

2. Type **Get-Command** for a list of PowerShell commands

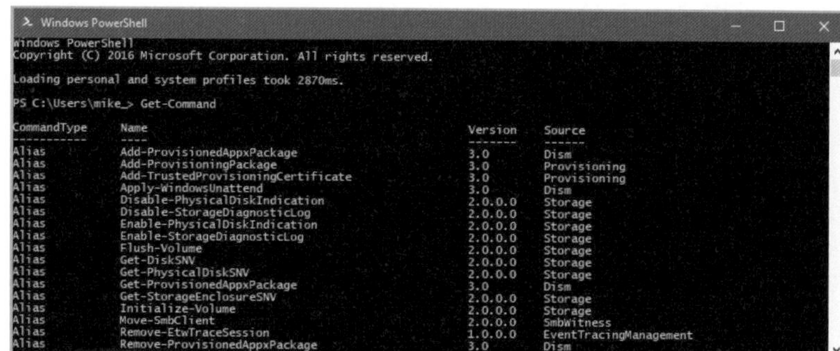

3. Now you can discover more about any command using the PowerShell help system – for example, to discover more about a particular alias, type **help Flush-Volume**

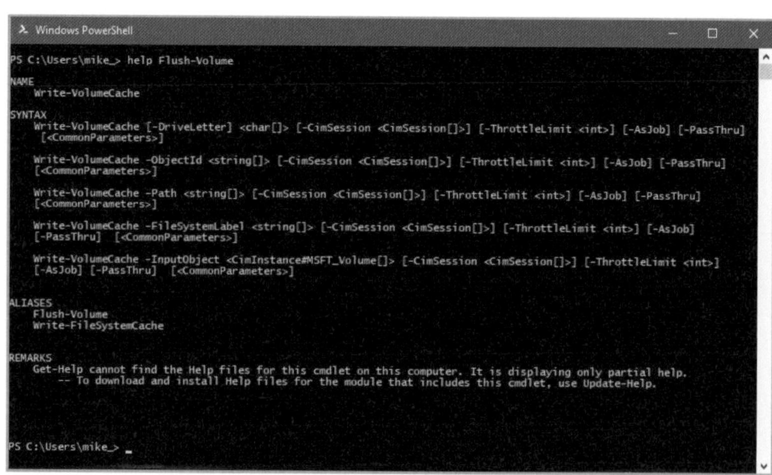

Windows PowerShell can execute "Cmdlets" (which are .NET programs), PowerShell scripts (file type **.ps1**), PowerShell functions, and executable programs.

4. The PowerShell help system can be updated online using the command "Update-Help", and further assistance can be found online at **msdn.microsoft.com/en-us/powershell**

Administrative tools

Administrative tools are intended for system administrators and advanced users. To see the list available on your system:

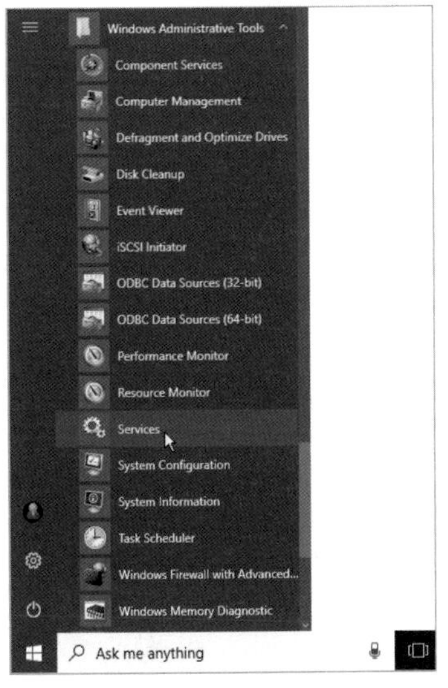

1. Open the Start menu then find all the tools under "Windows Administrative Tools"

2. Here you will see a range of tools that enable you to manage the way the PC is used

3. Click **Services** and you will see a list of all services available and running on the PC

You can use the **System Information** tool to discover details of the hardware, components, and the software environment of your entire system.

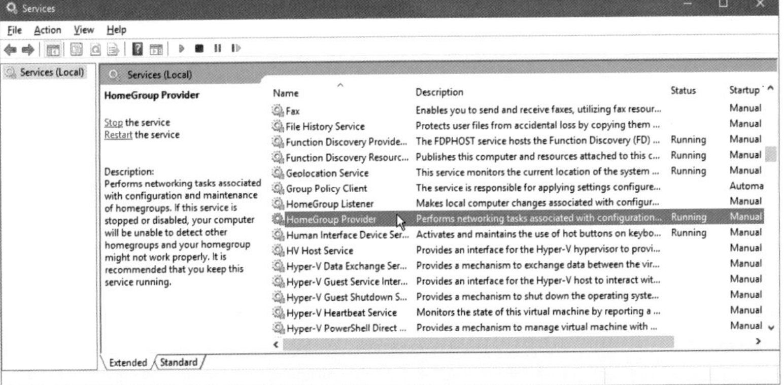

4. Double-clicking a service reveals options for starting and stopping the service. This enables you to disable the ones that aren't necessary. A typical example is network-related services – if you don't use networking, you can safely disable these and gain a small performance boost

Explore each item in **Windows Administrative Tools** to see how they might be useful to control your PC.

Unknown file types

A problem you may come across occasionally is trying to start a program, only to be greeted by a message like this one:

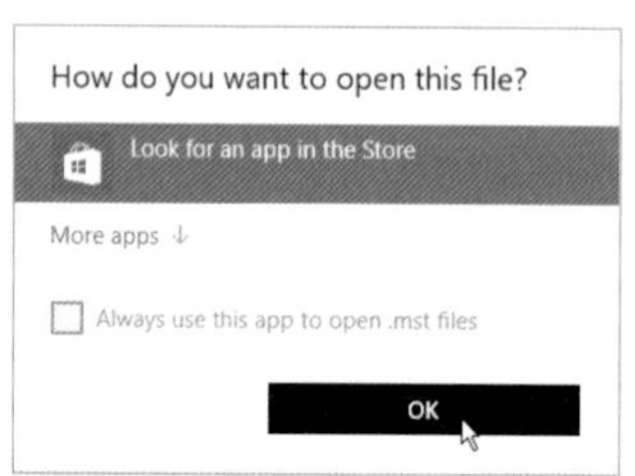

The reason for the message is that Windows cannot recognize what program is associated with the type of file you are trying to open – so has no idea how to open that file.

Initially, you are offered one option: Look for an app in the Store. Clicking this will take you to the Windows Store where, if you aren't already, you will have to log in with a Microsoft account. Once done, a search is made automatically for apps capable of opening the file in question. If one is found, you are offered the option of downloading it – remember, you may have to pay for it.

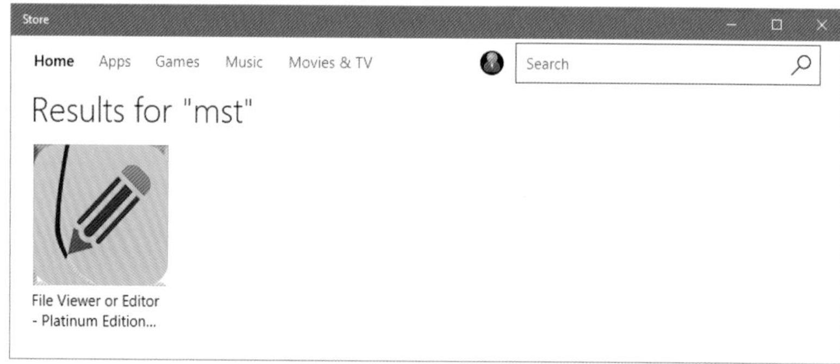

If the results inform you that a suitable app hasn't been found for this type of file, you can return to the message box to retry.

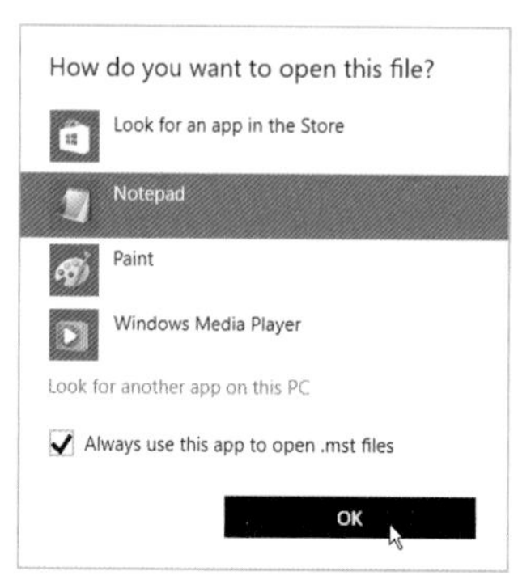

Clicking the "More apps" link will reveal a list of suggested programs. However, if none of these work either, your last recourse is the internet. There are quite a few sites that provide lists of file types and the programs associated with them. For example, you could try looking online at **filext.com**

If you try any of the suggested programs, make sure the "Always use this app to open XXX files" option is not selected – unless you are sure the program is the one you want.

Change default program

All files are designed to be opened with a specific type of program. For example, graphics files such as JPEG and GIF can only be opened by a graphics editing program, e.g. Paint, or with a web browser, such as Microsoft Edge.

A common problem that many users experience is when they install a program on their PC that automatically makes itself the default program for opening related files. If the user prefers the original program, he or she will have to reassociate the file type in question. Alternatively, the user might want to set a different program as the default:

If a newly-installed program has hijacked your files, you can reassociate them with your favored program.

1. Go to **Start**, **Settings**, **Apps**, **Default apps** then click **Choose default apps by file type**

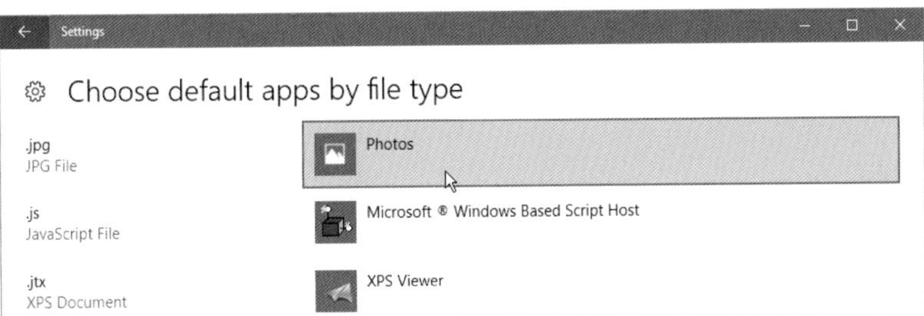

2. Select the file type you want to reassociate. For example, to open **JPG** files with a different app

3. You will now see a list of programs on the PC capable of opening that file type. Select the one you want to use, e.g. **Paint**

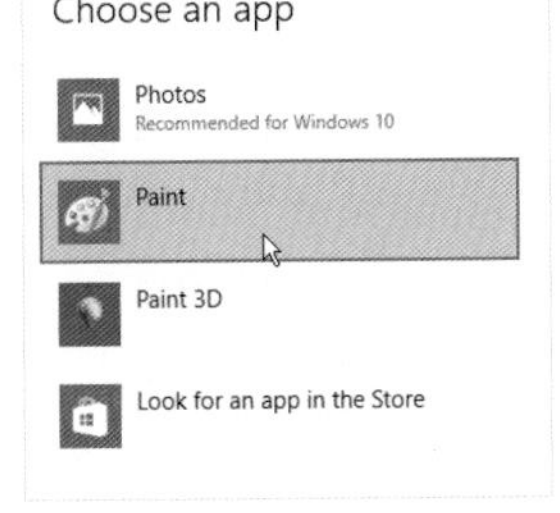

Another way is to right-click a file and then click **Properties**. Click the **General** tab and then click **Change**. Browse to find the program you want to open the file with and select it.

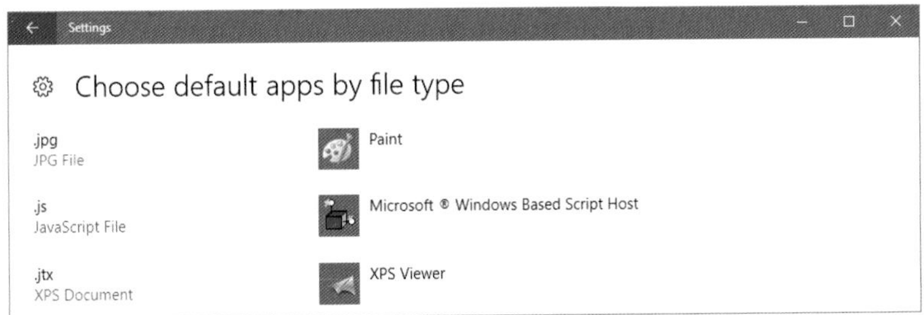

Search the web for software

There was a time when if you wanted a specific program, you either had to visit a store to buy it, or order it online – the instant downloads of today were very rare due to painfully slow internet connections. Because of this it was almost impossible to "trial" a program – you had to pay for it and hope it did the job.

When you need a certain program only temporarily, download a time-limited trial version for free.

Nowadays, thanks to broadband, the situation is completely different, and there are several very useful sources of software:

Manufacturers

Without doubt, the best source of software is the manufacturers' websites. The vast majority of them allow users to download time- or feature-limited versions of their products to try out before parting with the cash.

The big advantage here is that the software is guaranteed to be the real deal, and with no unwelcome attachments in the form of viruses and malware. The downside, of course, is that once the trial period is up, you have to pay for the program if you want to keep using it.

Watch out for phishing sites that imitate those of major manufacturers and rip you off.

Download sites

Software download sites are set up specifically to provide an outlet for the legions of small software developers. Many of these programs are free (freeware), others are time- or feature-limited, (shareware), while others require up-front payment.

Well-known download sites include **Download.com**, **Soft32**, **ZDNet Downloads**, and **Tucows**. The big advantage offered by these sites is variety – a vast number of programs of all types are available. However, you do have a risk of picking up viruses and malware hidden in the programs, and many of the freeware programs also come with irritating nag screens or ads.

Software acquired from download sites can be poorly coded and thus contain bugs. These can cause problems on your computer.

File sharing

File sharing is a common internet activity that makes use of peer-to-peer networks. Users install a program that connects to these networks and lets them share designated files on their PC with other users.

This enables all types of data (software, video, images, etc.) to be downloaded at no cost. The practice is quite legal. However, actually using the data is often illegal. There is also a high risk of virus and malware infection.

8 Windows downloads

This chapter explores some of the most popular Windows downloads to complement the great apps that come bundled with Windows 10.

Popular downloads

For every task, there will be many programs available to choose from, for free or for a fee.

If a program offers to create a Desktop shortcut during installation, accept the option.

Not every program offered on the internet is safe to use. Some are still under development; some may be infected with viruses or malware. Make sure that you check out programs at reliable sources before downloading.

There are a number of applications not included with Windows and not supplied by Microsoft that are used by thousands of people all over the world. They supplement the existing Windows applications or they fill in the gaps.

The reasons for their popularity are that they are free, good at their intended purpose, and generally well-behaved, i.e. they are free of bugs and malware.

There are, of course, many other programs that do the same things, but the ones we are going to highlight in the next few pages tick all the boxes – excellent performance, no malware and absolutely free to use.

Category:	Program:
PDF Viewer	**Adobe Reader**
Maintenance	**CCleaner**
CD/DVD Tool	**CDBurnerXP**
Photo Viewer	**IrfanView**
Text Editor	**Notepad++**
Office Apps	**Apache OpenOffice**
Photo Editor	**Paint.NET**
Utility	**7-Zip**
File Sharing	**uTorrent**

All of these programs are available over the internet, ready for download and installation. In the following pages you'll find the details needed to get started with each of the programs, including:

- Website address
- Brief description
- Installation notes
- Screenshot of application

After installation, each program can be accessed by typing its name into the Taskbar Search box.

Adobe Reader

get.adobe.com/reader

Adobe Reader is the worldwide standard for viewing, printing, and commenting on PDF documents of all types.

To install the application:

1. Browse to the website then click the **Install now** button

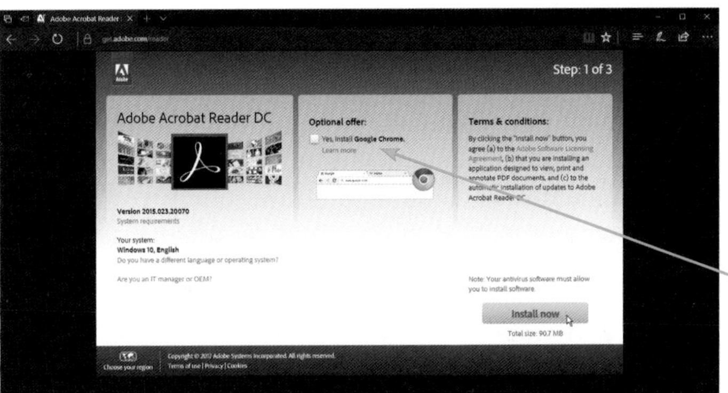

You may find extras such as **Google Chrome** and **Google Toolbar** being offered. You can usually uncheck these items unless you are sure they will be needed.

2. Follow the Setup Wizard to complete installation of the app, double-click any PDF file, then associate that file type with the Adobe Reader app as the default

3. Click **OK** to open the PDF file in Adobe Reader

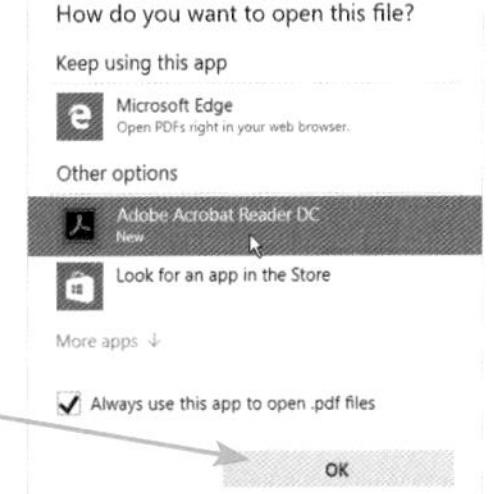

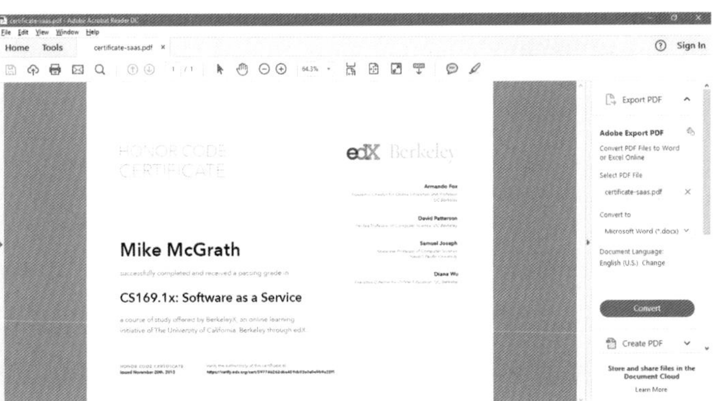

Adobe Reader is not just for viewing documents. Select **View**, **Read Out Loud** to set the Reader in narrative mode.

CCleaner

piriform.com/ccleaner

CCleaner is a utility that cleans out the junk that accumulates over time – temporary files, broken shortcuts, and other problems. The program also protects the user's privacy by clearing the contents of the history and temporary internet files folders.

1. At the website, scroll down the page and click the **Free Download** button

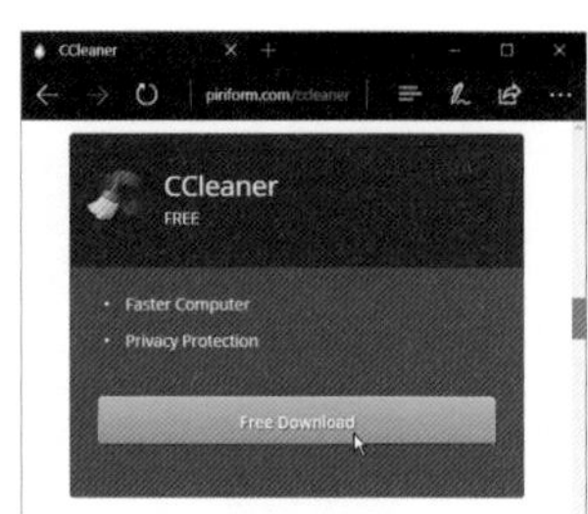

2. Next, click the link to download the free version of CCleaner

3. Click **Install** to run the Setup Wizard

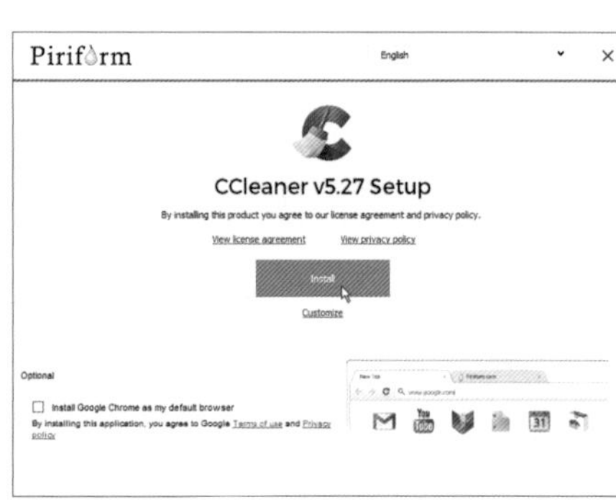

4. When the installation is complete, click the **Analyze** button to see a list of files that can be safely deleted

Uncheck the box on the Setup dialog to install **Google Chrome** unless that is what you want.

CCleaner also provides a **Registry Cleanup** tool that keeps the system's registry in good shape, and a **Drive Wiper** tool that lets you safely remove data from a drive.

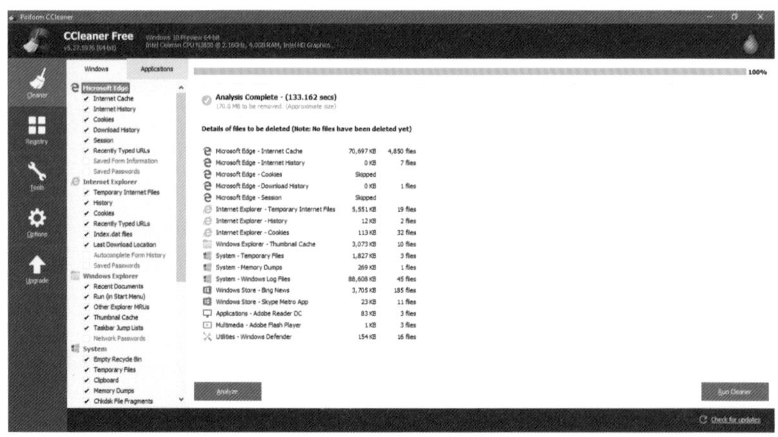

CDBurnerXP

cdburnerxp.se/en/home

CDBurnerXP is a burning utility that enables a wide variety of disks such as CDs, DVDs, Blu-ray and HD-DVDs to be created. Other useful options include the ability to create ISO image files and bootable disks.

1. At the website, click the **Free Download** button

2. Install the program by running the Setup Wizard

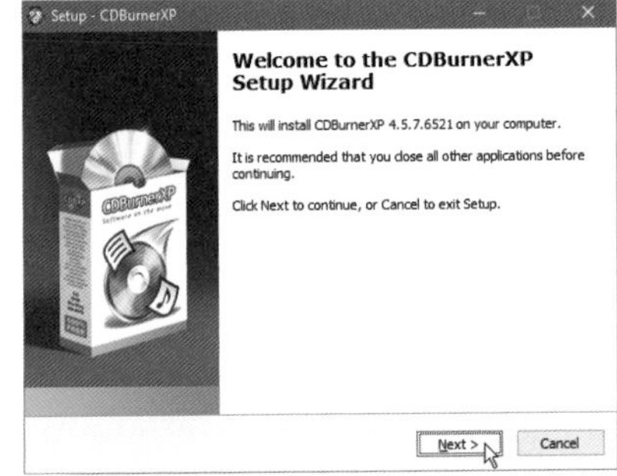

3. When the program is run, you are offered disk burner options to create a Data disk, Video DVD, Audio disk, Burn an ISO image, Copy a disk, or Erase a disk

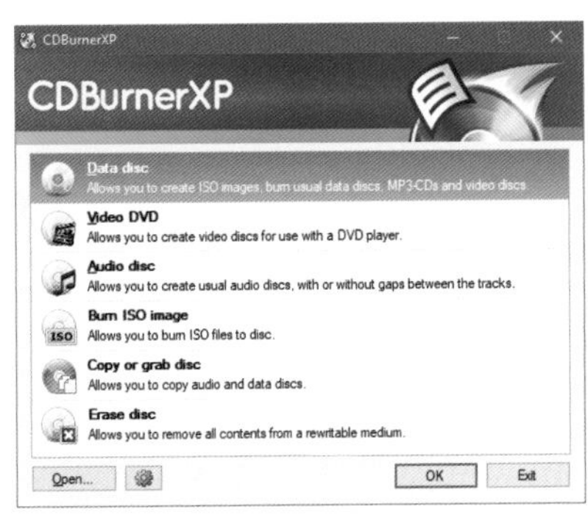

Another free disk authoring utility with a good reputation is **ImgBurn**, which you can download free from imgburn.com

IrfanView

irfanview.com

IrfanView is a very fast and compact graphic viewer for Windows that is freeware (for non-commercial use). It supports many graphics file formats, including multiple (animated) GIF, multi-page TIF and videos.

1. Visit the website and select the IrfanView **download** link

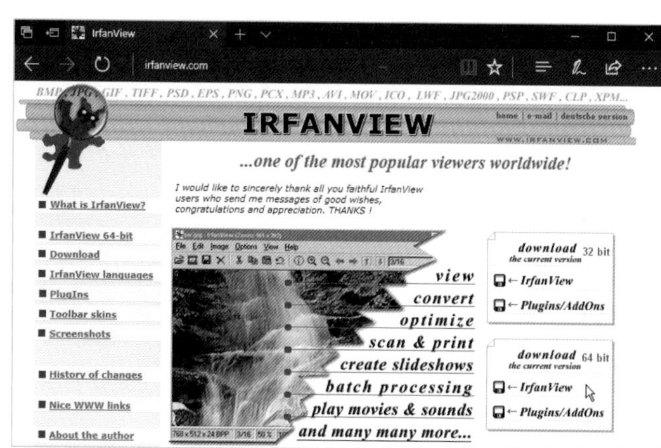

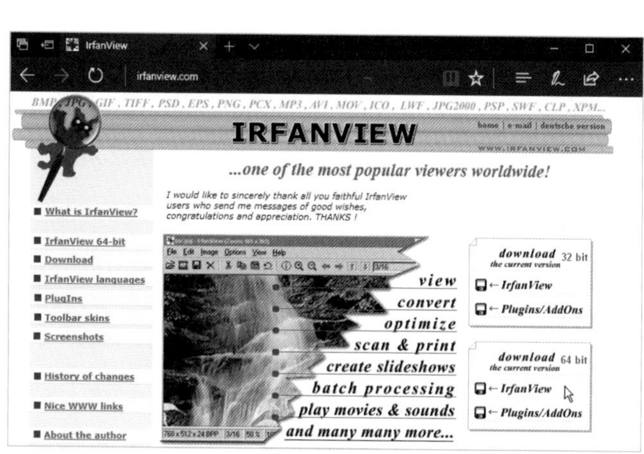

2. Follow the prompts to download and install IrfanView

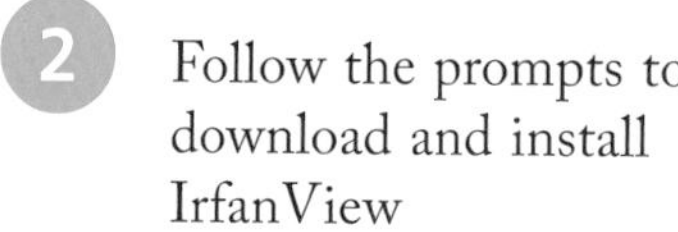

3. On completion, the FAQ web page is displayed and IrfanView starts up

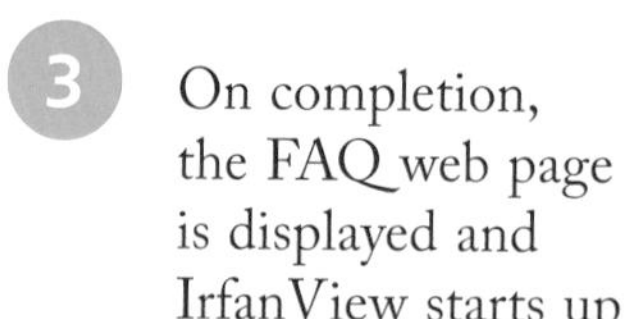

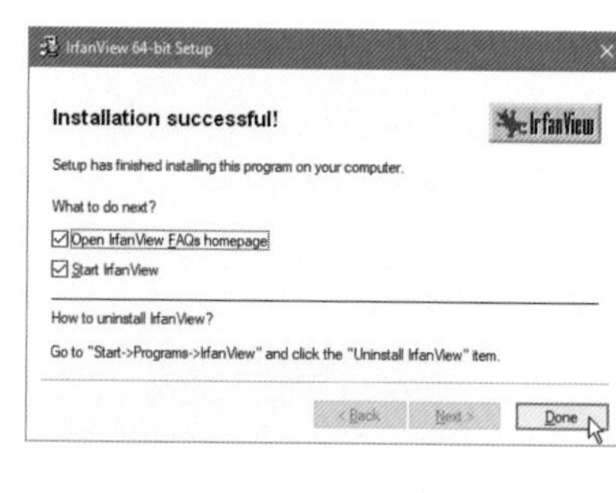

4. Click the forward or back buttons to scroll through all the images

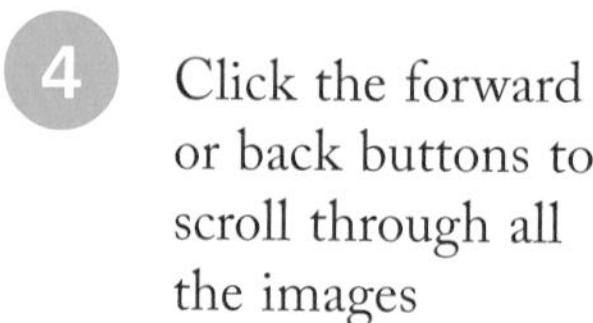

5. In this example, image 5 of 6 is showing

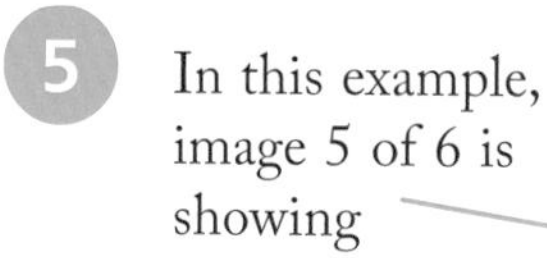

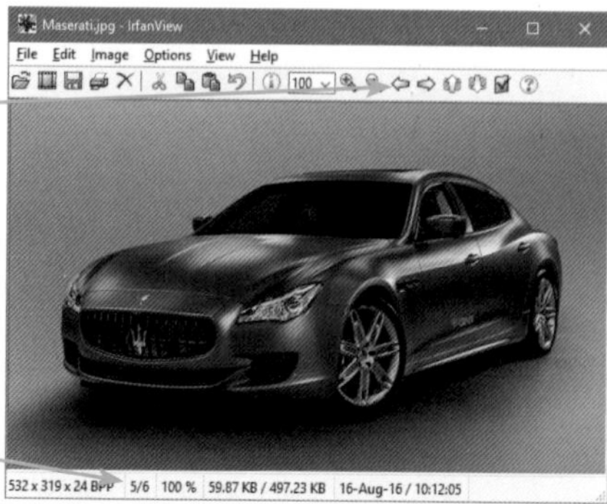

Don't forget

IrfanView is designed to be simple for beginners, and powerful for professionals. It also provides an extremely quick way to scroll through picture folders.

Hot tip

Select the download for **Plug-ins/AddOns** shown in the image in Step 1 to get support for the full set of file formats.

Notepad++

notepad-plus-plus.org

Notepad++ is a free text editor and Notepad replacement that is particularly designed for source code editing. It supports over 50 programming languages, including C, C++, CSS, HTML, Java, and Python.

1. On the website, make sure the current version is selected on the left of the screen then click **Download**

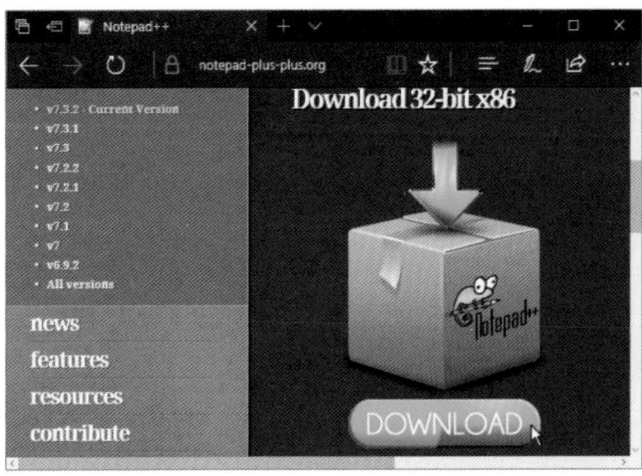

2. Follow the prompts to run the Setup Wizard and install Notepad++

3. The program opens with the Change Log, showing new features and fixes

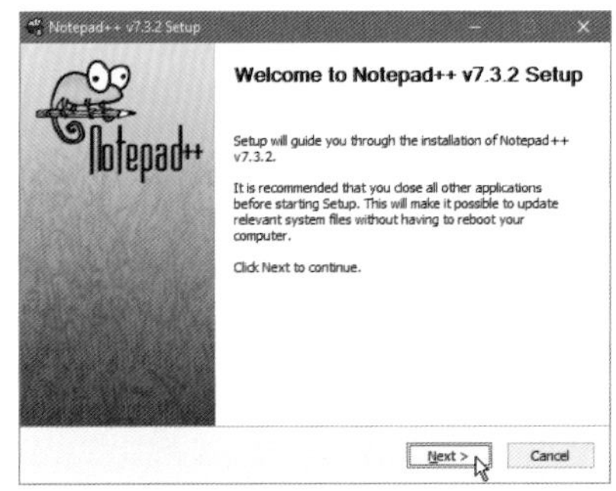

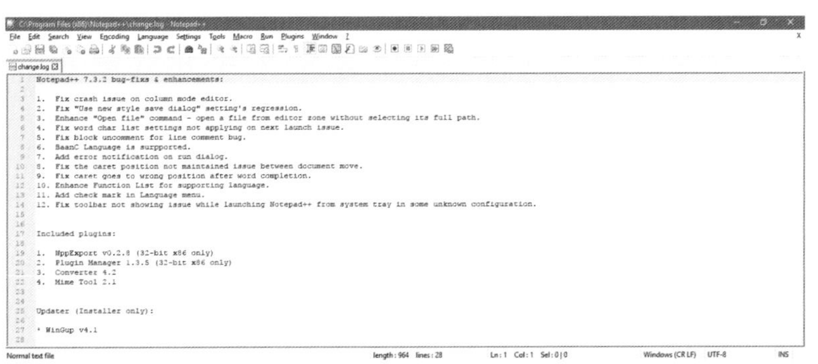

In addition to language support, the main advantage over the built-in Notepad is tabbed editing, which allows you to work with multiple open files.

If you are interested in programming, you can download the source code for this application.

Apache OpenOffice

openoffice.org

Apache OpenOffice is an open-source suite with a powerful set of applications that are very similar to those in Microsoft Office, and include techniques such as macros and templates, but have the advantage of being free to use.

1. Visit the website and select **I want to download...**

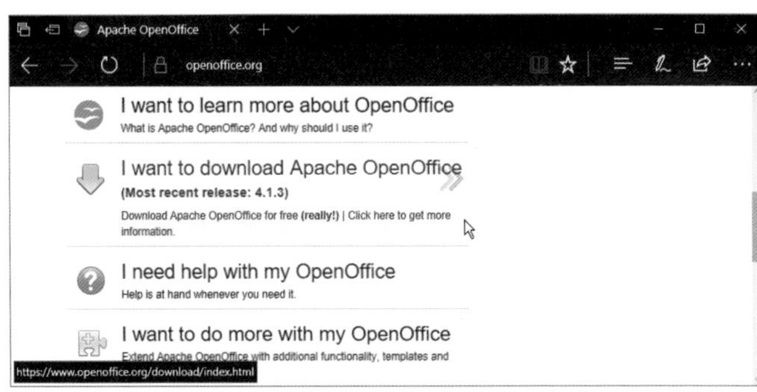

2. Select **Download full installation** for your system

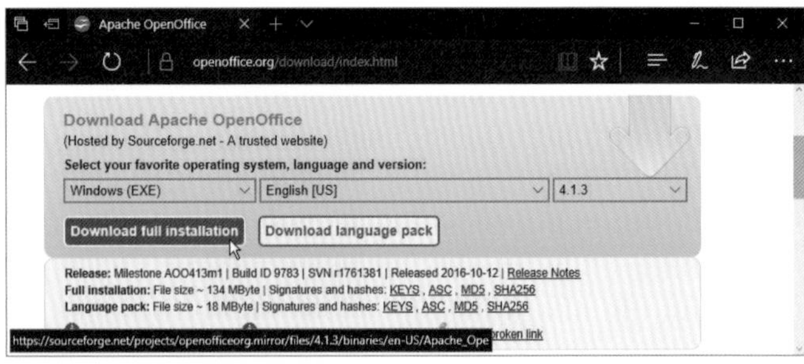

3. Follow the prompts to unpack and save the installation files ready for the actual installation

This website is the entry point for all aspects of Apache OpenOffice, with help, documentation, templates and clipart, as well as installation.

You'll be invited to contribute, but it's your time and effort they want, not your money, since the product is built on user participation.

4. Provide your name and, optionally, your organization, as they are to be used in OpenOffice documents

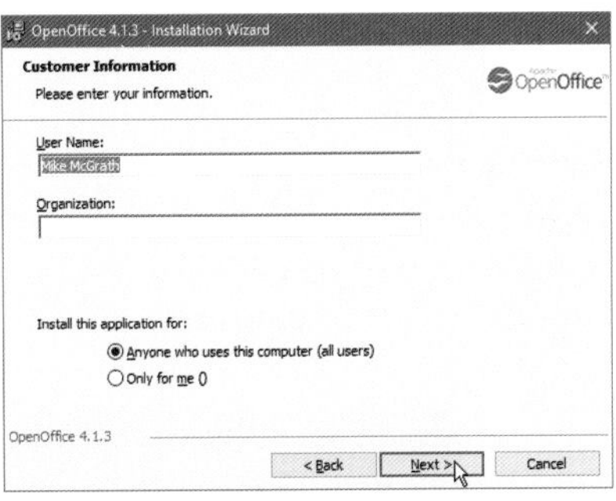

Don't forget

The first time you run Apache OpenOffice you will also be asked to register your details.

5. Select the **Typical** setup, and click Next to install all OpenOffice apps, or choose **Custom** and click Next if you prefer to install only specific apps

6. Upon completion, click **Finish** to end the Wizard

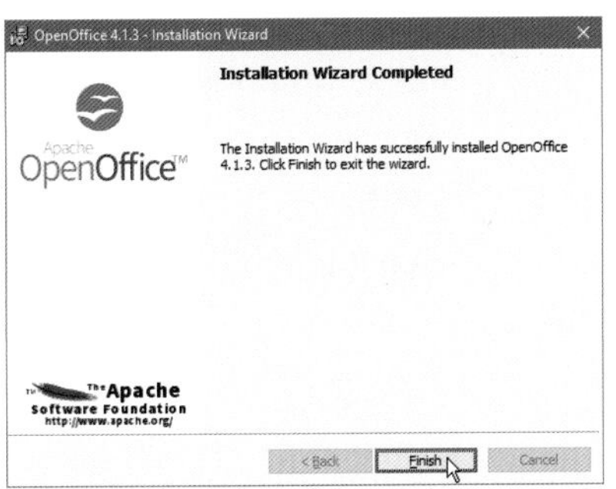

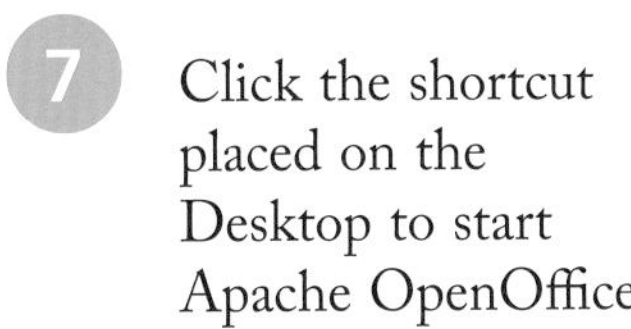

7. Click the shortcut placed on the Desktop to start Apache OpenOffice

Apache OpenOffice has these six components:
Writer (word processor)
Calc (spreadsheet)
Impress (presentations)
Draw (vector graphics)
Base (database) and
Math (formula editor)

Paint.NET

getpaint.net

Where the built-in Windows Paint app doesn't have the power you need, Paint.NET gives you more powerful editing facilities.

1. Click **Download** or click the **paint.net** link

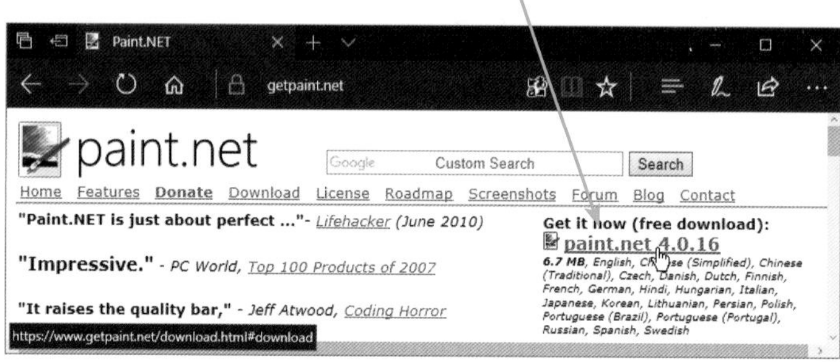

2. Click the **Download Now** button for Paint.NET

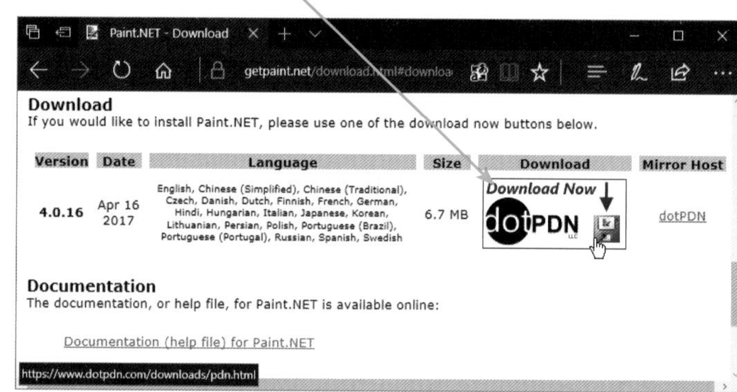

3. Choose to Open the compressed file Paint.NET.4.0.16.Install.zip

Free Download Now:
paint.net 4.0.16
System Requirements

4. This expands to the executable file Paint.NET.4.0.16.Install

It's not equivalent to the full Adobe Photoshop, but it is just what's needed for casual graphic design tasks.

There are many links to lots of programs, such as Facemoods, WhiteSmoke and FLV Player, so make sure that the link you choose does download Paint.NET itself.

5 Choose **Express** for the install method, then click **Next**

6 Agree terms and conditions, then continue

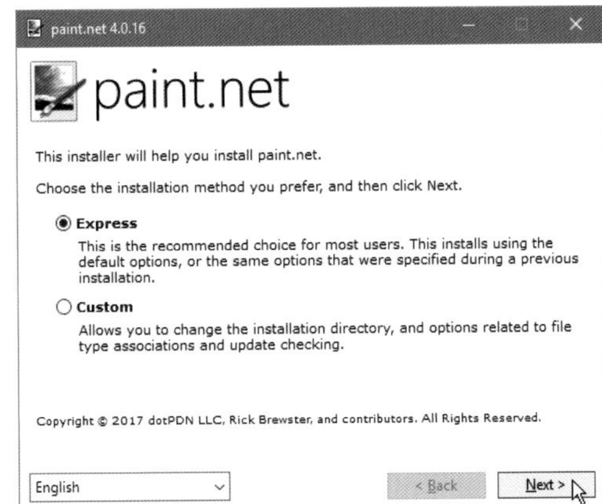

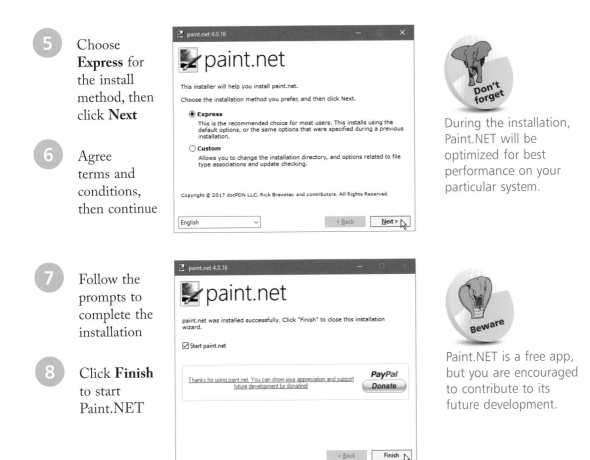

During the installation, Paint.NET will be optimized for best performance on your particular system.

7 Follow the prompts to complete the installation

8 Click **Finish** to start Paint.NET

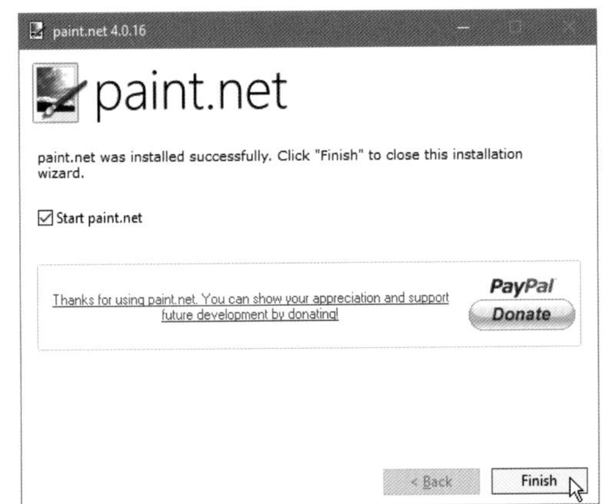

Paint.NET is a free app, but you are encouraged to contribute to its future development.

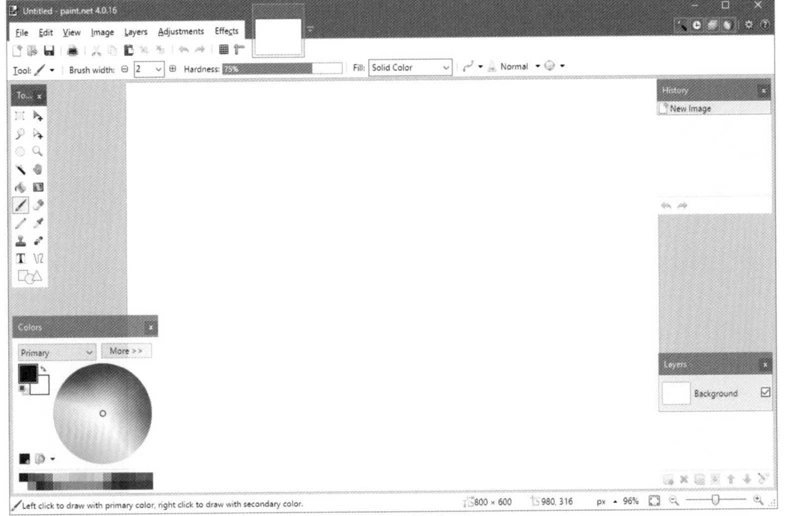

Select **Effects** to see the range offered: Photo, for example, with Glow, Sharpen and Soften, as well as Red Eye Removal. Adjustments also applies various changes to the appearance.

7-Zip

7-zip.org

7-Zip is a free file compression utility that can handle more compressed file formats than the built-in Windows 10 file compression tool. Additionally, it can compress large files into its own **.7z** file format, which produces smaller compressed archive files than the ubiquitous **.zip** file format:

1. Click **Download** and run the installer

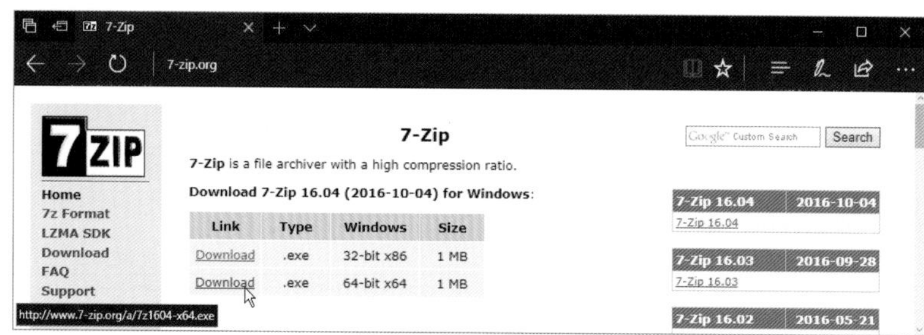

2. Right-click on a compressed archive file and see 7-Zip has been added to the context menu

3. To decompress the archive, choose **Extract Here** from the menu options

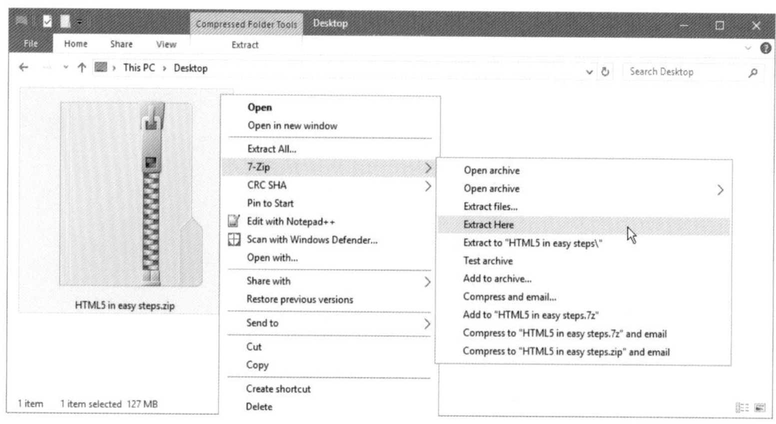

4. See 7-Zip decompress the archive and extract all of its contents alongside the compressed archive file

To use the Windows 10 file compression tool, right-click and choose **Send to**, **Compressed (zipped) folder** to create an archive file, or choose **Extract All...** to decompress an archive.

7-Zip can create archives in several formats including: **.zip**, **.7z**, and **.bzip2**, and extract many archive formats including: **.cab**, **.chm**, **.iso**, **.lzh**, **.rar**, and **.wim**.

5. In this example, notice that the compressed **.zip** archive of 127MB is expanded to 229MB when decompressed

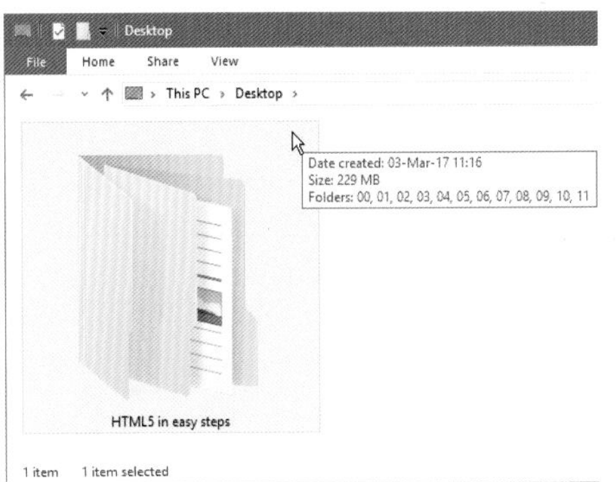

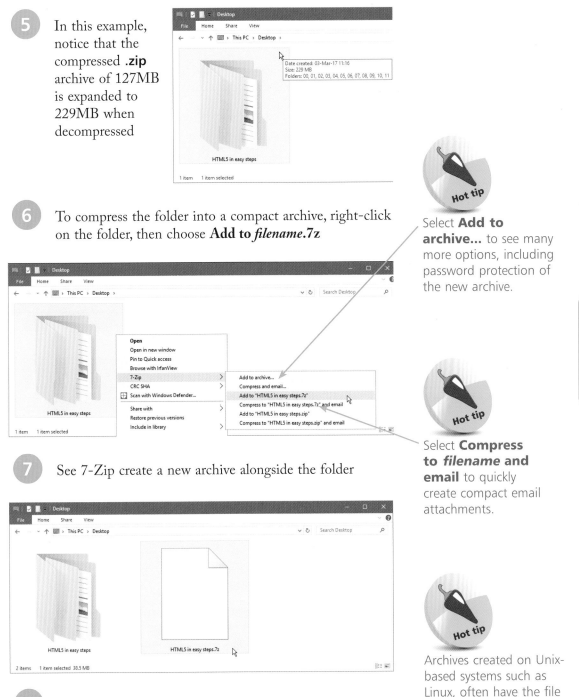

6. To compress the folder into a compact archive, right-click on the folder, then choose **Add to *filename*.7z**

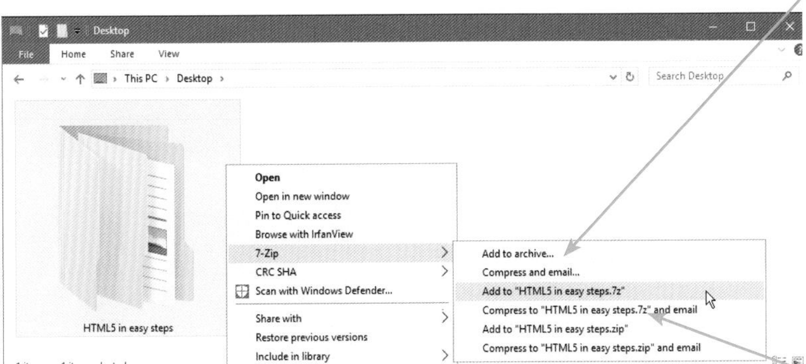

7. See 7-Zip create a new archive alongside the folder

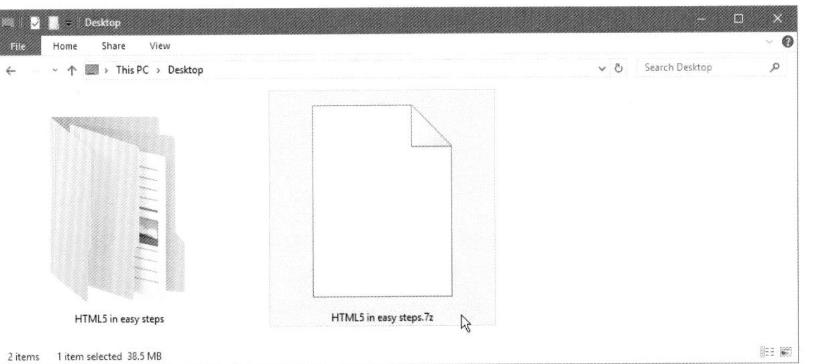

8. In this example, notice that the compressed **.7z** archive is just 38.5MB – considerably smaller than the **.zip** version!

Select **Add to archive...** to see many more options, including password protection of the new archive.

Select **Compress to *filename* and email** to quickly create compact email attachments.

Archives created on Unix-based systems such as Linux, often have the file extension **.tar.gz** – 7-Zip can handle those too.

μTorrent

utorrent.com

μTorrent (also referred to as uTorrent) is a freeware but closed-source BitTorrent client. The μ in its name implies the prefix micro, in deference to the program's small size, but it can handle very large downloads very rapidly.

1. At the μTorrent website, click the **Get μTorrent for Windows** button

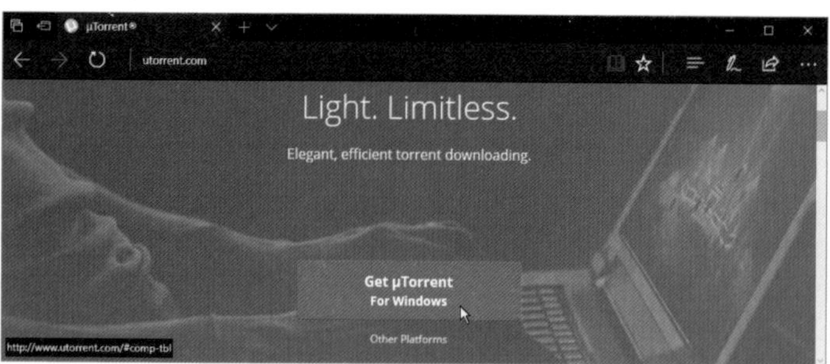

2. Again, click **Get μTorrent for Windows** and a free download will automatically start

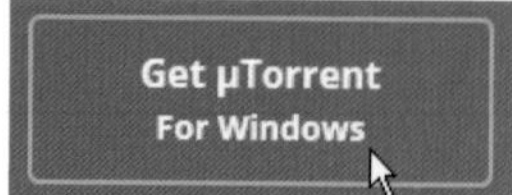

3. Follow prompts to download and run the Setup Wizard

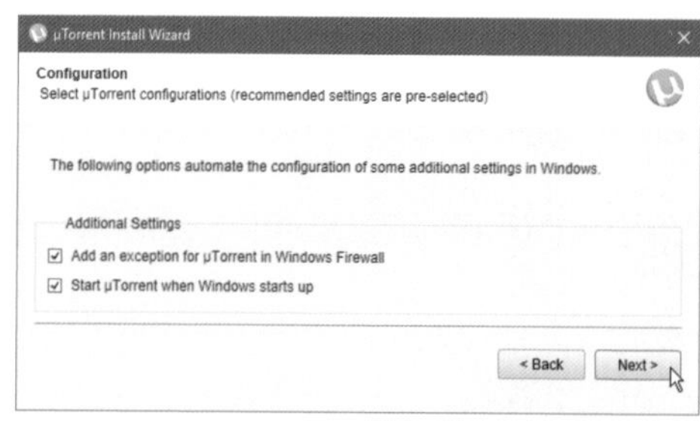

4. When the installation completes, μTorrent is launched

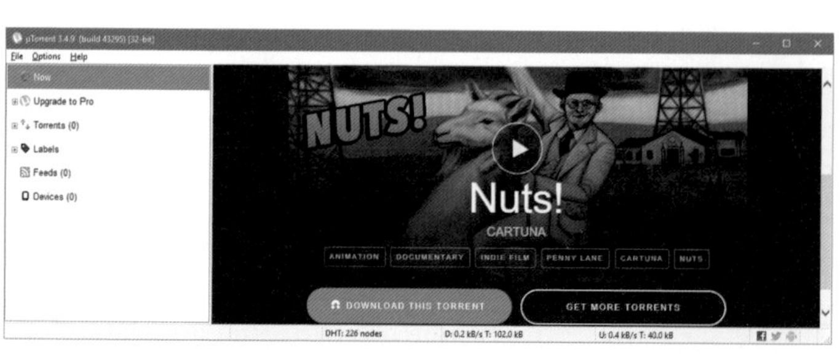

A BitTorrent client is a computer program that manages downloads and uploads using the BitTorrent protocol. This is used for peer-to-peer file sharing for distributing large amounts of data.

Make sure that files you select for downloading via μTorrent are in the public domain and not subject to copyright.

9 Windows Store

If you need apps to run on your Windows 10 devices, the Windows Store is the place to go. This chapter shows how to access, search and navigate the Store. You will also learn how to install apps, keep them updated, and how to manage them.

Accessing the Store

When you need apps, the Windows Store is the place to go. It is, in fact, the only place to go – official Windows 10 apps are not available from any other source. To access the Store:

Open the Start menu, then click any **Store** launcher

The Windows Store has been redesigned to be a one-stop-shop for all Windows 10 devices.

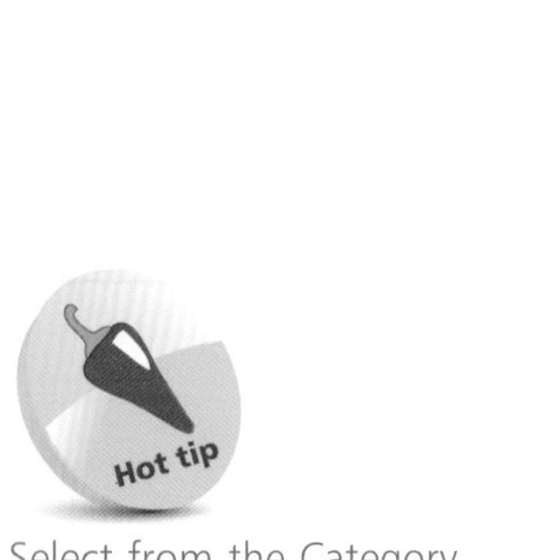

Select from the Category menu then scroll down the page to find the list of categories.

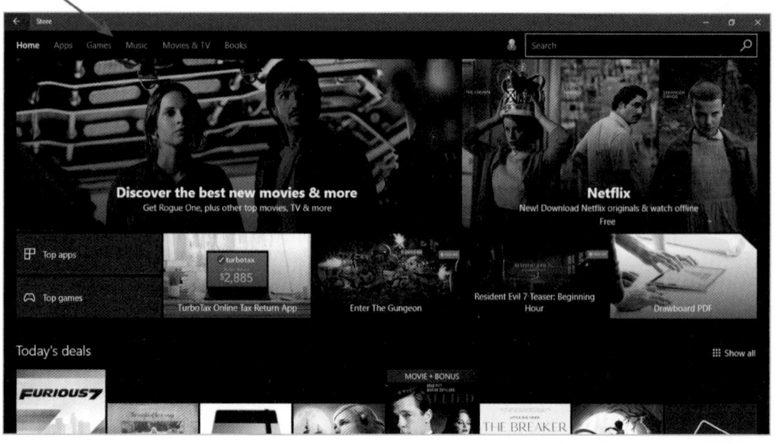

The Books category was added to the Windows Store when the Windows 10 Creators Update was released.

Store categories

The Windows Store organizes its products into specific categories to make it easier to find what you are looking for. These frequently change, but look like this at the time of writing:

Apps				
Books & reference	Food & dining	Medical	Personal finance	Shopping
Business	Government & politics	Multimedia design	Personalization	Social
Developer tools	Health & fitness	Music	Photo & video	Sports
Education	Kids & family	Navigation & maps	Productivity	Travel
Entertainment	Lifestyle	News & weather	Security	Utilities & tools
Games				
Action & adventure	Companion	Multi-player battle	Racing & flying	Sports
Avatar	Creators collection	Music	Role playing	Strategy
Card & board	Educational	Other	Shooter	Tools
Casino	Family & kids	Platformer	Simulation	Video
Classics	Fighting	Puzzle & trivia	Social	Word
Music				
Blues/Folk	Country	Kids	R&B/Soul	World
Christian/Gospel	Electronic/Dance	Latin	Reggae/Dancehall	
Classical	Hip Hop	More	Rock	
Comedy/ Spoken Word	Jazz	Pop	Soundtracks	
Movies & TV				
Action/Adventure	Documentary	Horror	Sci-Fi/Fantasy	
Animation	Drama	Other	Sports	
Anime	Family	Romance	Thriller/Mystery	
Comedy	Foreign/Independent	Romantic Comedy	TV Movies	
Books				
Arts & Entertainment	Computers & Internet	Health, Mind & Body	Politics, Law & Society	Sci-Fi & Fantasy
Biography & Memoirs	Cooking, Food & Wine	History	Reference & Language	Sports & Outdoors
Business & Finance	Education	Home & Garden	Religion & Spirituality	Travel
Children's eBooks	Engineering & Transportation	Mystery & Thrillers	Romance	Young Adult
Comics & Graphic Novels	Fiction & Literature	Parenting & Family	Science & Nature	

Navigating the Store

You can select the **Home** menu item at any time to return to the Store's Home page.

Category menu

Selection groups

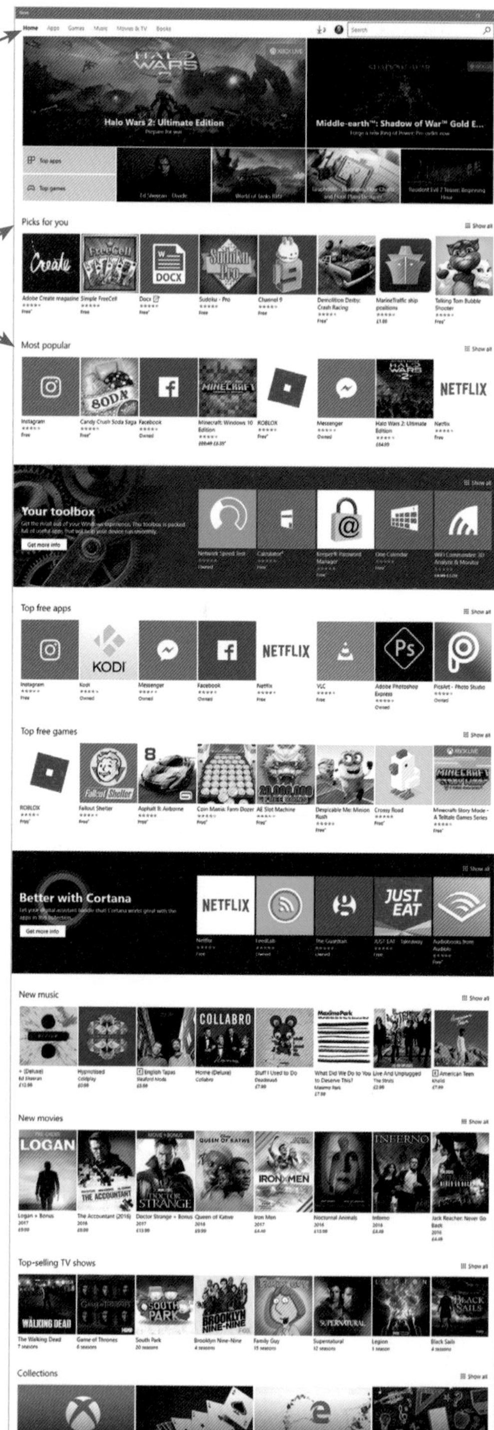

The Store's **Home** page is headed with recent promotional items. Scroll down the Home page of the Store to see these selection groups:

- **Picks for you**
- **Top free apps**
- **Top free games**
- **New music**
- **New movies**
- **Top-selling TV shows**
- **Collections**

Use the Store's category menu bar at the top-left of the Store window, to review categories of:

- **Apps**
- **Games**
- **Music**
- **Movies & TV**
- **Books**

Exploring categories

On the Home page, a small selection of featured apps are presented in selection groups, which can be accessed directly from the Home page.

If you can't see what you want here, then you need to dig deeper. Select a Store category, then refine your requirements.

1. To open a Store category, click its name on the category menu. For example, select the **Games** category

2. The category page will open and is laid out like the Home page, but features only items relevant to that category

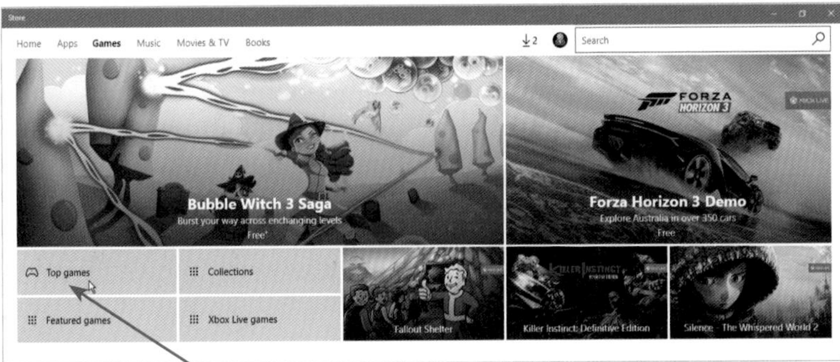

3. The category page also provides a menu with which to explore that category further. For example, on the Games category page, select the **Top games** menu item

4. Sub-categories are provided to refine your requirements

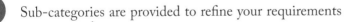

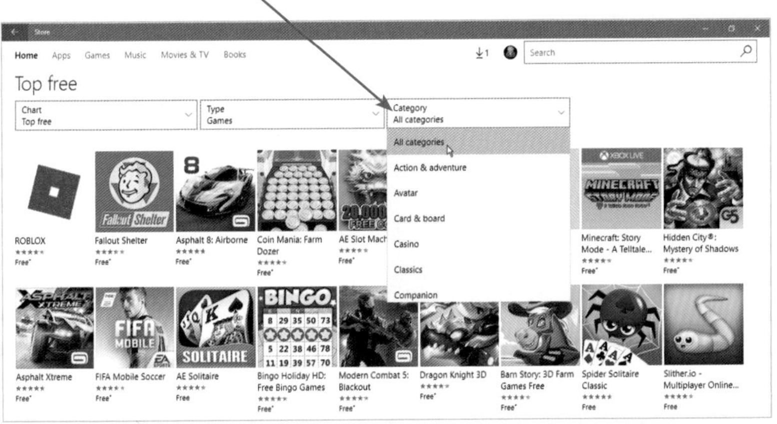

Use the **Back** button at the top-left of any Store window to return to previous pages.

Search the Store

Search is an extremely important component of modern user interfaces, and currently is one of the most common ways for customers to find things when browsing online stores.

In Windows 8, the Windows Store didn't have a Search box – you had to search using the Search charm, which many users found confusing. The revamped store in Windows 10 does provide a Search box, though, and this can be found at the top-right of any Store page, as shown below:

Search begins looking for results as soon as you type two characters into the Search box.

If you know the name of the app you want or are looking for apps by a specific publisher, enter the name into the Search box. In the page that opens, you'll see the results of your search, as in our "video" search below:

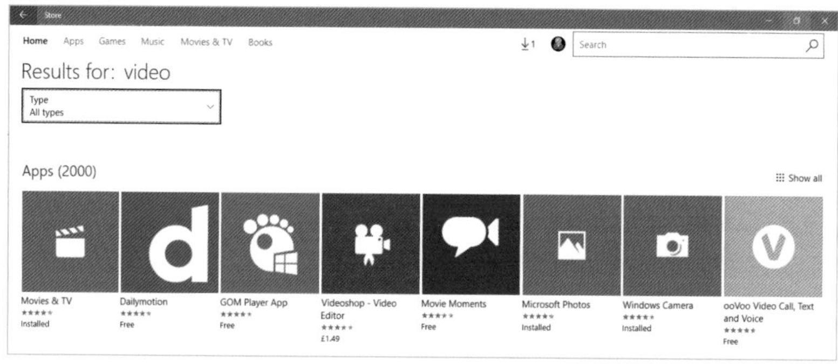

1. If any of the apps shown appear to be of interest, just left-click one to open it and get further details

An important aspect of the Windows 10 search is that it is universally accessible, meaning you can search for an app no matter where you are in the Windows 10 interface – you don't need to be in the Store. We see how this works on the next page.

In the example shown below, you're using the Microsoft Edge app to browse a site about Mahjong. This triggers in you a sudden curiosity to see if there are any Mahjong apps available.

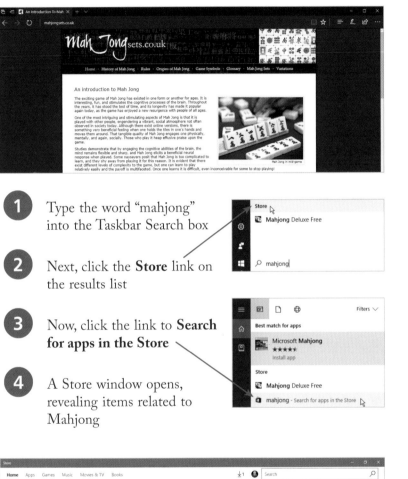

1. Type the word "mahjong" into the Taskbar Search box

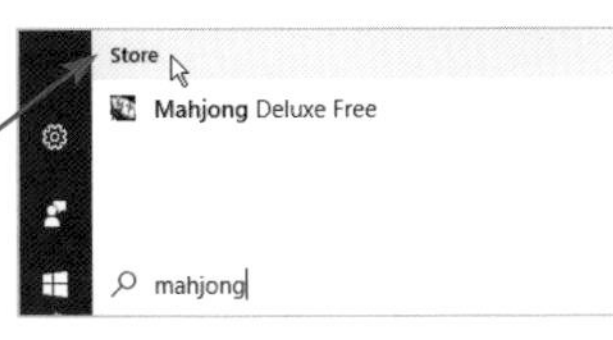

2. Next, click the **Store** link on the results list
3. Now, click the link to **Search for apps in the Store**

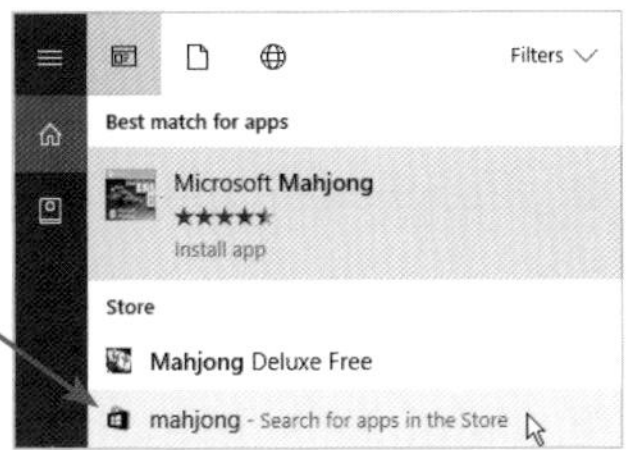

4. A Store window opens, revealing items related to Mahjong

As you type in the Taskbar Search box, suggestions immediately appear in the results list.

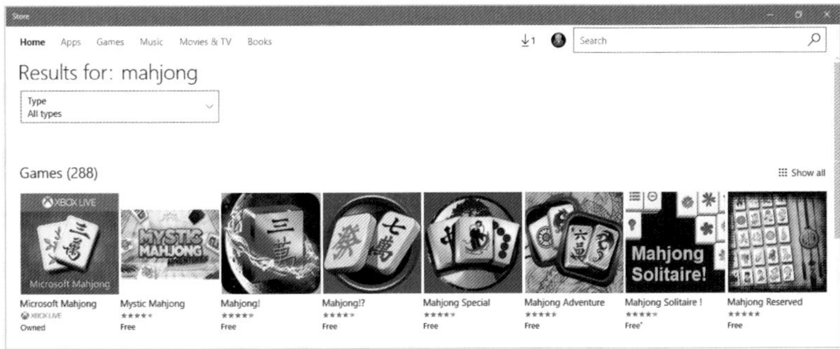

Select an app

To select an app, simply click on its tile. As an example, we have searched for the Netflix app as shown below:

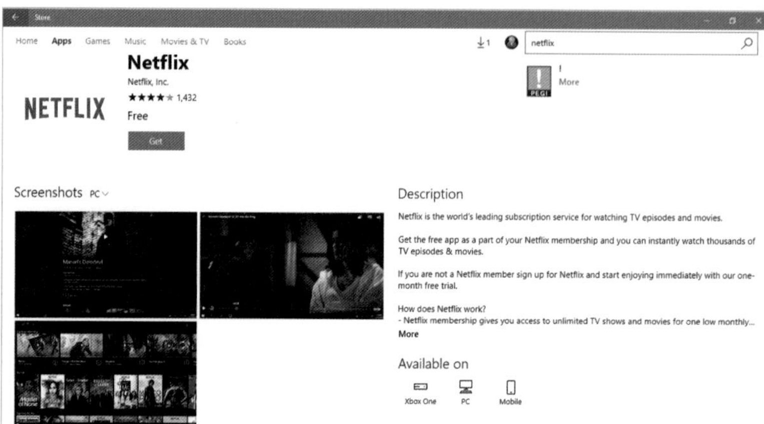

The **More** link shown here provides the age rating from PEGI (Pan European Gaming Information). Rating information for other regions may vary.

The page begins with a brief description of the app. Age rating information can be seen by clicking the **More** link. Below the description is a download button that will display the price if the app isn't free, or "Install" if you can download the app for free.

Moving down the page, there are four headings:

- **People also like** – similar apps that you may want to consider.
- **System Requirements** – operating system version needed.
- **Additional information** – typically informs you of the app's file size, required permissions, and the languages supported.
- **Ratings and reviews** – gives you the average rating figure, the total number of ratings and the total number of reviews.

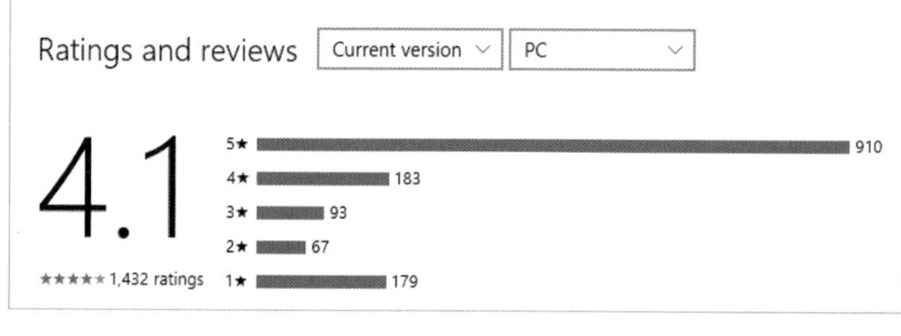

Before paying for an app it's worth checking out the reviews.

Download and install

Microsoft has made it simple to download and install apps from the Store in Windows 10:

1. Click the **Get** button below the app description

2. See the **Get** button change to a "Downloading..." label while the app installs

You must be logged in with a Microsoft account before you can download an app.

3. You will receive a notification when the installation is complete

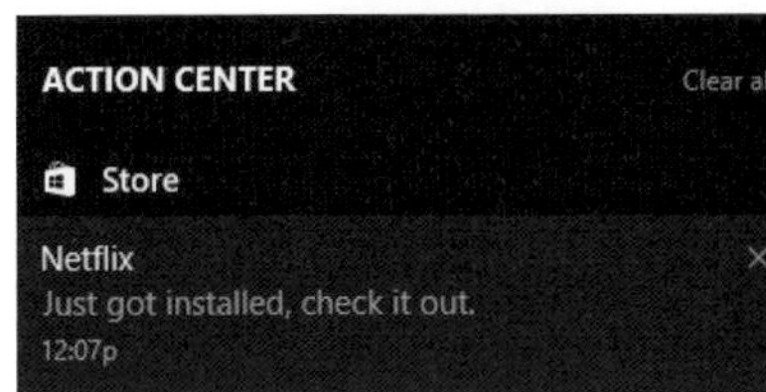

4. The app will now appear on the Start menu, under its alphabetic A-Z heading, and will also appear under the **Recently added** heading

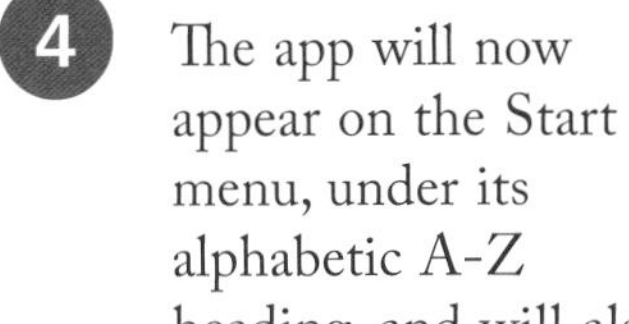

5. Click the menu item to launch the app as usual

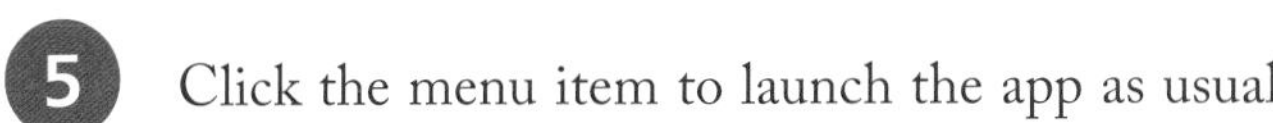

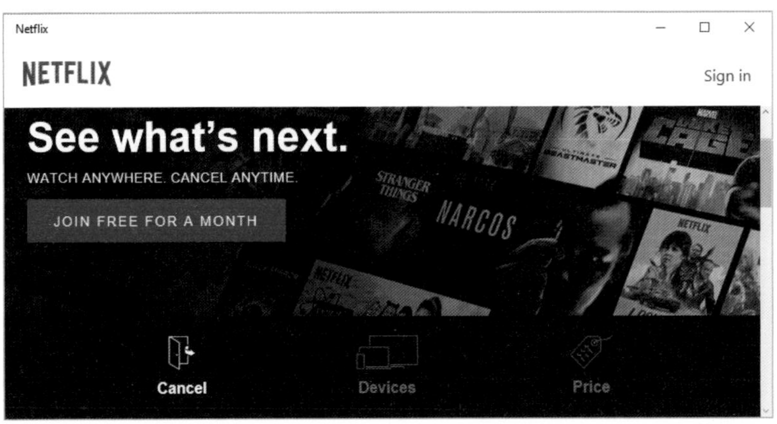

Skype app

Skype is a service that allows users to communicate by voice, video, and instant messaging. It can be found on the Store or bundled with Windows 10 and is launched from the Start menu:

1. Skype starts up displaying your recent activity

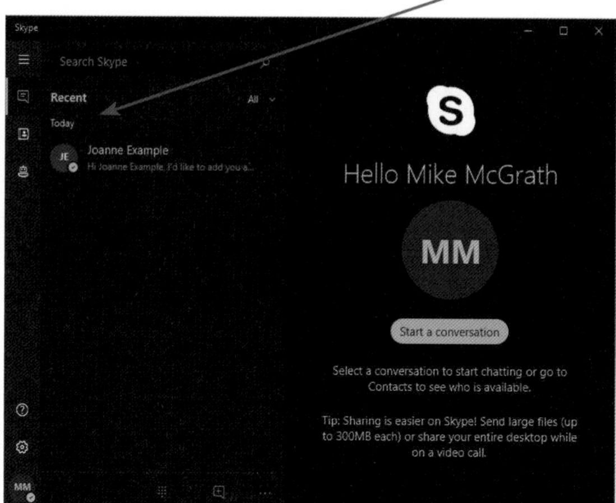

Calls to other users within the Skype service are free of charge, while calls via landline and mobile networks are charged via a debit-based user account system.

2. Click on **Contacts** in the left-hand pane, then choose a contact

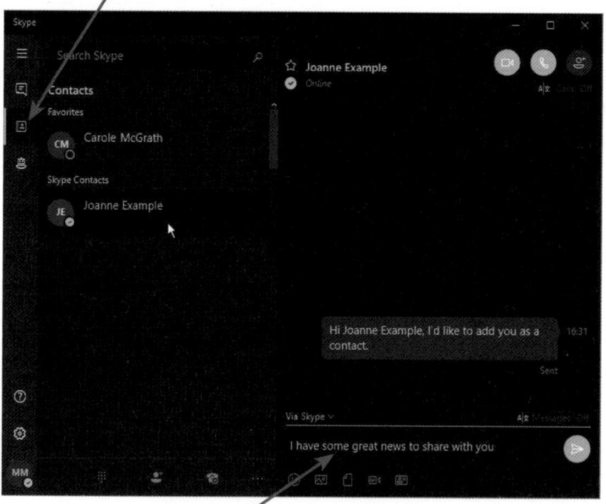

Skype provides additional features, such as file transfer, and video conferencing.

3. Type in the box then click [send] to send an instant message

4. Click the [video] button to make a Skype video call

5. Click the [call] button to make a Skype voice call

Skype can also make calls to regular phone numbers, but you will need credit to pay for these calls:

1. Click the button to open the call dialer

2. Enter the phone number you wish to call, then click the **Call** button on the dialer to see the attempt fail

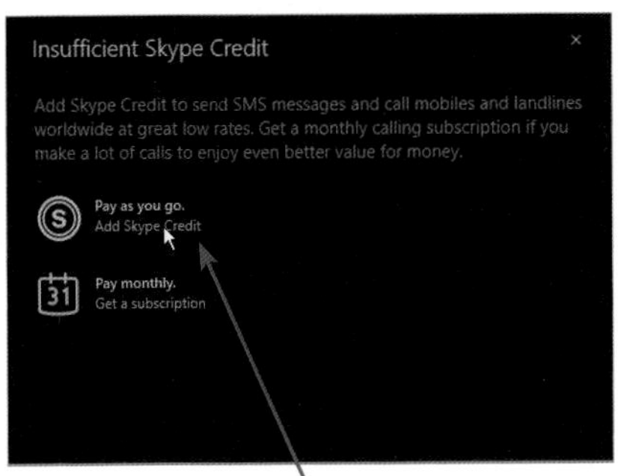

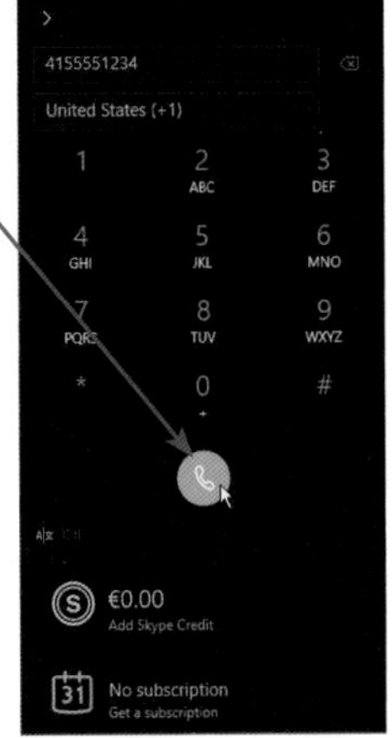

3. Select **Add Skype Credit** (or **Get a subscription**) and see a Microsoft Edge browser window open to add credit

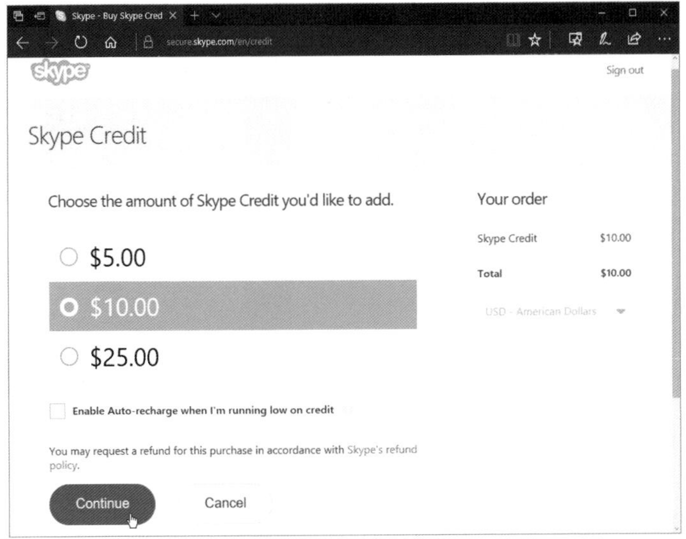

4. Add credit, then click the **Call** button to complete the call

The Skype app can be extremely useful when used with Windows 10's split-screen Snap feature. This enables a conversation to be had, while at the same time getting on with something else on the main part of the screen.

A feature of the Skype app is that it can be left running permanently without any adverse effect on the computer.

App account

One of the big advantages of logging in to all of your devices with the same Microsoft account is that any apps you have bought and installed on one device can be downloaded from the Cloud and installed on another device. For example, we have bought a game called "Riptide GP" and installed it on a desktop PC. To install it on other devices, all we have to do is:

1. On a tablet's Start menu, tap the **Store** item
2. In the **Store** Search box, enter "Riptide GP" to see that you already own this product

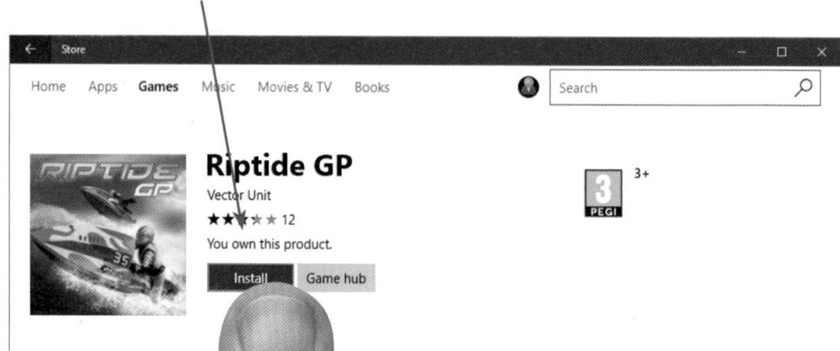
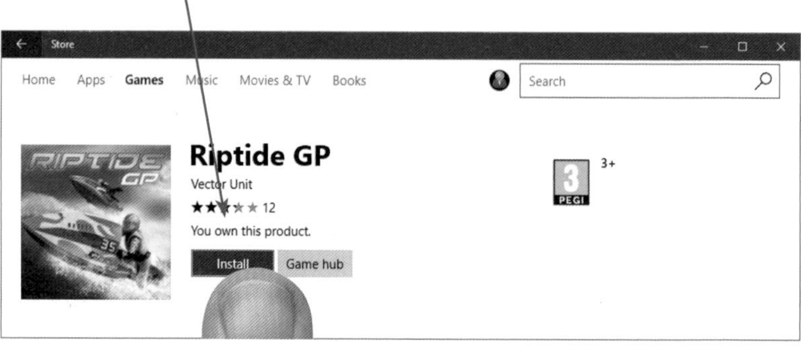

3. Tap the **Install** button to install this game on the tablet
4. In a laptop's Search box, enter "Riptide GP" to see the results offer related suggestions and a **Store** link
5. As you already own this game there is also an **Install app** option
6. Click the **Install app** option to install the game on the laptop

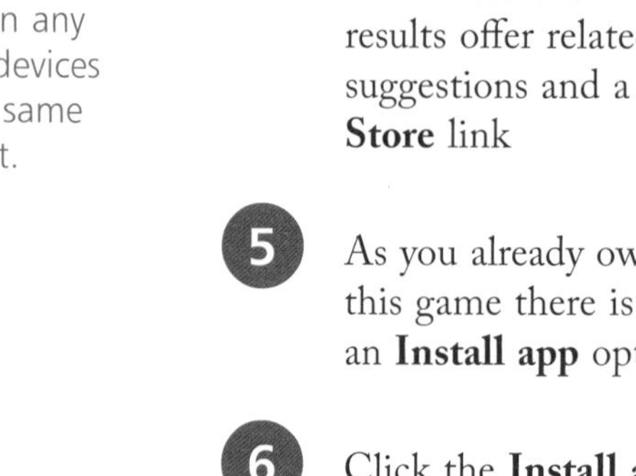
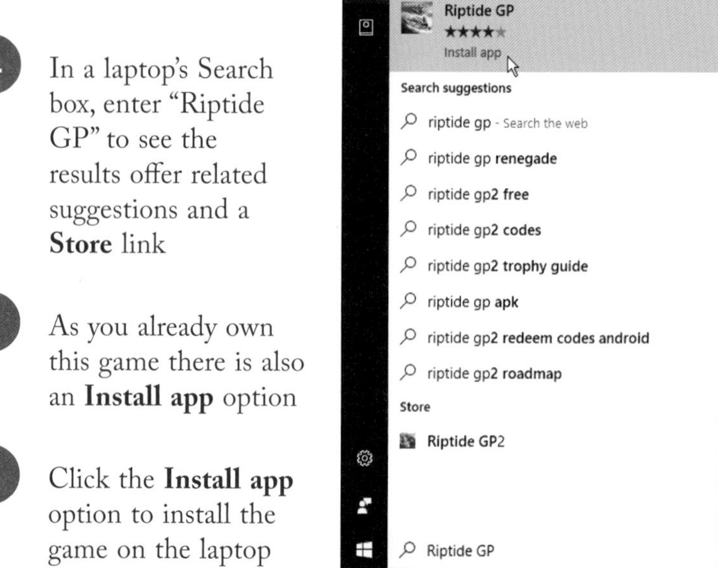

Hot tip

Because the app has already been paid for, the **Install** button is shown rather than the **Buy** button.

Don't forget

Having paid for an app you can install it from the Cloud on any other supported devices you use with the same Microsoft account.

Updates

It is important to keep your system updated. This applies not just to Windows itself, but also to the programs you use. App publishers sometimes update their apps to add new features and fix problems.

Windows 10 updates itself automatically. To set it up to update your apps automatically as well, do the following:

1. On the Start menu, click the **Store** item to open the Windows Store

2. Click your user profile icon to open the drop-down menu

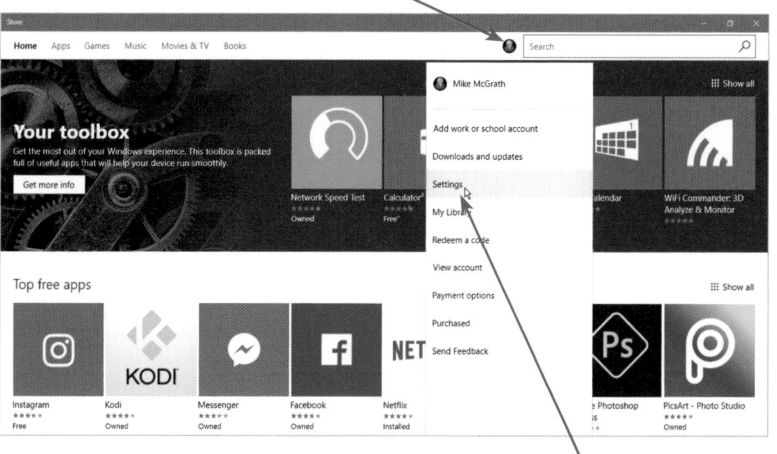

3. From the drop-down menu, select the **Settings** item

4. On the Settings menu, slide the button to set the "Update apps automatically" option to the **On** position

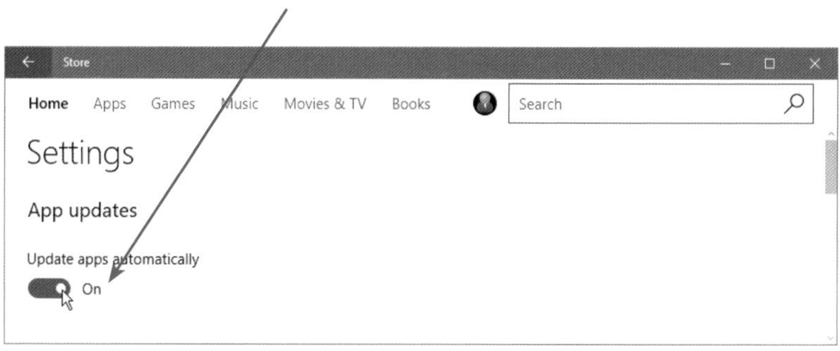

Unlike previous versions of Windows, the Windows 10 release is seen by Microsoft as "Windows-as-a-Service" – which will automatically receive free feature additions, improvements, and updates.

When you log in to Windows or the Store with a Microsoft account, your user profile icon automatically appears in the Store window.

Manage apps

App tiles on the right of the Start menu are much larger than the Start menu list items. The more congested the Start menu becomes, the more scrolling will be necessary to find an app, so it's a great idea to arrange the Start menu tiles conveniently. It's best to place your most frequently-accessed apps at the top of the Start menu tile area where they will be on view by default. To do this, just left-click on the tile, then drag it to where you want it.

An important aspect of organizing the Start menu is placing app tiles in related groups.

Create and organize groups

App tiles are automatically placed in groups, which can be moved around the Start menu in blocks. This makes it easier to arrange your Start menu, and having your apps in specific and related groups makes it much easier to locate them as and when required. At the top of each group is a bar bearing the name of that group. Drag this bar across the Start menu to move the group.

The customizable Start menu is a great new feature in Windows 10.

Tiles can be easily switched from one group to another group. Drag a tile from any group to see the other tiles move to accommodate that tile within a different group, as shown below. If you take any heading group bar and drag it across the Start menu you'll see other groups move to accommodate that group.

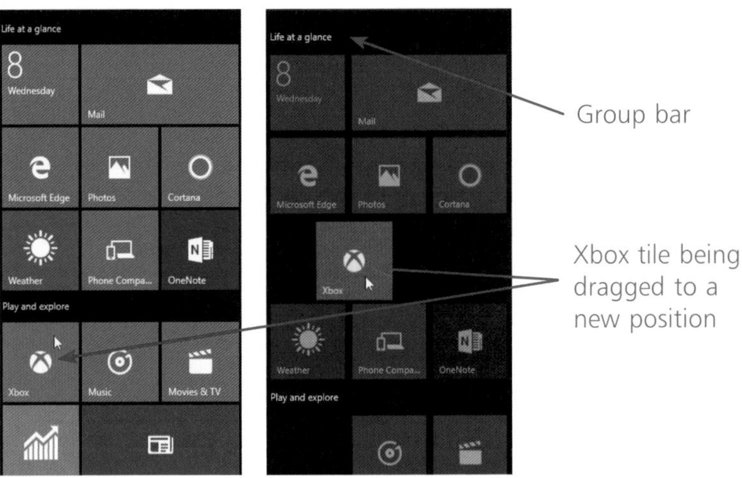

Another thing you can do is to reduce the size of the large tiles. This will create more space on the Start menu, which reduces the amount of scrolling necessary. Just right-click on a tile, select **Resize** and choose from the available options.

If you want to start a new group, drag an app item from the Start menu's A-Z list onto the right-hand part of the Start menu, and release it above an existing group bar – the new group is created. Add more tiles to it as already described.

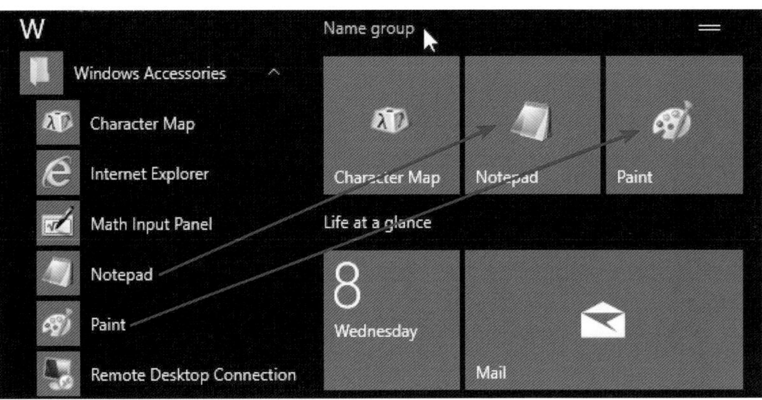

The group bar of a new group may not be visible until you place the mouse over its position.

Name a group

You can assign a name to a group by editing its group bar. Simply click on a group bar then type a name of your choice into the box.

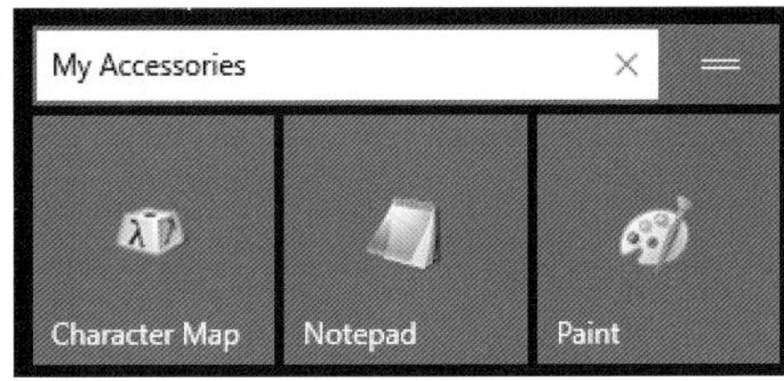

You can edit the name of any existing group using its Name group box.

Create Start menu folders

You can group the tiles on your Start menu into folders, too. Just drag a tile onto another, then drop it to create a folder that can contain multiple tiles. Click on the folder to see it expand to reveal the tiles it contains, then click again to collapse the folder:

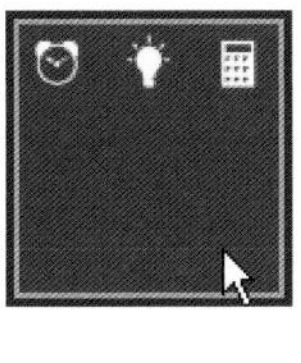

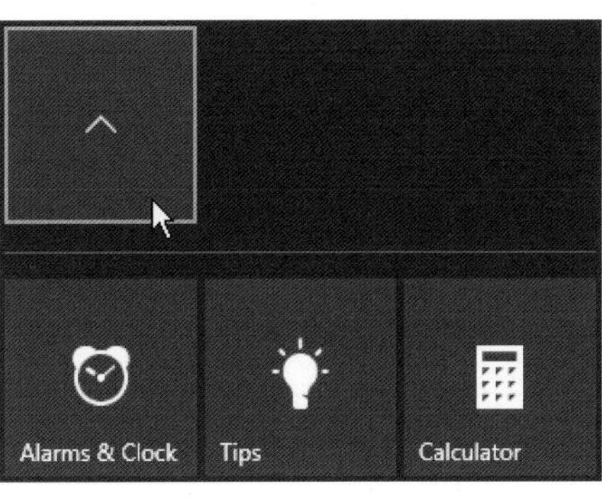

The ability to create Start menu folders was introduced in the Windows 10 Creators Update to add more Start menu flexibility.

Desktop apps

Although the Windows Store provides a huge range of apps, some traditional Desktop programs are not included and must be downloaded directly from the publisher's own website. For example, the popular Photoshop image editing program must be acquired directly from Adobe:

When you buy a Desktop program outside the Windows Store, don't forget that updates to the app must be downloaded from the publisher's website – they won't be provided through the Store.

1. Enter "adobe photoshop" in the Taskbar Search box, then select a link from the results to visit the Adobe website

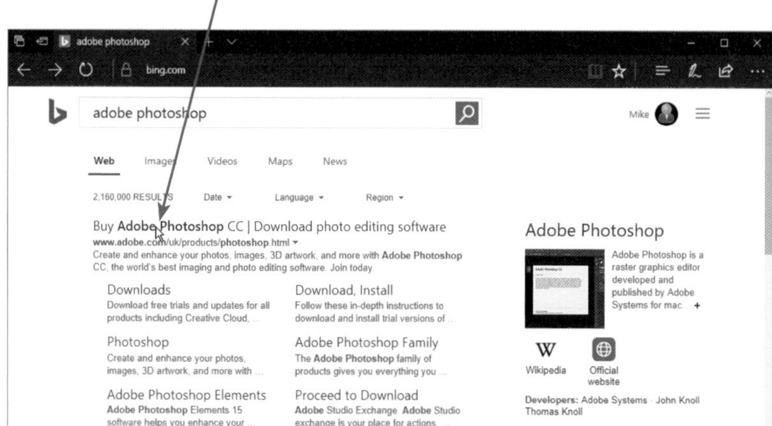

2. Click the **Buy now** button to download and install the program directly from Adobe

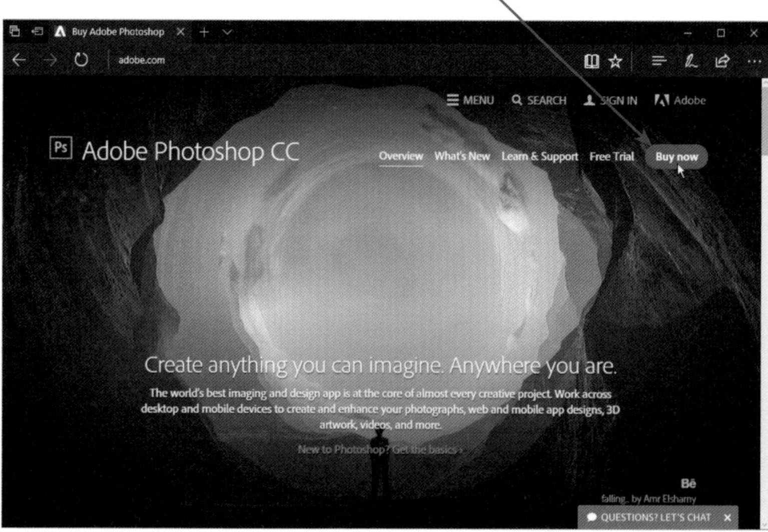

10 Search techniques

Windows 10 provides many ways to help you find the programs, utilities and information that you need. There's a Search box in every File Explorer folder, and the Taskbar Search box is always readily available.

Start screen search

When you need to search for something it's remarkably simple in Windows 10 – all you have to do is type what you want to find into the Search box located on the Desktop Taskbar.

By default, Windows 10 searches include your apps and folders.

Search box

As you begin to type, the search results will instantly update, displaying the search results in a list above the Search box:

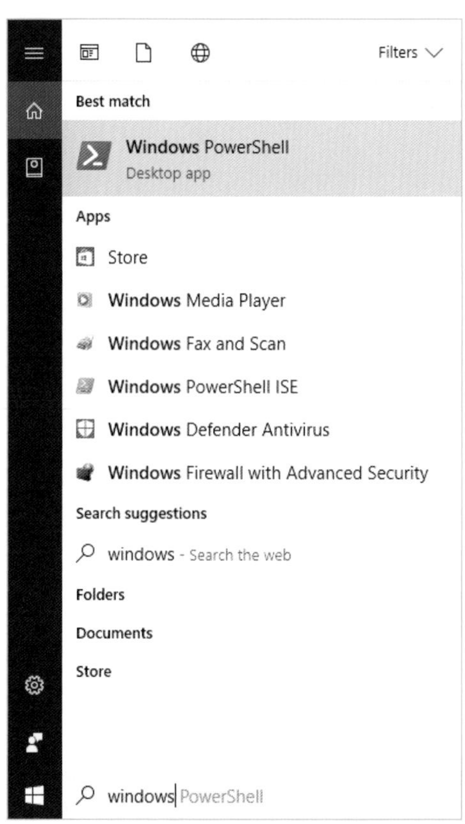

The Taskbar Search box is another great new feature in Windows 10.

In our example, we've searched for "windows". Due to its tight integration with Microsoft's Bing search engine, the results of the search allow to search further on the internet and in the Store.

Search filters

The default action of Windows 10's search function is to search the apps and folders on your PC. This can bring too many results, unrelated results, or not the desired results. There are three things you can do:

Apps filter

The first is to use the apps filter built in to the Search box to return only results related to applications:

1. In the results, choose the **Apps** button to limit results to apps on your PC and apps available in the Store

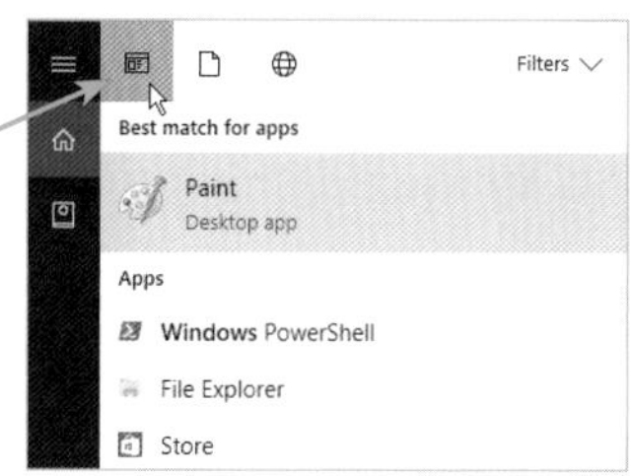

Documents filter

The second is to use the documents filter built in to the Search box to return only results related to documents:

2. In the results, choose the **Documents** button to limit results to document files on your PC and in your OneDrive folders

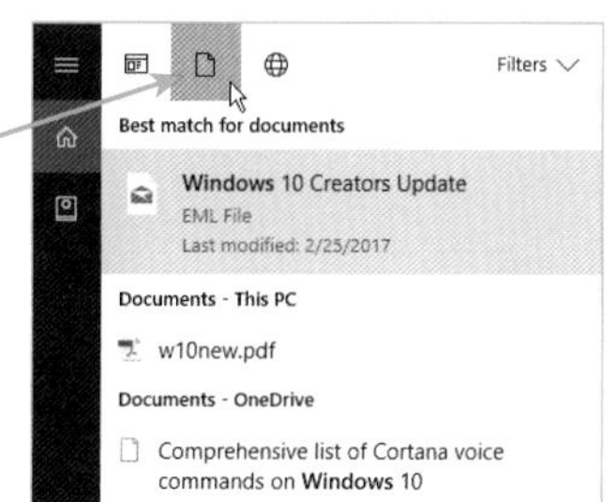

Windows 10 local search lets you sort results by **Most Relevant** or **Most Recent**, and it provides seven secondary filters – Documents, Folders, Apps, Settings, Photos, Videos, Music.

Web filter

The third is to use the web filter built in to the Search box to return only results related to internet items:

3. In the results, choose the **Web** button to limit results to a list of internet search suggestions and an option to search with Bing

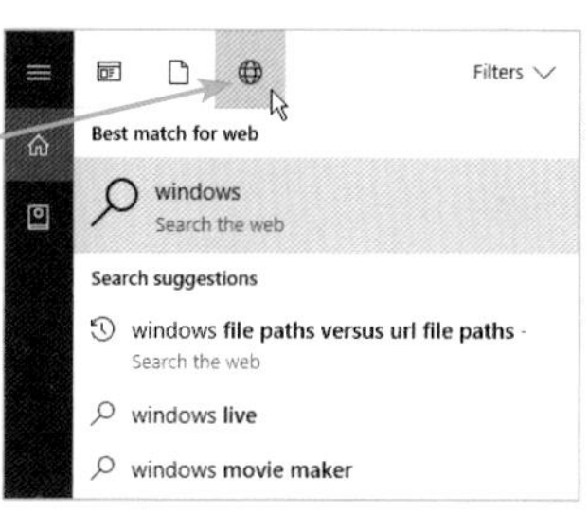

File Explorer search

The Search utility is considered by some to be one of the best features in Windows 10, and provides quick and very comprehensive search results – sometimes too many, in fact. While secondary local filters help to narrow searches down, general and system-wide searches can produce too many results.

The Search facility provided by File Explorer is extremely useful in situations such as these, as it enables searches to be restricted to specific parts of Windows, thus producing fewer, but more relevant results.

Don't forget

Results from a folder search will include any sub-folders the folder may contain.

Open a File Explorer window (it doesn't matter which)

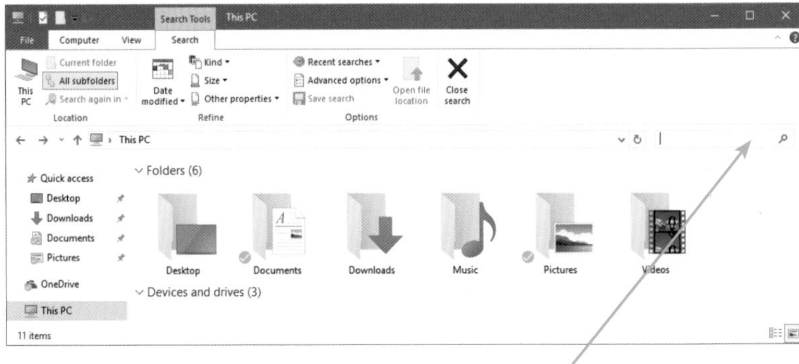

2. At the right, you will see a Search box. By default, searches made from this will be restricted to the contents of the folder, plus any sub-folders

Hot tip

You can change the location from any folder to search anywhere in the computer.

3. Clicking in the Search box also opens the **Recent searches** feature in the **Search** tab on the ribbon toolbar – here, you can repeat a search or clear the search history

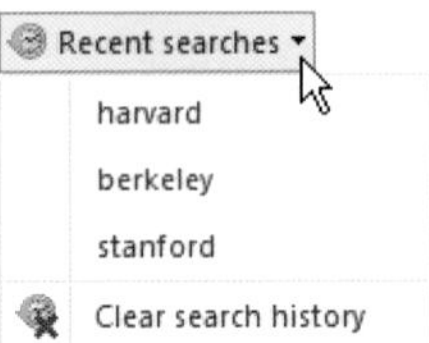

4. The **Search** tab provides **Advanced options** with which to refine your search – see page 170 for more details

Navigation pane

To the left of the File Explorer window, you'll see the Navigation pane. By default, this shows links for favorite folders such as Desktop, Documents, and Downloads. There are also links for OneDrive, Homegroup, This PC, and Network. These links enable any folder or drive on the computer to be accessed and thus searched. You can do this as follows:

1. Hover over the left-hand pane to see arrows beside the links

2. Click a right-arrow **>** to expand a list, or click a down-arrow **v** to collapse a list

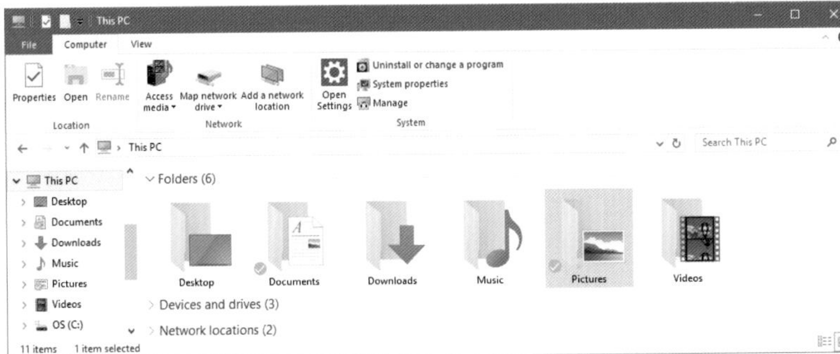

Double-click any folder name to expand that folder and display its contents with one action.

3. Select a folder name to display its contents and find files. For example, double-click the **Pictures** folder to explore the folders and files it contains

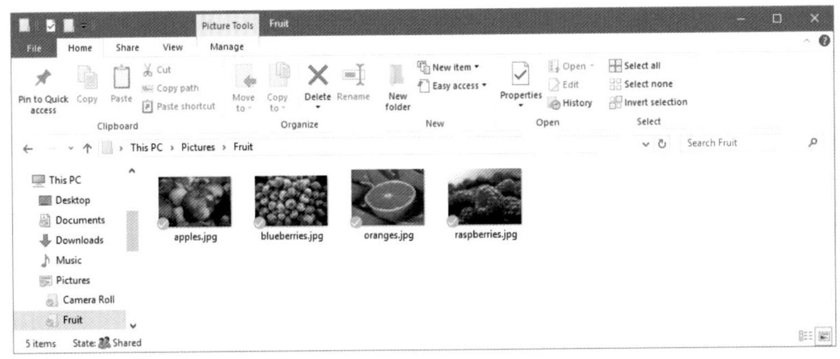

Click the arrows or double-click the names to expand and collapse the entries.

4. At any point you can use the folder Search box to search within a particular folder

Search tools

Windows provides a number of filters with which folder searches can be made even more relevant. These can be accessed from the ribbon toolbar found at the top of File Explorer folders.

This is a toolbar that provides options related to the task at hand, i.e. it is contextual. We'll take a closer look at this later on, but for now we'll see what it has to offer in the way of search options.

Open a folder you want to search and click in the Search box. The Search tab on the ribbon toolbar will immediately reveal the search tools. We'll take these as they appear on the toolbar:

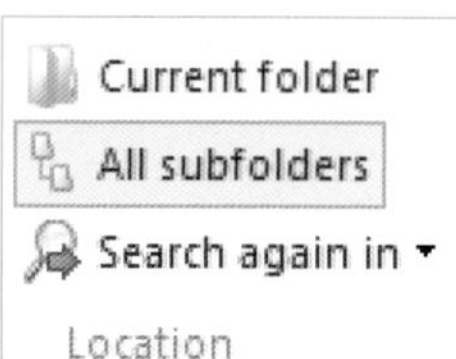

- **Current folder** – restricts the search to the current folder.
- **All subfolders** – includes sub-folders in the search.
- **Search again in** – list of locations in which to repeat the search.

- **Date modified** – allows you to search specific dates or ranges of dates. Options provided are: Today, Yesterday, This week, Last week, This month, Last month, This year, and Last year.

- **Kind** – choose the kind of file from a list of types, such as Movie or Program.
- **Size** – choose from a list of sizes ranging from Tiny to Gigantic.
- **Other properties** – choose from a list of properties for Date taken, Tags, Type, Name, Folder path or Rating.

Recent searches, and **Save search** items are not filters.

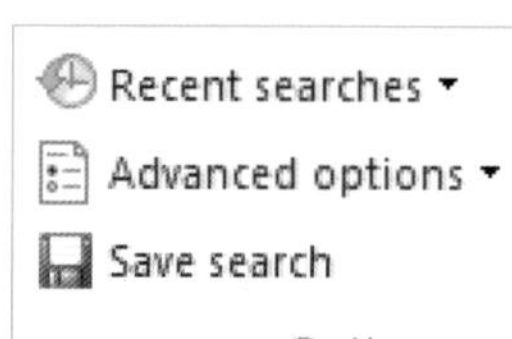

- **Advanced options** – lets you change the indexed locations to search, and allows searches to be limited to File contents, System files, or Zipped (compressed) folders in non-indexed locations.

Favorites

The Navigation pane includes a "Quick access" section where you can keep shortcuts to the locations on your system that you may often view. To view your File Explorer **Quick access** favorites:

1. Open File Explorer then click View, Navigation pane and ensure that **Navigation pane** is checked – to be visible

2. Now, click on the **Quick access** item at the top of the Navigation pane to reveal your current favorites

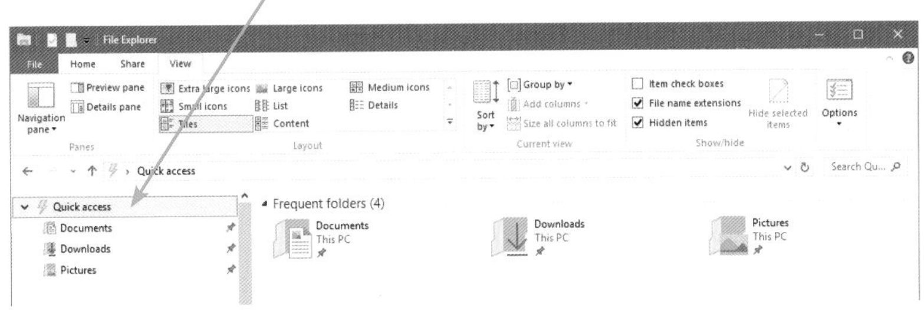

To remove a favorite location from the **Quick access** section, right-click on its folder icon and choose "Unpin from Quick access".

To add a folder location to your **Quick access** favorites:

3. Click on a folder in the Navigation pane – to select it ready to be added

4. Next, click the **Home** tab on the File Explorer ribbon

5. Now, click on the **Pin to Quick access** link on the ribbon to add the selected folder to your favorites

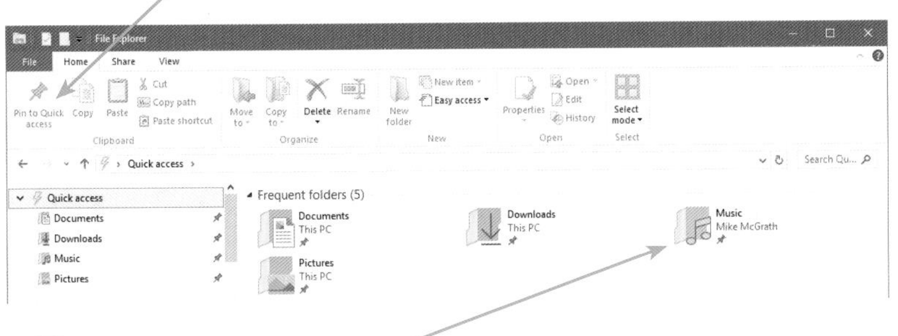

The **Quick access** favorites can also be returned to an earlier state by choosing "Restore previous versions" from the right-click context menu.

6. Our example, Music, is added to the **Quick access** favorites

Folder and search options

You can change the way files and folders function and how items are displayed on your computer using **Folder Options**.

1. Open a folder, click the **View** tab, click **Options** then click **Change folder and search options**

2. When **Folder Options** displays, select the **General** tab

From this panel you can:

- Choose to open each folder in the same window, or in its own window.
- Use double-click to open an item, or use the browser style single-click to point and select items.
- Control **Quick access** privacy.
- Restore Defaults after changes.

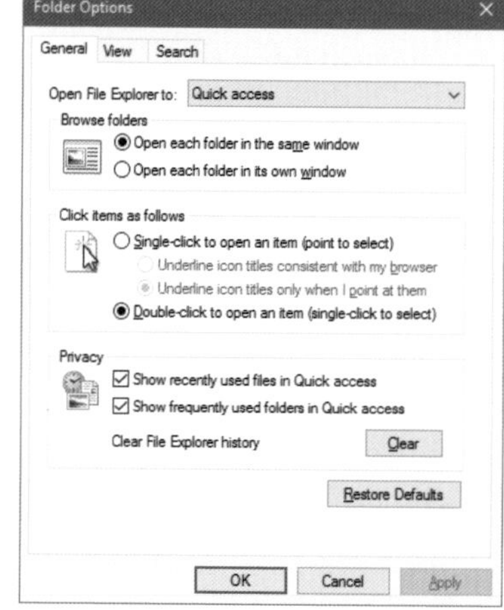

3. Select the **View** tab

From here you can:

- Apply the view for the current folder to all folders of the same type.
- Reset folders.
- Apply Advanced settings to files and folders.
- Restore Defaults after changes.
- Hide empty drives in the **This PC** folder.

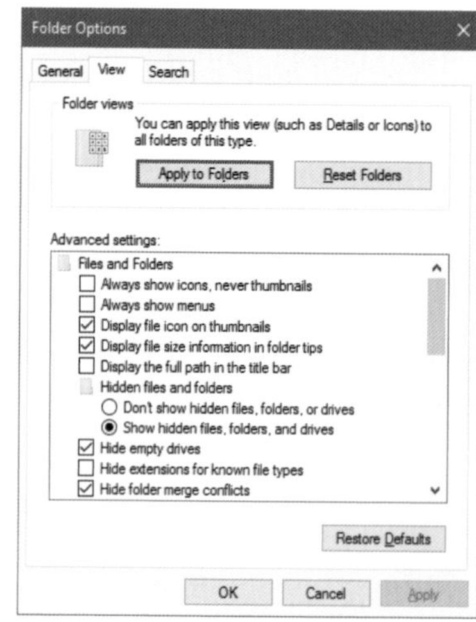

Don't forget

You will also find **Folder Options** under Appearance and Personalization, File Explorer Options in the Control Panel.

You can choose to hide or show hidden files, folders and drives. You can also hide or reveal file extensions.

4. Scroll down to reveal the remaining settings

Among these settings are options to:

- Automatically open the folders that you were using when you last shut down Windows whenever you start your computer, thus restoring your work session.
- Hide or show file tips that display when you point to files or folders.
- Use check boxes to select items.

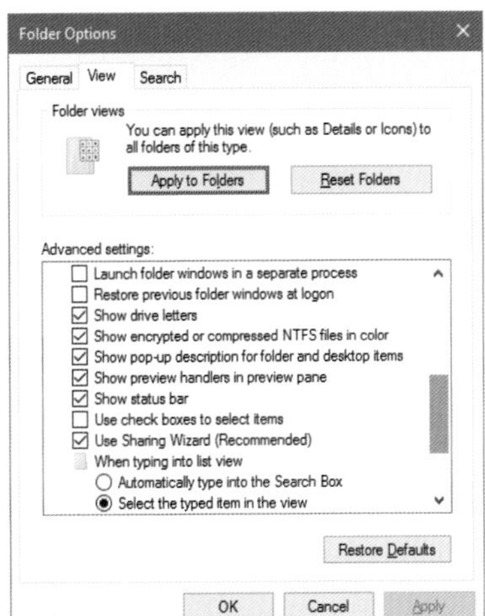

Make a note of the options that you would normally prefer, since the Restore Defaults will undo all changes, not just recent changes.

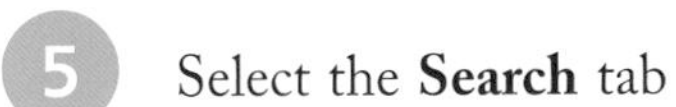

5. Select the **Search** tab

The Search settings let you manage what to search and how to search.

- Don't use the index when searching file folders for system files.
- Include system directories.
- Include compressed files.
- Search file names and contents.

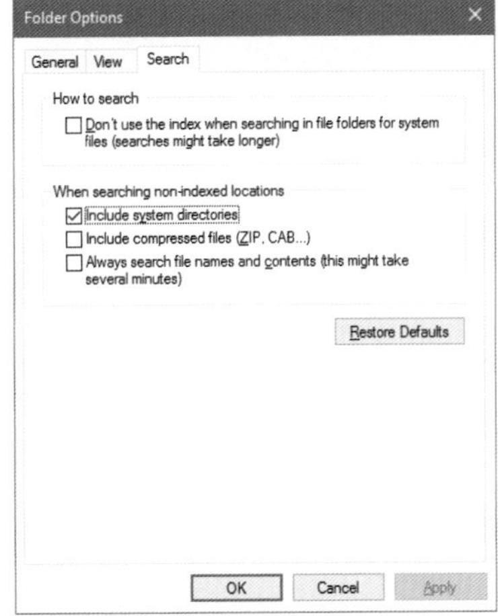

You can click the **Restore Defaults** button to undo any changes that might previously have been applied.

Indexing options

When you add a folder to one of the libraries, that folder will automatically be indexed. You can also add locations to the index without using libraries.

Windows uses the index for fast searches of the most common files on your computer. By default, folders in libraries, email and offline files are indexed, but program and system files are not.

Go to Settings and search for **Indexing Options**

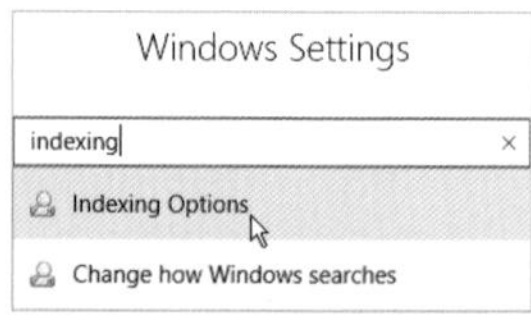

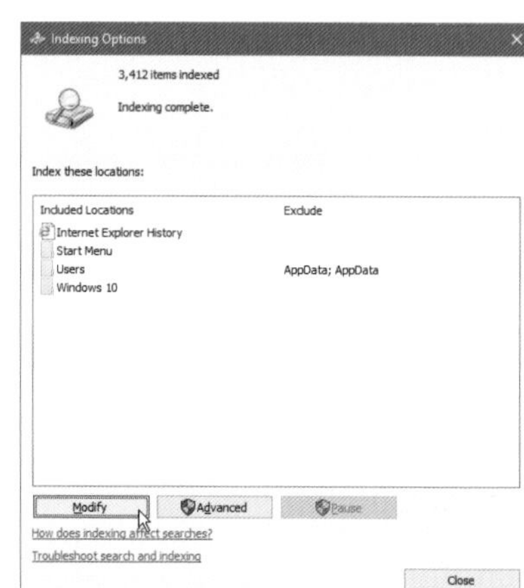

2 Click **Modify** then expand the folder lists and select new locations to index, for example a USB drive, and click **OK**

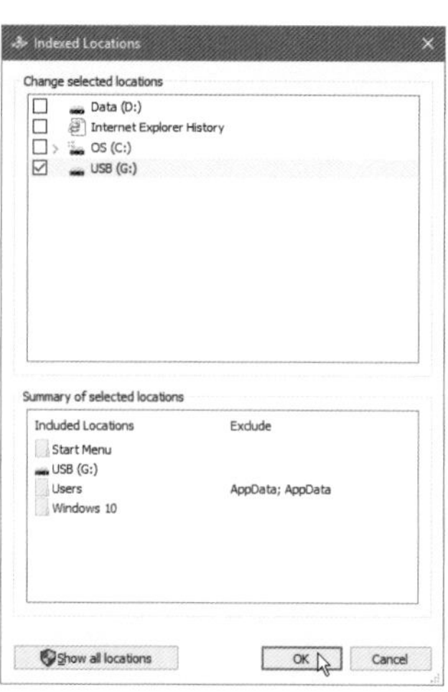

Indexing proceeds in the background, and may slow down during periods of user activity.

3. The contents of the new locations are added to the index

You can press **Pause** to suspend indexing, but you are recommended to do this for no more than 15 minutes at a time.

4. To make changes to the settings for indexing, click the **Advanced** button and select the **Index Settings** or **File Types** tab

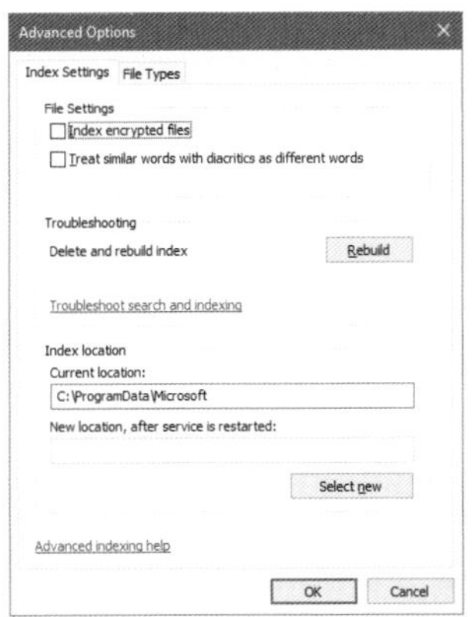

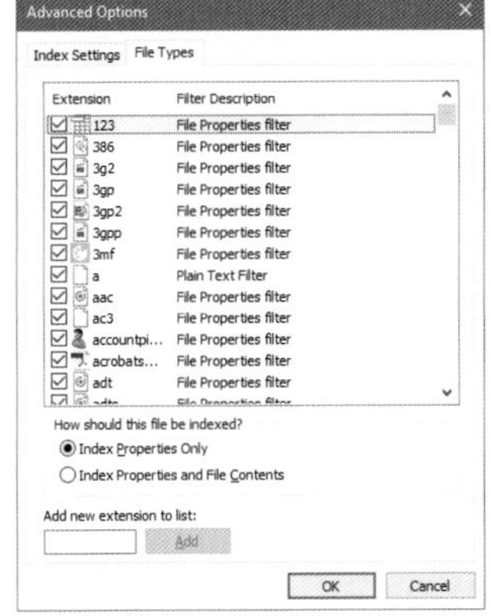

You can choose to index encrypted files, ignore accents on characters for matching, change the index location, or delete and rebuild the index. You can also specify file types that are indexed by Properties only or Contents plus Properties.

Address bar

The address bar at the top of the folder contains the location path of the folder or library, and you can use this to check the actual folder path and to switch to other libraries and folders.

1. Click the space in the address bar to the right of the location names (and left of the down-arrow)

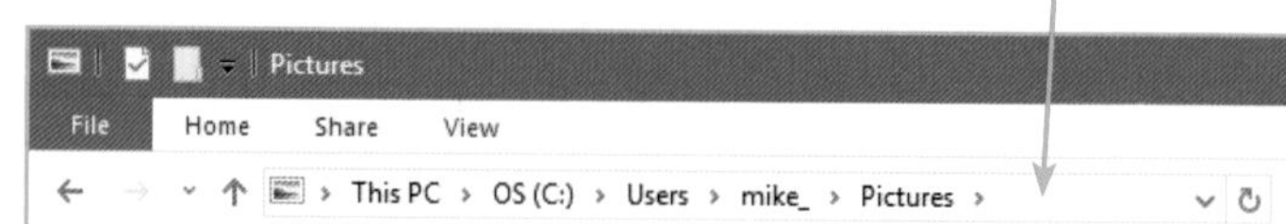

If a library rather than a folder is being displayed, you'll see a library path rather than a drive.

2. The current location is shown in the standard drive and folder path format

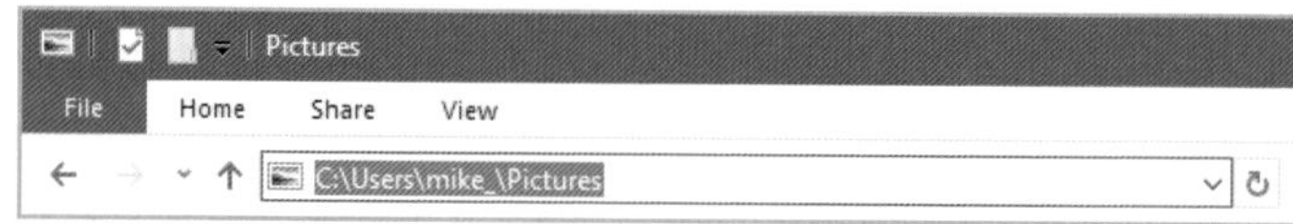

3. Click anywhere in the folder to revert to the location path

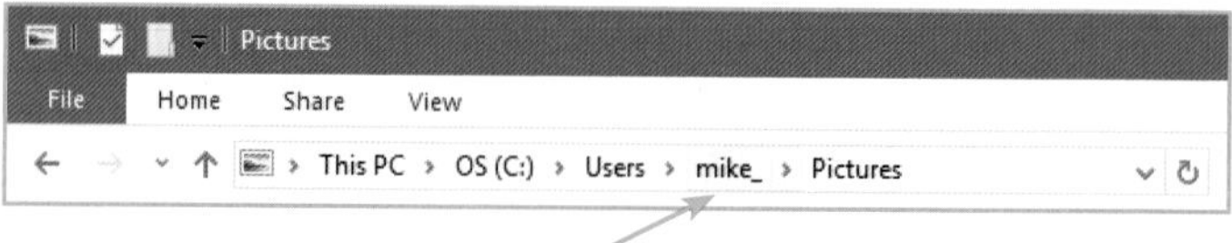

4. Click a location name, for example the user name, to switch to that location

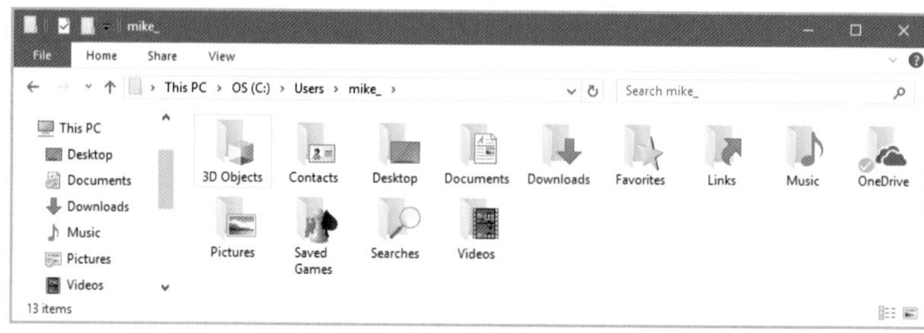

Click the arrow to the right of the location name to show all the folders that are stored within that location.

5. Click the arrow to the right of a location name, for example **Users**, to display all the user folders

6. When the folders are displayed, you can select any folder to switch to that location

7. Click the back arrow to redisplay the previous folder visited

8. Click the arrow at the left to see the top-level locations

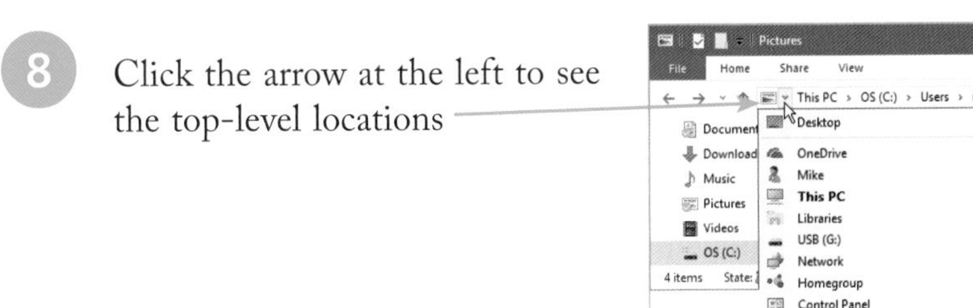

The libraries, user folders, network folders, etc. are included as special folders in Desktop, along with **This PC** and any Desktop icons. Note that File Explorer is also used to display the Control Panel.

9. Select **Desktop** in the Navigation pane to see the complete structure of your system components

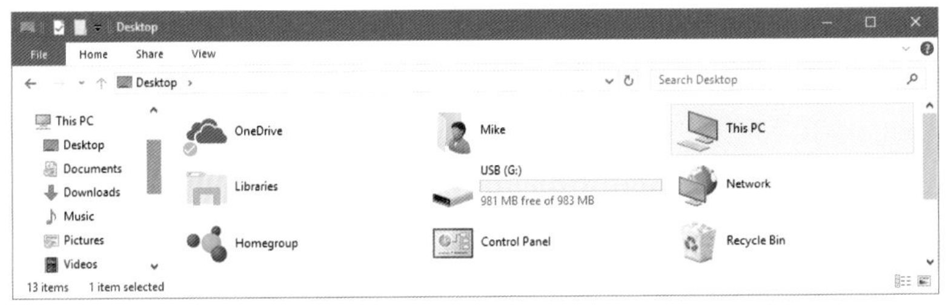

Save searches

If you regularly search for a certain group of files, it might be useful to save your search. To save a search:

1. Carry out a search as previously described

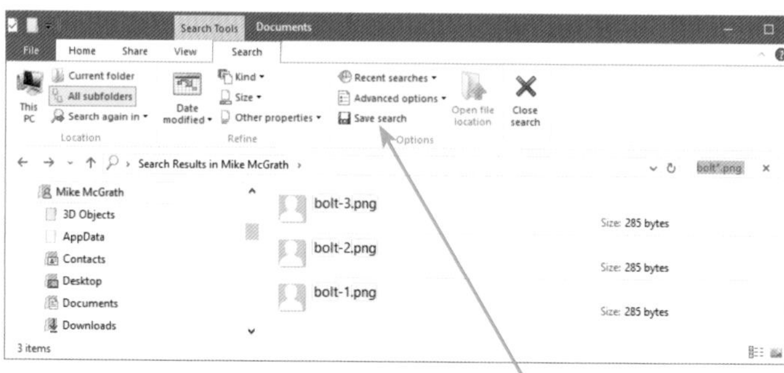

2. When the search is complete, click **Save search**

3. Type a name for the search, and then click **Save**

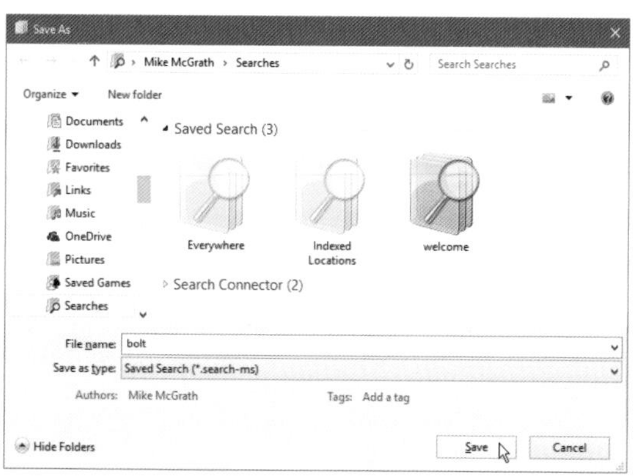

4. The search itself will be saved in your Searches folder

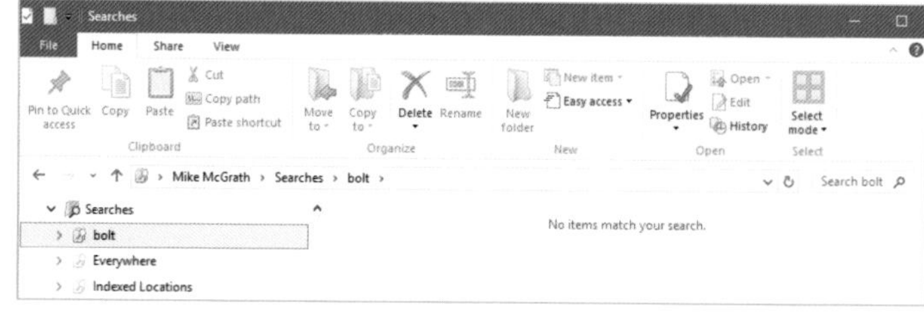

Save a search, and the next time you want to use it, you just open the saved search, and you'll see the most current files that match the original search.

The Searches folder may be hidden unless you have checked **View**, **Hidden items**.

Move and copy

You can use the search results and the Navigation pane to help move or copy files and folders from their original locations.

1. Use Search to display the items you wish to copy or move (in this case all Word files named "Minutes" within Users)

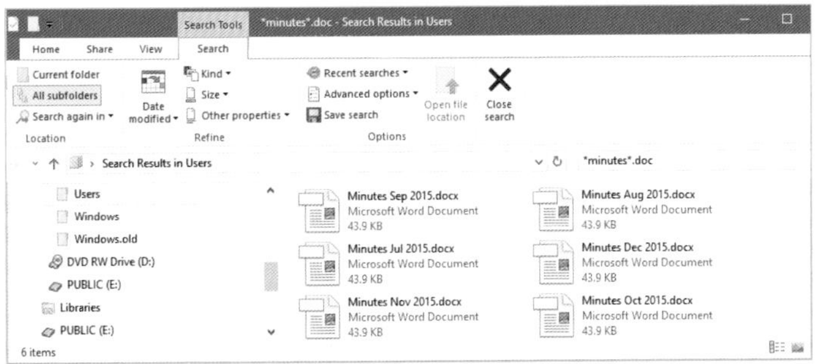

Select the first item, then press **Shift** and select the last in a range, or press **Ctrl** and add individual items to the selection.

2. Select the items to copy, using **Shift** or **Ctrl** as necessary

3. Expand the Navigation pane (clicking the arrows, not the folder names) to show the target folder

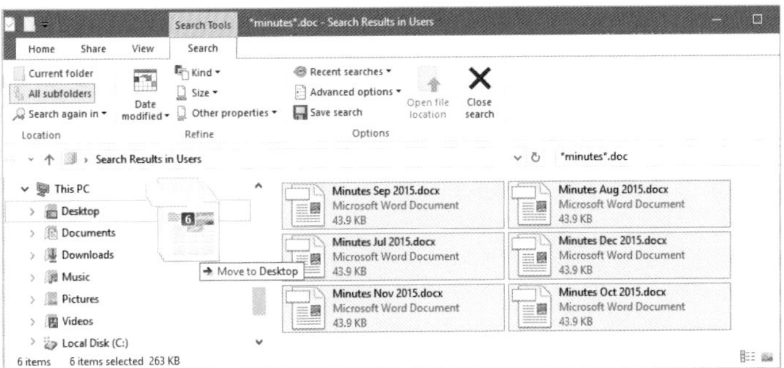

If the destination is on the same drive as the selected items, the default is Move, otherwise the default becomes Copy. However, you can still make your preferred selection.

4. Right-click part of the selection and drag the items onto the Navigation pane, over the name of the target folder

5. Release the mouse and click **Move here** or **Copy here** as appropriate, and the files are added to the destination

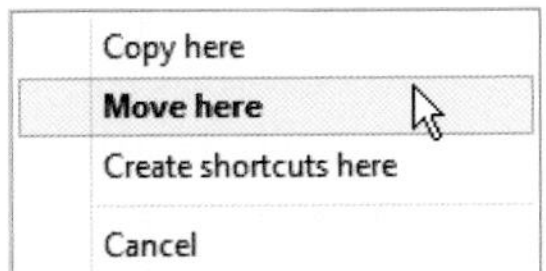

...cont'd

6. As soon as the move takes place, Windows Search adjusts the search results, in this case showing Public documents

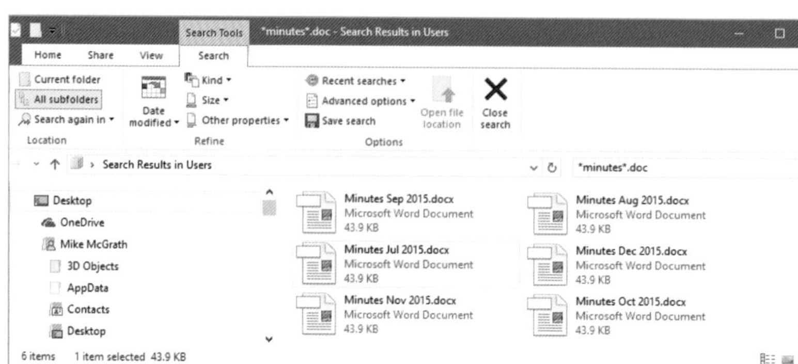

You don't have to use Search; you can Move or Copy from the original location using the same techniques.

7. Select the target folder, and you'll see all the items added

You can simply click and drag any selected items to your preferred destination then release the mouse button to have Windows Move or Copy them there immediately, with no menu.

Force move or copy

With either a left-click or right-click, you can force the action you want, whether the same or different drives are involved:

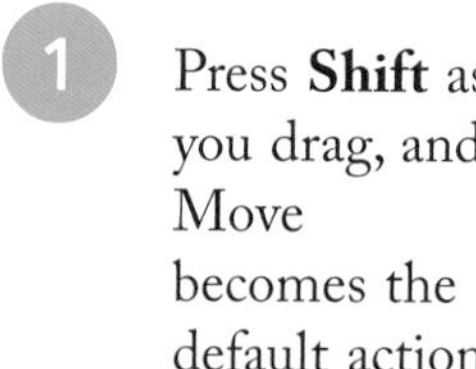

1. Press **Shift** as you drag, and Move becomes the default action

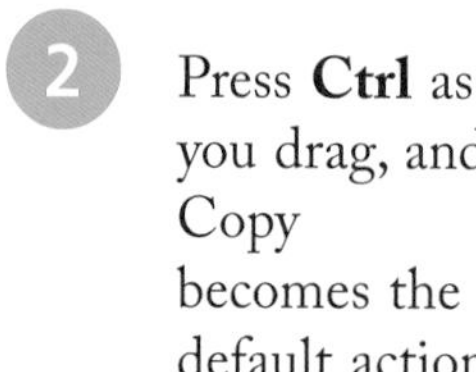

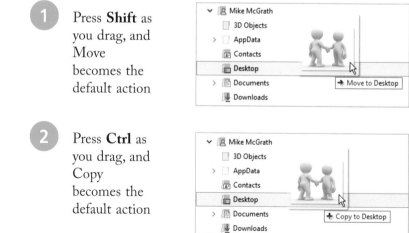

2. Press **Ctrl** as you drag, and Copy becomes the default action

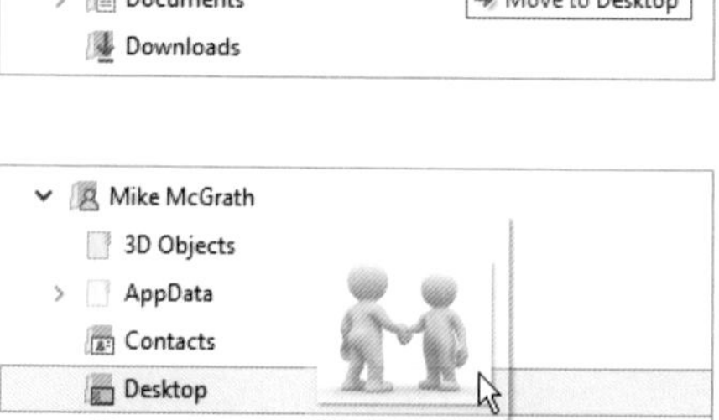

Don't use the left-click option unless you are very familiar with it, since there's no opportunity to confirm the action.

11 Manage files and folders

Use File Explorer to manage your files, folders and libraries, sorting and organizing the contents. Windows 10 provides libraries for documents, music, pictures and videos but you can define your own libraries for your projects or to manage information.

Files, folders and libraries

Data storage devices are defined as blocks of fixed-size sectors. These are managed by the file system, which defines a root drive directory containing folders and files. Each folder can contain further folders and files. This gives a hierarchical structure.

Files of the same or related types will usually be stored in the same folder. For example, the **Users** folder within the root drive directory will be organized along the following lines:

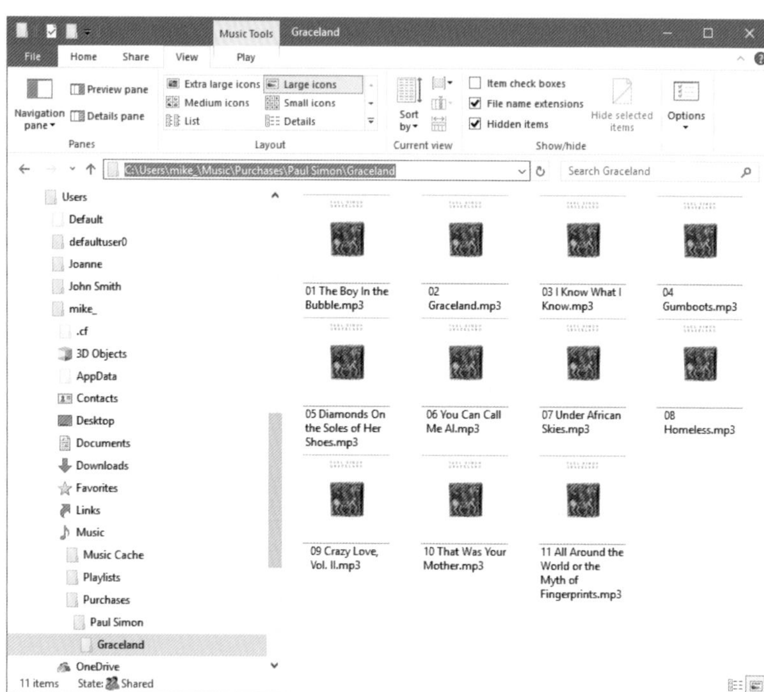

Windows uses the NTFS file system for disks and large storage devices. One of the older FAT file systems is normally used for smaller storage devices such as memory cards and flash drives.

The root drive directory includes the **Program Files** folder which contains applications installed on your system, and the **Users** folder which contains the folders and files associated with each user account. In your user account folder, you will see a number of folders, including your **Music** folder. The example above shows the MP3 music files within a purchased album of a particular artist.

Windows 10 goes a stage further and associates folders with similar content into libraries. The folders included in the library may be stored separately on the disk, or may be on a different disk on the computer or elsewhere on the network. To manage the files, folders and libraries, Windows uses the File Explorer application.

Each file has a starting block and links to the subsequent blocks, with the last link being the end of file marker. The blocks are not necessarily allocated in sequence, hence the potential for fragmentation.

File Explorer

There are several different ways to start File Explorer or change the particular files and folders being displayed.

Quick access is new in Windows 10, replacing the classic Favorites of previous versions. You can also press **WinKey** + **E** to open File Explorer to see **Quick access**.

1. Click the **File Explorer** icon on the Taskbar or open the Power User Menu and select **File Explorer**

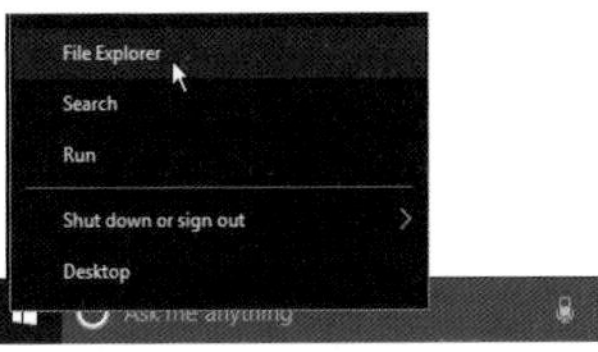

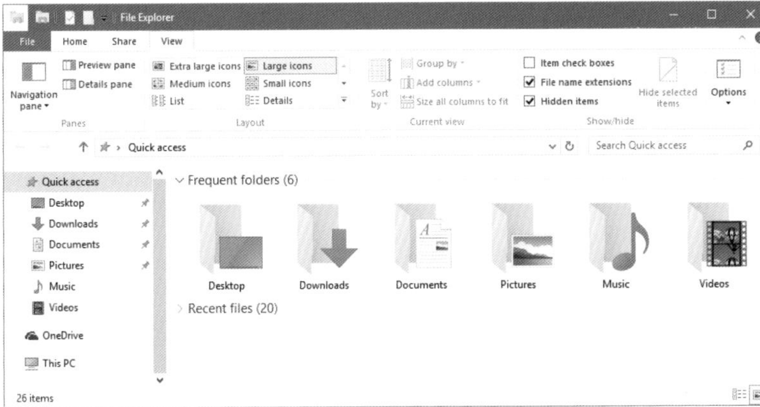

2. The **Quick access** feature displays your **Frequent folders**

3. Click an entry on the Navigation pane to display those contents instead, for example select the **Music** folder

If you don't want to have File Explorer start in **Quick access**, click View, Options, **Change folder and search options**, then on the General tab choose **Open File Explorer to: This PC**.

4. To retain the current entry and open another, right-click the newly-required entry and choose **Open in new window**

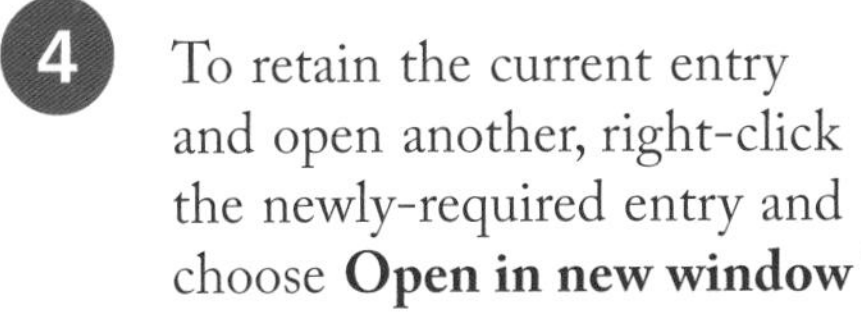

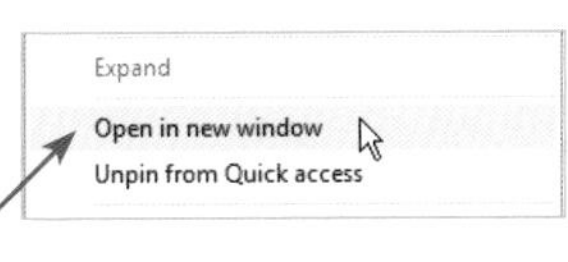

...cont'd

The Taskbar button for the program initially shows a single icon. When you open another window, or more, a second icon gets stacked alongside the first icon – to indicate that multiple File Explorer windows are currently open. To use the Taskbar:

1. Move the mouse pointer over the Taskbar button, and thumbnails for the open windows are displayed, as shown below:

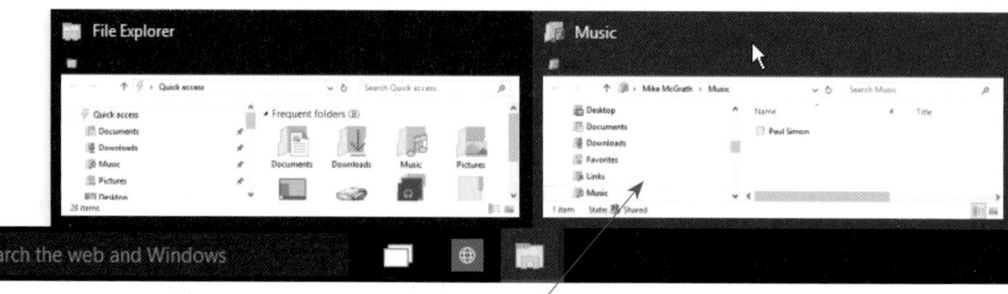

2. Click on a thumbnail to open that window in File Explorer

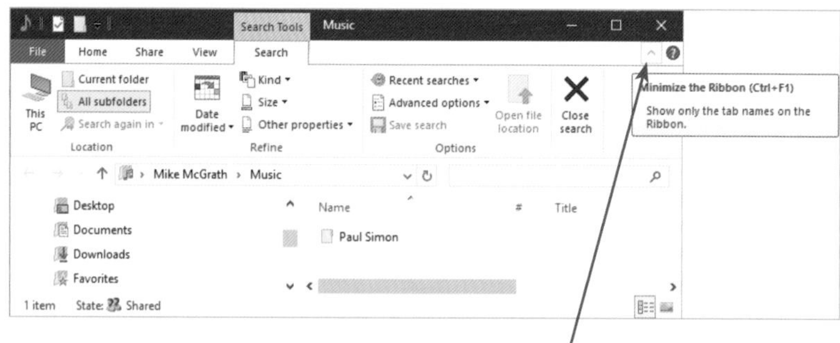

3. Click the down-arrow to open (or up-arrow to close) the File Explorer ribbon toolbar

You can also open the ribbon toolbar by clicking a File Explorer tab – Home, Share, or View.

File Explorer layout

This shows all the elements for File Explorer, apart from the ribbon toolbar, which we look at on page 186.

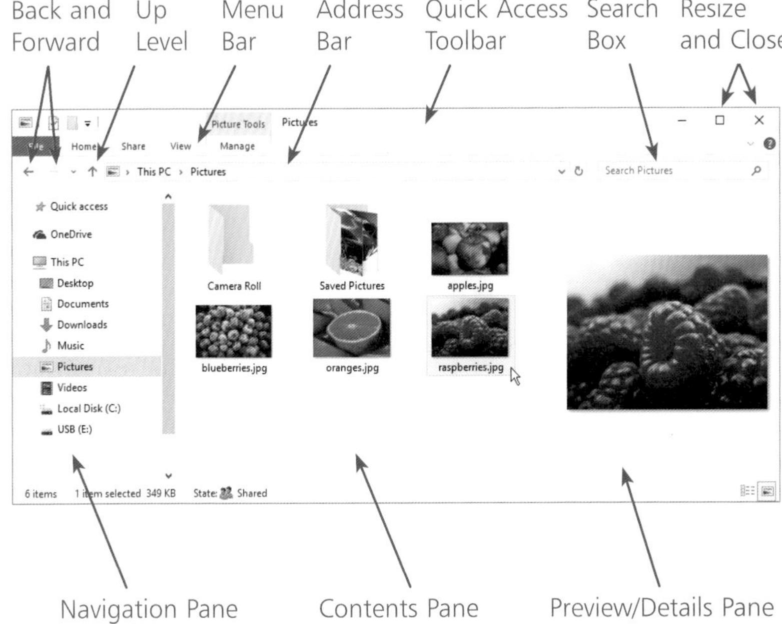

File Explorer preview

The type of preview displayed depends on the file type. For recognized document types, you will see part of the first page.

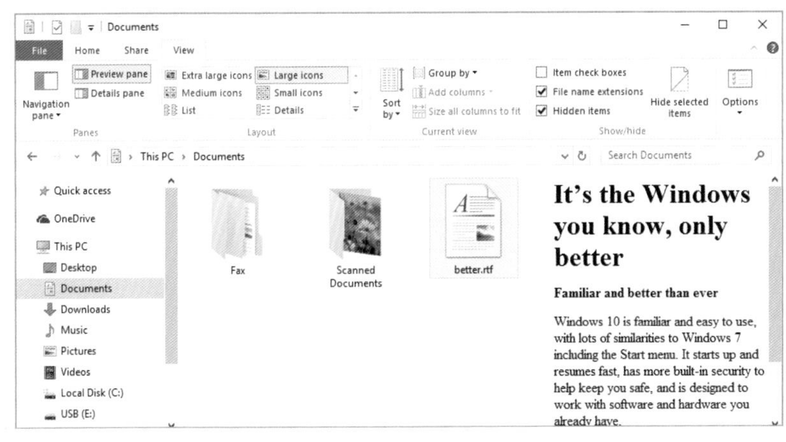

For file types Windows does not recognize, or when a folder is selected, you will see a message saying: No preview available.

File Explorer ribbon

Hot tip

The File tab offers a variety of options:

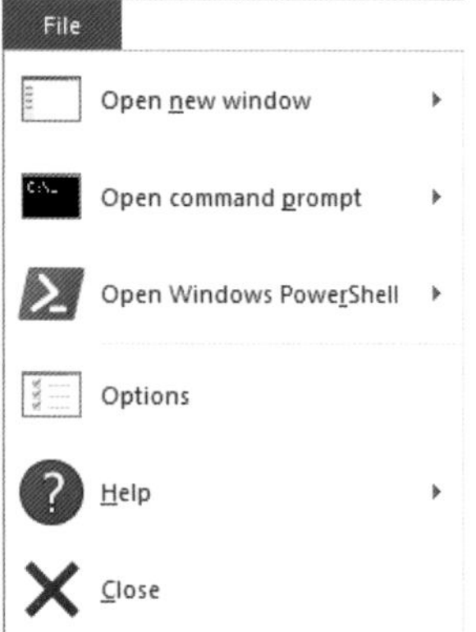

A feature in Windows 10 is the File Explorer ribbon toolbar, which is situated at the top of every File Explorer folder. By default, it is hidden – to reveal it just click the down-arrow located under the red **X** close button at the top-right.

In essence, the ribbon consists of a File menu plus three core tabs – Home, Share and View – that are always visible. Other tabs include Manage, Computer and Network. The ribbon also shows colored contextual tabs, the display of which depends on the type of object selected by the user. For example, when a video folder is opened or a video file is selected, the Video Tools tab appears and provides related options, such as Play, Stop, and Pause.

This system of core and contextual tabs enables the ribbon toolbar to offer some 200 different management commands. The user gets the required options as and when required without having to wade through unrelated toolbar menus, right-click menus, etc.

Home tab

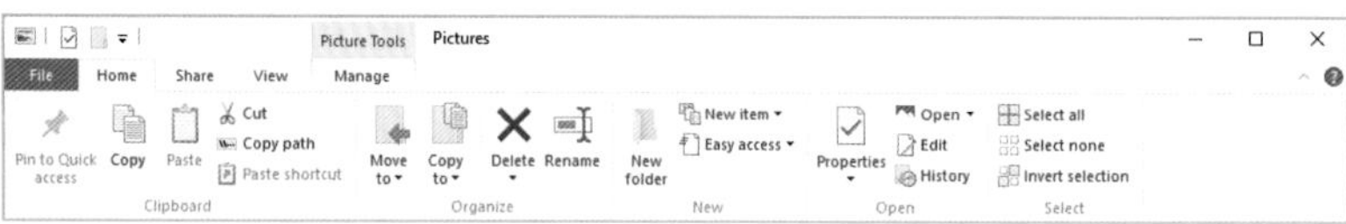

View tab

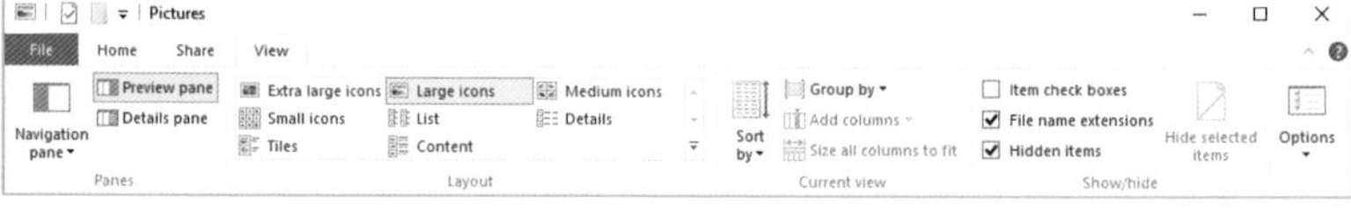

Share tab

Computer tab

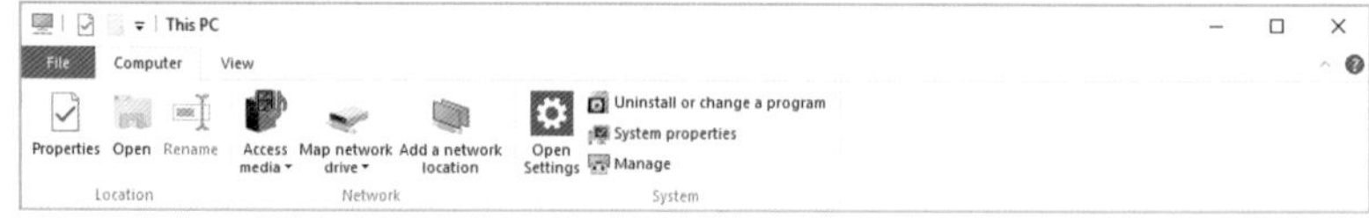

Manage tab

Folder contents

You'll also find that the way in which the contents of folders are displayed varies depending on the type of file involved.

In these example views, the Navigation, Details, and Library panes have been hidden, to put the emphasis on the Contents pane.

Documents

Details view:
- Name
- Date modified
- Type
- Size

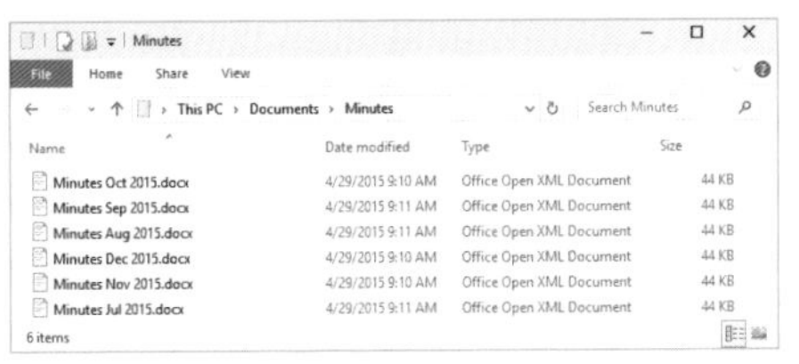

Documents and Music both use the Details view, but the fields displayed are appropriate to the particular file type.

Music

Details view:
- Name
- Contributing artists
- Album
- Track number
- Title

Pictures

Large Icons view

Program Files

Medium Icons view

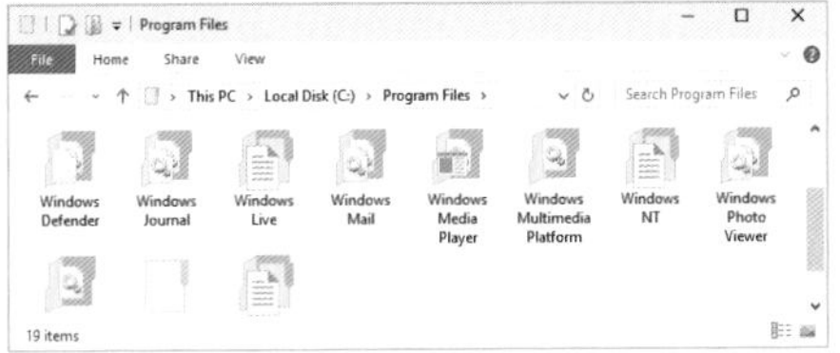

The Videos library also uses the Large Icons view, while Network and Computers use the Tiles view, the same as Libraries.

Libraries

Tiles view

Since views can easily be varied, you may find the setup for some of the folders on your system may be different.

Change view

1. Open the folder whose view you want to change, and then right-click in an empty part of the folder

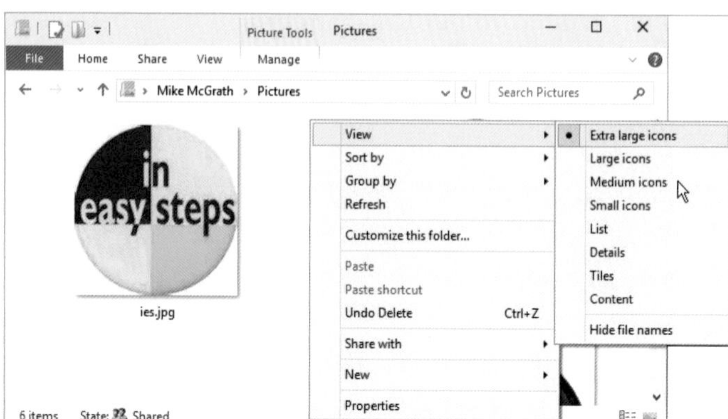

The View menu option, available by right-clicking in an open folder, provides a quick way to change a folder's view, but the **View** menu on the ribbon toolbar offers more, and more easily accessible, options.

2. Hover the mouse on the **View** menu option and then select the required view. Using our example above, we are changing the view from **Extra large icons** to **Medium icons**. You can see how the view has changed below

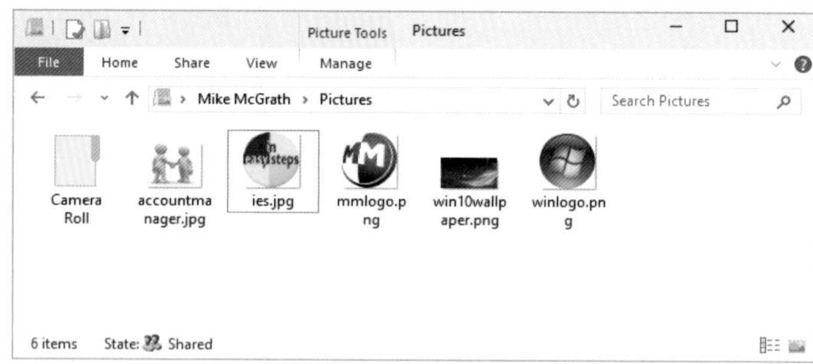

The information provided in the **Content** view depends on the file type. For example, Pictures has **Date taken**, and Music has **Track length**.

3. The same commands, and more, are also available from the **View** tab on the File Explorer ribbon toolbar

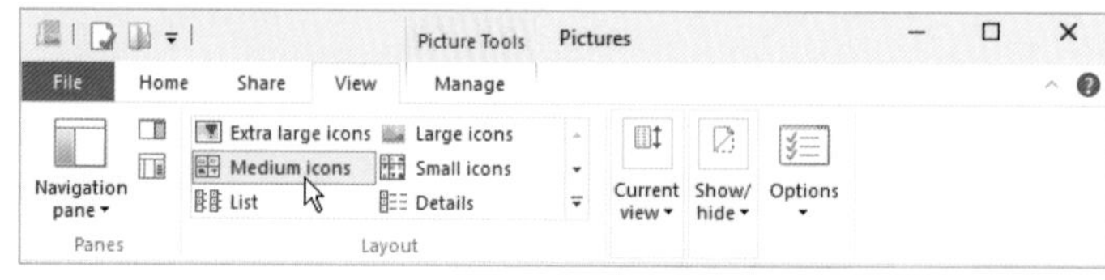

Sort contents

You can sort the contents of any folder by name, date, size or other attributes, using the **Details** view. You can also group or filter the contents.

1. Open the folder and select the **Details** view

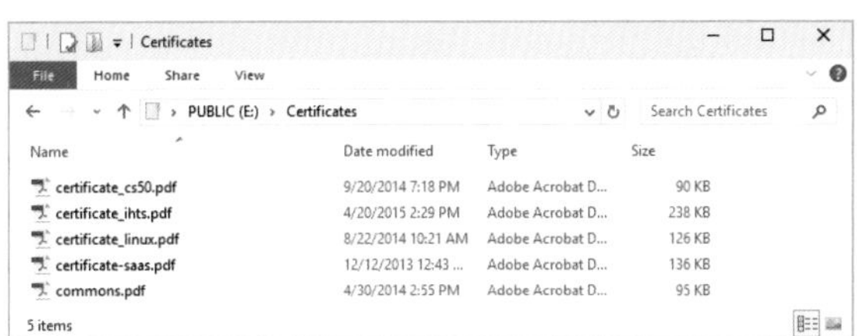

2. Click on a header such as **Size**, and the entries are sorted

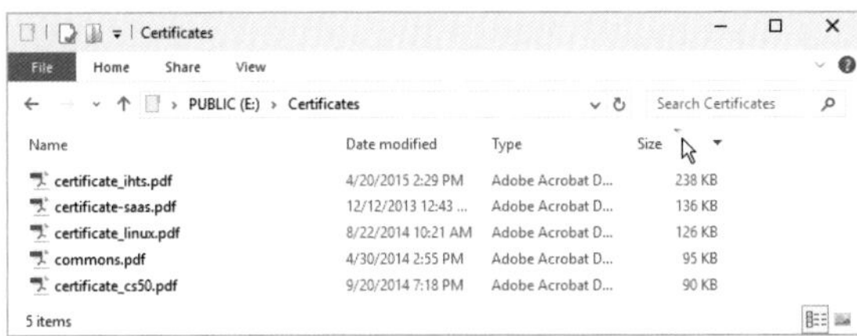

3. Click the header again, and the sequence is reversed

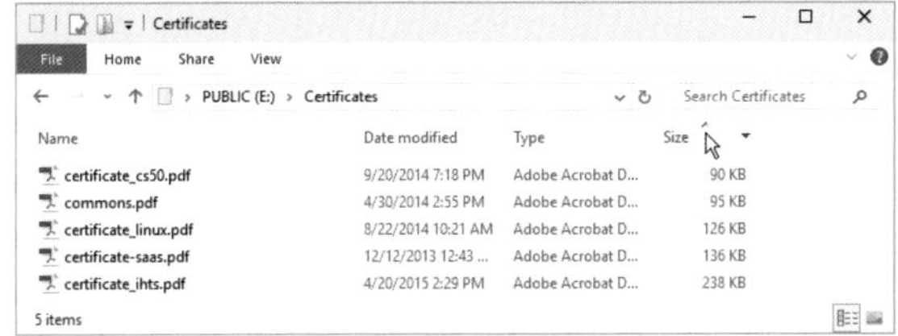

4. Change the view, and the sequencing that you have set up will be retained for the new view

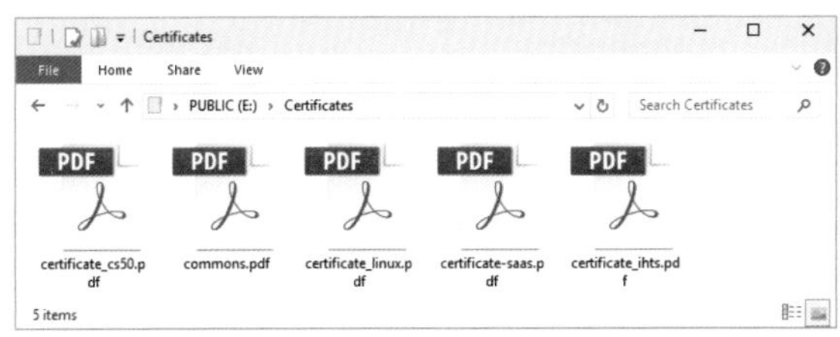

On the first selection, alphabetic fields such as Name or File Type are sorted in ascending order. Number fields such as Date or Size are sorted in descending order.

Click the arrow that appears when you hover over any header, to group the entries in ranges. By excluding some of the ranges, you can filter the contents displayed.

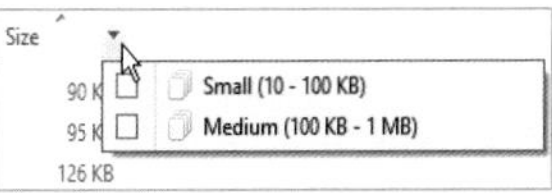

...cont'd

You can reorganize the contents from views other than Details.

1. Open the folder, and right-click an empty part of the contents, being sure to avoid the icon borders

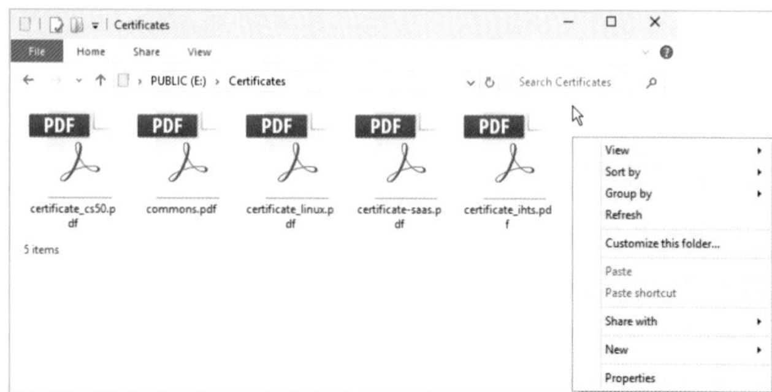

The space between icons can be very narrow, so you must take care to choose an empty area.

2. Select **Sort by**, to change the sort field or sequence

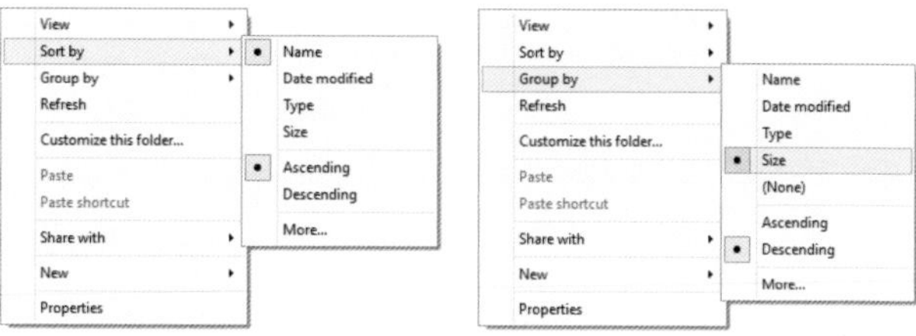

3. Select **Group by**, and select the field (**Size,** for example) by which you want to arrange the entries in ranges

4. To remove the grouping, select **Group by**, then **(None)**

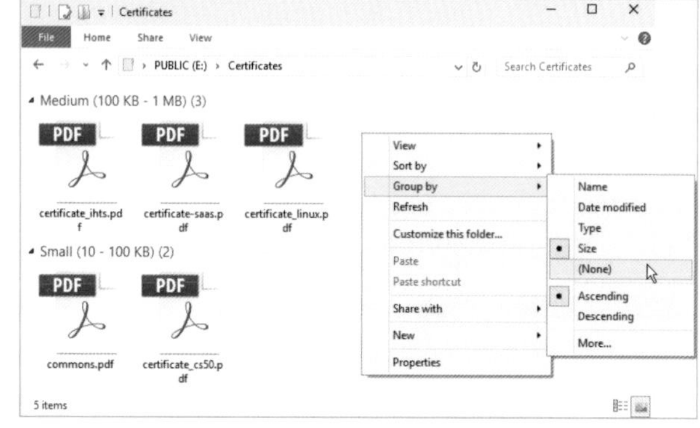

Click **More** to add other attributes that can be used for grouping or sorting. The selected fields would also appear on the Details view.

Windows 10 libraries

Windows 10 comes with default libraries such as Camera Roll, Documents, Music, Pictures, Saved Pictures, and Videos. You can add them to the Navigation pane by clicking the View tab in any folder, clicking Navigation pane and then clicking Show libraries.

1. Click **Libraries** on the Navigation pane

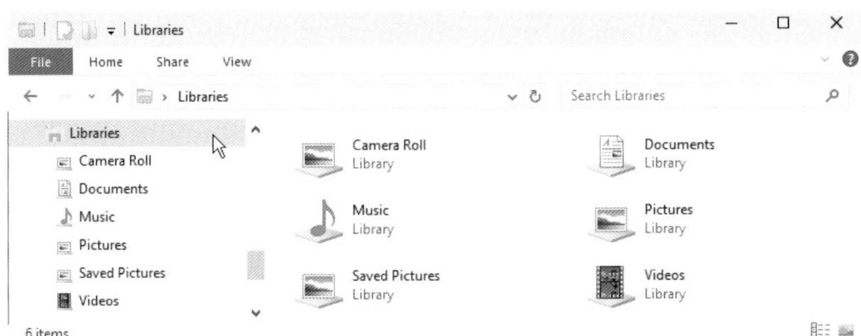

You can include other locations in the existing libraries, and you can also create your own libraries.

2. Double-click a library (Pictures, for example) to open it

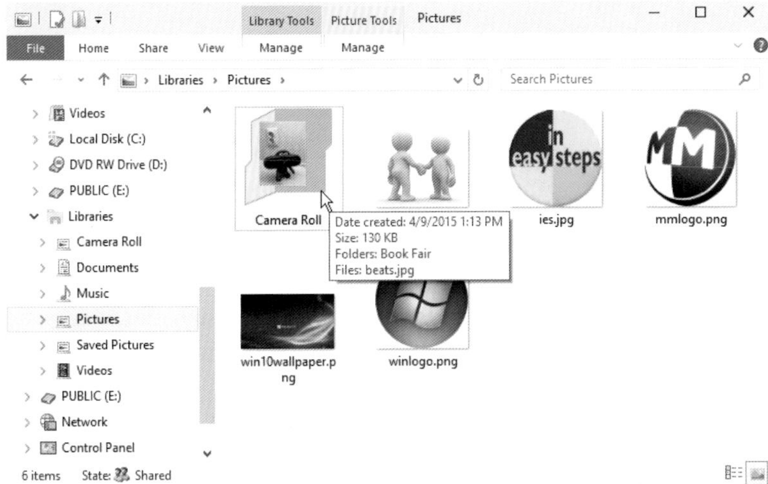

3. Here we can see the library includes the Camera Roll location. The files and folders at that location are listed when you hover over the Camera Roll icon

Manage library

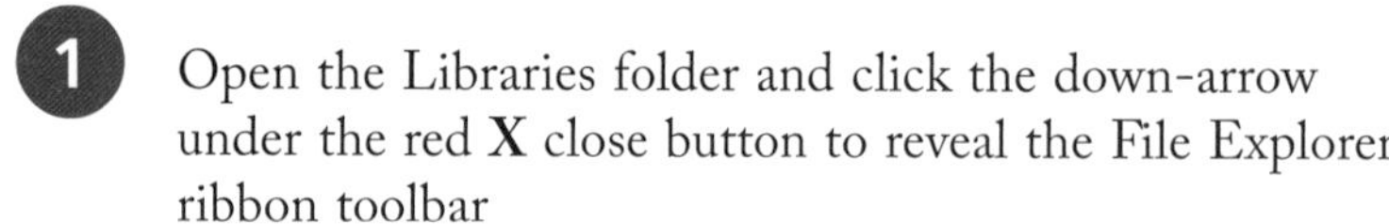
1 Open the Libraries folder and click the down-arrow under the red **X** close button to reveal the File Explorer ribbon toolbar

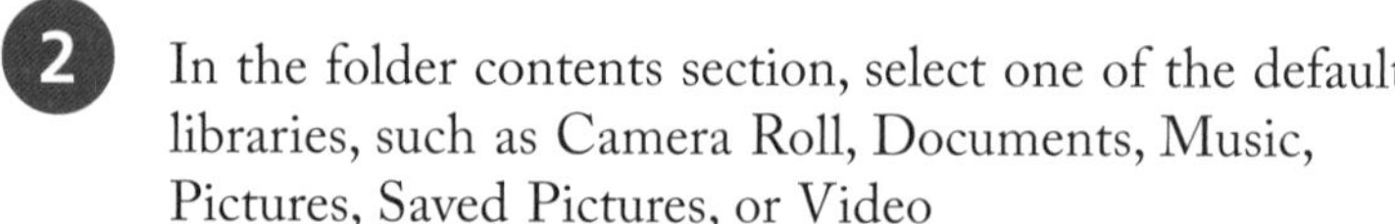
2 In the folder contents section, select one of the default libraries, such as Camera Roll, Documents, Music, Pictures, Saved Pictures, or Video

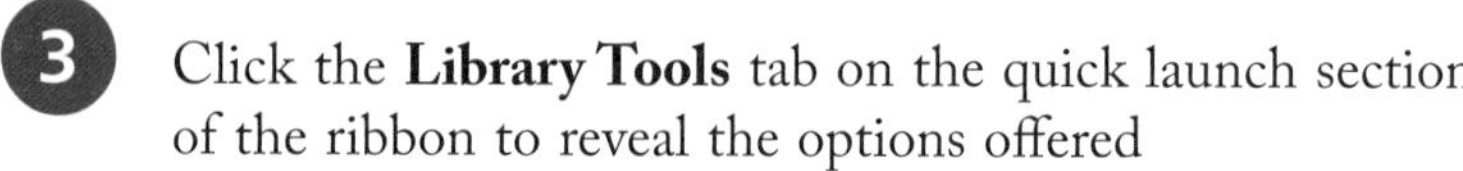
3 Click the **Library Tools** tab on the quick launch section of the ribbon to reveal the options offered

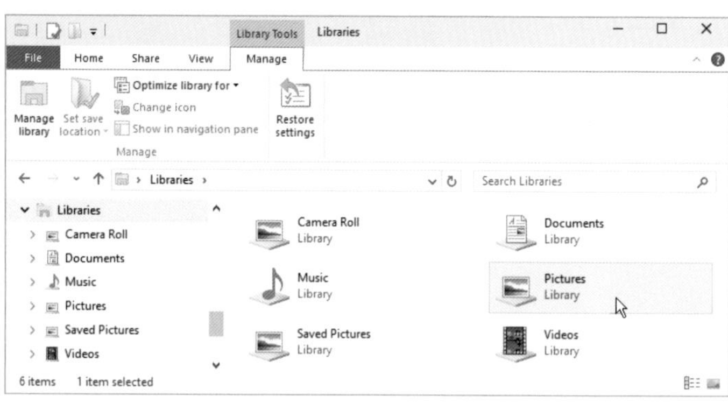

The File Explorer ribbon Library options don't appear automatically – you have to select a library and then click the **Library Tools** tab.

Manage library – the Manage library link enables you to add new locations to an existing library – see pages 193-194 where we look at how to do this.

Set save location – this allows you to specify a default save location within a library. For example, if one of your libraries has two or more locations, you can set one of them as the default.

Optimize library for – the six default libraries all have different arrangement options appropriate for their respective contents. Should you create a new library, the Optimize library for link enables you to quickly set suitable arrangement options for the content of that library.

Show in navigation pane – this lets you hide or show the Libraries link in the Navigation pane.

Restore settings – Click this link to undo all configuration changes made to the Libraries feature.

Right-click in any library and choose **Arrange by** to see its arrangement options.

Add a location

1. Open the Libraries folder and access Library Tools as described on page 192, then click **Manage library**

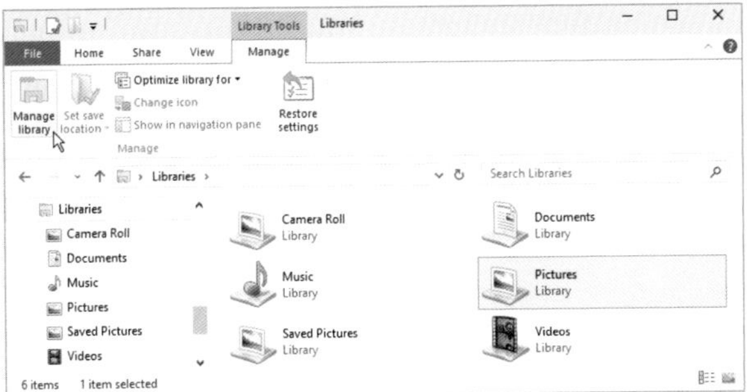

This lists the currently-defined locations and indicates the default save location, where new files would be added.

2. Click the **Add...** button next to Library locations

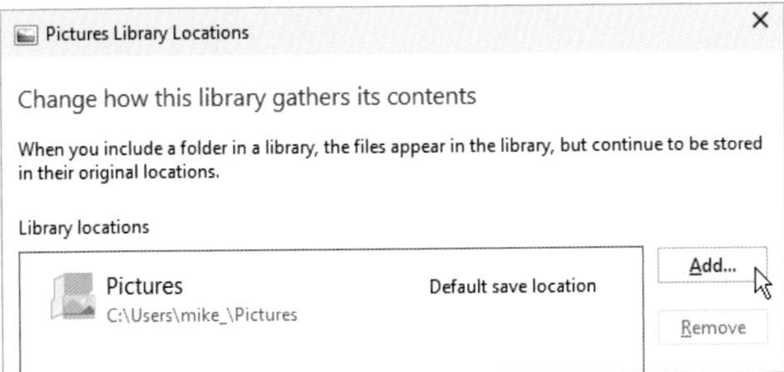

3. Open the drive the required folder is located on

4. Select the folder and then click **Include Folder**

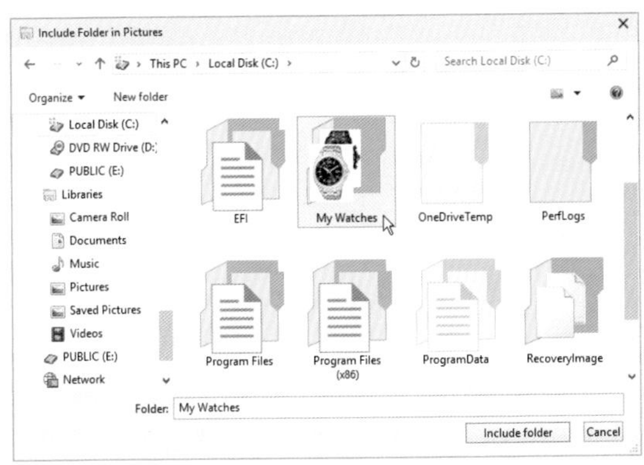

You could select folders from your hard drive, as in this example, or from a second internal hard drive, or from an external hard drive.

...cont'd

You cannot use folders from devices with removable storage. You can add folders from removable drives, but only if they appear in the hard disk drive section.

5. The selected folder becomes a new location in the library

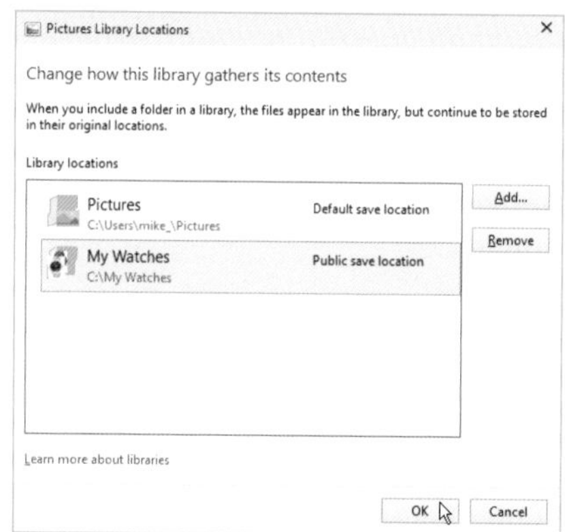

6. Click **OK** to see the added folder content

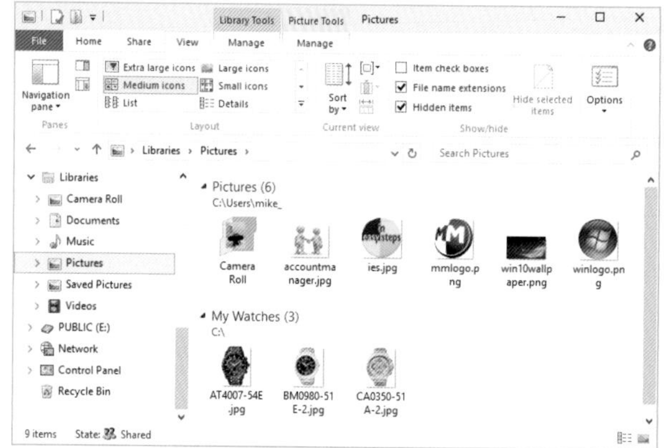

7. Right-click on the library's icon and choose **Share with** then select an option if you want to share this library

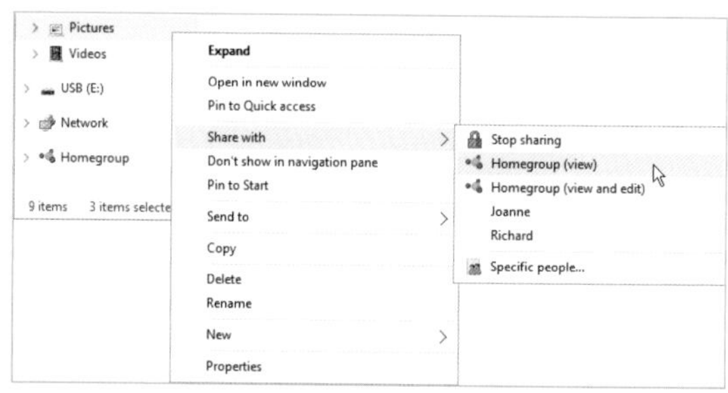

Arrange library contents

Library contents are usually organized by location and folder, but you can change this.

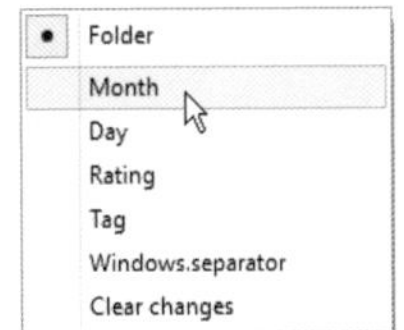

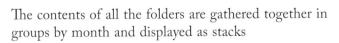

1. Right-click in the library files window, then choose **Arrange by** and select an alternative to Folder, e.g. **Month**

2. The contents of all the folders are gathered together in groups by month and displayed as stacks

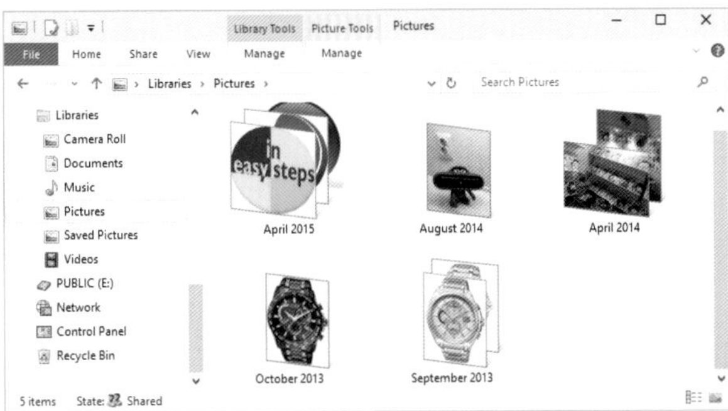

3. Right-click in the library files window and choose **Arrange by** again, then select another alternative, e.g. **Rating**

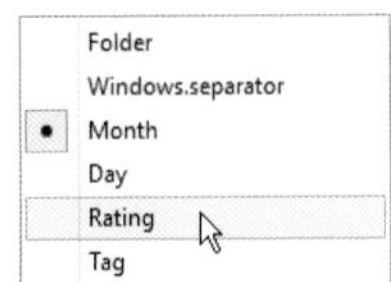

4. The contents of all the folders are gathered together in groups by their star rating, or as "unspecified" if unrated

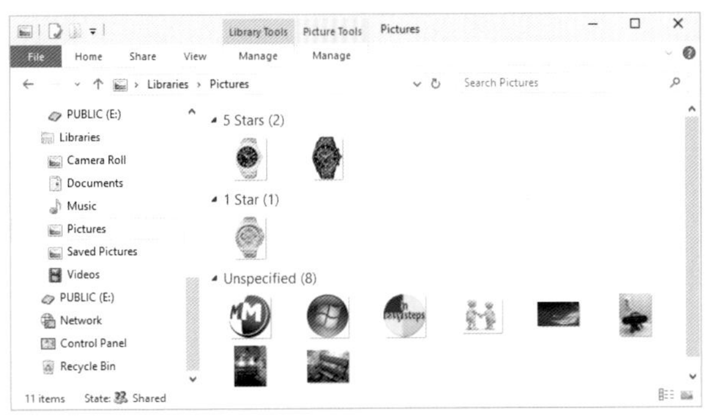

Files can be given star Rating and Tag names using the Details tab on their Properties dialog. Right-click on a file icon and choose the Properties item on the context menu, then select the Details tab and edit its star Rating or Tag name values there.

Create a library

1. Open the Libraries folder, right-click in the folder and select **New**, **Library**

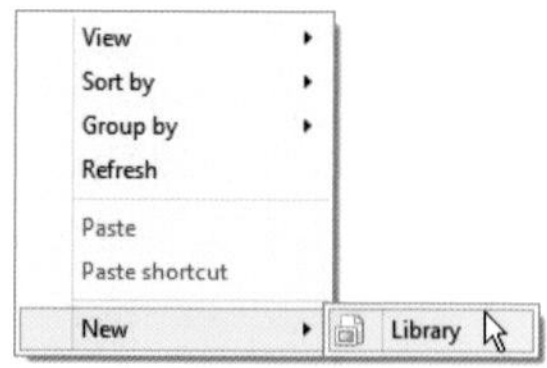

You can create a library of your own to manage other collections, for example project plans, or family history.

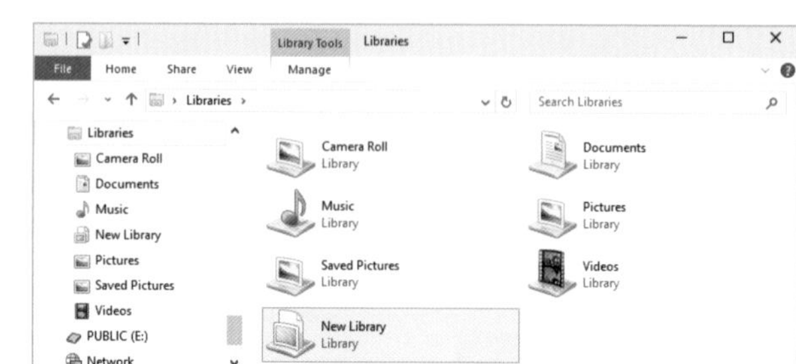

2. Edit the library name, e.g. "Projects", and press **Enter**

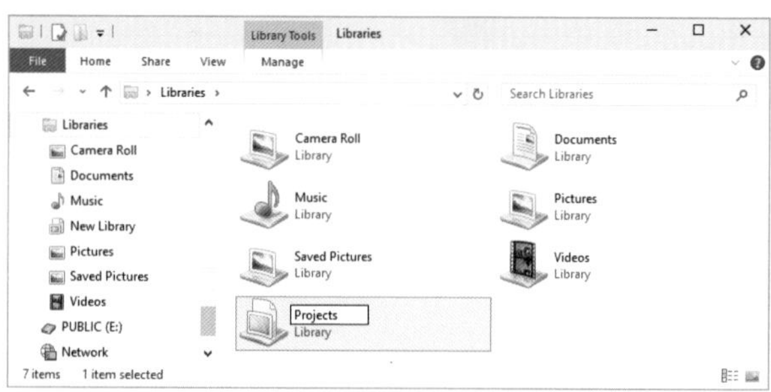

The first folder that you add will be assigned as the save location, but you can change this later if you wish.

3. Double-click the new library to open it, and you'll be invited to add folders

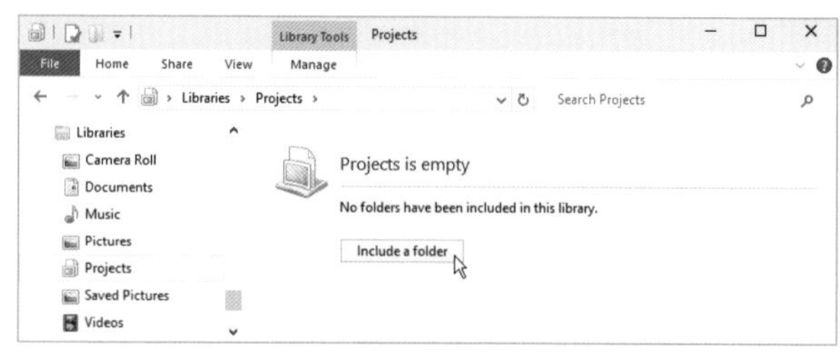

Adjust properties

When you've added folders, the library appears on the Navigation pane and shows locations and folders, just like default libraries.

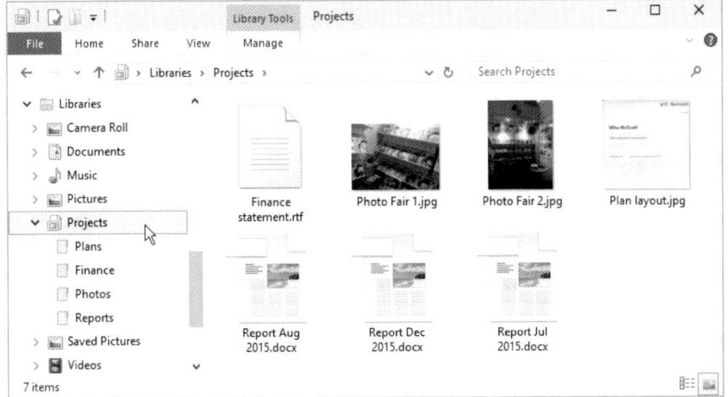

From the right-click menu you can open the library in a new window, share it with other users, and hide or show it in the Navigation pane, as well as displaying properties.

1. Right-click the library name in the Navigation pane or in the Libraries folder and select **Properties**

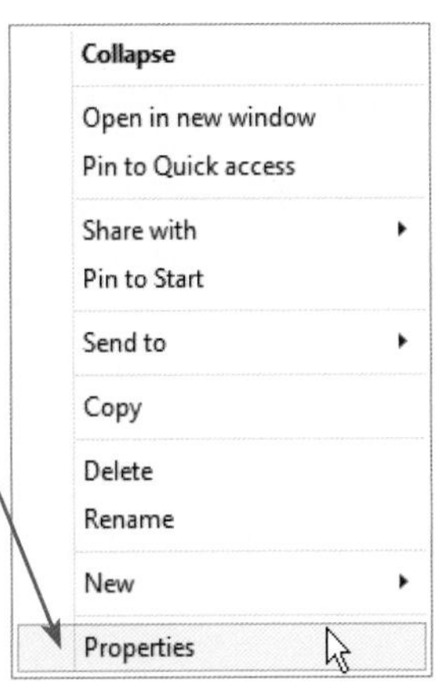

From here you can:

- Select a location and click **Set save location**
- **Add** a new folder or location
- **Remove** an existing location
- Hide or show in **Navigation pane**
- Check **Shared** status
- **Restore Defaults** after making changes
- **Apply** the changes you make

2. Click **OK** to save your changes, or click **Cancel** to abandon your changes

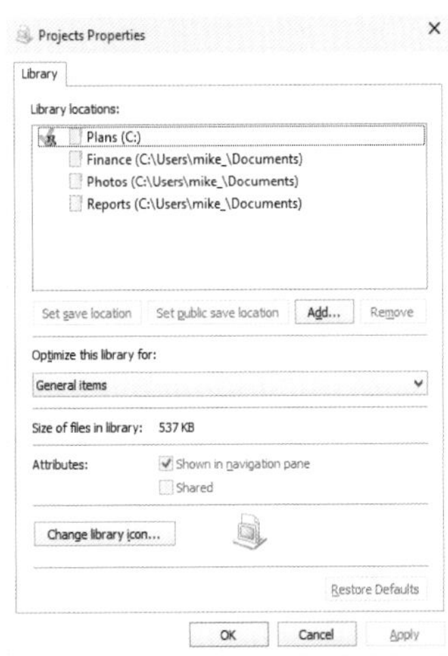

By default, the library will be optimized for the type of file it contains, or for general items if the file types are mixed. However, you can choose a particular file type if you prefer.

Customize folders

1. Right-click the folder and select **Properties**

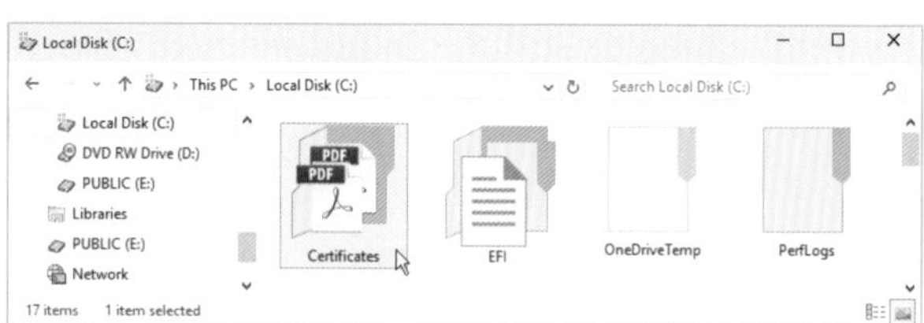

2. Click the **Customize** tab on the Properties panel

3. To specify a folder picture, click the **Choose File** button

4. Find and select the picture image and click **Open**

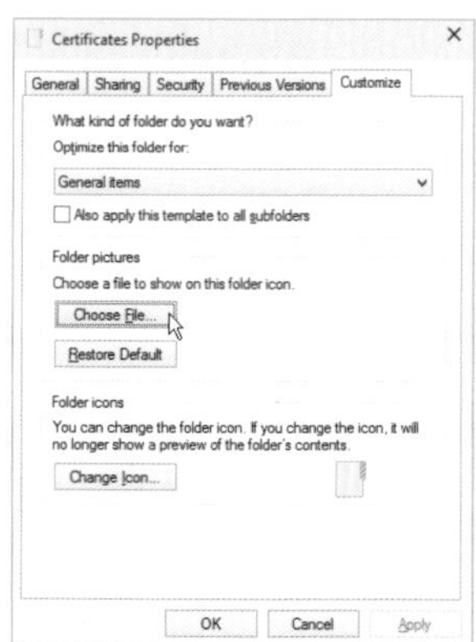

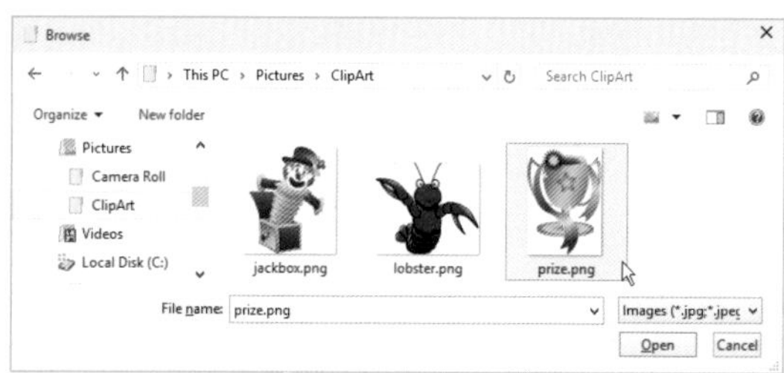

5. Click **Apply, OK** on the Properties panel to add the image as the custom folder image

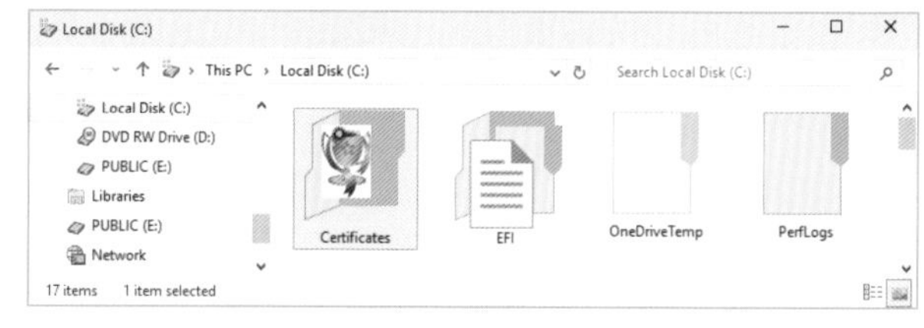

To customize a folder in a library, access it from your hard disk, or right-click its folder and select Open file location.

By default, the folder will be optimized for general items, but you can choose a specific file type if you wish.

You can only add images on drives defined with the NTFS file system with its extended attributes. They cannot be added to drives defined with a FAT file system.

12 Email messaging

The communication tools built into Windows 10 let you communicate with others, sending messages and attachments to individuals or groups of contacts, and the Calendar facility helps you manage your schedule.

Mail app

The Mail app was introduced in the initial release of Windows 10 but was greatly improved for the Creators Update.

Windows 10 provides an app named simply "Mail" for all your email requirements. This has plenty of great features and can be easily configured for multiple email accounts:

1. Go to Start, **Mail** to launch the email app for the first time, and you will be asked to add an email account. Click the **Add account** link

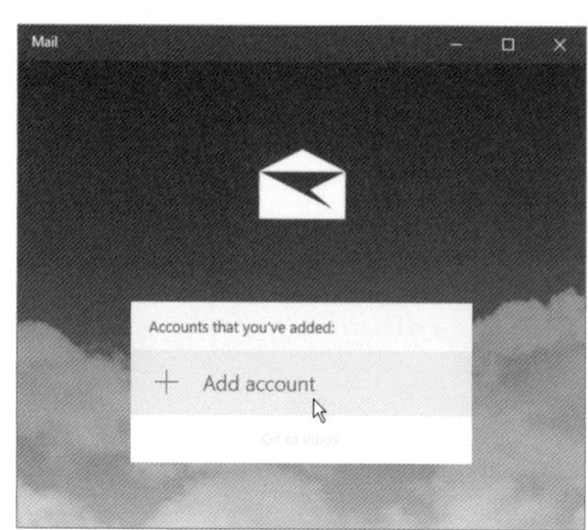

2. Next, you are offered a variety of email services on a "Choose an account" list. Select the type of email account you wish to add. For example, choose **Outlook.com**

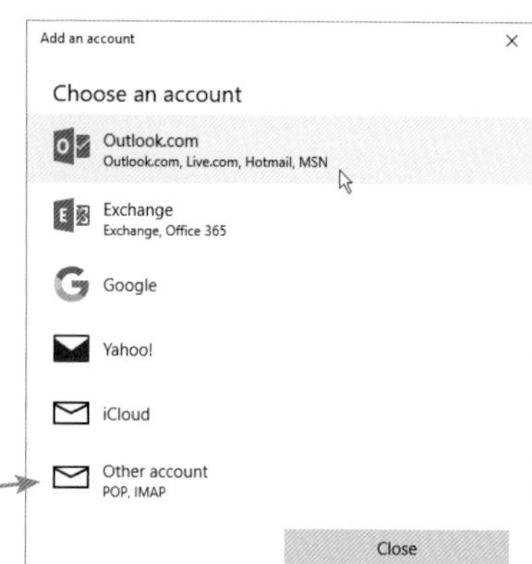

You can choose the **Other account** option if you don't see the email service you want to add.

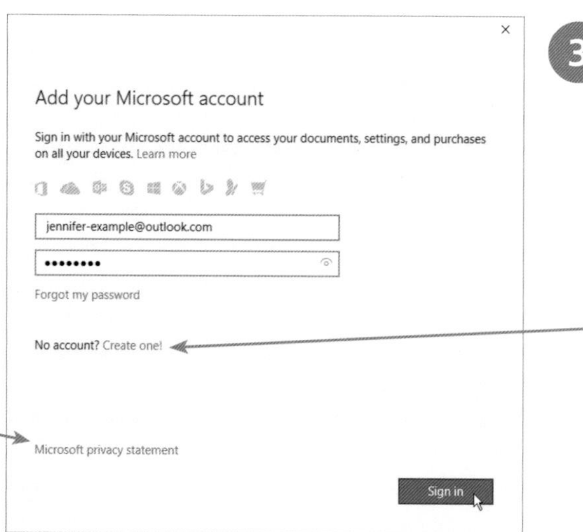

3. Now, enter details of your Microsoft account and click **Sign in**, or click the **Create one** link then follow the Wizard to get an account

Consult the **Microsoft privacy statement** to discover how your personal data may be collected and used.

4. The Outlook account is now added to the **Mail** app and is ready to use. Click the **Add account** link once more if you want to add further accounts – for example a **Yahoo!** email account

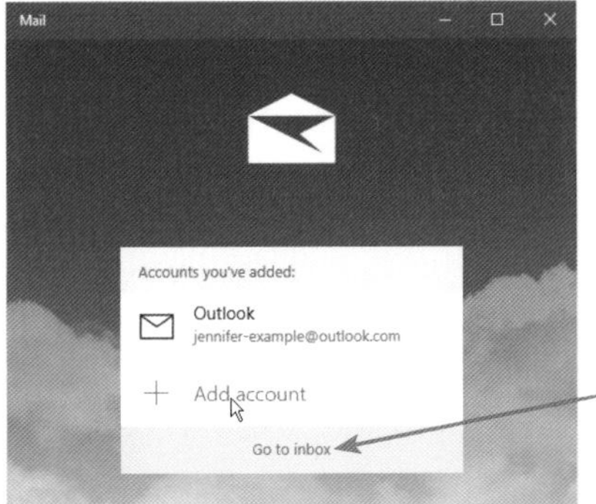

If you don't want to add further accounts simply click the **Go to inbox** link to open the Mail app immediately.

5. Select **Yahoo!** from the "Choose an account" list, then **Sign in** to the Yahoo! email account

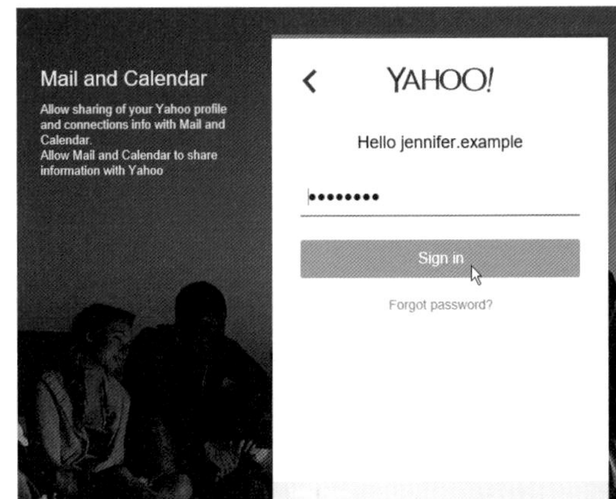

6. The Yahoo! account is now added, and the **Mail** app opens, listing the added accounts in the left-hand pane

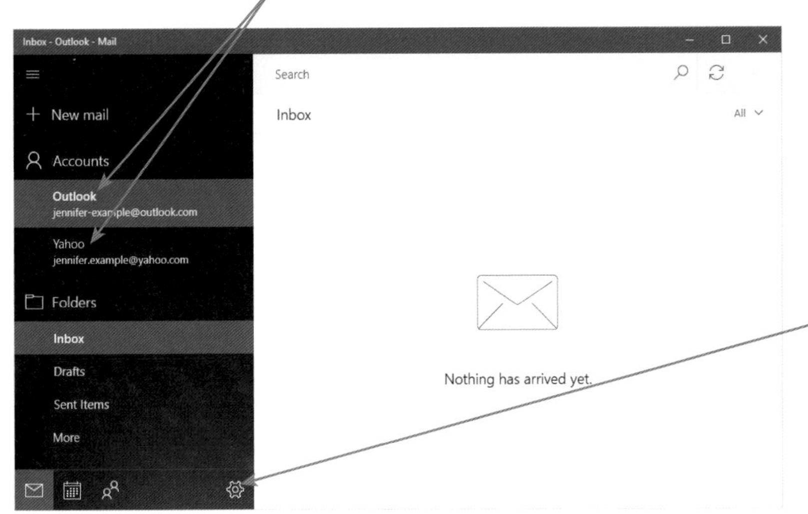

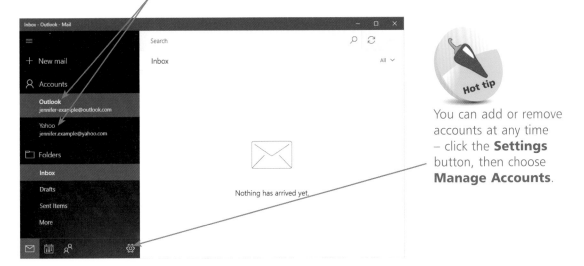

You can add or remove accounts at any time – click the **Settings** button, then choose **Manage Accounts**.

Reading messages

Messages received by any accounts added to the Mail app accumulate in the account's "Inbox" folder, waiting to be read. The left-hand pane of the Mail app screen contains navigation buttons to select an account and folder. Selecting the **Inbox** folder in the left-hand pane displays a list of received messages in the center pane, for the currently selected account. Selecting any message from the list in the center pane displays its contents in the right-hand pane.

Hot tip

Messages that the Mail app considers suspicious are automatically placed in a **Junk Email** folder.

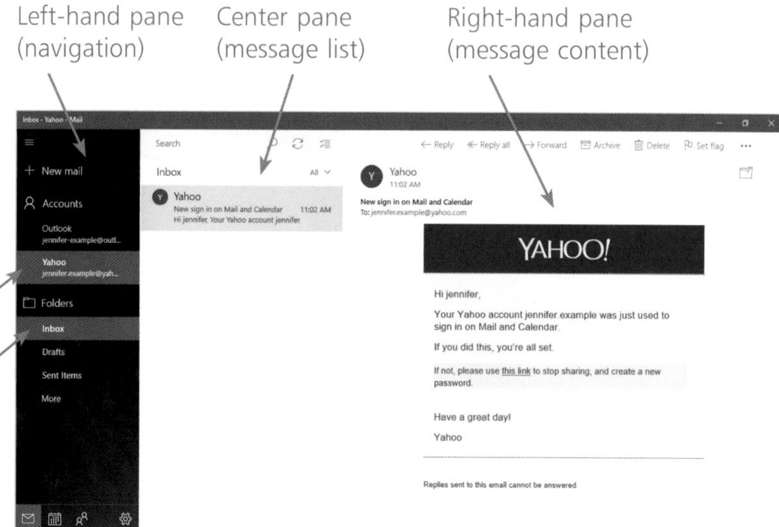

The currently selected items in the left-hand pane remain highlighted to identify the account and the folder that is open.

With the Inbox folder selected, you can click on a different account to see received messages for that account:

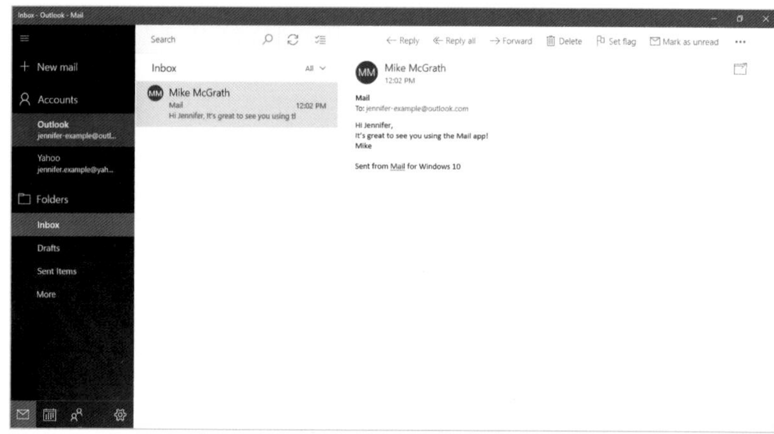

Notice that the messages are automatically given colored icons displaying initials – for easy identification of the message sender.

The Mail app learns from your email habits and begins to separate received messages in the Inbox message list. Important messages are placed under a **Focused** tab, and lower priority messages are placed under an **Other** tab. This lets you focus on important messages and helps you keep an uncluttered Inbox.

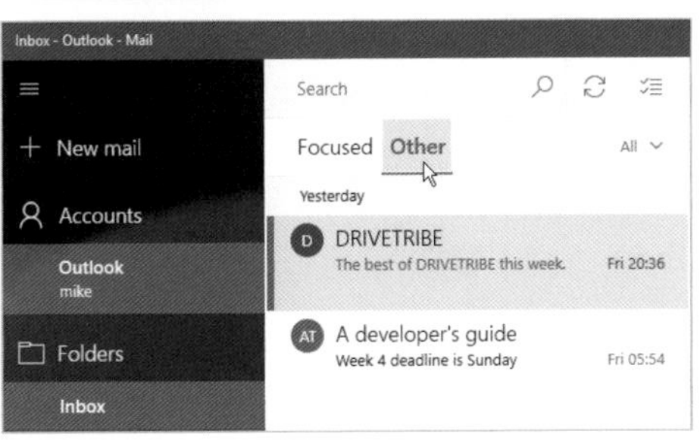

You can turn off the Focused Inbox feature if you don't like it – see page 215.

While you are reading a message you will see a number of links appear above the contents in the right-hand pane:

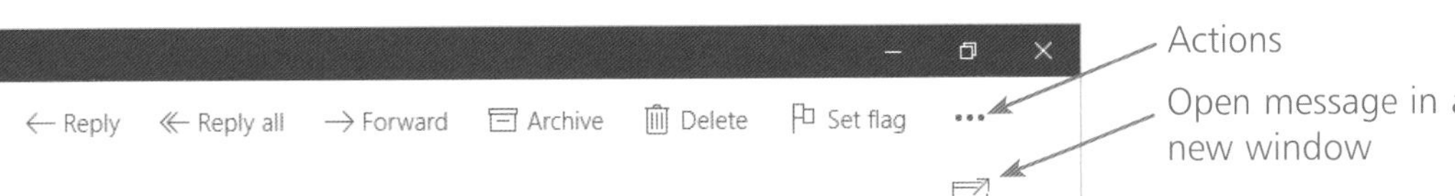

The links are mostly self-explanatory and let you perform various tasks with the message. For example, click the **Delete** link to remove a message after you have read it and need not save it. More options are available if you click the **...** ellipsis button to reveal the **Actions** menu. The **Find** action is particularly useful to search a lengthy message. It opens a search box above the message content where you can type a word to seek. Results are highlighted in the message, and a count of matches is provided:

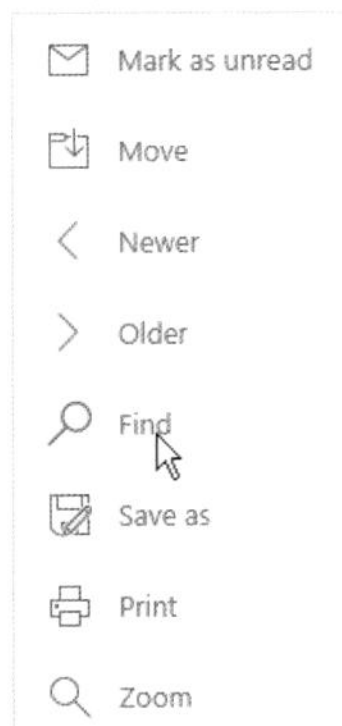

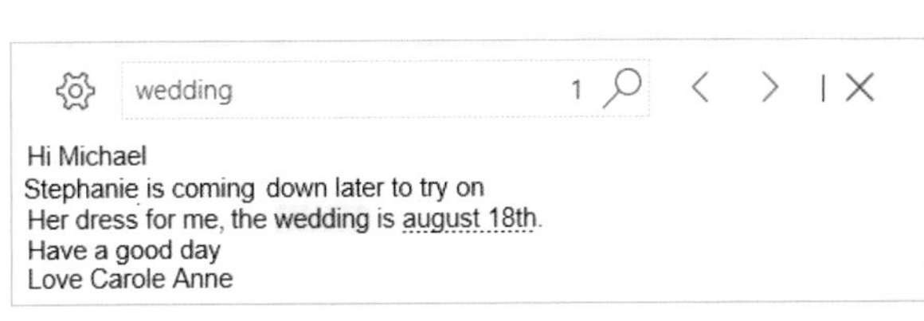

wedding
1
Hi Michael
Stephanie is coming down later to try on
Her dress for me, the wedding is august 18th.
Have a good day
Love Carole Anne

Some messages may arrive with small print – use the **Zoom** option to read those clearly.

Saving messages

When you want to retain email messages, the Mail app provides a number of solutions. Most simply, the app provides an "Archive" folder in which to save your received messages:

1. With a message open for reading, click the **Archive** link to instantly move that message to the Archive folder

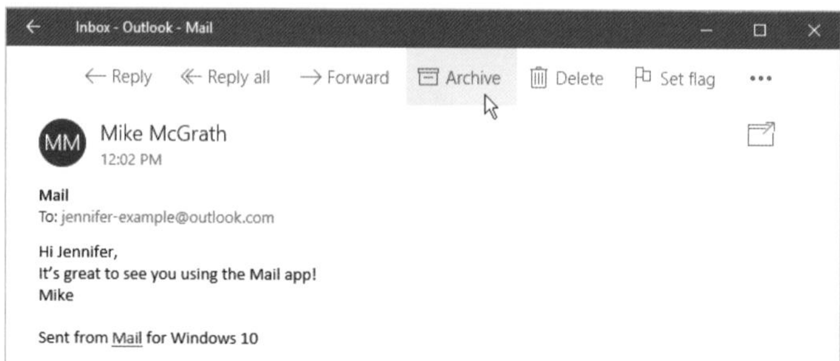

2. Alternatively, select the message in the Inbox list then click the **Archive** button to move the message instantly

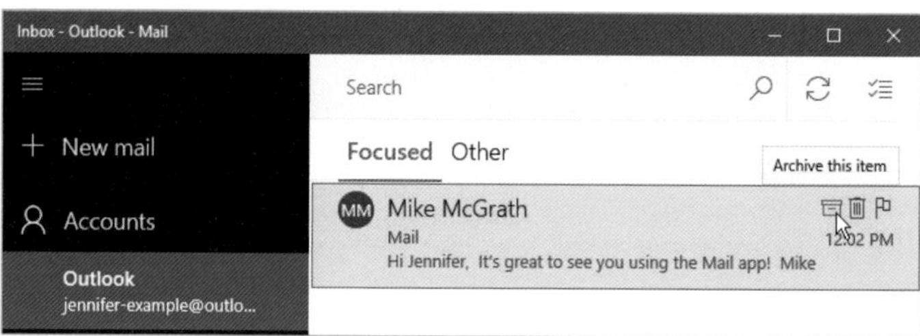

3. Now, in the left-hand pane, click **More**, then choose **Archive** in the pop-up **All folders** list to see your saved messages

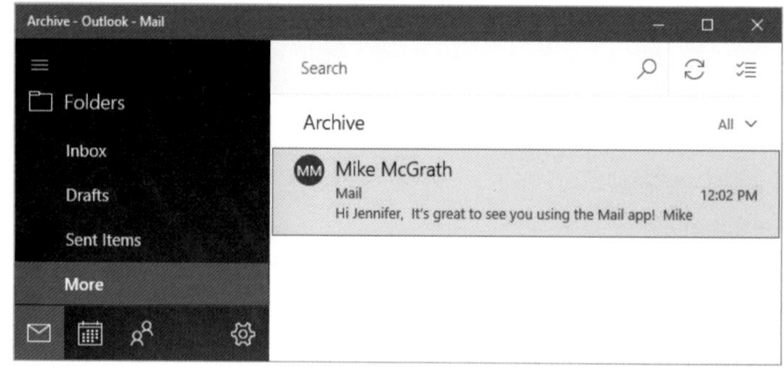

You can click the button to open a message in a new window, without the navigation pane and folder pane.

You can also right-click on a selected message in the Inbox list to see this context menu appear, which provides options including Archive, Move, or Delete the message.

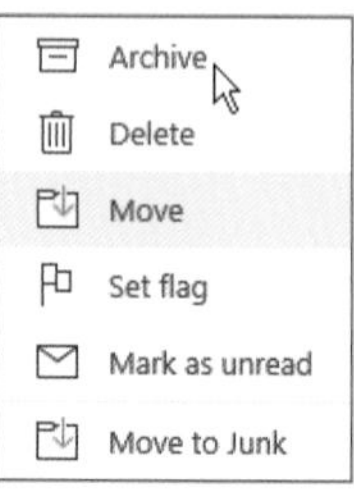

As the **Archive** folder fills up pretty quickly, you may prefer to create your own individual folders in which to save messages:

1. In the Inbox list, click the **Enter selection mode** button

2. Next, click the **Move** button, to open the "Move to..." list

3. Click the + button and type a folder name

Move to...
Mike's Messages

4. Now, hit enter to see your new folder appear in the list

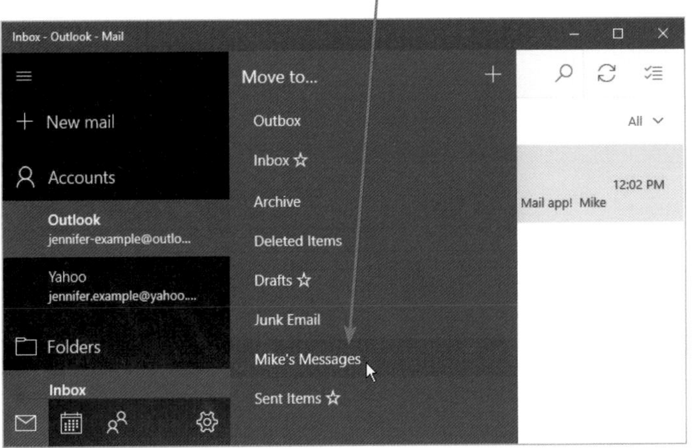

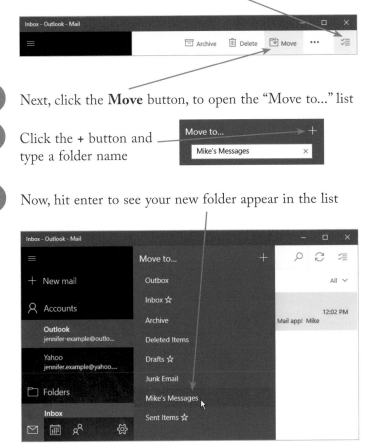

5. Click on the new folder in the list to move the message

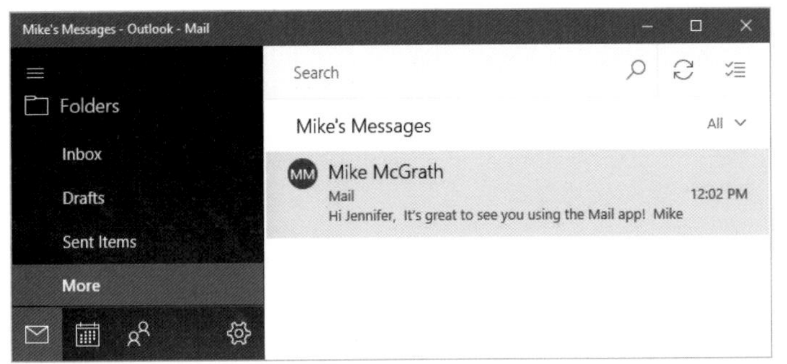

If you save lots of email messages you can create a hierarchy of folders. Right-click on a folder, then choose **Create new subfolder** to add a nested folder inside the selected folder.

Click **More** in the left-hand pane at any time to see the **All folders** list.

Writing messages

The Mail app allows you to easily format the messages you write and check their spelling before you send them, then automatically stores a copy in its **Sent Items** folder for reference later:

Contacts that appear in the list in Step 2 are contacts you have added in the People app (see pages 216-217).

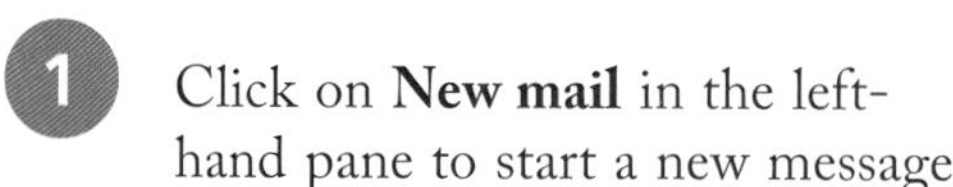

1. Click on **New mail** in the left-hand pane to start a new message

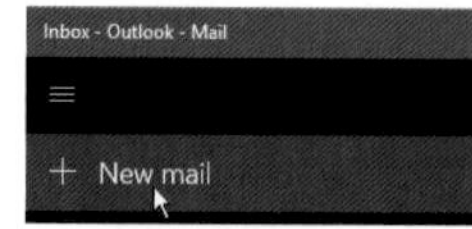

2. In the right-hand pane, type the recipient's email address in the "To:" box – you may select a recipient from a list of contacts that appears as you begin to type

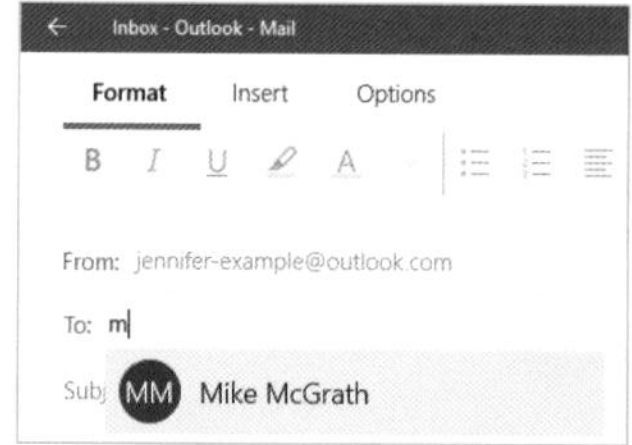

The **@mentions** feature was introduced in the Windows 10 Creators Update.

3. Add a subject, then type your message. Much like the tags in social media you can use **@mentions** to tag a contact within the message – type "@" and a list of contacts will appear. Select a contact to tag them in the message body so they will get a copy of your message

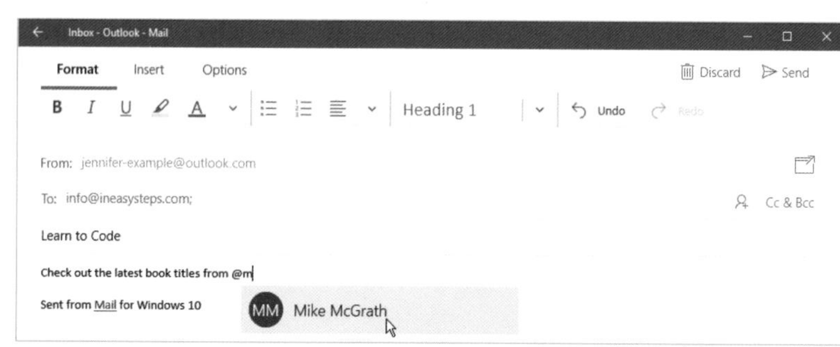

4. Complete the message, then add style with **Format** tools

The **Format** tools let you style and decorate the font, create bulleted or numbered lists, and create indented blocks.

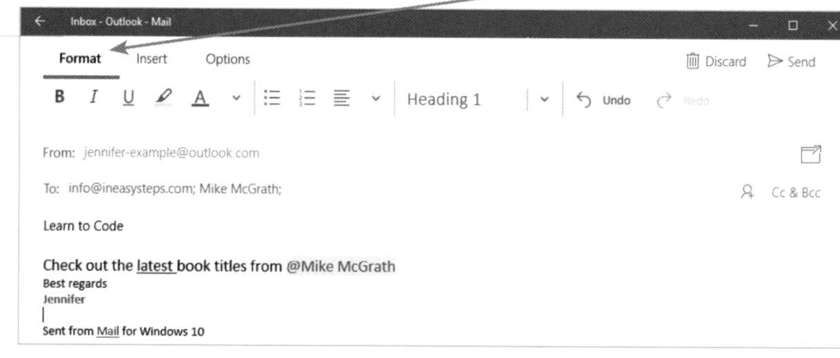

5 Next, select the **Options** item on the toolbar

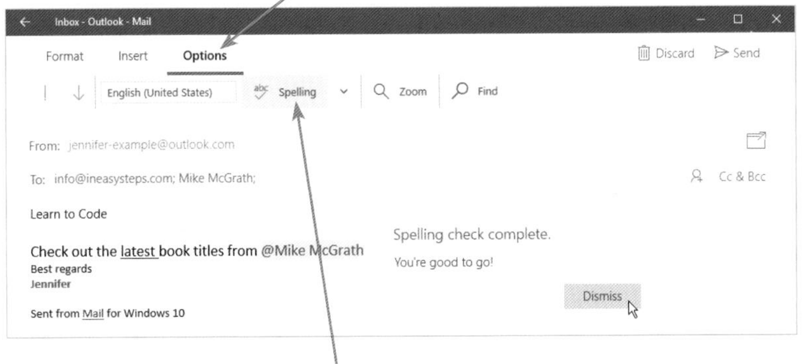

Adjust the language for appropriate spellings in the recipient's location.

6 Now, click the **Spelling** tool to check your message for spelling errors. Click **Dismiss** if none are found

7 When you are entirely happy with your message, click the **Send** button to deliver it to your chosen recipients

If you decide not to send the message, simply click the **Discard** button to remove it from the app. If you don't send or discard the message, it will automatically be saved as a draft.

8 To review your message later, click on the **Sent Items** folder in the left-hand pane, then open a copy from the list there

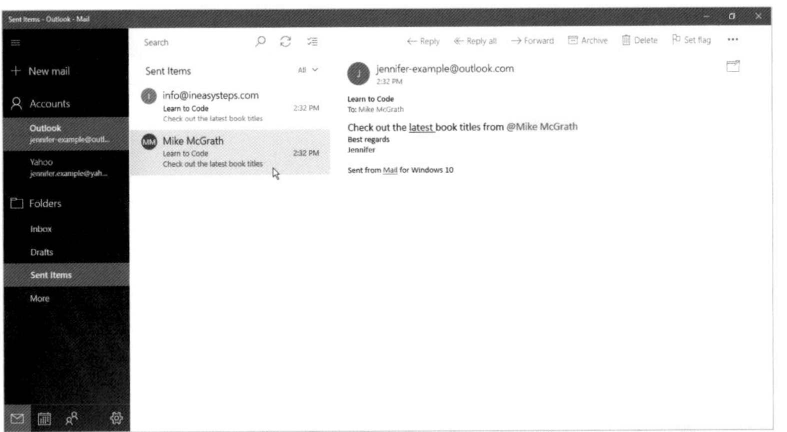

You can also use the keyboard shortcuts **Alt** + **S** or **Ctrl** + **Enter** to send a message from the Mail app.

Adding attachments

They say a picture paints a thousand words, so attaching images to your email messages can mean a lot. The **Mail** app in Windows 10 makes it easy to include any type of file with your messages. You can insert images within your email to enhance the message, and clip attachments alongside the message for further reading:

1. Type your message, then click the **Insert** menu item

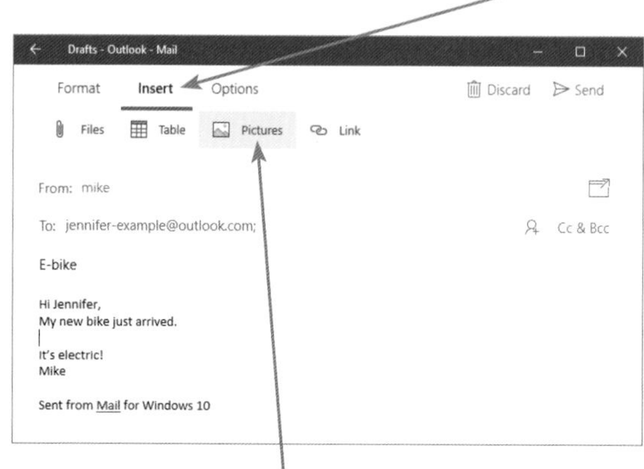

2. Next, choose the **Pictures** option, then browse to a picture you would like to include in your message

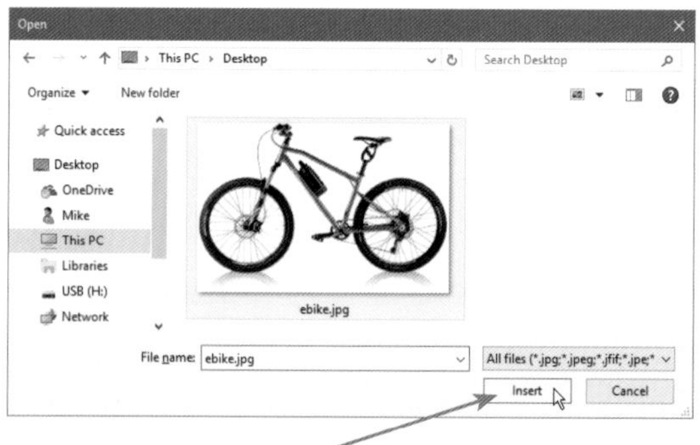

3. Click the **Insert** button to include the picture in your message, then click the **Insert**, **Files** menu item

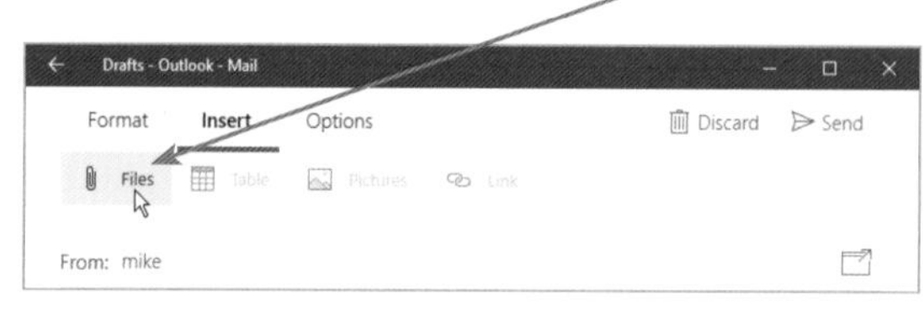

You can also include links to online images and files in your email messages using the Mail app's **Link** menu item.

Use an image editor to reduce the file size of images you include in your emails to minimize the download for the recipients – they may receive your message on a metered connection where charges could apply.

4. Now, browse to a file you would like to attach to your email message

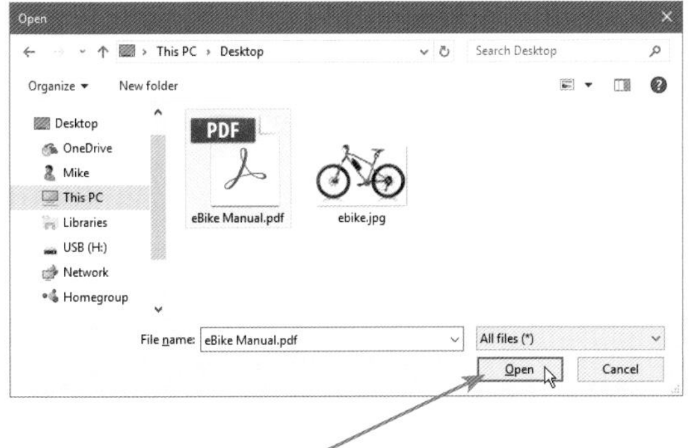

You can drag a file onto the Mail app and drop it onto a message you have written to attach that file to the message.

5. Click the **Open** button to attach the file to your message, then click the **Send** button

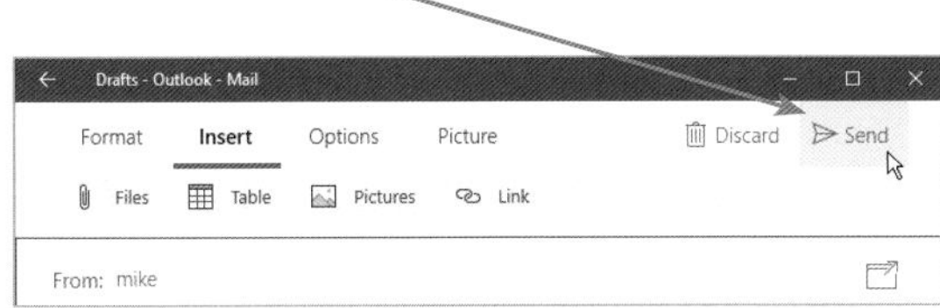

6. Your message is received with the selected picture inserted and the selected file attached

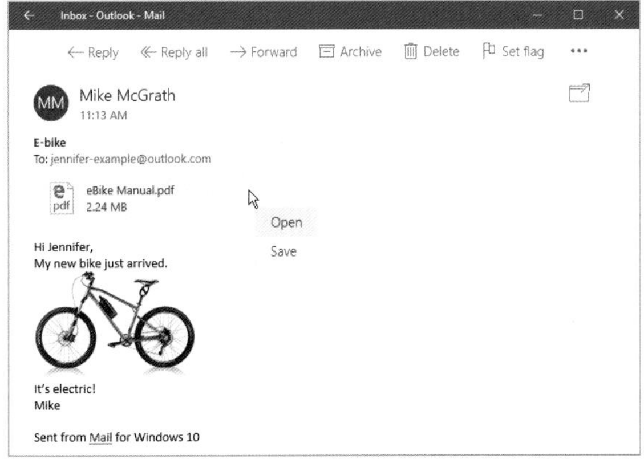

The recipient's email app must allow automatic inclusion of images to see them in your message. Some people prefer to deny this due to security concerns.

7. The recipient can right-click the attachment and choose to **Open** or **Save** the file you sent

Syncing options

If you often use a metered internet connection, you might like to configure the frequency at which the Mail app checks for the arrival of new email messages:

1. Launch the Mail app, then click its **Settings** button and choose the **Manage Accounts** option

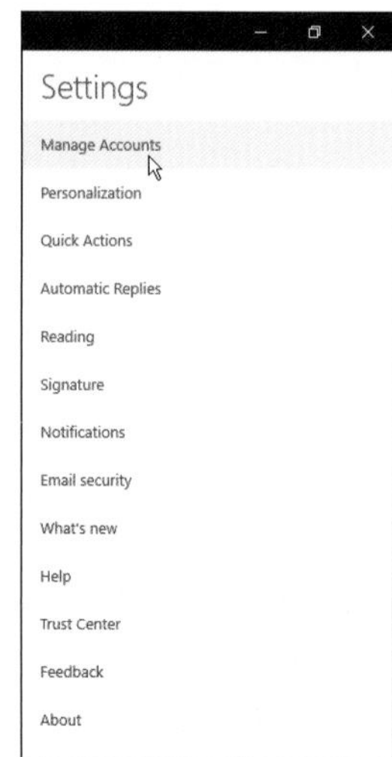

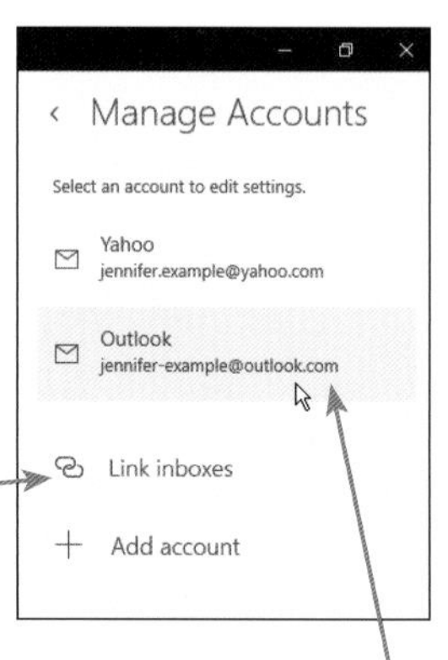

You can unify multiple email accounts into a single Inbox by clicking the **Link inboxes** option.

2. Next, select the account you want to configure and see its **Account settings** dialog open

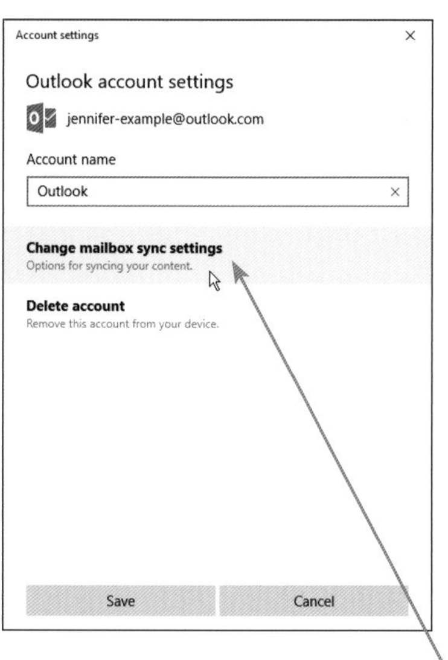

3. Now, click the **Change mailbox sync settings** option to see the account's current synchronization settings

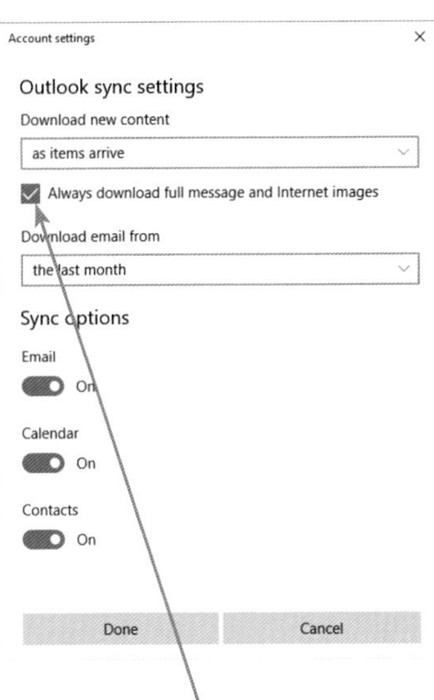

Different mail accounts may provide differing syncing options.

4 Uncheck the checkbox if you prefer to receive only previews of your messages

5 Open the top drop-down menu and select an option to check for messages less frequently

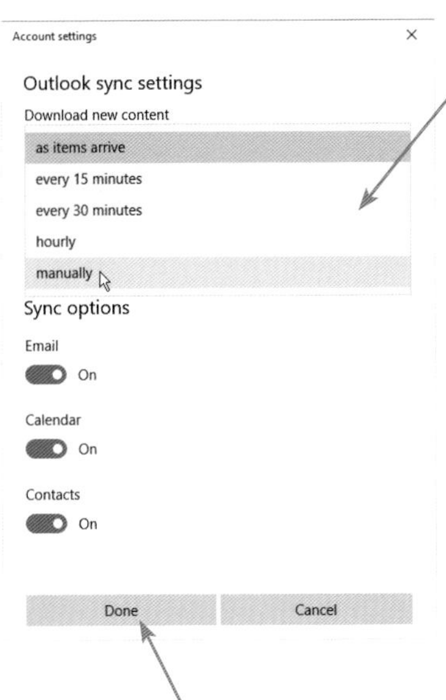

If you choose the option to download messages **manually**, the Mail app will never check for messages automatically. Choose an interval such as **every 30 minutes**, to avoid manual syncing.

6 Click the **Done** button to close sync settings, then click **Save** on the Account settings dialog to apply the changes

Automating responses

The Mail app can be configured to automatically send replies to email it receives. This is useful when you cannot respond in person but want to ensure the message sender does not feel ignored:

1. Launch the Mail app, then click its **Settings** button and choose the **Automatic Replies** option

2. If you have more than one email account, choose the one you want to automate in the drop-down box

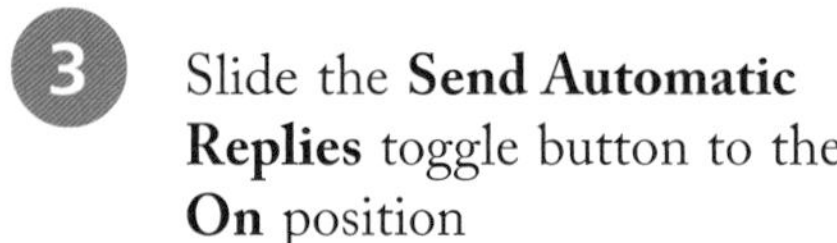

3. Slide the **Send Automatic Replies** toggle button to the **On** position

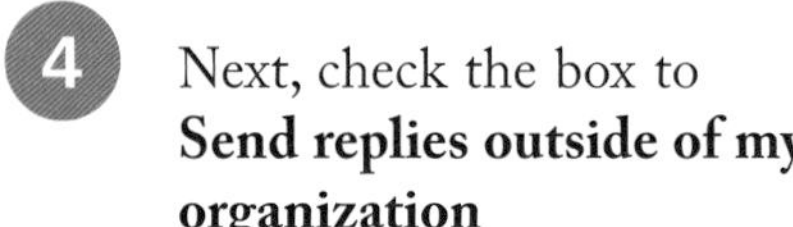

4. Next, check the box to **Send replies outside of my organization**

5. Type your automated message in the text box below the checkbox

6. Senders of email to your account will now receive automatic replies

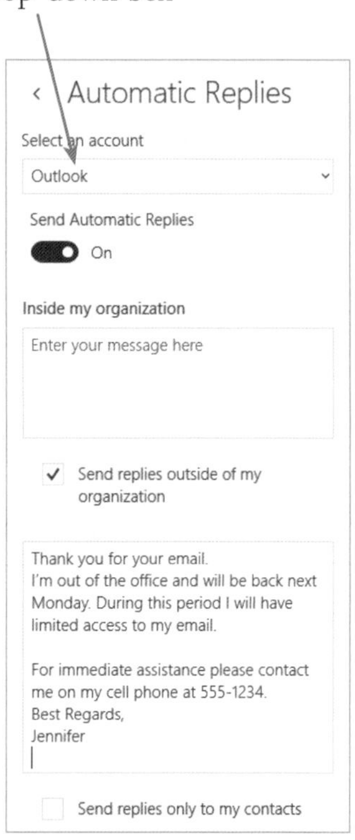

Automatic Replies
Select an account
Outlook
Send Automatic Replies
On
Inside my organization
Enter your message here
Send replies outside of my organization
Thank you for your email.
I'm out of the office and will be back next Monday. During this period I will have limited access to my email.
For immediate assistance please contact me on my cell phone at 555-1234.
Best Regards,
Jennifer
Send replies only to my contacts

Automatic replies should advise the length of your absence and provide an alternative method of contacting yourself or a colleague.

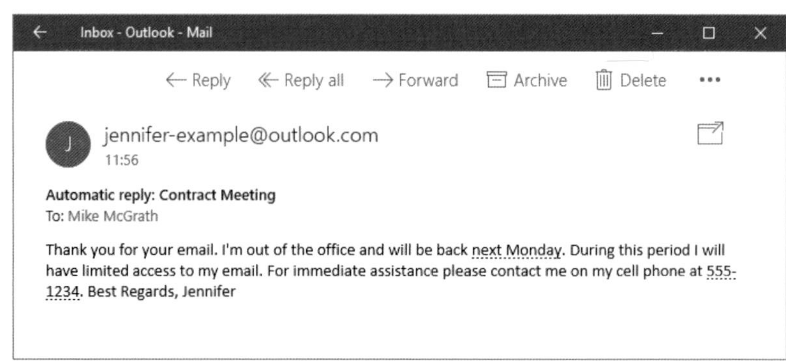

Inbox - Outlook - Mail
Reply
Reply all
Forward
Archive
Delete
jennifer-example@outlook.com
11:56
Automatic reply: Contract Meeting
To: Mike McGrath
Thank you for your email. I'm out of the office and will be back next Monday. During this period I will have limited access to my email. For immediate assistance please contact me on my cell phone at 555-1234. Best Regards, Jennifer

The automatic reply does not maintain formatting of line breaks or paragraphs.

You can also automate your signature at the end of every email so you need not type it manually. This is also useful if you would like to append a disclaimer at the end of each message:

1. Launch the Mail app, then click its Settings button and choose the **Signature** option

2. If you have more than one email account choose the one you want to append a signature to in the drop-down box, or check the box to **Apply to all accounts**

3. Slide the **Use an email signature** toggle button to the **On** position

4. Type your signature or disclaimer message in the text box below the toggle button

5. Your signature or disclaimer will now be automatically appended to each new email message you write

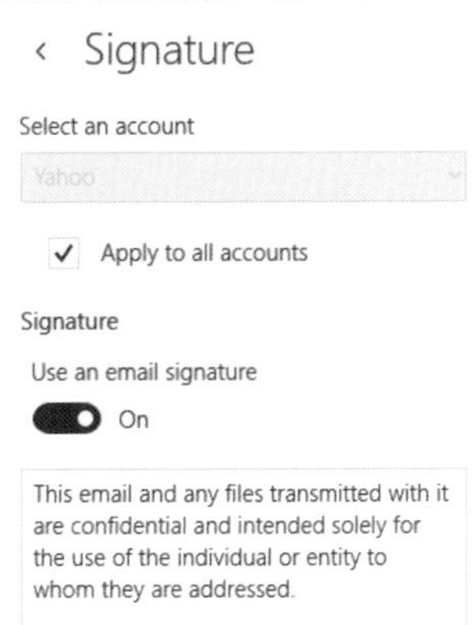

Your signature will not be appended to automatic replies.

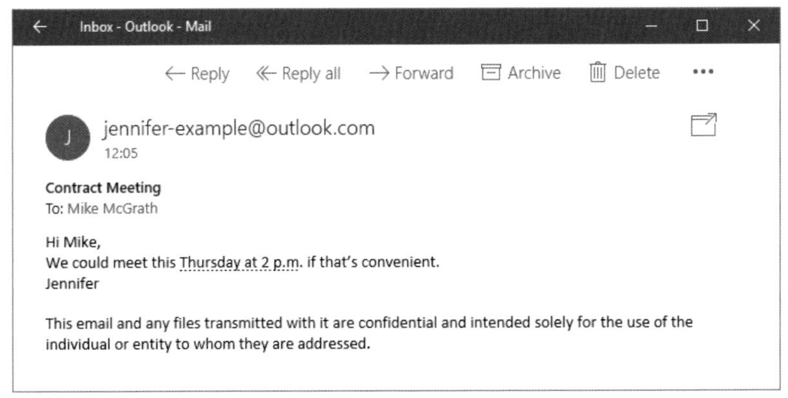

Inbox - Outlook - Mail
Reply
Reply all
Forward
Archive
Delete
jennifer-example@outlook.com
12:05
Contract Meeting
To: Mike McGrath
Hi Mike,
We could meet this Thursday at 2 p.m. if that's convenient.
Jennifer
This email and any files transmitted with it are confidential and intended solely for the use of the individual or entity to whom they are addressed.

Disclaimers in email messages may not be legally enforceable, but they are in common use to underline confidentiality.

Choosing preferences

The Mail app settings provide various options to customize appearance and performance to suit your personal preference:

Personalization

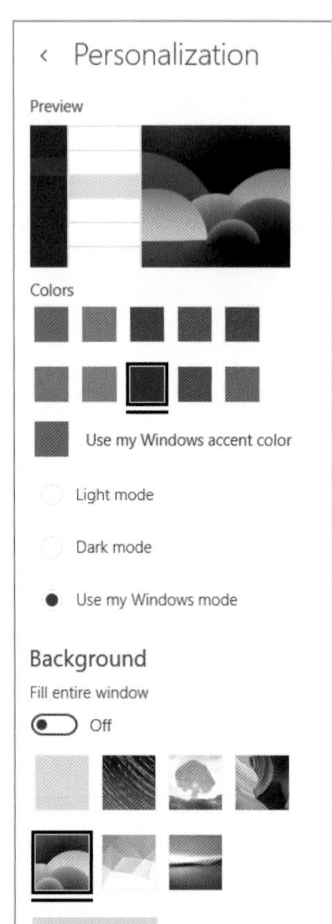

- **Colors** – choose from a selection of 10 colors, or choose to use your Windows accent color, to customize both the Mail and Calendar apps instantly.
- **Modes** – choose Light mode for a white background in the folder and message list panes, or choose Dark mode for a black background in those panes.
- **Backgrounds** – choose from a selection of several default background images, or browse to find a suitable background image on your computer. The background image will appear in the content pane when you are not viewing a message. A portion of the background image can also appear in the left-hand pane but is faded so you can see the items.

Turn off the option to **Fill entire window** if you prefer to only see a background image in the content pane – when you are not viewing a message.

Quick actions

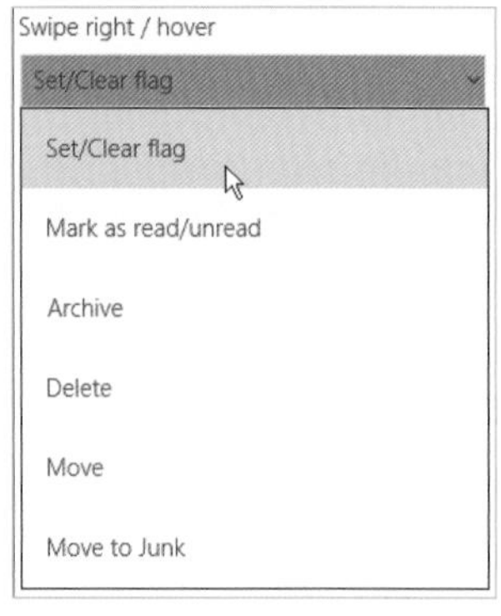

- **Swipe actions** – choose what will appear when you hover the mouse over a message in the message list. When swipe actions are turned on, a Set/Clear flag button and a Delete button will appear by default when you hover over a message in the list.

Swipe actions determine what will appear when touchscreen users swipe left or swipe right.

Reading

- **Mark item as read** – choose when to internally denote that you have read a message.
- **Caret Browsing** – choose to turn On the option to navigate through messages using the keyboard arrow keys if you're a fan of Caret Browsing.
- **External content** – choose to turn Off the option to automatically download external images if you want to limit data costs over a metered connection.
- **Conversation** – choose whether to see the beginning of messages in the message list, and choose whether to display user icons in the message list.
- **Focused Inbox** – choose to turn Off the option to sort messages into Focused and Other if you don't want to see these separate tabs in the message list.

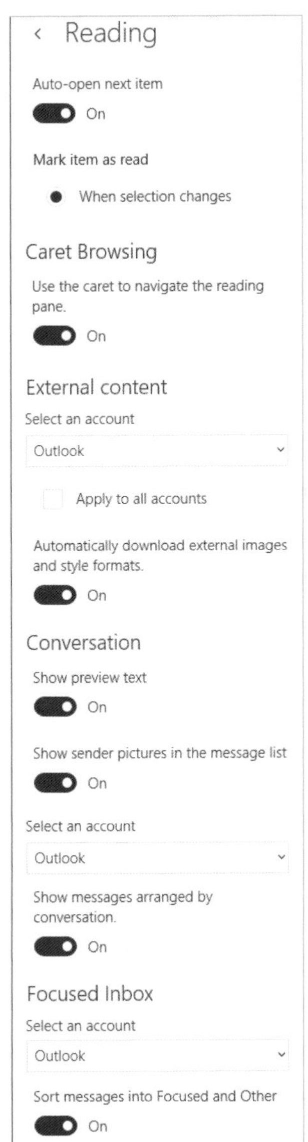

You can discover more about Caret Browsing on page 242.

The Mail settings also provides a **What's new** option that opens a web page in your browser detailing the latest developments in the Mail and Calendar apps.

Notifications

- **Show notifications in the action center** – choose if you want to see a banner and hear a sound when a message arrives.

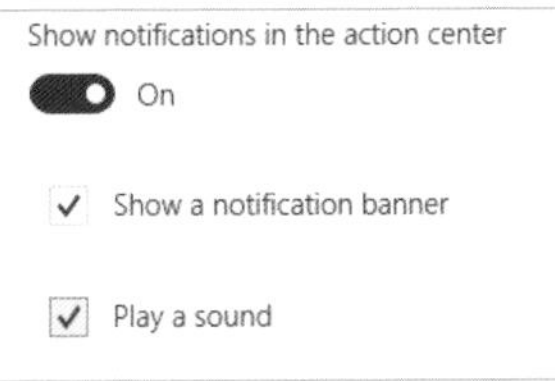

People app

The **People** app is a new Universal Windows App in Windows 10.

Windows 10 provides a contacts manager called the **People** app that is closely integrated with the Mail app and the Maps app. The People app is useful for storing information such as email addresses, phone numbers, and physical addresses.

The People app has the ability to amalgamate all of your contacts across a range of different email services and social media websites. It allows you to easily call a contact from a phone, send an email to a contact, or retrieve a map of the contact's location:

1. Go to Start, People, or click the button in the Mail app, to launch the **People** app

2. If you are signed in to the computer with a Microsoft account, the **Contacts** page will open, otherwise you are asked to connect accounts from which to gather contacts

People lets you access your contacts, regardless of where they are, from one convenient location.

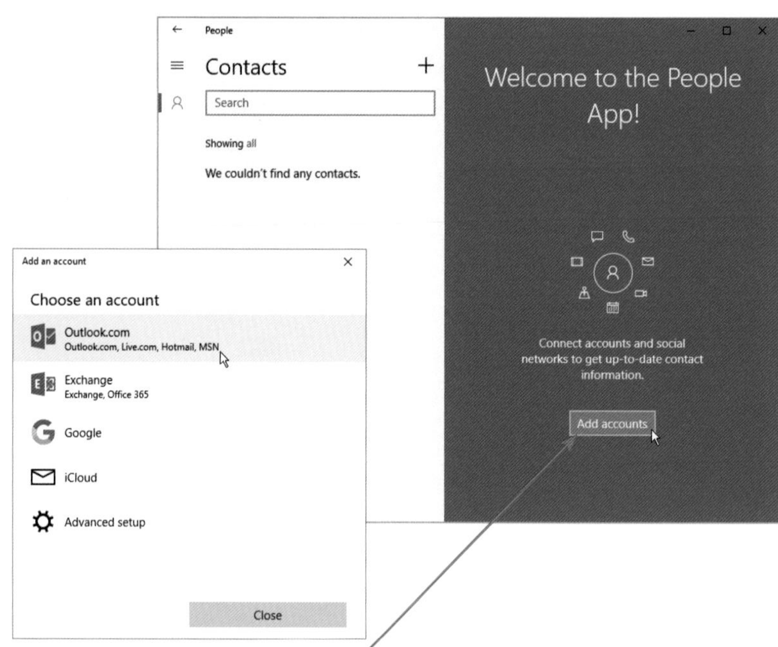

People can link the same contacts from different networks under one profile. There is also an option that allows you to link contacts manually.

3. Click the **Add accounts** button, then choose an account. For example, choose **Outlook.com** to add that account

4. Sign in to the account to add contacts to the People app

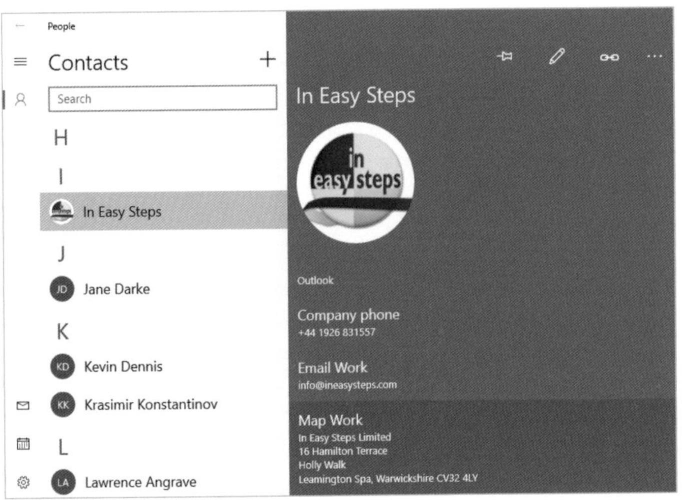

5. Scroll down the contacts list and select any one to see their profile details

6. Click an email address in a profile to launch the **Mail** app, ready to send that contact a message

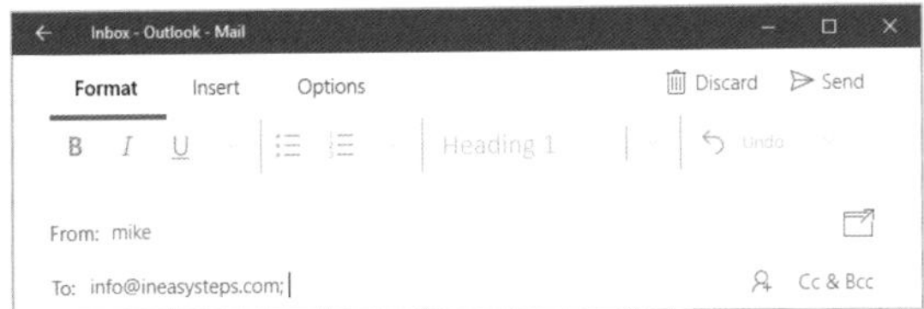

7. Click a location address in a profile to launch the **Maps** app, to see that contact's physical address

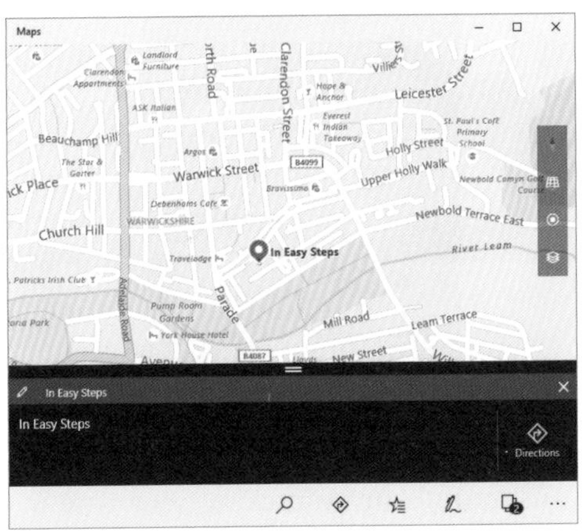

On a phone or call-enabled tablet you can tap the telephone number in the contact's profile to call that contact, or to make a Skype call.

The People app can be used with the Maps app to plan a route to a contact's address.

Calendar app

The **Calendar** app is a new Universal Windows App in Windows 10.

Windows 10 provides a useful Calendar app in which to keep track of forthcoming events. The app is powered by Exchange ActiveSync (EAS) technology that is the backbone of Microsoft services such as Hotmail, Exchange, and Office 365. It can also connect to other EAS-based calendars, such as Google Calendar.

As with many Windows 10 apps, Calendar uses a browser-like form of navigation. When using a mouse, you'll see small navigational arrows appear near the top-left of the calendar. Or you can use the keyboard – **Ctrl** + **Up arrow**, **Ctrl** + **Down arrow**, **Ctrl** + **Left arrow**, and **Ctrl** + **Right arrow** for calendar navigation.

A cool feature is that moving backwards or forwards in time is done within the context of the current view. For example, going back while in Week view takes you back a week. Going forward while in Day view takes you forward to tomorrow:

You move around the Calendar app using the arrow buttons.

1. Go to Start, Calendar, or click the button in the Mail app, to launch the **Calendar** app

2. If you are not signed in to the computer with a Microsoft account you will be asked to sign in, otherwise the Calendar will open in Month view

You can import calendars into the Calendar app from Hotmail, Outlook and Google by clicking the Calendar app's Settings button then Manage Accounts, **Add an account**.

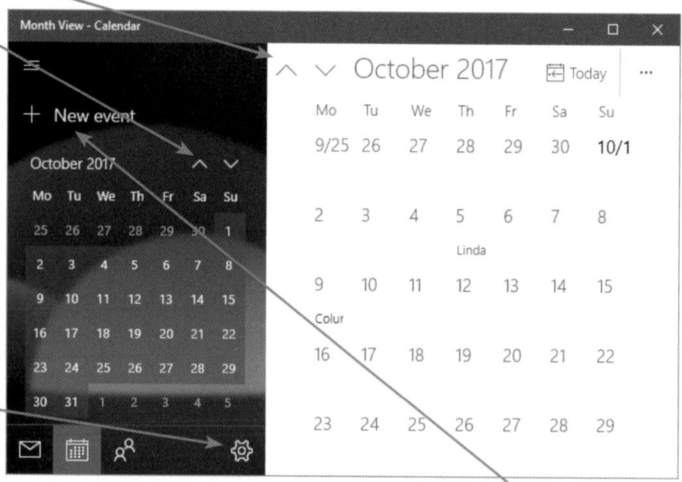

3. Add an entry to the calendar by clicking the **New event** link, or by clicking on a date in the calendar to open the event **Home** page

4. On the event Home page, enter details of the event name, location, and duration

5. If you would like Cortana to remind you of the event in advance, specify a notice period on the toolbar

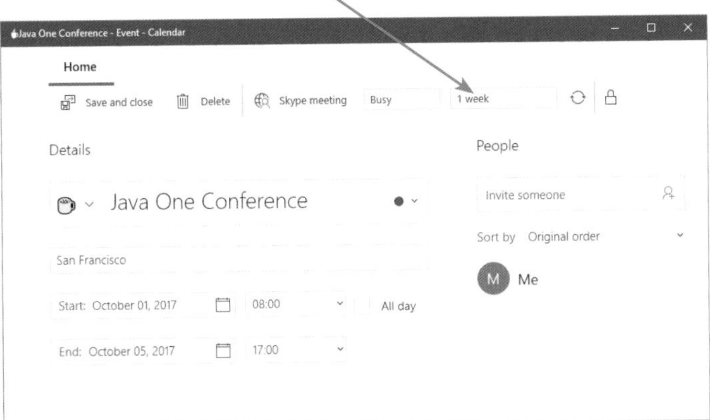

6. Click the **Save and close** button to return to the calendar view and see the event has now been added

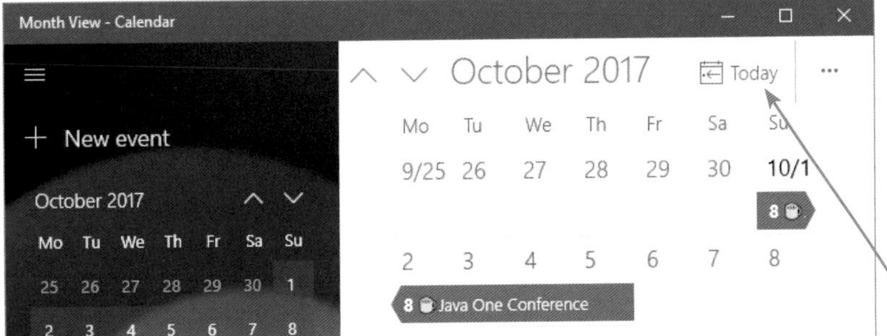

7. You will receive a Cortana notification reminding you of the forthcoming event at the time specified by the notice period

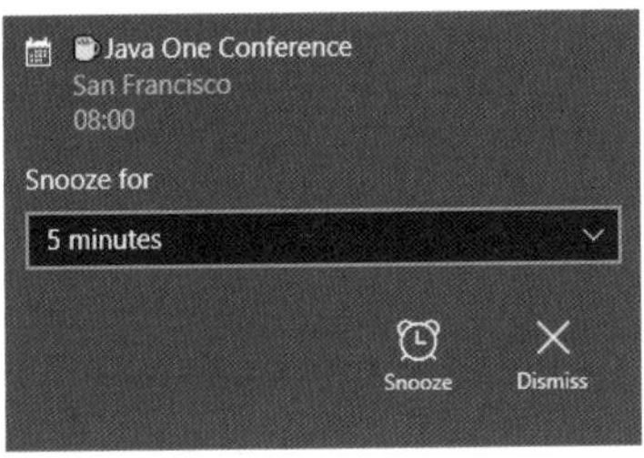

Hot tip

Options to enable Cortana reminders and additional calendars are provided at the bottom of the left-hand pane.

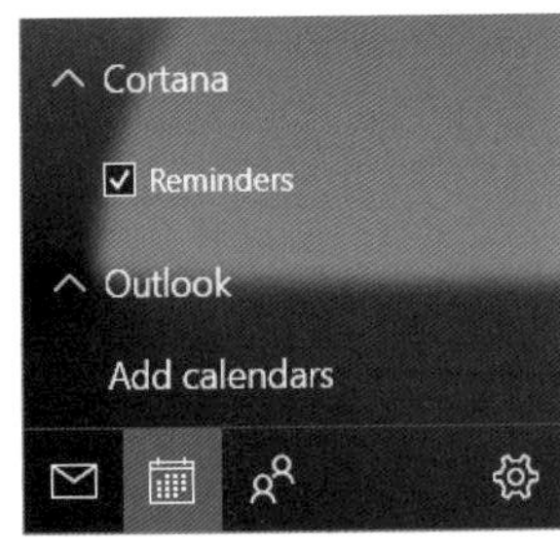

Beware

Some of the options may be hidden if the Calendar is viewed in a small window. The options to select Day, Week, Month, or Year view are located to the right of the **Today** option, but are not visible in these screenshots.

...cont'd

The Calendar app toolbar options let you choose to view **Today**, **Day**, **Week**, **Month**, or **Year**, to change the calendar view as required. Other options (like **Work week**) are available from the Day and Week drop-downs. Changing from Month view to Week view provides rows for each hour under each day's column. This is useful for noting daily agenda schedules of events for each day. The hamburger button collapses the left-hand pane for extra space.

The **Work week** view shows a five day week.

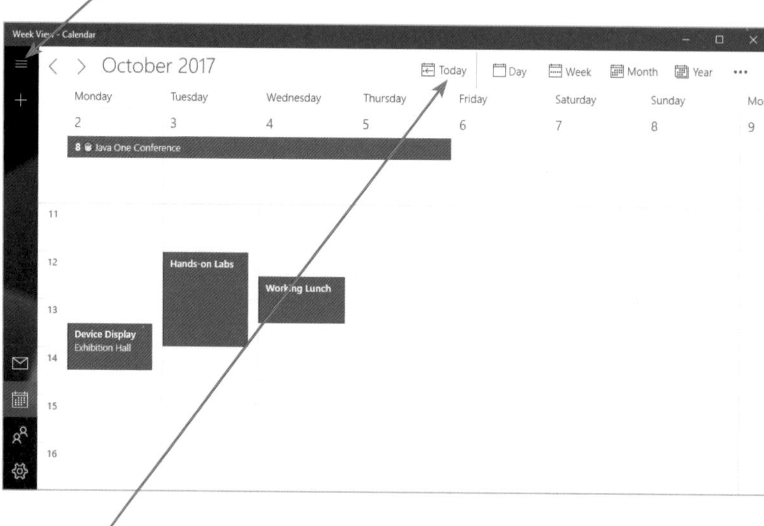

Calendar can show detailed information regarding your next event on the Lock screen.

The **Today** button returns the Calendar view to the current date and retains the left-hand pane position – full or collapsed.

The Calendar app has buttons for the Mail app, People app, and for Calendar settings.

13 Microsoft Edge

Windows 10 includes Microsoft Edge as the default web browser. Here, we explore its features and discover the innovations it brings to web browsing.

Better browsing

Windows 10 introduces the next-generation web browser named Microsoft Edge. This replaces the Internet Explorer web browser that has been around for many years. Microsoft Edge is a brand new, faster, more streamlined web browser.

Microsoft Edge has a new rendering engine called EdgeHTML that replaces the Trident rendering engine used in Internet Explorer. The new browser doesn't support old "legacy" technologies, such as ActiveX, but instead uses an extension system similar to those in the Chrome and Firefox web browsers. There is, however, a version of Internet Explorer included with Windows 10 for backward compatibility. Not supporting legacy technologies in Microsoft Edge has a number of benefits:

- Better interoperability with other modern browsers.
- Enhanced performance.
- Improved security and reliability.
- Reduced code complexity.

The Microsoft Edge web browser app is a new Universal Windows App in Windows 10.

In addition to these benefits, there are several great innovations in the Microsoft Edge web browser:

- Integration with the Cortana Personal Digital Assistant for voice control, search, and personalized information.
- Annotation of web pages that can then be easily stored on OneDrive for sharing with other users.
- Compilation of web pages into a Reading list that synchronizes content between devices.
- Elimination of formatting distractions in Reading view mode that allows web pages to be read more easily.

If you need to view a web page that uses legacy technology, you can find Internet Explorer under Windows Accessories on the A-Z Start menu.

The Microsoft Edge web browser is uncluttered in appearance, as its design intends to emphasize web page content. Browsing the web simply requires use of the familiar "navigation buttons":

Interface layout

When the Microsoft Edge web browser is launched it shows just the Start page and provides the interface features shown below:

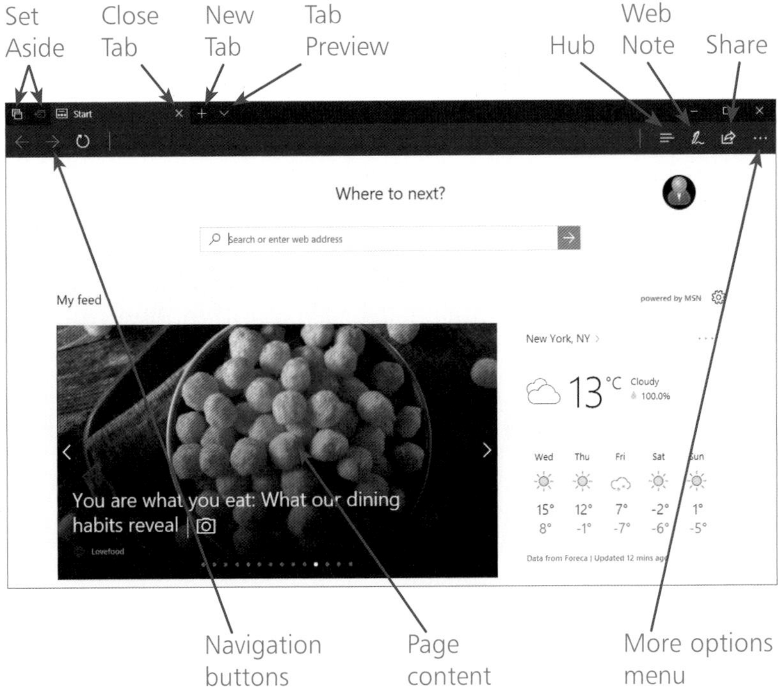

The Hub is a new feature of Microsoft Edge in Windows 10.

Additional interface features of the Address Bar, the Favorites button, and the Reading View button are initially hidden, but will appear to the left of the Hub button as you begin to browse web pages.

Clicking the **+ New Tab** button opens a new tab containing a Search box and, by default, an intelligent selection of **Top sites** tiles that may be of interest to you.

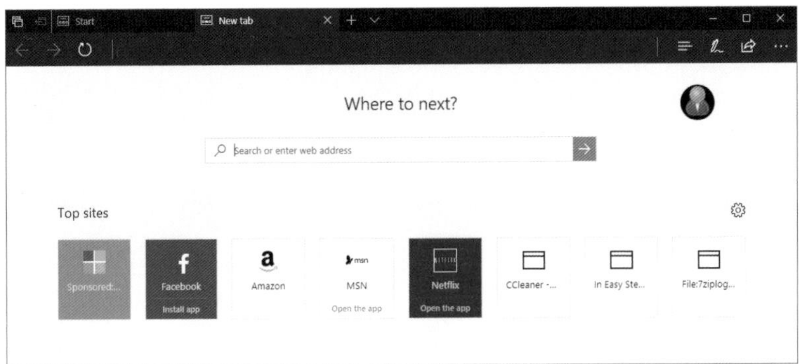

Use the **Customize** option on the new tab page if you wish to include your news feed or wish to exclude the Top sites list.

Tabbing pages

The ability to open multiple pages on separate "tabs" is available in other modern browsers, but Microsoft Edge provides great additional features to better control your open tabs.

NEW

The **Tab Preview** feature was introduced in the Windows 10 Creators Update.

Tab Preview

To quickly view the pages you have opened on multiple tabs:

1. Click the **Tab Preview** button to the right of the final tab

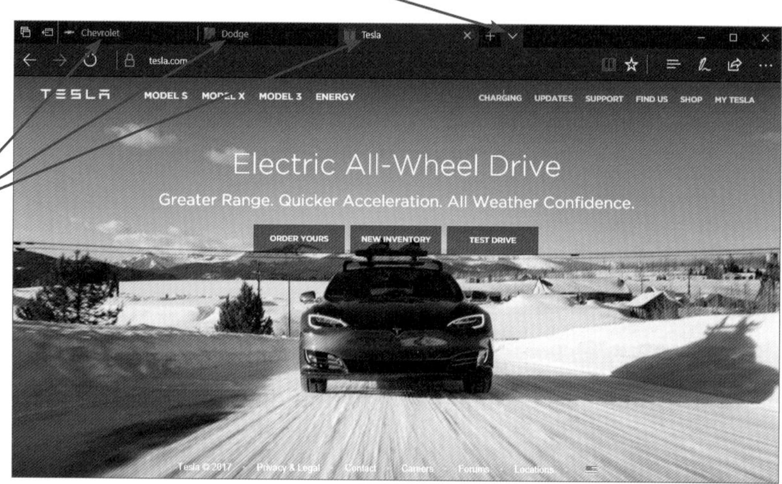

Don't forget

Simply select any tab to view the page that is open on that tab.

2. See the Tab Preview panel open at the top of the window

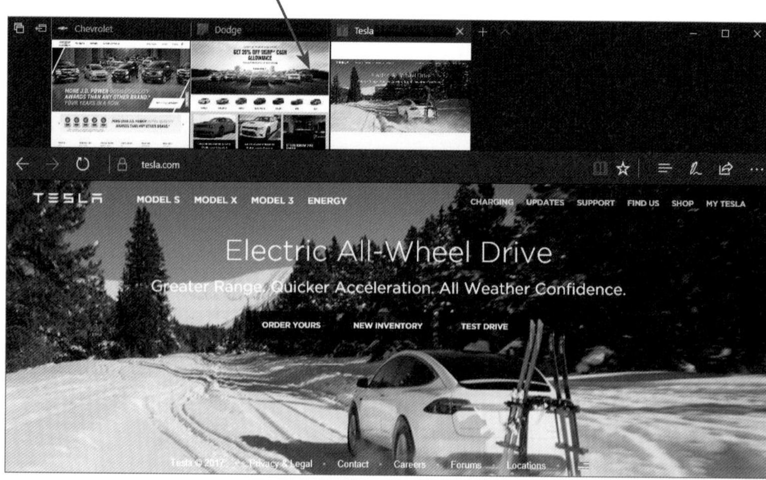

Hot tip

You can also right-click on any Tab Preview to choose an option from this context menu.

Close tab
Reopen closed tab
Close other tabs
Close tabs to the right
Refresh all
Duplicate
Move to new window
Pin

3. Click any preview to switch to that page, or click the Tab Preview button once more to close the preview panel

Set Aside

As you add more tabs, the Tab Preview panel provides Forward/Back scroll buttons for navigation, but you can clear the panel by setting aside all open tabs for later:

The **Set Aside** feature was introduced in the Windows 10 Creators Update.

1. Click the **Set Aside** button on the Edge toolbar

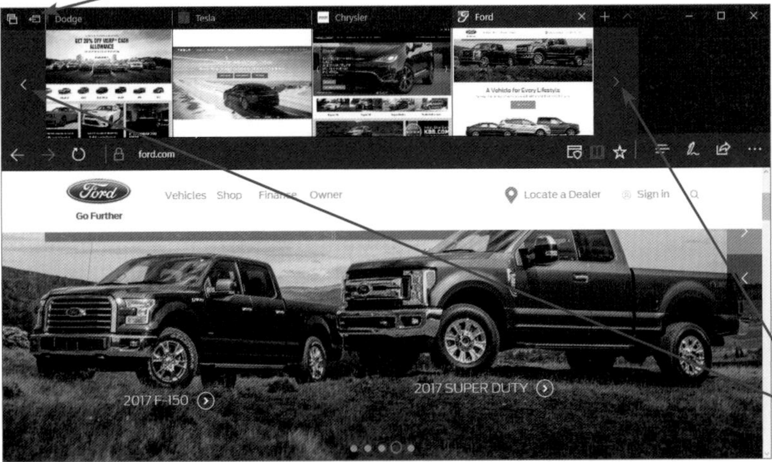

You can use the Forward/Back buttons to scroll through the Tab Preview.

2. See only a New Tab now appear in the Tab Preview panel

3. Click the **Tabs** button to reveal the tabs you've set aside

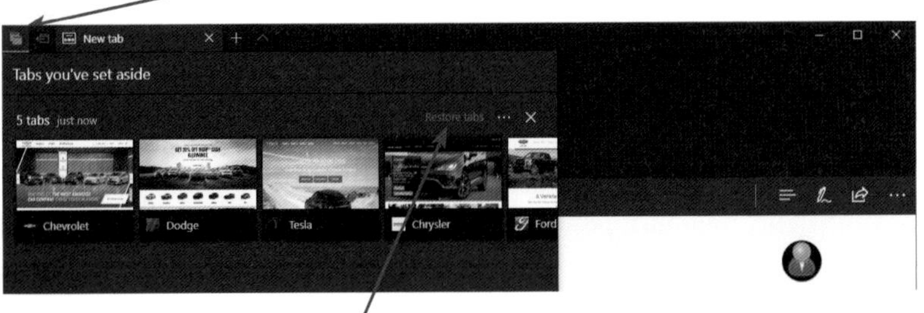

You can right-click any tab from the **Tabs you've set aside** preview and choose Remove to delete that individual tab.

4. Click the **Restore tabs** link to see the tabs you've set aside reappear in the Tabs Preview panel

Search and navigation

The Search box on the Start page contains a text message inviting you to "Search or enter web address". This indicates its multi-purpose function for both web search and for address navigation:

Type a word or phrase into the box to see a list of suggestions instantly appear. For example, type "kadaza"

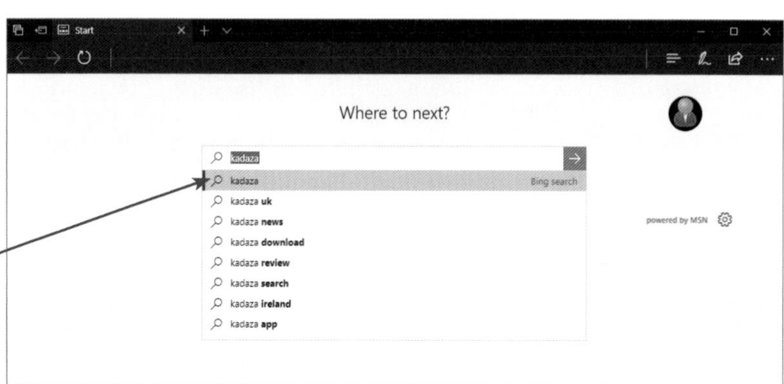

Search suggestions are denoted by the magnifying glass icon.

2 Now, hit **Enter**, or press the Search box arrow button, to see search engine results for the entered word or phrase

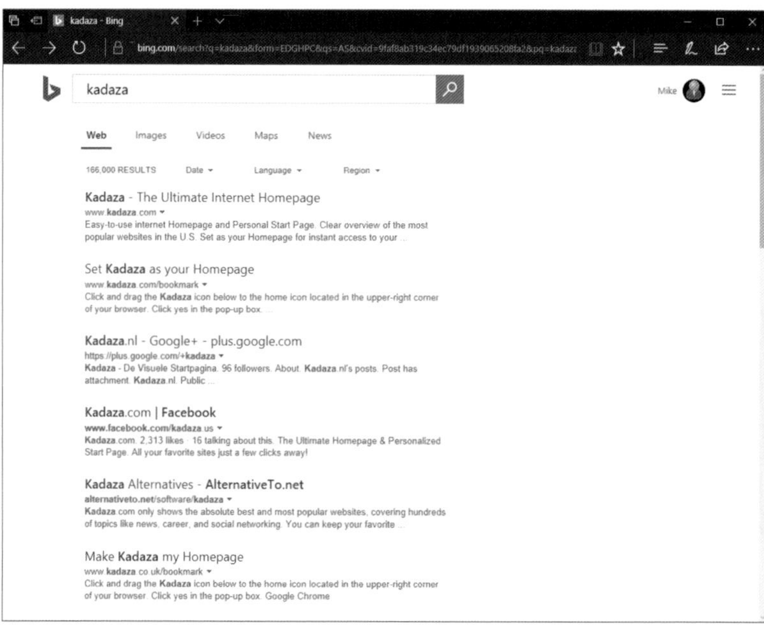

Notice that an Address Bar, Reading View button, and Favorites button now appear in the browser interface.

By default, the Bing search engine will provide results, but you can choose an alternative default by selecting **(...) More actions**, **Settings**, **View advanced settings**, **Change search engine**.

3. Next, hit the browser's back-arrow navigation button to reload the Start page once more

4. Then, type a URL address into the box to see a result appear containing a recognized website

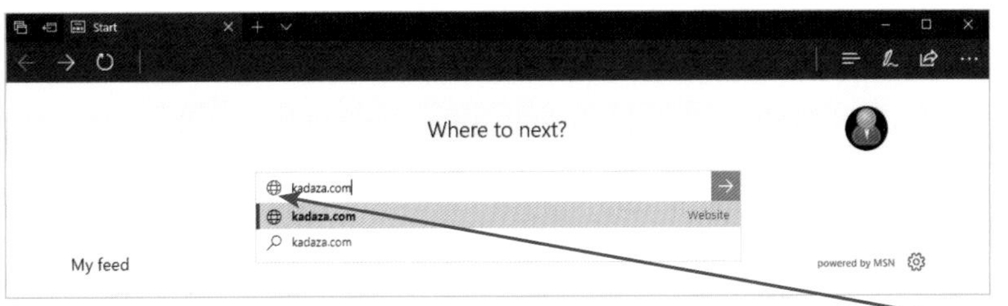

Recognized websites are denoted by the globe icon.

5. Hit **Enter**, or press the Search box arrow button, to load the recognized website

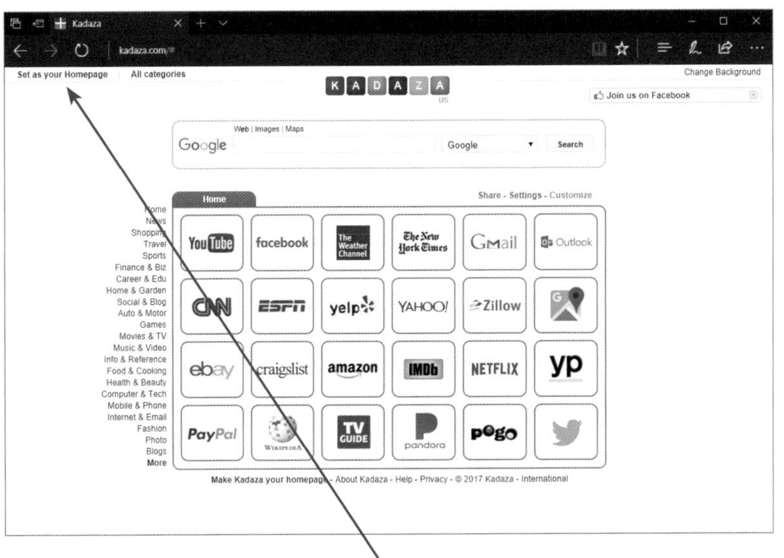

Click on the Address Bar to make it active, then enter a search phrase or URL address – it works just like the Search box.

6. Optionally, select the **Set as your Homepage** to load this website whenever you start Microsoft Edge

Opening options

Typing a URL address or search phrase into Microsoft Edge's Search box or Address Bar will, by default, display the search results or specified website in the current window area. It is, however, often preferable to retain the current window and open search results or specified websites in other tabs or windows:

1. Click on the Address Bar to make it active, then type in a search phrase and hit **Enter** to see the search results

If the Address Bar is hidden, you can click to the right of the navigation buttons to make it appear.

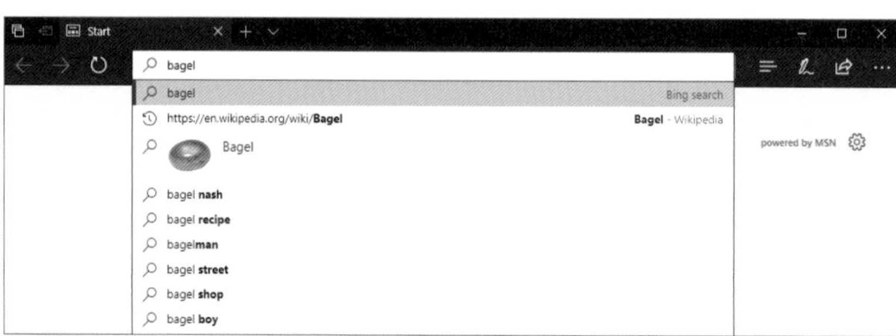

2. Now, place the mouse cursor over one of the result links and right-click to see a context menu appear

3. Select the menu option to **Open in new tab**

The **Copy link** menu option copies the URL address of the selected link onto the clipboard.

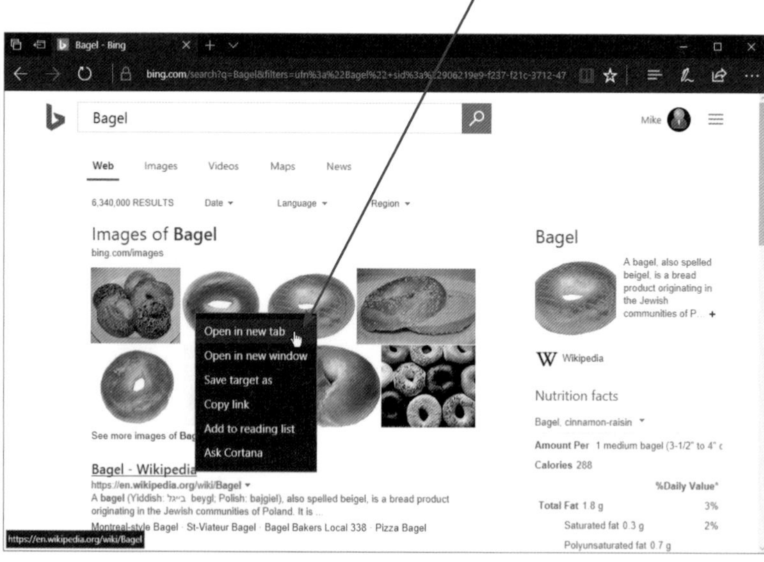

4. Now, click the new tab that appears, to see the page contents of the link displayed in that tab

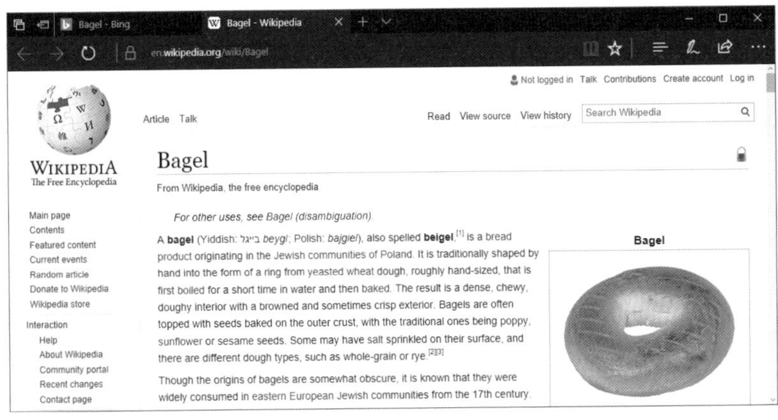

You can also use the keyboard shortcut **Ctrl** + **Tab** to move forwards and backwards between tabs.

5. Click the original tab to see the search results once more

6. Place the mouse cursor over a different result link, and right-click to see the context menu appear

7. Select the menu option to **Open in new window**

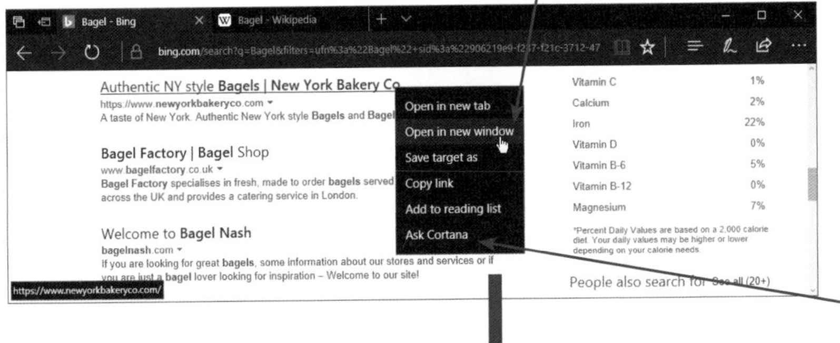

Select the **Ask Cortana** option to see further links related to a particular search result.

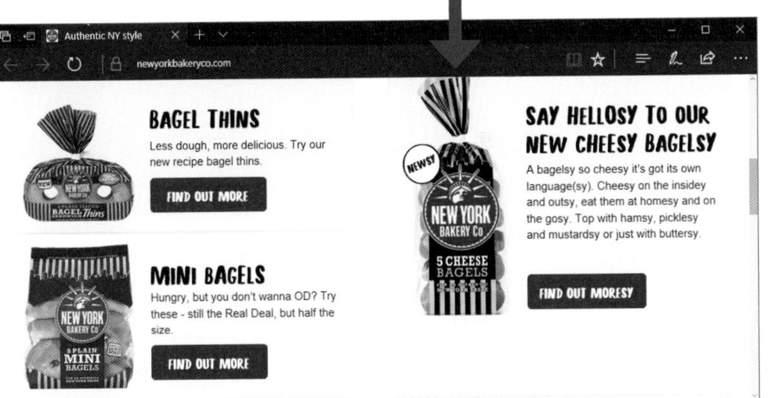

Saving favorites

If you've found a website that you are likely to visit frequently, it can be made quickly accessible as a saved Favorite:

1. Open the website then navigate to a page of interest

2. On the toolbar, click the **Favorites** star icon

3. Edit the favorite **Name**, if desired, then choose **Favorites** from the **Save in** drop-down menu, and click the **Add** button

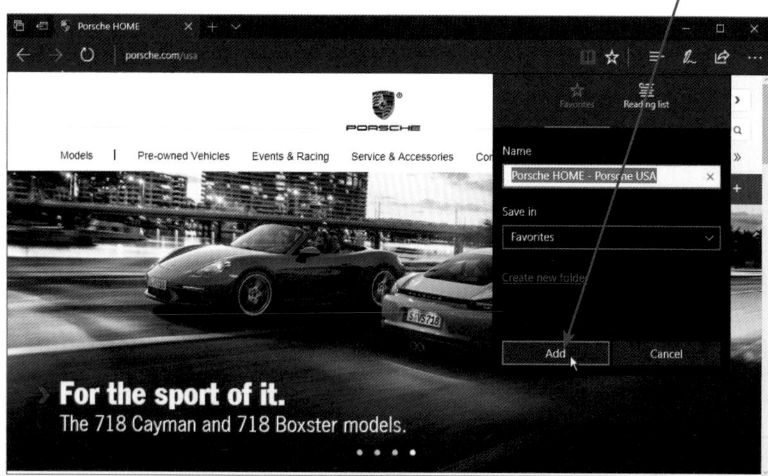

4. To open a saved Favorite, if the Favorites Bar is not enabled, first launch Microsoft Edge then click the **Hub** button

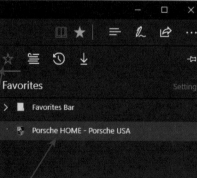

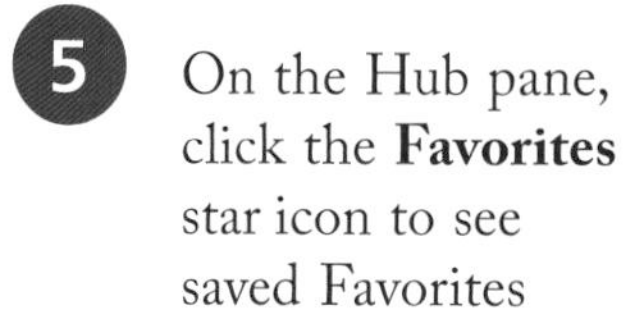

5. On the Hub pane, click the **Favorites** star icon to see saved Favorites

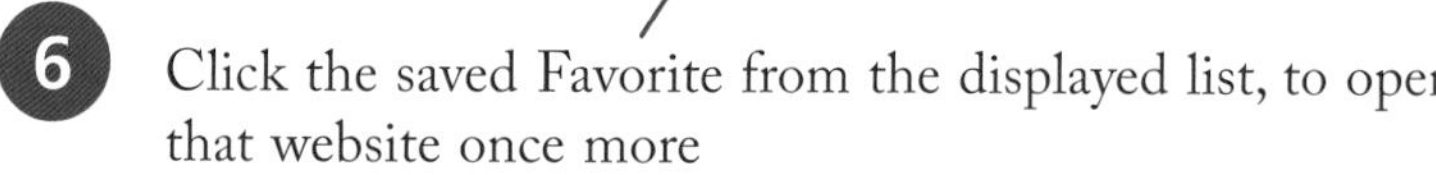

6. Click the saved Favorite from the displayed list, to open that website once more

The Favorites Bar is hidden unless enabled in **More actions** (**...**), Settings (see page 240).

Remove a saved Favorite from the list by right-clicking on it and choosing **Delete** from the context menu.

Pinning websites

A website that you are likely to visit frequently can alternatively be made quickly accessible as a link pinned to the Start menu:

1. Open the website in the Microsoft Edge browser
2. Click the ellipsis (...) **More actions** button
3. On the **More actions** menu, choose the **Pin this page to Start** option to create a link to the current website

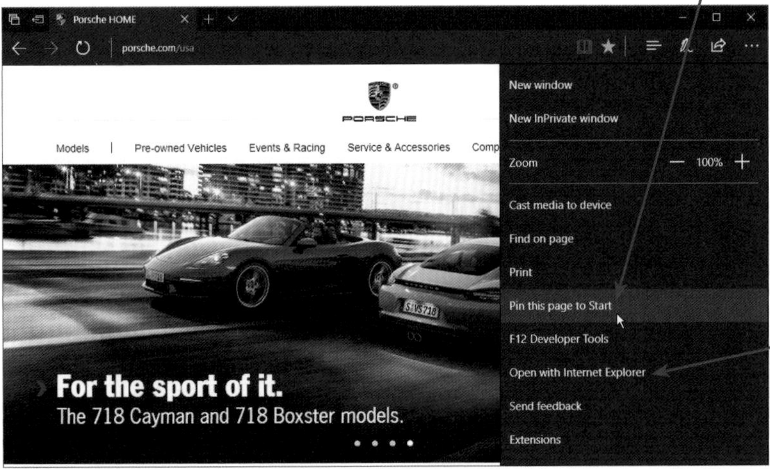

4. Confirm you want to pin this tile to the Start menu by clicking the **Yes** button

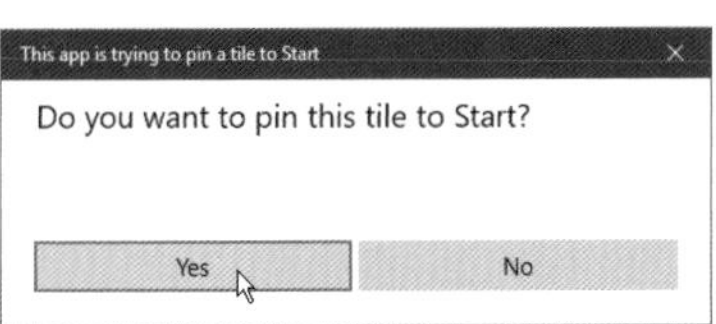

5. Open the Start menu, then click on the link tile to launch Microsoft Edge and open that website once more

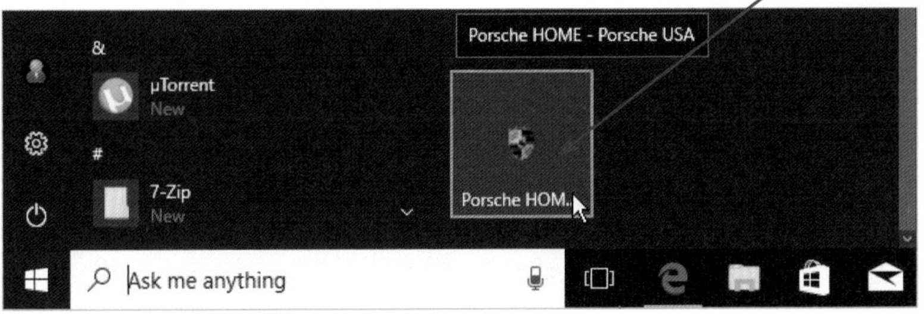

See pages 240-241 for more functions of the **More actions** button.

Notice the option here to **Open with Internet Explorer** for legacy websites that do not perform well in the Microsoft Edge browser.

You can remove any tile from the Start menu, including a pinned link, by right-clicking on it then choosing **Unpin from Start** from the context menu.

Reading articles

When you discover an article of interest that you don't have time to read right away, you can save it to your Reading list for later:

Reading list is a new feature of Microsoft Edge in Windows 10.

1. Open the website, then click the **Favorites** star icon on the Address Bar

2. On the panel that opens, click the **Reading list** icon

3. Edit the article Name, then click the **Add** button

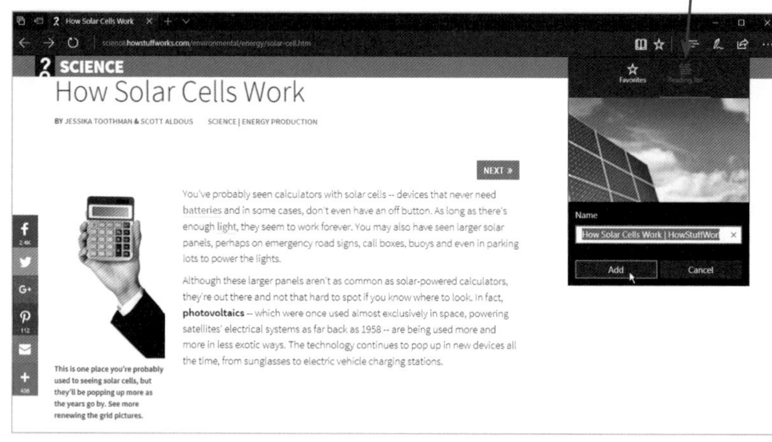

Remove a saved article from the Reading list by right-clicking on it and choosing **Delete** from the context menu.

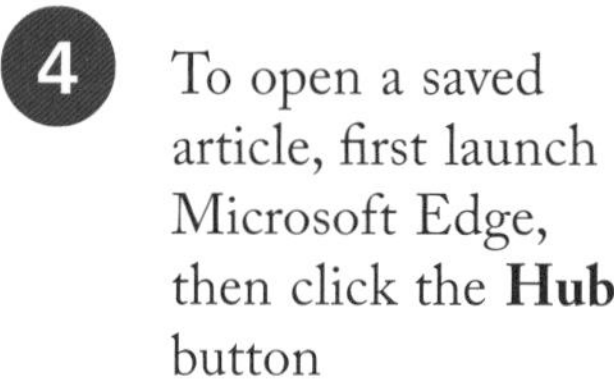

4. To open a saved article, first launch Microsoft Edge, then click the **Hub** button

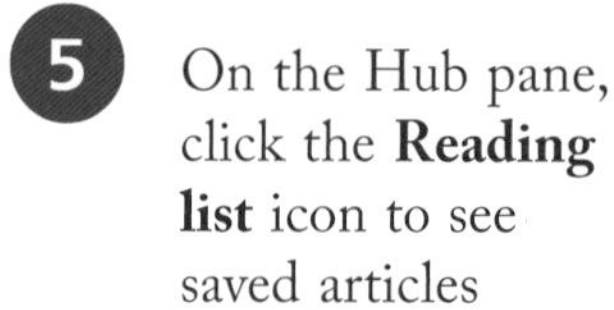

5. On the Hub pane, click the **Reading list** icon to see saved articles

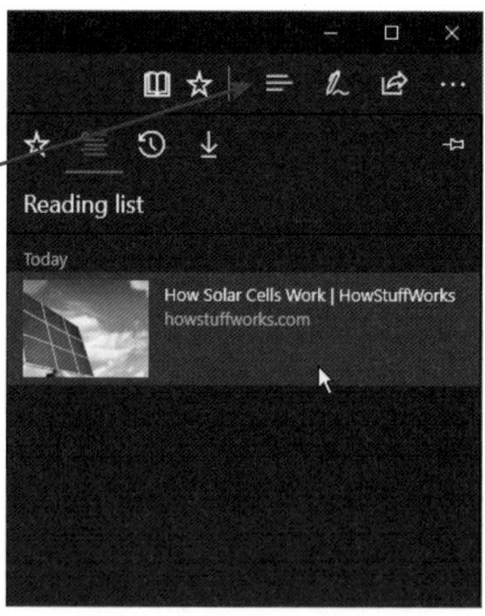

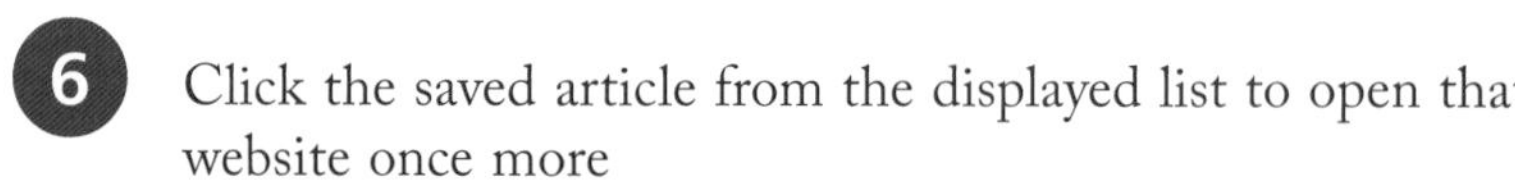

6. Click the saved article from the displayed list to open that website once more

Reading view

Microsoft Edge provides a Reading view option that lets you read articles in a distraction-free format that you can customize:

1. Open the website then click the **Reading view** icon to switch to the default textual content display mode

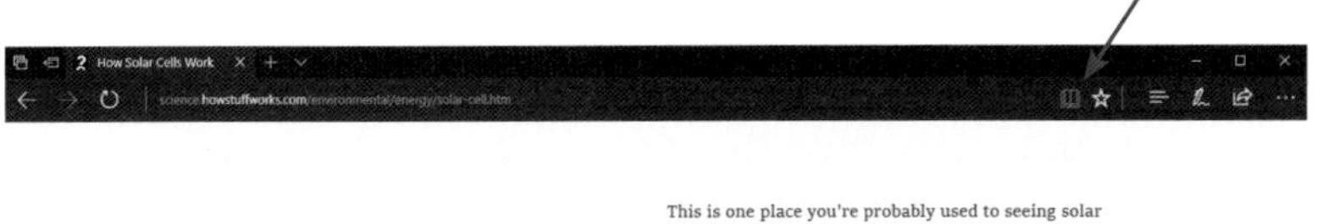

How Solar Cells Work

science.howstuffworks.com
19 mins read

This is one place you're probably used to seeing solar cells, but they'll be popping up more as the years go by. See more renewing the grid pictures.
©iStockphoto.com/blackred

You've probably seen calculators with solar cells -- devices that never need batteries and in some cases, don't even have an off button. As long as there's enough light, they seem to work forever. You may also have seen larger solar panels, perhaps on emergency road signs, call boxes, buoys and even in parking lots to power the lights.

Although these larger panels aren't as common as solar-powered calculators, they're out there and not that hard to spot if you know where to look. In fact, **photovoltaics** -- which were once used almost exclusively in space, powering satellites' electrical systems as far back as 1958 --

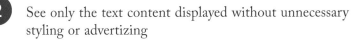

Don't confuse the **Reading list** (for saved articles) with the **Reading view** – for easy viewing.

2. See only the text content displayed without unnecessary styling or advertizing

3. Read through the clearly displayed content using the **Back** or **Forward** buttons to move between pages

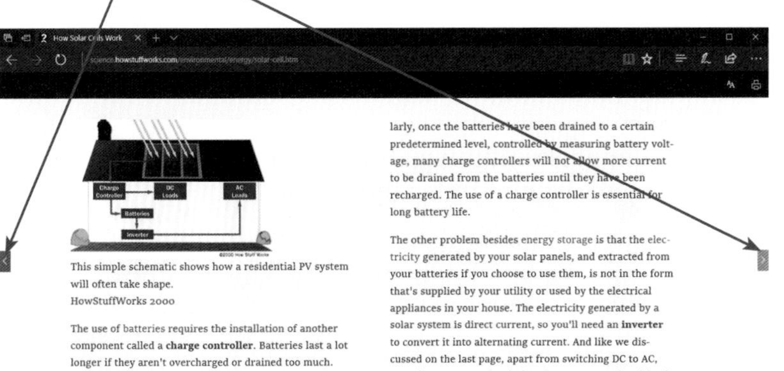

This simple schematic shows how a residential PV system will often take shape.
HowStuffWorks 2000

The use of batteries requires the installation of another component called a **charge controller**. Batteries last a lot longer if they aren't overcharged or drained too much. That's what a charge controller does. Once the batteries are fully charged, the charge controller doesn't let current from the PV modules continue to flow into them. Similarly, once the batteries have been drained to a certain predetermined level, controlled by measuring battery voltage, many charge controllers will not allow more current to be drained from the batteries until they have been recharged. The use of a charge controller is essential for long battery life.

The other problem besides energy storage is that the electricity generated by your solar panels, and extracted from your batteries if you choose to use them, is not in the form that's supplied by your utility or used by the electrical appliances in your house. The electricity generated by a solar system is direct current, so you'll need an **inverter** to convert it into alternating current. And like we discussed on the last page, apart from switching DC to AC, some inverters are also designed to protect against islanding if your system is hooked up to the power grid.

Reading view is a new feature of Microsoft Edge in Windows 10.

Reviewing history

As you are browsing the web, Microsoft Edge automatically saves a link to each web page you visit. This means you can easily revisit any page by recalling your browsing history and choosing its link:

1. Launch Microsoft Edge then click the **Hub** button

2. On the Hub pane, click the **History** (clock) icon to see links to web pages you visited earlier

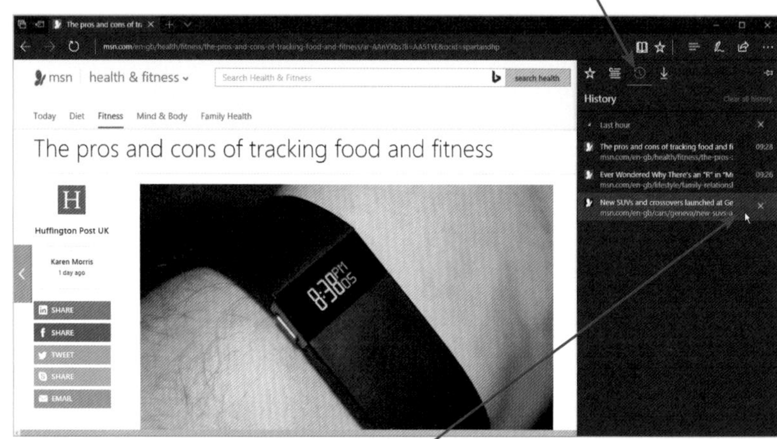

3. Click any history link to re-open that web page

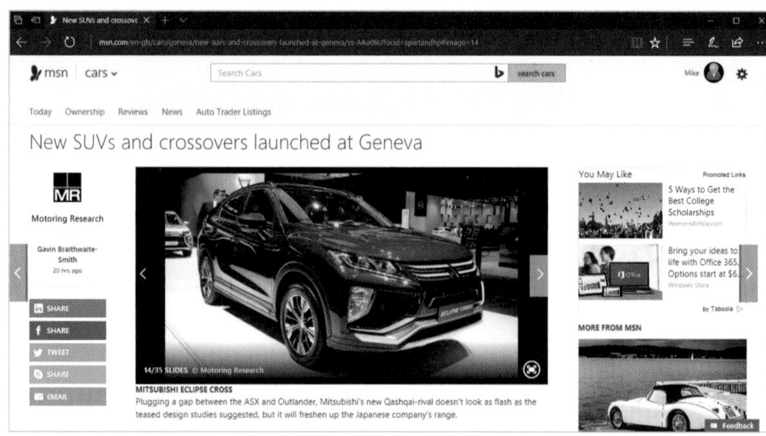

You can also use the keyboard shortcut **Ctrl** + **H** to see your browsing history.

Click the **Clear all history** link on the History list to clear your browsing data.

Managing downloads

Microsoft Edge includes a simple download manager facility. This allows you to easily monitor, pause, resume, or cancel downloads from the web. Upon completion, downloaded items can be found in your Downloads folder:

1. Start to download an item then click the **Hub** button

2. On the Hub pane, click the **Downloads** arrow icon to see the progression of your downloading item

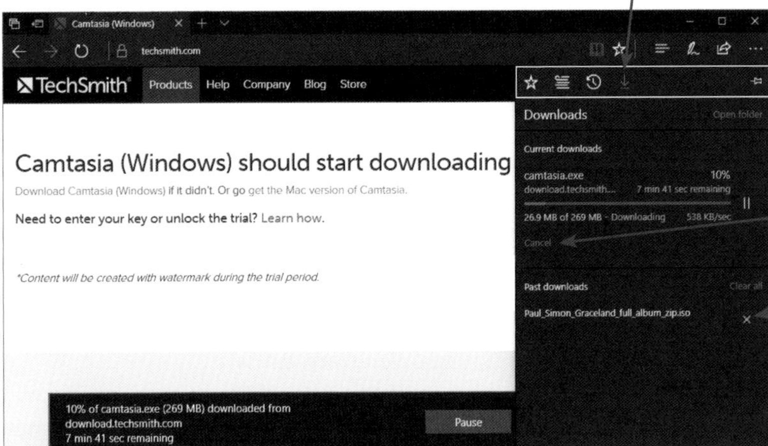

You can click the **Cancel** link to terminate a download in progress and click the **X** button against an item to remove it from the list of completed downloads.

3. Click the || button if you want to pause or resume progress of the download

4. To launch File Explorer in the Downloads folder, click the **Open folder** link to find your downloaded items

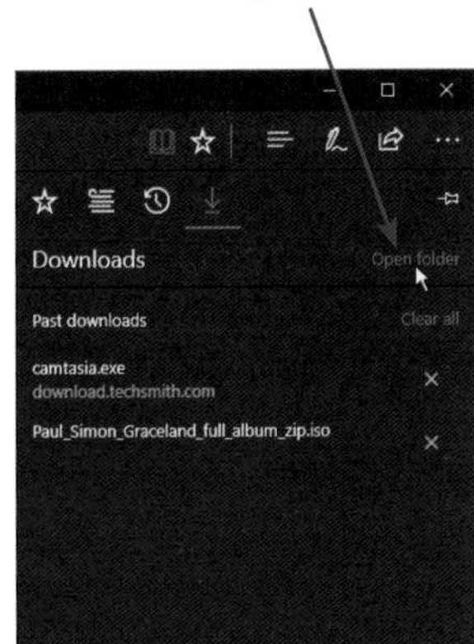

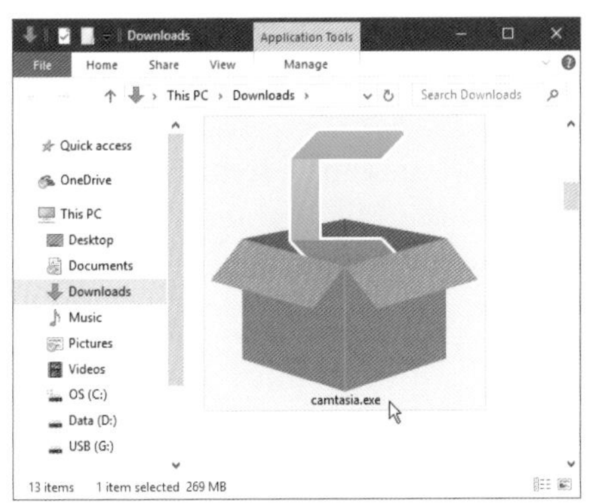

You can also use the keyboard shortcut **Ctrl** + **J** to see the Downloads list.

Making Web Notes

Microsoft Edge lets you make notes and highlight important text directly within web pages, creating your own "Web Notes" that can be saved and shared:

Web Notes are a great new feature of Microsoft Edge in Windows 10.

1. Open a page in Microsoft Edge, then click the Web Note button to see the toolbar switch to Web Note mode

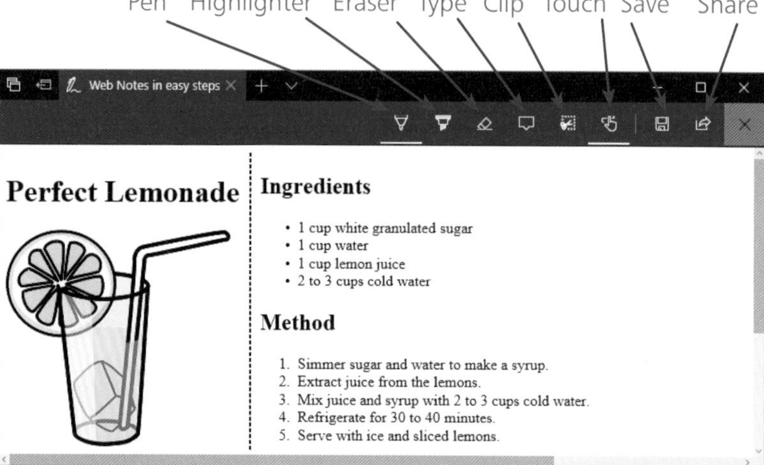

The Clip tool simply copies a selected area to the clipboard so you can paste it into another app, such as Paint.

2. Click the Pen icon to select the Pen tool, then choose a color and nib size

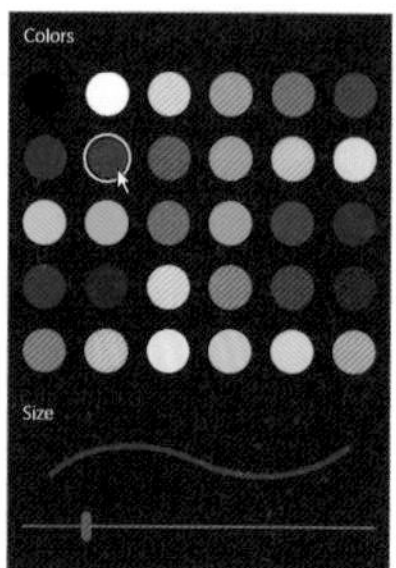

3. Now, use the cursor to scribble a web note onto the page, using your chosen color and nib size

4. Click the Eraser icon, then drag the cursor across your note if you want to erase individual written characters

5. Click the Highlighter icon to select the Highlighter tool, then choose a color and shape

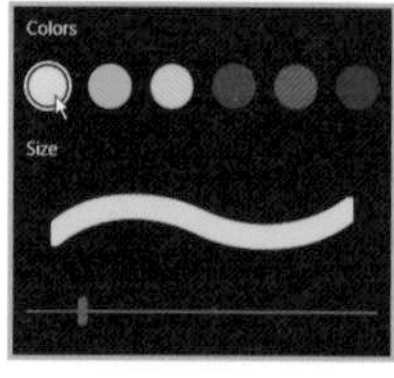

6. Now, use the cursor to highlight any items of particular importance

You can double-click the Eraser icon and select **Erase all ink** to remove all highlights and pen notes.

7. Click the Type icon then click on the page at a point where you want to type a note

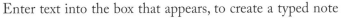

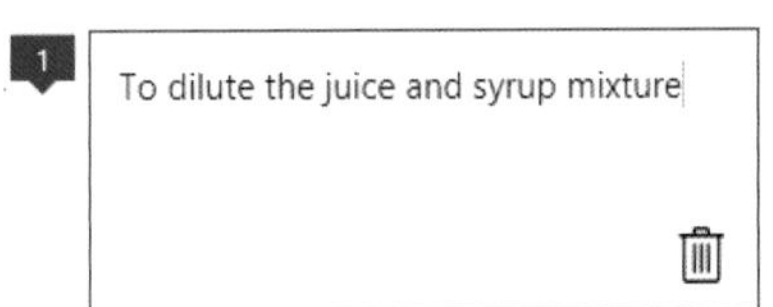
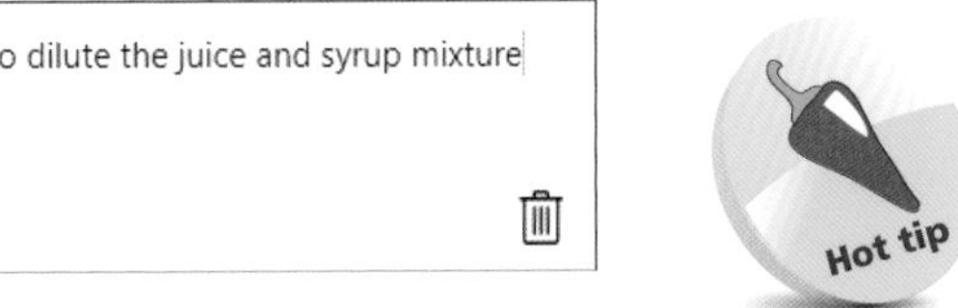

Click the numbered icon beside a typed note to collapse or expand that typed note.

8. Enter text into the box that appears, to create a typed note

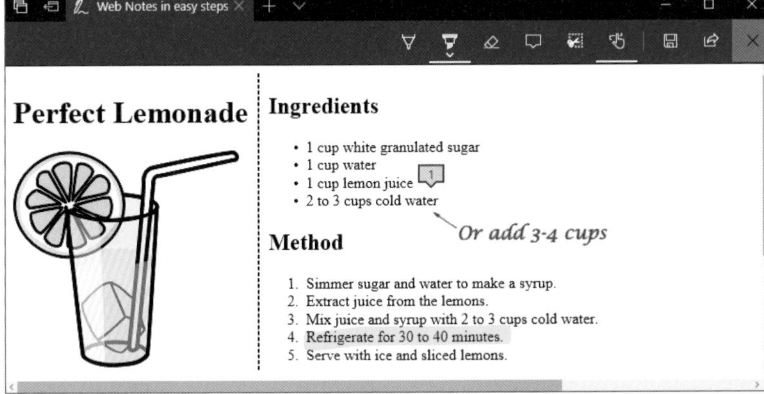

9. Click the Save icon, then choose to save the complete noted page in OneNote – and it will also be sent to OneDrive

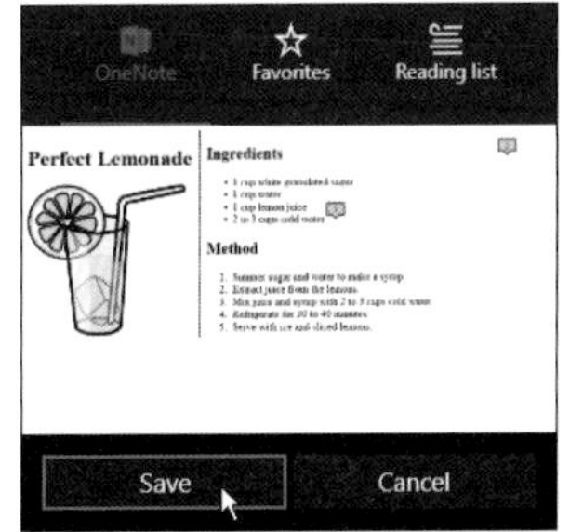

10. Open the OneNote app on any device to see the page, complete with your notes

You can also save to your Favorites or Reading list, and use the Share button to send the noted page to another location.

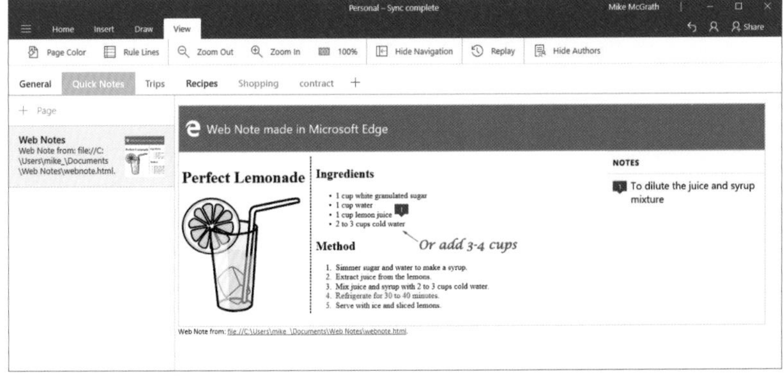

Sharing pages

When you want to share a web page of interest, Microsoft Edge provides the ability to share a link to that page's URL address:

1. Click the **Share** button – to open the Share panel

2. Select the **OneNote** option on the Share panel

3. Add a note if desired, then click **Send** to share the link with your OneNote app

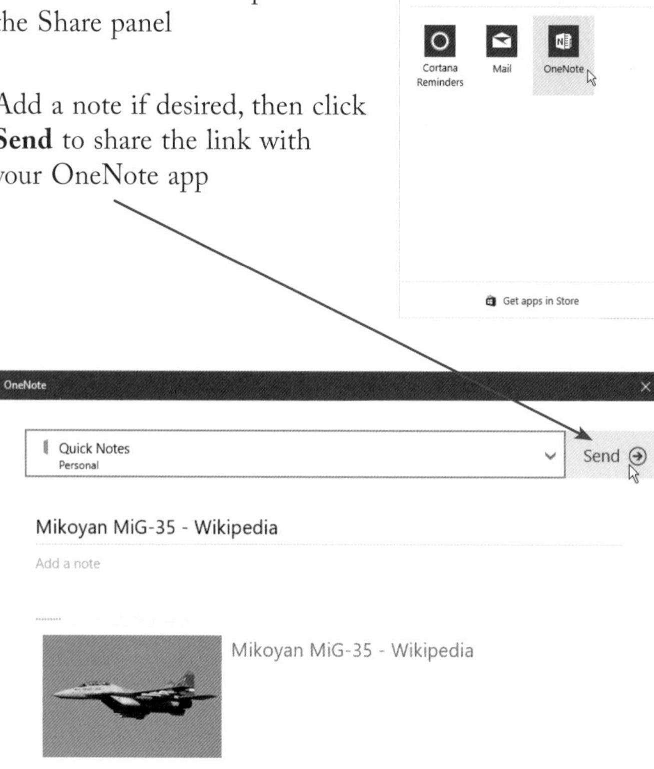

You can send the link to Cortana if you want to be reminded about it later.

4. Open the OneNote app on any device to see the shared link

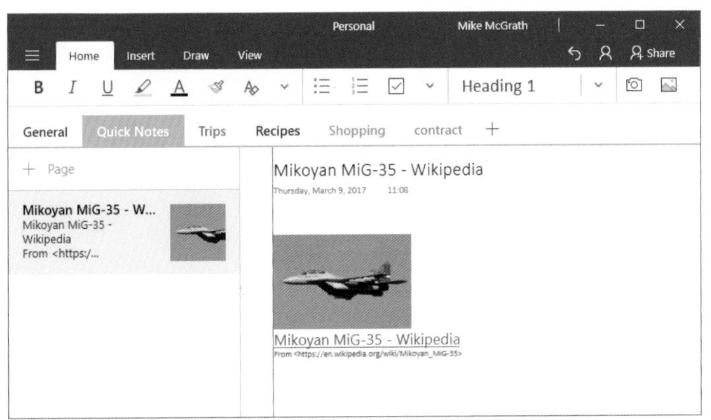

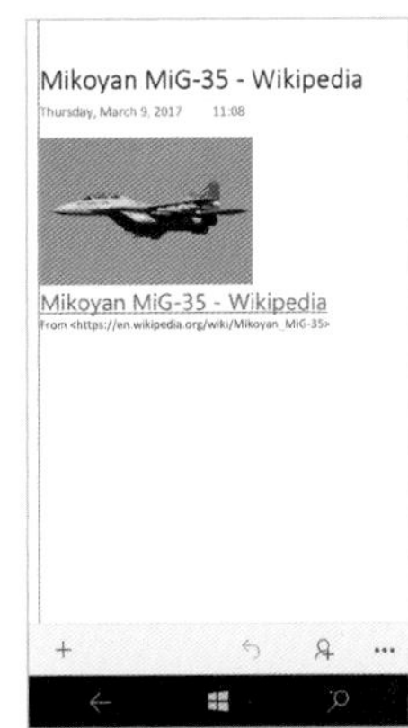

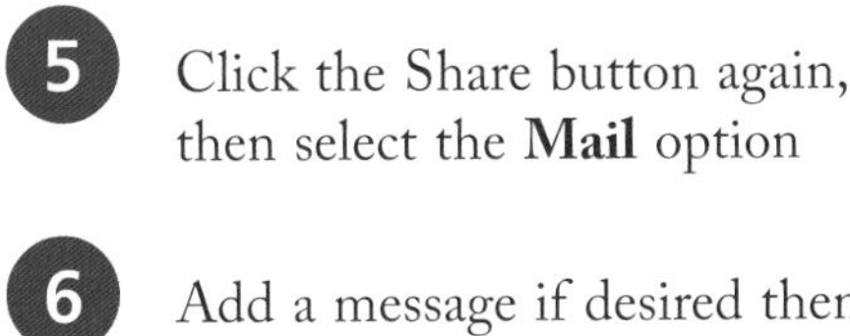

5. Click the Share button again, then select the **Mail** option

6. Add a message if desired then click **Send** to share the link with a chosen email recipient

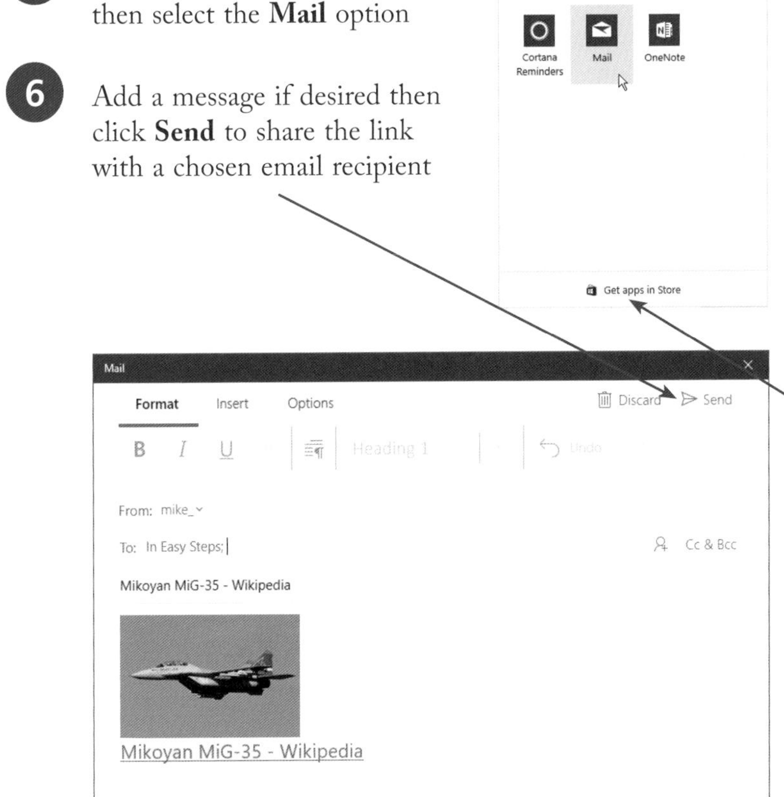

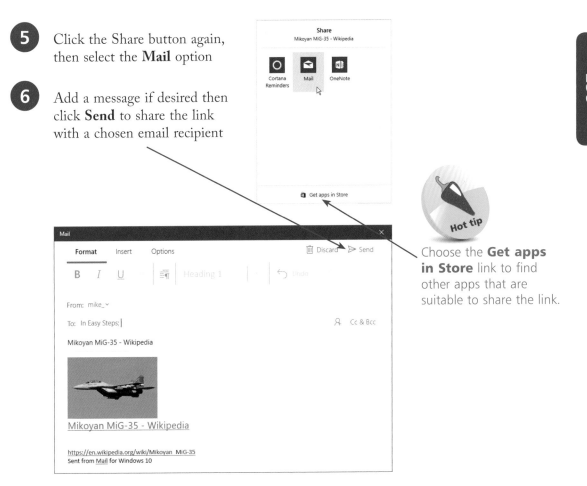

Choose the **Get apps in Store** link to find other apps that are suitable to share the link.

Customizing Edge

Hot tip

You can open the current web page in Internet Explorer from this menu if the page uses any legacy technologies not supported by the Microsoft Edge browser.

Hot tip

Click More actions, Extensions, then choose **Get extensions from the Store** to add features to the Microsoft Edge browser – the Translator extension is particularly useful when viewing foreign language websites.

Hot tip

You can start Edge with multiple pages if you click the **+ Add new page link** after adding a URL as shown in Step 4, then add more URLs.

The drop-down menu from the (...) **More actions** button in Microsoft Edge provides typical options to **Zoom** the page view, **Find** text within the page, or **Print** the page. It lets you open a **New window** or, if you prefer, a **New InPrivate window** that does not store cookies, history, or temporary files on your PC. The **F12 Developer Tools** option provides a suite of tools to build or debug web pages, and the **Settings** option provides several customization possibilities:

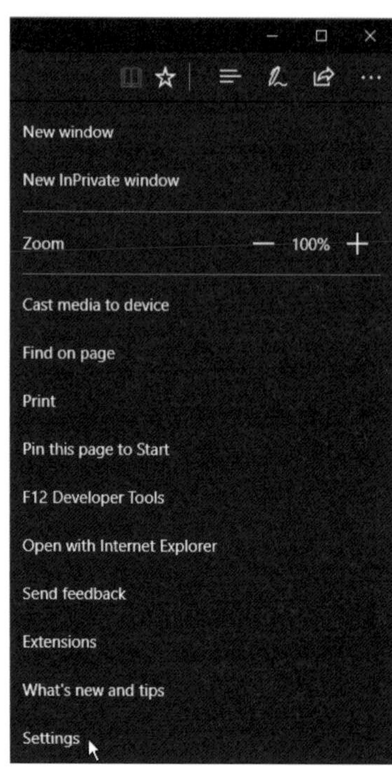

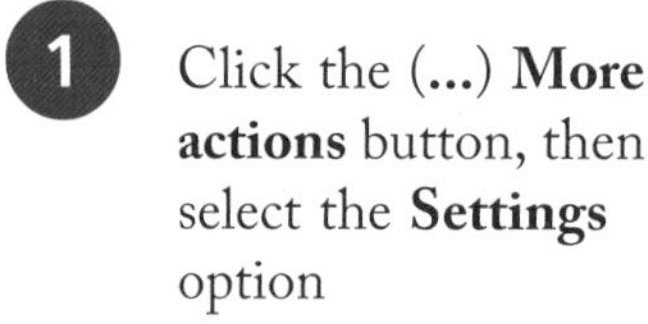

1. Click the (...) **More actions** button, then select the **Settings** option

2. In Settings, under the **Choose a theme** section, click the down arrow and select the **Dark** option from the drop-down that appears

3. In Settings, **Open Microsoft Edge with**, select **A specific page or pages**

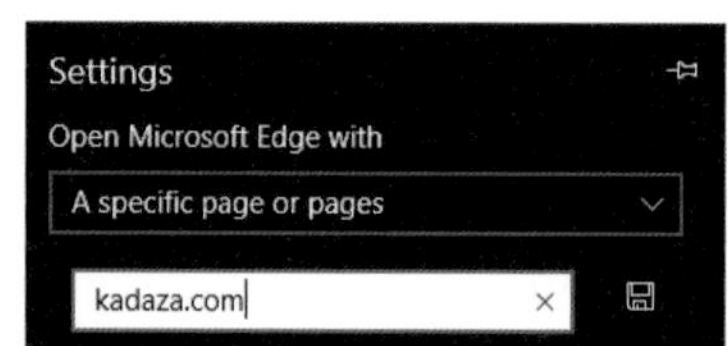

4. Next, enter the URL of a preferred start page

5. Next, click the **Import from another browser** link, and select a browser from the list that appears

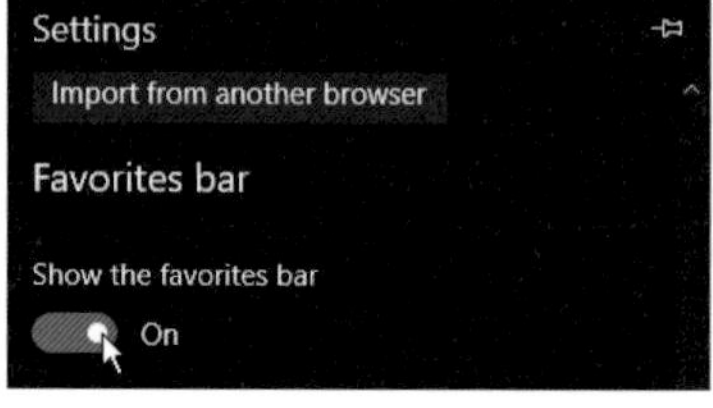

6. Now, slide the **Show the favorites bar** toggle button into the **On** position

7. Now, in Settings, choose the **View advanced settings** button

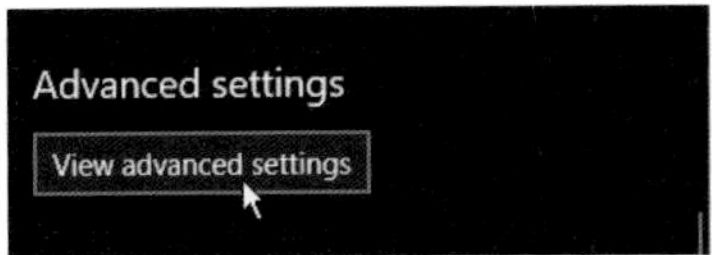

8. Slide the **Show the home button** toggle button into the **On** position – to add a **Home** button on the toolbar

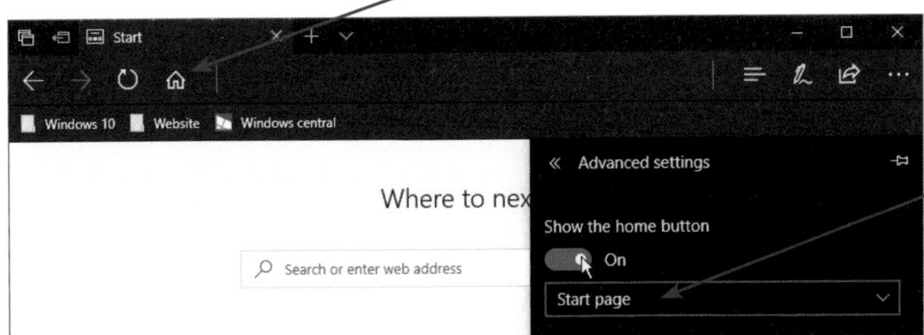

You can add the URL of a Start page to open when you click the Home button, or leave this blank to use the default Start page.

9. Scroll down **Advanced settings** and slide the **Block pop-ups** button to the **On** position – to block annoying pop-up dialogs

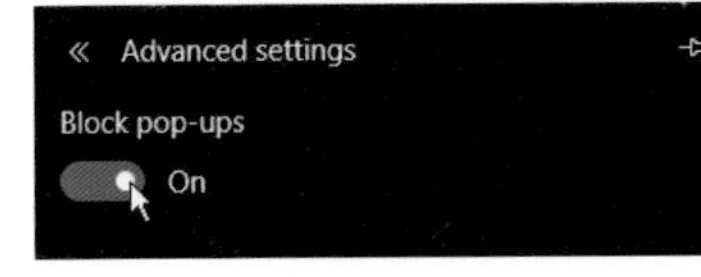

10. Scroll down again and be sure to slide the **Use Adobe Flash Player** button to the **Off** position – to avoid malicious website content, unless you are absolutely sure that the content is safe

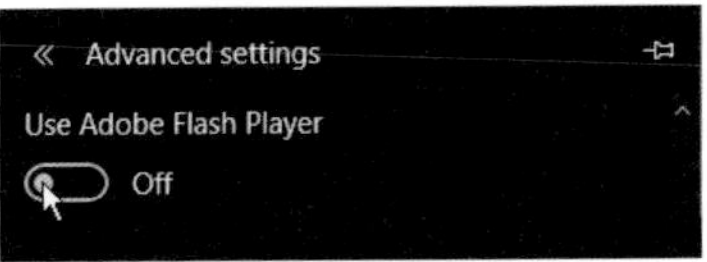

The Adobe Flash Player plugin is a known security risk. It became disabled by default in the Windows 10 Creators Update – it is strongly recommended you do not enable this feature.

11. Scroll to the bottom of **Advanced settings** and edit your **Privacy and services** settings to suit your preferences

Selecting text

When selecting text in a web page it can be difficult to select precisely what you want without also selecting adjacent text and images, as shown below:

Hot tip

If you find Caret Browsing useful you may want to enable it permanently by checking this box. It can be temporarily disabled by pressing **F7** at any time.

With Microsoft Edge, the Caret Browsing feature helps solve this problem. This lets you use the keyboard instead of the mouse to make selections, and it offers much more precise control.

To activate Caret Browsing:

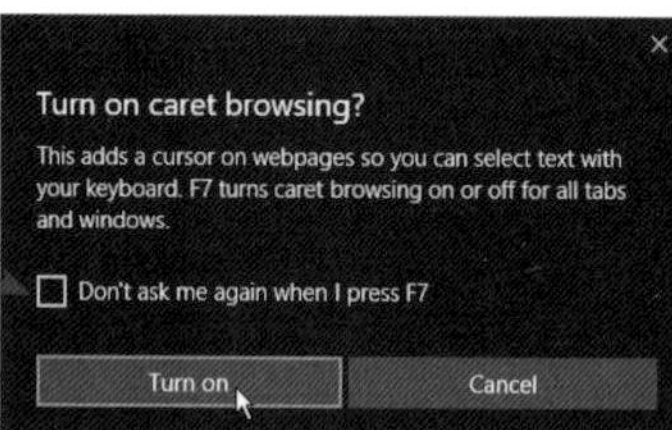

1. Press the **F7** key to see a dialog box appear
2. Click the **Turn on** button

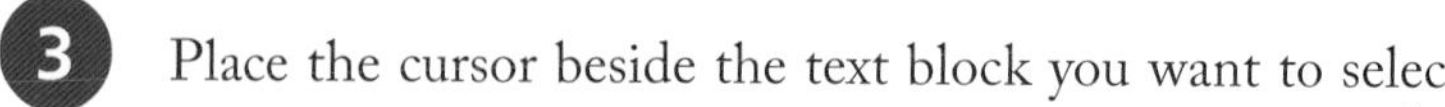

3. Place the cursor beside the text block you want to select

Beware

You will not be able to select text that appears within an image – you can only select actual text content in a document.

4. Hold down the **Shift** key and use the arrow keys (the < left arrow key in this example) to highlight the text you want

14 Digital images

Windows 10 helps you easily manage and organize digital images that you can display on your TV and share with your family, friends, and colleagues.

Digital images

Digital images may be created in a graphical application, using a scanner or with digital still and movie cameras. The images are defined in terms of picture elements or pixels. The location, color and intensity of each pixel is stored in the image file. The images can then be displayed, enhanced, printed and shared using software on your computer or on specialized websites.

The size of the file depends on the image resolution (the number of pixels used to represent the image) and the color depth (the number of color variations defined). For example:

Pixel size	Bytes	No. Colors	Name
8-bit	1	256	System
16-bit	2	65,536	HighColor
24-bit	3	16,777,216	TrueColor

Cameras also have Digital zoom, which magnifies the picture by cropping it to select only the specific area after it has captured it as pixels. This would reduce the saved image size. However, it is usually better to edit and crop on your computer, using software supplied with the camera or included in Windows.

Another factor that influences the image size is the degree of zoom that the camera utilizes. Cameras use the capabilities of the camera lens to bring the subject closer, enlarging the image before it is stored as pixels. This is known as Optical zoom.

High-resolution cameras can take images of, say, 4000 x 3000 pixels in TrueColor. This works out at 36 million bytes per picture. Various image file formats have been developed to store such large images. These incorporate image compression algorithms to decrease the size of the file. The algorithms used are of two types: lossless and lossy.

Lossless compression algorithms reduce the file size without losing image quality, though they will not be compressed into as small a file as a lossy compression file.

Lossy compression algorithms take advantage of the inherent limitations of the human eye, and discard information that does not contribute to the visible effect. Most lossy compression algorithms allow for variable quality levels (compression), and as these levels are increased, the file size is reduced. At the highest compression levels, the deterioration in the image may become noticeable, and give undesirable effects.

Image file formats

BMP (Windows bitmap)

This handles graphics files within Windows. The files are uncompressed, and therefore large, but they are widely accepted in Windows applications so are simple to use.

GIF (Graphics Interchange Format)

This is limited to 256 colors. It is useful for graphics with relatively few colors such as diagrams, shapes, logos and cartoon-style images. The GIF format supports animation. It also uses a lossless compression that is effective when large areas have a single color, but ineffective for detailed images or dithered images.

These are the main image file format types you will encounter in dealing with digital photographs and website images.

JPEG (Joint Photographic Experts Group)

The JPEG/JFIF filename extension is JPG or JPEG, and it uses lossy compression. Nearly every digital camera can save images in the JPEG format, which supports 24-bit color depth and produces relatively small files. JPEG files suffer generational degradation when repeatedly edited and saved.

PNG (Portable Network Graphics)

This was created as the successor to GIF, supporting TrueColor and providing a lossless format that is best suited for editing pictures, whereas lossy formats like JPG are best for final distribution of photographic images, since JPG files are usually smaller than PNG. PNG works well with web browsers.

TIFF (Tagged Image File Format)

This is a flexible format that saves 24-bit and 48-bit color, and uses the TIFF or TIF filename extension. TIFFs can be lossy and lossless, with some digital cameras using the LZW compression algorithm for lossless storage. TIFF is not well supported by browsers, but is a photograph file standard for printing.

You should save originals in the least lossy format, and use formats such as PNG or TIFF to edit the images. JPEG is good for sending images or posting them on the internet.

Raw image format

This is used on some digital cameras to provide lossless or nearly-lossless compression, with much smaller file sizes than the TIFF formats from the same cameras. Raw formats used by most cameras are not standardized or documented, and differ among camera manufacturers. Graphics programs and image editors may not accept some or all of them, so you should use the software supplied with the camera to convert the images for editing, and retain the Raw files as originals and backup.

Photos app

The Photos app is a new Universal Windows App in Windows 10.

The Photos app provides links to the photo collection on your PC, as well as your photos on OneDrive, plus any other connected PCs and devices. As with the People app, which can amalgamate all your contacts from a variety of sources, the Photos app does the same with all your pictures. So, while they may be scattered around on various websites, computers, portable drives, etc., the app pulls them all together so they can be quickly accessed.

1. Click the **Photos** item on the Start menu to launch it displaying **Collection** view – grouping photos by month

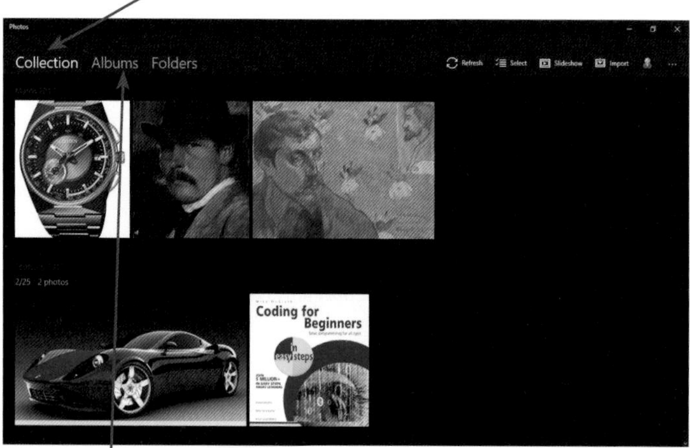

The default view of the Photos app displays your collection of images grouped by month.

2. Click **Albums** to see related photos automatically grouped

3. To discover the source locations from where the Photos app is gathering your images, click **Folders**

You can also choose **Albums** view to create your own albums.

4. Choose a source location to explore the folders there. For example, choose your **OneDrive** source

Only local folders will be presented if you have not enabled OneDrive.

5 Next, select a folder to explore the images it contains

Notice that folder options appear on the toolbar in this view – select **Slideshow** to view each photo within the folder in turn.

6 Now, select a photo to view, then click the **...** (ellipsis) button and choose **File info** from the menu to see details

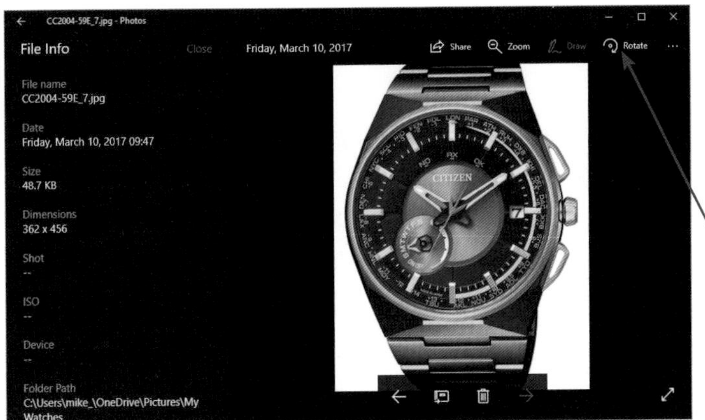

Notice that photo options appear on the toolbar in this view – select **Rotate** to switch between portrait and landscape orientation.

Import photos

Pictures can easily be imported into Windows 10 from different types of device, using the Photos app:

If you import two or more picture folders, the folders themselves will not be imported – just the pictures. These will be "lumped together" and placed in the Pictures library.

1. Connect the device containing the pictures to your computer

2. Launch the **Photos** app from the Start menu, then click the **Import** button at the top-right of the window

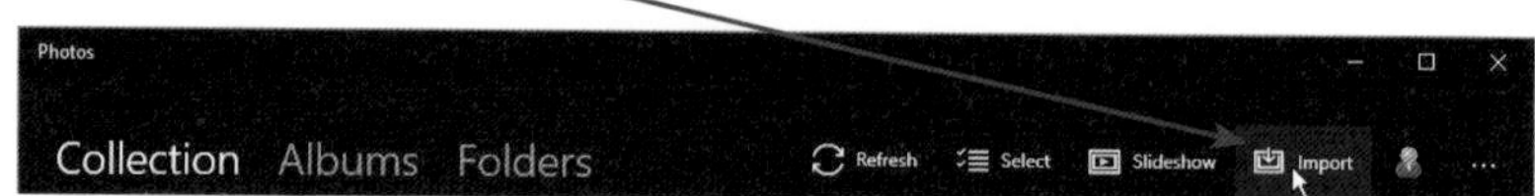

3. Select the items to be imported by checking the box on each thumbnail, then click the **Continue** button

If you first see a list of devices connected to your computer, you will need to select the one that contains the pictures to be imported.

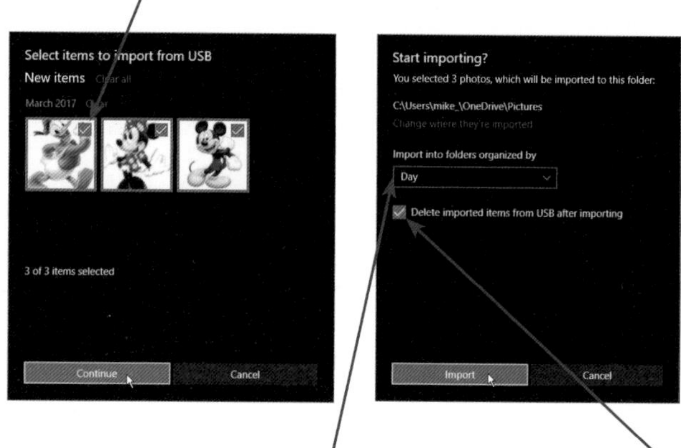

4. Choose how to organize the items and whether to delete them from the connected device, then click **Import**

By default, images will be imported into the Pictures folder on your OneDrive so they will be instantly accessible across all your devices.

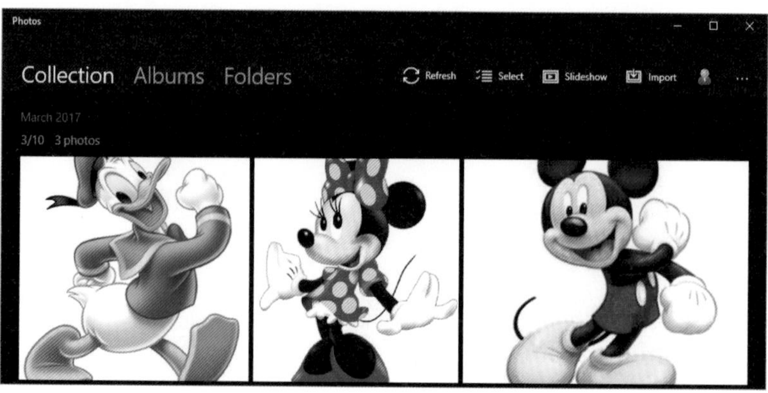

Import with Windows

Windows AutoPlay offers another method of importing pictures to a computer.

1. Connect a device to the PC, such as a camera fitted with a memory card, then click the notification banner which appears near the System Tray

2. Windows AutoPlay will open at the top-right of the screen and ask what you want to do with the device. Click the option to **Import photos and videos**

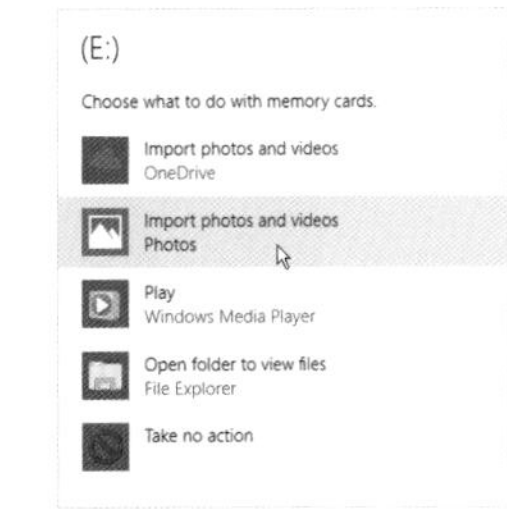

Go to Settings, Devices, **AutoPlay** to choose options for how the AutoPlay feature will respond when devices get connected to the PC.

3. This opens the Photos app, asking you to choose a device – the camera is selected in this example

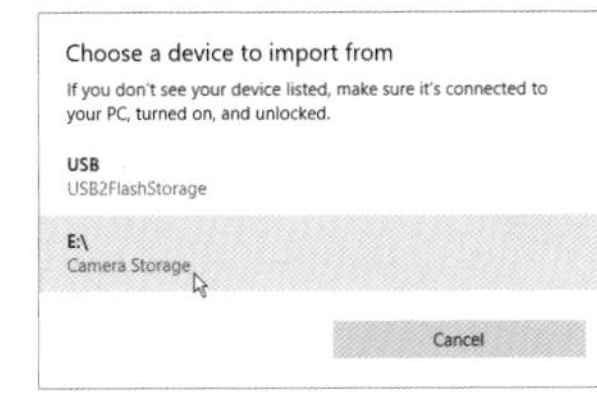

4. Next, you are asked to select items to import, or simply click **Continue** to import all

5. Now choose where to place the imports, how to organize them, and whether to delete the originals from the camera – then click the **Import** button

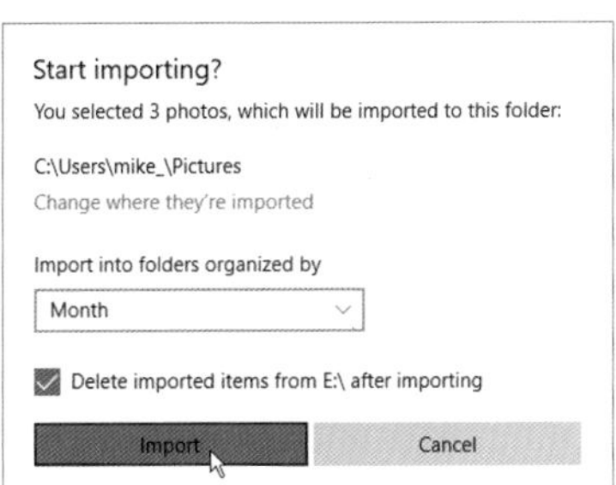

The Import process will tell you when there is nothing to transfer.

6. The pictures are imported and saved in the chosen folder

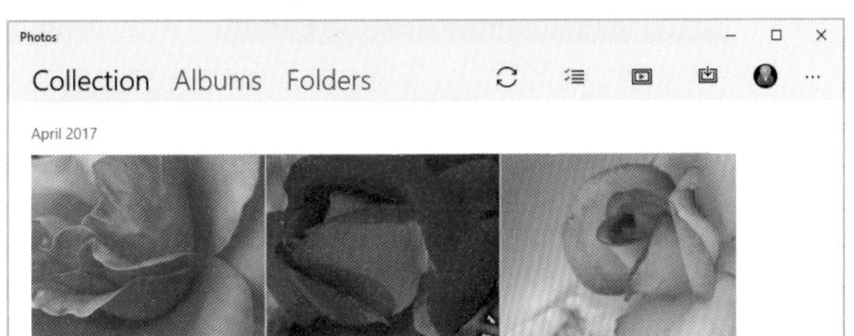

The next time that you import from this device, Windows will only select new items.

Edit photos

The Photos app in Windows 10 provides some great tools that let you edit your photos in a variety of ways:

A Light mode and other improvements were added to the Photos app in the Windows 10 Creators Update.

1. Open a picture in the **Photos** app, then click at the top of the window to see a pop-up toolbar appear

You can choose the **Draw** menu to annotate the picture.

2. Next, click the **Edit** menu on the toolbar to see a panel appear offering a wide range of editing options

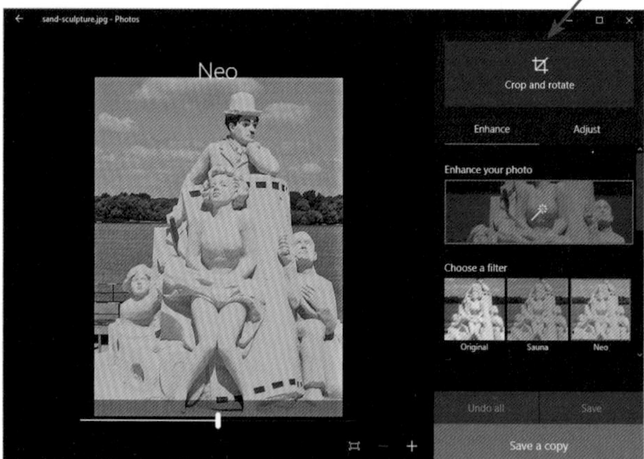

Edit possibilities include **Crop**, **Enhance**, a wide range of **Filter** options, and **Adjust** for Light, Color, Clarity, Vignette, Red-eye, and Spot fix.

3. Apply edits to see the preview change in real time

4. When you are happy with the result, click the **Save** button to apply the edits to the original image

Share photos

The Photos app provides a **Share** button on the pop-up toolbar, so you can quickly post a copy of any selected picture to friends or colleagues by a variety of methods:

1. Click the **Share** button to see a Share dialog listing installed apps that you can use to share the photo

2. Select the app you want to share the photo with, such as **Facebook** to share with your friends on social media

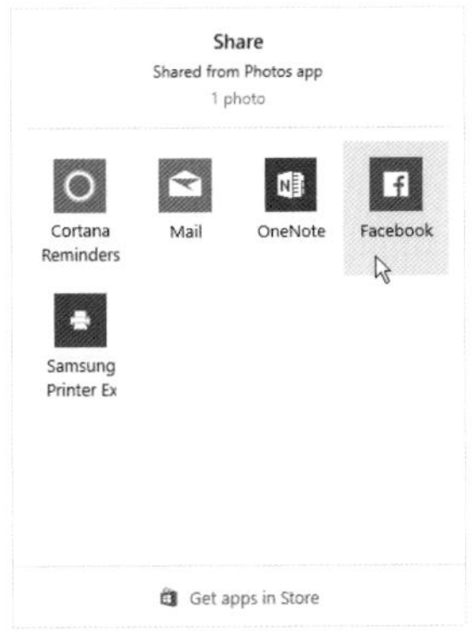

The **Facebook** option will not be available unless the Facebook app has previously been installed from the Store.

3. When the Facebook app opens, add a message, then click the **Post** button to share your photo

4. If you prefer to email your photo, choose the **Mail** app on the Share dialog

5. If you prefer to print your photo, choose the printer app on the Share dialog – a **Samsung** printer in this example

6. Select the printer preferences, then click the **Print** button

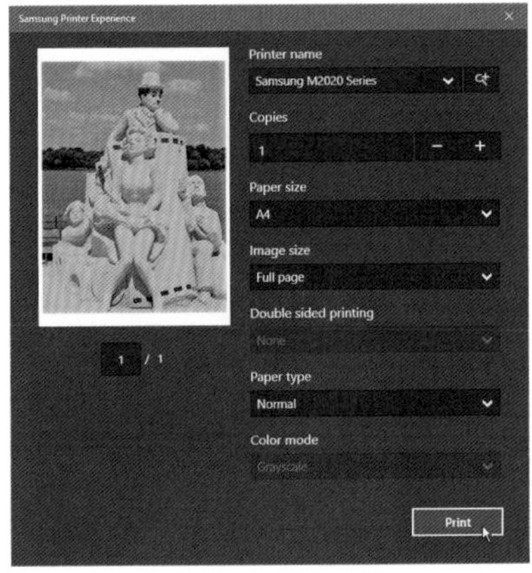

The printer option will not be available unless you have installed a printer which supplies an app.

Camera app

The Camera app is a new Universal Windows App in Windows 10.

You cannot use a digital camera with the Camera app – it only works with webcams.

The Photo and Video buttons become larger and white when selected.

To get the best picture, set up your device in Camera options.

Of all the apps bundled with Windows 10, the Camera app is one of the most basic. The first thing to note here, and it's something that confuses many users, is that the app only works with webcams – connect a digital camera to it and absolutely nothing will happen.

1. Connect your webcam to the PC, or enable your laptop webcam
2. Open the **Camera** app from the Start screen
3. You may be asked to approve the app using your location
4. When the camera is on, you will see two buttons at the right-hand side of the window offering options for **Video** and **Photo**

5. Click the **Video** button to start making a video, then click it again to stop recording – the completed video will then be automatically added to your Camera Roll folder
6. Now click the **Photo** button to take a picture – the photo will then be added to your Camera Roll folder

7. Before you start using the app though, you may want to change some settings. Unfortunately, the app is very limited in this respect, but settings can be accessed by clicking the **Settings** button in the Camera window

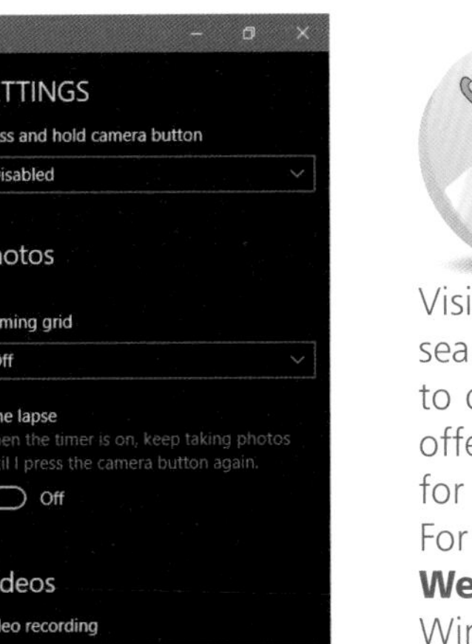

Visit the Store and search for "webcam" to discover apps that offer further possibilities for your web camera. For example, try **My Webcam** to turn your Windows 10 device into a remote camera for your local network.

8. When you have taken some pictures or videos, back- and forward-arrow buttons appear at the edges of the Camera window. These let you view your work

9. You can also click on the Gallery button at the bottom-right of the Camera window to view your image in the Photos app

Note that once taken by the Camera app, your photos are actually handled (viewed and edited as explained above) in the Photos app. If you'd rather not use the Photos app for viewing your images, you can open them with a viewer of your choice from the **Camera Roll** within the Pictures folder:

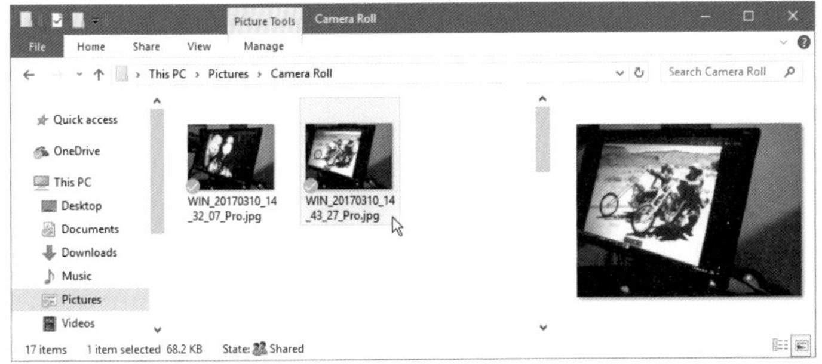

Pictures and videos taken by the Camera app are saved by default in the user's Camera Roll within the Pictures folder.

10. Right-click on the photo, then select **Open with** and choose your app

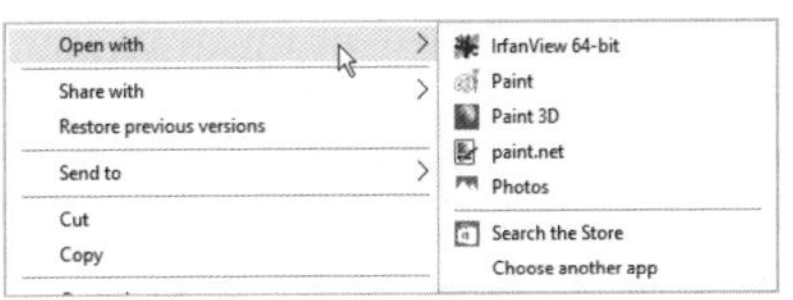

Movies & TV app

Windows 10 provides two video players – the Windows Media Player app and the **Movies & TV** (Films & TV) app. The new **Movies & TV** video app is what we're going to look at here. We're assuming at this point that you're signed in to the PC with a Microsoft account.

The **Movies & TV** app is a new Universal Windows App in Windows 10. It may be called **Films & TV** in your region.

1. Open the app by clicking the **Movies & TV** item on the Start menu. If you don't have any videos in your **Personal** video gallery folder, the screen prompts you to add some

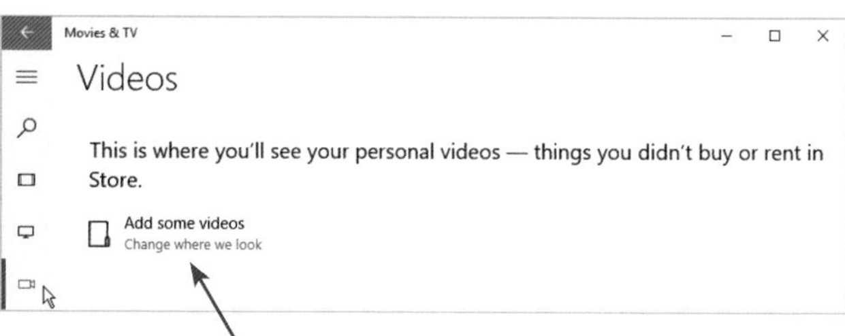

Only videos placed in the Videos folder will be accessible from the **Movies & TV** app initially.

2. Click **Change where we look**, then click the + button to specify a folder other than the default Videos folder

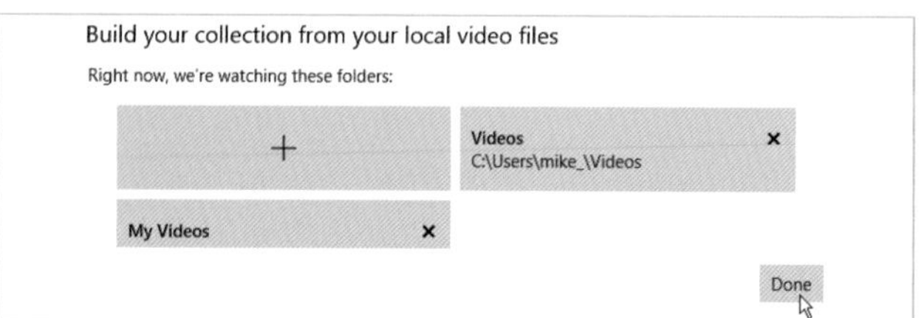

3. Icons will then appear for each video at your specified location – click any icon to start playing that video

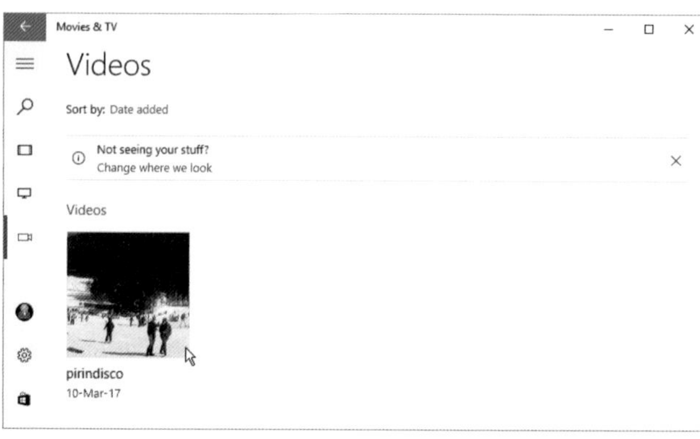

You will need to be signed in with a Microsoft account to rent or buy videos.

4. Play/Pause, back 10 seconds, and forward 30 seconds controls can be accessed from the bar at the bottom of the app window

The **Movies & TV** app isn't just about your personal videos, though. If you click the **Movie gallery** button or the **TV show gallery** button on the app window, you will be offered a selection of movies or television shows that you may buy or rent.

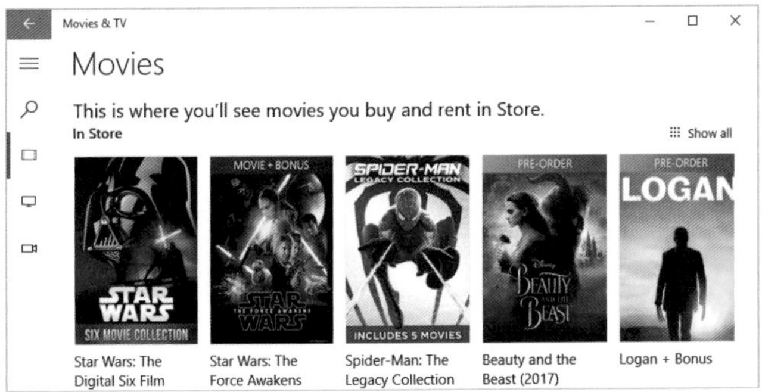

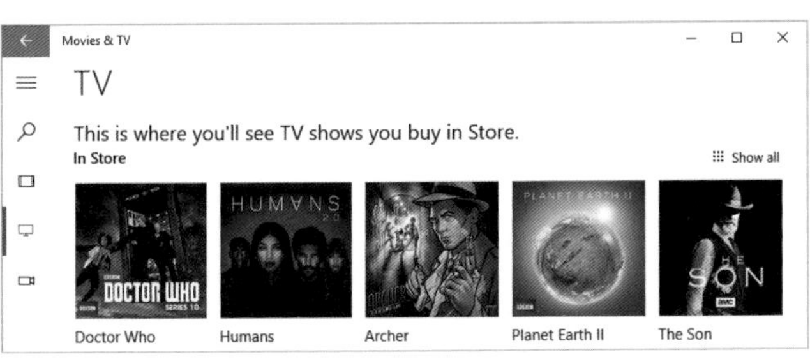

Free trailers are available for most movies.

Photo apps in the Store

If the Photos app described on pages 246-251 does not meet your requirements, a large selection of other photo apps are available in the Windows Store.

1. Open the **Store** from the Start menu
2. Type "photos" into the Search box then hit **Enter**
3. Select the **Apps** filter from the "Type" options

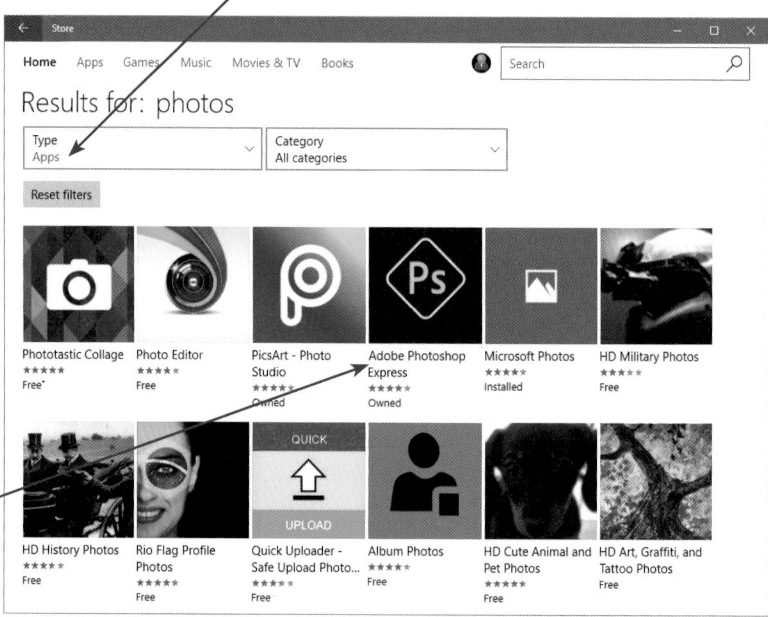

Hot tip

Adobe Photoshop Express is a popular free photo-editing app.

Many of these apps provide image-related options other than just organizing and sharing. For example, you will find apps that:

- Map pictures to specific locations – i.e. geotagging
- Create photo albums
- Provide editing tools
- Provide camera functions
- Import pictures from other devices
- Create slideshows

15 Windows games

Traditional Windows games such as FreeCell Solitaire are included with Windows 10 and there are a huge number of games available in the Windows Store. We take a look at some popular ones.

Games support

Gaming has always been a very popular use of computers and, in recognition of this, Windows operating systems have traditionally provided a selection of games with which users can amuse themselves. No games were included with the Windows 8 operating system by default, but a selection of games is bundled with the Windows 10 operating system. The Microsoft Solitaire Collection is available on the Start menu, and contains a selection of popular traditional Windows card games re-done as modern apps.

If you want to play more games in Windows 10, you can download them from the Windows Store.

The Microsoft Solitaire Collection in the Windows 10 Creators Update includes guaranteed solvable decks for the Klondike, Spider, and FreeCell Solitaire games.

Surprisingly, the standard edition of the Microsoft Solitaire Collection supplied with Windows 10 now contains advertisements. You can, however, upgrade to the Premium edition (at a cost) to remove the adverts and receive other game benefits. The Menu button produces a menu that includes an **Upgrade to Premium** option.

Not all the traditional Windows games are available in Universal Windows App versions.

Upgrade to Premium on Windows

Upgrade now to the Microsoft Solitaire Collection Premium Edition on Windows and receive these great features:

- No advertisements
- More coins for completing Daily Challenges
- Get a boost for every game of TriPeaks and Pyramid.
- NOTE: this will not grant Premium on iOS or Android devices

Upgrade for 1 month | Upgrade for 1 year | No, thanks

FreeCell is, perhaps, the most popular Solitaire card game in the Microsoft Solitaire Collection.

1. Open the Microsoft Solitaire Collection app, then click on the **FreeCell** tile to begin the game

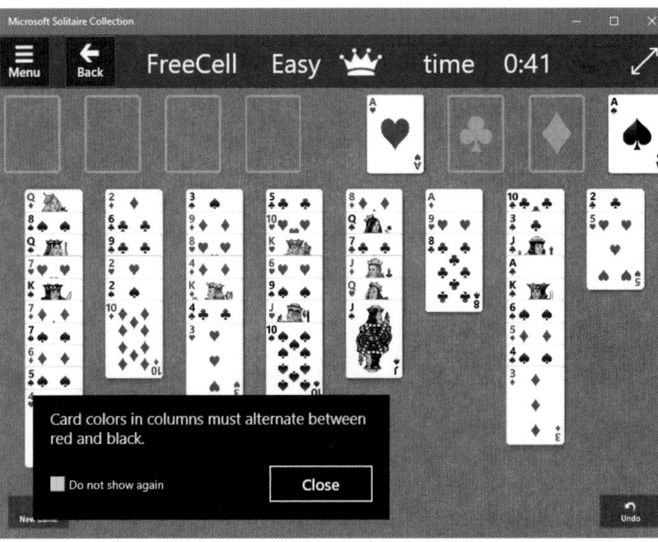

As shown here, you are notified if you attempt to make an invalid move.

2. Click the Menu button then choose the **? How to play** option to see the game instructions

3. Arrange the cards to create four stacks of card suits

4. On completion you can review your gameplay statistics

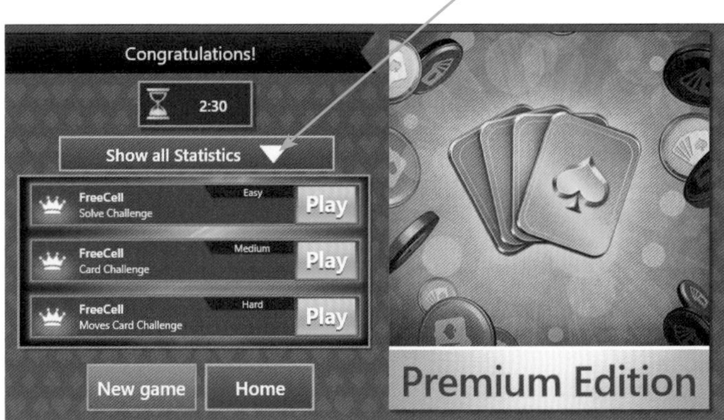

If you quit a game before completion it is counted as a loss in your game statistics.

Candy Crush Soda Saga

The highly addictive and popular Candy Crush Soda Saga match-3 game is available as a Universal Windows App on Windows 10.

NEW

Candy Crush Soda Saga from game-maker "King" is new in Windows 10 – more King game titles will be available later.

1. Launch the Candy Crush Soda Saga app from the Start menu, then click on the **Play** button to begin the game

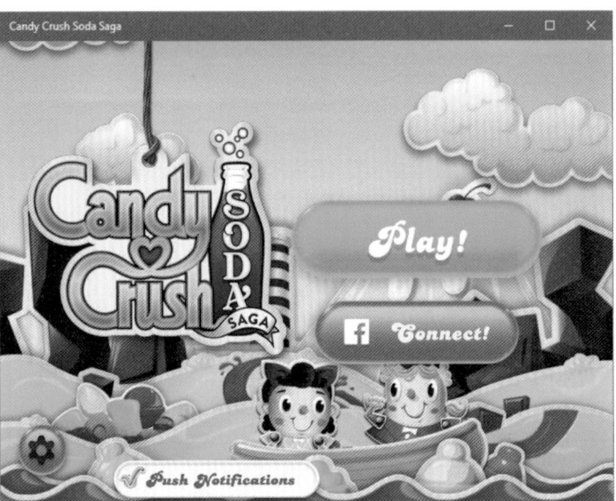

Candy Crush Soda Saga has many levels, and game instructions are provided on screen during the early levels.

2. Match three or more candies to meet the target score within the limited number of available moves

3. On success you will see and hear the phrase "Soda Crush", then follow the options and the game will proceed to the next level

Click the arrow icon in the bottom-left corner of the app for options to control the music and sound effects.

Xbox app

The new Xbox app on Windows 10 now makes Xbox features available on PCs and tablets. It allows you to keep track of friends on Xbox Live, record game play clips using its Game DVR, join in an Xbox One multi-player game without leaving your desk, and easily acquire Windows 10 games.

The Xbox app is a new Universal Windows App in Windows 10.

1. Launch the Xbox app from the Start menu, then click on the **My Games** button
2. Now, to search for a game, click on the **Find games in the Store** link 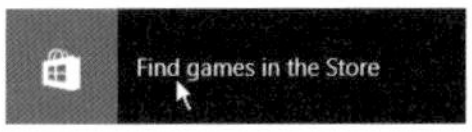
3. Choose a game, such as "Farmville 2: Country Escape"

4. When the game is installed it appears in your "My games" list, with a **Play** button you can click to launch that game

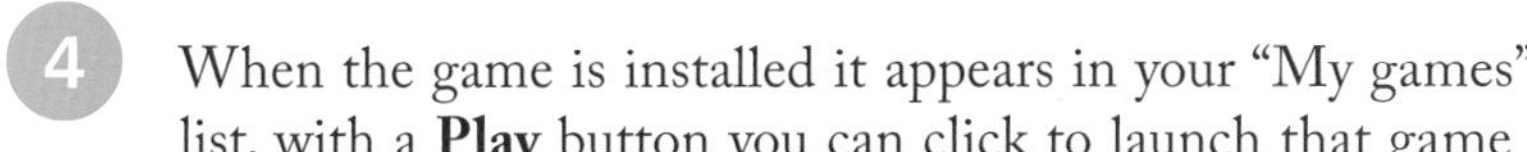

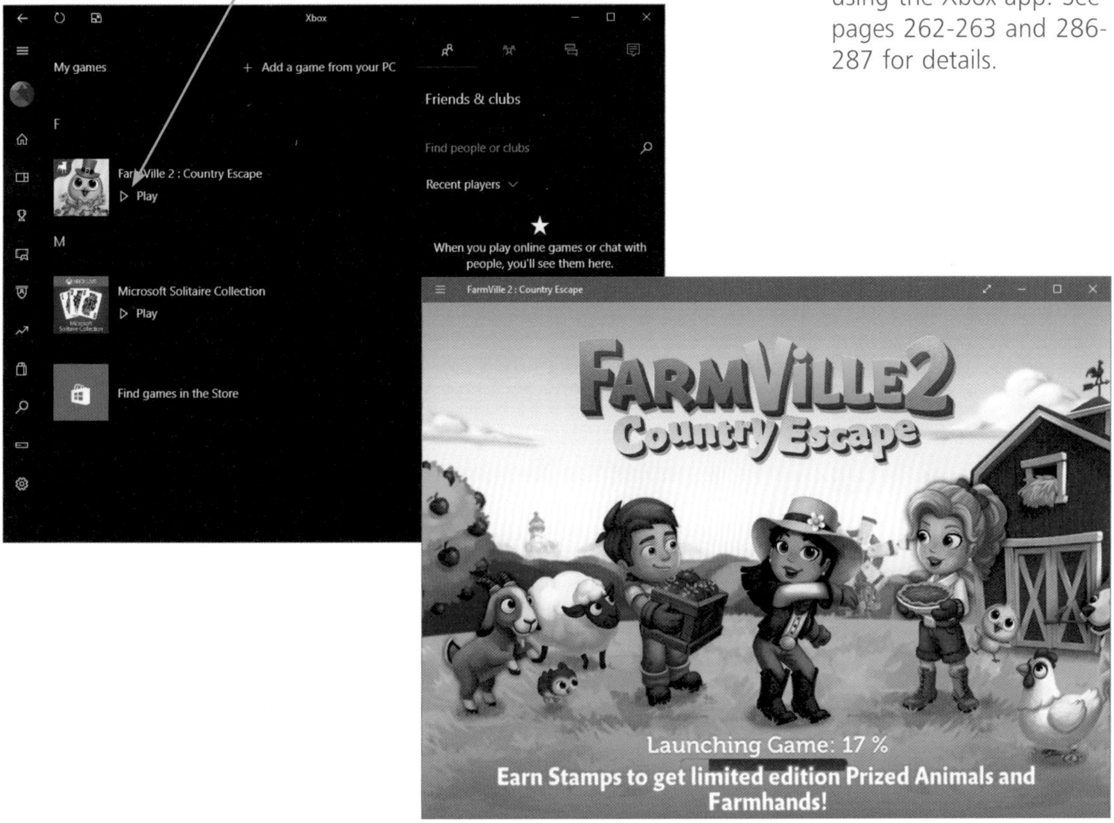

Xbox One consoles can stream games and media to your Windows 10 PC using the Xbox app. See pages 262-263 and 286-287 for details.

Streaming Xbox games

The Xbox app is a great new Universal Windows App in Windows 10 that brings Xbox gaming to your PC.

You must sign in to both the Xbox console and Xbox app using the same Microsoft account.

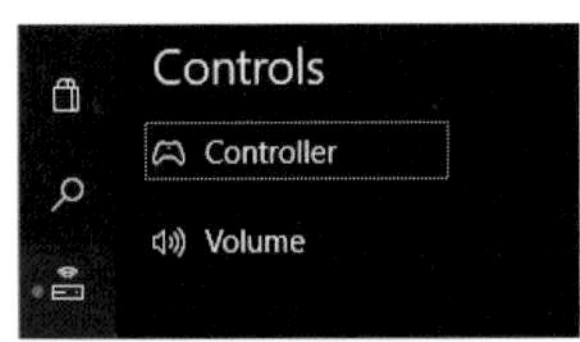

If you have an Xbox console on the same network you can stream games, video, and music to your PC:

1. Turn on your Xbox console and controller, then sign in using your Microsoft account
2. On your PC, launch the Xbox app from the Start menu, then sign in using the same Microsoft account
3. To have the Xbox app search for your Xbox device, click the **Connect** button in the left-hand toolbar

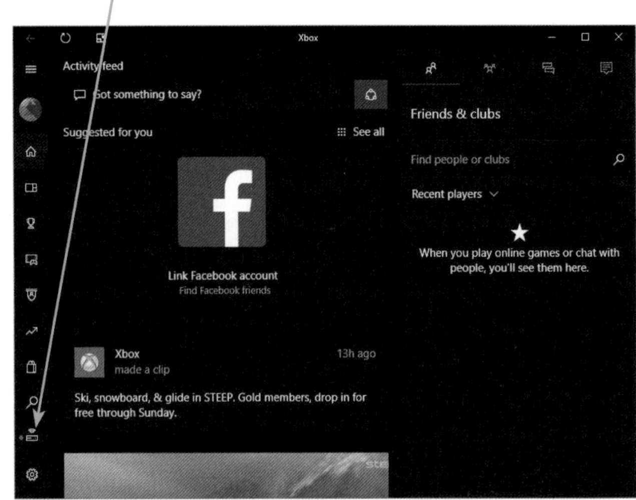

4. Connect an Xbox controller to your PC using a USB to micro-USB cable, so you can interact with your Xbox app
5. Select the Xbox console with which to connect, then click the **Stream** link

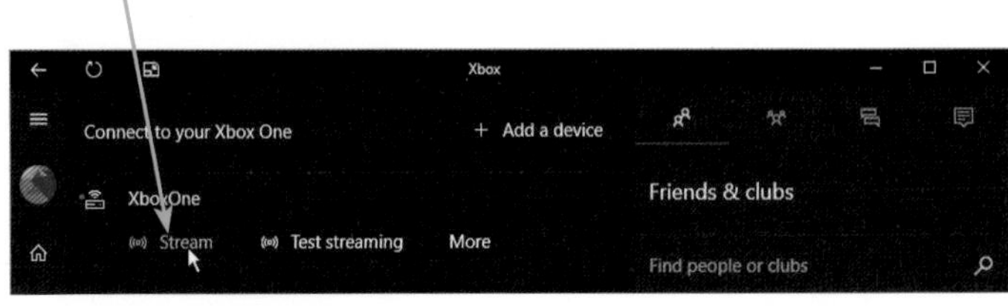

6 Your Xbox console screen now loads in the Xbox app

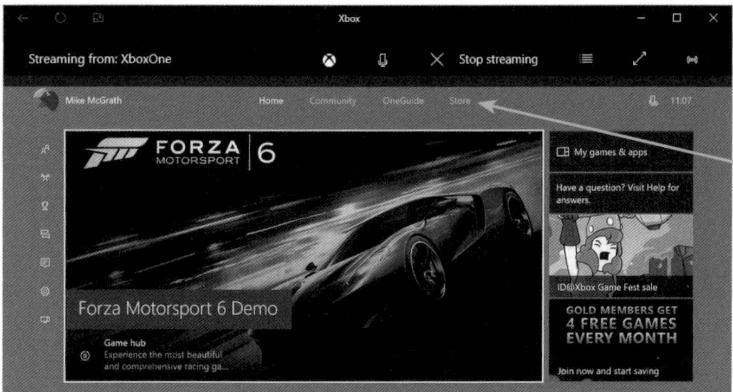

You can search the Store for Xbox game demos to play on a trial basis.

7 Use the Xbox controller to select a game to stream to your PC, then play – just like on your Xbox

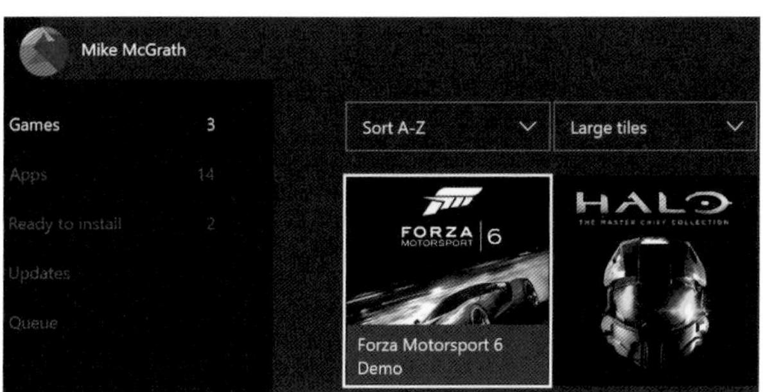

To use a wireless Xbox controller after using it on your PC you will have to re-sync the controller, using the console's Sync button or a USB cable.

Games in the Windows Store

The Windows Store contains many different categories of software. Let's see what it has to offer to gamers.

1. On the Home page is a menu bar – Apps, Games, Music, Movies & TV, and Books. Click on the **Games** item

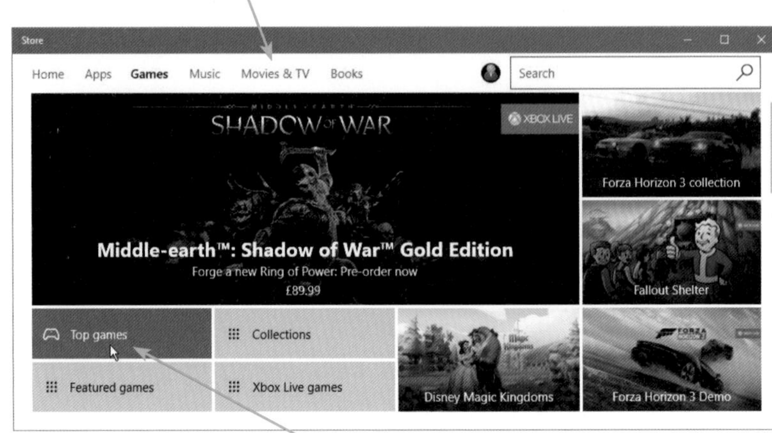

The Store app is a new Universal Windows App in Windows 10.

2. Now, click on the **Top games** tile, then choose from the list of filters to narrow your search, such as **Top free**

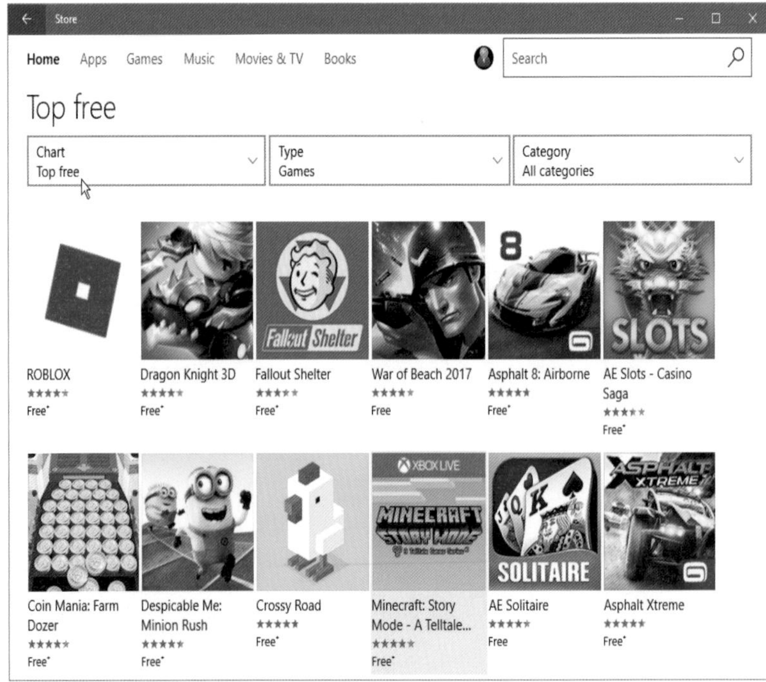

Many free games contain "in-app purchases" that you may need to fully enjoy the game.

Explore Pinball FX2

Let's take a look at some of the free games available in the Windows Store. One of the most popular is Pinball FX2, which can be played on a Windows 10 PC, on an Xbox, and online.

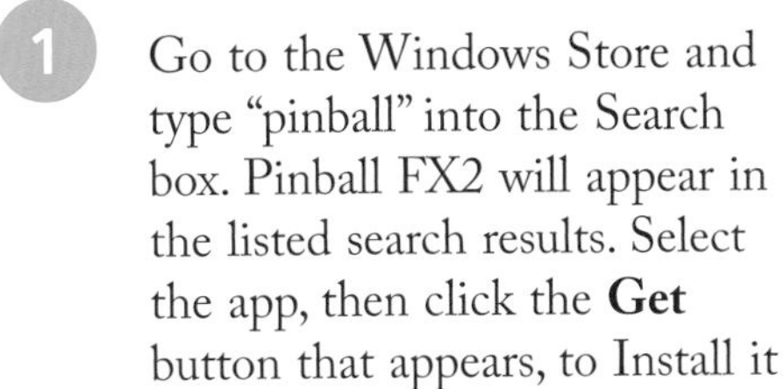

1. Go to the Windows Store and type "pinball" into the Search box. Pinball FX2 will appear in the listed search results. Select the app, then click the **Get** button that appears, to Install it

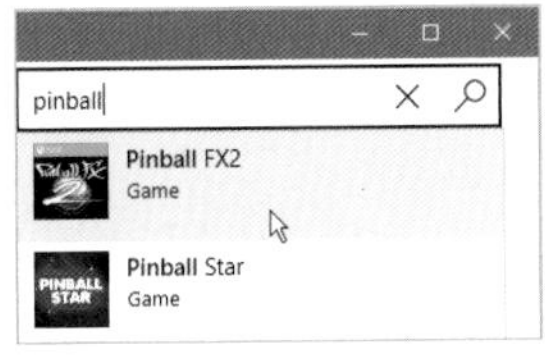

2. On the game's Home page you will see several tiles under **Collection**, each of which represents a different pinball table. Some tiles are grayed out, which means they are not active, so select an active table such as "Mars"

3. Next, choose to **Buy Now** or **Play Free! With Ads** to launch the selected table

4. Click the hamburger button at the top-left of the window and select **Settings** to see a list of options, including: **How to Play**, **Video**, **Audio**, and **Controls**

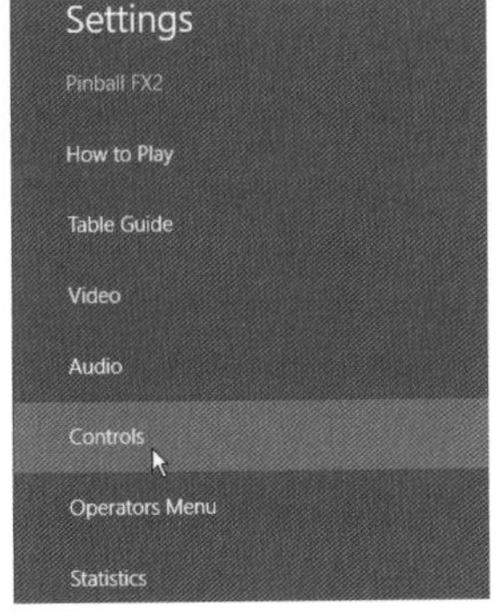

As you click on each pinball table tile in the left-hand panel, an overview of that table is given in the right-hand panel.

Many of the options in Pinball FX2 relate to online play.

...cont'd

5 From the Settings options choose the **Controls** item to see the default set of controls provided. For example, the left flipper is operated with the left **Shift** key. However, if the default key for any particular control doesn't suit you, you can click on the down arrow against the control and choose an alternative key from the drop-down list that appears

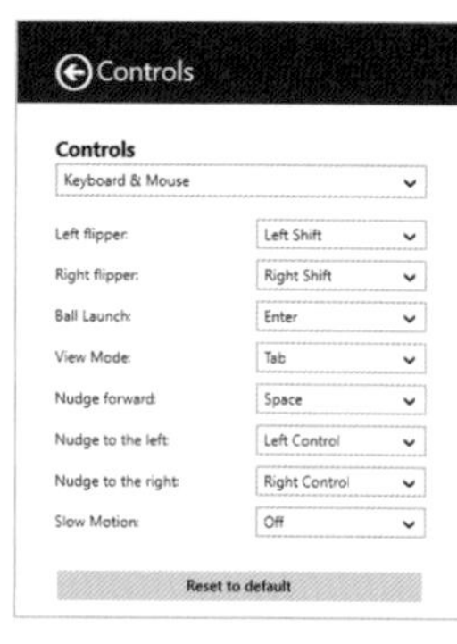

Don't forget

By clicking on a control, you can select the key that activates it. For example, for Ball Launch you can choose from the down arrow, Space, number 2, number 0, Right Control, and Enter.

6 Settings provides three main options – **Audio**, **Video** and **Graphics**. On the right we see the audio settings. Slide or click the bar to adjust volume controls for different types of sound used in the game

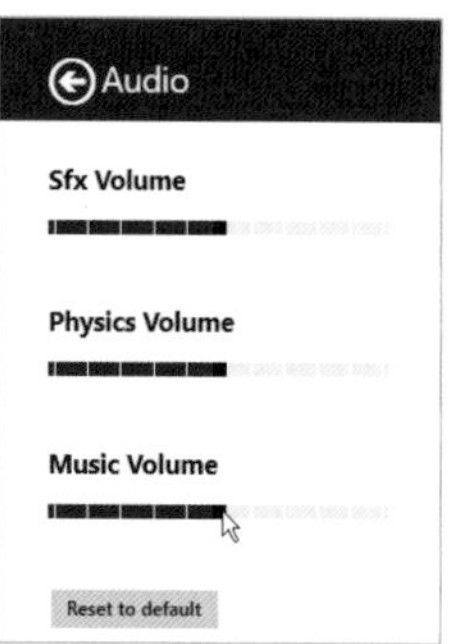

7 When you are ready to play, you can choose from **Single Player** or **Hotseat** mode. The latter enables two, three or four players to play a game

Hot tip

During a game, you can zoom in and out. Tables can be viewed from different angles as well, by pressing the **C** key to change the View Mode.

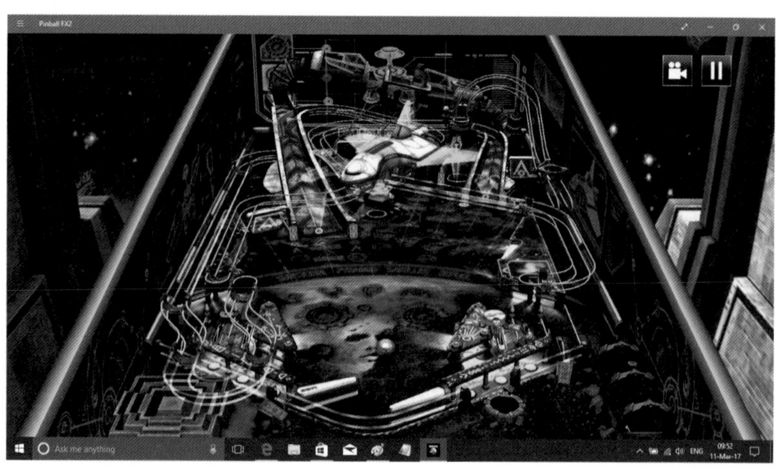

PuzzleTouch

PuzzleTouch is all about jigsaws, and is a game that will appeal to jigsaw buffs and children. A number of jigsaws are supplied with the program but you can also create them from your own pictures.

1. Download the app from the Windows Store, as described in Step 1 on page 265
2. The Home page presents sets of puzzles, some of which are free and others which have to be paid for
3. Click on a jigsaw to open the set

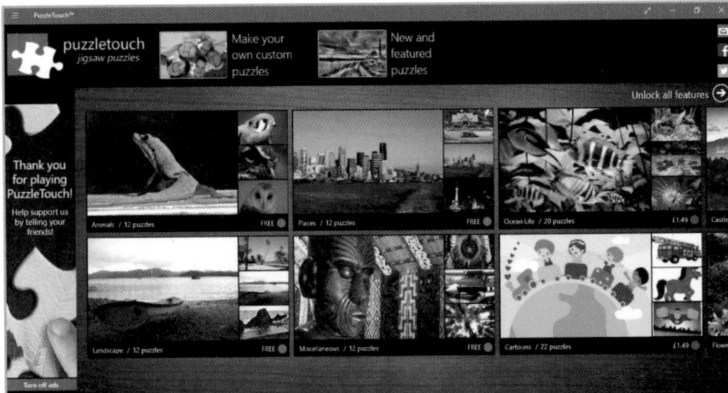

If you lose your way in the jigsaw, right-click on the screen. From the app bar that opens, click Sneak peek to see a complete picture of the jigsaw.

4. You will now see all the puzzles in the set. Select the one you want, and in the next screen choose the level of difficulty

To access the more advanced features of PuzzleTouch you will have to pay.

5. Drag and drop the pieces to complete the puzzle

Microsoft Mahjong

Microsoft Mahjong is a tile-based game that can be played on the PC, a tablet or online. The purpose of the game is to remove all the tiles from the board by matching them with identical tiles.

1. Download the app from the Windows Store, as described in Step 1 on page 265

2. The Home page shows a number of sections – select from **Choose Puzzle**, **Daily Challenges**, **Themes**, **How to Play**, **Awards and Achievements**, and **Statistics**

3. If you are new to Mahjong, click **How to Play** to discover how to play the game, then click **Choose Puzzle**

4. Next, select your skill level. Initially, you are restricted to the first game in each level – when you have completed this, you can move up to the next one

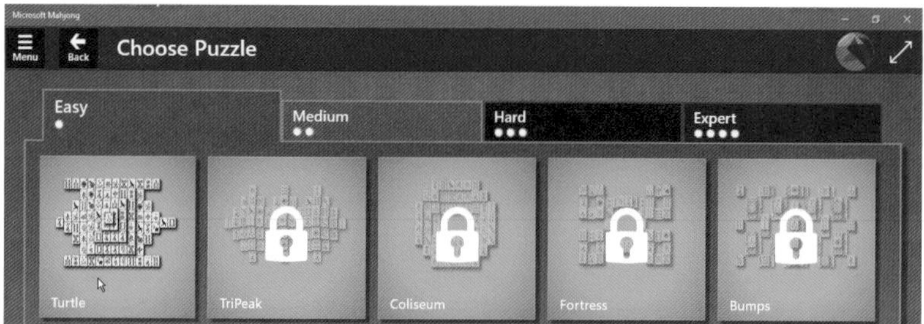

5. Click pairs of matching tiles to remove them from the board. Clear the board completely to win

Microsoft Mahjong has been redesigned as a Universal Windows App for Windows 10.

If you play a lot, the **Statistics** section on the Home page will be interesting.

Hot tip

If you get stuck or just want to take a break, click the **Menu** button – the **Hint** option will reveal a matching pair and **Pause** will stop play until you choose to resume.

Minesweeper

Microsoft Minesweeper is another fun and tactical game. The purpose is to uncover all empty squares in a grid while avoiding the mines.

1. On the Home page, select your skill level – **Easy**, **Medium**, or **Expert**. There is also a **Custom** option, which allows you to set your own degree of difficulty

2. At the top of the screen there is a timer and the number of mines on the board

3. As you reveal empty squares, numbers appear on them. These indicate how many mines are touching that square, and thus help you determine which squares are mines

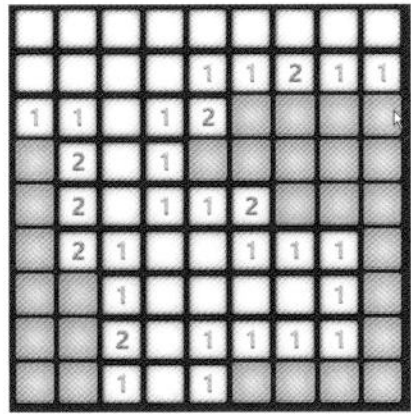

4. If you hit a mine, that's it – the game is over

5. When all the empty squares are uncovered, you win

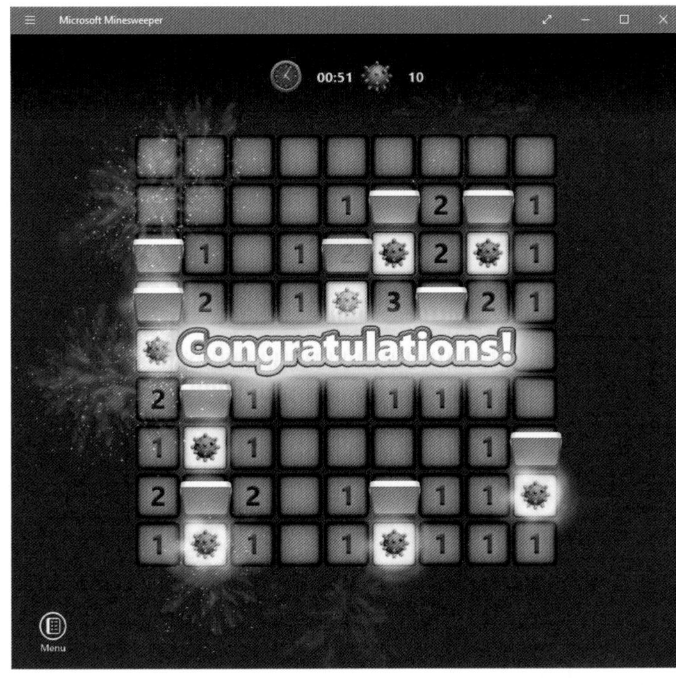

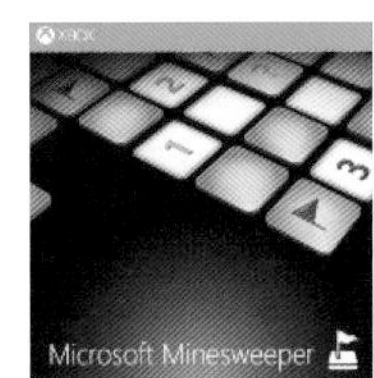

Microsoft Minesweeper has been redesigned as a Universal Windows App for Windows 10.

The more difficult the skill level you choose, the more squares and mines there are on the board.

Right-clicking on a square that you suspect contains a mine will put a warning flag on the square.

Sudoku

If you're a fan of logic puzzles you can play the popular game of Sudoku – to fill a 9x9 grid so that each column and row, and each of the nine 3x3 sub-grids, contain all of the digits from 1 to 9.

1. Download the app from the Windows Store, as described in Step 1 on page 265
2. On the Home page, select your skill level – **Very Easy**, **Easy**, **Medium**, **Hard**, or **Expert**
3. The grid is partly filled with digits. Click an empty square, or use the arrow keys to select an empty square

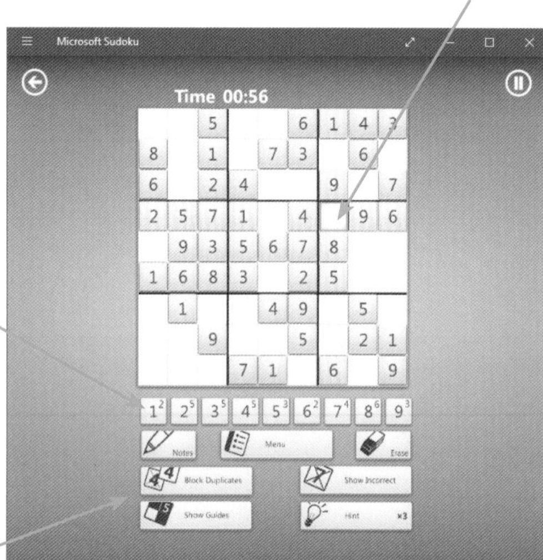

4. Type a digit that is not already present in the selected row, column, or grid
5. Complete the grid with the missing digits to win

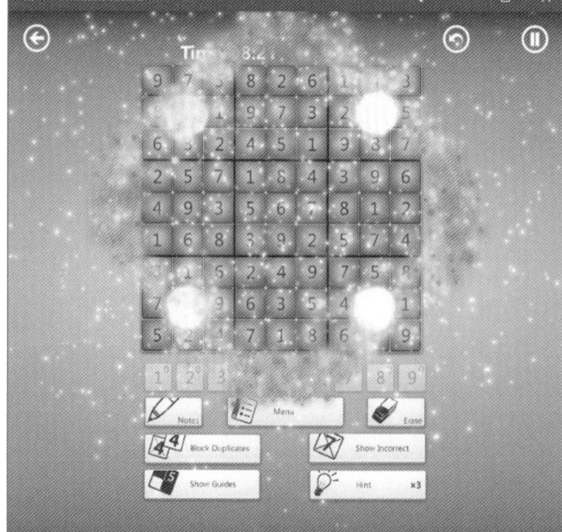

The quantity of each remaining digit is shown on these tiles, in the top right-hand corner of each number.

Use the **Block Duplicates**, **Show Guides**, and **Show Incorrect** buttons for assistance if you are new to the Sudoku game.

16 Music and sound

The sound card in your computer lets you play music, listen to internet radio, or play videos with audio tracks. You can also share your media files with others on your network. With a microphone you can dictate to your computer. You need suitable software, for which Windows 10 provides the Groove Music app and Windows Media Player.

Audio connections

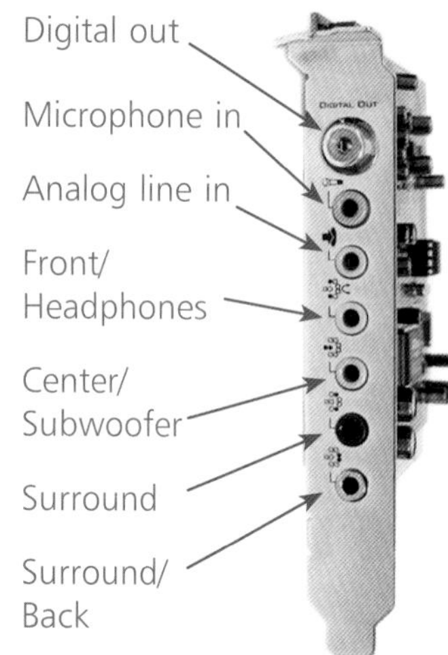

Desktop and laptop computers are equipped with audio facilities that can produce high-fidelity audio playback. On desktop machines, the sound card can provide the connections for various types of speakers, ranging from simple stereo speakers to multiple speaker sets with surround sound.

For a laptop or notebook the options are often limited to microphone and headset sockets, though some laptops include more sophisticated connections, such as the SPDIF (Sony Philips Digital Interface) used for home theater connections.

On a desktop computer, the sound card may be incorporated into the motherboard or provided as a separate adapter card, as shown here.

You may have speakers attached to your computer, or built into the casing of portable computers. To check the configuration:

1. Go to Settings, Devices, and then under **Related settings** choose **Sound settings**

2. On the Playback tab, select **Speakers** and click **Configure**, then select your configuration and click **Test** to check

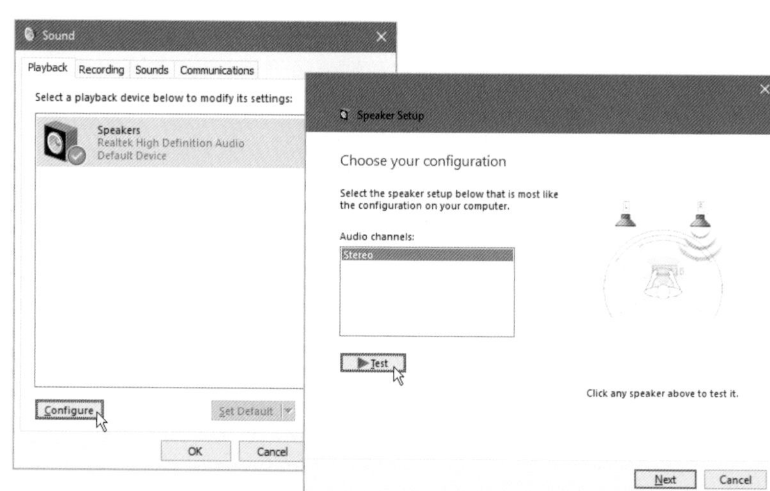

The configurations listed depend on the features of your sound card. To check the operation of each of your speakers, click the **Test** button. Note that some software will only use the main speakers, especially with tracks that are two-channel stereo only.

Groove Music app

The Groove Music app in Windows 10 not only allows you to play your own music, it also lets you access a huge range of artists and genres from the Microsoft Store.

The Groove Music app is a great new Universal Windows App in Windows 10.

1. The first thing to do is place all your music in **My Music** folder. It will then be accessible in the app

2. Open the Groove Music app and click the buttons to see your music listed as **Albums**, **Artists**, or **Songs**

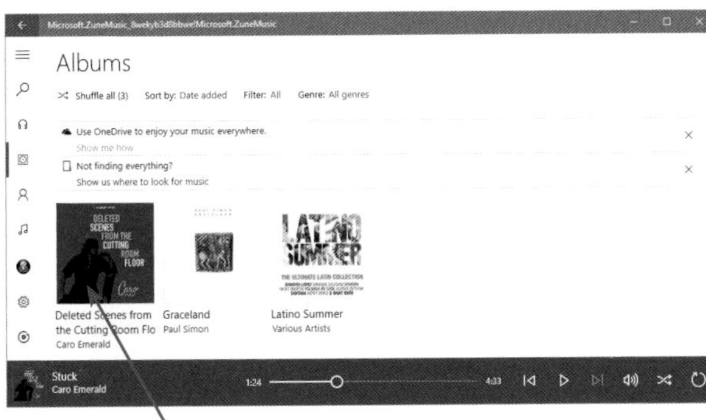

3. Click a music tile to open an Album

4. Double-click a music track to play it, or click the track to select it, then click the Play button below the album title

5. Explore the playback controls at the bottom of the screen

The **+ Add to** option allows you to create playlists by adding tracks.

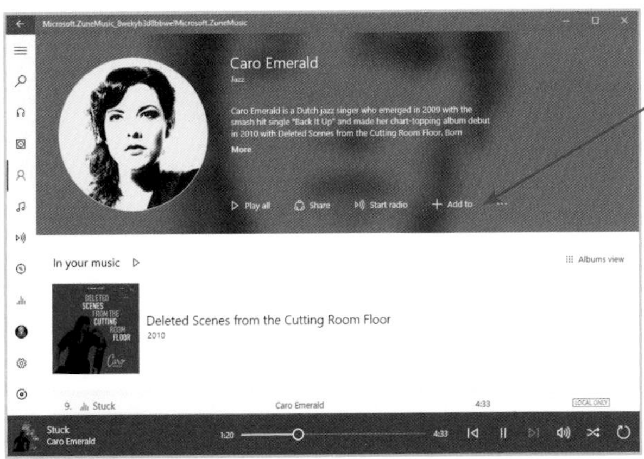

Download media files

Due to the quantity and variety of music available through the Microsoft Store (accessible via the Groove Music app), you may find your own music taking a back seat.

Hot tip

You can use the Search box in the Groove Music app to find music you have on your computer.

1. Open Groove Music and search for an album, artist, or song. For example, search for the artist "Caro Emerald"
2. The results include items you own in **In your music**
3. Select **Full catalog** to find other items

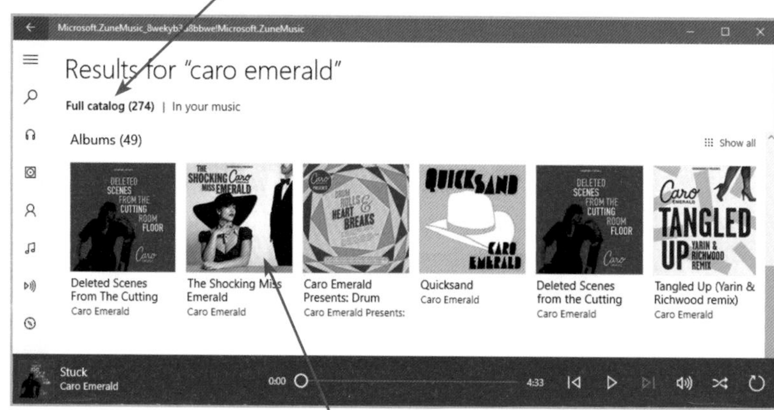

4. Click any item of interest to discover more. For example, select one of the Caro Emerald albums listed here to see a descriptive summary

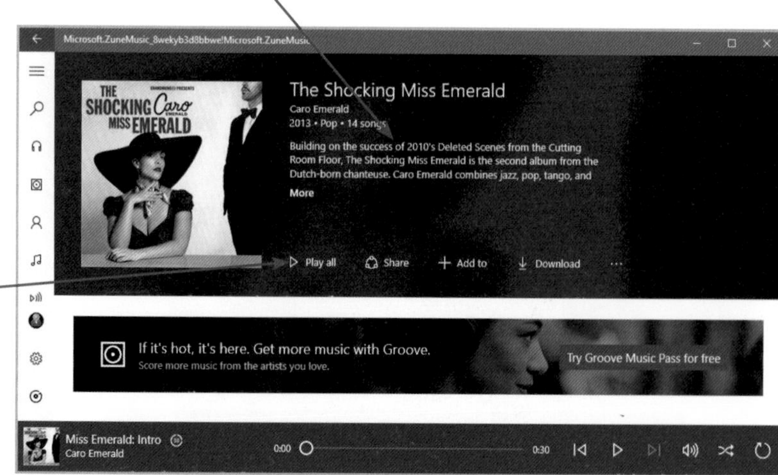

Beware

You will not be able to **Play all** tracks on the album unless you have paid for a Groove Music Pass (see Step 8 on the next page).

5. Scroll down the results page to see a list of tracks contained on the selected album

6. Check the box against any track to select the song

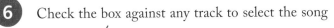

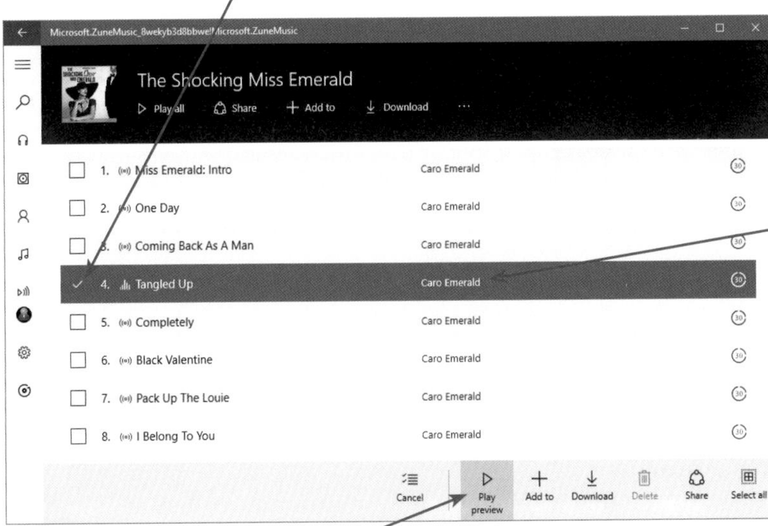

Click the artist name in the songs list to see information on the artist.

7. Click the **Play preview** button to hear a 30-second snippet of the selected song

8. If you decide you would like to own the song, click the **Download** button and confirm your Groove Music Pass

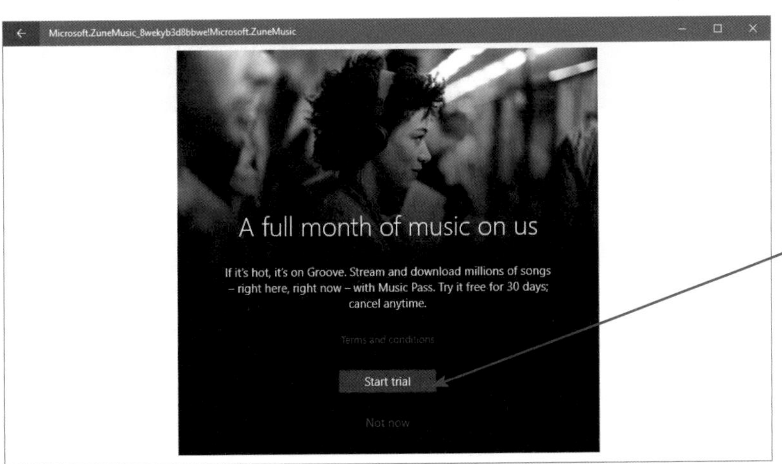

Microsoft.ZuneMusic_8wekyb3d8bbwe!Microsoft.ZuneMusic
A full month of music on us
If it's hot, it's on Groove. Stream and download millions of songs – right here, right now – with Music Pass. Try it free for 30 days; cancel anytime.
Terms and conditions
Start trial
Not now

Here, you can accept the offer of a free 30-day trial to Groove Music by clicking the **Start trial** button. At the end of the trial period you will automatically be charged a monthly subscription fee unless you cancel your subscription.

Windows Media Player

Windows Media Player (WMP) has long been one of the best applications in Windows, and the version supplied in Windows 10 is no exception. Windows Media Player can handle just about any media-related task.

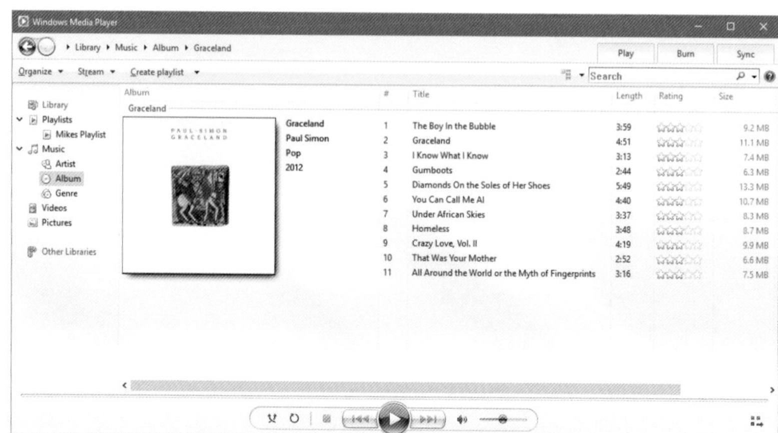

Hot tip

Windows Media Player supports an extensive list of media codecs. This ensures it will play most types of media.

These include:

- Playing music
- Viewing your pictures in a slideshow
- Playing video
- Streaming media on home networks
- Ripping music
- Burning media to disks
- Downloading media files
- Listening to music on the internet
- Creating playlists
- Synchronizing media on your devices
- Accessing online media sources to rent or buy music

Windows Media Player features brightness, contrast, saturation and hue adjustment controls. It also provides a 10-band graphic equalizer with presets, and an SRS WOW audio post-processing system to personalize audio to your preferences for rich listening experience.

Play CDs

Assuming you have a CD/DVD drive on your computer, you can use your sound card and speakers to play an audio CD.

1. Insert the disk in the drive, and AutoPlay asks what you want to do

DVD RW Drive (D:) Audio CD
Tap to choose what happens with audio CDs.

2. Select **Play audio CD** Windows Media Player

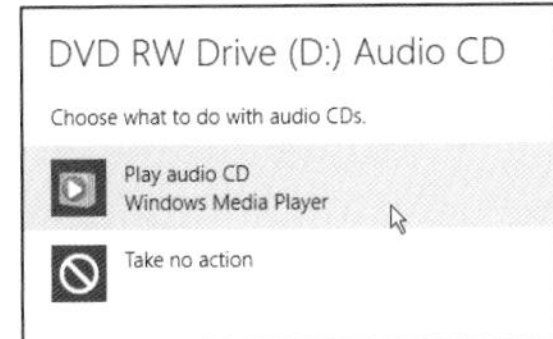

The CD begins to play, as an unknown album and showing no details other than the track numbers and their durations.

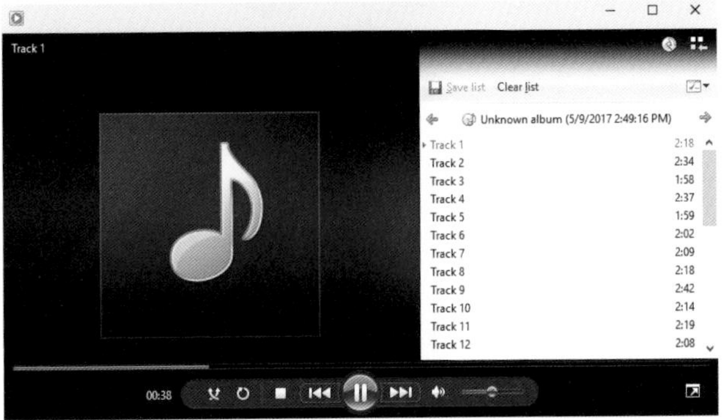

If you are connected to the internet, Windows Media Player will locate and download information about the CD, and display the album and track titles. You can also change the Visualization to display the album cover image.

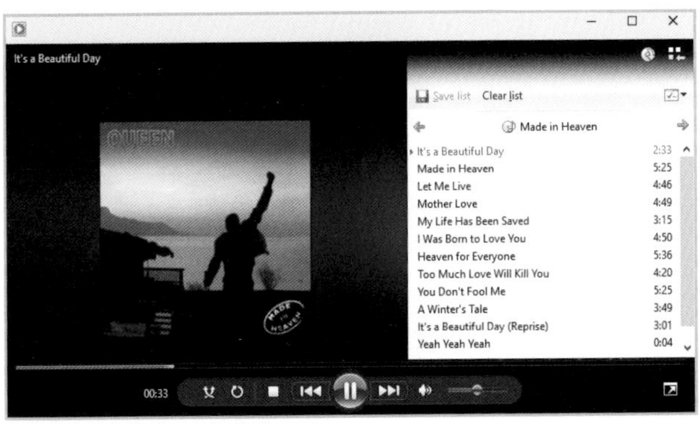

Click the box **Always do this for audio CDs**, and the selected option is carried out automatically in future, whenever an audio CD is identified.

Right-click the window and select **Visualization** to choose the effects to display, for example Album art (cover image).

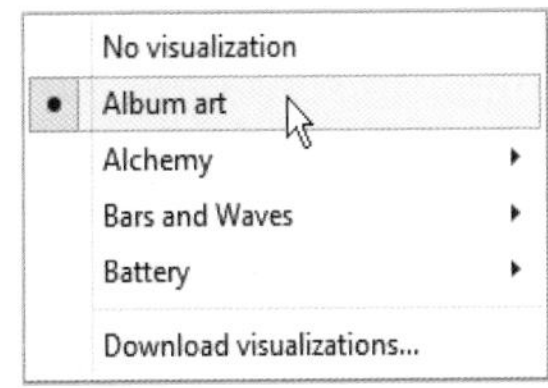

Copy CD tracks

You can copy songs from an audio CD, an action known as "Ripping" the CD, where Media Player makes file copies that get added to your library. To specify the type of copy:

Beware

Your Media Player may be set to automatically begin ripping when you insert an audio CD – choose the format before inserting the CD.

1. Right-click the Media Player window and select **More options...**

2. Click the **Rip Music** tab

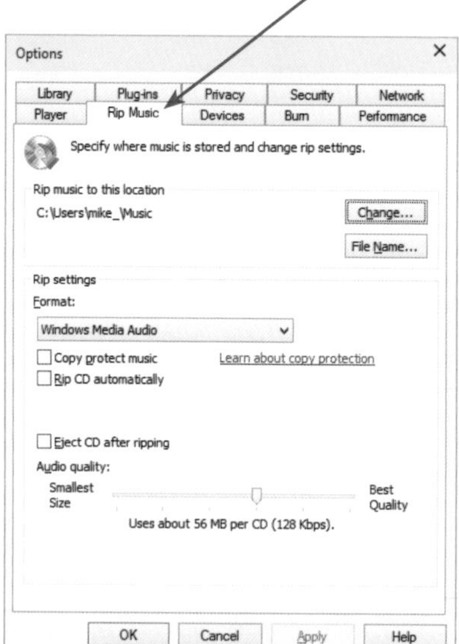

You can listen to the CD while you are ripping it, or play other content from your library. To cut short the copy, click the **Stop rip** button.

3. Set Format as one of the Windows Media Audio (WMA) file formats, or select the MP3 format for greater flexibility

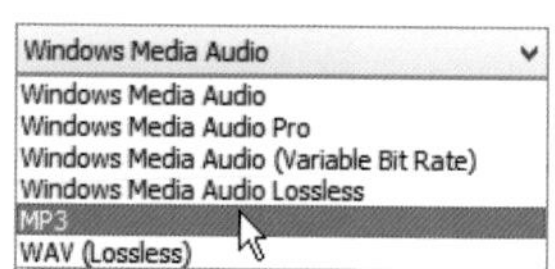

4. Select the bit rate – higher bit rates will give much better quality, but will use up more disk space

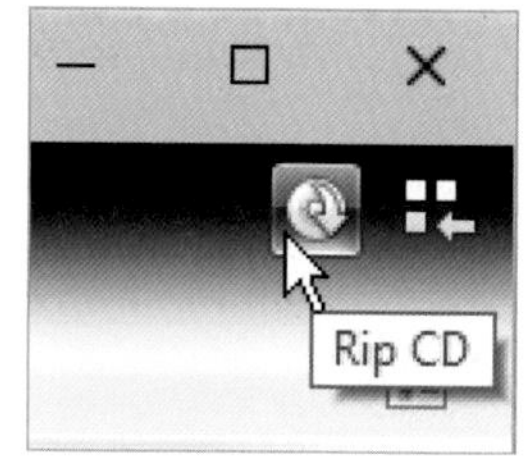

5. Click the **Rip CD** button to extract and compress the tracks

You are offered the option to copy-protect your files, restricting playback to one computer. Choose "No" to allow playback by any computer.

6. The tracks are added to your Music library, and stored with a folder for each artist, and a sub-folder for each of their albums

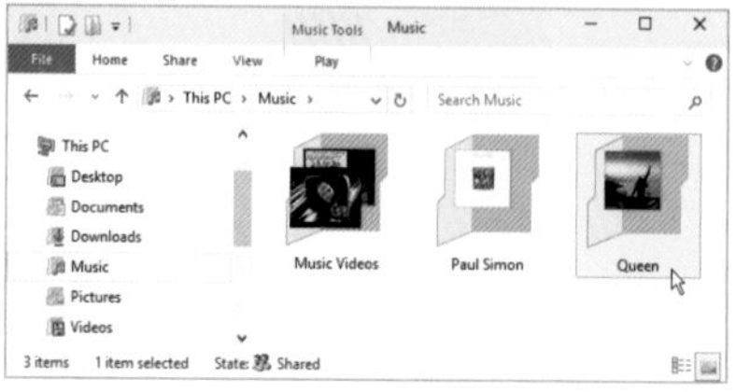

Media Player library

1. When the CD has been copied, select **Go to Library** (or click the **Switch to Library** button)

2. Select **Music** to display the Music library, by artist and track

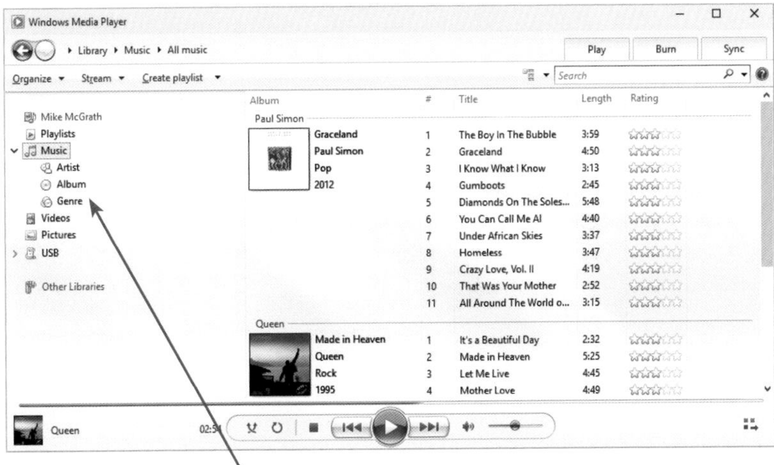

3. Select **Artist**, **Genre**, or **Album** to group all the associated albums by your preference

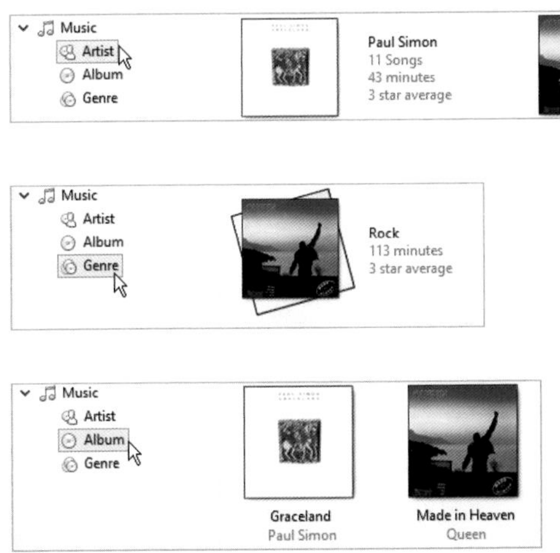

The Windows Media Player library displays content of the current user's Music, Videos and Pictures libraries, plus links to the libraries of users who are online or HomeGroup members.

Click Organize, **Customize navigation pane...**, to group music by other properties, such as Year, Rating or Composer.

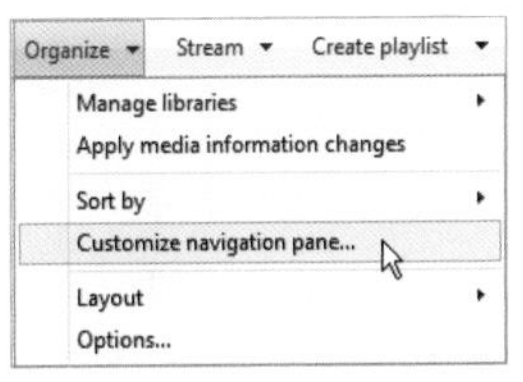

Double-click a group to display the individual tracks that it contains, arranged by album.

Internet radio

Around 60,000 stations worldwide are available via the TuneIn Radio app.

The ability to listen to internet radio stations is no longer available in Windows Media Player. The solution, therefore, is to download a third-party program. Go to the Windows Store, and search for "internet radio". You'll see a number of results. One we have tried and can recommend is TuneIn Radio, shown below:

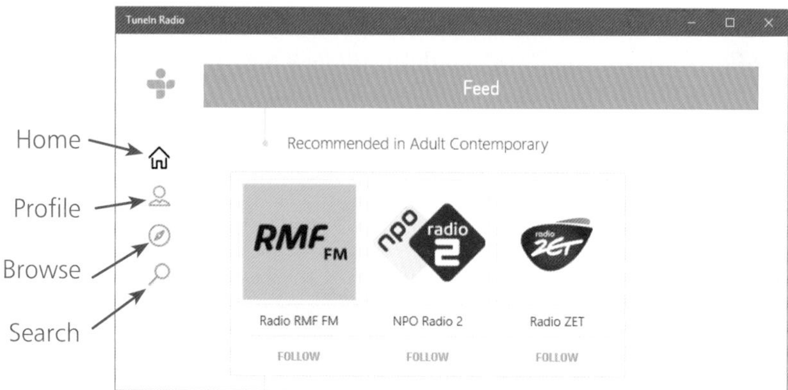

Beware

Searching by song may return mentions of the song, rather than the song itself.

The **Home** screen will show recommended stations listed by various categories. Scroll through the list and click on any station to listen, or click the **Browse** button to further filter categories. You can also search for songs, artists, and stations:

1. Click the **Search** button, then enter the name of a station. For example, the UK station, "BBC Radio 2"

You can also **Browse** for podcasts of pre-recorded audio programs that are available on the internet.

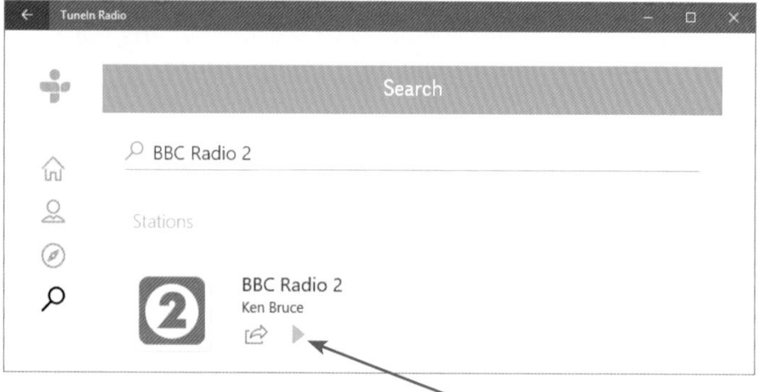

2. When the station is found, simply click on the **Play** button to begin listening to the live broadcast

Home media streaming

Anything that you can play in Windows Media Player, you can share with other computers and devices on your home network.

1. Open Windows Media Player, select the Library view and click the **Stream** button

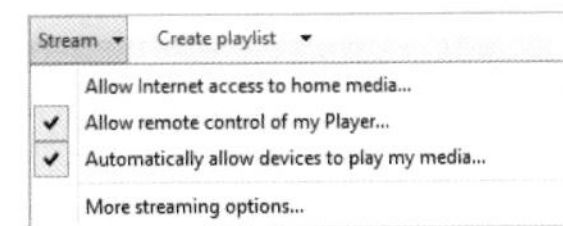

2. Check the options to **Allow Internet access to home media...**, **Allow remote control...**, **Automatically allow devices to play my media...**, and **More streaming options...**

With these settings, your Windows Media Player will have access to **Other Libraries**, in particular the media libraries that were shared when the computers on your network joined the HomeGroup (see Chapter 18).

3. Select one of the computer/user combinations to see what's available – in this example Music, Videos, Pictures, Recorded TV, and Playlists

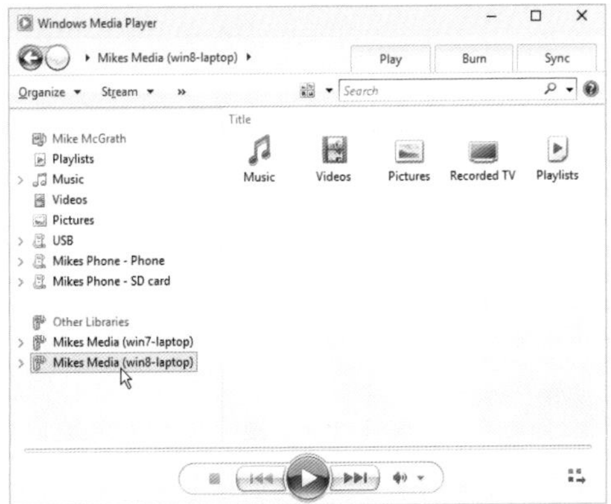

4. Expand the Music available on the other computer, and you will be able to play these on your computer

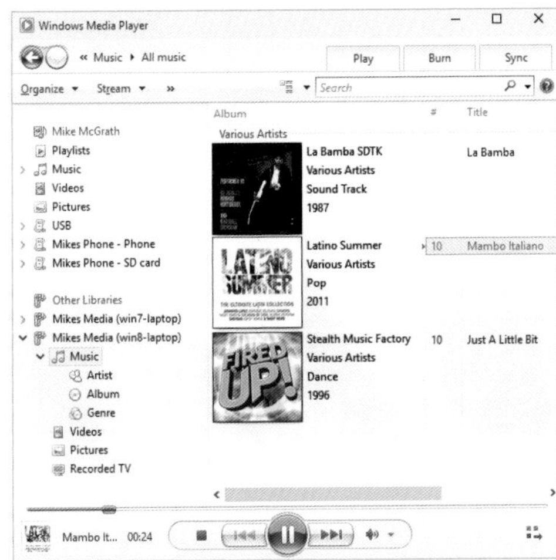

These are the default settings for Windows Media Player and HomeGroup, but if necessary, turn on media streaming and select the options to **Allow remote control** and **Automatically allow devices to play my media**.

You may have to wait a few moments as the list of contents is transferred from the other computer.

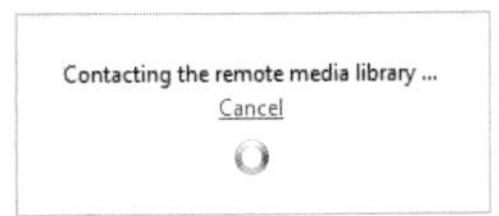

Play to device or computer

You can also use media streaming to play items from your computer on another computer or device on the network.

1. Start by turning on the networked device or start Windows Media Player on the target computer

2. Open Windows Media Player and drag a track from your Music onto the **Playlist**

3. Hit the **Pause** button to stop playback on your computer

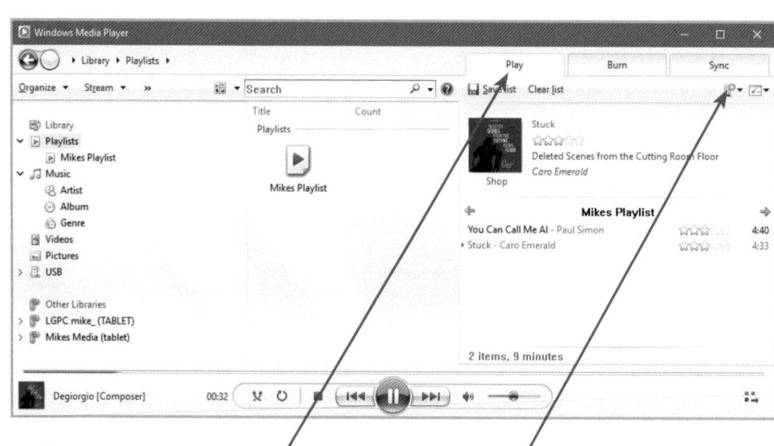

4. Now, on the **Play** tab, click the **Play to** button

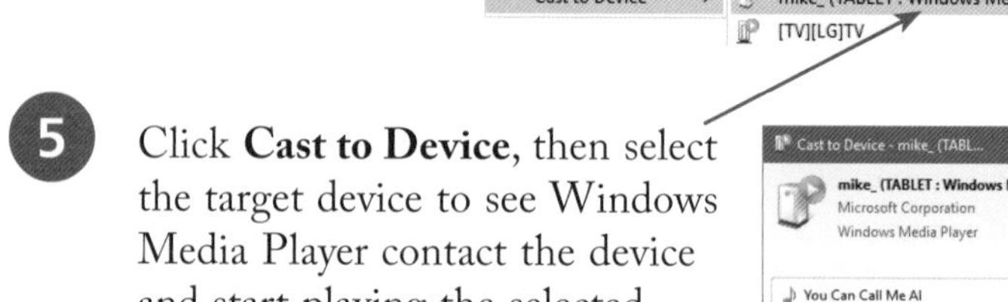

5. Click **Cast to Device**, then select the target device to see Windows Media Player contact the device and start playing the selected media files

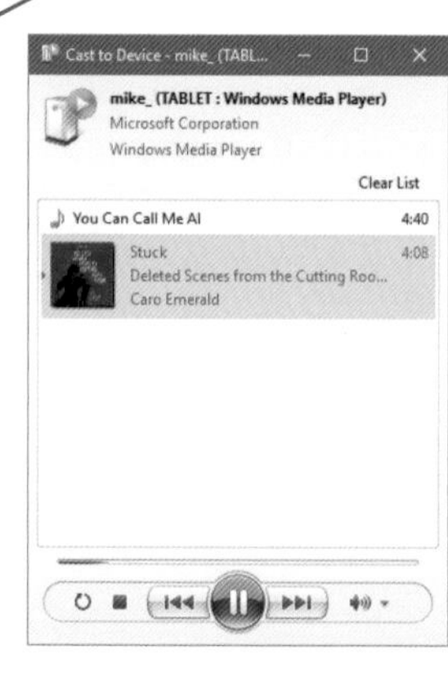

6. You can then control the operation from either computer

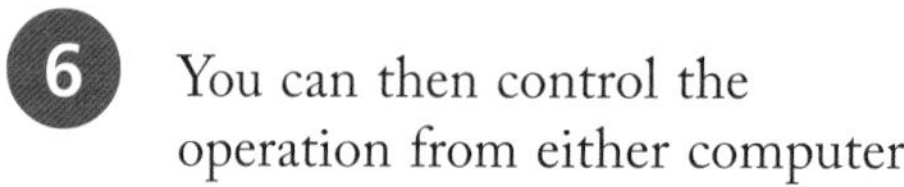

The **Play to** function is supported by Windows 10 Mobile, which can also stream media files to networked devices or computers running Windows Media Player.

You don't have to use Windows Media Player to initiate **Play to**. You can simply highlight a group of files in one of the library folders, then right-click the files, select **Cast to Device** and click the target device.

Dictate to your computer

One way to interact with your computer is to simply tell it what you want to do, with Windows Speech Recognition.

1. Go to the Start menu, then in the Windows Ease of Access folder choose **Windows Speech Recognition**, then click **Next**

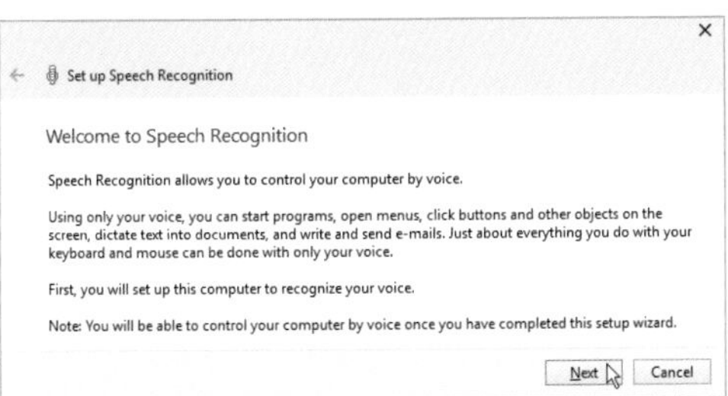

2. Select the type of microphone that you'll be using; a headset microphone being best for speech recognition, then click **Next**

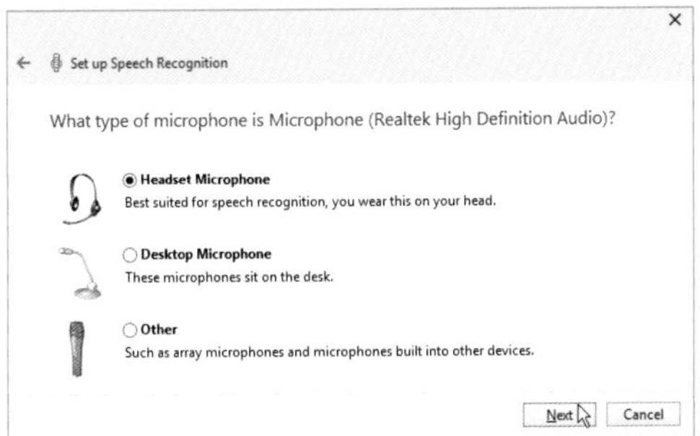

3. Follow the advice to position the microphone effectively, then read text aloud so the microphone volume can be set, then click **Next**

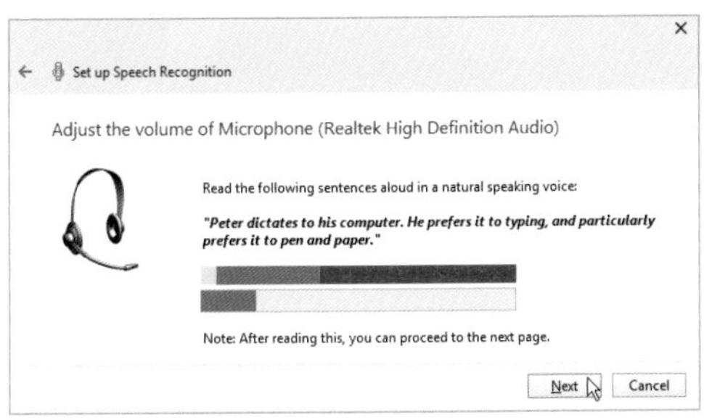

Speech Recognition is supported in all editions of Windows 10 and is available in the English, German, French, Spanish, Japanese and Chinese languages.

The Wizard takes you through all of the steps that are required to set up Speech Recognition on your computer.

...cont'd

Use Manual activation mode unless you are planning to always control your computer by voice.

All the users on the computer should carry out their own training sessions, so that each has a separate profile.

4. Following the prompts, choose **Manual** or **Voice activation** mode, and run Speech Recognition when Windows starts

5. Click **Start Tutorial** to learn about the basic features and to train your computer to better understand you

Now, when you start Windows, Speech Recognition will start up and switch itself into **Sleeping mode**, or **Turn listening off** (depending on the activation mode you have set).

1. If it is Off, right-click the Speech Recognition bar and select **Sleep**

2. Say "Start listening" (or click the mic button on the bar)

3. Say "What can I say?" to view the Speech Reference Card

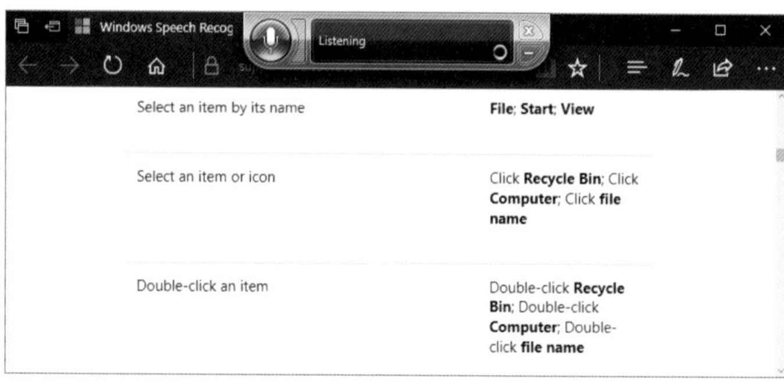

You can print the Speech Reference Card so that you have it to hand when you are practicing with the system.

Text to speech

You can let the computer talk to you, using the text to speech facilities of the Narrator application.

1. Go to the Start menu, then in the Windows Ease of Access folder choose **Narrator**

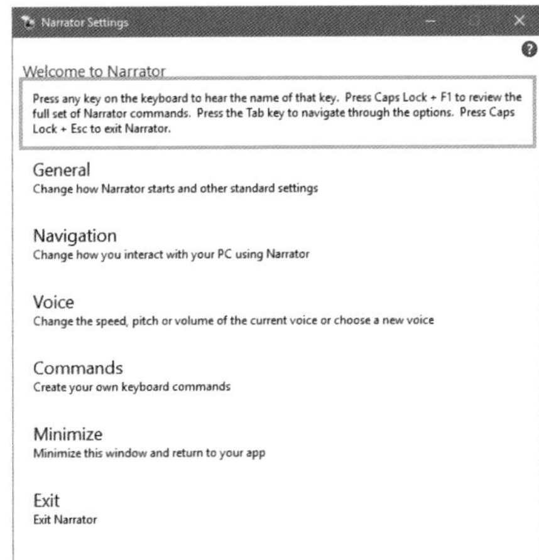

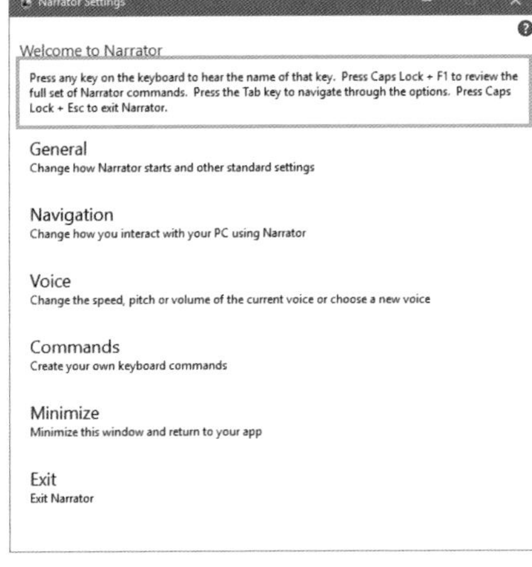

2. Narrator starts up and you can configure the main settings to set up the program

3. Click **Voice** to adjust the voice settings. Adjust the speed, volume and pitch to suit your preferences and maybe select a different voice. Narrator will read the contents of the screen, including the text content of programs such as Notepad, WordPad, and Windows Help and Support

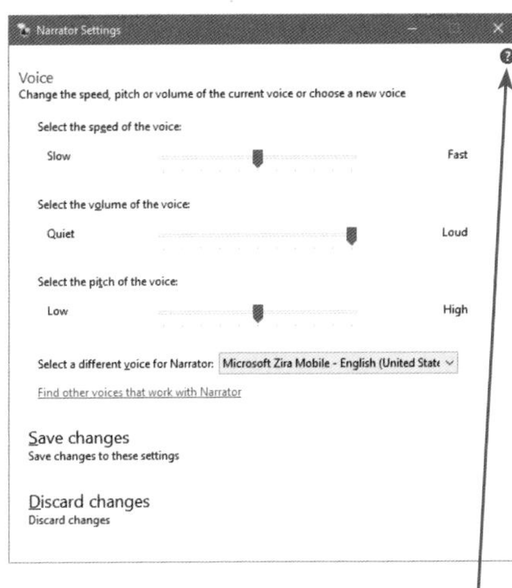

4. Click **Save changes** to keep the new voice settings, or click **Discard changes** to revert to previous settings

5. Click the **?** Help icon at the top-right of the Narrator window to get some useful hints

Open Settings, Ease of Access and slide the **Start Narrator automatically** toggle button to the **On** position to have the program start automatically when you start Windows.

Narrator does not read the text content of all programs, so its value is somewhat limited in comparison with Speech Recognition.

Streaming Xbox Music

If you have an Xbox console on the same network you can stream games, video, and music to your PC:

You must sign in to both the Xbox console and Xbox app using the same Microsoft account.

1. Turn on your Xbox console and controller, then sign in using your Microsoft account

2. On your PC, launch the Xbox app from the Start menu, then sign in using the same Microsoft account

3. To have the Xbox app search for your Xbox device, click the **Connect** button in the left toolbar

The Xbox app is a great new Universal Windows App on Windows 10 that brings Xbox gaming to your PC.

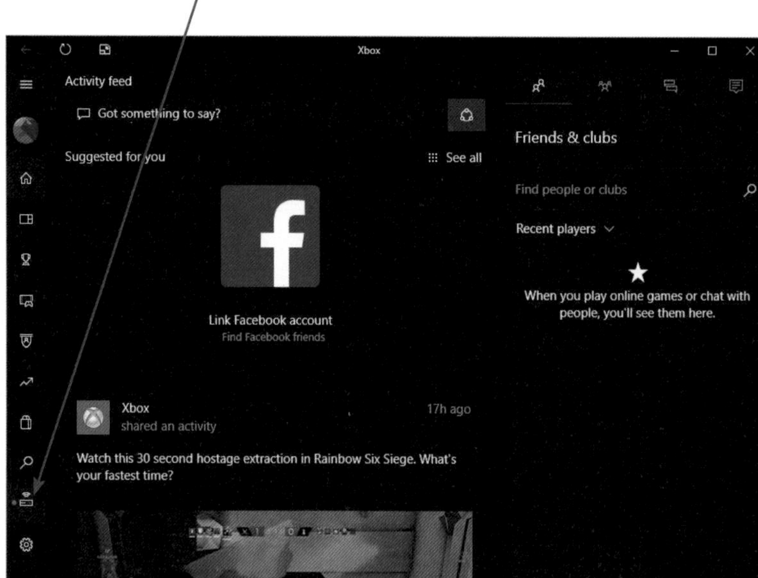

4. Connect an Xbox controller to your PC using a USB to micro-USB cable, so you can interact with your Xbox app

5. Select the Xbox console with which to connect, then click the **Stream** link

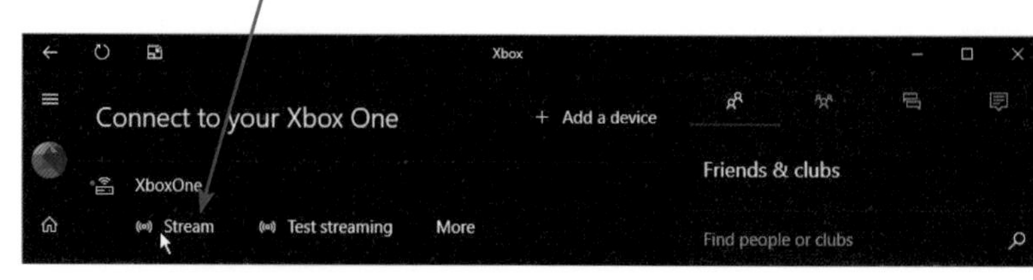

6. Your Xbox console screen now loads in the Xbox app

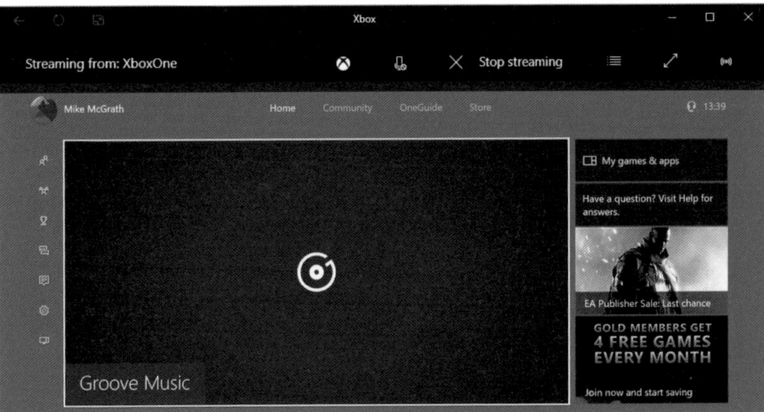

Groove Music is a subscription service, but you can try it free on a limited-time trial basis (see page 275).

7. Use the Xbox controller to select the **Groove Music** tile and choose **Explore** from the hamburger button menu

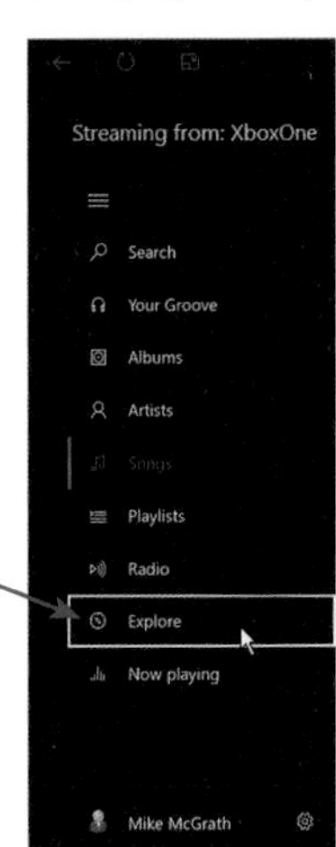

8. Browse through the various current offerings, then select an item to hear it play. For example, select the current number one item in the **Top songs** category

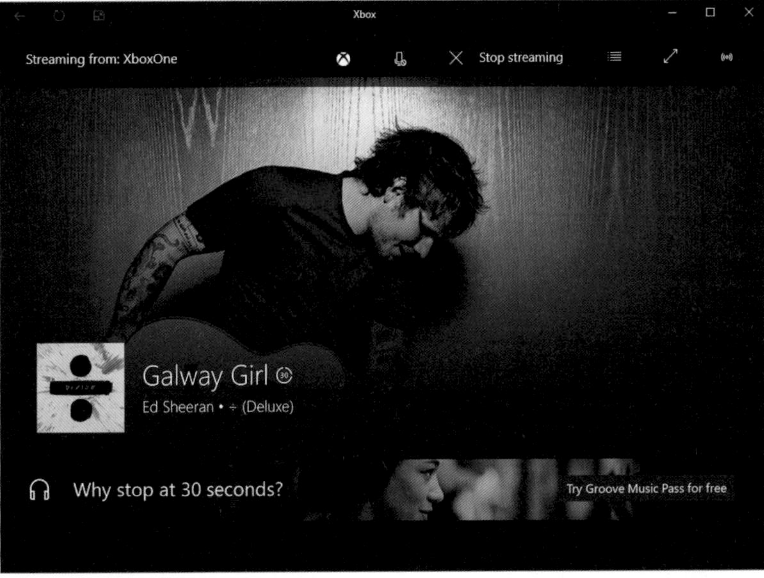

To use a wireless Xbox controller after using it on your PC you will have to re-sync the controller, using the console's sync button or a USB cable.

Recording

To record stuff on your computer, you need a working microphone and the Microsoft Voice Recorder app that is included with the Windows 10 operating system:

The Voice Recorder app is a new Universal Windows App in Windows 10.

1. Open the **Voice Recorder** app from the Start menu, then click its microphone icon to begin recording – this starts the timer

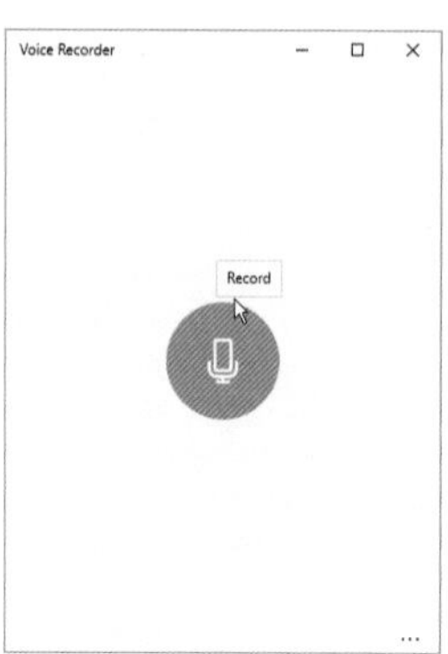

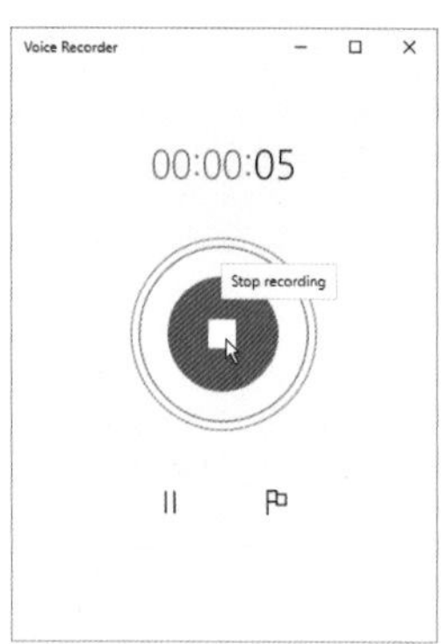

2. Click the icon again to stop recording – the recording is saved as a file in your **Documents**, **Sound recordings** folder and gets added to the Recording list in the app screen

3. Click an item in the **Recording** list to select it – the app screen changes to display the playback controls

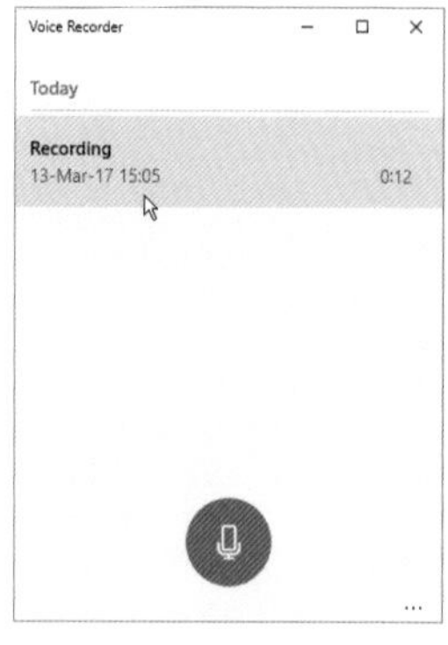

On the playback screen use the Share button to email your recording, or the Trim button to edit the recording length. You can use the Delete button to remove recordings, and the Rename button to give your recording a descriptive title.

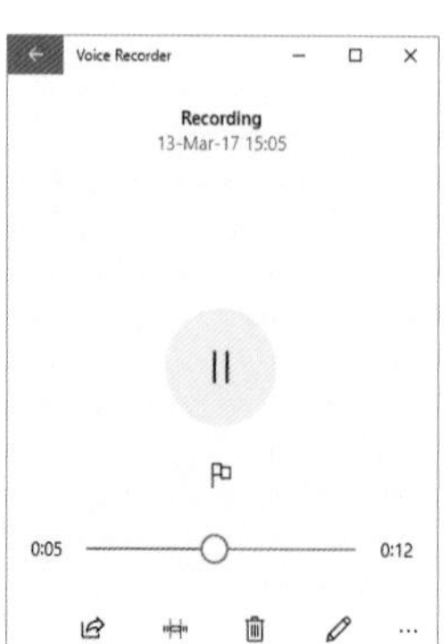

4. Click the || **Pause** button to halt the voice recording – the button changes to a > **Play** button so you can resume playback

17 Devices and printers

Learn how to manage your devices in Windows 10. You can add various types of printers and scanners to your PC, and Windows usually provides the drivers needed to manage the devices.

PC settings – devices

The Settings menu is new in Windows 10. Here, you change most of your PC's settings.

Windows has always provided a device management utility called Device Manager with which users can manage devices on their computer. The Windows 10 interface provides a simpler option to add and remove devices, troubleshoot device issues, and more:

1. Click the Start button, then select **Settings**
2. In the Settings window, choose **Devices**

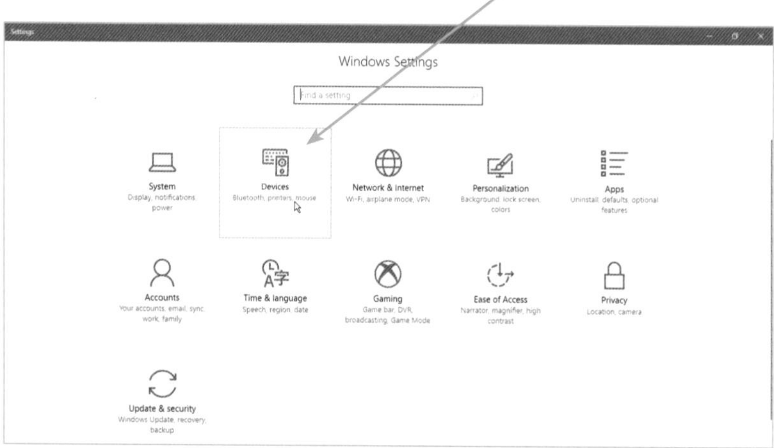

You can also manage your devices from the older Control Panel app – via Start, Windows System, Control Panel, **Devices and Printers**.

3. Now, choose **Bluetooth & other devices** and you will see a list of all the devices connected to your computer

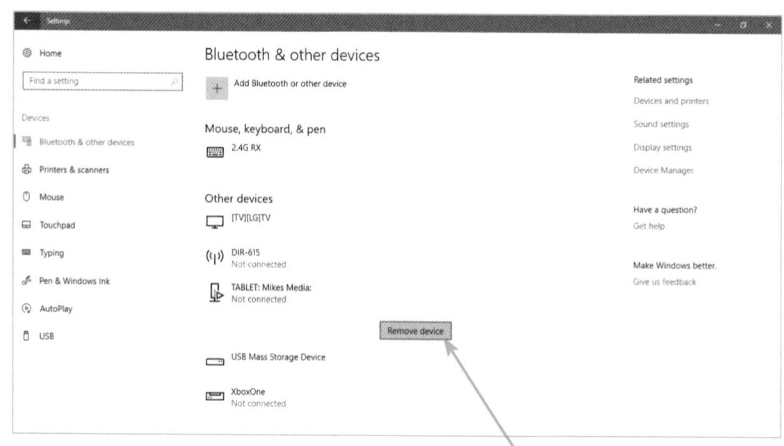

It is important to remove devices from your PC in the correct way. Simply disconnecting them can cause problems.

4. Clicking on a device reveals a **Remove device** option, which can be used to uninstall the device safely

Add a device

Modern hardware devices are very easy to install. Simply connect one to the computer and switch on. Windows will see the device as a new addition to the system, locate the drivers from its in-built driver database, and then install it automatically. If you experience any problems you can try to add the device manually:

1. Open **Bluetooth & other devices** as described on the previous page

2. Check if the device you are trying to install is listed under **Other devices**

3. If you don't see your device in the list, click **Add Bluetooth or other device** at the top of the screen

4. Select the category of device to seek from **Bluetooth**, **Wireless display or dock**, or **Everything else**

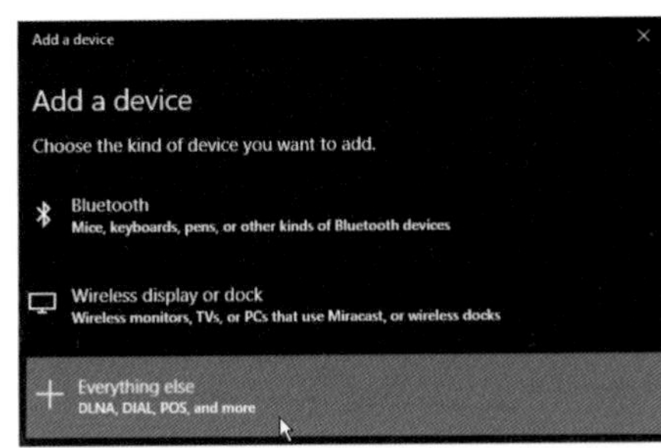

5. Select the item to add from the detected devices

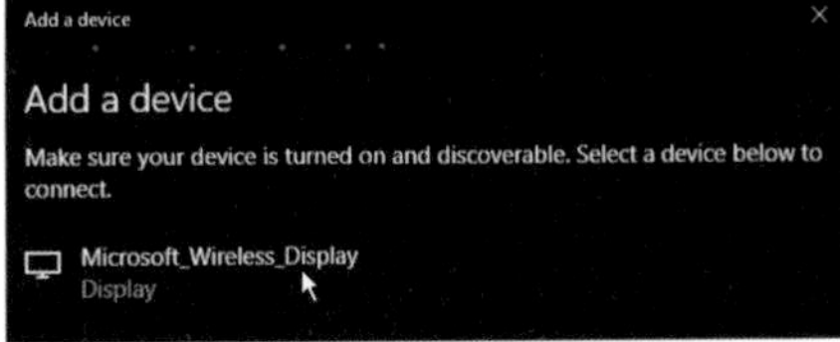

6. Windows 10 will now attempt to add the device by seeking a suitable device driver from those bundled with the operating system. If none are found locally, Windows will try to find a driver online if you are connected to the internet. If that fails too, you may have to visit the device maker's website and search for a suitable driver to install manually

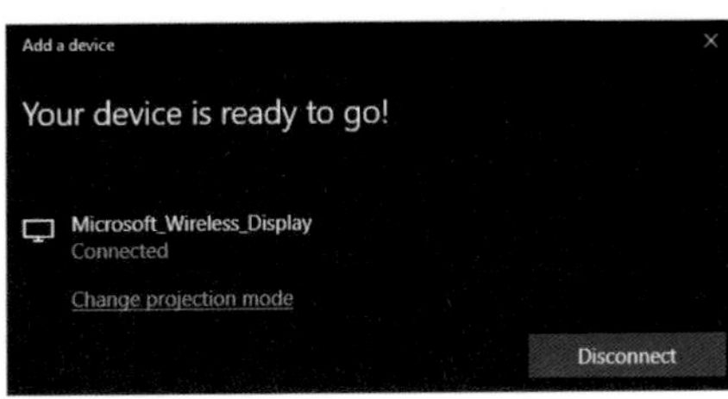

The most common reason for Windows not seeing a device is that it simply hasn't been switched on.

Microsoft's Wireless Display Adapter plugs into a Smart TV so you can broadcast your PC Desktop to the TV screen.

Control Panel devices

Device management can also be carried out via the Control Panel, if you prefer.

1. Go to Start, Windows System, Control Panel and click **Devices and Printers** to see all devices on your computer

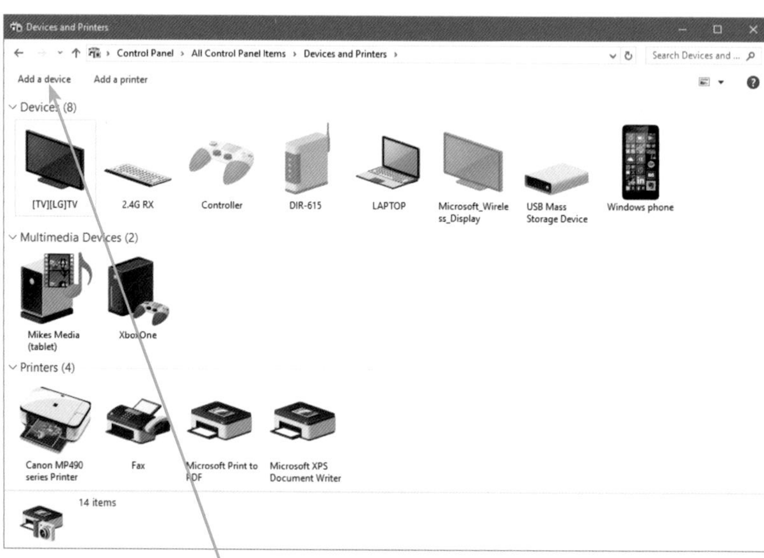

2. Click **Add a device** to install a new hardware device. If the device being added is a printer, click **Add a printer**

3. Left-click a device to see its Properties, or right-click a device to see a menu with options for that device

4. Here, we see right-click options for a printer. Other devices will have different options

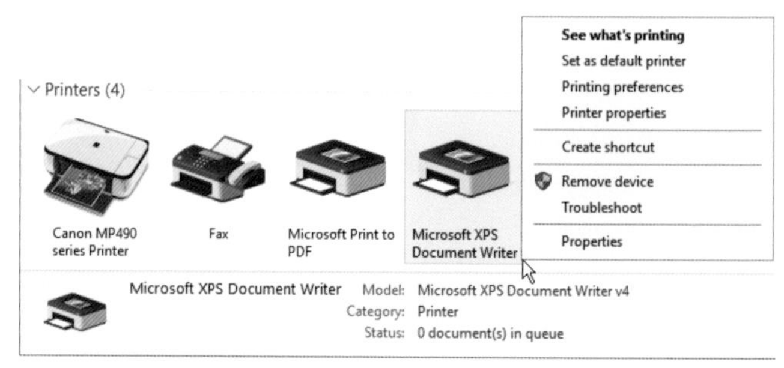

The Control Panel offers more management options.

Update device driver

To check the date for your printer driver:

1. Go to the Control Panel and open **Devices and Printers**. Right-click the printer and select **Properties**, **Hardware** tab, **Properties** and then the **Driver** tab

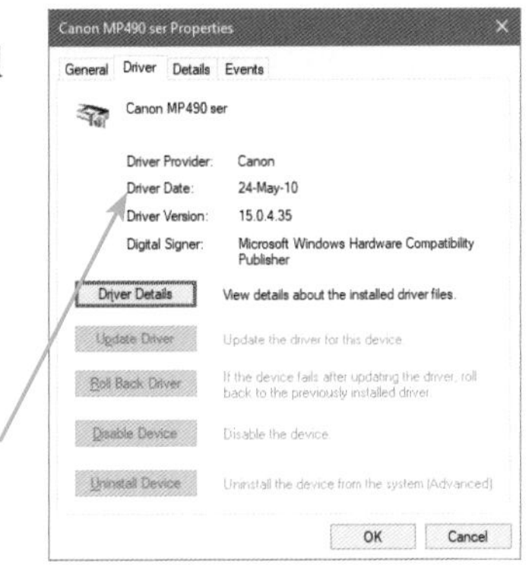

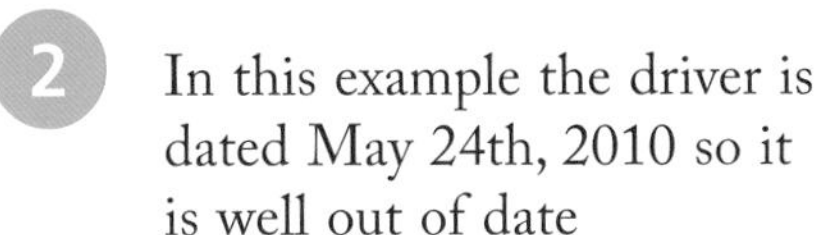

2. In this example the driver is dated May 24th, 2010 so it is well out of date

Normally, Windows will have an up-to-date driver for the printer, but this is not always the case, so if in doubt, check with the manufacturer.

3. To check for the latest driver, visit the manufacturer's website, e.g. go to **canon.com** then choose your region and select **Support**

4. Choose the device's model name and model number to look for an appropriate driver

5. If the results indicate that there is a more recent driver for this printer, click the **Download** button to grab the installer for that driver

Follow a similar process at the website for your printer's manufacturer. Search **Support** for possible updates to the driver.

6. When the download completes, run the installer and follow the Wizard's steps to update the device driver

Wireless printer

1 Go to Start, Windows System, Control Panel and click **Devices and Printers**, then click **Add a Printer**

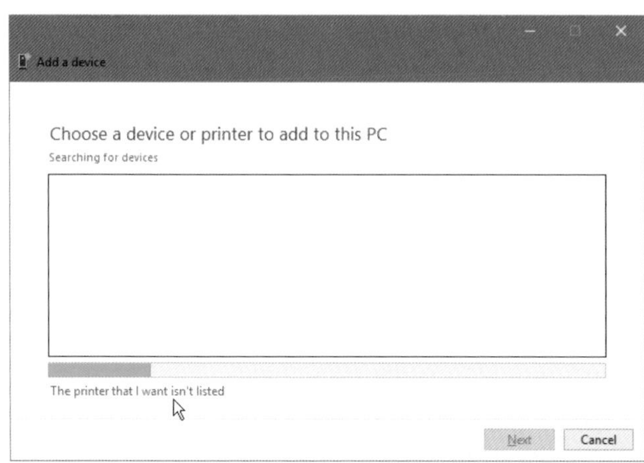

2 Windows will attempt to find your networked printer. If it does, select it and click **Next** to install it. If it doesn't, however, you will see a blank dialog box. In this case, click **The printer that I want isn't listed**

If you have a wireless printer set up on your network, you can add it to your Windows 10 computer.

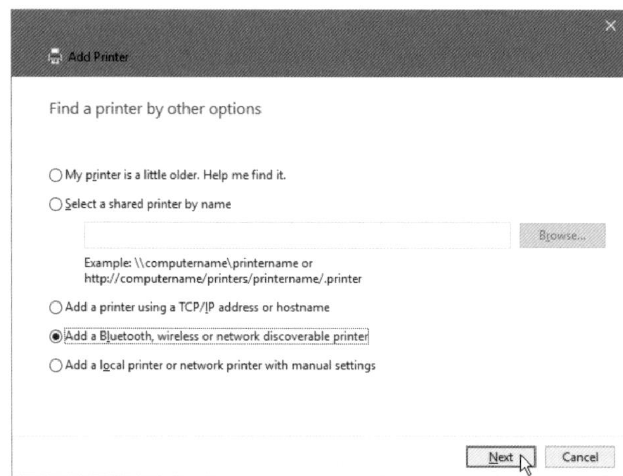

3 Select **Add a Bluetooth, wireless or network discoverable printer** and click **Next**

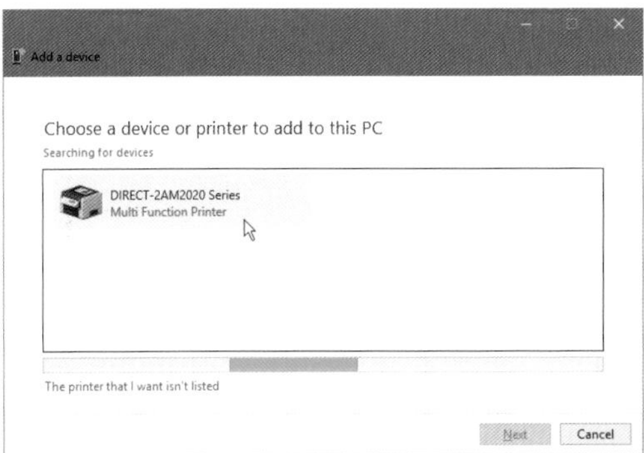

4. This time, Windows should find the printer. Select it and click **Next** to install the printer

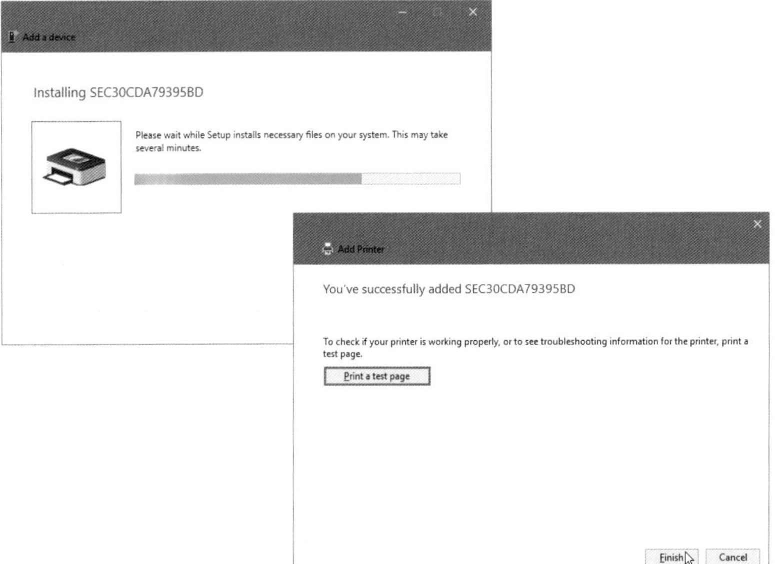

5. Click **Finish** to see it added to the printers on your PC

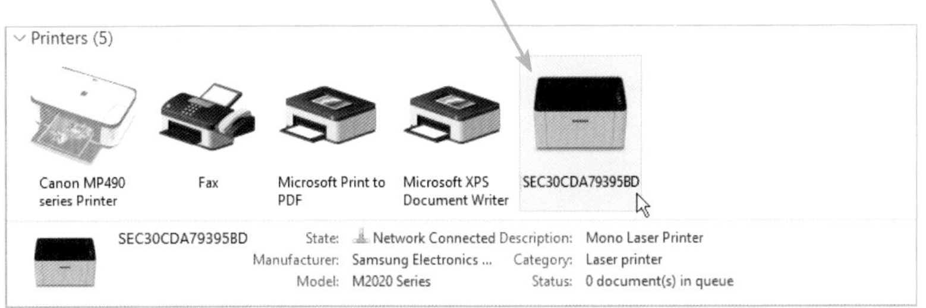

You may also be prompted to enter a PIN code to configure WPS (Wi-Fi Protected Setup). Refer to your printer manual on how to find the WPS PIN code for your wireless printer.

Adding a new printer often results in a change to the default printer, so you need to check this and ensure the right printer is specified.

Virtual printers

You may have some items in **Devices and Printers** that are not physical devices but are software programs that act as virtual printers. To see how these could be used:

Fax

Microsoft Print to PDF

Microsoft XPS Document Writer

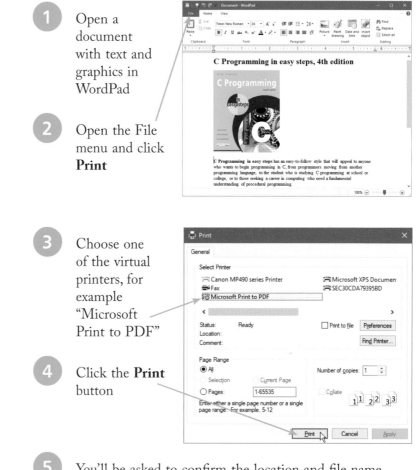

1. Open a document with text and graphics in WordPad

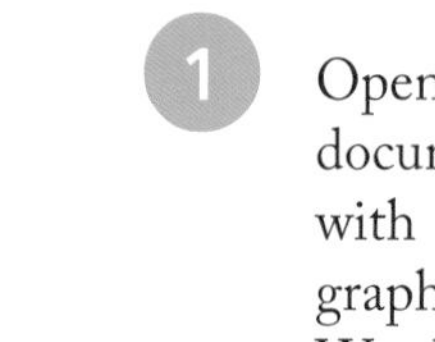

2. Open the File menu and click **Print**

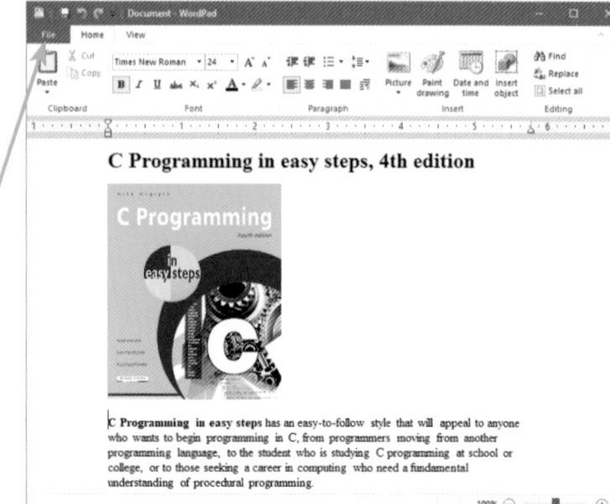

3. Choose one of the virtual printers, for example "Microsoft Print to PDF"

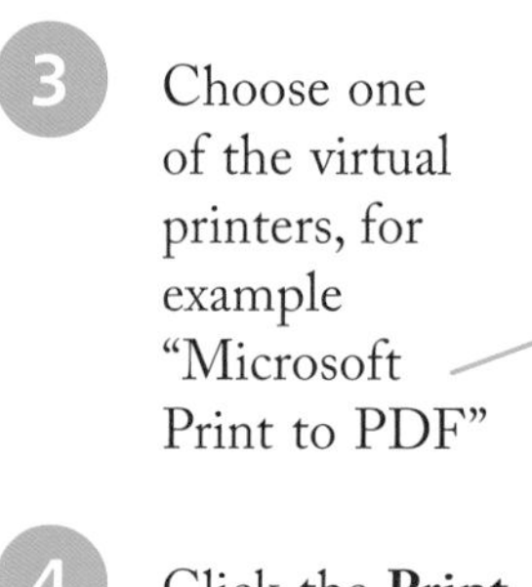

4. Click the **Print** button

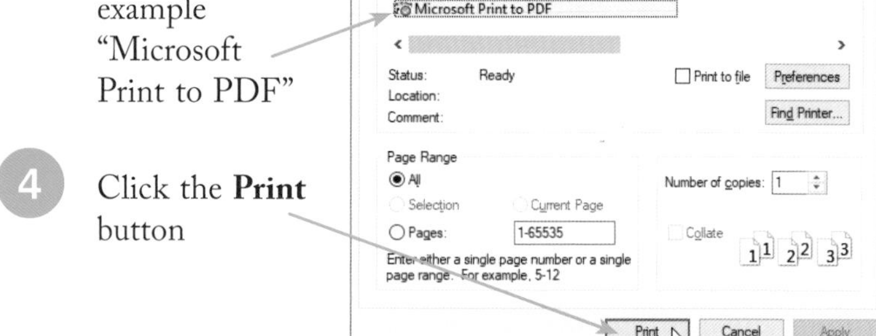

5. You'll be asked to confirm the location and file name, then click Save, and a PDF version of the document is saved

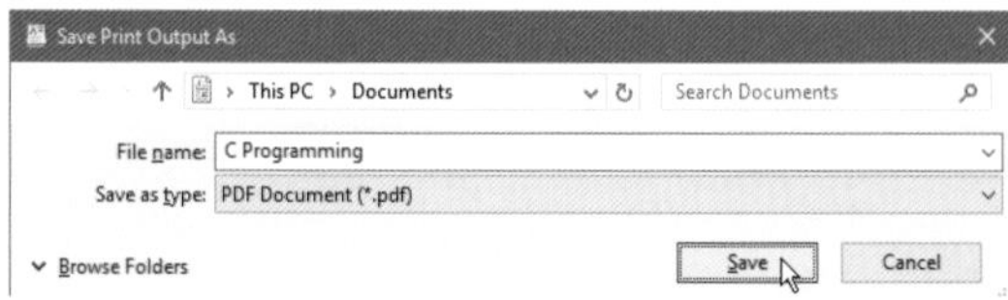

Don't forget

WordPad is chosen here since it supports text and graphics, but you could use almost any Windows program that prints.

Alternatively:

1. Select **Microsoft XPS Document Writer** as the printer
2. Provide a name, and save in Open XPS document format

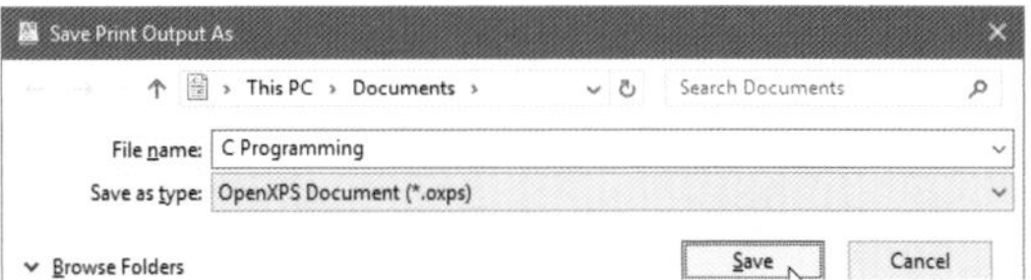

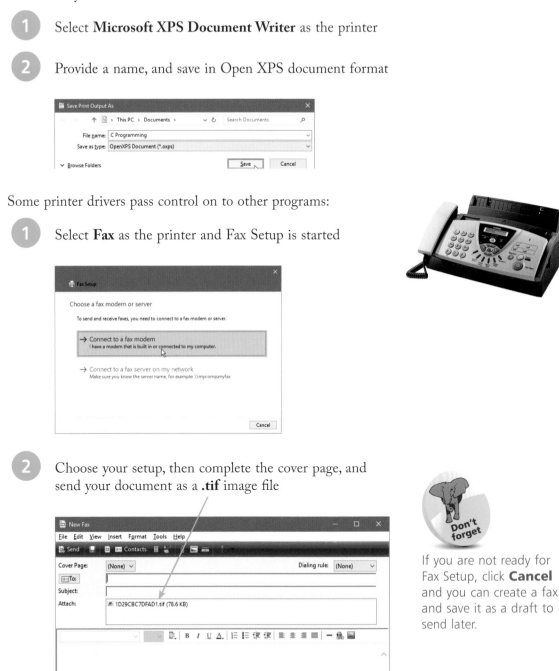

Some printer drivers pass control on to other programs:

1. Select **Fax** as the printer and Fax Setup is started

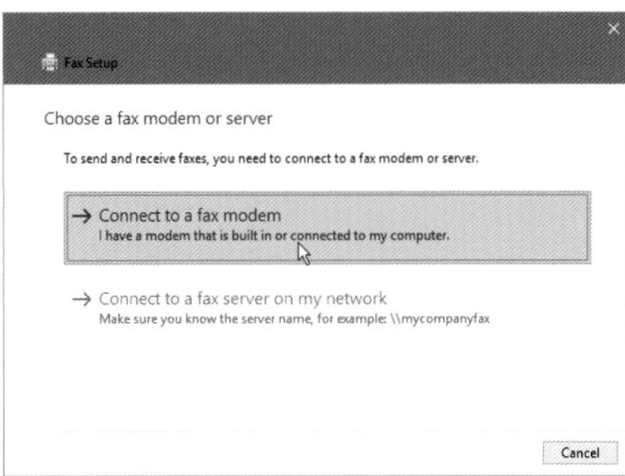

2. Choose your setup, then complete the cover page, and send your document as a **.tif** image file

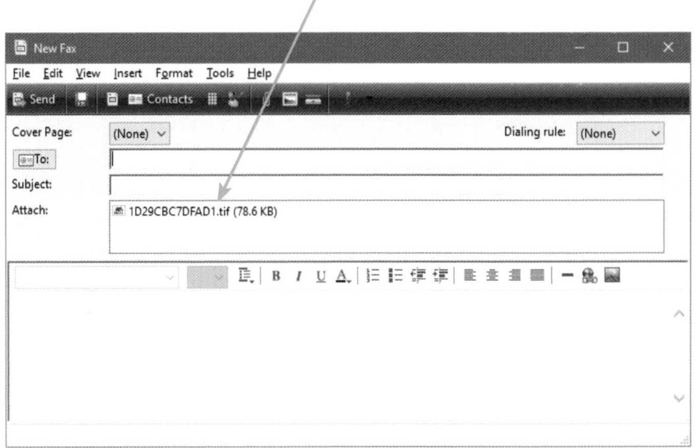

If you are not ready for Fax Setup, click **Cancel** and you can create a fax and save it as a draft to send later.

Generic/text only printer

To create a generic/text only printer:

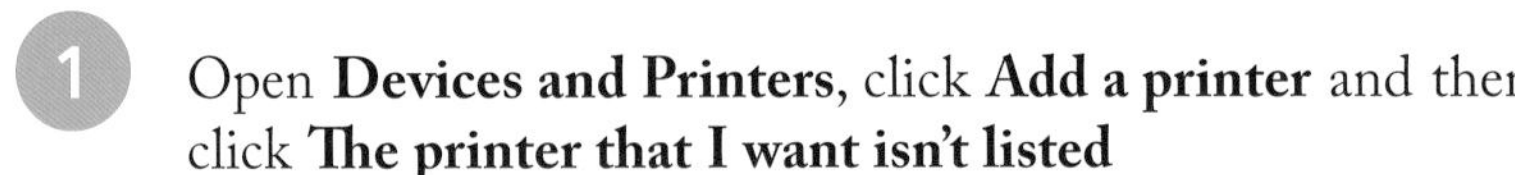

1. Open **Devices and Printers**, click **Add a printer** and then click **The printer that I want isn't listed**

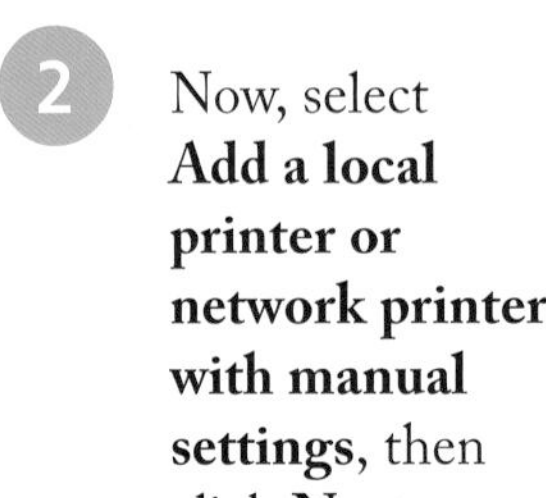

2. Now, select **Add a local printer or network printer with manual settings**, then click **Next**

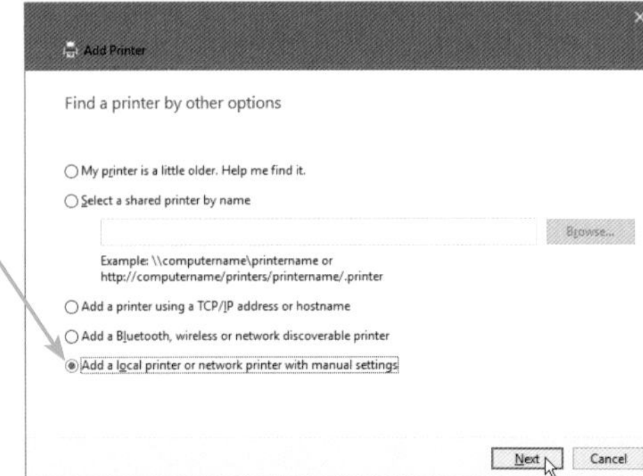

Don't forget

You can install a generic/text only printer driver in Windows 10 as a way to capture text information in a file, or for use with an application that requires this type of printer driver.

3. Select **Use an existing port** and choose the drop-down menu option of **FILE: (Print to File)**, then click **Next**

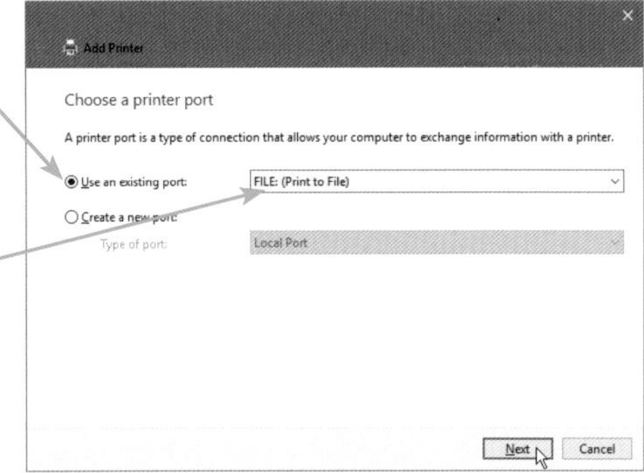

Hot tip

If you are creating support for an old printer, you'd choose the port it uses, **COM1** for example.

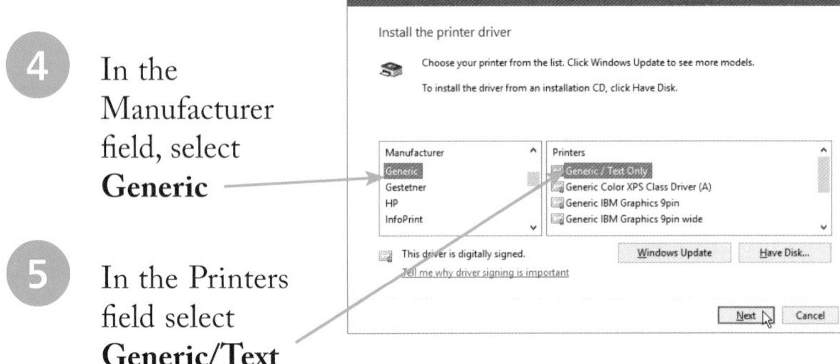

4. In the Manufacturer field, select **Generic**

5. In the Printers field select **Generic/Text Only**, then click **Next**

6. Accept or amend the suggested name, then click **Next**

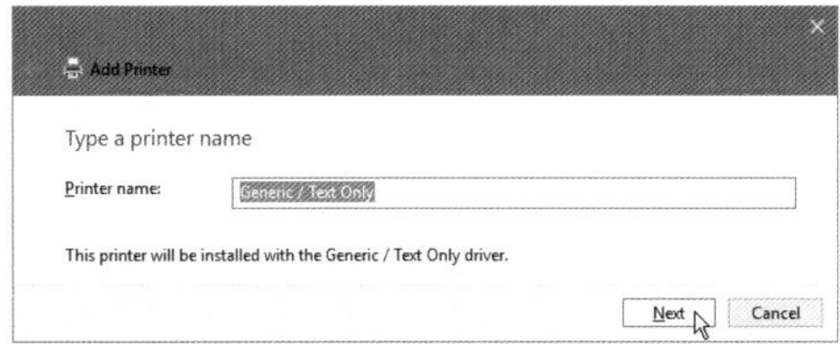

7. Select **Do not share this printer**, then click **Next**

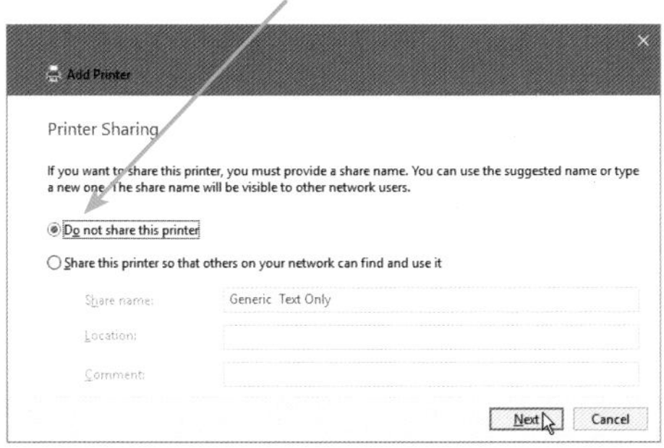

8. Finally, click **Finish** to see the printer is added to the list of Printers in **Devices and Printers**

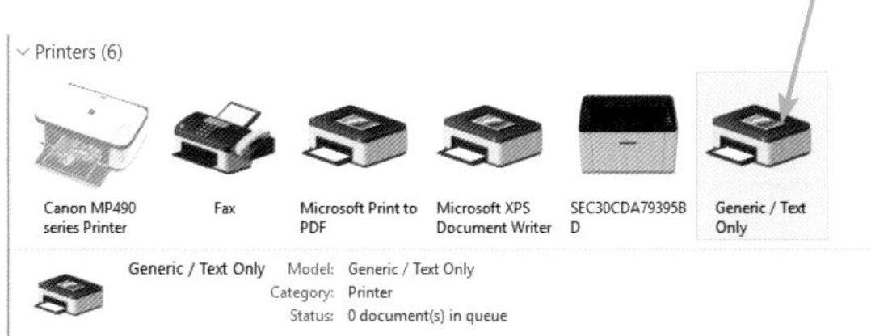

Since this printer creates files on your system, it is best to avoid making it shareable.

To check out the operation of this printer:

1. Create a simple plain text document using Notepad

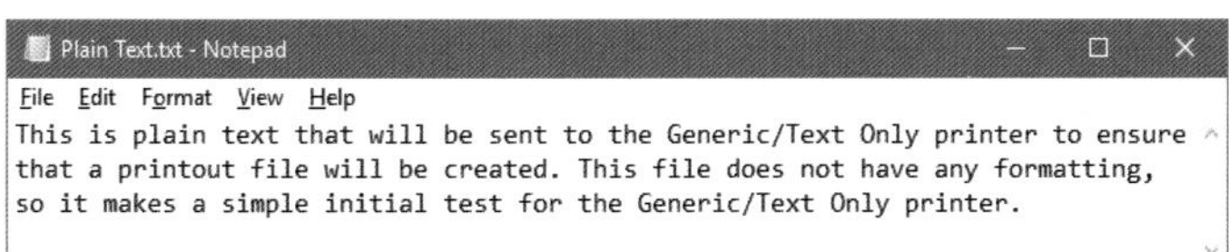

2. Select **File**, **Print** and choose the **Generic/Text Only** printer

3. Provide the file name (type **.prn**) and click **OK**

When you print from a formatted source, the graphics and formatting will be stripped out. You may find the resulting text disorganized, as a default line of 80 characters is assumed.

Add a scanner

You can install a scanner to the **Devices and Printers** folder.

1. To install a USB-connected scanner such as the Canon CanoScan, insert the USB cable and switch on

2. If the driver is available, the scanner will be installed. If the driver is missing, an **Action Center** error message may be displayed, helping you to download the driver

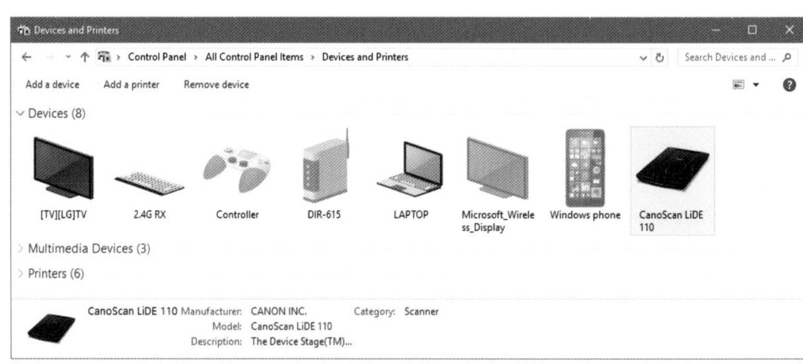

Windows 10 will have the drivers for many scanners, but may not include older devices.

To test the operation of this scanner:

1. Right-click on the scanner in **Devices and Printers**, then choose **Scan Properties** to open the Properties dialog

2. Select the **General** tab, then click the **Test Scanner** button

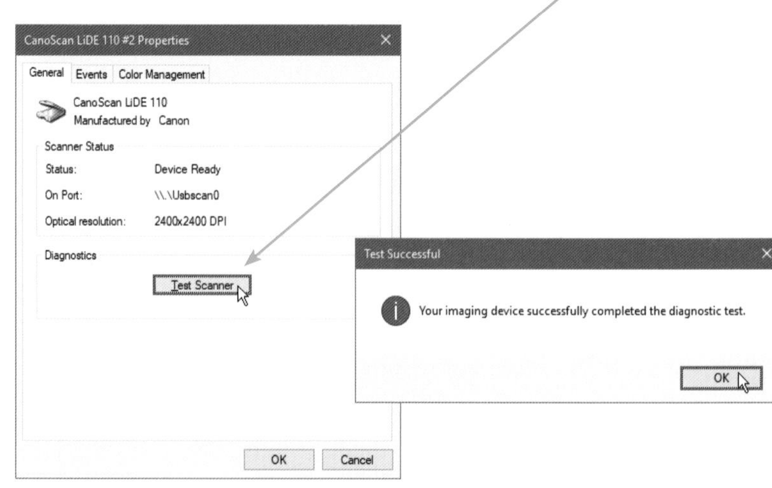

Windows checks its compatibility database and identifies where to find the missing driver.

Using the scanner

There are several ways to access images from your scanner, such as with the traditional **Windows Fax and Scan** program. Microsoft also provides a new easy-to-use free app called "Scan".

The **Scan** app is a new Universal Windows App, listed in the Store as "Windows Scan".

1. Connect your scanner and insert an item to be scanned
2. Go to the Store and install the free Windows **Scan** app
3. Launch the **Scan** app, then click the **Show more** link to see scanning options

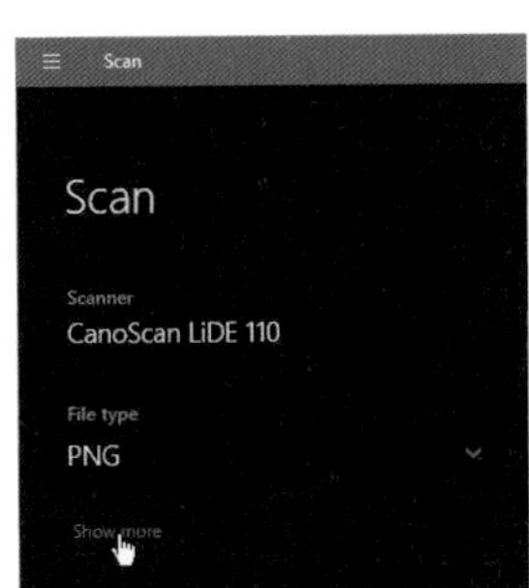

4. Choose your preferences for file type, etc. then click the **Preview** button to see how your item looks in the scanner
5. Drag the handles in the **Scan** window to fit your item
6. Click the **Scan** button to save the image as a file of your specified type, color mode, resolution, and location

The **Scan** app saves the image files with the name set to the date they were scanned.

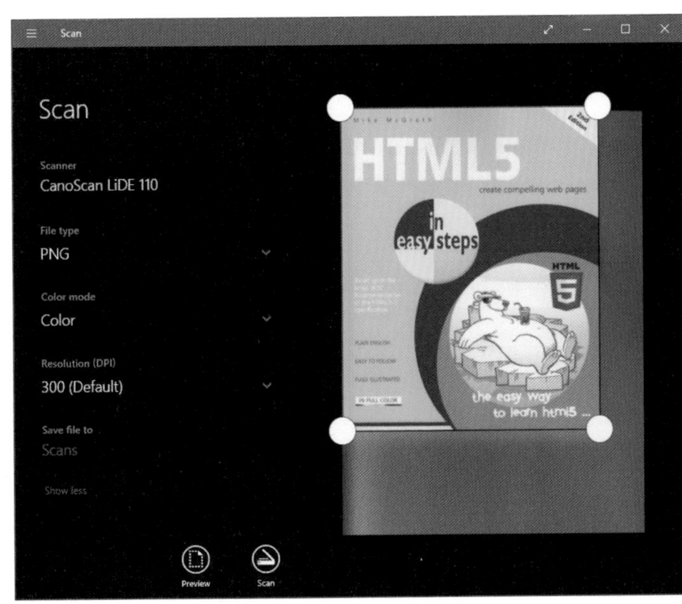

...cont'd

Image editing programs, such as Paint, provide the ability to import an image directly into the program for manipulation.

1. Connect your scanner and insert an item to be scanned
2. Go to the Start menu and launch the **Paint** program

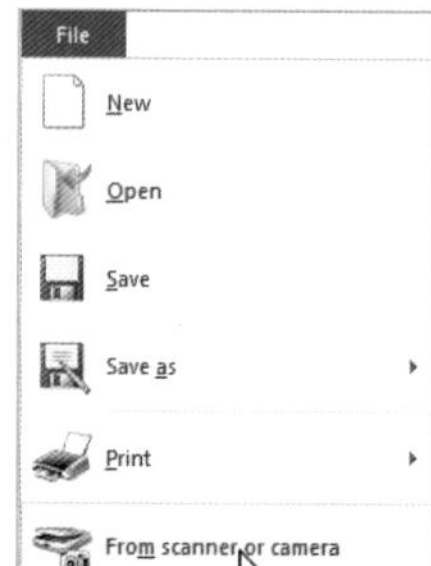

3. Click **File**, **From scanner or camera**, to open the scanner dialog box
4. Choose your option preferences

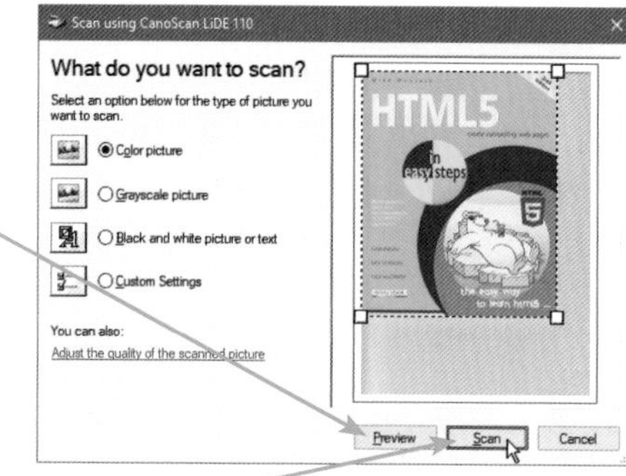

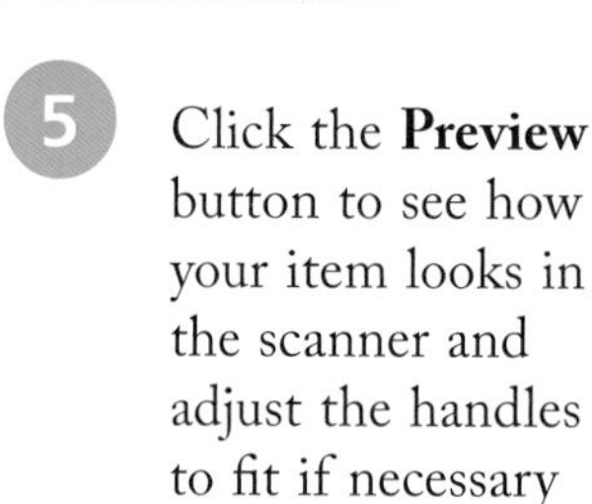

5. Click the **Preview** button to see how your item looks in the scanner and adjust the handles to fit if necessary
6. Click the **Scan** button to import the image into Paint, where you can modify it and save it as an image file

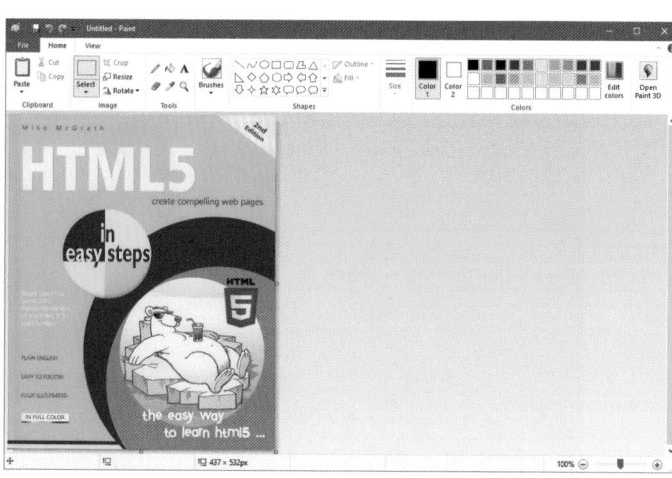

Hot tip

Some scanners are supplied with OCR (optical character recognition) software that can read text from a scanned document and save it as a text file.

Don't forget

The physical size of the imported image is large for high quality resolution – it is shown here reduced to 40%.

Add Bluetooth

You can connect to an external device that supports Bluetooth wireless technology, such as a Beats Pill speaker, using a Bluetooth USB dongle and the Control Panel in Windows 10:

1. Insert a Bluetooth dongle into a USB socket on your PC

2. Switch on your Bluetooth device and activate it to make it discoverable

3. Open the Control Panel and select **Devices and Printers** then choose to **Add a device** to have Windows 10 look for devices

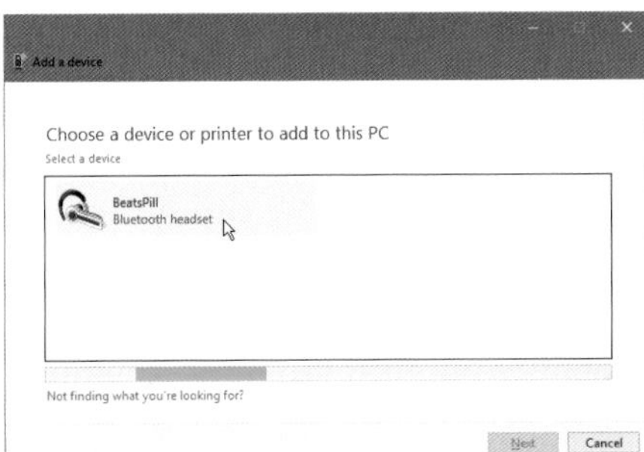

4. When Windows finds your Bluetooth device, click **Next** to install the drivers for your device

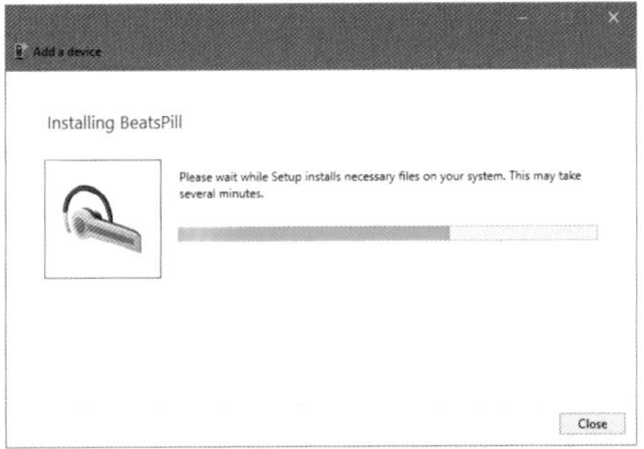

5. Now, in **Devices and Printers** you see that your Bluetooth device is now connected and ready to use

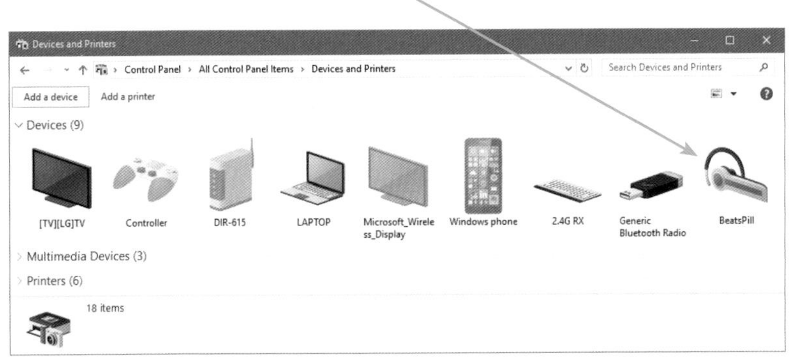

After installing the drivers you can control the connection using the Bluetooth tile that appears in the Action Center when you insert the Bluetooth dongle.

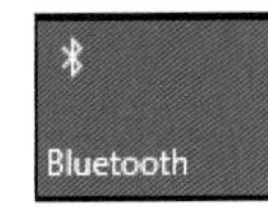

Add a storage device

Adding a storage device to a Windows 10 computer couldn't be easier – Windows does the hardware configuration for you. In this example we are adding a 2.5" External Hard Disk Drive to the system. As with most current devices, the drive uses a USB connection. If your device uses USB 3.0, connect it to a USB 3.0 socket (if available) rather than USB 2.0. (USB 3.0 is much faster than USB 2.0 so the drive will perform much better.)

You can run a USB 3.0 device from a USB 2.0 socket but it will not operate at its maximum performance level.

1. Connect the device to a USB socket, then switch on the drive if required

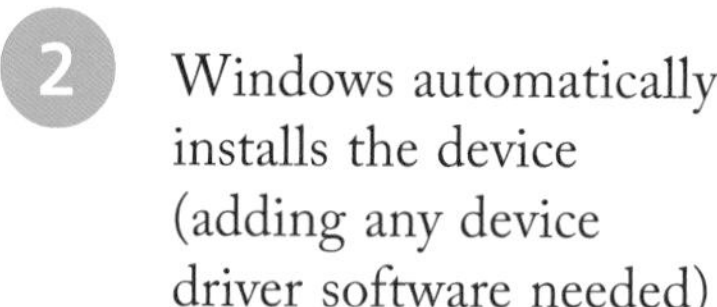

2. Windows automatically installs the device (adding any device driver software needed)

3. Go to **Devices and Printers** to see the device is added

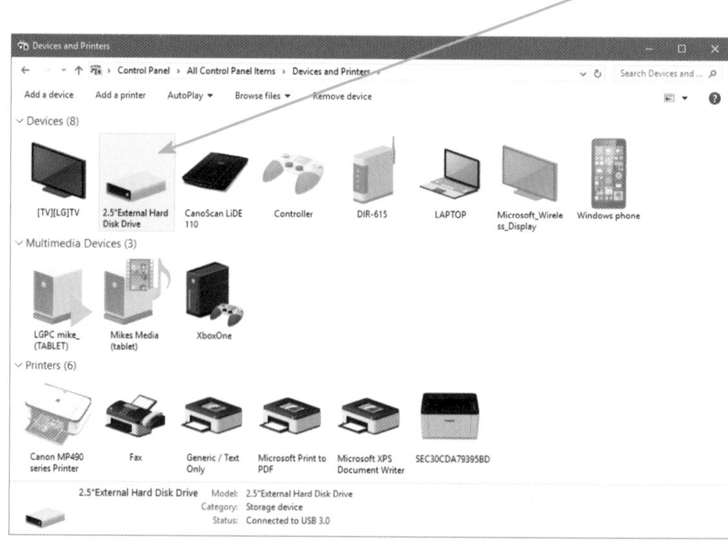

If you are unsure which of your USB sockets are USB 3.0, look for any that are colored blue – these are USB 3.0; USB 2.0 are black.

18 Networking Windows

If you have more than one computer, even just a laptop and a desktop machine, you can connect them with cables or wirelessly, and share information between them. Windows 10 makes it easy to set up and manage the network you create.

Create a network

A network consists of several devices that exchange information over cables or Wi-Fi. A computer and an internet router form a small network. If you have other computers, they can be added to share the internet connection and perhaps share data information with each other, creating a larger network. In order to connect to the network, each computer requires an Ethernet (wired) network adapter and cable, or a wireless network adapter. The flow of data between the computers and the router is managed by Windows.

Most routers will offer both wired and wireless connections, as well as internet access, or you may have individual devices for each of these functions.

To start a new network using a wired network adapter:

1. Install a network adapter in the computer (if required)

2. Start (or restart) the computer, and on the Start menu click **Settings** and then the **Network & Internet** icon

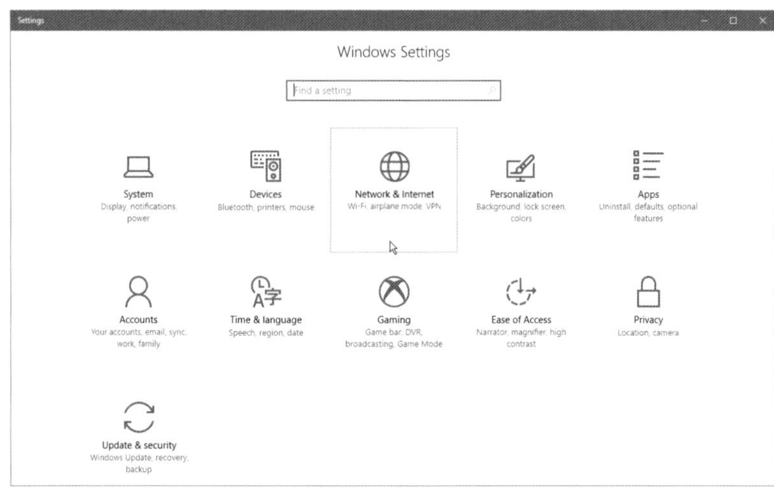

There is no built-in option to create an ad hoc network in Windows 10 but you may find third-party tools online for creating ad hoc networks, if you need to do this.

3. Click on the **Ethernet** item in the left-hand pane to see wired connections

Ethernet
Not connected

4. Now, connect the adapter to the router using a network cable (Ethernet cable)

5. Windows will then automatically detect and identify the new network

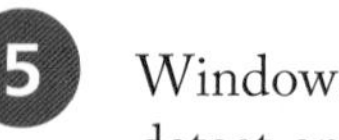

6. To discover the status of your network, click on the **Status** item in the left-hand pane, then choose **Sharing options**

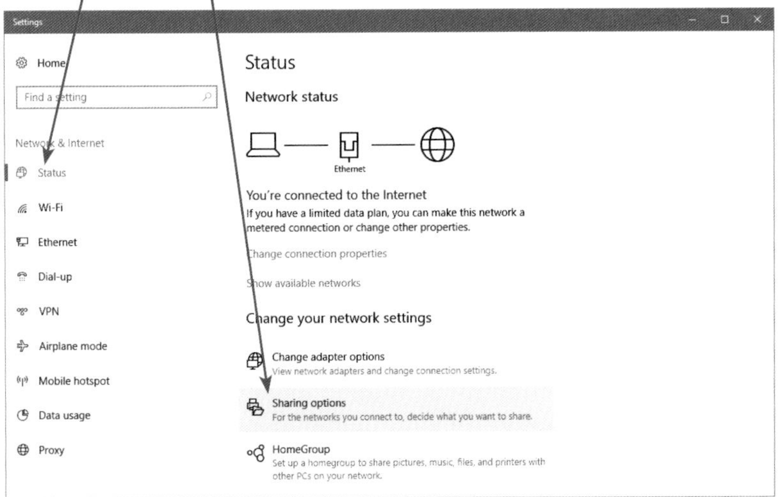

The settings formerly known as network location (Private/Public or Home/Work/Domain) are now called **Sharing options**. You can turn these settings on or off as required.

7. For your Private profile, choose to **Turn on network discovery** to see other devices on the network – and to allow this device to be seen by them

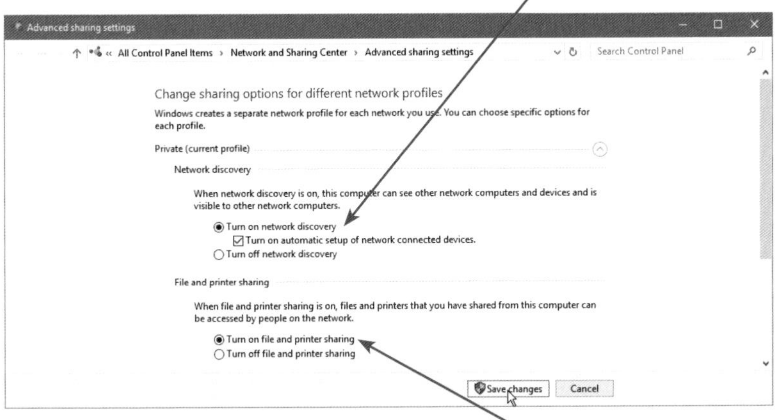

Sharing options automatically set the appropriate firewall and security settings for the network that you are connected to.

8. For your Private profile, also choose to **Turn on file and printer sharing** to allow other devices on the network access to files and printers that share from this device

9. Click the **Save changes** button to apply your choices

Network classification

Two main types of network are possible in Windows 10 – Public and Private. If you are going to get involved in networking, it is important to understand the differences between them.

Network Location Awareness allows programs that use network connections to apply different behaviors based on how the computer connects to the network. In conjunction with Windows Firewall with advanced security, you can configure specific firewall rules that apply only when connected to a specific network type. By default, the first time you connect to any network, the network is designated as Public unless you assign it to another category.

Public

A public network is one that is directly connected to the internet. Typical examples include your computer, and airport, coffee shop, and library wireless networks. Because they use public internet Protocol (IP) addresses, devices on these networks are visible to other devices on the same network, and also on other networks.

This has advantages and disadvantages. The main advantage is that their "openness" allows data to be freely and easily shared between connected devices. This is the basis of the internet. The disadvantage is that the lack of security makes it very easy for these networks to be hacked.

Private

Private networks tend to be smaller and much more exclusive. Examples are home networks and corporate intranets. Because members of these types of network are usually known to each other, and often are not connected to the internet, security is much less of an issue.

The most common use of private networks is in the home, since most Internet Service Providers (ISPs) only allocate a single IP address to each residential customer. In homes that need to have several computers connected to the internet, the answer is to network them so they can all share a single internet connection.

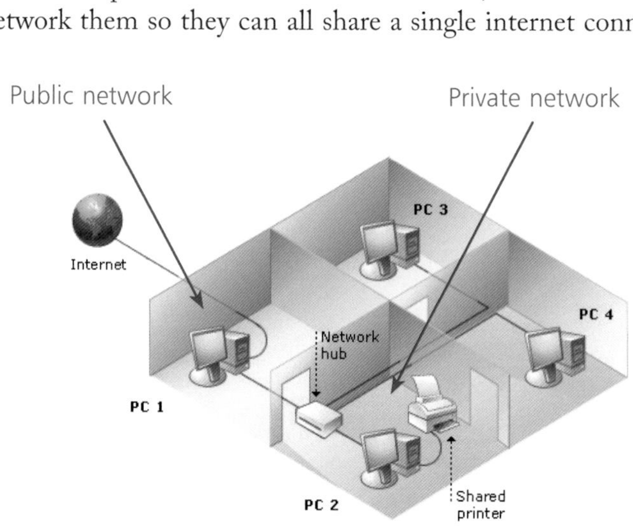

Create a HomeGroup

1. Go to Start, Settings, Network & Internet, Status, then click on the **HomeGroup** item

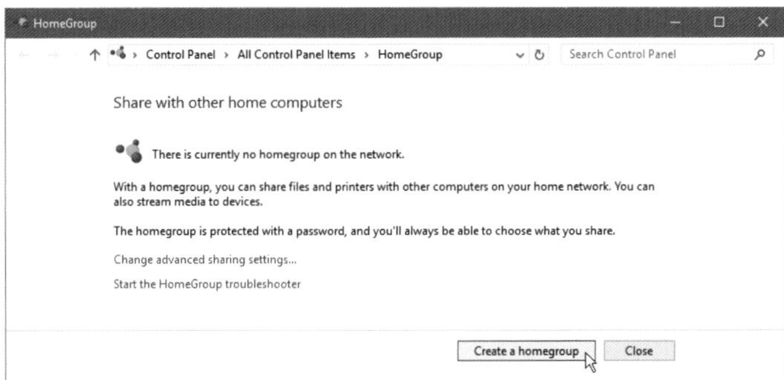

When there is already a HomeGroup on the network, you will be invited to join.

2. Click **Create a homegroup** and in the next window, click **Next**. You'll then see the window below, from where you can choose what to share on the network

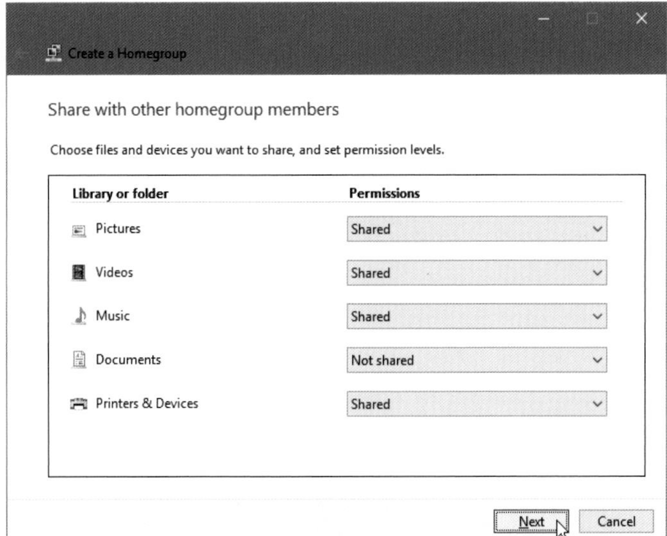

You can view or change the password from the **Network and Sharing Center** or from the Control Panel.

3. You will now see a screen that provides the password needed for other computers to join the HomeGroup

4. Record the password and click **Finish**. A HomeGroup has been created

Join the HomeGroup

When you connect to a Home network which already has a HomeGroup, you are invited to join.

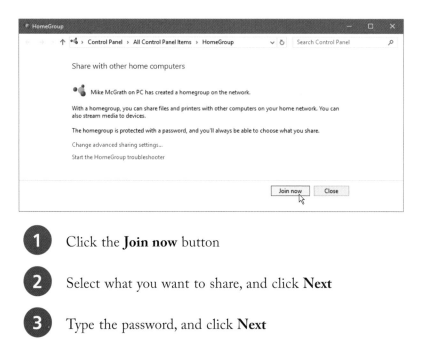

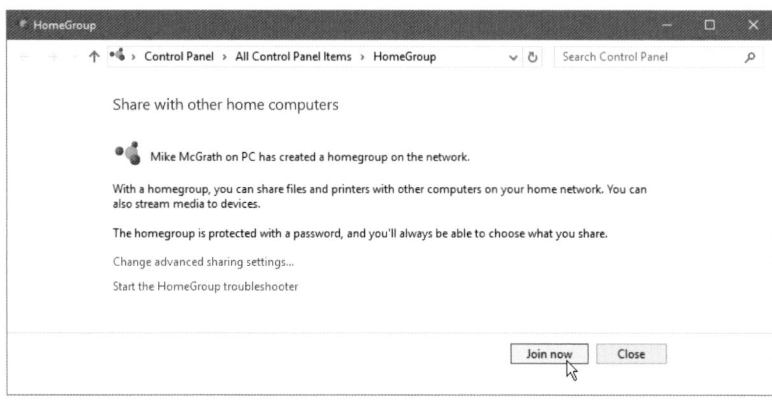

1. Click the **Join now** button
2. Select what you want to share, and click **Next**
3. Type the password, and click **Next**

4. You have joined the HomeGroup

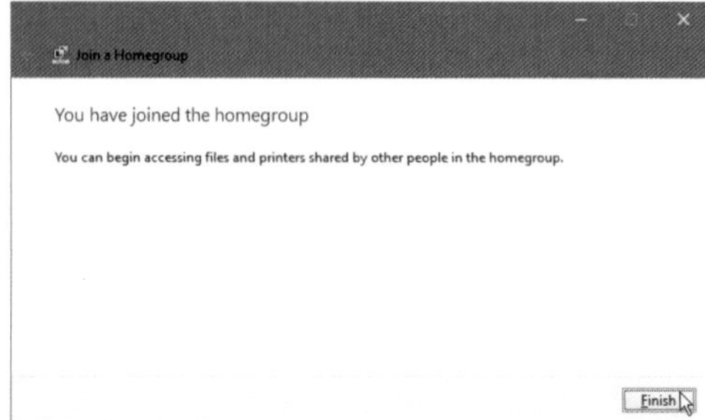

You will only be invited to join the HomeGroup if you specify your network location as **Home** when you connect to the network.

If the HomeGroup was created by another user on the network, you must be given the password to join.

Everyone on the network who joins the HomeGroup will be able to share everything that they make available.

Network settings

Settings related to networking can also be found via the Network icon in the System Tray.

1. Place the cursor over the Network icon to see the network name and status

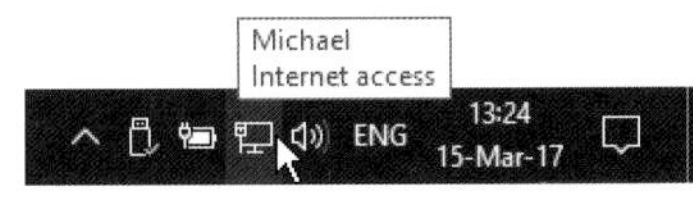

2. Click the Network icon to see connection details. In this example, the network connection is by Ethernet cable, but there is also a Wi-Fi connection available

3. Next, click the **Airplane mode** button to disable all wireless communication, and see that connection become unavailable

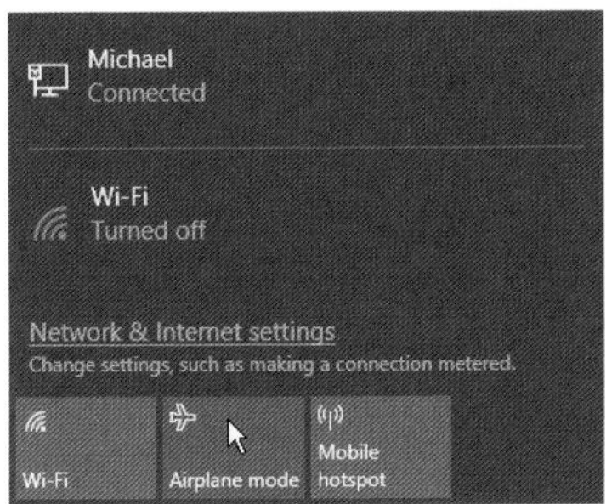

4. Click the **Airplane mode** button again to enable wireless communication once more

5. Now, click the **Wi-Fi** button to disable Wi-Fi connectivity

6. Click the **Wi-Fi** button again to enable Wi-Fi connectivity once more, and choose how you wish to re-connect

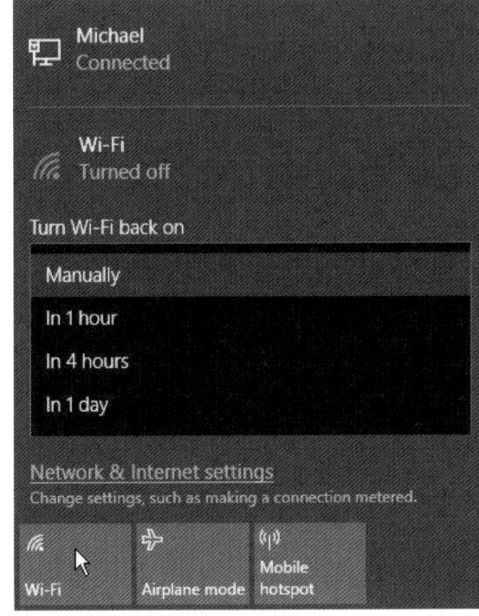

The button color indicates the active state.

Click on the **Network & Internet settings** link in this panel to open the Settings window for the current connection.

The ability to configure Wi-Fi to automatically turn on after a chosen interval is a new feature introduced in the Windows 10 Creators Update.

Connect to a wireless network

1. Go to Start, Settings, Network & Internet, then click on the **Wi-Fi** item in the left-hand pane

2. Slide the Wi-Fi toggle button to the **On** position, then click the **Show available networks** option to see available wireless networks

3. To connect whenever the network is in range, check the **Connect automatically** box, then click **Connect**

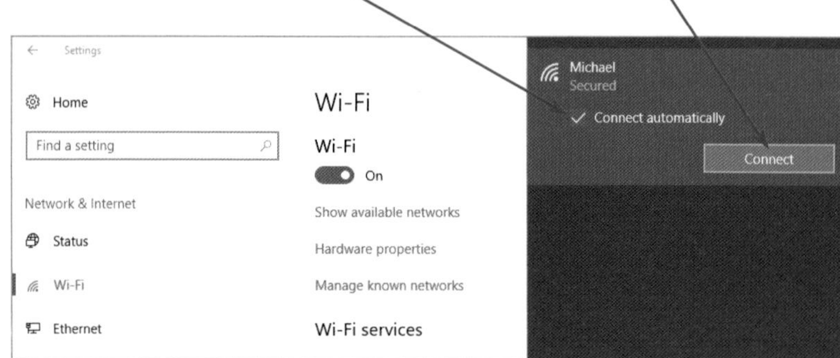

4. Enter the security key when prompted, then click **Next** to continue

5. Windows validates the security key then connects to the network and confirms you now have a connection

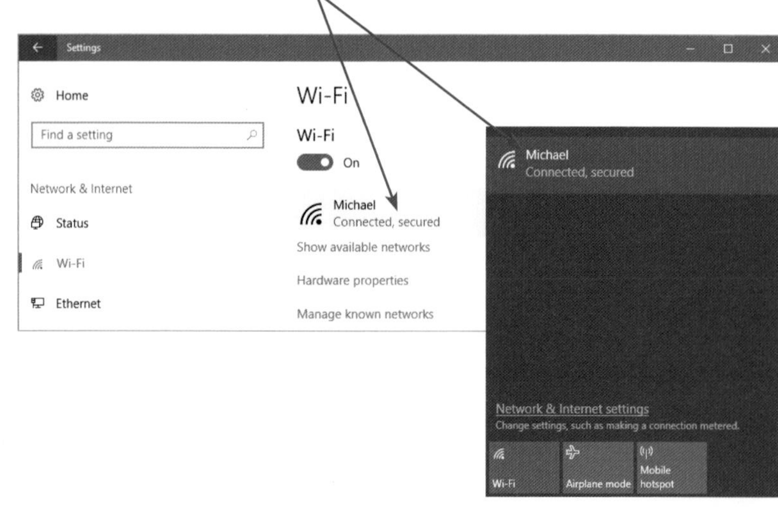

If you have a netbook or laptop PC, and your router supports wireless access, you can connect to a wireless network.

You can temporarily disconnect then re-connect to the wireless network by clicking the **Wi-Fi** tile or **Airplane mode** in the Action Center.

6. Go back to Start, Settings, Network & Internet, Wi-Fi, then click **Network and Sharing Center** in the far right-hand pane

7. Network information for the PC's networks is displayed

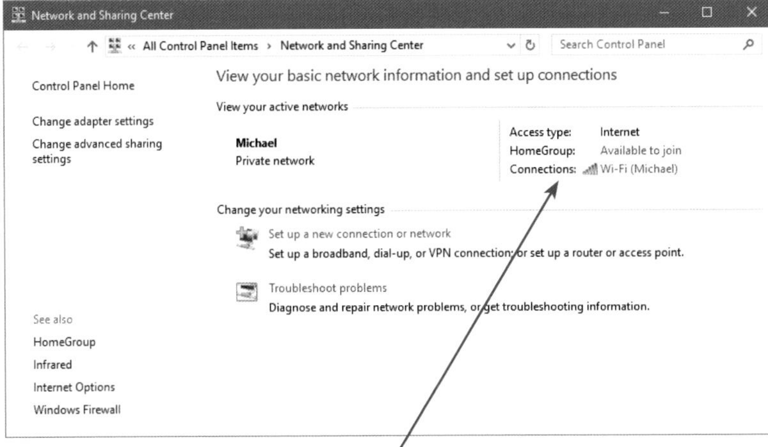

8. Click the Wi-Fi connection to display the status of the wireless network

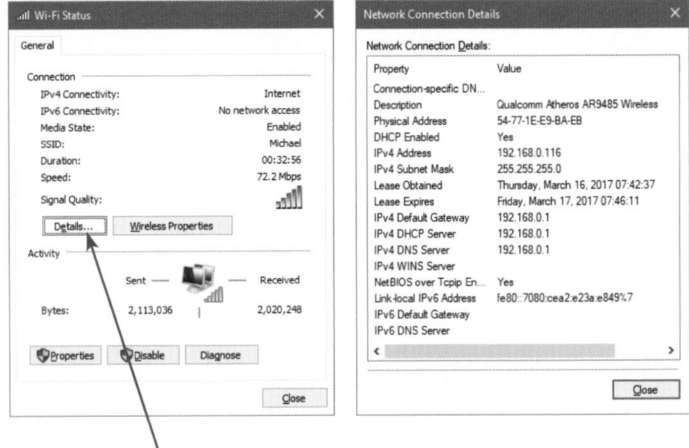

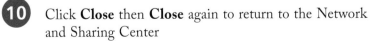

9. Click the **Details...** button for the wireless network connection details

10. Click **Close** then **Close** again to return to the Network and Sharing Center

Notice the useful link here to **Troubleshoot problems** that will perform connection diagnostics if you have network problems.

View network devices

Many networks contain a lot of devices, and keeping track of them all can be somewhat tricky. To assist with this, Windows provides a location that lets you view all the devices on your network.

Open any File Explorer window and select **Network** at the bottom of the Navigation pane to see network devices

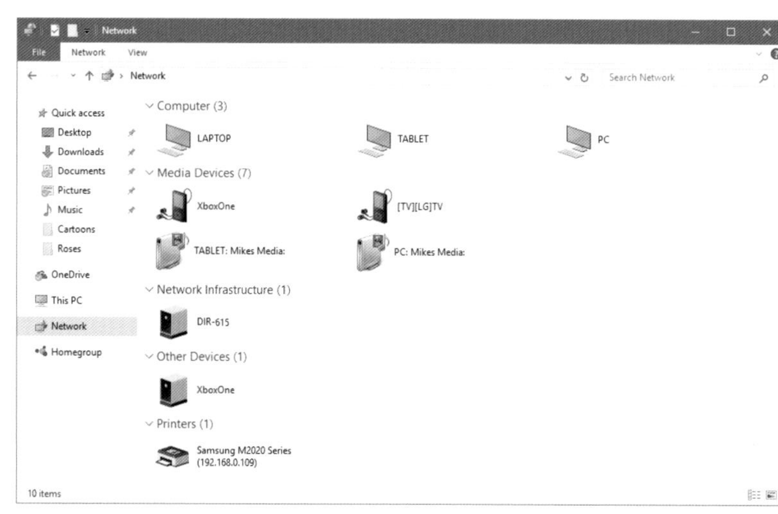

The Network dialog box can also be opened by searching for "View network computers and devices" from the Taskbar Search box.

In the network shown above, at the top are the three networked computers. Click on any of these and you see all the files on the respective computers that have been designated for sharing. Below that are media devices, a wireless router, a game console, and a printer. Right-clicking on the various devices reveals related options:

- **Computer** – provides a **Pin to Start** option to pin it to the Start menu for quick access.
- **Media Devices** – provides an **Open Media Player** option to select and play content if an item displays a media indicator.
- **Network Infrastructure** – provides a **View device webpage** option to open the router's configuration web page.
- **Printer** – provides a **View device webpage** option to open the printer's configuration web page.

If you need to know exactly what devices are on your network, Network is the place to find out.

At the very top of the window, you can open the ribbon toolbar to see further network-related options.

View the HomeGroup

Another way of seeing what is being shared on the network is by viewing the networked computers in the HomeGroup.

1. Open any File Explorer window and select **Homegroup** on the Navigation pane

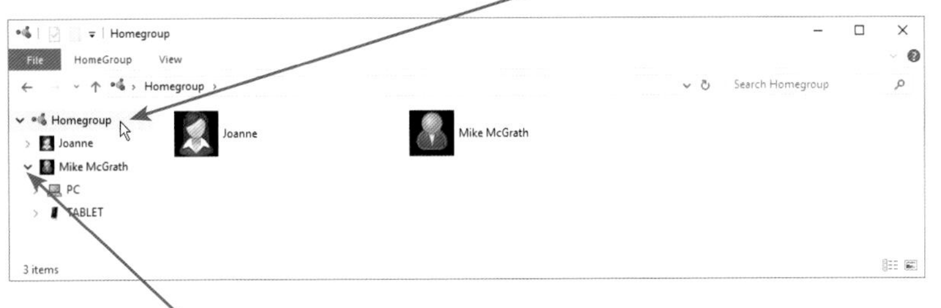

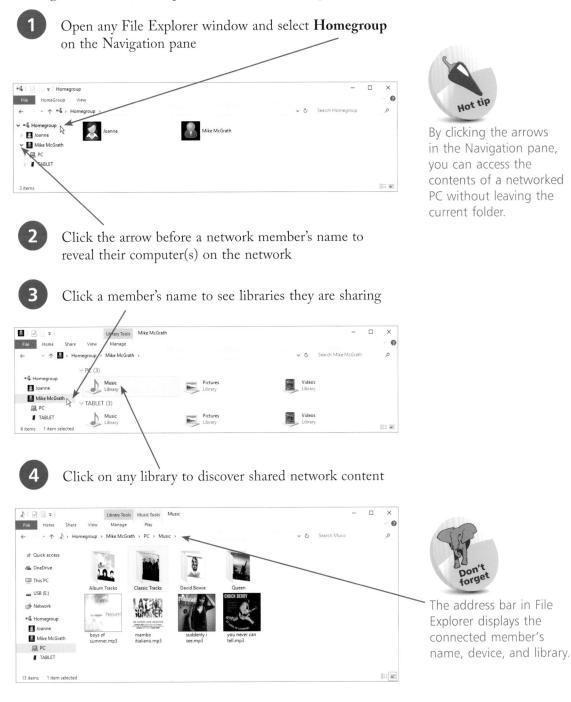

By clicking the arrows in the Navigation pane, you can access the contents of a networked PC without leaving the current folder.

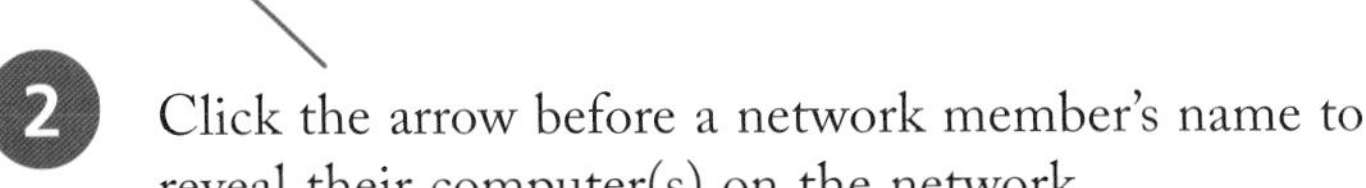

2. Click the arrow before a network member's name to reveal their computer(s) on the network

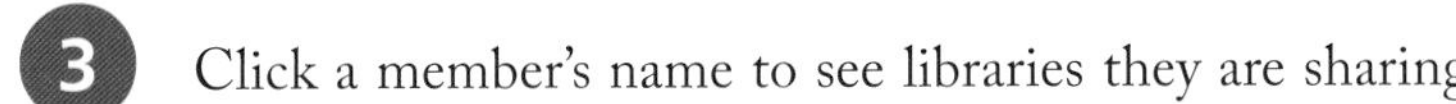

3. Click a member's name to see libraries they are sharing

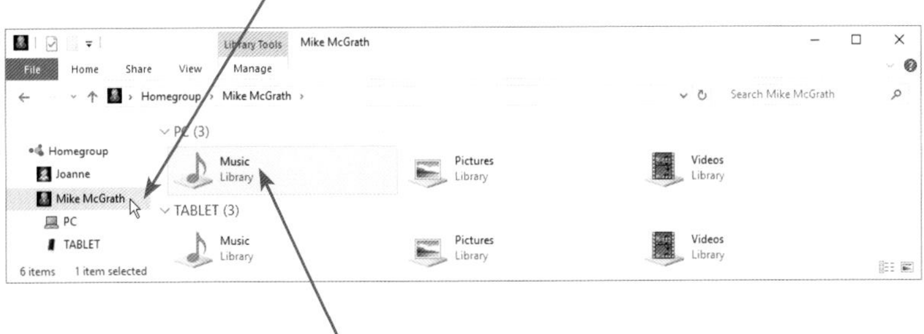

4. Click on any library to discover shared network content

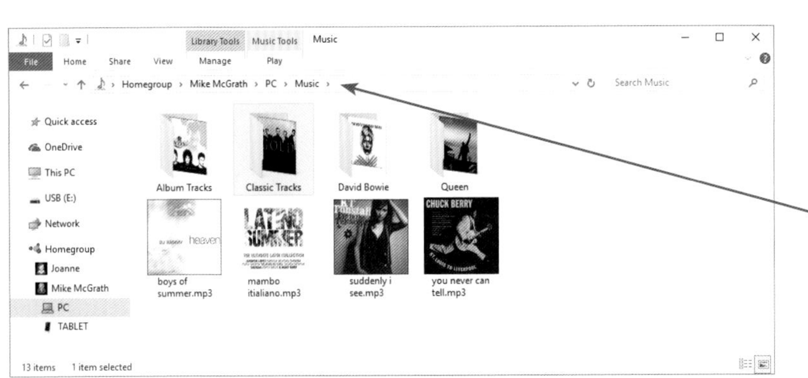

The address bar in File Explorer displays the connected member's name, device, and library.

Network and Sharing Center

Select the Network location, in this case Private network, if you need to switch to an alternative network location.

1. Right-click the **Network** icon in the Notification area and click **Open Network and Sharing Center**

Troubleshoot problems
Open Network and Sharing Center

2. Your basic network information is displayed

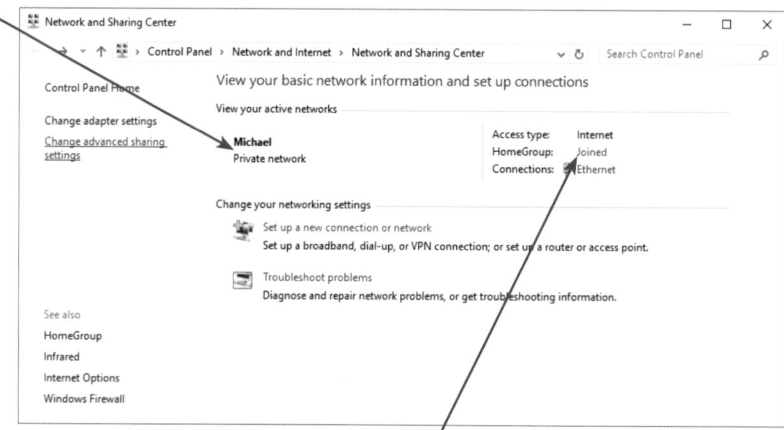

3. Click the HomeGroup **Joined** connection status link to see the libraries and devices you are sharing with the HomeGroup network

Select **View or print the homegroup password** if you need a reminder or if you want to share it with another user on the network.

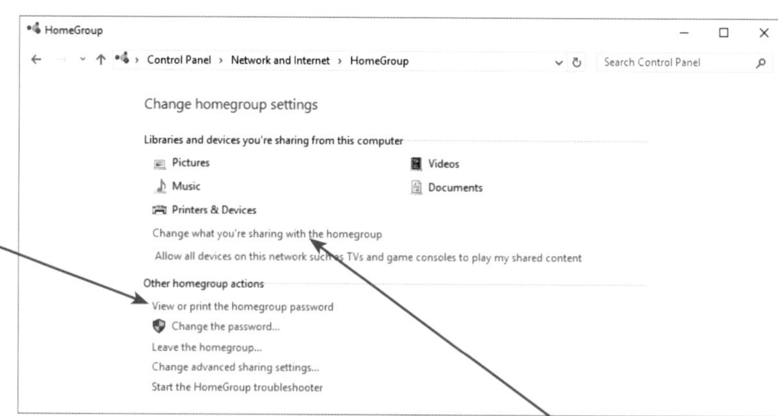

4. Select **Change what you're sharing with the homegroup** if you want to edit the list of shared libraries

5. For detailed information, click the **Ethernet** link

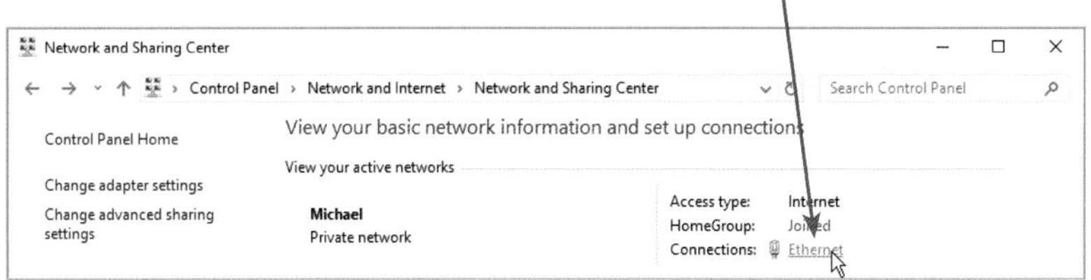

6. The connection status is displayed. Click the **Details...** button for Network Connection Details, including addresses

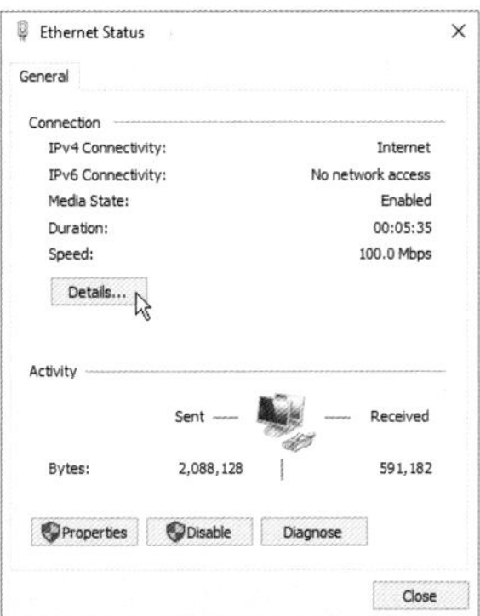

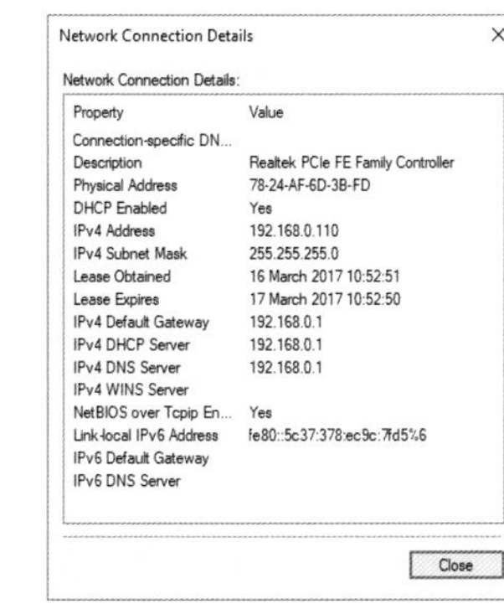

The **Status** dialog shows the adapter speed and the amount of data transfer activity. The **Details** dialog shows the addresses for the adapter and router components.

7. Click **Close** to return to the Center then click **Change adapter settings**, on the left-hand menu

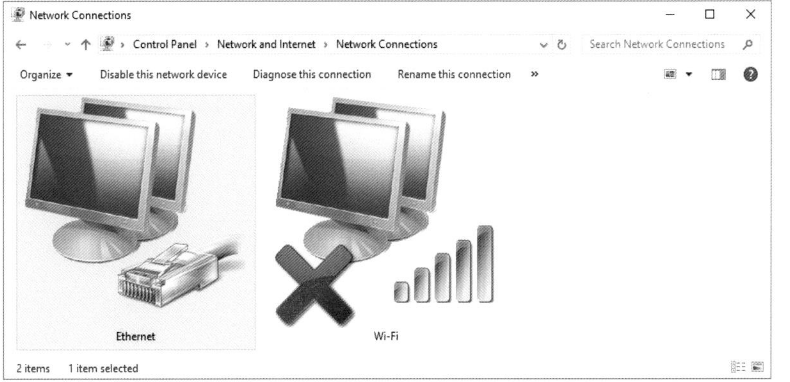

You can also view the local area connection properties from the **Status** dialog.

8. Click the toolbar buttons, or right-click the adapter icon to select one of the options or to view the properties

PC settings

HomeGroup and network sharing options are available from the Windows 10 **Settings** interface:

1. Launch **Settings** from the Start menu then choose the **Network & Internet** icon and select **HomeGroup**

2. Here, you can view or change the HomeGroup password, choose to leave the HomeGroup, or change sharing settings within the HomeGroup

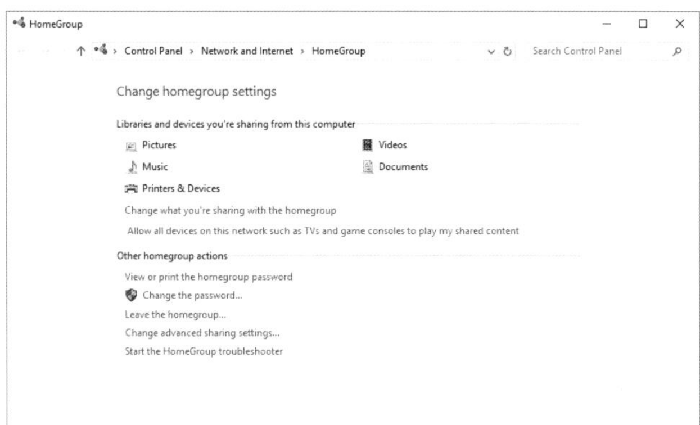

If someone wants to join the network they will need its password.

3. Click the link to **Change what you're sharing with the homegroup**

4. Sharing can be turned on and off for Pictures, Videos, Music, Documents, and Printers & Devices. To do this, just click the drop-down boxes

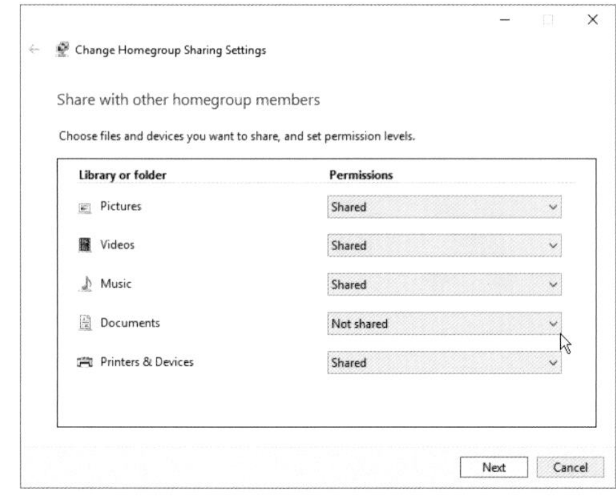

If you are not part of the network you will not see these options but simply be invited to join.

Monitor network

Windows provides several tools to monitor the activities on your network.

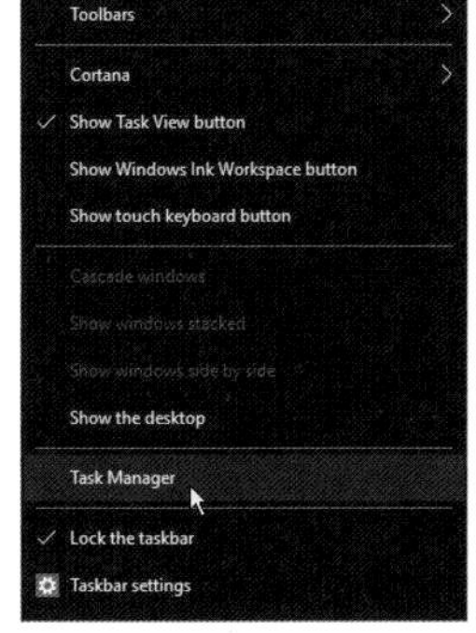

1. Right-click on the Taskbar and select **Task Manager**

2. Select the **More details**, **Performance** tab to see activity charts for the network adapter or adapters (wireless and wired)

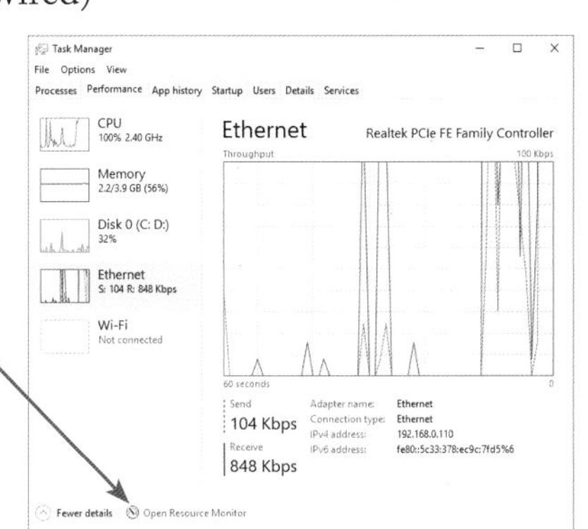

3. At the bottom of the window, click **Open Resource Monitor**

4. Comprehensive tables and charts are displayed, giving a real-time view of all networking activity

Network monitors can help you identify the causes of unexpected or excessive network activity on your system.

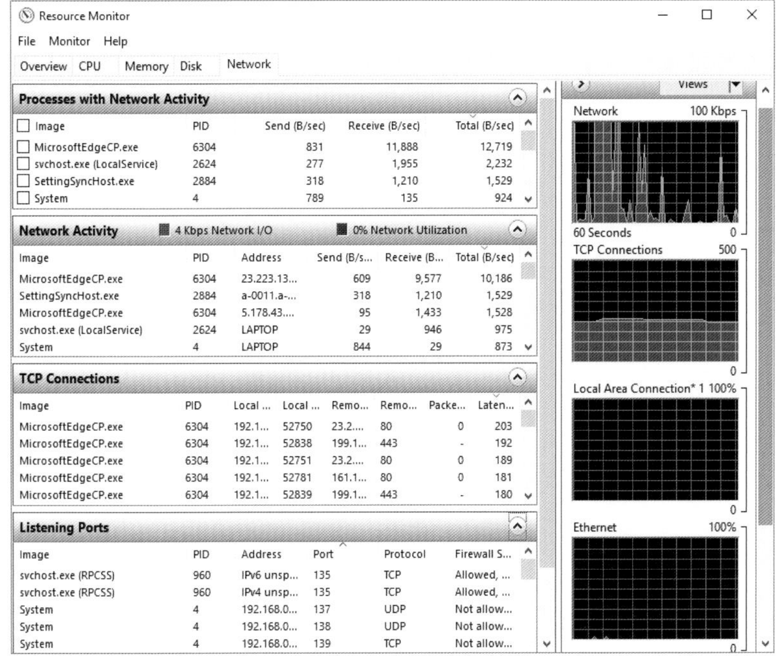

Sharing folders

If you want to share a file or folder that is not in a library, or if you want to share with computers running other operating systems, you need the File Sharing Wizard.

1. Open **File Explorer** and locate the folder or file you would like to share

2. On the ribbon toolbar, click the **Share** tab and select **Specific people...**

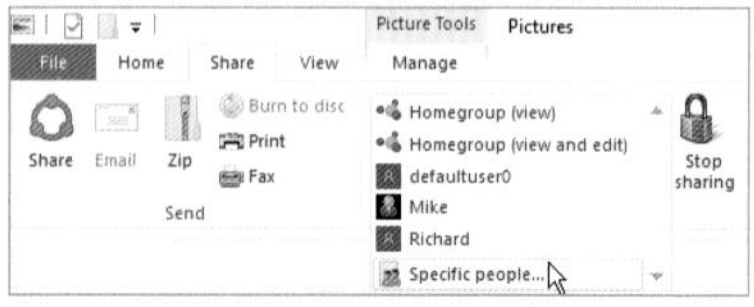

3. Choose a member name from the drop-down list, then click **Add** to include that user

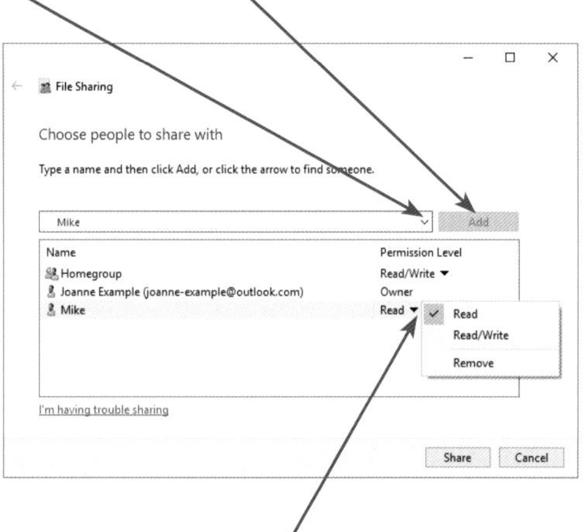

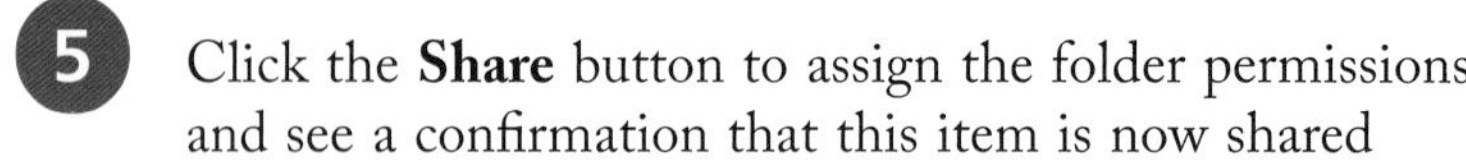

4. Click the member name to change the permission from the default **Read** to **Read/Write** (or **Remove**) as desired

5. Click the **Share** button to assign the folder permissions and see a confirmation that this item is now shared

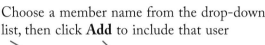

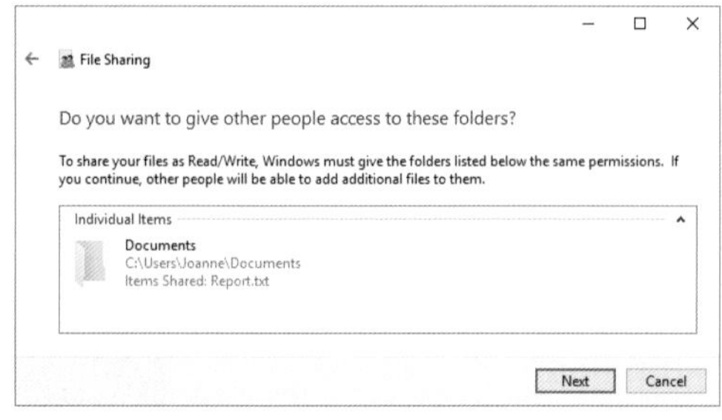

You can type a member name that you know is defined in the HomeGroup, or click the down-arrow and select from the list.

The HomeGroup makes it easy to share libraries and printers with other computers on the network, but there are some situations it doesn't cover – for example, when logged in to more than one computer on the network using the same credentials.

19 Protection and Ease of Access

This chapter demonstrates how Windows 10 offers protection for yourself and family members. It also describes Ease of Access options and the Windows Mobility Center that is especially useful for portable computer owners.

Guard your privacy

Microsoft recognizes that some users have privacy concerns when using Windows 10, so has provided a Privacy settings page where you can determine what to make public or private. You can also see the information stored about you and delete it if preferred:

The **Privacy** settings page is a welcome new feature introduced in the Windows 10 Creators Update.

1. Go to Start, Settings, **Privacy**, then choose **General**
2. If you prefer not to have your app usage tracked to provide relevant content, move the toggle buttons to **Off** here

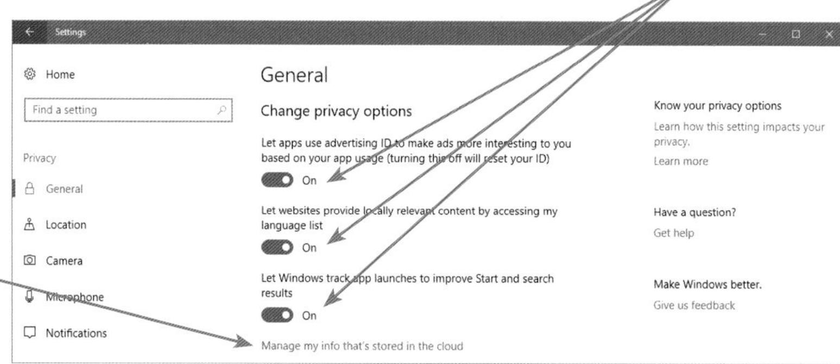

You can click the link here to discover what info is stored online.

3. Next, choose **Location** in the left-hand pane
4. If you prefer not to reveal your location for local content, click **Change** then move the pop-up toggle button to **Off**

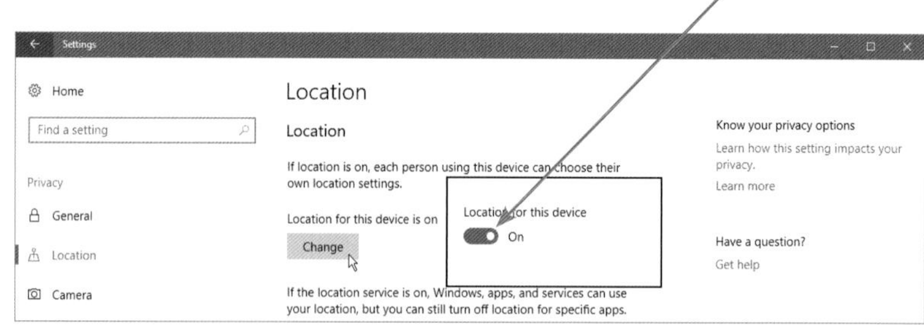

Some apps such as Weather can only supply local information easily if your **Location** is known.

5. Now, choose **Camera** in the left-hand pane
6. If you prefer not to allow apps to use your web camera, move the toggle button to **Off** here

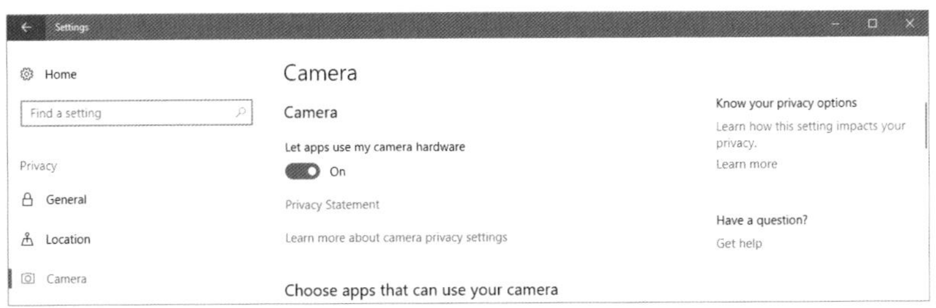

7. Choose **Microphone** in the left-hand pane

8. If you prefer not to allow apps to use your microphone, move the toggle button to **Off** here

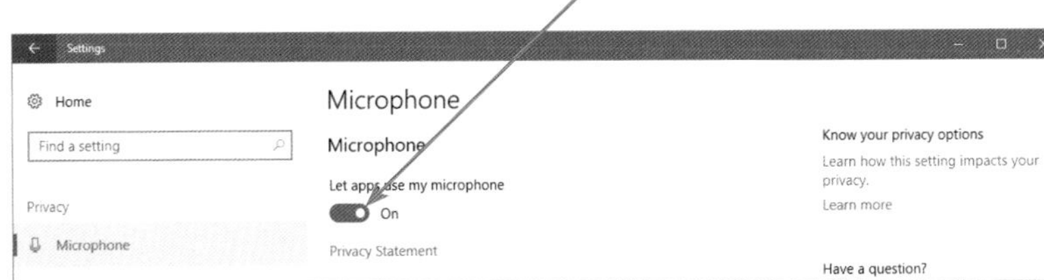

9. Choose **Account info** in the left-hand pane

10. If you prefer not to allow apps to access your name, picture, etc., move the toggle button to **Off** here

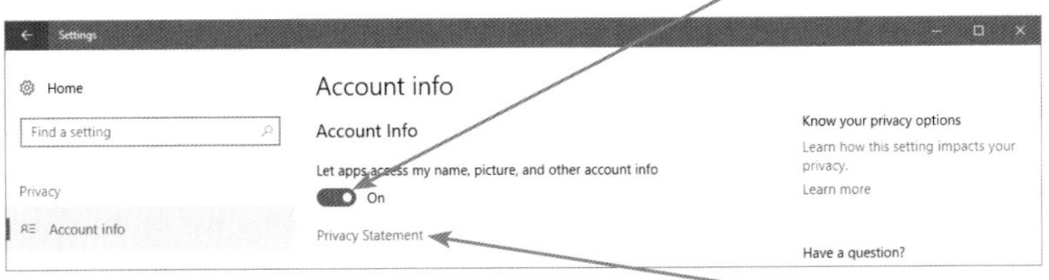

We suggest you also investigate each of the many other options in the left-hand pane on the **Privacy** page to set each individual option to suit your personal preference. If you want to discover more about any selected option, you can follow the links in the far right-hand pane under the **Know your privacy options** heading.

You can leave the toggle button set to **On** for **Camera** and **Location**, then scroll down and choose individual apps you want to allow to access your camera.

Choose **App diagnostics** in the left-hand pane and select **Basic** to limit how much data you send to Microsoft.

You can click the **Privacy Statement** link here to discover how Microsoft uses your personal data.

Account management

When Windows 10 is installed on a computer, an administrator account is created by default. However, the user has the option of creating and using a standard account instead. Let's take a look at both types and see what the pros and cons are:

A Windows 10 computer must have at least one administrator account.

Administrator account

The administrator account has complete access to the computer and can make any desired changes.

Most people use it for two reasons:

- It's already there
- It allows them to do whatever they want on the computer

Note that any program that is run on an administrator account also has complete access to the computer. This is how malware, viruses and rootkits get on to a user's system. It is also possible for the user to cause unintentional damage to their system due to having access to system tools like the Windows Registry and the System Configuration utility.

Standard accounts

Standard accounts are much safer as they do not allow users to make unauthorized changes that affect the system. If a standard account user tries to install a program, for example, they will get a User Account Control (UAC) prompt to provide an administrator password before being allowed to do so.

Doing your day-to-day computing with a standard account will help protect your PC from viruses and malware.

However, while they may not be able to install programs, make changes to global settings, etc., they will be able to do just about anything else. Therefore, on a day-to-day basis, using a standard account will present no problems to the average user.

The ideal setup then, is to create a standard account for daily use. This helps protect the user from viruses and malware as they are not allowed to run. Should the user need to make a change that requires administrator permission, they don't even need to log out and then log back in as an administrator – they simply provide the administrator password in the UAC dialog box that appears.

It is also possible to run programs under the administrator account by right-clicking the file to be run and selecting **Run as administrator** from the context menu.

Before you can use a standard account, you need to create one. Do it as described below:

1. Go to the Start menu and open Settings, Accounts, and then click **Family & other people**. In the new window, under "Other people", click **Add someone else to this PC**

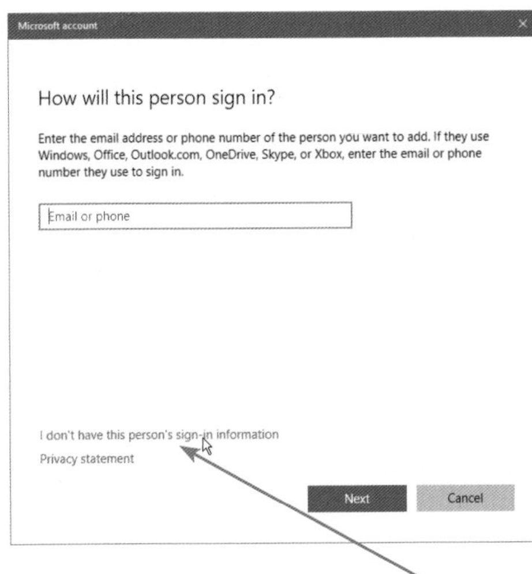

Microsoft account
How will this person sign in?
Enter the email address or phone number of the person you want to add. If they use Windows, Office, Outlook.com, OneDrive, Skype, or Xbox, enter the email or phone number they use to sign in.
Email or phone
I don't have this person's sign-in information
Privacy statement
Next
Cancel

2. Select the option at the bottom **I don't have this person's sign-in information**. In the next screen, select **Add a user without a Microsoft account** then click **Next**

3. Next, enter the **User name**, **Password** (twice), and a **Password hint** reminder

4. The new account is created. By default it is a standard account

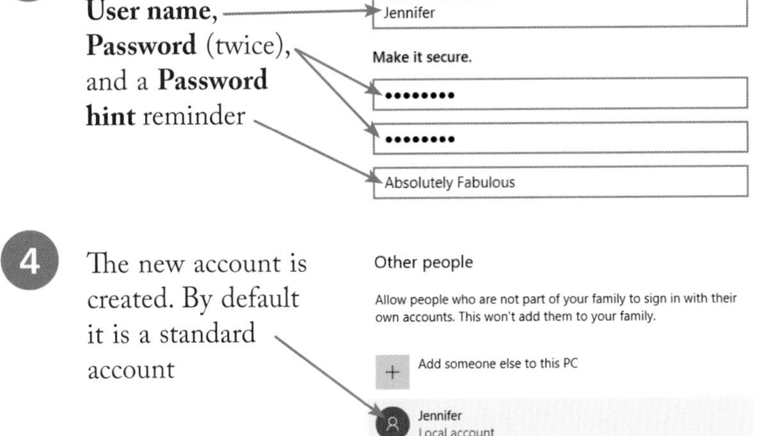

Make it secure.

Absolutely Fabulous

Allow people who are not part of your family to sign in with their own accounts. This won't add them to your family.

You must complete all fields in the **Who's going to use this PC?** screen, including the **Password hint** box.

...cont'd

You may at some point wish to change an administrator account to a standard account, or vice versa.

1. Go to Settings, then click Accounts, **Family & other people**

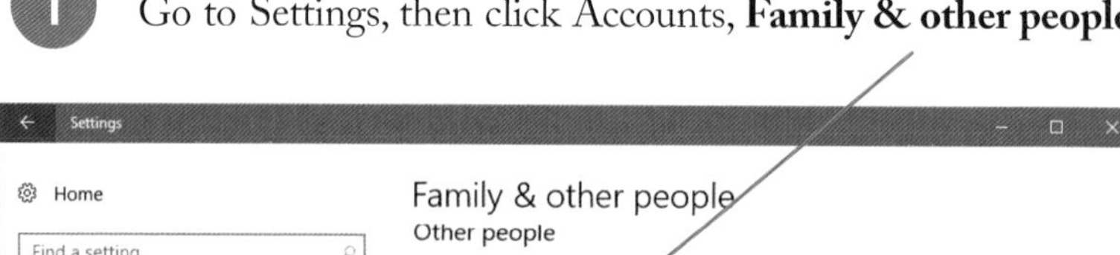

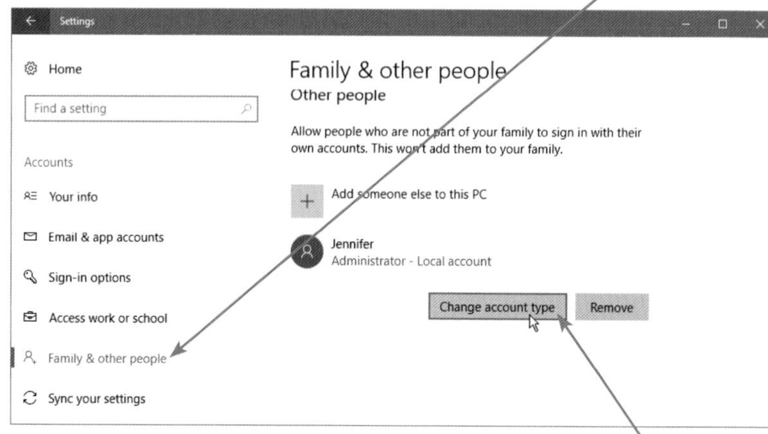

Standard account holders cannot make changes to other user accounts.

2. Choose the user account, then click **Change account type**

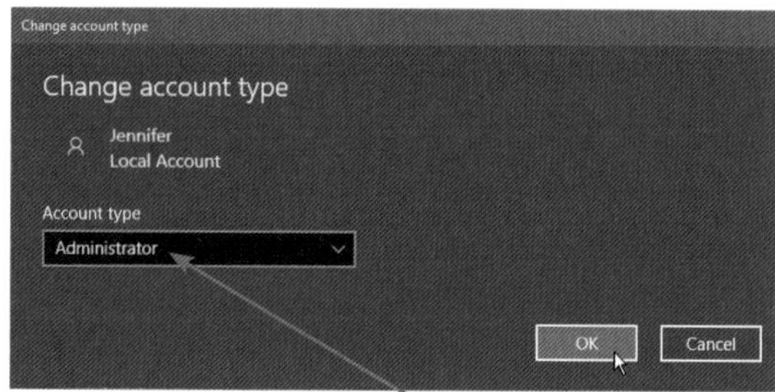

3. Select **Administrator** from the drop-down menu, then click the **OK** button to apply the change

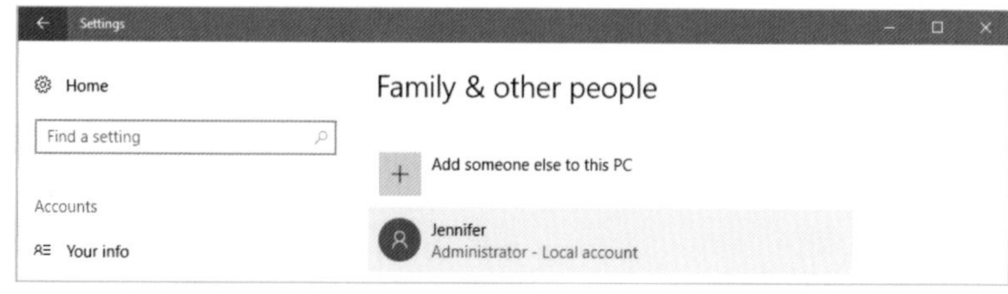

In this example, "Jennifer" is now an administrator.

Set up Family Safety

With Windows 8, child protection was achieved by creating a standard account and then activating the Family Safety utility for that account. Windows 10 simplifies the procedure by offering a Child account option, which is simply a standard account for which the Family Safety utility has already been activated.

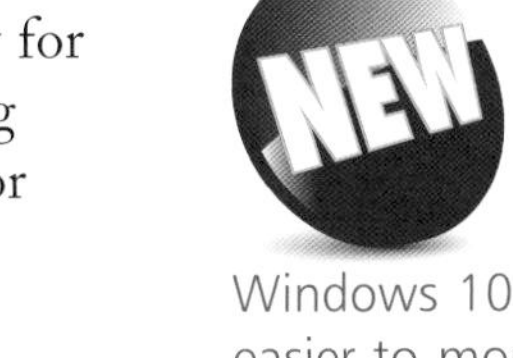

Windows 10 makes it easier to monitor your children's online activity.

1. Go to Start, Settings, Accounts, then click **Family & other people**. In the new window, click **Add a family member** and select the option to **Add a child**

2. Enter the child's existing email address, then click **Next**, or click **The person I want to add doesn't have an email address**, to create one

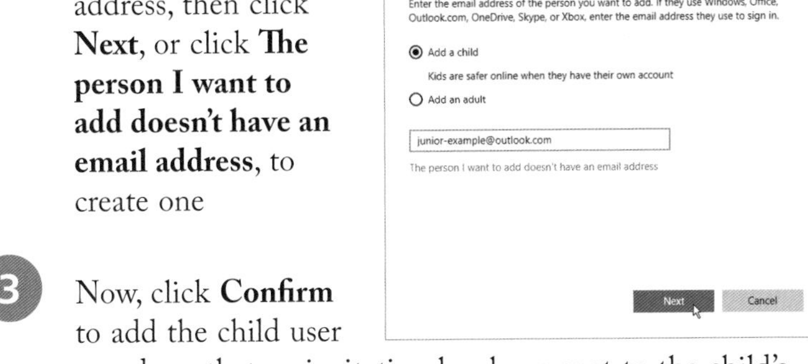

Existing standard accounts can be converted to Child accounts.

3. Now, click **Confirm** to add the child user – and see that an invitation has been sent to the child's email address

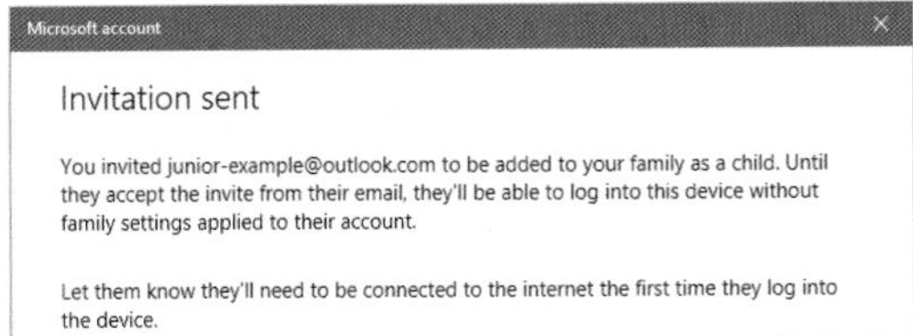

4. The new Child account is created, and Family Safety begins monitoring it automatically

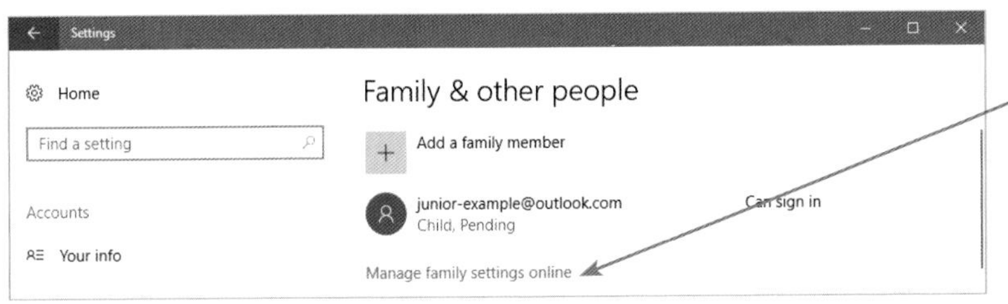

You can monitor and control your children's internet activities from the **Manage family settings online** link, or remotely by accessing the Family Safety website at account.microsoft.com/family

Defend the system

Windows Defender Security Center is a convenient new feature introduced in the Windows 10 Creators Update.

Windows 10 provides a central location where you can easily manage all your device's security settings:

1. Go to Start, **Windows Defender Security Center**

2. The status of five security categories is indicated by check marks over the category icons

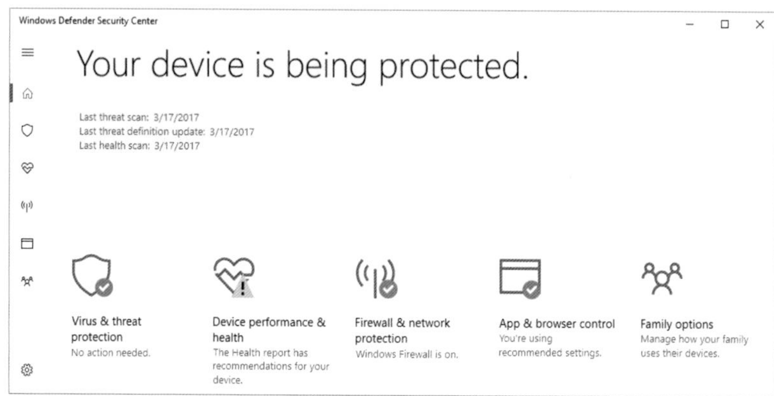

3. Click the **Virus & threat protection** icon to see the status and history of your Windows 10 antivirus protection

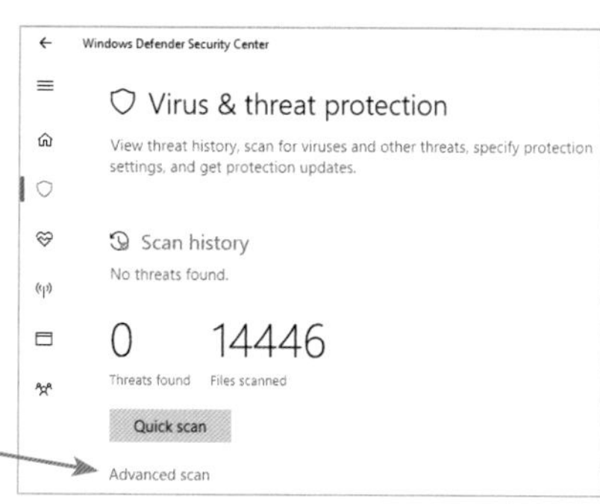

Choose **Advanced scan**, **Windows Defender Offline scan** if you are having difficulty removing malicious software.

4. Click the **Device performance & health** icon to check for issues and system recommendations – click to see the recommendation ("reduce screen brightness" here)

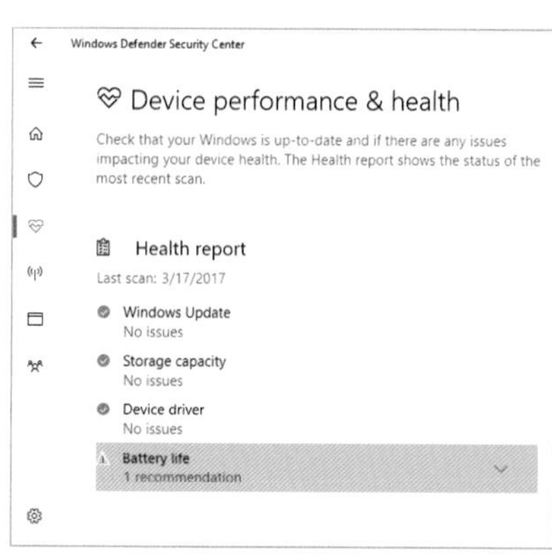

Below the **Health report** is a **Fresh start** option to start over with a clean installation of Windows 10 – as good as new.

5. Click the **Firewall & network protection** icon to see the status and network, and to troubleshoot network problems

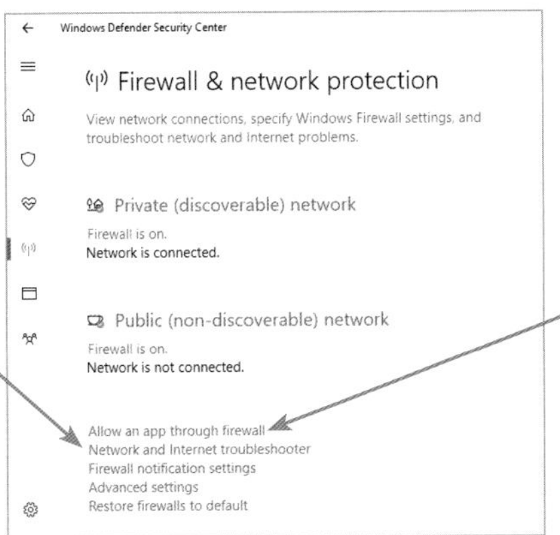

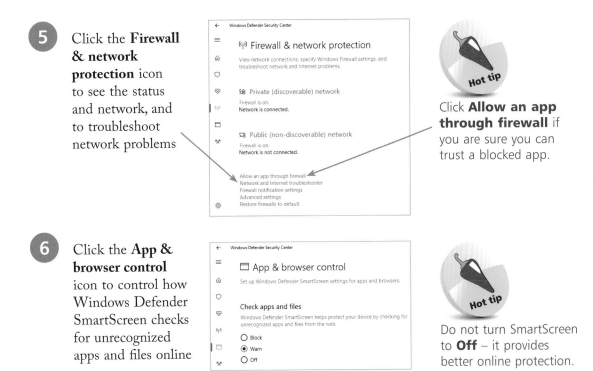

Click **Allow an app through firewall** if you are sure you can trust a blocked app.

6. Click the **App & browser control** icon to control how Windows Defender SmartScreen checks for unrecognized apps and files online

Do not turn SmartScreen to **Off** – it provides better online protection.

7. Click the **Family options** icon to configure your **Parental controls** – to specify which websites your children can visit, when and for how long your children can use their devices, and which apps they can purchase for their devices

You can click the **View family settings** link to visit the Family Safety website at **account.microsoft.com/family**

Ease of Access

Windows 10 provides a number of accessibility options designed to help users see, hear, and use their computers. These options are all available in the **Ease of Access** settings:

Ease of Access tools are not just for those with disabilities. PC users with no impairments may find some of these tools useful in everyday computing.

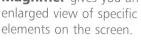

1. Go to Start, Settings, and click **Ease of Access**

2. Click **Narrator** and slide the toggle button to the **On** position – to hear the screen reader say "Starting Narrator"

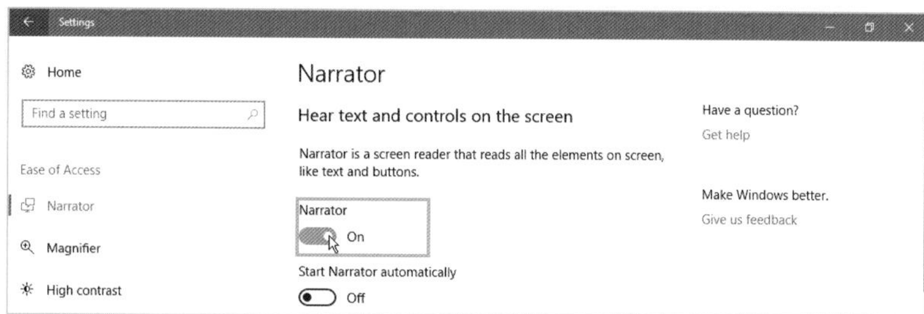

Magnifier gives you an enlarged view of specific elements on the screen.

3. Click **Magnifier** and slide the toggle button to the **On** position – choose your zoom level

4. Click **Keyboard** and slide the toggle button to the **On** position – click the on-screen keys to type

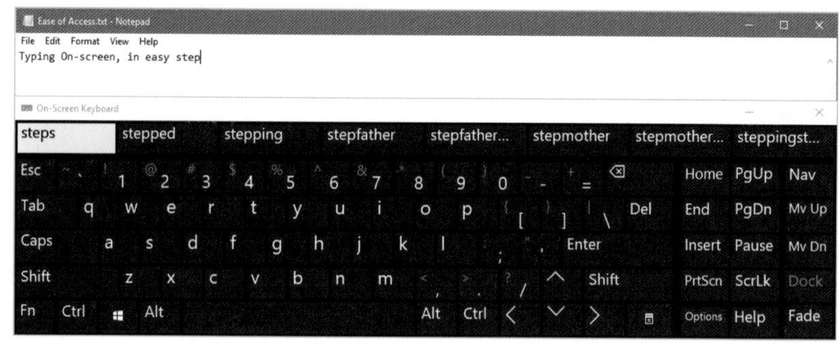

Ease of Access **Mouse** settings are a particularly useful tool as they can also keep you going if your mouse stops working for some reason – under **Mouse keys** turn **On** the option to use the numeric keypad to move the mouse around the screen.

5. Explore more Ease of Access settings for **High contrast**, **Closed captions**, **Mouse**, and **Other options**

Start Mobility Center

You'll find Windows Mobility Center (WMC) on any portable computer, though not usually on a desktop or all-in-one computer. The utility is basically a control panel that provides all the Windows options specific to portable computers in one easily-accessed location.

There are several ways to open Windows Mobility Center. These include:

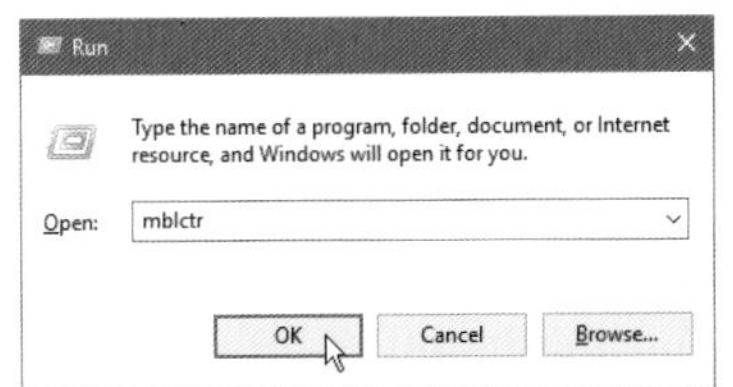

- Press **WinKey** + **R** to open the Run box. Type "mblctr", then press **Enter**.
- Go to the Control Panel, Hardware and Sound. Then, click **Windows Mobility Center**.
- You get a link to Windows Mobility Center when you right-click the Battery icon in the System Tray.

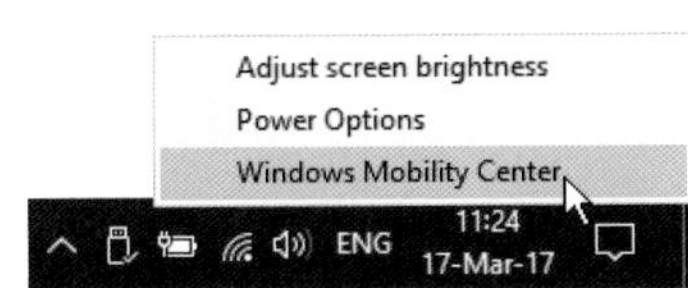

If you are using a desktop PC, Windows Mobility Center will not be accessible.

When the utility opens, you will see the following window:

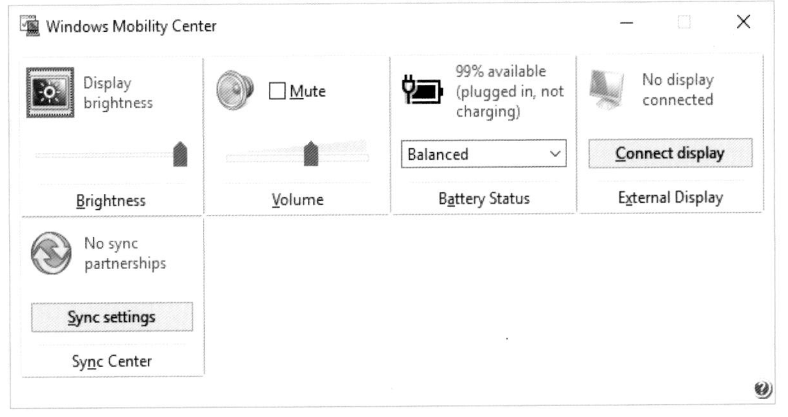

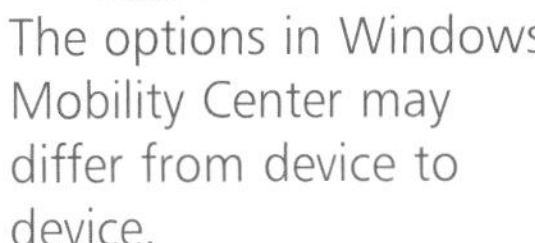

The options in Windows Mobility Center may differ from device to device.

The options offered depend on the type of computer and the hardware it is using.

Screen management

Windows Mobility Center provides several options related to screen management, via slider controls and icon buttons.

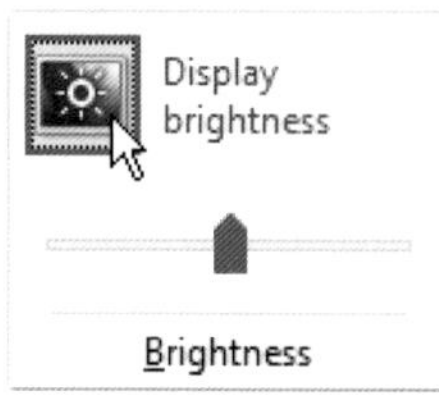

Brightness

The first is Display brightness. This is an important setting with laptops, as the higher it is set, the quicker the battery will run down. The Mobility Center provides a quickly-accessible way of adjusting this setting. If you click on the icon button, you will open the computer's **Power Options** utility, from where you can make changes to various settings including the display brightness.

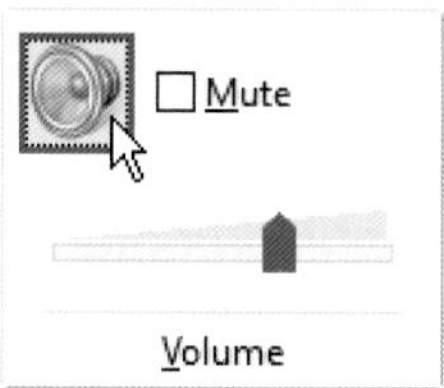

Volume

As with the brightness setting, the higher the PC's volume level, the greater the load on the battery. You can adjust it with the slider, check the Mute box, or click the icon button to open the **Sound** utility for more options.

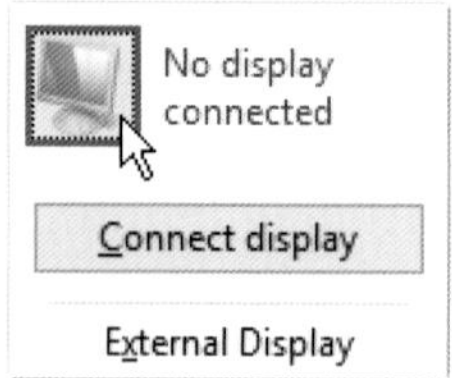

External Display

The External Display option allows you to connect your laptop to a different monitor, duplicate the display, or extend the display. Click the icon button to open the **Screen Resolution** utility. If you click **Connect display**, you will open **Project** options in the Windows interface. Both offer the options mentioned above.

Presentation Settings

Laptops are often used in business to give presentations. With this in mind, the **Presentation Settings** option makes it possible to pre-configure a laptop's settings in terms of volume, screen saver, and background so that they will not detract from the presentation. To do this, click the icon and make your adjustments as shown on the right. Click **OK**, and then click the **Turn on** button.

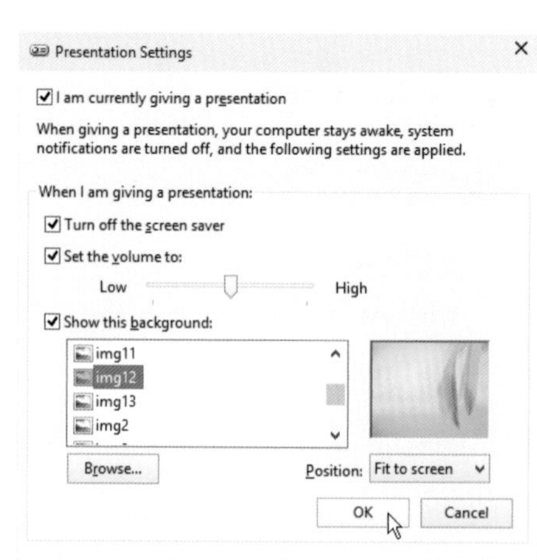

When the presentation is finished, you can revert to the normal settings by clicking the **Turn off** button.

Many people connect their laptops to their main PC monitor to take advantage of the larger and usually better displays these offer.

Battery status

The main drawback with portable computers such as laptops is the constant need to conserve battery power. To this end, Windows Mobility Center provides options that help to manage this aspect of portable computing. All the settings described on page 332 affect to some degree the length of time the battery will last. Users looking to conserve battery power will benefit by lowering these settings as far as possible.

A related option provided by Windows Mobility Center is battery power monitoring, or status. This tells the user the percentage of power remaining in the battery.

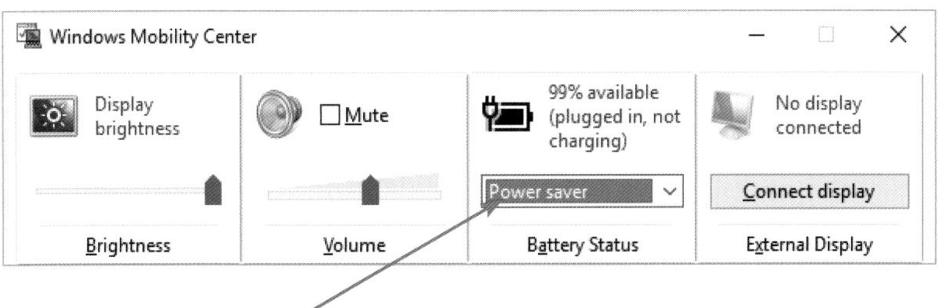

The drop-down menu provides three basic options:

- **Power saver** – this option will extend battery life.
- **High performance** – this option reduces battery life.
- **Balanced** – this option is a compromise between performance and battery life.

Clicking the Battery icon opens the **Power Options** dialog box, which provides settings with which to fine-tune the **Power saver**, **High performance** and **Balanced** options.

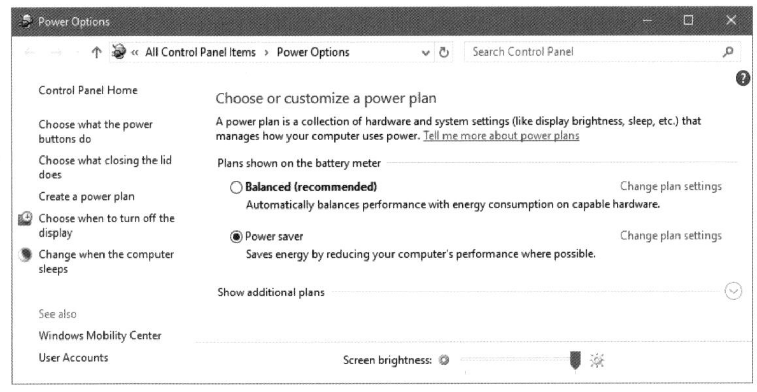

You can also see the battery status from the Battery icon in the System Tray. If the battery is fully charged, the icon will look like this:

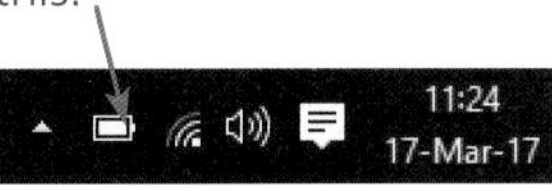

If it is running low, it will look like this:

Hover over the icon and you will see the percentage of power remaining:

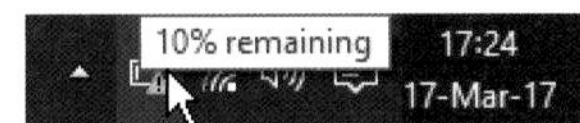

Power options

This feature is provided for all types of computer, though it takes on particular significance for battery-powered PCs:

1. Go to Start, Settings, System, then click **Power & sleep**

2. You can select when to turn off the PC, and when to send the PC to sleep, when powered by mains or battery

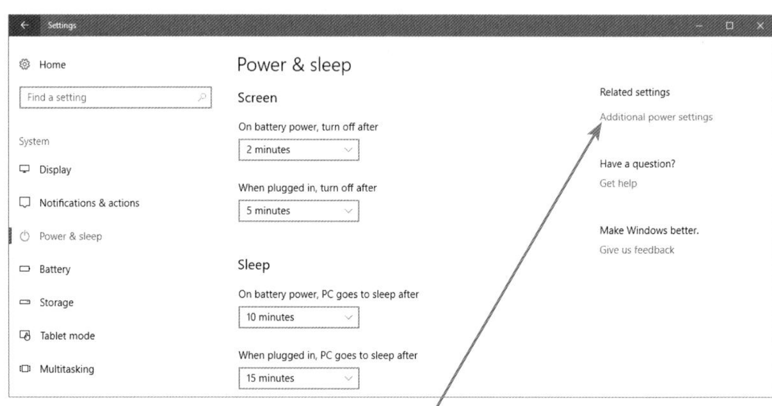

3. Click the **Additional power settings** option, then select **Choose what the power buttons do**

4. From the drop-down menus select **Do nothing, Sleep, Hibernate, Shut down** or **Turn off the display** for when you perform various actions on your computer

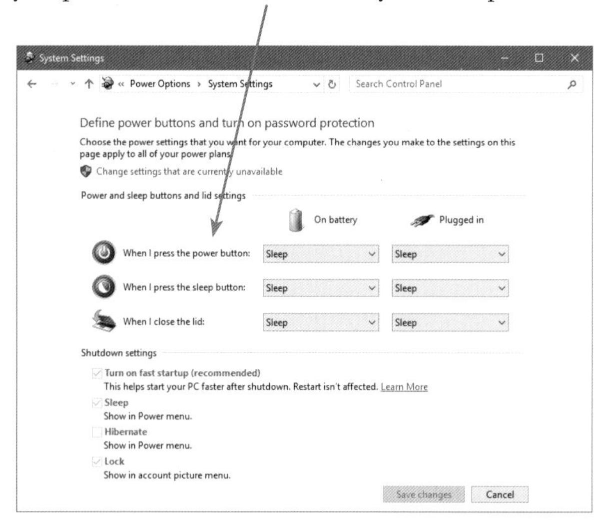

Additional power settings also lets you create **Power plans** to set the idle time after which the display is turned off or the computer is put to sleep – for your custom **High performance** or **Power saver** preference.

Not all computers support Hibernation, so this option is not always available.

20 Troubleshooting

When an error occurs on your PC, Windows 10 attempts to identify the issue. It also provides a set of troubleshooters and a Problem Steps Recorder. Other facilities include allowing a friend to remotely connect to your computer. There is also support for improving program compatibility.

Windows error reporting

Windows 10 constantly sends data over the internet to check your PC for security and maintenance problems, and sends back a message when a problem is discovered. Windows' User Account Control also notifies you when potentially harmful programs attempt to make changes to your computer. Additionally, the Windows SmartScreen feature warns you before running any unrecognized apps and files downloaded from the internet.

You can set the level of reporting you want for each one of these:

Go to Start, Windows System, Control Panel (View by: Large icons), then select **Security and Maintenance**

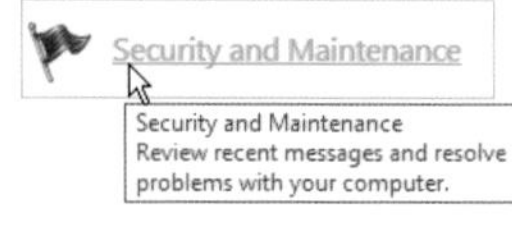

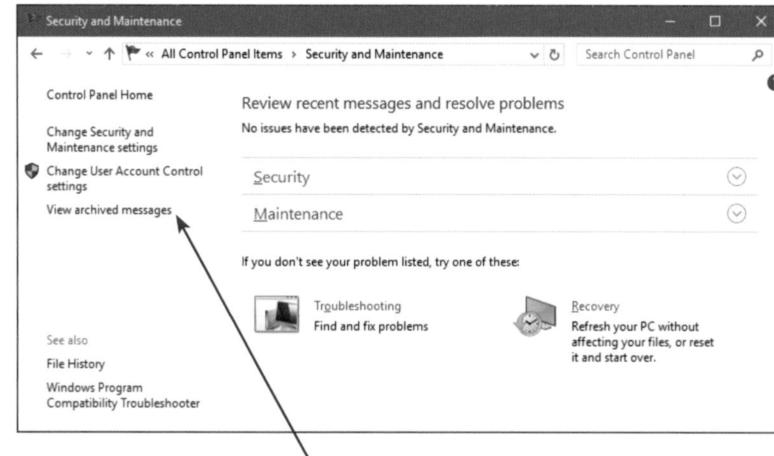

2 Here, you can review messages and resolve problems, and select **View archived messages** to see problem messages

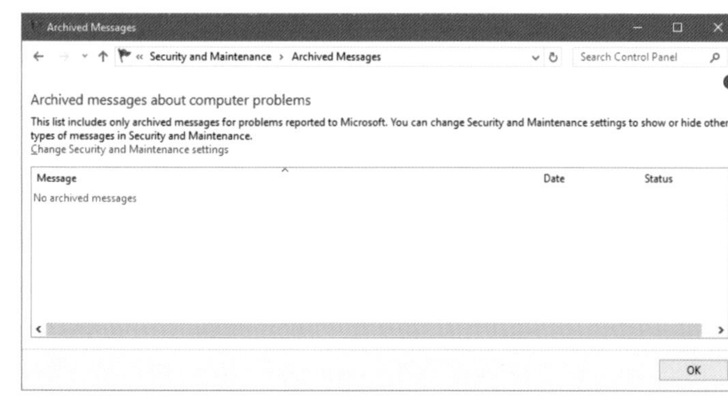

Windows identifies errors and problems, and attempts to find solutions for you.

Archived messages only keeps a copy of error problems reported to Microsoft – no earlier problems have been reported in this example.

3. Next, select **Change User Account Control settings** then choose an option to set the notification level for potentially harmful programs

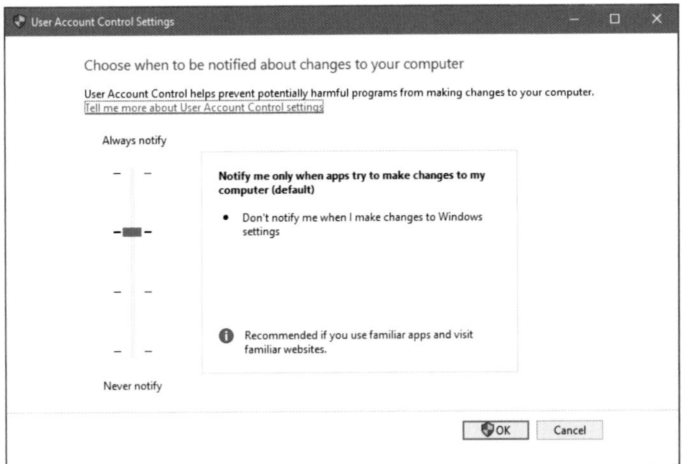
User Account Control Settings
Choose when to be notified about changes to your computer
User Account Control helps prevent potentially harmful programs from making changes to your computer.
Tell me more about User Account Control settings
Always notify
Notify me only when apps try to make changes to my computer (default)
Don't notify me when I make changes to Windows settings
Recommended if you use familiar apps and visit familiar websites.
Never notify
OK
Cancel

Don't forget

The settings shown here for **User Account Control**, and for **Security and Maintenance**, are the default (recommended) settings.

4. Now, select **Change Security and Maintenance settings** then choose the items for which you would like to receive messages when problems are discovered by Windows

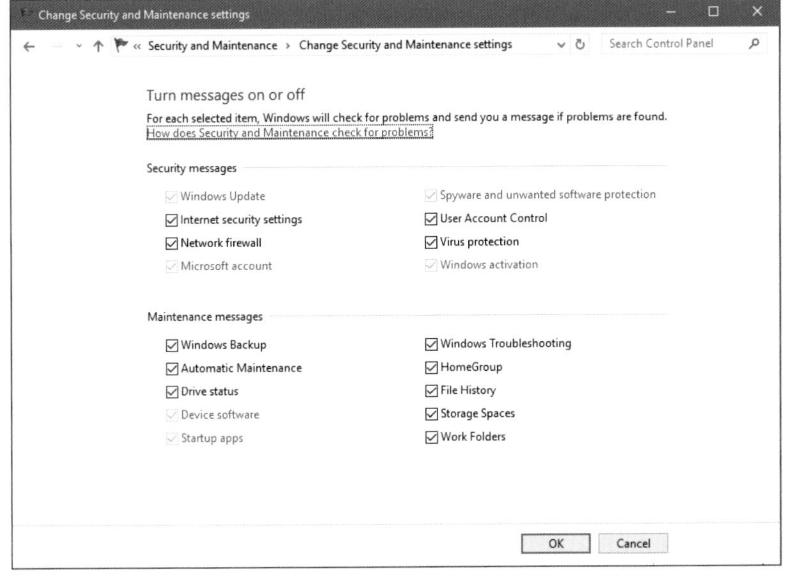
Change Security and Maintenance settings
Security and Maintenance › Change Security and Maintenance settings
Search Control Panel
Turn messages on or off
For each selected item, Windows will check for problems and send you a message if problems are found.
How does Security and Maintenance check for problems?
Security messages
Windows Update
Internet security settings
Network firewall
Microsoft account
Spyware and unwanted software protection
User Account Control
Virus protection
Windows activation
Maintenance messages
Windows Backup
Automatic Maintenance
Drive status
Device software
Startup apps
Windows Troubleshooting
HomeGroup
File History
Storage Spaces
Work Folders
OK
Cancel

Hot tip

Security and Maintenance monitors security issues as well as the maintenance and troubleshooting issues discussed in this chapter.

Troubleshooting settings

1. Expand the **Maintenance** section to review the status of the monitoring that is being applied

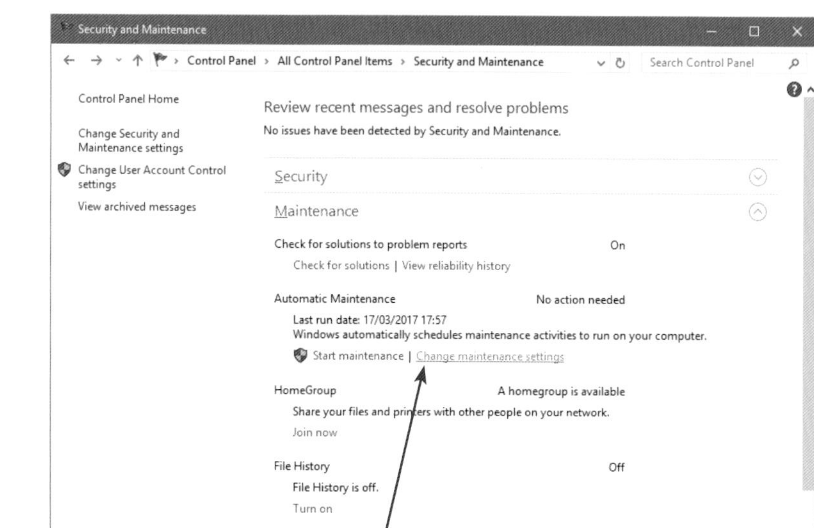

Entries will only appear here when there are problems that Windows has identified and for which solutions are available.

2. Click **Change maintenance settings** to specify the scope of problem analysis and maintenance on your system

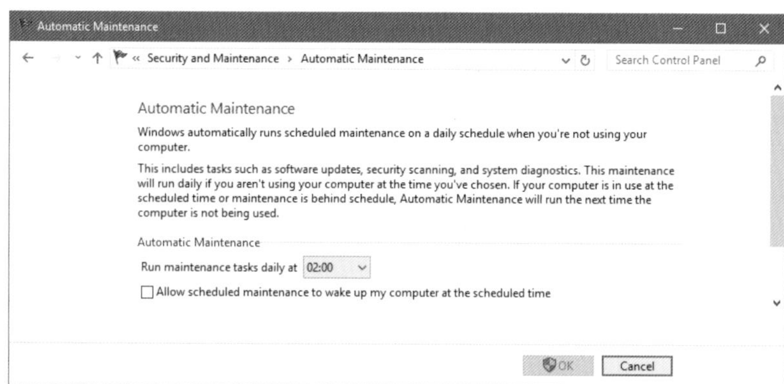

You may want to turn off these options for a system that is being operated by an inexperienced user, so they won't have to deal with troubleshooting responses.

3. By default, Windows will remind you when the System Maintenance troubleshooter can help fix problems, and will also allow users to browse for online troubleshooters

Windows troubleshooters

1. Open **Security and Maintenance, Troubleshooting** to see a list of categories and the troubleshooters available within these to handle common problems

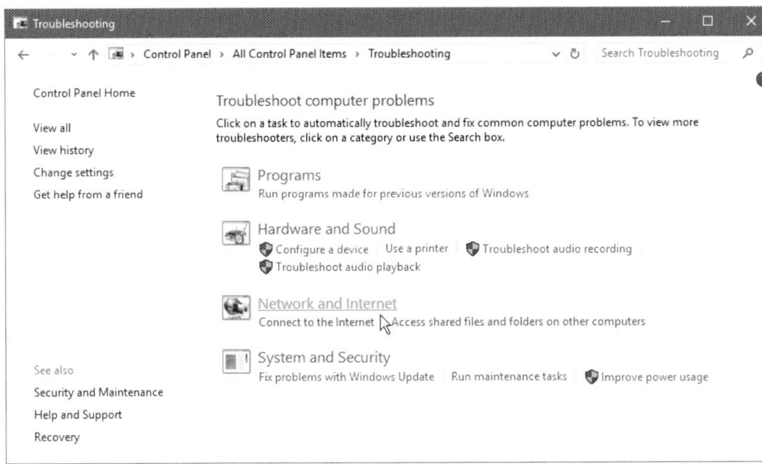

If you encounter a problem, and find no related messages in **Security and Maintenance**, you can try the troubleshooters provided by Windows.

2. Select a task that appears to match the problem you have, or click the most appropriate category

3. Windows searches online to find any troubleshooting packs in that category

4. The troubleshooters are listed by their sub-categories

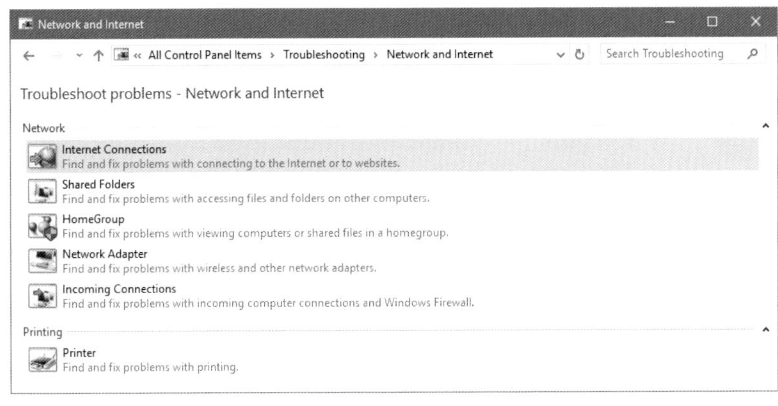

Hot tip

Depending on the category you select, you should find one or more troubleshooters online, ensuring that you have the latest support for the problem area.

Troubleshooter in action

You can also troubleshoot problems by going to Start, Settings, then search for "Troubleshoot" and select this option. Select the problem category then click the **Run the troubleshooter** button that appears.

1. To illustrate, select **Connect to the Internet**, in the **Network and Internet** category

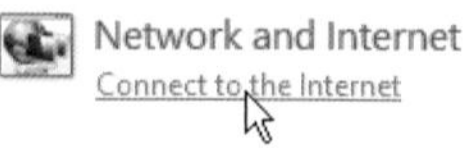

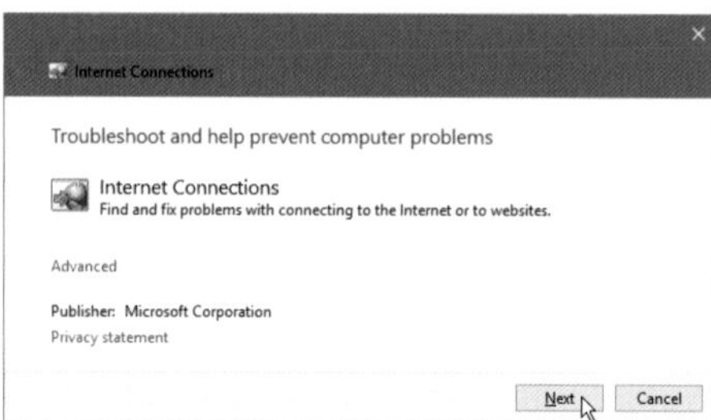

2. Click **Next** to run the troubleshooter, which carries out a series of checks to detect any internet connection issues

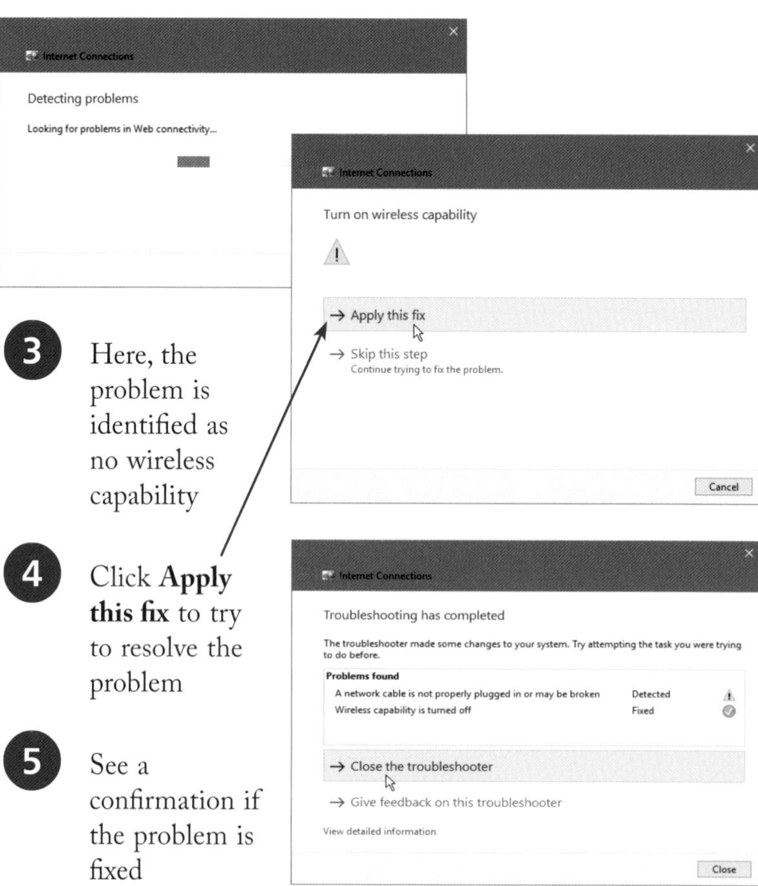

3. Here, the problem is identified as no wireless capability

4. Click **Apply this fix** to try to resolve the problem

5. See a confirmation if the problem is fixed

Problem Steps Recorder

If troubleshooting doesn't help, and you need to report the problem, you can use the Problem Steps Recorder to automatically capture the steps you take, including a text description of where you clicked and a screenshot during each click. You can save the data to a file that can be used by a support professional or a friend helping you with the problem.

To record and save the steps:

1. Go to Start, Windows Accessories, **Steps Recorder**

2. When the Problem Steps Recorder has opened, click its **Start Record** button, then go through the steps to reproduce the problem

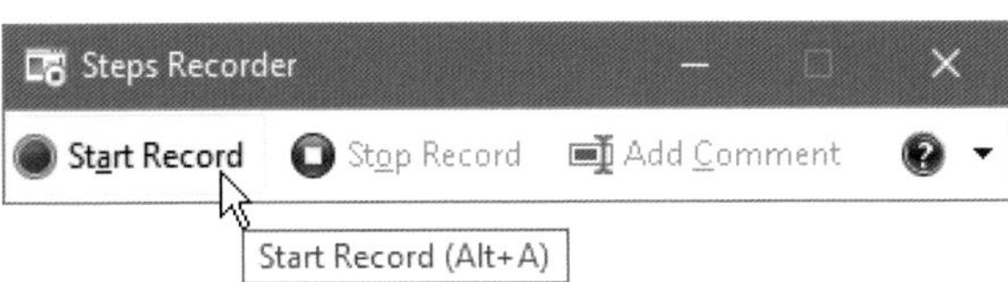

3. You will see that the Start Record button label has changed to **Pause** – click this to pause recording

4. The Start Record button label has now changed to **Resume** – click this to resume recording

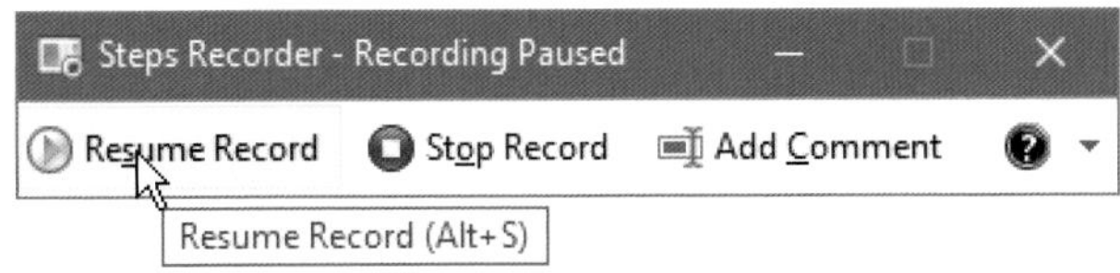

5. Click **Add Comment** whenever you want to make notes about any step in the process you are recording

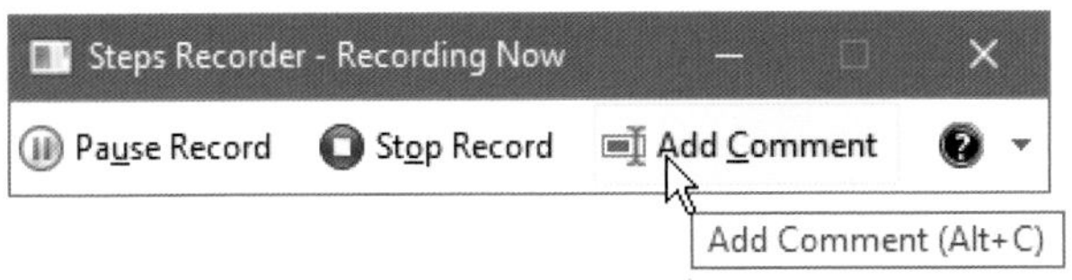

Some programs, for example a full-screen game, might not be captured accurately or might not provide useful details.

If you want to record any activities that need administrator authority, you must run the **Steps Recorder** as an administrator.

...cont'd

6. Type your comments in the box that opens at the bottom-right of the screen

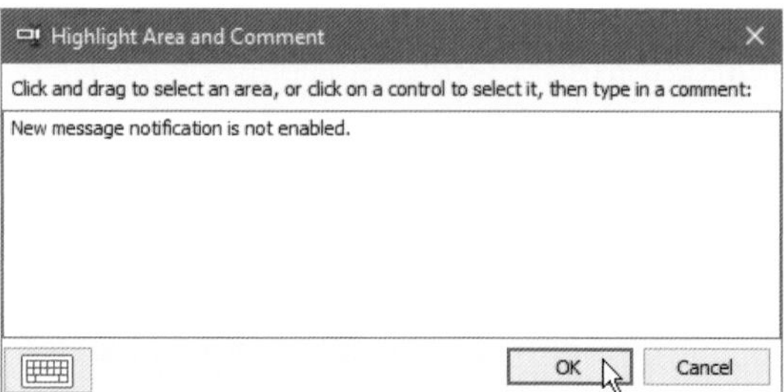

When you record steps, anything you type will not be recorded. If it is relevant to the problem, use the comment option to note what you type.

7. Click **Stop Record** when you finish all the steps

8. Click **Save**, then choose a name and location for the report, e.g. "MyProblemReport" and your Desktop

9. The report is saved as a compressed Zip file in your chosen location

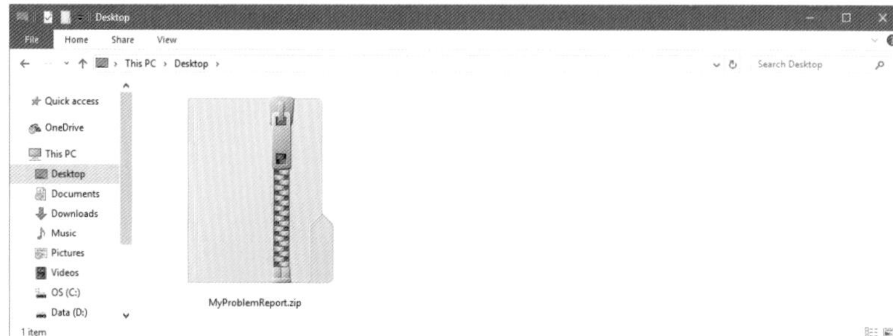

View the report

1. Double-click the compressed Zip file, then double-click the MHTML document (**.mht**) that it contains

2. The report opens in a web browser window

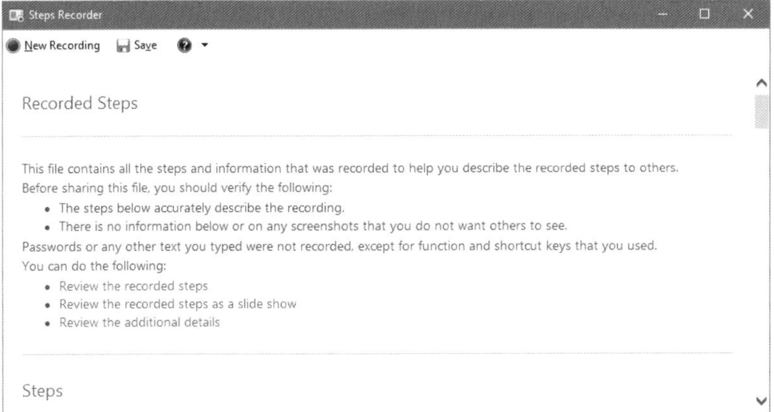

Steps Recorder
New Recording
Save
Step 2: (18-Mar-17 11:56:52) User left click on "Network Connections (window)" in "Network Connections"
Recorded Steps
This file contains all the steps and information that was recorded to help you describe the recorded steps to others.
Before sharing this file, you should verify the following:
The steps below accurately describe the recording.
There is no information below or on any screenshots that you do not want others to see.
Passwords or any other text you typed were not recorded, except for function and shortcut keys that you used.
You can do the following:
Review the recorded steps
Review the recorded steps as a slide show
Review the additional details
Steps

There is a summary of the contents and links to the individual steps, and to additional details which contain technical information intended for advanced users.

3. Each step has a description of the action taken, plus a screenshot of the full screen at that point

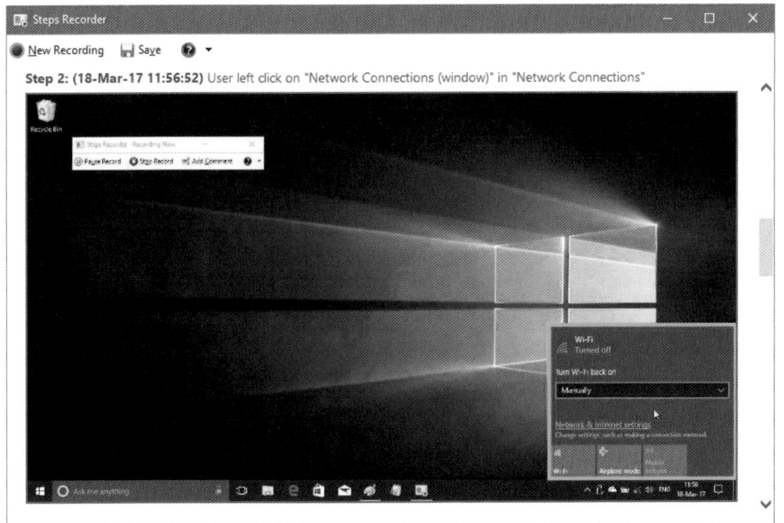

You can view the actions and screenshots as a slide show, which proceeds automatically, showing a new step every few seconds.

Get help from a friend

You can ask a friend to look at how your system is working, even if they are away from you, by connecting your computers.

1. Go to Start, Windows System, Control Panel, **Troubleshooting** and choose **Get help from a friend**

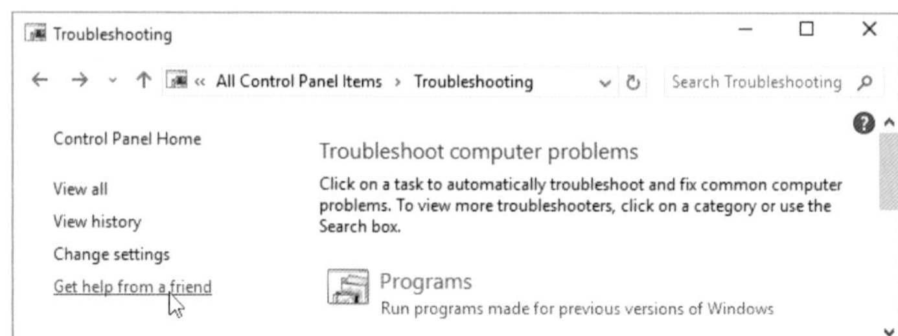

2. Click the option to **Invite someone to help you**

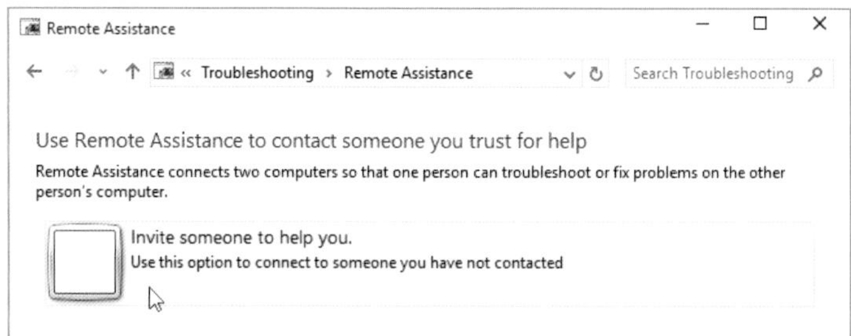

3. Select, for example, **Use email to send an invitation**

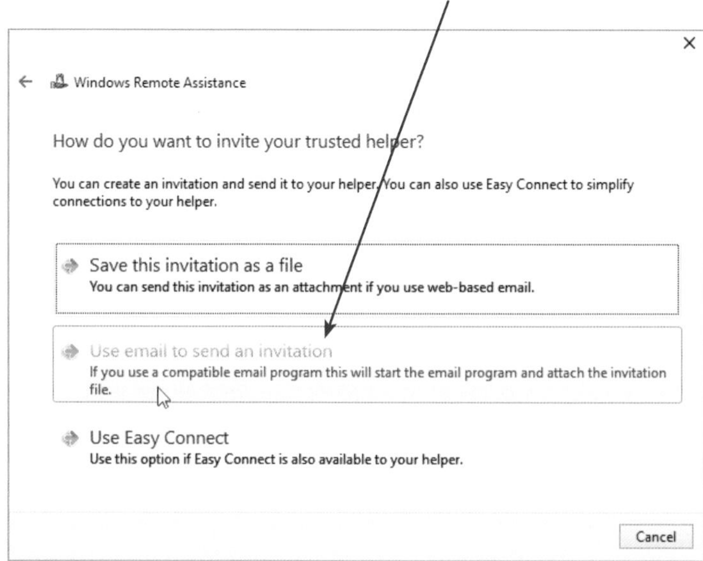

4. Amend the message, adding the helper's name and email address, and click the **Send** button

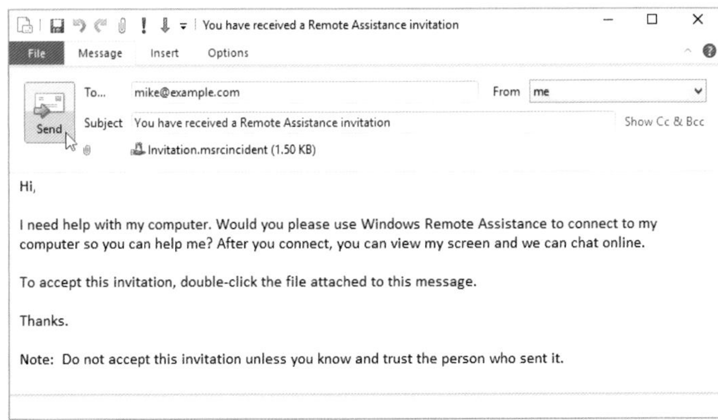
You have received a Remote Assistance invitation
File Message Insert Options
Send
To... mike@example.com
From me
Subject You have received a Remote Assistance invitation
Show Cc & Bcc
Invitation.msrcincident (1.50 KB)
Hi,
I need help with my computer. Would you please use Windows Remote Assistance to connect to my computer so you can help me? After you connect, you can view my screen and we can chat online.
To accept this invitation, double-click the file attached to this message.
Thanks.
Note: Do not accept this invitation unless you know and trust the person who sent it.

Don't forget

You can change the contents of the message however you wish, to make it appropriate for the person you are contacting.

5. Windows Remote Assistance provides a password for you to share, then waits for an incoming connection

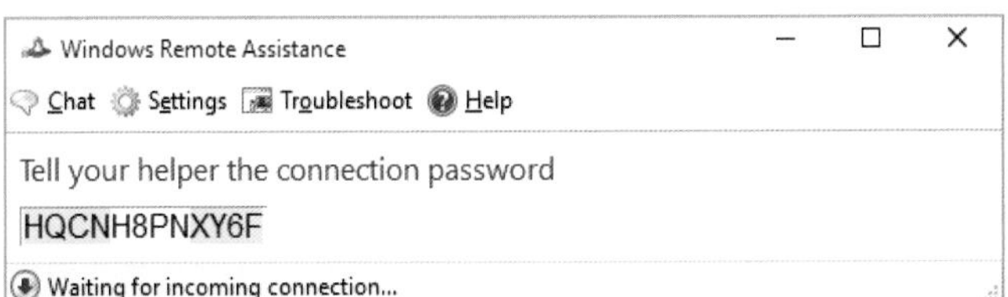
Windows Remote Assistance
Chat Settings Troubleshoot Help
Tell your helper the connection password
HQCNH8PNXY6F
Waiting for incoming connection...

6. Your helper receives and opens the message and, if willing to help you, double-clicks the attached invitation file

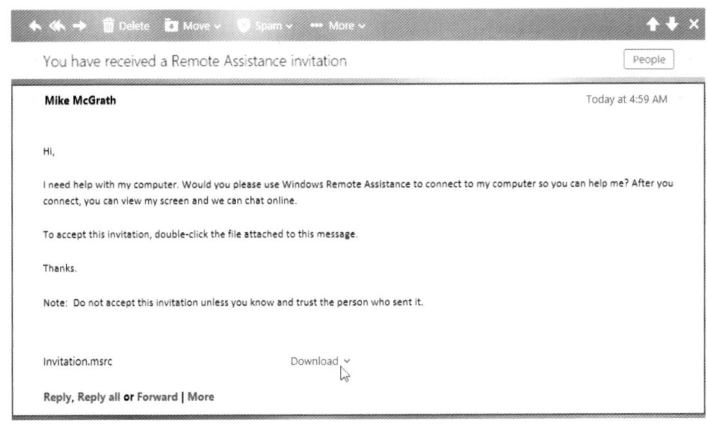
Delete Move Spam More
You have received a Remote Assistance invitation
People
Mike McGrath
Today at 4:59 AM
Hi,
I need help with my computer. Would you please use Windows Remote Assistance to connect to my computer so you can help me? After you connect, you can view my screen and we can chat online.
To accept this invitation, double-click the file attached to this message.
Thanks.
Note: Do not accept this invitation unless you know and trust the person who sent it.
Invitation.msrc
Download
Reply, Reply all or Forward | More

Hot tip

You'll need to tell your helper the connection password, perhaps via a separate email message, or via instant messaging.

Send and respond

1. Your helper opens the invitation file and enters the connection password

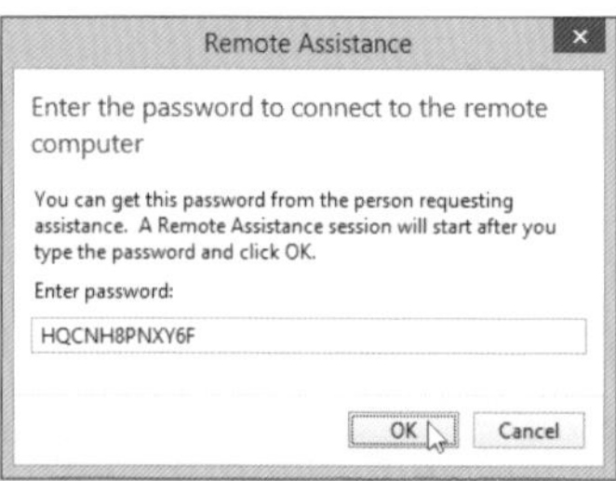

Beware

When your computer is connected this way, you are giving full access, so you should be sure it is a trusted friend that you have contacted.

2. You are notified of the acceptance, and asked to confirm you will allow the helper to connect to your computer

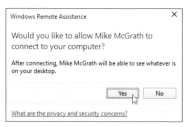

3. Your helper can now see your Desktop on his/her monitor, and observe any actions

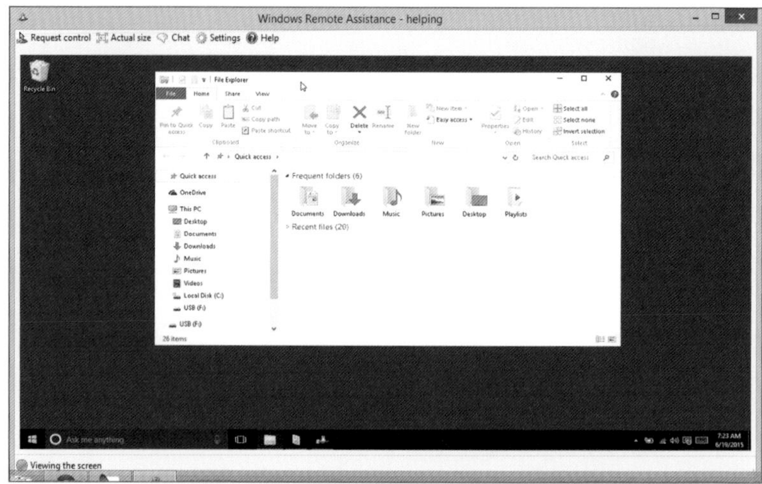

4. Your helper can click **Request control**, asking to operate your computer using his/her mouse and keyboard

5. When you receive the request, click **Yes** to allow your helper to share control of your Desktop

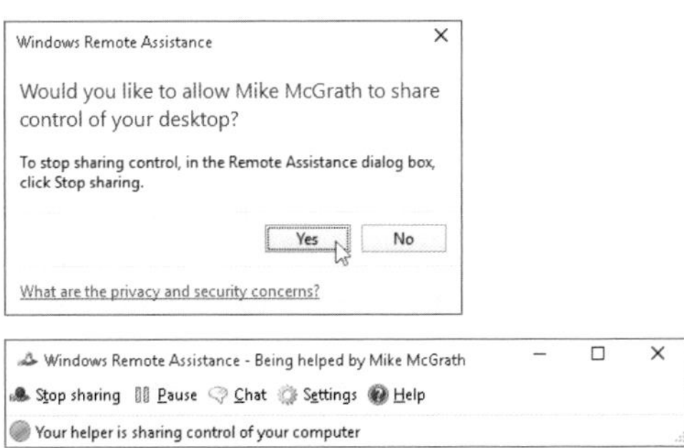

6. Now, either you or your helper can operate the computer using mouse and keyboard

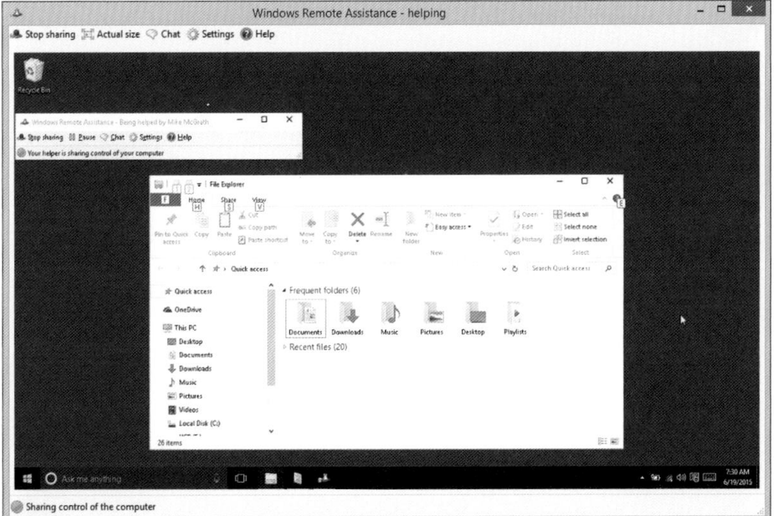

7. Click **Chat** to communicate via instant messaging, or click **Stop sharing** to return full control to you alone

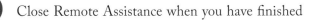

8. Close Remote Assistance when you have finished

Click the **Yes** button in Step 5 to allow your helper to respond to User Account Control prompts.

Don't forget

Click **Pause** if you want to temporarily stop the Remote Assistance session, for example to carry out a separate task.

Use Easy Connect

If you believe you are likely to connect with the same computer on a frequent basis then you can try the Easy Connect method:

1. Invite someone to help you (see page 344) and select **Use Easy Connect**

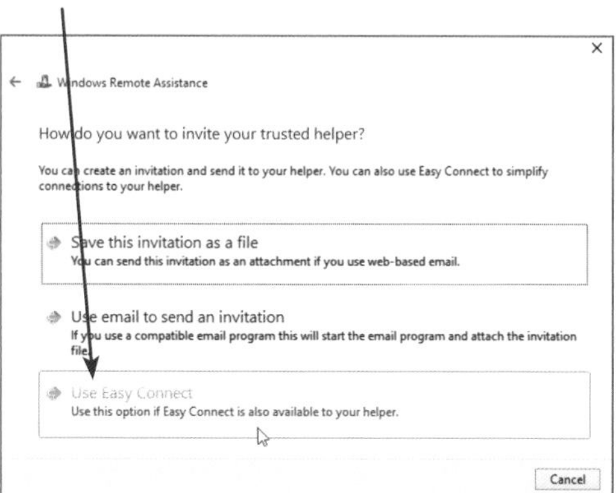

2. Remote Assistance will generate an Easy Connect password which you must supply to your helper

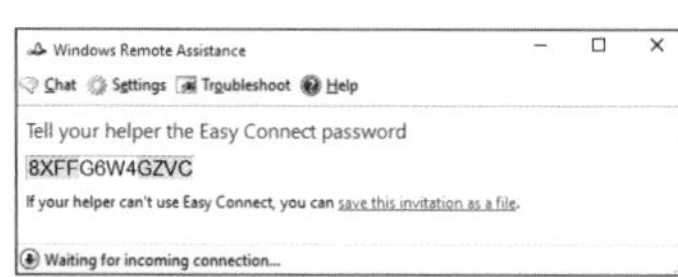

3. Your helper will open Troubleshooting and select **Offer Remote Assistance to help someone**, then select **Use Easy Connect** and enter the password provided

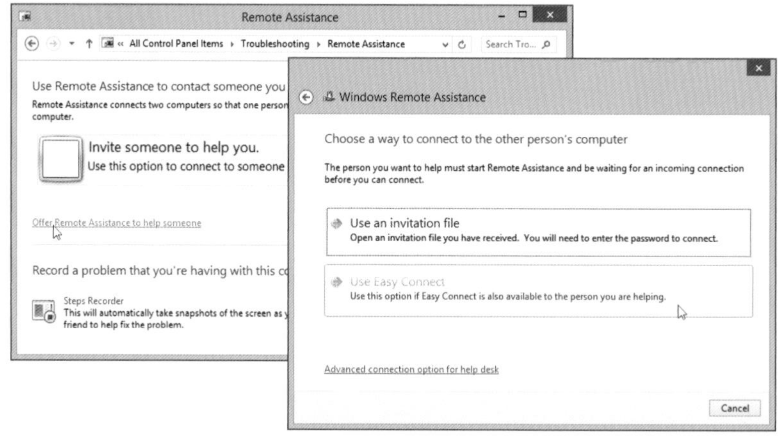

When the connection is made, contact information is exchanged between your computer and your helper's computer that will allow you to quickly connect in the future without using the password.

If you have problems connecting, such as issues with the firewall or router, try the Troubleshooting option at either computer for suggestions, or switch to the Invitation method.

System Restore

If problems arise due to recently-added drivers or updates, you can use System Restore to return the computer to an earlier position.

1. Go to Start, Windows System, Control Panel, (View by: Large icons), System and Security, **Security and Maintenance** then select **Recovery**

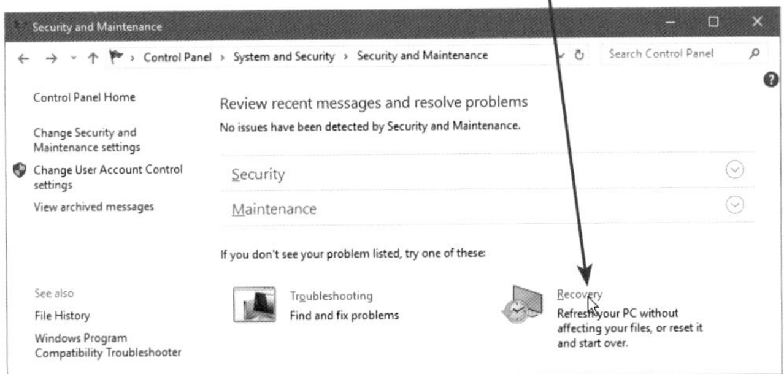

2. Click **Open System Restore**, then click **Next**

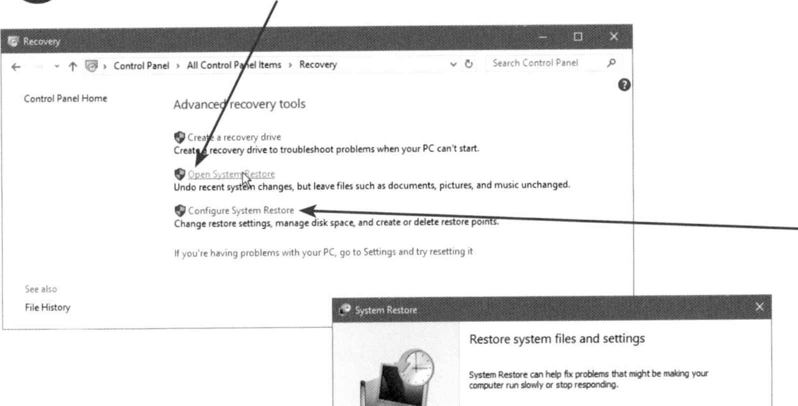

3. Choose the recommended restore point, or choose a different restore point to go back to an earlier state, and click **Next**

System Restore will suggest the option to undo the latest change to your system. Choose this if problems have only just appeared. You can still try another restore point later.

System Protection must be enabled to use the System Restore feature – select **Configure System Restore**, choose a disk drive, click **Configure**, then check **Turn on system protection**.

If more restore points are displayed, select the one that immediately pre-dates the problems, then click **Next**.

...cont'd

If System Restore is being run in Safe Mode or from the System Recovery Options menu, it cannot be undone.

4. Confirm your restore point, then click **Finish**

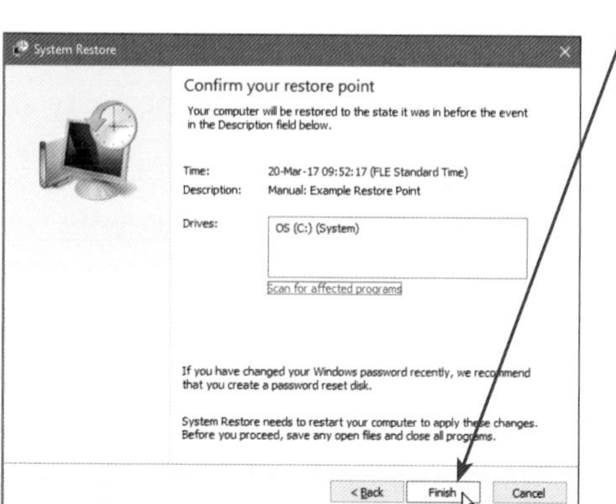

5. Click **Yes** to continue and carry out the System Restore

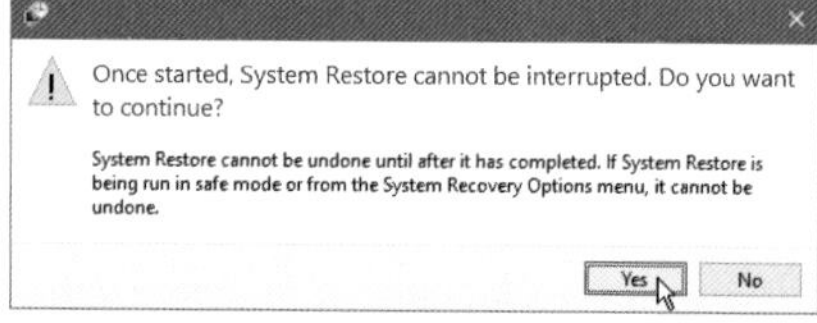

6. Windows will close down and restart, and the system files are restored to the required versions

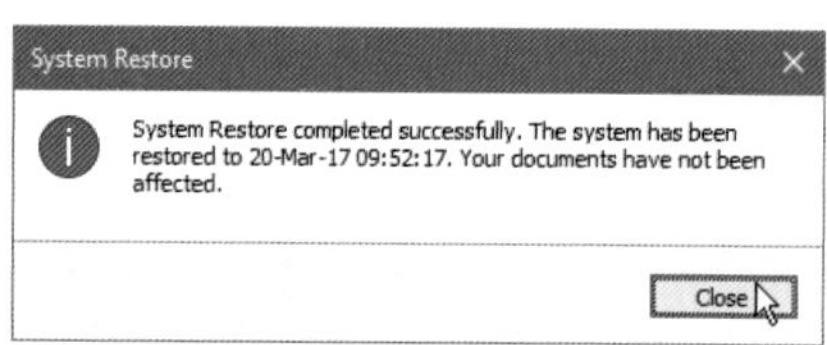

Once started, you must allow System Restore to complete. You can then Open System Restore and select Undo, if you want to revert to the initial state.

7. If this does not fix the problem, you can **Undo System Restore**, or **Choose a different restore point**

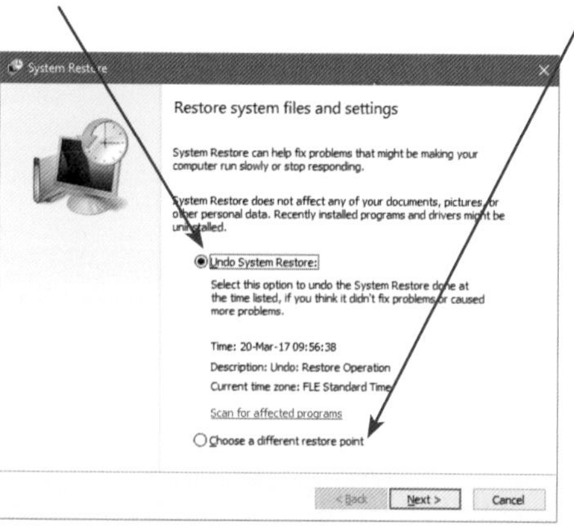

Start in Safe Mode

1. Open Settings, then select **Update & security**
2. Click **Recovery** on the left-hand pane
3. Under "Advanced start-up" on the right, click **Restart now**
4. The computer will reboot and ask you to "Choose an option" – choose **Troubleshoot**

   Troubleshoot
   Reset your PC or see advanced options

5. In the "Troubleshoot" screen, choose **Advanced options**

   Advanced options

6. Next, choose **Startup Settings**, then click the **Restart** button you will find there

   Startup Settings
   Change Windows startup behavior

7. When the "Startup Settings" screen appears, press the **F4** key or the number 4 key to enable Safe Mode. The computer will now reboot into Safe Mode

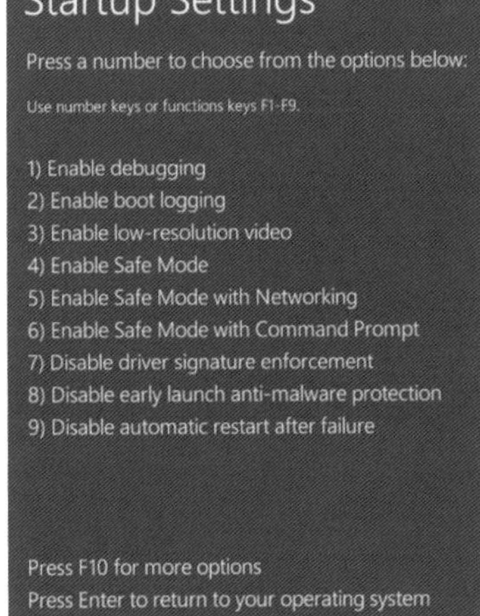

Note that Startup Settings replaces the Advanced Boot menu found in earlier versions of Windows. Unlike the Advanced Boot menu, Startup Settings cannot be initiated while the PC is booting by pressing the **F8** key. It can only be initiated from within Windows as described above, from a Windows 10 installation disk, or a Windows 10 Recovery drive. Also, the **Startup Settings** options cannot be selected with the mouse or keyboard – a specific key is allocated to each option.

Safe Mode starts Windows with a limited set of files and device drivers, without the usual startup programs and services. This validates the basic settings.

Safe Mode cannot be initiated by pressing the **F8** key as with previous versions of Windows.

Startup Settings is a new feature in Windows 10.

Program compatibility

When you install programs on your Windows 10 PC, you may come across one or two that refuse to run – this could be due to an incompatibility issue with Windows 10. A possible solution is the Program Compatibility Troubleshooter. This will recreate the Windows environment for which they were designed and may get them running.

1. Go to Start, Windows System, Control Panel, (View by: Category), Programs, **Run programs made for previous versions of Windows**

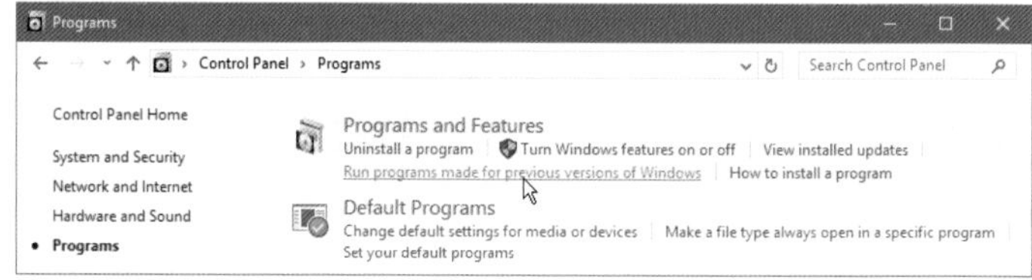

2. Click **Next**, and after a few moments you will see a dialog box showing you a list of all the programs on the PC

3. Select the one you're having trouble with and click **Next**, then select **Troubleshoot program**

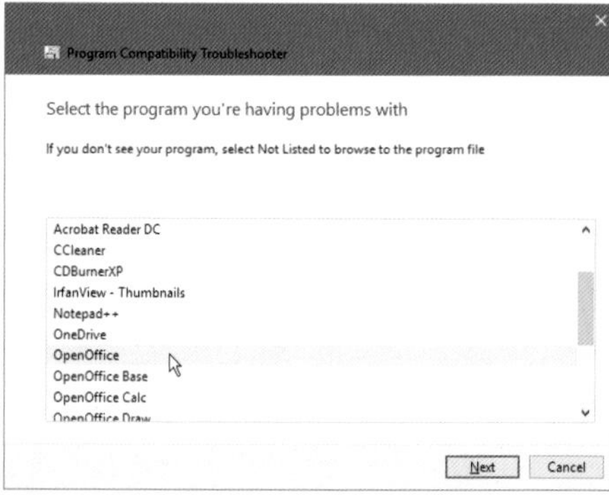

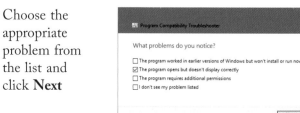

4. Choose the appropriate problem from the list and click **Next**

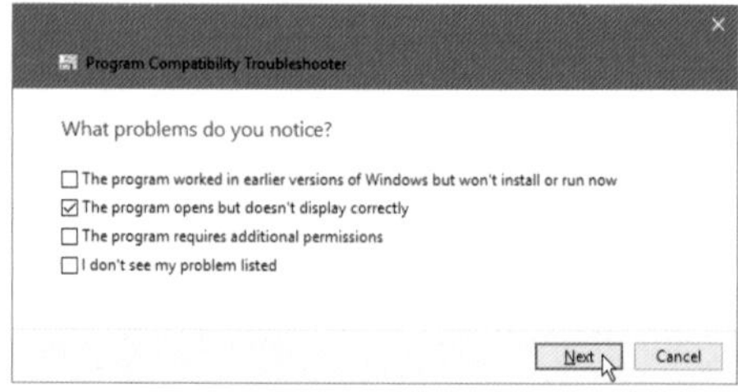

5. Windows will try to fix the issue. If the problem hasn't been resolved, click **No, try again** with different settings to repeat the procedure with other possible causes

Another way of applying compatibility settings is to right-click the program's executable (setup) file. Click **Properties** and then open the **Compatibility** tab. From here, you can choose an operating system that the program is known to work with.

If a program won't install at all, the method described on the right won't work. In this case, do it as described above.

Once a program has been successfully set up, it will use the compatibility settings every time it is run.

21 Backup and recovery

You need to keep copies of your data so that if you have problems you can recover your system. Windows 10 provides ways to make backups and helps you restore the copies, should it be necessary.

Sync settings

With synchronization turned on, your data is accessible on all the devices you are logged in to with a Microsoft account. Your settings, such as Wallpaper, can also be replicated on all devices.

In Windows 10, sync settings are consolidated in the Accounts category.

If you have critical or confidential files on OneDrive, you may want to think carefully about synchronizing passwords.

An important feature in Windows 10 is the ability to synchronize your settings across all your devices. This means that when you change your Desktop background, for example, the change is replicated on all your devices.

Because your settings are stored in the Cloud, not only are they synchronized, they are thus also automatically backed up. Furthermore, the backup is dynamic as it is done in realtime.

The synchronization feature is enabled by default, so you may wish to review exactly what is being synchronized, and thus backed up.

1. Open Settings, Accounts, then click **Sync your settings** in the left-hand panel

2. In the right-hand panel, you'll see all the settings on your PC that can be synchronized. At the top, under "Sync your settings" you can turn synchronization on or off altogether

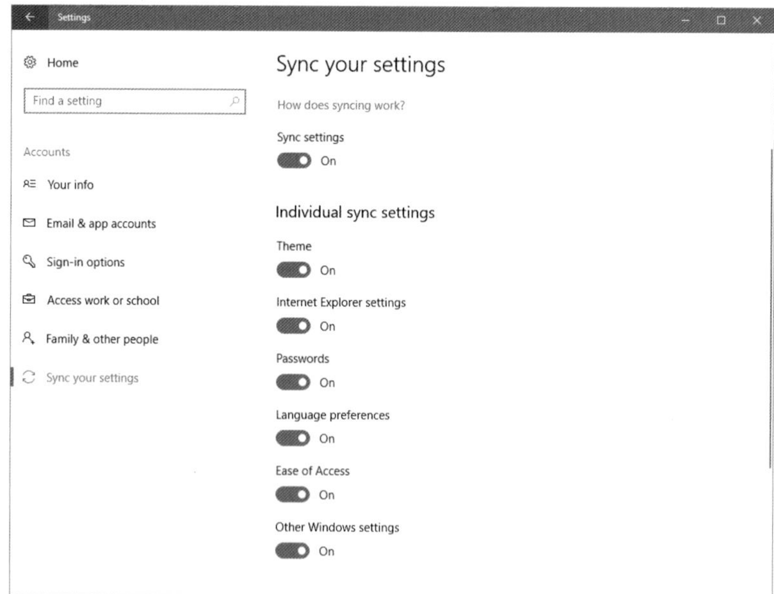

3. You can toggle individual settings on and off by clicking on them

Sync to OneDrive

While the synchronization feature makes it possible to automatically back up your settings, it cannot back up your files and folders. For this, you need the OneDrive feature that is built into Windows 10.

1. Open any File Explorer window and on the left-hand side, you'll see a OneDrive item in the Navigation pane

2. Click on the **OneDrive** item to see all your folders whose contents are stored as duplicates in "the Cloud"

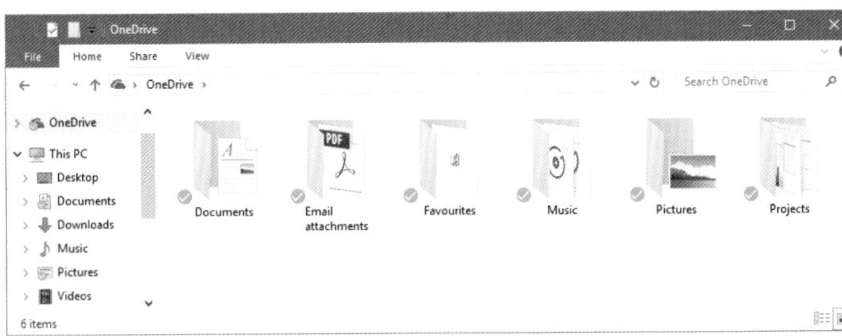

3. You can keep this selection of folders as they are, add more, delete them, or create your own folder structure

4. To back up a file or folder, just save it within OneDrive – it will be automatically duplicated on the Cloud

5. You can save files to the OneDrive folder from a program's **Save As** menu

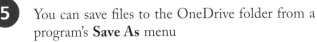

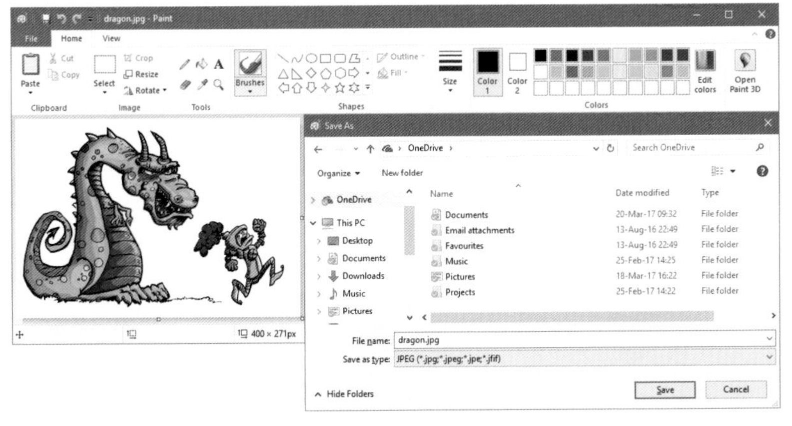

The OneDrive folder works like any other folder – files can be added, deleted, renamed, etc.

Some programs provide a Save to OneDrive menu option. An example is Microsoft Office 2016.

Save As

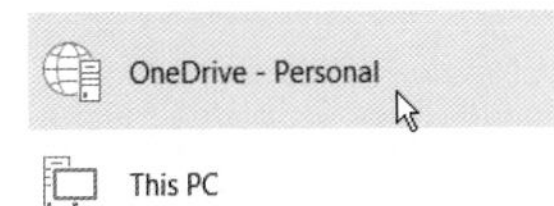

Copy data

When you create documents or other files on your computer, it is wise to take precautions to protect your work in case problems arise with the original version.

To illustrate the options and the considerations, we'll look at the drives and users on an example computer:

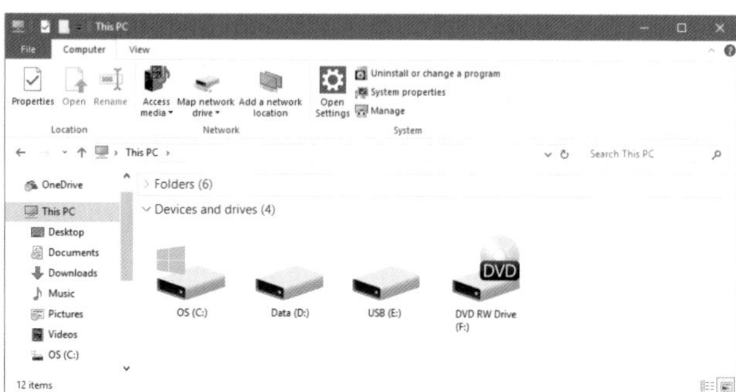

Protecting your files can be as simple as copying the files onto a USB flash drive, but there are more sophisticated methods available.

1. Press **WinKey** + **X** and select File Explorer, then choose **This PC** to view the storage devices:

   - Local Disk (C:) containing the system and the library files.
   - A second hard drive Local Disk (D:).
   - USB Drive (E:).
   - A DVD RW Drive (F:).

2. Go to Start, Windows System, Control Panel, **User Accounts** then click the **Change account type** link to see the accounts

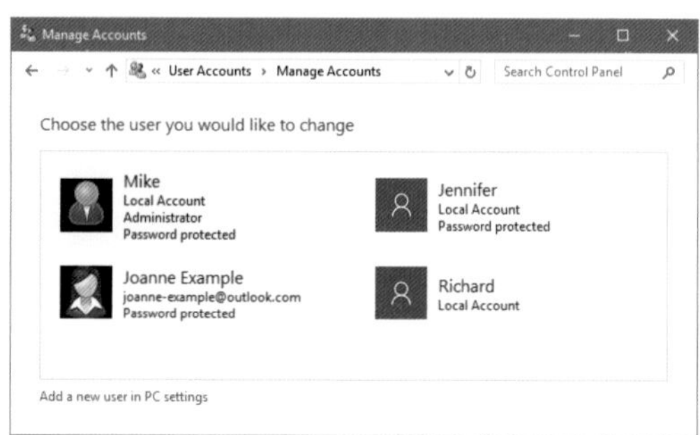

The Standard user account shown here for the user named Richard has no password assigned. As administrator, you could select accounts from this panel and create passwords for them.

To make a copy of a file on the USB drive:

1. Navigate to the folder containing the file

2. Left-click on the file and drag it onto the drive name in the Navigation pane, then release it there

You could also right-click a file or folder and select **Copy**, then right-click the destination drive and select **Paste** (or use the **Ctrl** + **C** and **Ctrl** + **V** keyboard shortcuts).

3. You can also drag a folder to copy the complete contents using the same technique

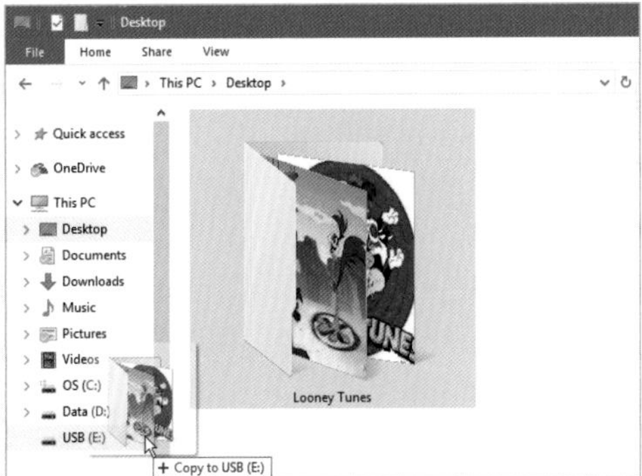

Repeated copies

Note that a repeated copy at a later date to the same removable drive would over-write the initial copy. To keep a history of changes, you need to copy to a folder, perhaps named as the copy date, or use a separate removable drive each time.

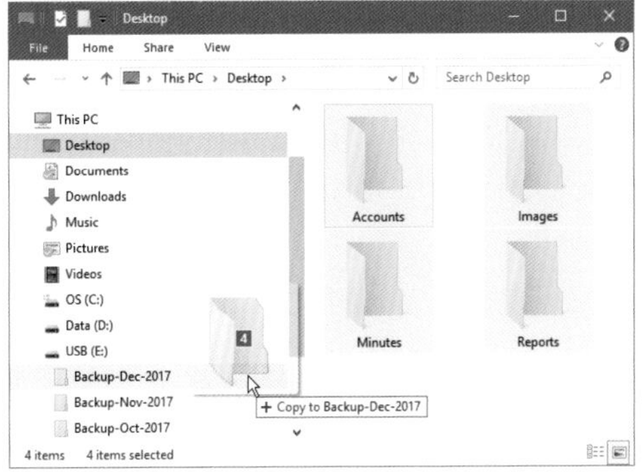

If you right-click as you drag, you will Move rather than Copy the files to the destination drive.

Copy libraries

Suppose you want to save the entire contents of your libraries:

1. Open Libraries in **File Explorer** (see page 191)

2. Rather than drag and drop, right-click the **Libraries** folder and select the **Copy** option

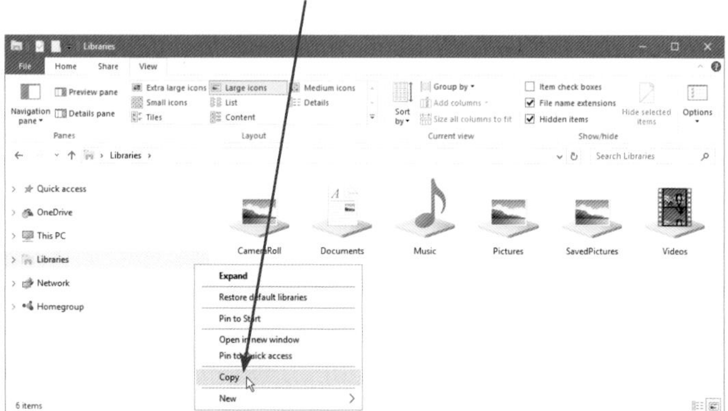

On the ribbon choose View, Navigation pane, **Show all folders** – to display the Desktop and the Libraries folder in the Navigation pane.

3. In the Navigation pane, select the removable drive to open it

4. Right-click the Contents pane and select the **Paste** option

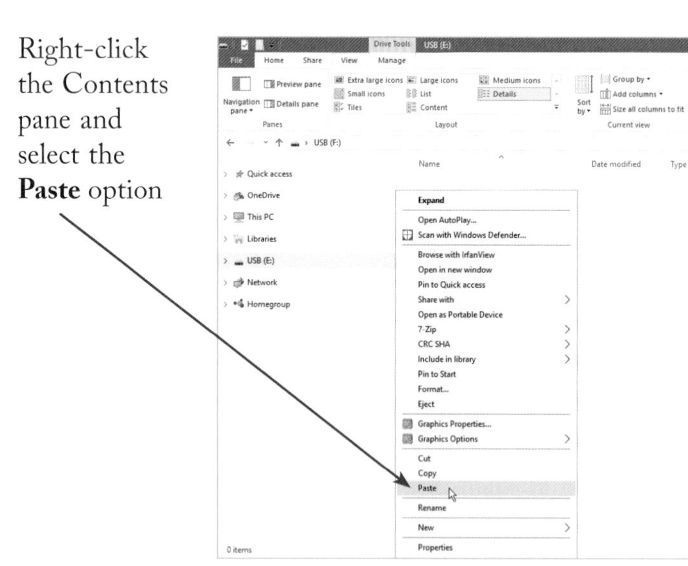

Dragging and dropping the Libraries folder creates a link to the original folder, rather than making actual copies of the files and folders.

5. The contents of the libraries then begin copying to the removable drive – click **More details** to see the progress

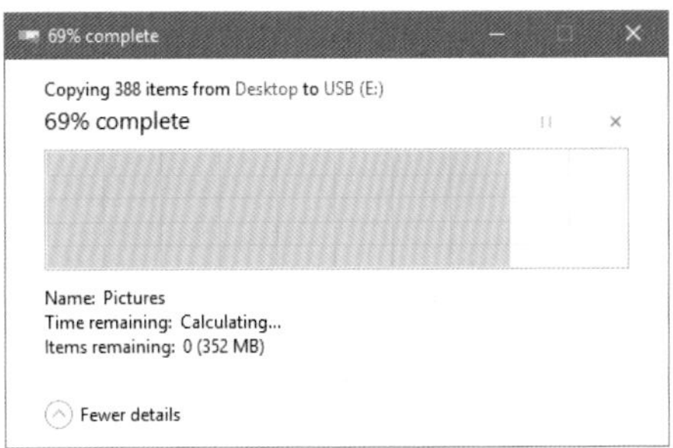

6. Expand the Navigation pane entry for the removable drive, and you'll see how the contents are arranged

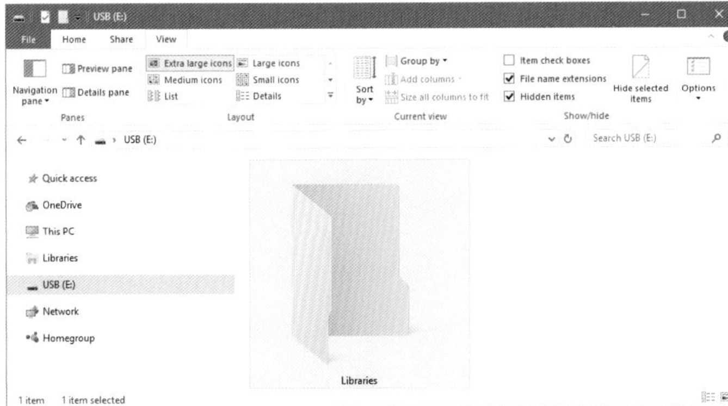

The files and folders that are listed in the libraries may be stored in separate locations on your disk.

Note that each library folder in the copy contains the merged contents of the Current user and the Public libraries. This can lead to difficulties when restoring files and folders.

When you copy libraries, you'll also have problems with over-writing older copies with new copies.

Other users

You may encounter problems accessing user folders if you are required to make backup copies on behalf of other users with accounts on your computer.

Reset your system

Like many things in life, Windows depreciates with use. It develops faults, slows down and may become unstable. Windows 10 provides a utility that will quickly restore it to an "as new" condition.

Virtually all problems that occur with Windows can be repaired. However, it is almost always easier to simply revert the system to a state prior to the fault manifesting itself. The reset process is one way of doing this.

1. Go to Settings, **Update & security**, then choose **Recovery** in the left-hand pane

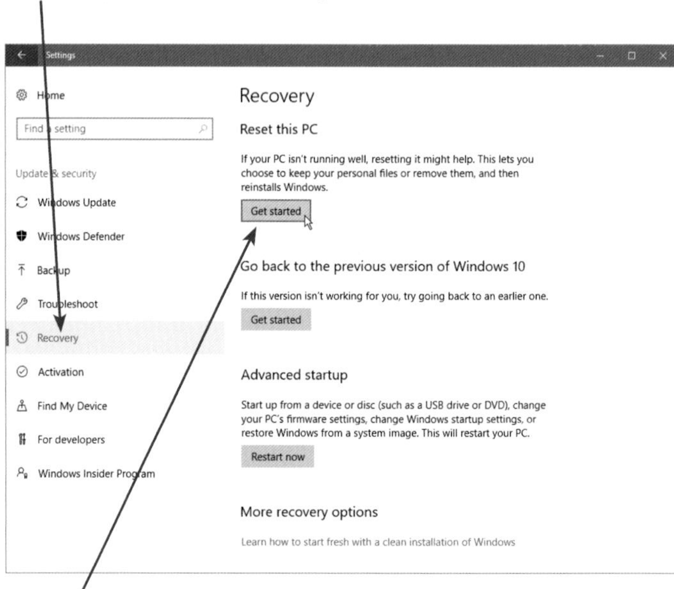
Settings
Home
Find a setting
Update & security
Windows Update
Windows Defender
Backup
Troubleshoot
Recovery
Activation
Find My Device
For developers
Windows Insider Program
Recovery
Reset this PC
If your PC isn't running well, resetting it might help. This lets you choose to keep your personal files or remove them, and then reinstalls Windows.
Get started
Go back to the previous version of Windows 10
If this version isn't working for you, try going back to an earlier one.
Get started
Advanced startup
Start up from a device or disc (such as a USB drive or DVD), change your PC's firmware settings, change Windows startup settings, or restore Windows from a system image. This will restart your PC.
Restart now
More recovery options
Learn how to start fresh with a clean installation of Windows

You might be prompted to insert your Windows 10 installation disk or recovery media that came with your PC.

2. Now, in the right-hand pane, under "Reset this PC", click the **Get started** button

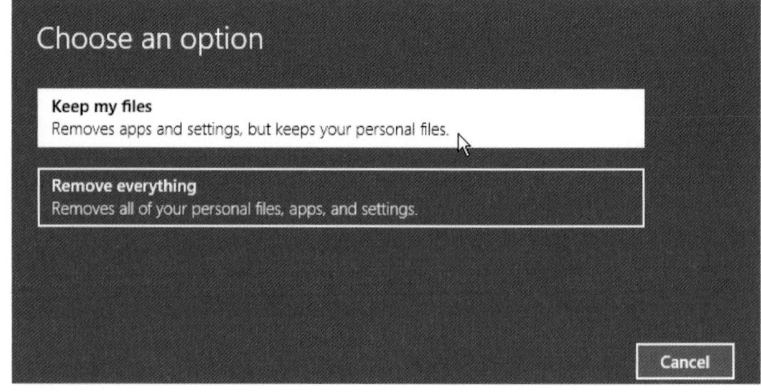
Choose an option
Keep my files
Removes apps and settings, but keeps your personal files.
Remove everything
Removes all of your personal files, apps, and settings.
Cancel

You are then asked to choose an option. If you choose the option to **Keep my files**, here is what will happen:

- **Your files and personalization settings won't change** – this means that your data will not be deleted, and that any changes you have made to the default personalization settings will be retained. The former is the big plus here, as it means you do not have to make a backup of your data and then reinstall it afterwards.
- **Your PC settings will be changed back to their defaults** – this means that Windows 10 will be deleted and replaced by a new copy. Any configuration changes made to Windows settings will be lost.
- **Apps from the Windows Store will be kept** – Windows 10 apps installed from the Windows Store will not be deleted.
- **Apps you installed from disks or websites will be removed** – all third-party software will be deleted.
- **After the reset, a document will appear on the Desktop** – listing the applications that have been removed.

One advantage of the reset process is that it will reinstall Windows in less time than taken for the original installation.

3. Having read and understood what the utility will do, click **Keep my files**

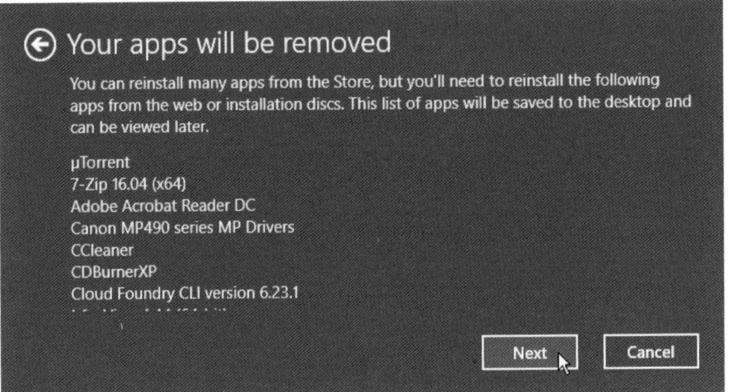

Your apps will be removed
You can reinstall many apps from the Store, but you'll need to reinstall the following apps from the web or installation discs. This list of apps will be saved to the desktop and can be viewed later.
µTorrent
7-Zip 16.04 (x64)
Adobe Acrobat Reader DC
Canon MP490 series MP Drivers
CCleaner
CDBurnerXP
Cloud Foundry CLI version 6.23.1
Next
Cancel

You may want to make a note of the applications to be deleted.

4. You'll now see a list of applications that will be deleted during the reset procedure. Click **Next**

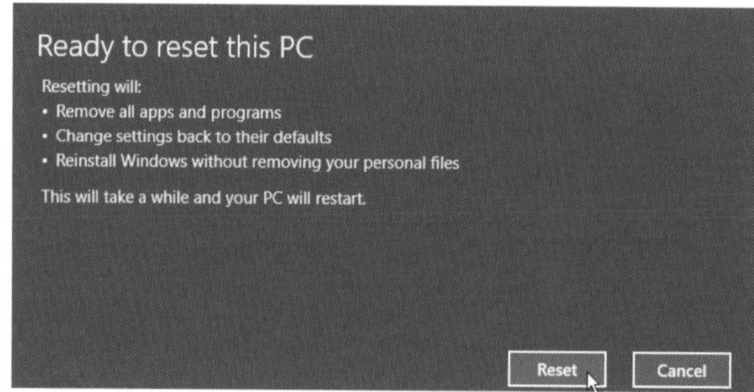

The reset process will install a new copy of Windows 10 while retaining the user's Windows apps, data and personalization settings. Everything else will be deleted.

5. Click **Next** on the warning screen, then on the next screen, click **Reset** – the computer will reboot and reset

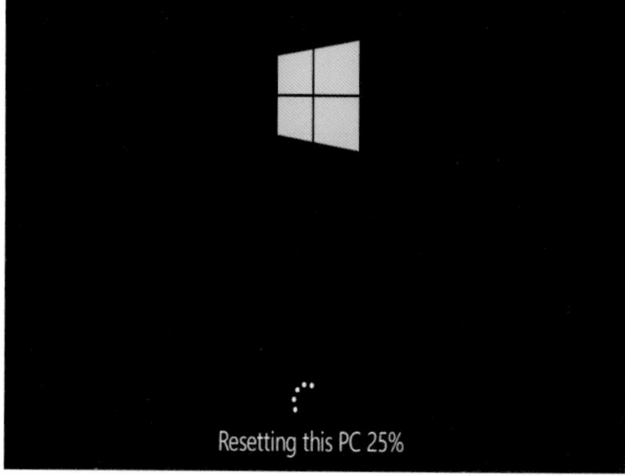

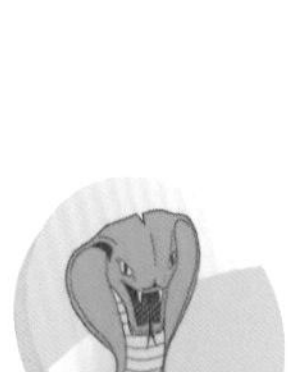

The big drawback is that users will probably have to reinstall/reconfigure most of their software, and reconfigure various Windows settings.

6. When the computer has been reset, Windows begins its setup routine. When that's done, you're back in business

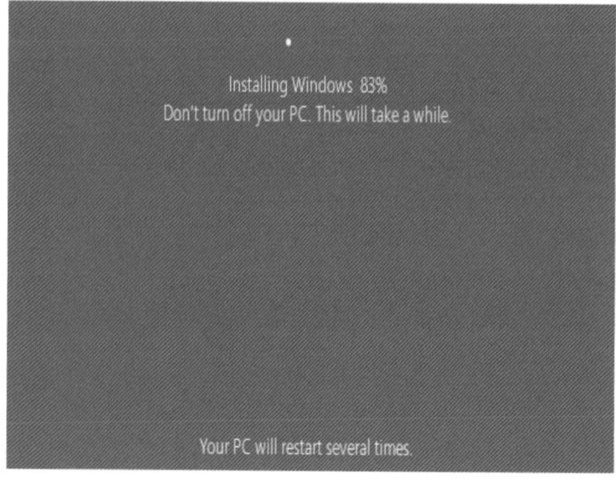

Reinstall your system

The traditional method of completely restoring a Windows PC to its factory settings is to do a clean installation. This wipes the drive clean of all data, after which a new copy of Windows is installed. The procedure is done by booting the PC from the installation disk and is something many will be wary of trying. Windows 10 provides a much simpler method of restoring Windows to its factory settings, courtesy of its Reset utility. It works as described below:

Hot tip

The Reset utility also provides an ideal way of securely deleting your data on a computer you are going to sell or scrap.

1. Go to Settings, Update & security, and choose **Recovery**

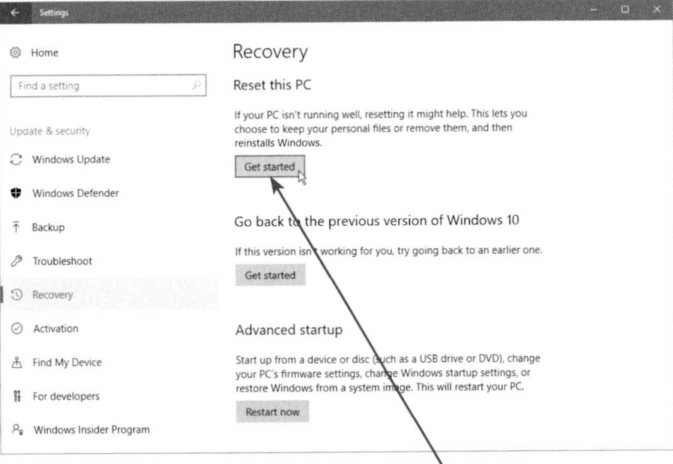
Settings
Home
Find a setting
Update & security
Windows Update
Windows Defender
Backup
Troubleshoot
Recovery
Activation
Find My Device
For developers
Windows Insider Program
Recovery
Reset this PC
If your PC isn't running well, resetting it might help. This lets you choose to keep your personal files or remove them, and then reinstalls Windows.
Get started
Go back to the previous version of Windows 10
If this version isn't working for you, try going back to an earlier one.
Get started
Advanced startup
Start up from a device or disc (such as a USB drive or DVD), change your PC's firmware settings, change Windows startup settings, or restore Windows from a system image. This will restart your PC.
Restart now

2. Under "Reset this PC", click the **Get started** button

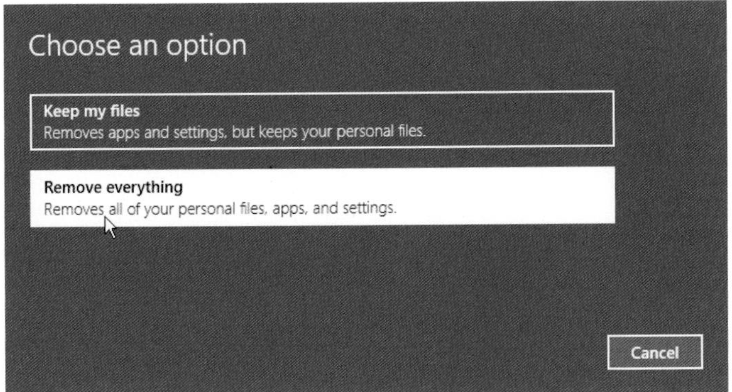
Choose an option
Keep my files
Removes apps and settings, but keeps your personal files.
Remove everything
Removes all of your personal files, apps, and settings.
Cancel

3. When asked to choose an option, choose the option to **Remove everything** to completely reset Windows 10

...cont'd

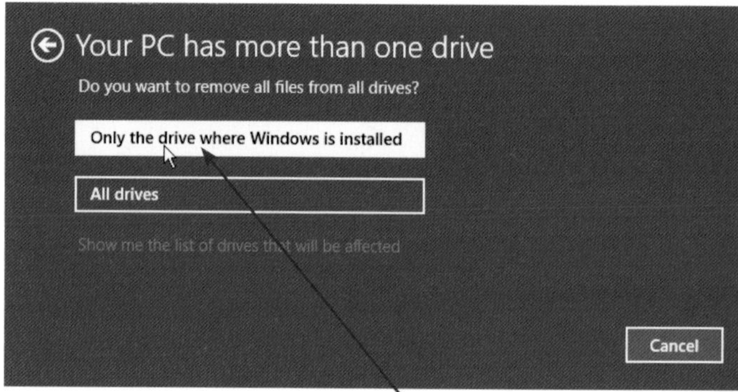

4. Elect to only remove files from your Windows drive

5. Next, choose **Just remove my files** if you just want to start again from scratch – all data you have put on the PC will be deleted, leaving you with an "as new" copy of Windows

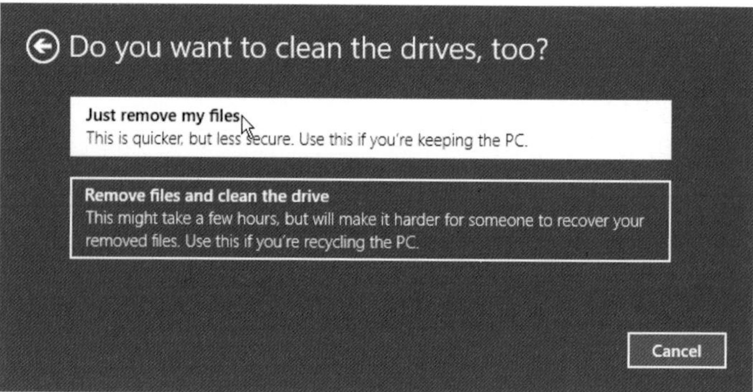

The **Remove files and clean the drive** option does the same as **Just remove my files** but also wipes the drive securely so the data cannot be recovered later.

6. Now, click the **Reset** button to begin the procedure

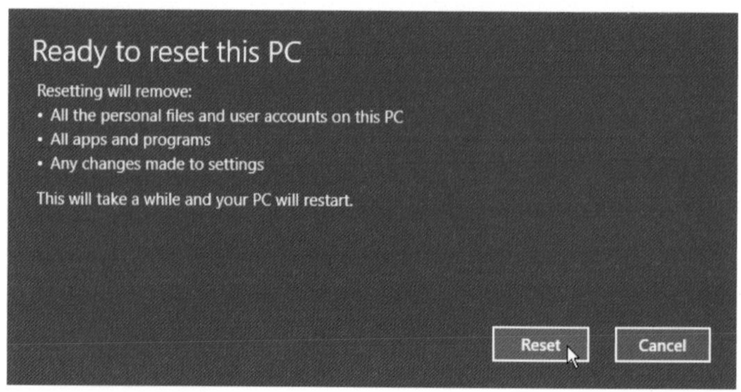

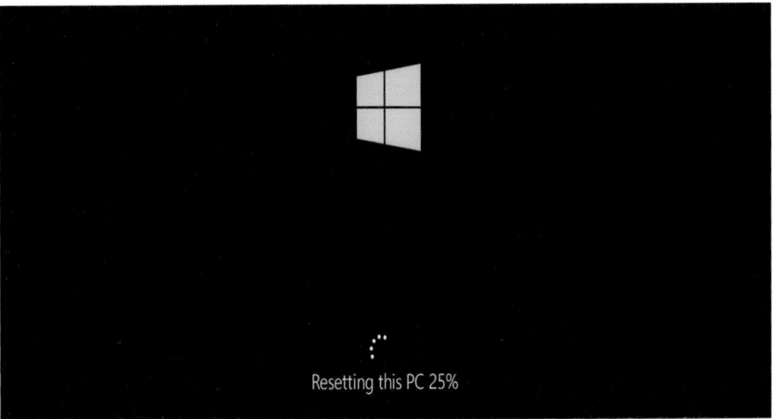

7. The computer will now reboot and you will see the screen above as the Reset procedure begins

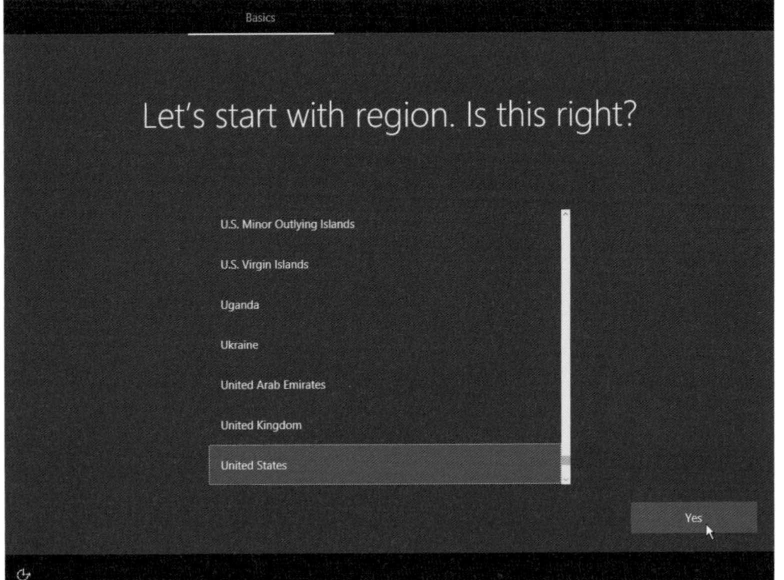

8. When the Reset is done, Windows goes through its setting-up routine, just like the first time it was installed

At the end of the Reset, your computer will be exactly how it was when you first installed Windows 10.

Enable File History

Windows 10 provides some very useful backup utilities. One of these is File History, with which users are able to quickly restore individual files that have been modified, damaged or even deleted.

It works by making automatic backups (every hour by default) of all files stored in the following folders – Contacts, Desktop, Favorites, and the Documents, Music, Pictures and Video libraries. By default, File History is turned off. Enable it as follows:

You will need to connect a second drive to your PC before you can use File History.

1. Go to Settings, Update & security, Backup, then under "Back up using File History", click **+ Add a drive**

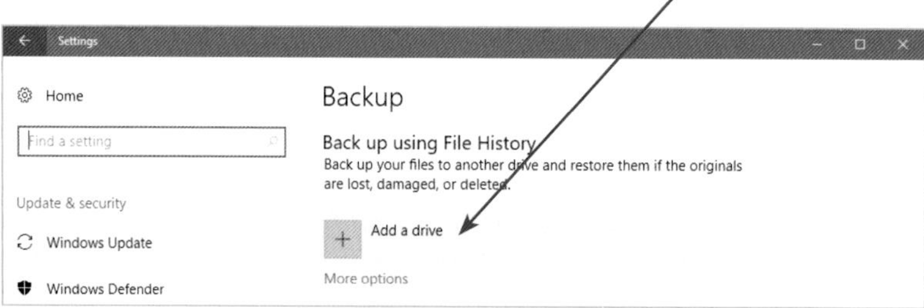

2. The utility will search your computer for a suitable backup drive

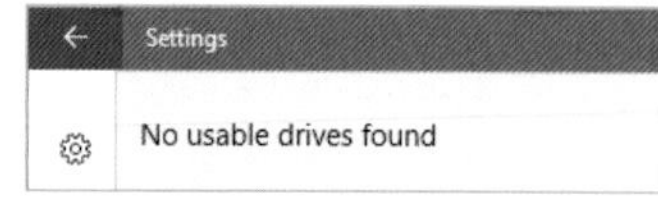

Note that existing backups are not overwritten by new ones – each backup is kept so, over a period of time, a file history is created. This enables a file to be restored from a unique backup created at a specific time and date.

3. Connect a second drive to your computer. This must be a separate drive to the main system drive and can be of any type – an external hard drive, a USB hard drive or a USB flash drive. Once done, run the utility again; this time your second drive will be recognized, as we see below:

4. Click the drive to turn on automatic backups – you will see a new toggle button appear

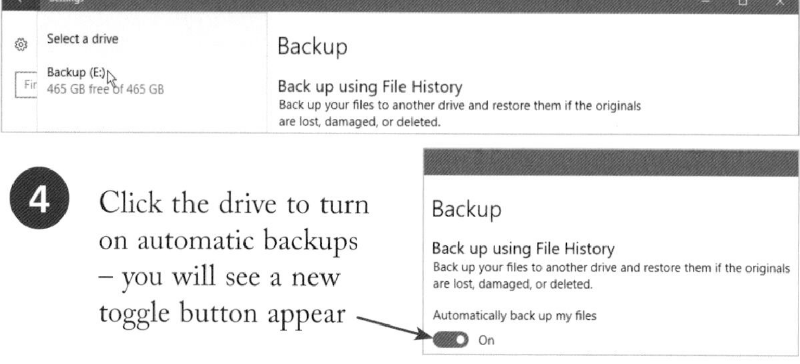

5. Next, click **Back up now** to create an initial backup on the chosen drive

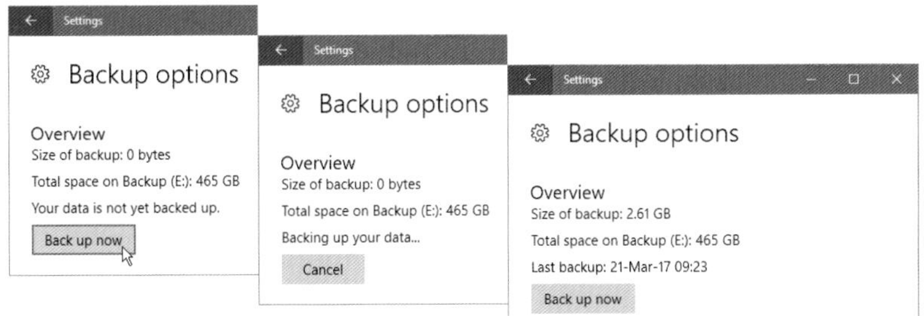

The only way to back up folders other than with File History is to add them to a library.

6. Now, scroll down the Backup options page to see the default collection of folders that are being backed up automatically

7. If you want to add a folder to the collection of folders listed, click the + **Add a folder** button then select the folder to be added

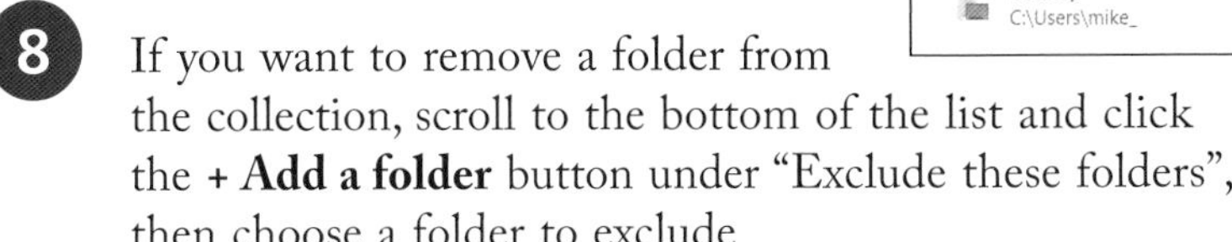

8. If you want to remove a folder from the collection, scroll to the bottom of the list and click the + **Add a folder** button under "Exclude these folders", then choose a folder to exclude

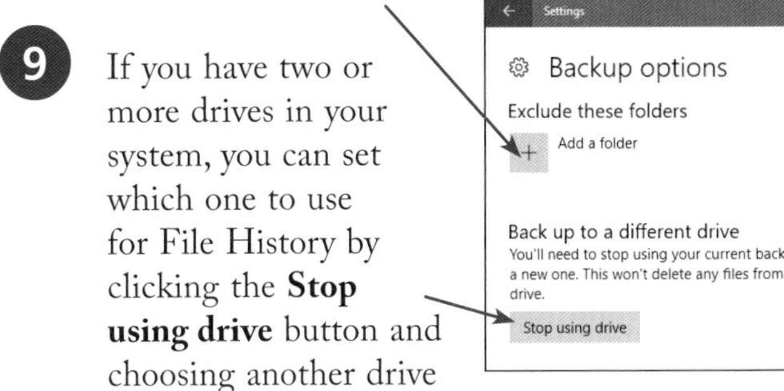

9. If you have two or more drives in your system, you can set which one to use for File History by clicking the **Stop using drive** button and choosing another drive

...cont'd

By default, backups are made every hour and backups are kept forever.

On the "Backup options" page, the **Back up my files** option lets you specify how often your files are backed up – from every 10 minutes to Daily. Consider this option carefully as the more frequent your backups, the more space is used on your backup drive.

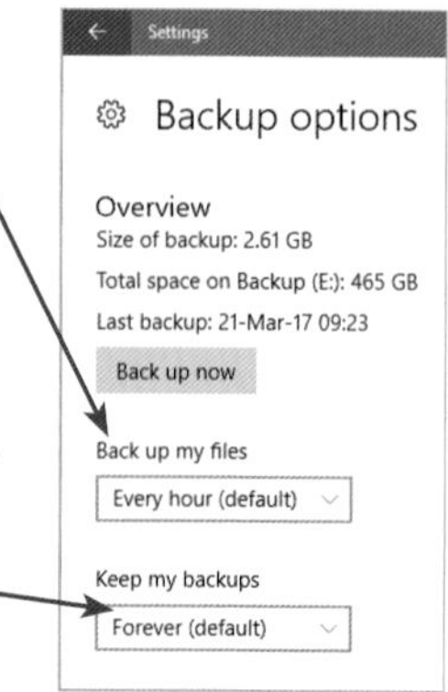

The **Keep my backups** option lets you specify how long your backups are kept – from one month to forever, or until space is needed.

To back up your system by the default settings, or restore personal files, the backup drive must be attached.

Restoring personal files

To restore a file or folder: scroll down to "Related settings", then click the option to **Restore files from a current backup**. This opens a window showing all your backed-up folders. To restore an entire folder, select that folder, then click the green **Restore** button.

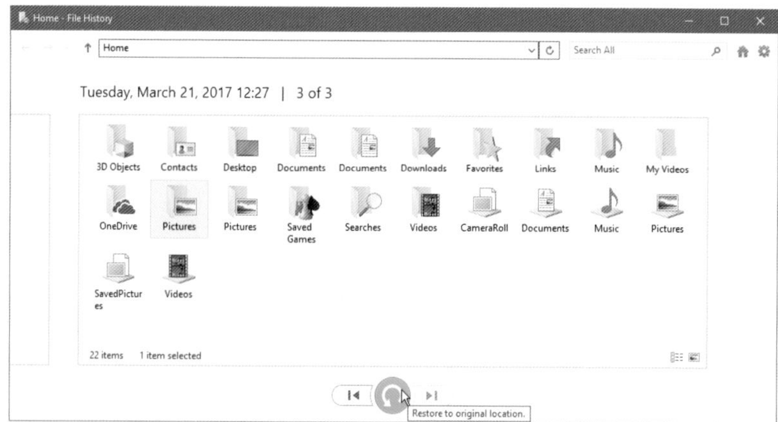

Enable automatic backups now – so you won't regret it later.

If you just want to restore a specific file or files within a folder, open the folder, select the file(s), then click the **Restore** button.

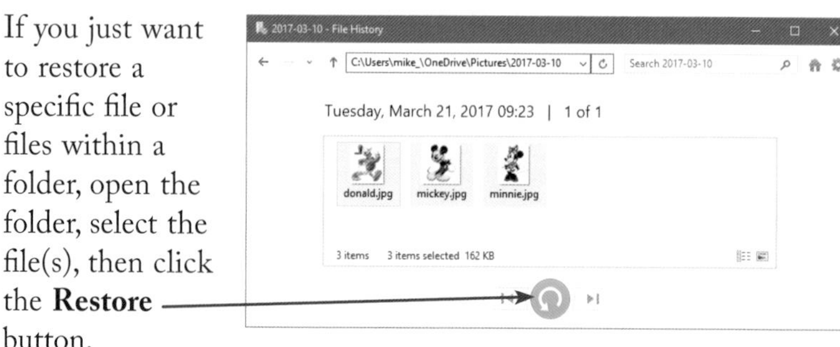

Create a system image

A system image is an exact copy of a drive and, by default, it includes the drives required for Windows to run. It includes Windows and your system settings, programs, and files. If desired, it can be configured to include other drives as well.

Should the imaged computer subsequently develop a problem that cannot be repaired, it can be restored from the image.

There are many third-party utilities of this type; a well-known one being Acronis True Image, but Windows 10 provides its own.

1. Go to Settings, Update & security, Backup, then under "Backup using File History" click **More options**

2. Scroll down to "Related settings" and click **See advanced settings** – to open the "File History" dialog:

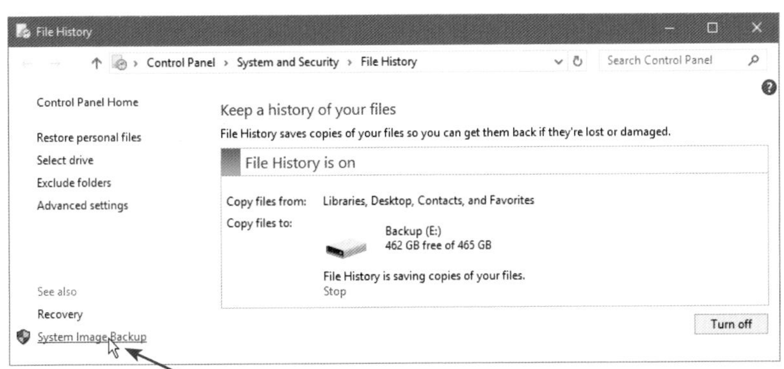

A system image will restore the PC to the state it was in when the image was built.

3. Next, click the **System Image Backup** link – to open the "Backup and Restore" dialog

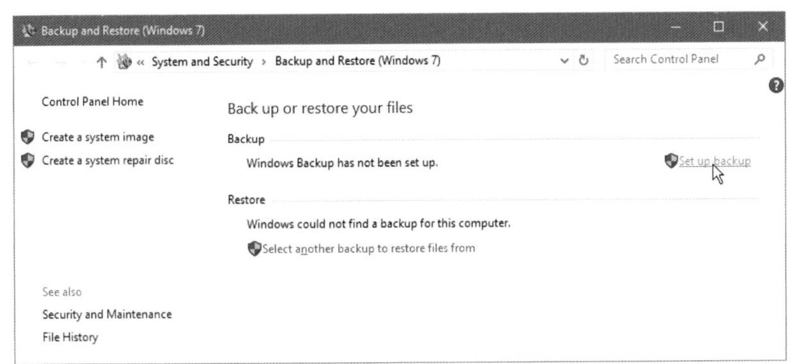

Any type of medium can be used for the image backup. It has to be separate to the main system drive, though.

...cont'd

A system image of Windows 10 will be at least 15GB or so in size, so if you use a USB flash drive make sure its capacity is adequate.

4. On the "Backup and Restore" dialog click the **Set up backup** link, and the utility will search your computer for suitable backup mediums. These have to be separate to the main system drive and can be internal hard drives or removable media drives such as external hard drives, or USB flash drives

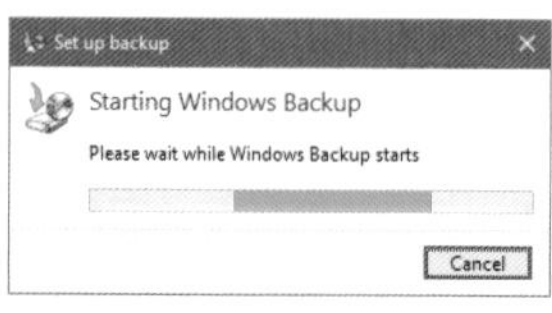

The utility will automatically recommend a separate hard drive for backups – if one is available on your system.

5. Accept the recommended backup medium or choose an alternative, and click **Next**

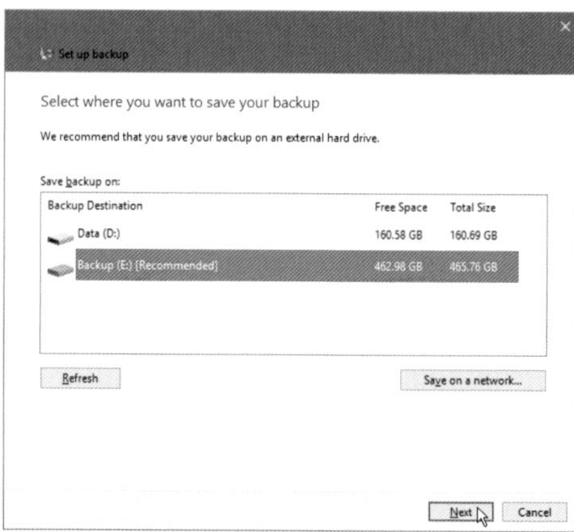

6. Opt to **Let Windows choose (recommended)**, then click the **Next** button

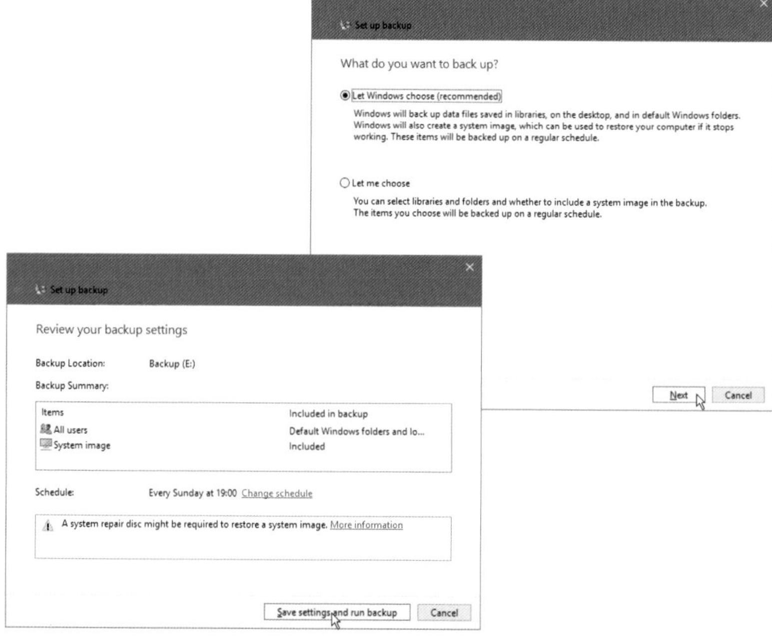

The image can include any number of drives.

7. Review your settings, then click the **Save settings and run backup** button

8. Windows creates the system image – this can take a while

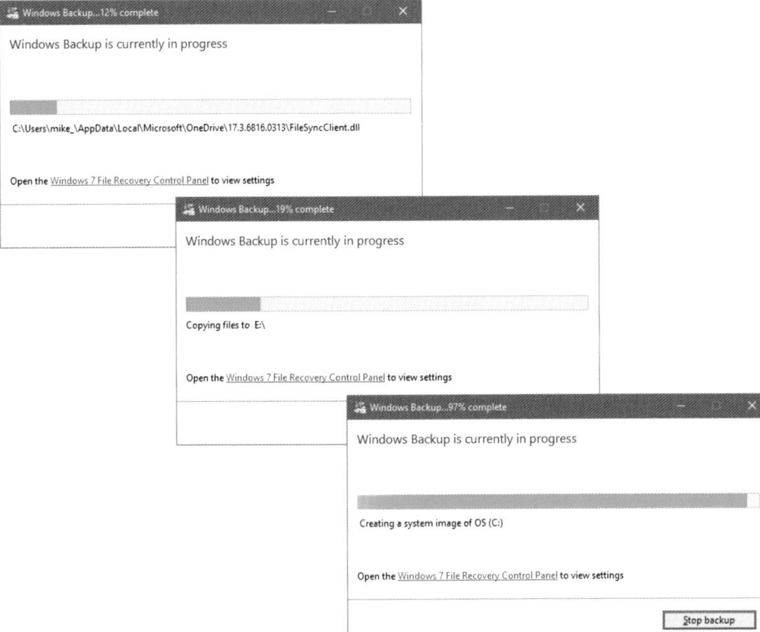

9. The image is added as a folder in the separate drive

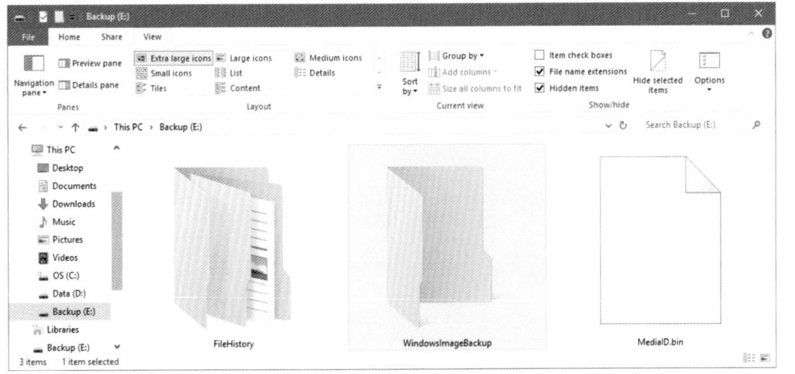

Images cannot be saved on the boot disk (where Windows is installed). You must use a different drive or partition.

If you need to move the **WindowsImageBackup** be sure to also move the **MediaID.bin** file alongside it to preserve the system image.

...cont'd

Restoring your system from an image

When you use an image backup to restore your system, be aware that, when done, your system will be exactly the same as when the backup was made. Any changes made to the computer after the backup was made will be lost – this includes files, settings and applications.

If you can't get Windows to start, you'll need a recovery drive to restore your system from an image.

How you go about restoring depends on your reason for doing it. If it's because your system is so damaged that you cannot get Windows to start at all, you'll need the aid of a Recovery drive, as we explain on pages 375-376. If it's for some other reason and Windows is working, you can do it from within Windows, as we explain below:

1. Go to Settings, **Update & security**, then choose **Recovery** in the left-hand pane

2. Now, in the right-hand pane, under "Advanced startup", click **Restart now**

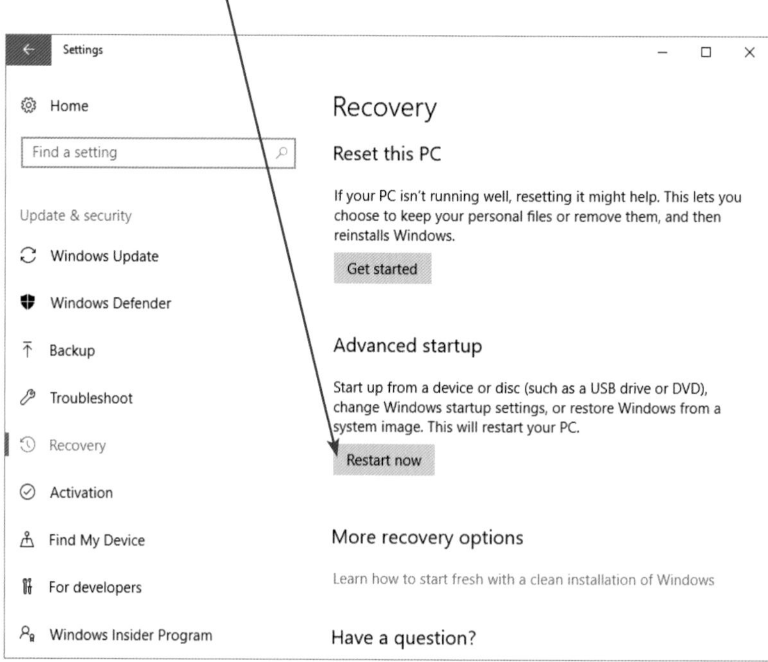
Settings
Home
Find a setting
Update & security
Windows Update
Windows Defender
Backup
Troubleshoot
Recovery
Activation
Find My Device
For developers
Windows Insider Program
Recovery
Reset this PC
If your PC isn't running well, resetting it might help. This lets you choose to keep your personal files or remove them, and then reinstalls Windows.
Get started
Advanced startup
Start up from a device or disc (such as a USB drive or DVD), change Windows startup settings, or restore Windows from a system image. This will restart your PC.
Restart now
More recovery options
Learn how to start fresh with a clean installation of Windows
Have a question?

Create a system recovery drive now – if you leave it until you need it, it will be too late.

3. When asked to "Choose an option", choose **Troubleshoot**

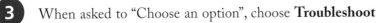

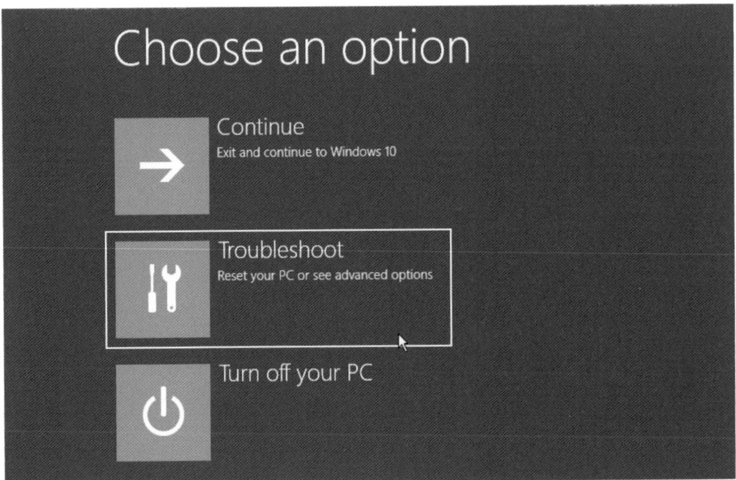

Advanced options also includes System Restore, Start-up Repair, Command Prompt and Start-up Settings. These can all be useful depending on the circumstances.

4. On the "Troubleshoot" page, select **Advanced options**

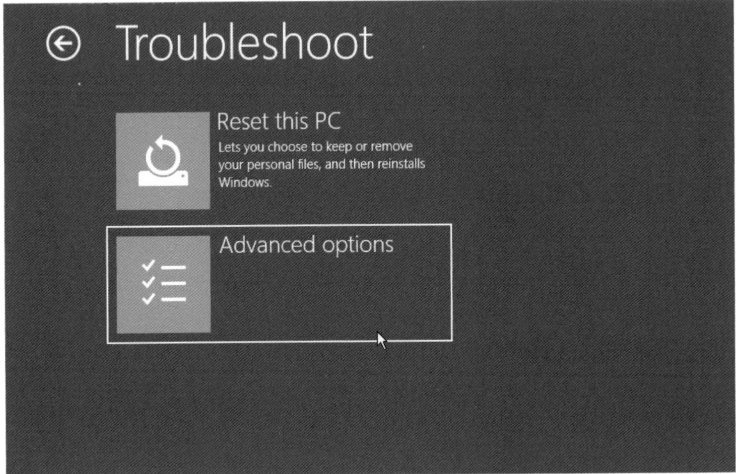

The restore procedure cannot take place while Windows is running.

5. Now, select **System Image Recovery**. The PC will reboot and the recovery configuration procedure will begin

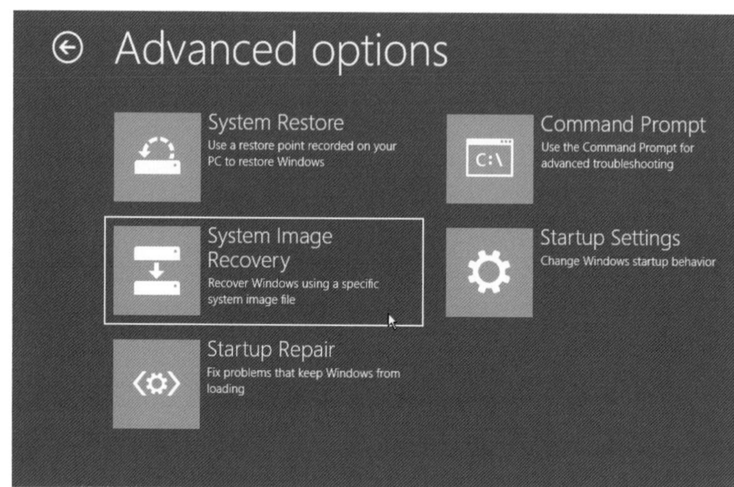

If you have several image backups, Windows will select the most recent one by default.

6. Enter your account password, then select the required image – if you only have one system image, Windows will select it automatically

7. Click **Next**, **Finish** to restore from the image backup

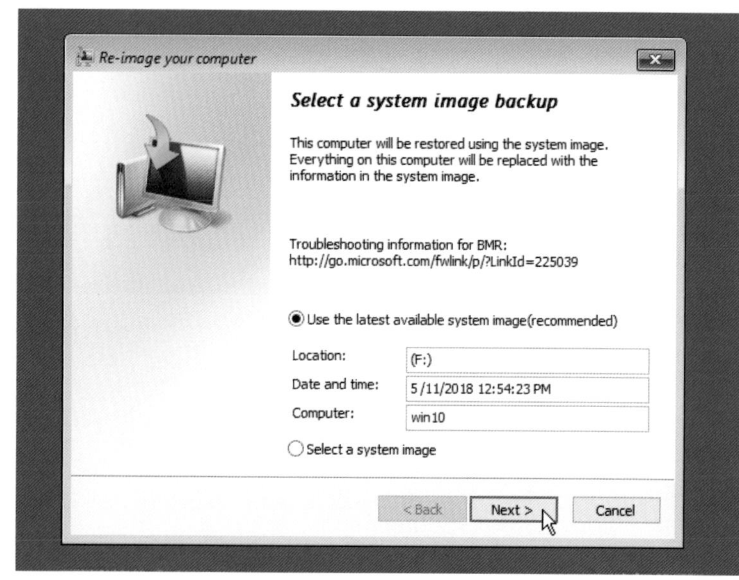

When the image has been restored, the computer will restart and boot into your newly-restored Windows.

System recovery drive

There will be occasions when it is impossible to get into Windows for some reason – damaged startup files is a typical example. For this reason, recovery and troubleshooting utilities have to be accessible from outside the Windows environment.

To be able to use the Windows utilities in this type of situation, they have to be first placed on removable media.

All the backups in the world are no good to you if you cannot get into the system. Make your recovery drive now.

1. Go to the Control Panel, (View by: Large icons), and open **File History**

2. In the File History window, click the **Recovery** link at the bottom-left of the window

3. Now, choose the option to **Create a recovery drive**

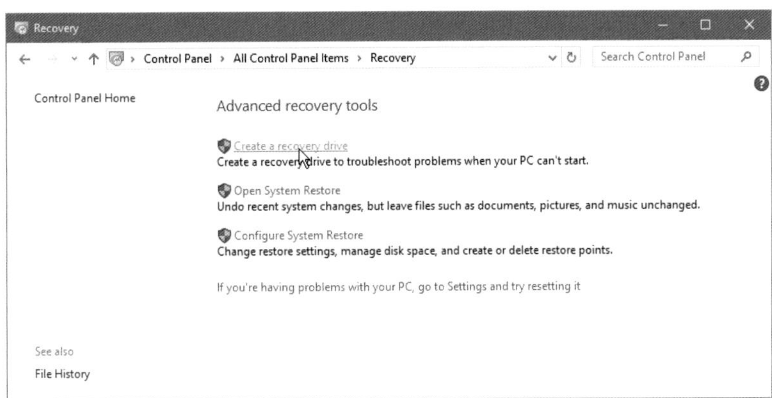

4. Follow the prompts to create a Windows recovery drive

Note that you will need a USB flash drive for this procedure. Also, it will erase anything already stored on the drive. So either use an empty drive or make sure you transfer any important data to another storage device.

Using your recovery drive

The time to use your recovery drive is when you are unable to boot your computer into Windows. When you find yourself in this situation, do the following:

...cont'd

1. Connect the recovery drive to your computer

2. Start the PC and go into the BIOS where you need to set the recovery drive as the boot drive – see page 43, where we explain how to do this. The procedure here is the same, apart from the fact that you want to set the recovery drive as the boot drive rather than the CD/DVD drive

3. Restart the computer

4. When the "Choose an option" screen opens, select **Troubleshoot**. This opens "Advanced options"

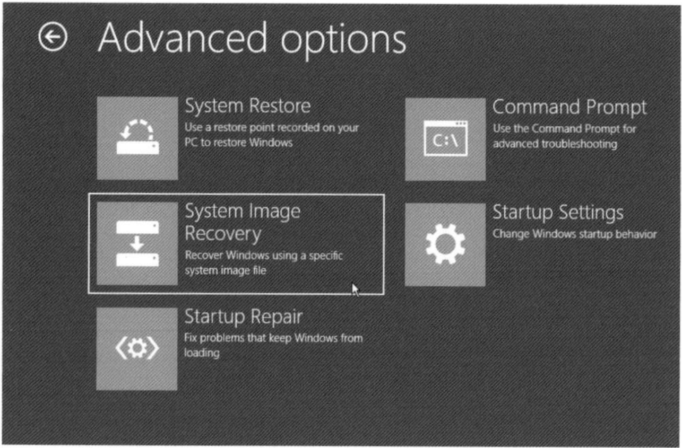

Here, you have five troubleshooting and recovery tools that will enable you to resolve most of the issues that are likely to occur.

The first option, **System Restore**, will undo any changes made to a system by installing software. So, if you've inadvertently downloaded a virus or malware, System Restore will fix it.

System Image Recovery we've already looked at on pages 372-374, while **Startup Repair** will fix issues that prevent Windows from booting.

Command Prompt is a troubleshooting tool for advanced users who know diagnostic commands.

Finally, **Startup Settings** enables you to start Windows in various troubleshooting modes that can help you fix a range of problems.

Choosing the Command Prompt option restarts the PC in the Windows Recovery Environment that is available before Windows loads. System administrators can enter commands at a prompt to diagnose problems.

22 Security and encryption

If your system or your storage devices contain sensitive information, you can protect the data even if the device is lost or stolen, using the various encryption facilities that are included in Windows 10.

User account management

There are several ways to manage user accounts on your computer. The traditional option is **User Accounts** in the Control Panel. Here, you can create or remove accounts, change account types, modify passwords, or change the pictures associated with accounts.

The traditional **User Accounts** applet is in the Control Panel.

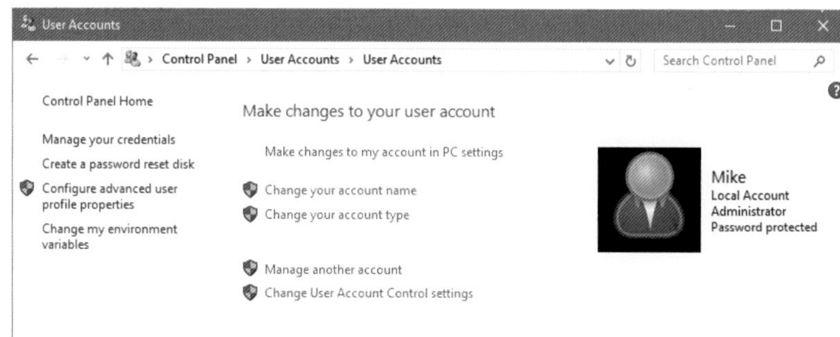

If several users share your computer, you may want to enable **Secure sign-in**, using the alternative User Accounts dialog:

This alternative **User Accounts** is very powerful and should only be used with caution.

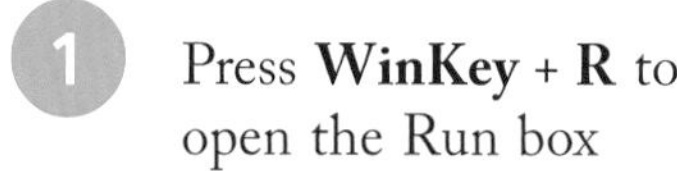

1. Press **WinKey** + **R** to open the Run box

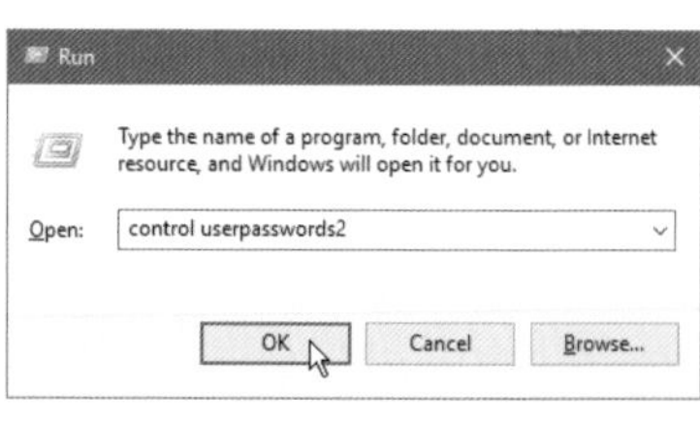

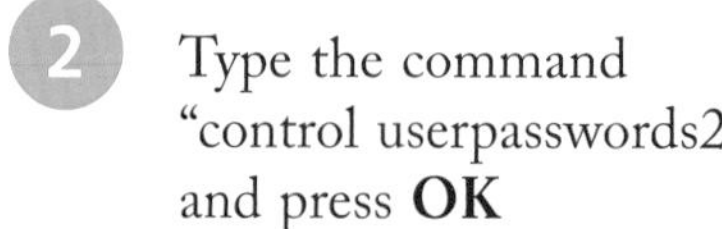

2. Type the command "control userpasswords2" and press **OK**

3. Select the **Advanced** tab to show **Secure sign-in**

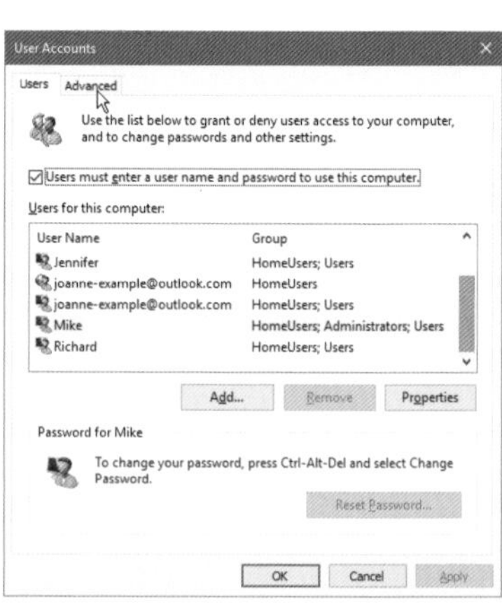

Setting **Secure sign-in** guarantees that the sign-in prompt is genuine, not an external program trying to discover your password.

4. Check the box that will **Require users to press Ctrl + Alt + Delete**

In the Pro and Enterprise editions of Windows 10, you can manage user accounts with the Local Users and Groups policy editor. There are several ways to display this. For example:

1. From the "Advanced" tab of the second User Accounts option, click the **Advanced** button

2. Press **WinKey** + **R**, type "lusrmgr.msc" then hit **Enter**

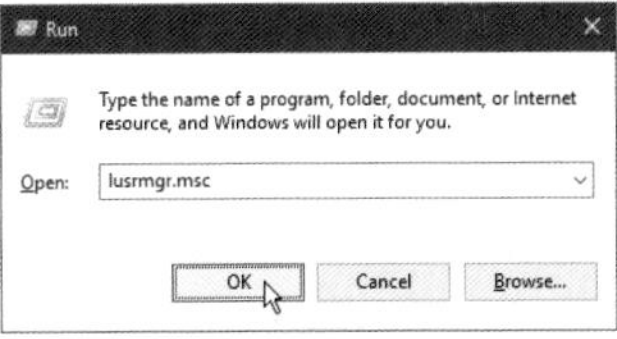

3. When the panel opens, click **Users** and you will see an extra user, **Administrator**, not shown in User Accounts

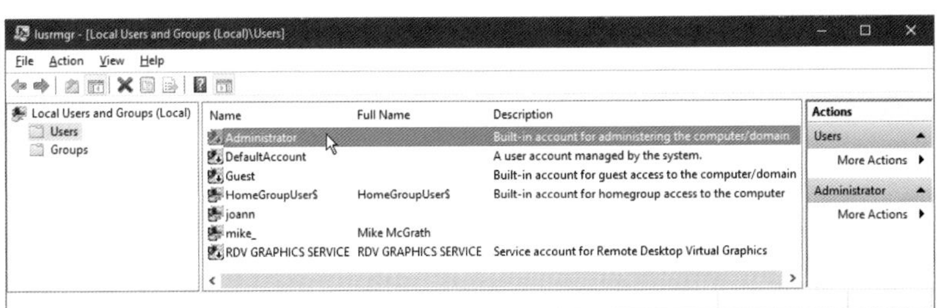

4. Double-click user account **Administrator** to display its Properties, and you'll see it is disabled by default

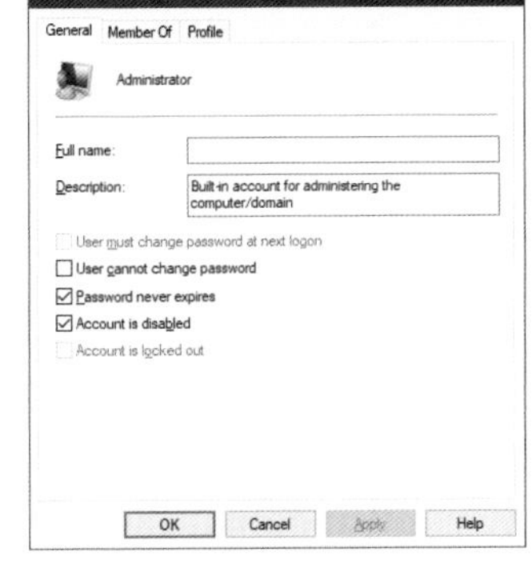

This is a built-in account that is automatically created but not normally used. If you do choose to use it, make sure to set a password.

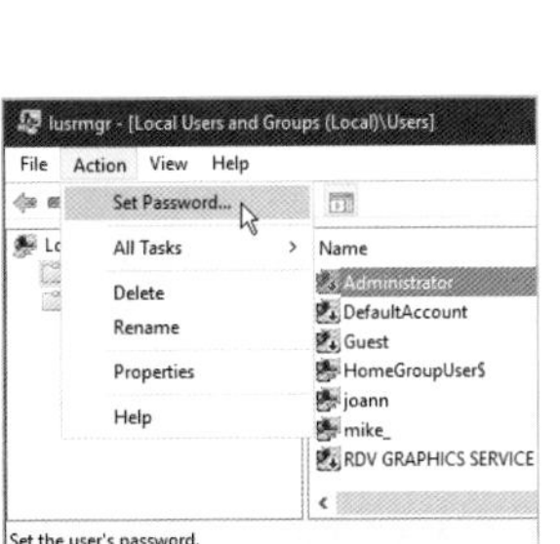

5. If you do enable this account, make sure to select **Action**, then **Set Password...**

Set password to expire

By default, your password can remain the same forever, but you are recommended to change it on a regular basis. Windows can be set to ensure that this happens for Local accounts:

1. Open "Local Users and Groups" (see page 379), select your username and click **More Actions**, **Properties**

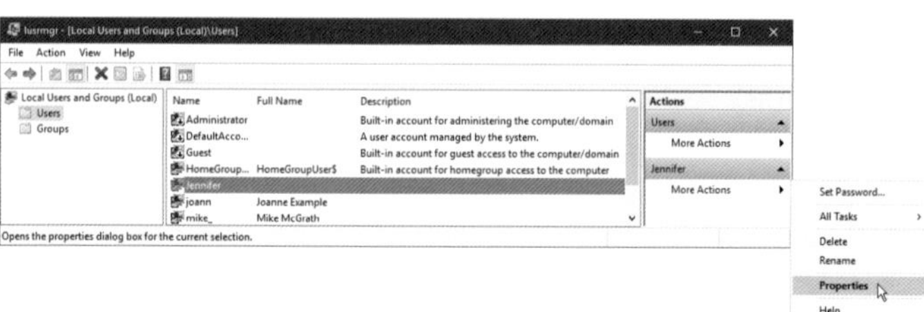

You can also double-click the username to open Properties.

2. Clear the box for "Password never expires" and click **User must change password at next logon**, then **Apply**, **OK**

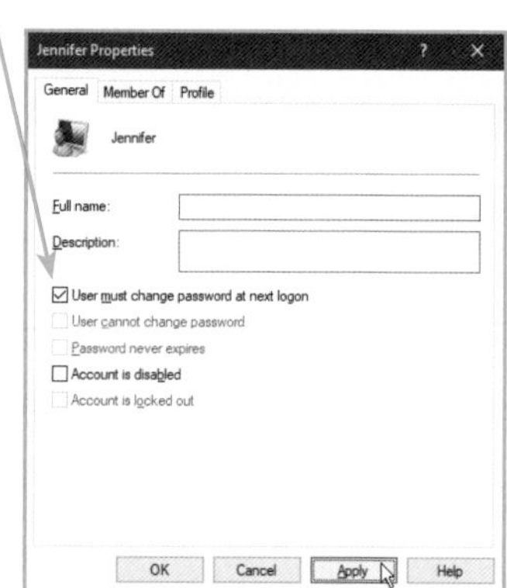

Local Security Policy is in Windows 10 Pro and Windows 10 Enterprise editions, but not available in the Windows 10 Home edition.

3. Close Local Users and Groups, then open "Local Security Policy" (see page 382) and expand **Account Policies**

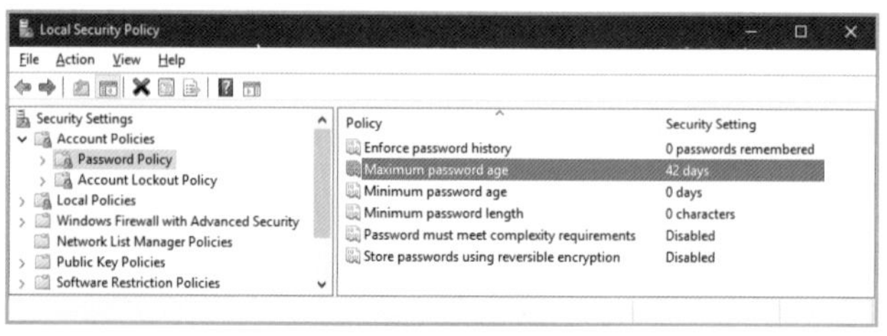

You could change the maximum password age to 182 days, and then you would get a new password twice a year.

4. Select **Password Policy**, then **Maximum password age** to discover the length of password validity

5 When you next sign in to the computer, select your account name as usual and enter your current password

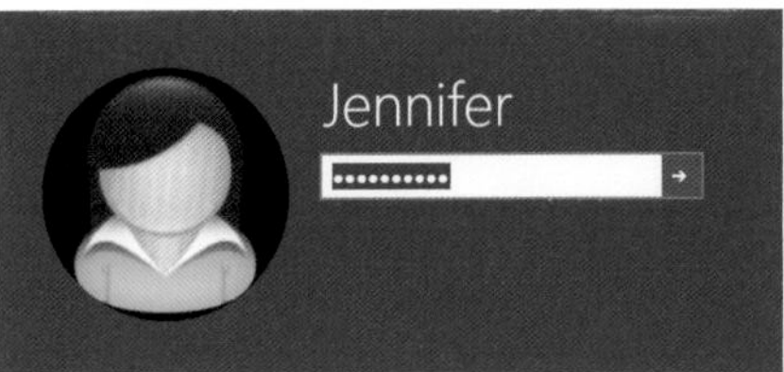

6 Your password needs to be changed. Click **OK**

7 Enter your existing password, then the new password, then confirm the new password and continue

8 Windows changes the password and confirms the change

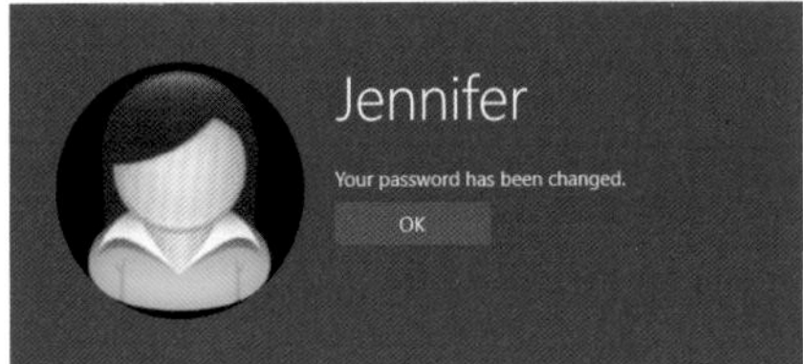

9 Click **OK** and Windows starts. The password is reset, and future sign-ins will proceed without interruption

When you enter a new password, Windows reminds you that you can create a password reset disk. However, it is only needed once, not every time you change your password.

When the specified period has passed, Windows will again notify you that the password has expired and require you to provide a new password.

Hide user list

Whenever you start Windows or switch users, the "Sign-in" screen lists all usernames defined for that computer by default.

You'd make changes like this if you had to leave your computer unattended. For example, when running a presentation at a meeting or show.

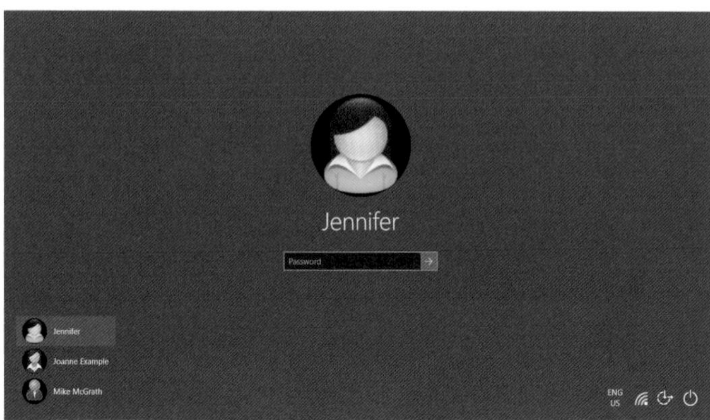

You might feel it would be more secure for the names to remain hidden, especially if you are using your computer in a public area. You can do this using the Local Security Policy.

1. Press **WinKey** + **R** and type "secpol.msc", then click **OK** or press **Enter** to open "Local Security Policy"

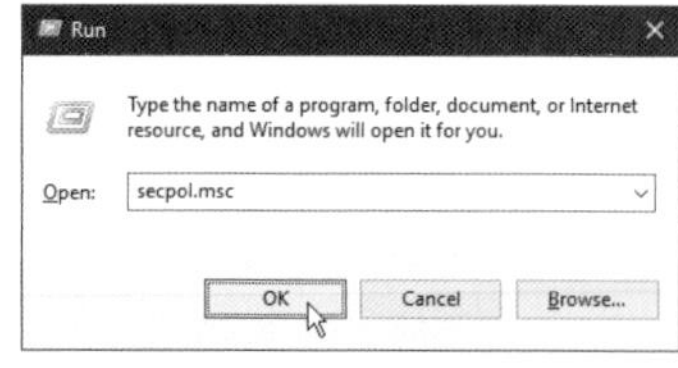

2. Expand **Local Policies**, select **Security Options** and locate **Interactive logon: Don't display last signed-in**

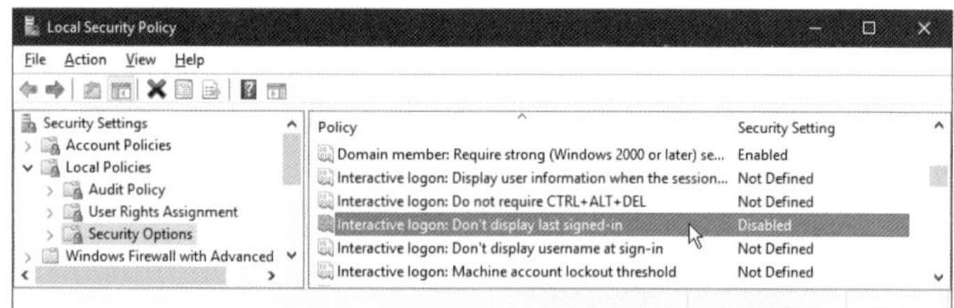

Local Security Policy is in Windows 10 Pro and Windows 10 Enterprise editions, but not available in the Windows 10 Home edition.

3. Double-click the entry to display the Properties, select **Enabled**, and then click **OK**

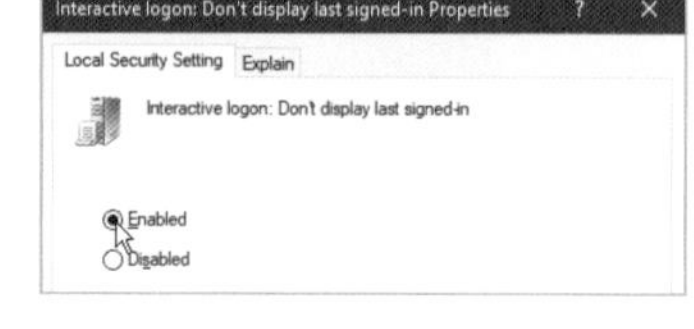

4. The entry will now be shown as Enabled, so click **File**, **Close** to save the change

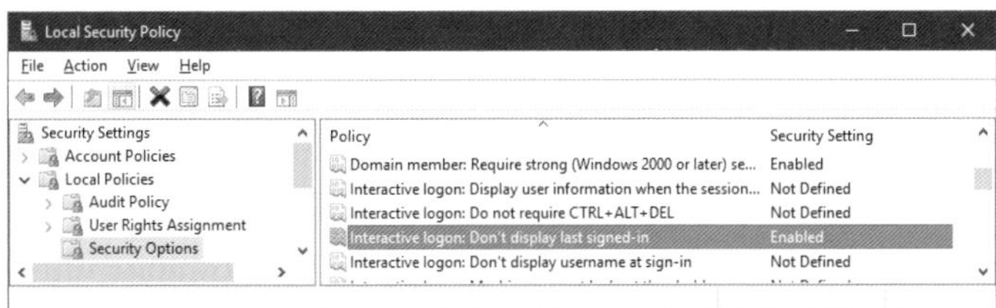

5. The next time you start Windows or switch users, the "Sign-in" screen is displayed without usernames

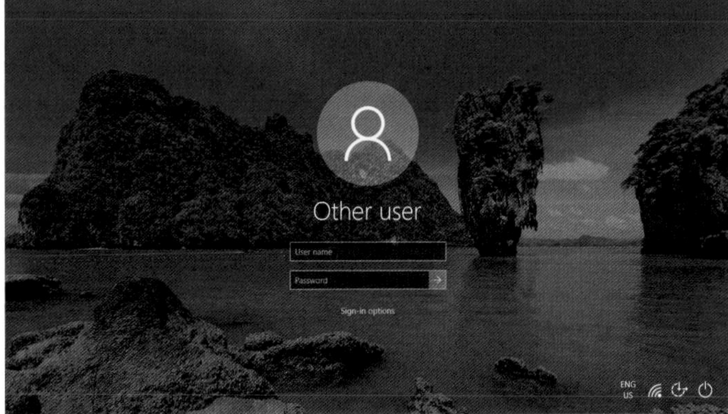

6. Type your username and your password to sign in

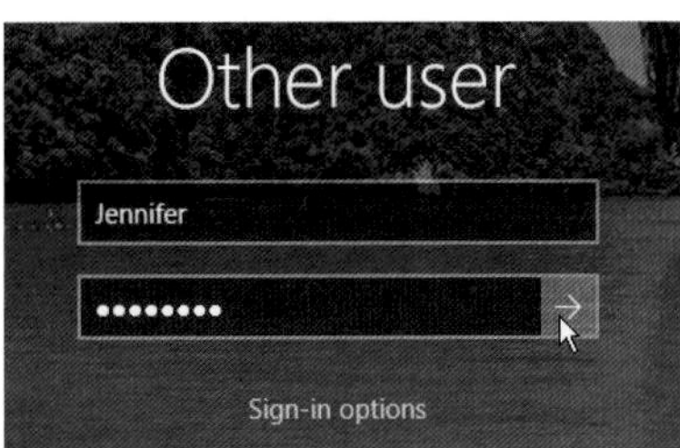

7. If you make a mistake, you are just told the username or password is incorrect, and you must click **OK** and try again

If you have other users on the computer with administrator accounts, they can, of course, view the list of users in **User Accounts**, or make changes to Security Options to reverse the setting.

There's no user picture, and no **Switch Users** button. If you enter a wrong value, there's no clue and the password reminder is not offered, to preserve the security.

Encrypting files

Anyone getting hold of a copy of the files won't be able to access their contents. Even another user logged on to your computer is unable to access the files.

You might be storing personal, financial or other information on your computer that you wouldn't want others to read. Some editions of Windows include encryption tools that can help protect confidential data. There are three components:

- **Encrypting File System (EFS)** – with this, your sensitive files and folders can be encoded so they can only be read when you log on to the computer with the associated user account.
- **BitLocker Drive Encryption** – this is used to encrypt an entire hard disk volume. The encryption is linked to a key stored in a Trusted Platform Module (TPM) or USB flash drive.
- **BitLocker To Go** – this provides BitLocker encryption for removable media.

TPM hardware will normally be found on business machines rather than home computers. However, a USB flash drive can be used in place of TPM.

Windows editions with encryption

EFS is available in the Pro and Enterprise versions of Windows 10, 8 and 8.1, and the Professional, Enterprise and Ultimate editions of Windows 7. You must have Pro or Enterprise versions of Windows 10, Windows 8 or 8.1, Windows 7 Enterprise or Windows 7 Ultimate to use BitLocker or BitLocker To Go.

There are no facilities to encrypt files in the Home Premium, Home Basic or Starter editions. However, when you encrypt a USB flash drive with BitLocker To Go, you can add, delete, and change files on that drive using any edition of Windows 7.

Systems running Windows XP and Windows Vista can, with the appropriate authentication, open and read the files on an encrypted drive using the reader program that is included on the drive itself. However, files cannot be changed or added.

You need a system partition in addition to the Windows volume. This system partition is normally set up when Windows is installed.

Hardware requirements

For BitLocker drive encryption of the whole system, the Windows partition and the System partition must both have NTFS (New Technology File System) format. You can use BitLocker to encrypt additional fixed data drives, and BitLocker To Go to encrypt your removable drives. These drives must have at least 64MB of available space, and can be formatted using FAT (File Allocation Table) format or NTFS format – unless intended for Windows XP or Windows Vista, where FAT format is required.

Using EFS

You can encrypt individual files, whole folders, or entire drives using EFS. However, it is best to encrypt by folder (or by drive) rather than by individual file. This means that the existing files would be encrypted, and new files that get created in that folder or drive will also be encrypted – including any temporary files that applications might generate.

To encrypt the contents of a folder on your hard drive:

1. Locate the folder in File Explorer, then right-click the folder icon and select **Properties**

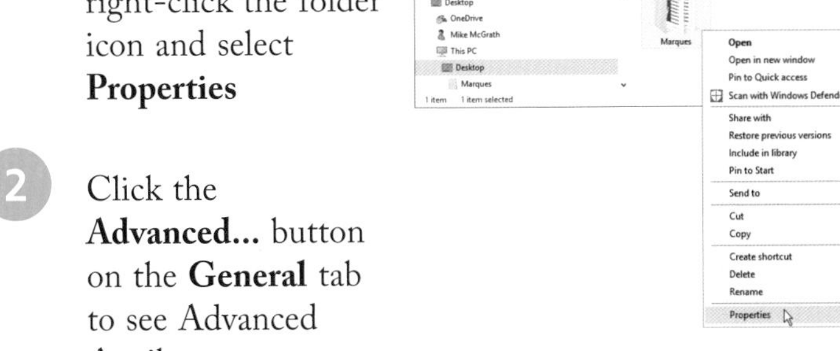

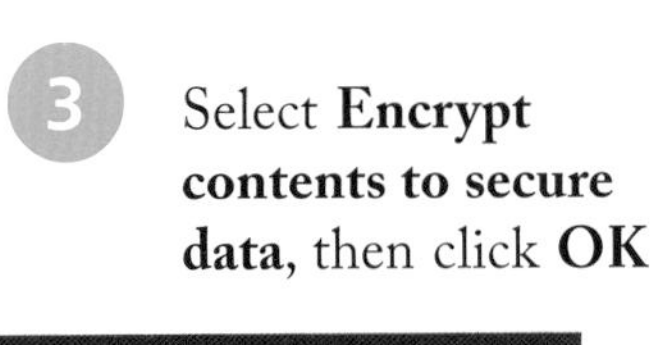

2. Click the **Advanced...** button on the **General** tab to see Advanced Attributes

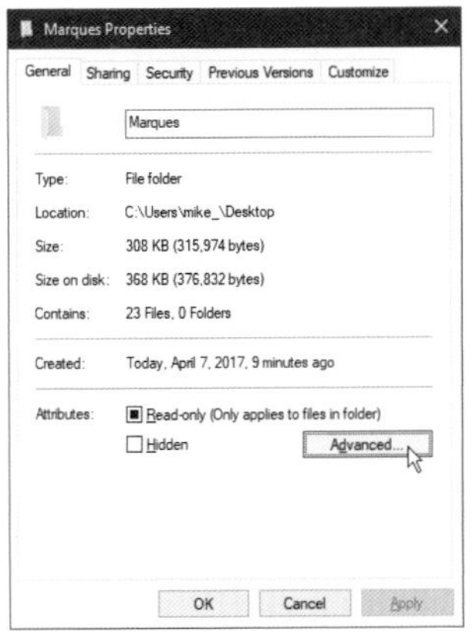

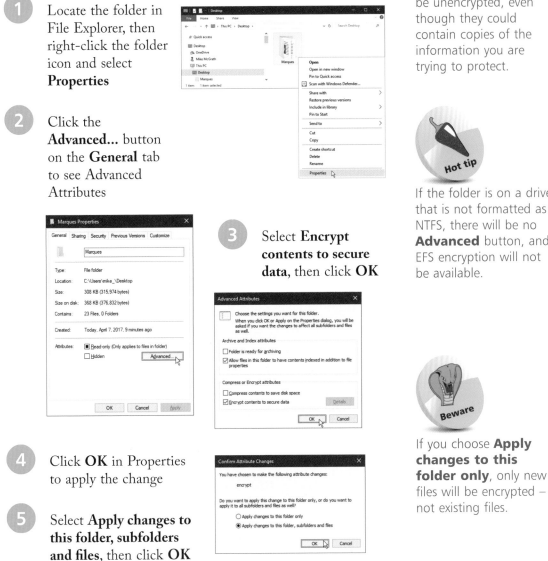

3. Select **Encrypt contents to secure data**, then click **OK**

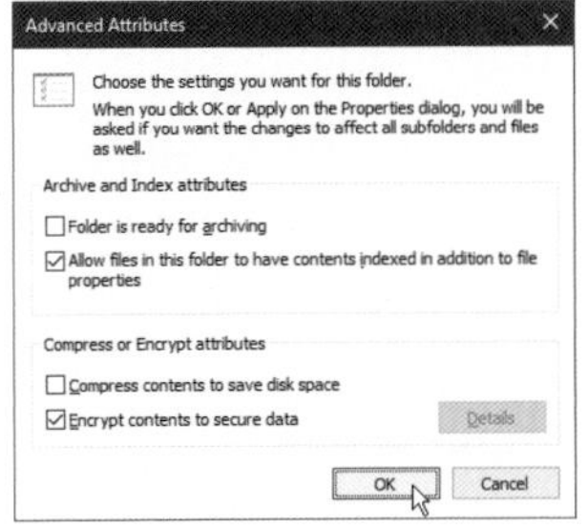

4. Click **OK** in Properties to apply the change

5. Select **Apply changes to this folder, subfolders and files**, then click **OK** to continue

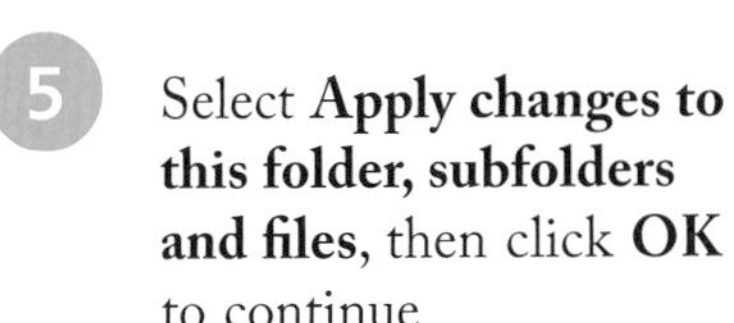

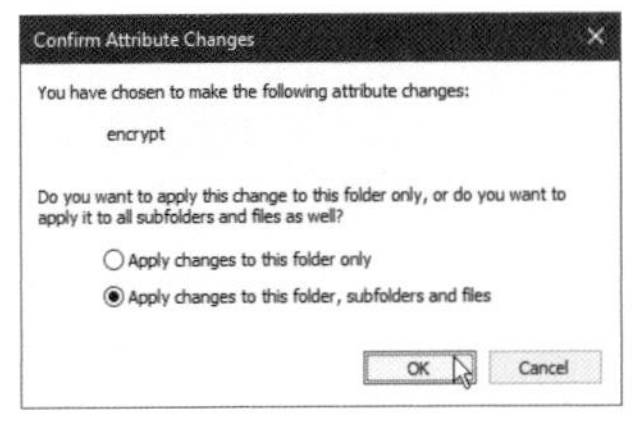

If you allowed encryption of individual files in a folder, temporary files created there would be unencrypted, even though they could contain copies of the information you are trying to protect.

If the folder is on a drive that is not formatted as NTFS, there will be no **Advanced** button, and EFS encryption will not be available.

If you choose **Apply changes to this folder only**, only new files will be encrypted – not existing files.

...cont'd

6. Your encryption certificate is created, and the folder and its contents are encrypted

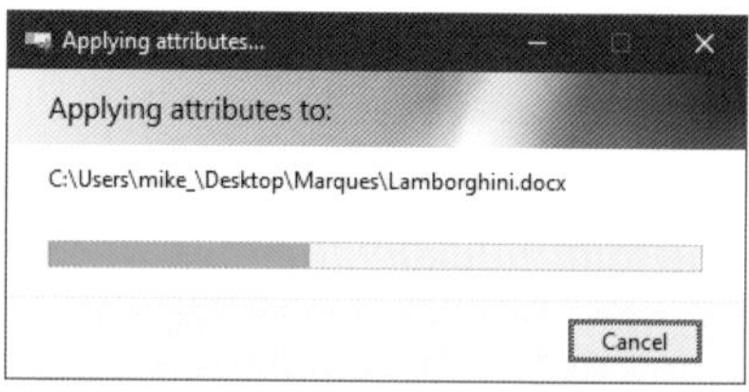

When encryption completes, check the folder in File Explorer, and you'll see the folder and its files now have an added Lock icon:

If you'd chosen the other mutually-exclusive attribute **Compress contents to save space**, you would see the folder and files would have blue arrow icons added.

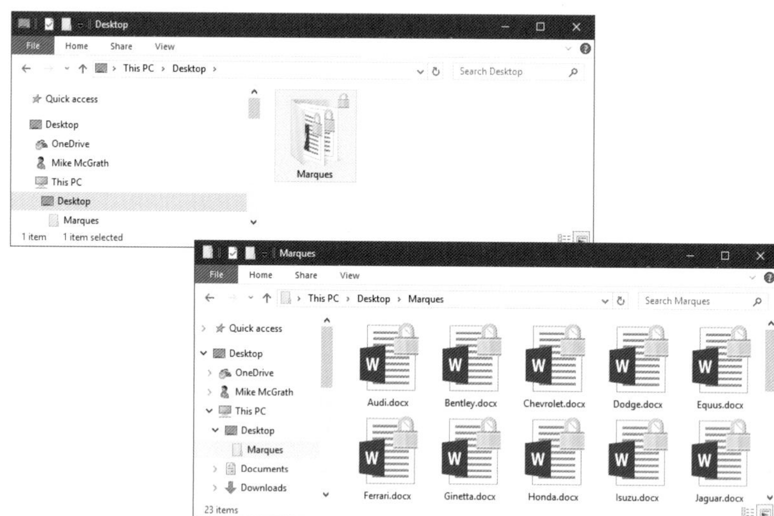

When you work with encrypted files from your user account, that's the only visible difference. Windows will decrypt your files as you use them and will re-encrypt them when you save, and it is all fully automatic.

The unauthorized user may be able to delete encrypted files from the folder. They will be transferred to the Recycle Bin, but will still be classed as encrypted.

Another user logging on to your system may be able to see the folder and open it to display the contents. However, any attempt to access the files will give an error message from the associated application, saying that access is denied.

Similarly, copying or moving of encrypted files will be denied. Even administrator user accounts will be denied access.

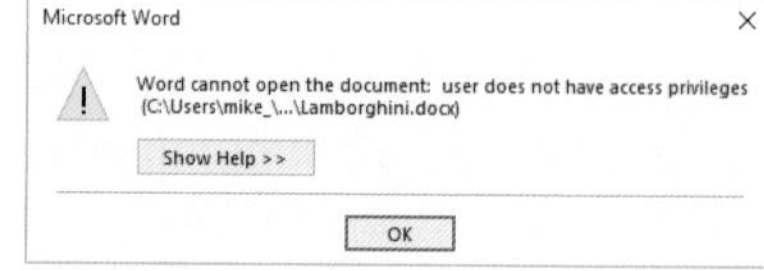

Backup encryption key

1. Press **WinKey** + **R**, and enter "certmgr.msc"

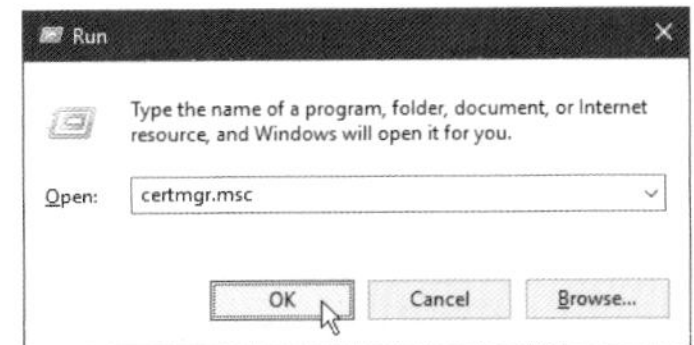

2. Expand **Personal** and select **Certificates**

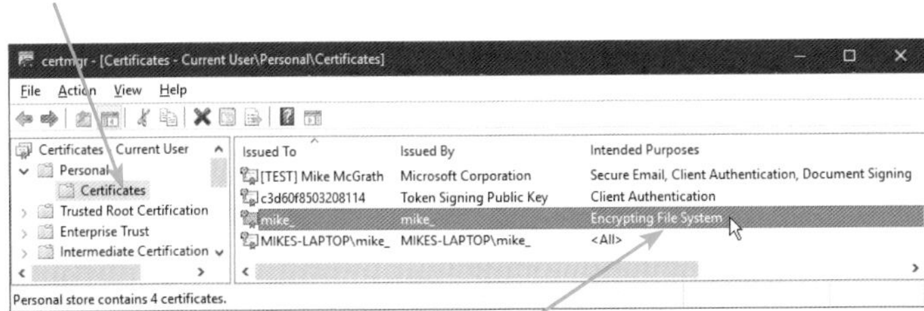

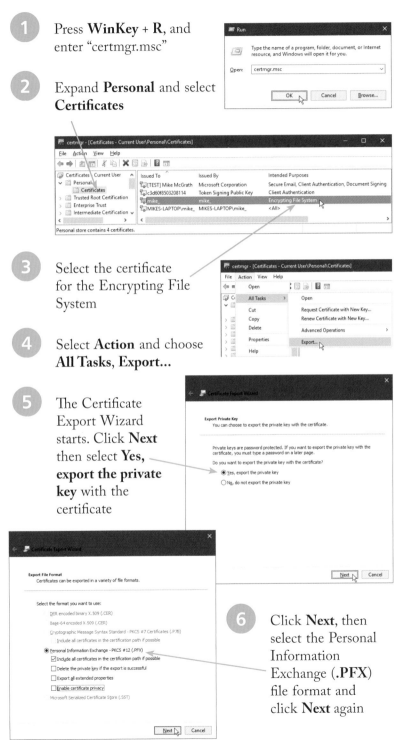

3. Select the certificate for the Encrypting File System

4. Select **Action** and choose **All Tasks, Export...**

5. The Certificate Export Wizard starts. Click **Next** then select **Yes, export the private key** with the certificate

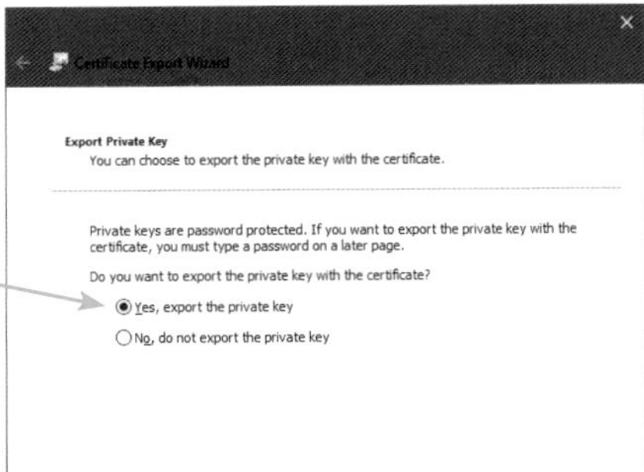

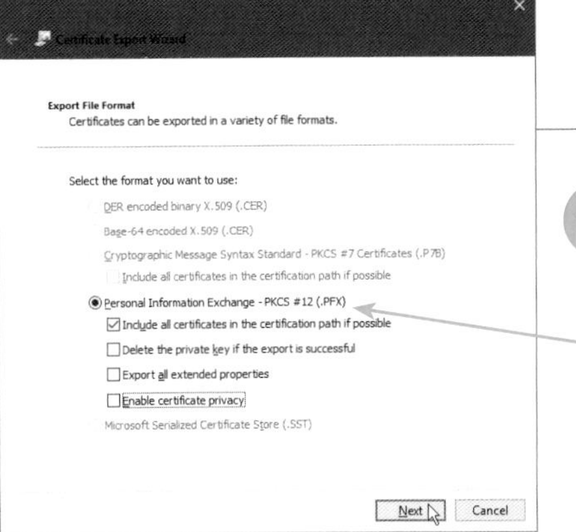

6. Click **Next**, then select the Personal Information Exchange (**.PFX**) file format and click **Next** again

If you lose the certificate, perhaps due to a hard disk failure, you won't be able to use your encrypted files. That's why you are advised to create a backup.

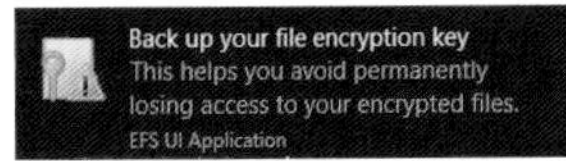

Back up your file encryption key
This helps you avoid permanently losing access to your encrypted files.
EFS UI Application

You'll need a removable device such as a USB flash drive, which is not encrypted and which can be kept physically secure.

...cont'd

You could use the same device as you used to create a password reset disk, since it has the same security requirements.

7. Provide a password, and re-enter it to confirm. Click **Next**

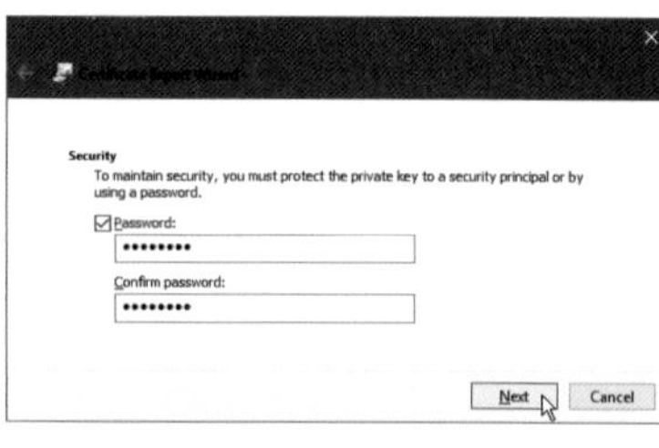

8. Click **Browse** to choose the destination drive

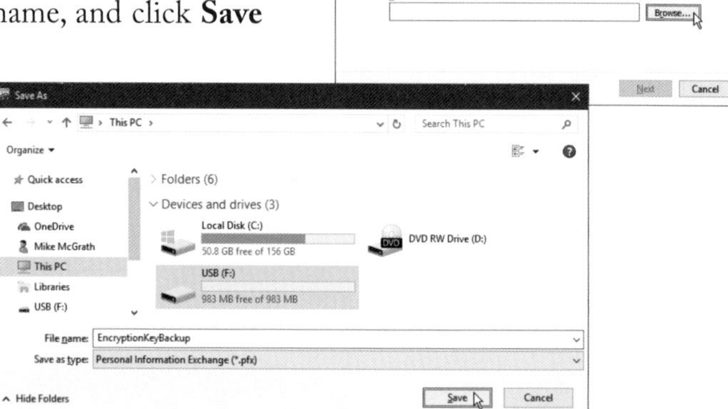

9. Select the storage device, enter the file name, and click **Save**

Remove the storage media and store it in a safe location, since it can enable anyone to access your encrypted files.

10. Click **Next** to confirm name and location

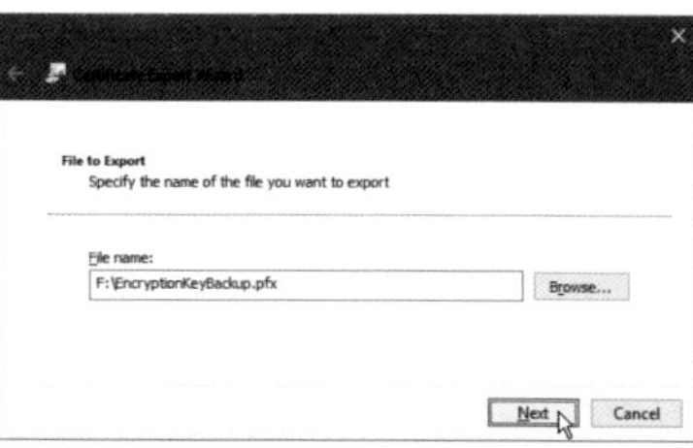

11. Click **Finish** to complete the Wizard

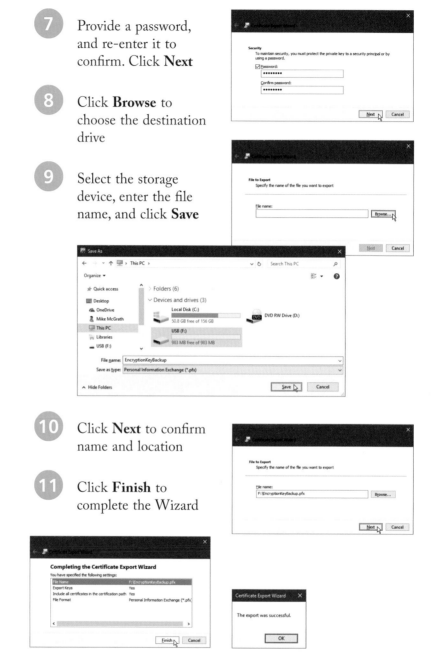

To restore the certificate, insert the backup media, run **certmgr.msc** to open Certificate Manager, select Personal, Action, All Tasks, Import, then follow the Certificate Import Wizard.

BitLocker To Go

To encrypt a removable drive with Windows Pro or Enterprise:

1. Connect the drive and press **WinKey** + **X** to open the Power User Menu. Select **File Explorer**

2. Right-click the drive icon and select **Turn on BitLocker**

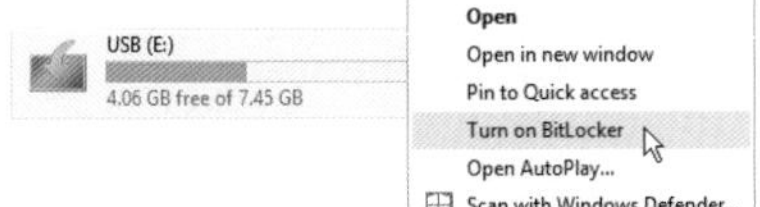

3. Choose to unlock this drive using a password or smart card. E.g. select **Use a password to unlock the drive**, then enter your password twice and click **Next**

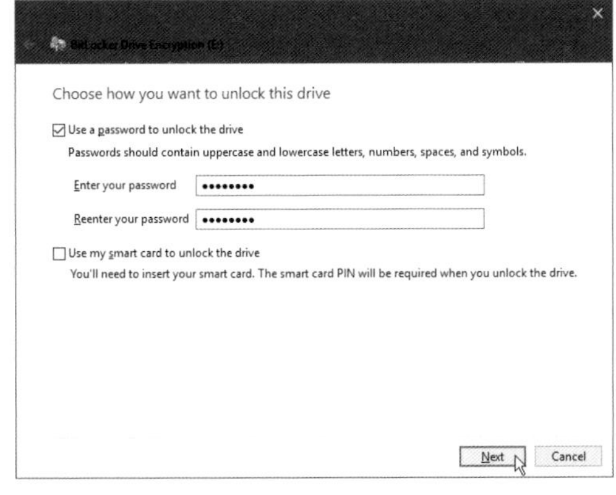

Large organizations use smart cards for network authentication and have computers with smart card readers that can access the cards and store information there.

4. Click **Save to a file**, and you will see that a file name is automatically generated

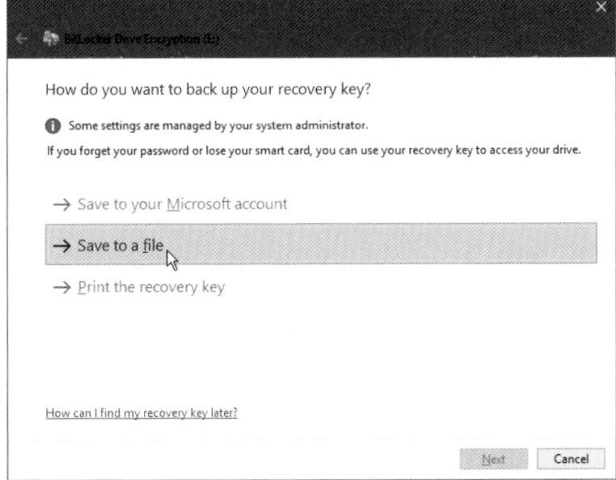

A good choice might be to use the USB flash drive as the password reset disk and for your EFS certificate.

5. Specify the folder and click **Save**

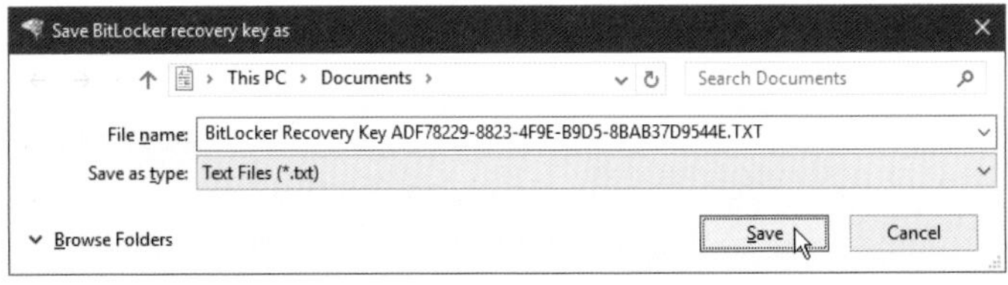

...cont'd

The **Next** button is grayed out until you save or print the recovery key, then it is enabled and becomes ready to use.

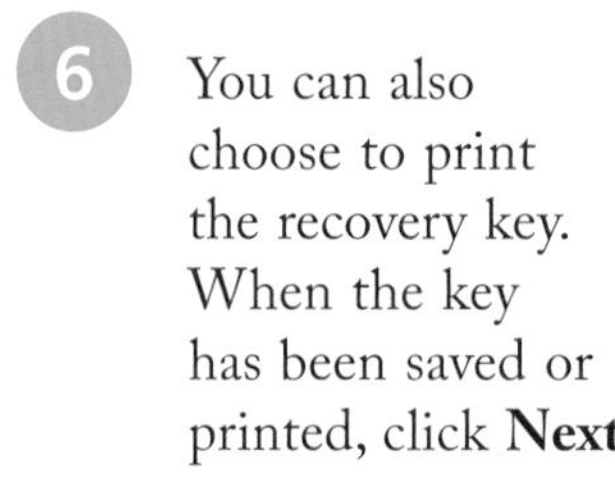

6. You can also choose to print the recovery key. When the key has been saved or printed, click **Next**

7. Choose how much of the drive to encrypt, e.g. the entire drive, then click **Next**

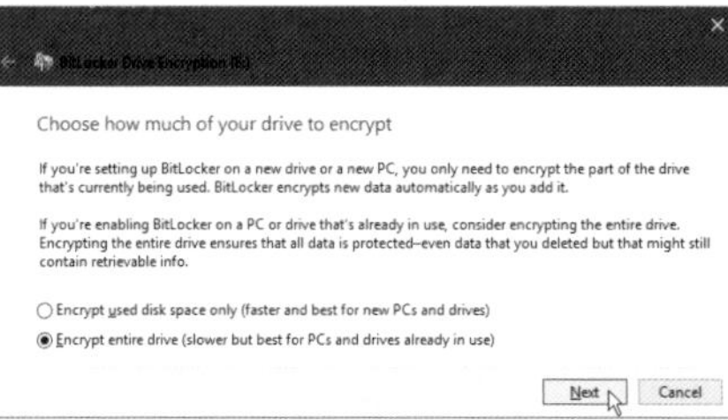

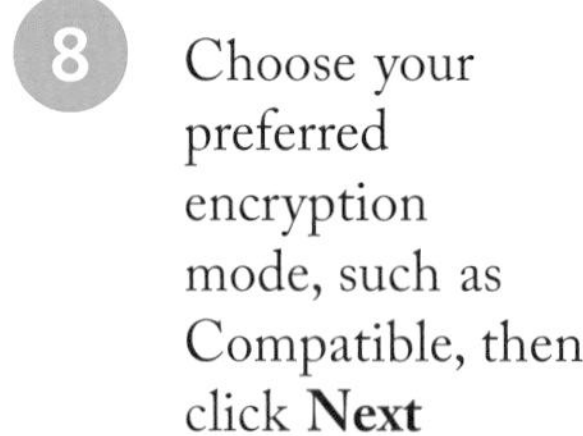

A more secure encryption mode was introduced in Windows 10 – but this is not compatible with previous versions of Windows.

8. Choose your preferred encryption mode, such as Compatible, then click **Next**

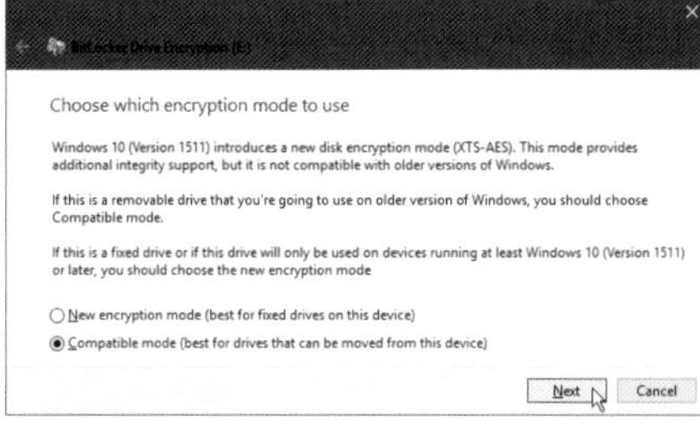

9. Click **Start encrypting** and the files on the removable device are processed

If, for any reason, you need to remove the drive before completion, click **Pause** to interrupt the processing, or else files could be damaged.

10. On completion, a Lock icon is added to the drive to indicate it is now protected by encryption

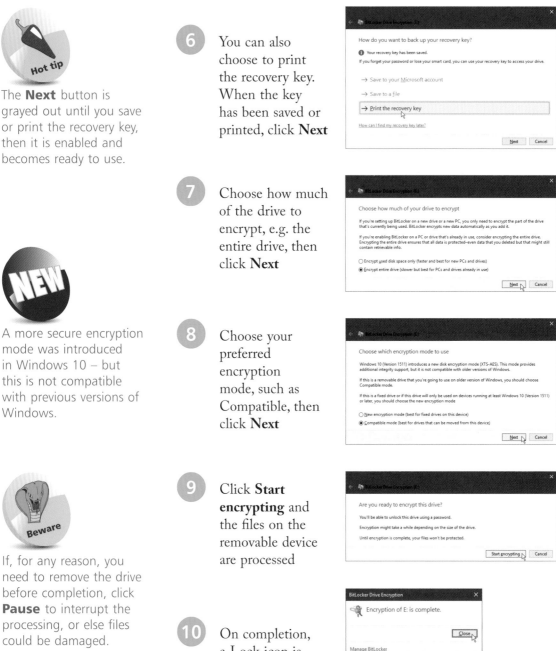

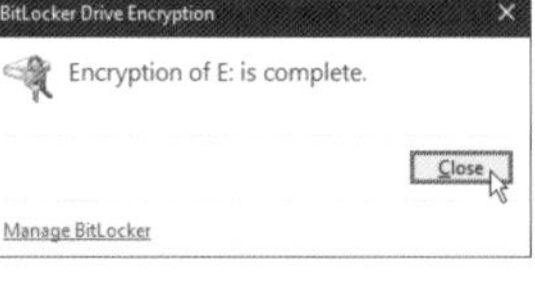

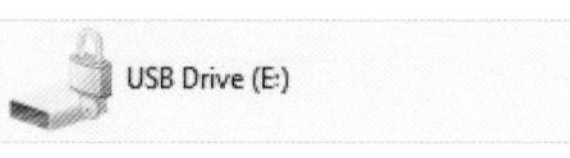

Access the encrypted drive

To access the drive:

1. Insert the removable device and BitLocker will tell you the device is protected

2. Click on the banner to open the password screen

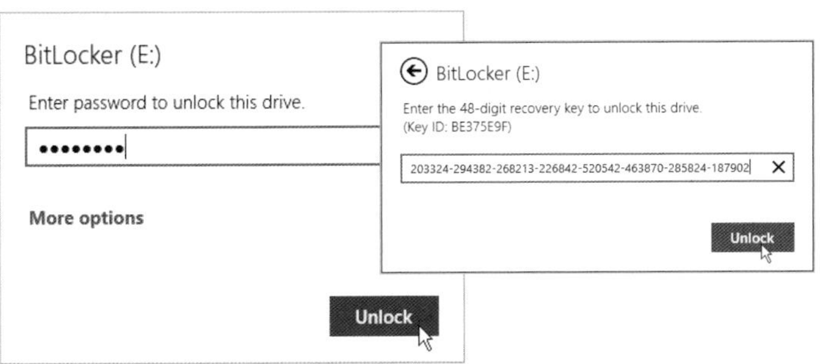

3. Unlock the drive by entering the password and clicking the **Unlock** button, or if you cannot remember the password click **More options** and enter the recovery key

4. The drive opens. You can open, edit and save files or create new files on this drive, and they will be encrypted

5. Right-click on the drive icon and choose **Manage BitLocker**, then click **Turn off BitLocker** if you want to decrypt the drive back to its original state

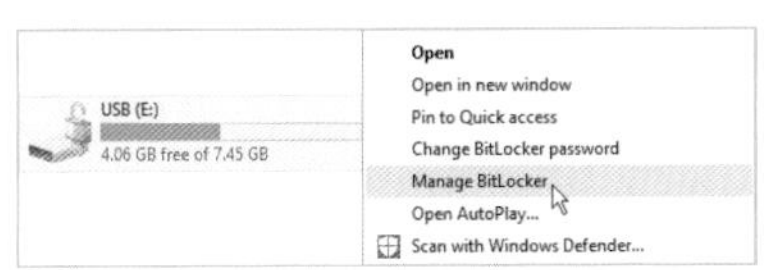

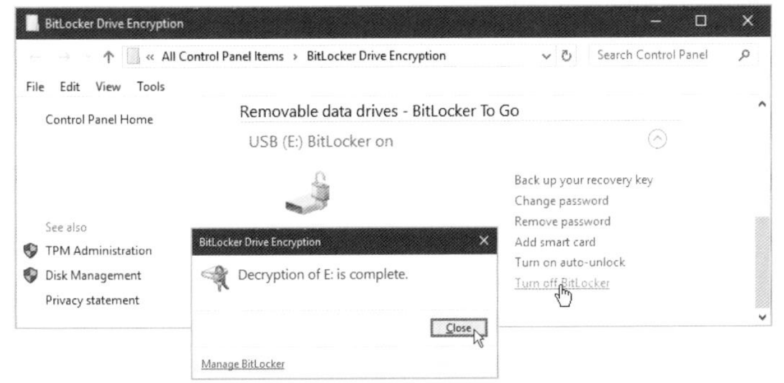

Click **More options** (see Step 3) and you will be able to select **Automatically unlock on this PC** to have Windows remember the password for you.

Remember to always use **Safely Remove Hardware** before removing a USB drive.

Whole system encryption

Hot tip

To completely protect your computer and prevent access to your data, you can use BitLocker to encrypt the Windows boot drive and internal data drives.

The TPM Management Console can also be opened by running a "tpm.msc" command.

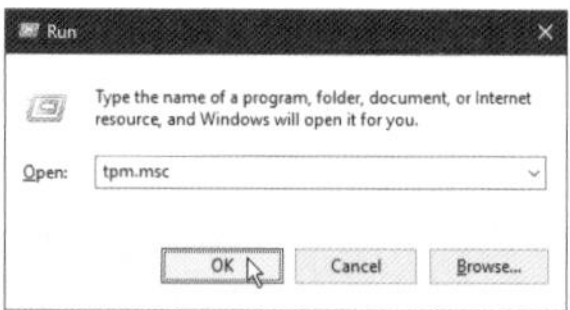

You can enable TPM in the BIOS, or you can configure BitLocker to use a USB drive instead. However, problems with BitLocker could make your system inaccessible, so only proceed with this if you have adequate technical support.

1. Go to the Control Panel, (View by: Category), **System and Security**, and open **BitLocker Drive Encryption**

2. Select **Turn on BitLocker** for the system or data drive and then follow the prompts to encrypt the drive

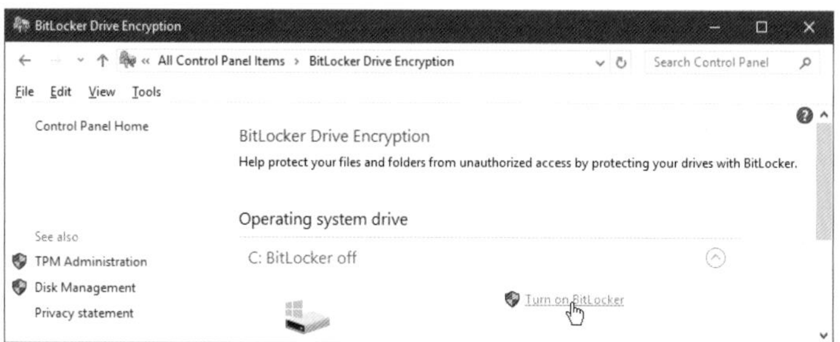

3. Any problems with the computer setup will now be detected. For example, you may see this message dialog appear regarding a "Trusted Platform Module" (TPM)

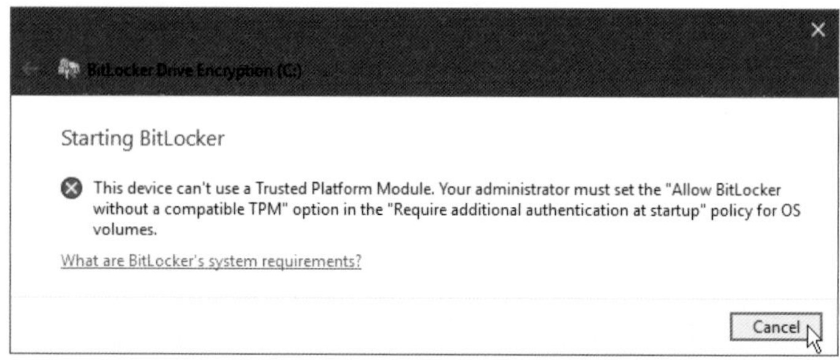

4. Click **Cancel**, then click the **TPM Administration** link to discover that the TPM module cannot be found

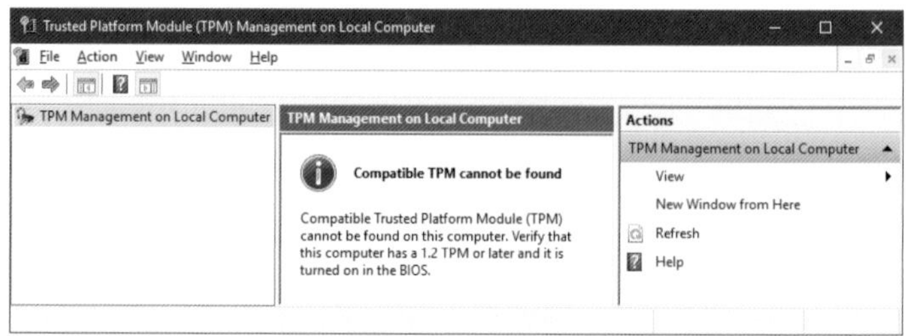

23 Windows PowerShell

The PowerShell command line in Windows 10 is a powerful tool that can be useful in certain situations. It has an administrator mode that can be used to perform system tasks.

Opening PowerShell

All editions of Windows 10 include the Windows PowerShell environment, where you can run commands, and batch files and applications by typing statements at a console command line.

There are a number of ways to start a PowerShell session:

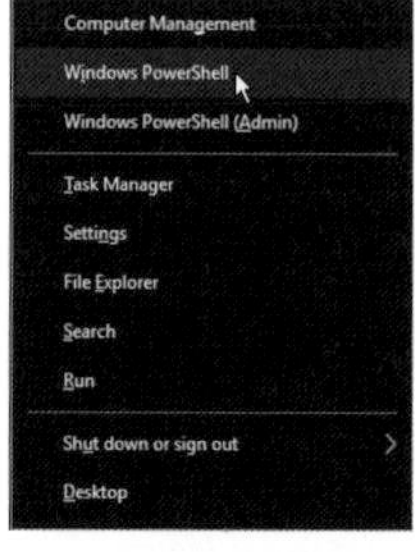

- Press **WinKey** + **X** to open the Power User Menu. Select **Windows PowerShell**.

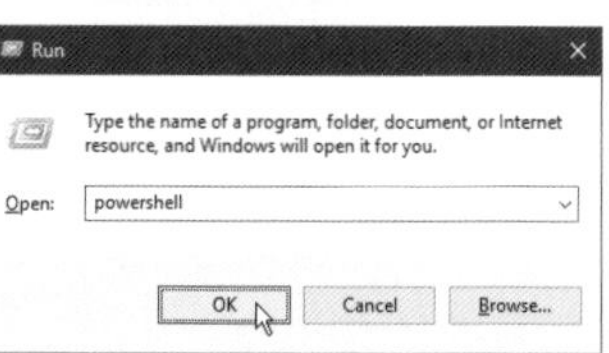

- Press **WinKey** + **R** to open the Run box. Type “powershell”, then click **OK**.

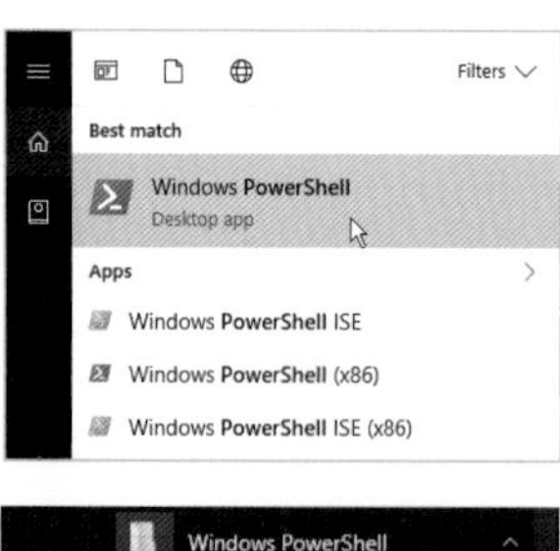

- In the Taskbar Search box type “powershell”, then hit the **Enter** key.

- On the Apps menu click **Windows PowerShell** in the “Windows PowerShell” group folder.

- Double-click any shortcut to the **powershell.exe** program.

Any method will start a Windows PowerShell session, open at the path location **C:\Users*username*** ready to accept commands.

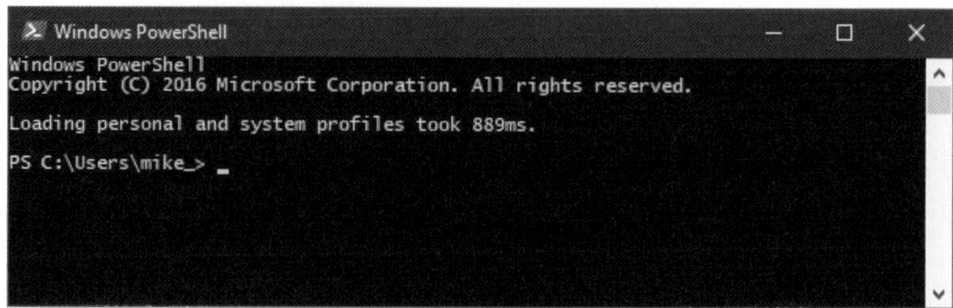

Don't forget

The Run box will display the last program run, and you can click the down-arrow and select from the list of previously-run programs.

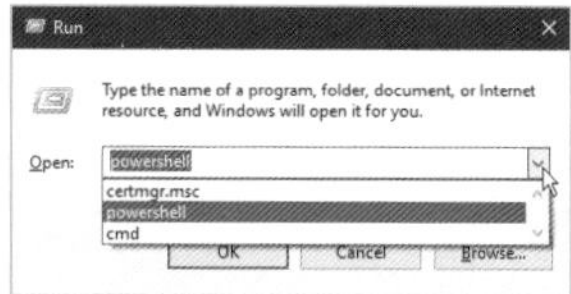

Windows PowerShell Integrated Scripting Environment (ISE) combines a PowerShell console window and scripting pane for advanced users. The X86 versions are only provided for backward compatibility and are best avoided.

To create a shortcut, right-click the program icon and select **Create Shortcut**. The shortcut icon will be placed on the Desktop.

- You can open additional independent PowerShell sessions, using the same methods or, from an existing session, type **start powershell** on the command line and press **Enter**.

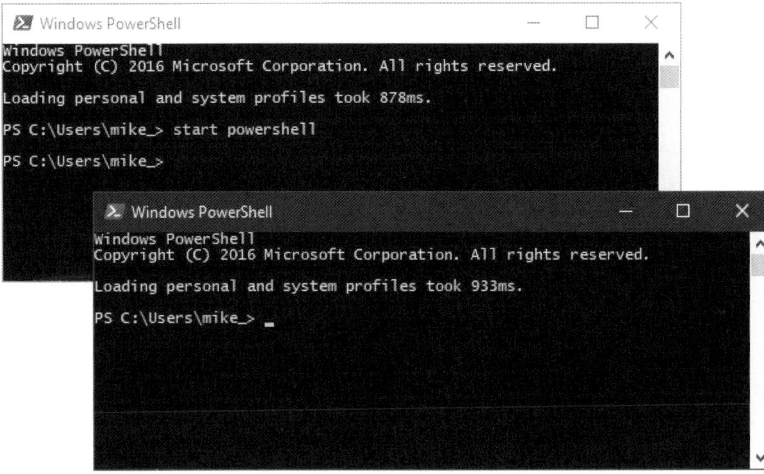

- You can also navigate to **C:\Windows\System32\WindowsPowerShell\v1.0** and click the **powershell.exe** file icon to open a PowerShell console session.

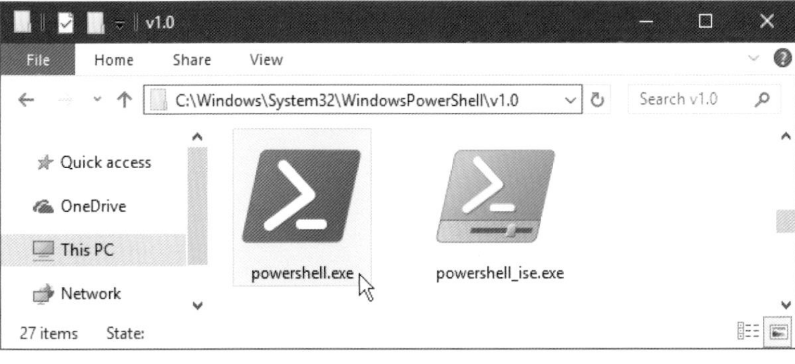

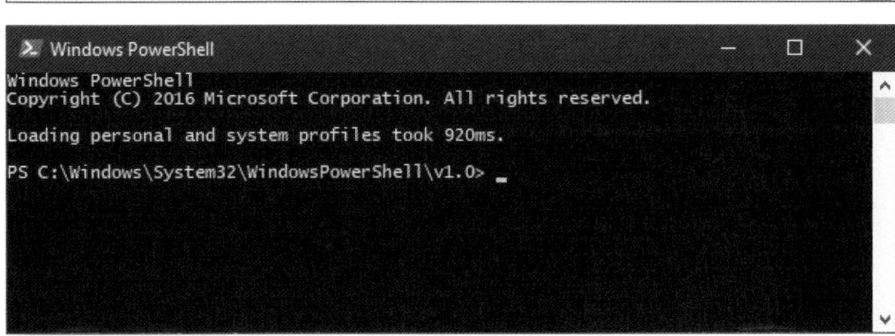

You might use multiple sessions to compare the contents of two or more folders.

Windows PowerShell became the default console application with the introduction of the Windows 10 Creators Update, but you can still find the Command Prompt console application in the Windows System folder on the Apps menu.

If you have a different folder or drive specified for your Windows system, folder paths will be adjusted accordingly.

Selecting a folder

You can switch folders in a Windows PowerShell console session using the CD (Change Directory) command. For example, to open the current user's Pictures folder, starting from anywhere:

Note that case does not matter. When there are spaces in the file or folder names, you should enclose those names within quotation marks.

1. On the Command Line, type these four CD commands, pressing **Enter** after each command:
cd ** **cd users **cd "john smith"** **cd pictures**

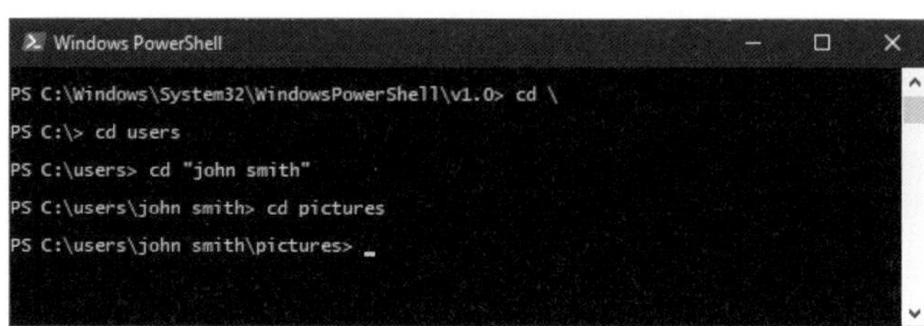

Windows PowerShell
PS C:\Windows\System32\WindowsPowerShell\v1.0> cd \
PS C:\> cd users
PS C:\users> cd "john smith"
PS C:\users\john smith> cd pictures
PS C:\users\john smith\pictures>

To avoid problems with long or complex file names, you can open a PowerShell session directly at the required folder.

1. Open File Explorer and use the normal Windows search methods to find the desired folder – from either the Contents pane or the Navigation pane

2. Press and hold **Shift**, then right-click the folder

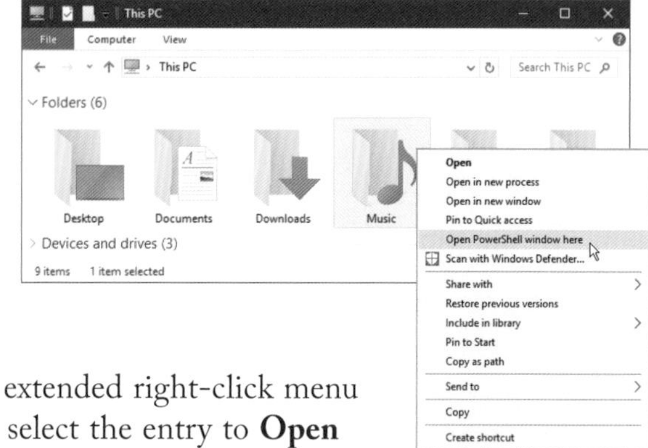

The PowerShell session is opened and switched to the required folder.

3. From the extended right-click menu displayed, select the entry to **Open PowerShell window here**

Running as administrator

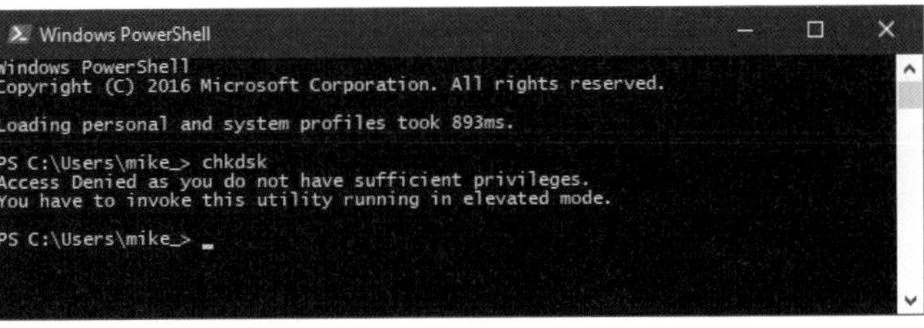

Commands that have a system-wide effect are restricted to run only in the elevated administrator mode.

The Windows PowerShell session opened has, by default, the standard user level of privilege. If some commands that you want to run require administrator privilege, you can open an elevated session using the following methods:

- Navigate to **C:\Windows\System32\WindowsPowerShell\v1.0**, right-click **powershell.exe** and select **Run as administrator**.

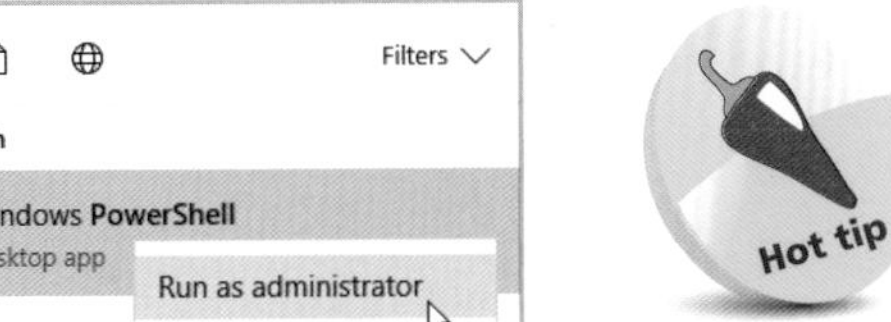

- Enter "powershell" in the Taskbar Search box then right-click on Windows PowerShell and select **Run as administrator**.

You can also type **start powershell** on the command line of an existing administrator session to get another administrator session – no UAC required.

Windows PowerShell

Windows PowerShell (Admin)

- Right-click on the Start button, or press **WinKey** + X, then choose **Windows PowerShell (Admin)** from the Power User Menu.

- Click **Yes** in the **User Account Control (UAC)** dialog box – to start a Windows PowerShell session with an "Administrator" window title:

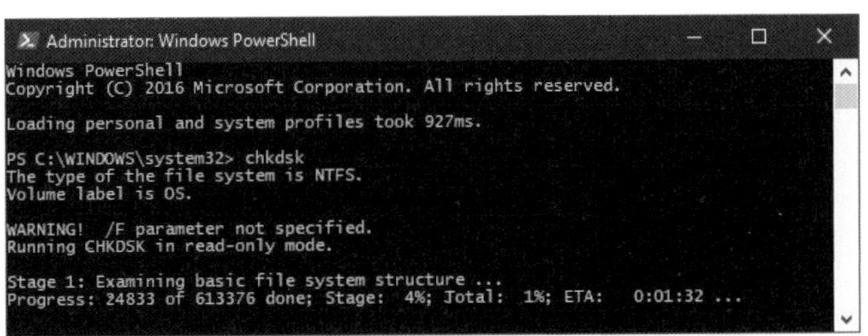

Notice that each Administrator PowerShell session starts in the **C:\Windows/System32** folder.

Creating shortcuts

You can configure a shortcut to **powershell.exe** to always start in administrator mode:

The modified shortcut can be saved to the Desktop or the Taskbar.

1. Create a shortcut to the **powershell.exe** program file (at **C:\Windows\System32\WindowsPowerShell\v1.0\powershell.exe**)

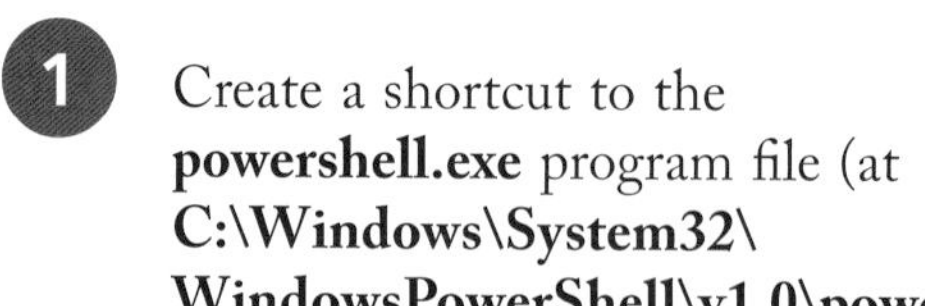
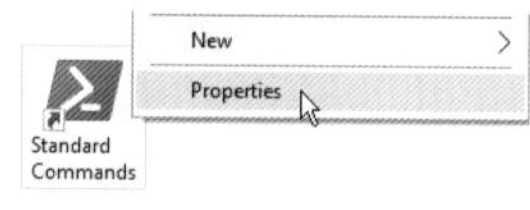

2. Right-click the shortcut and select the **Properties** item

3. Select the **Shortcut** tab and click the **Advanced...** button

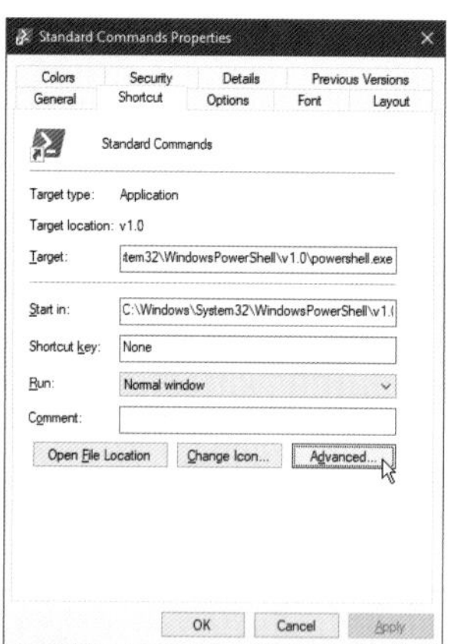

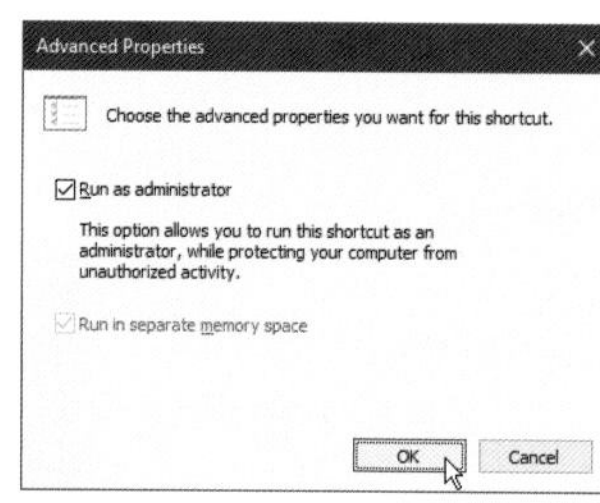

4. Check the box **Run as administrator** and click **OK**, then **OK** again

The name that you give the shortcut appears as part of the title for the session, along with the word **Administrator** for elevated sessions.

5. Right-click the shortcut icon, select **Rename** and give it a meaningful name

6. For example, you could rename "Standard Commands" to "Elevated Commands"

7. Double-click the renamed shortcut to start the administrator session

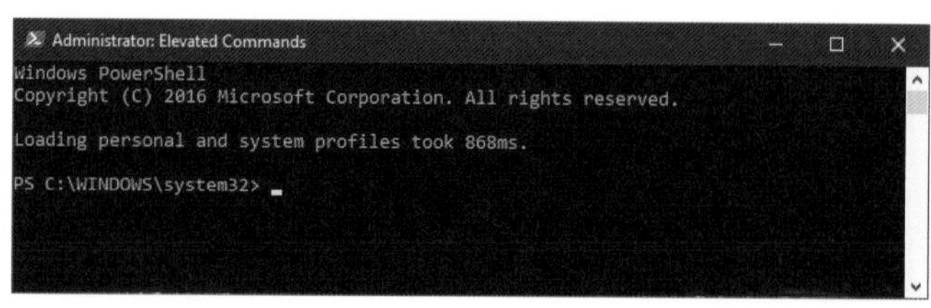

Adjusting appearance

You can adjust the Properties shortcut to control the appearance of the PowerShell window that is launched by that shortcut:

1. Right-click the shortcut icon and click **Properties**

2. Select the **Options** tab

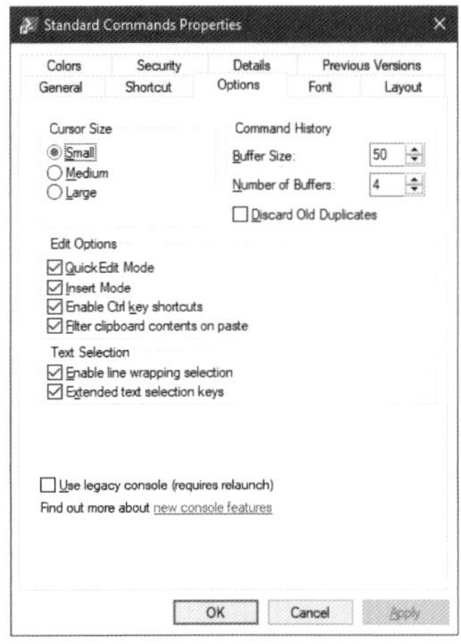

From here, you can adjust the size of the flashing cursor, change how the command history is managed, and change edit options.

3. Select the **Font** tab to choose a different font

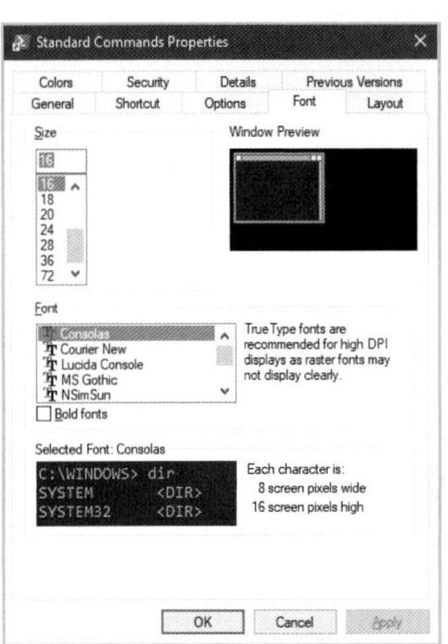

4. The recommended font is Consolas, since this is a ClearType font that will be more readable in the window

5. Select **Layout** to change the buffer size and screen size

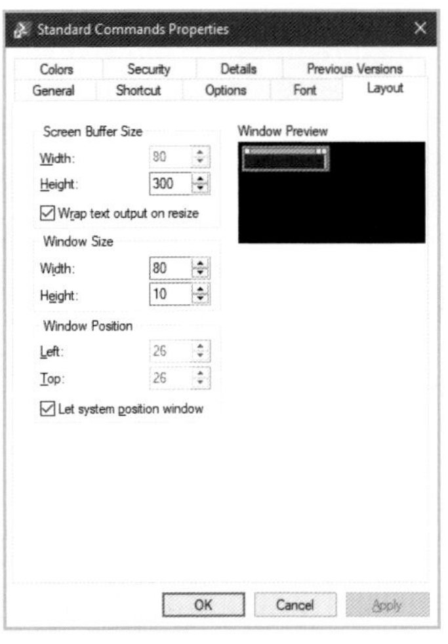

Adjust the width if the default 80 characters is not enough, and change the height (in this case from the default 25 lines to 10 lines). A vertical scrollbar allows you to view the whole buffer of information.

You can also adjust the properties from the Windows PowerShell window – right-click on the title bar then choose **Properties** from the context menu.

As PowerShell provides automatic syntax coloring, it is best to avoid changing the default window colors.

The fonts for the Windows PowerShell window must be fixed-pitch – i.e. the letters and characters each occupy the same amount of horizontal space.

Using PowerShell

You'll use Windows PowerShell to carry out tasks that are not easily achieved using the normal Windows functions. A typical example is to create a text file containing the names of all the files of a particular type in a folder:

1. Open a prompt at the required folder, using the Shift + right-click menu option **Open PowerShell window here**

2. Type this command at the prompt, then press the **Enter** key **dir *.jpg > filelist.txt**

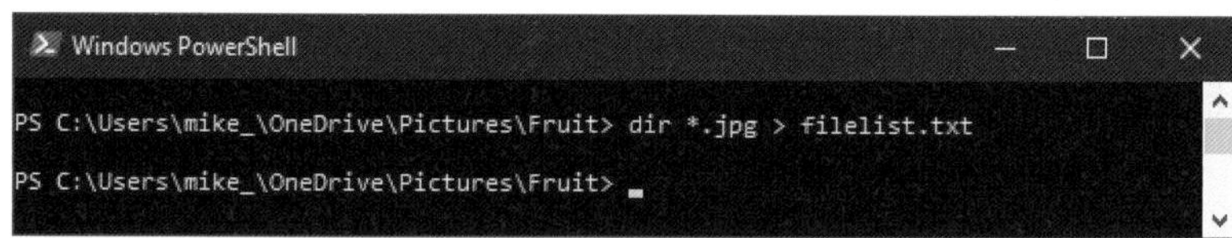

3. Open the folder to see a new file called "filelist.txt", then open that file to see a list of all the JPG files it contains

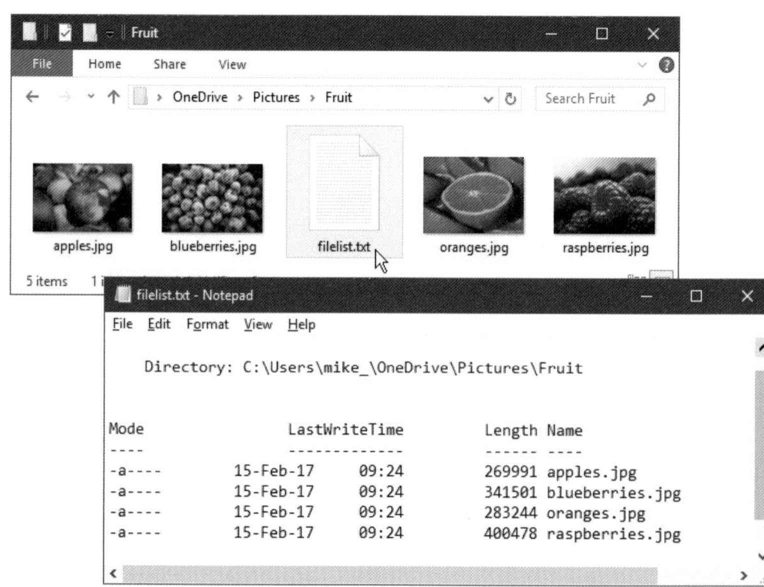

To list a different type of file, just change .jpg to the required file type, e.g. .doc. You can also list more than one file type, for example: **dir *.jpg *.tif > filelist.txt**.

If your Windows PowerShell session is already open, you need to switch directories to get to the required folder. Here, you can use Windows features to assist the PowerShell operation.

1. Open the required folder in File Explorer

2. Click the Address bar to show the path, and press **Ctrl** + **C**

3. Switch to the Windows PowerShell console and type the command **cd** (followed by a single space)

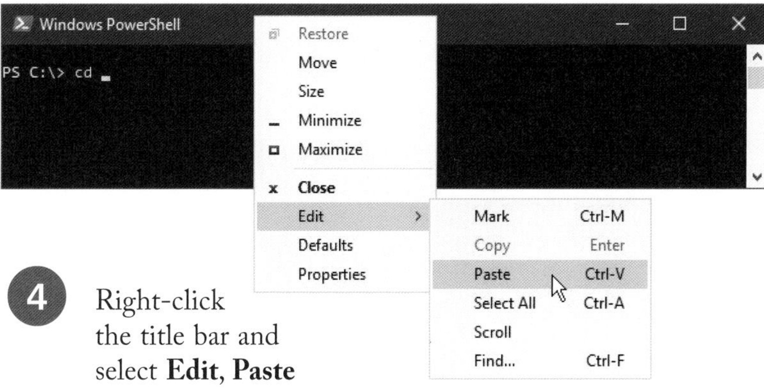

4. Right-click the title bar and select **Edit**, **Paste**

5. Press **Enter** to run the command and switch directories

When you select Paste, the contents of the Clipboard are copied to the command line, thus completing the CD command already started.

Discovering cmdlets

DOS (Disk Operating System) commands have been around since the days of MS-DOS – before computers were available with a Graphical User Interface (GUI).

The Windows PowerShell console recognizes the familiar DOS commands that are available in the older Command Prompt console, such as **cd**, **dir**, **cp**, **mv**, **rm**, or **cls**, but these are merely aliases to PowerShell "cmdlets" (command-lets). More importantly, Windows PowerShell has many additional cmdlets that make it much more powerful than Command Prompt.

Each cmdlet is named as a hyphenated verb-noun pair. For example, there is a cmdlet named **Get-Alias**. This can be used to discover the name of the cmdlet represented by a DOS alias.

You can see a list of all PowerShell aliases, functions, and cmdlets by typing **Get-Command**. Usefully, every cmdlet has its own individual help file that can be seen by typing **Get-Help** followed by the name of the cmdlet you are seeking help with.

Cmdlets that **Get** return an object that has methods and properties, which you can use to work with PowerShell most effectively. Methods and properties can be listed by "piping" the returned object through to a **Get-Member** cmdlet and can be filtered by adding a -**MemberType** parameter:

1. Open PowerShell, then enter this command to discover the name of the cmdlet representing the **cd** DOS alias
Get-Alias cd

Some cmdlets have multiple aliases. For example, **Get-Help** reveals that **Set-Location** has aliases of **cd**, **sl**, and **chdir**.

2. Next, enter this command to see a long list of all Windows PowerShell aliases, functions, and cmdlets
Get-Command

3. Scroll through the list to discover a **Get-Date** cmdlet

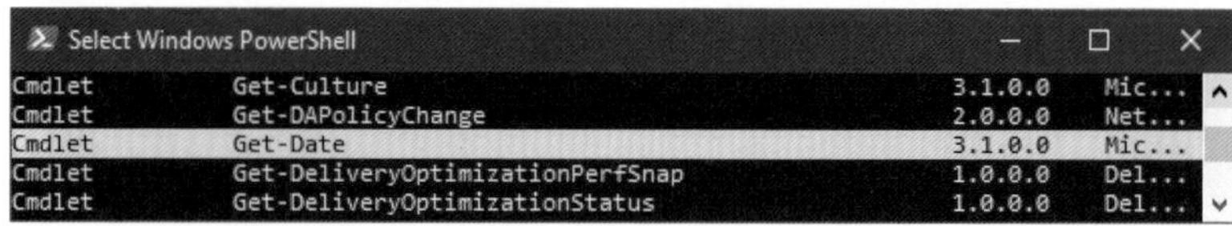

4. Enter this command to discover more about the cmdlet
Get-Help Get-Date

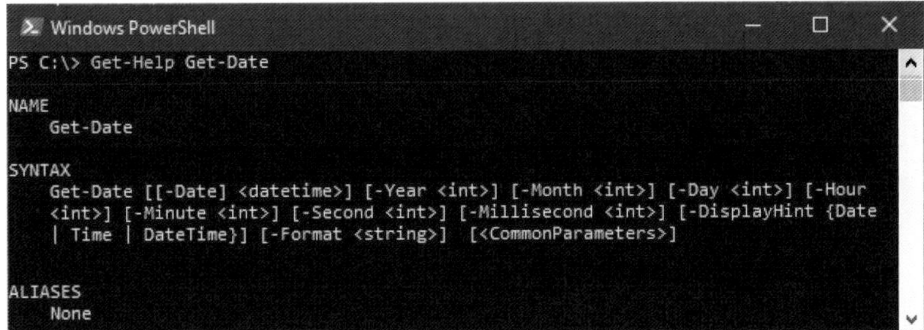

Windows PowerShell
PS C:\> Get-Help Get-Date
NAME
Get-Date
SYNTAX
Get-Date [[-Date] <datetime>] [-Year <int>] [-Month <int>] [-Day <int>] [-Hour <int>] [-Minute <int>] [-Second <int>] [-Millisecond <int>] [-DisplayHint {Date | Time | DateTime}] [-Format <string>] [<CommonParameters>]
ALIASES
None

PowerShell is not case-sensitive so **Get-Help** could be written in lowercase as **get-help** — but mixed case aids readability.

5. Enter this command to discover the cmdlet properties
Get-Date | Get-Member -MemberType Property

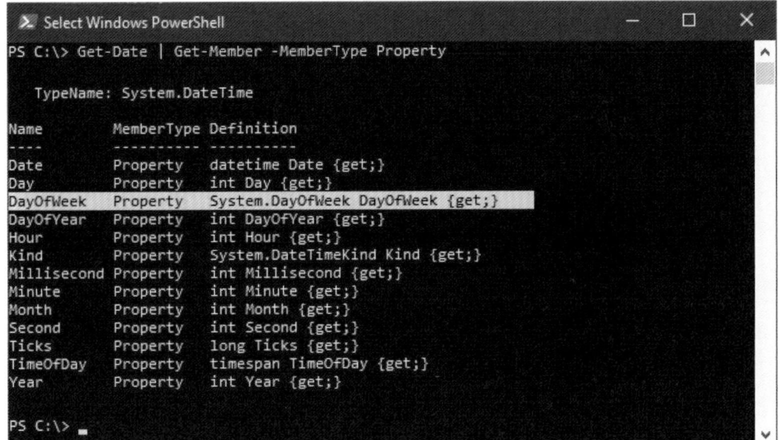

Select Windows PowerShell
PS C:\> Get-Date | Get-Member -MemberType Property
TypeName: System.DateTime
Name MemberType Definition
Date Property datetime Date {get;}
Day Property int Day {get;}
DayOfWeek Property System.DayOfWeek DayOfWeek {get;}
DayOfYear Property int DayOfYear {get;}
Hour Property int Hour {get;}
Kind Property System.DateTimeKind Kind {get;}
Millisecond Property int Millisecond {get;}
Minute Property int Minute {get;}
Month Property int Month {get;}
Second Property int Second {get;}
Ticks Property long Ticks {get;}
TimeOfDay Property timespan TimeOfDay {get;}
Year Property int Year {get;}
PS C:\>

With the piped command, **Get-Date** first returns a Date object, then passes that to the **Get-Member** cmdlet to extract only its properties. Change "Property" to "Method" to see only its methods.

6. Enter these commands in turn to discover the current date and time, and the value of a specific property
Get-Date
(Get-Date).DayOfWeek

The parentheses are required around the cmdlet name to ensure the Date object is first returned before the **DayOfWeek** property value can be extracted.

Combining commands

The true power of Windows PowerShell can be unleashed by combining several commands in a "pipeline". Lines can be broken after each "|" pipe character, and multiple commands can be separated by a ";" semicolon character:

1. Open PowerShell, and type this command, then press **Enter**
   Write-Output "tr:nth-child(even){background:yellow}" |

2. Next, type this command at the >> continuation prompt, then hit **Enter** to create a style sheet file
   Set-Content stripe.css

3. Now, type these commands to create and display a HTML table of date properties styled by the CSS file
   Get-Date |
   ConvertTo-Html -As List -CssUri stripe.css |
   Set-Content date.html ; Invoke-Item date.html

The **Write-Output** and **ConvertTo-Html** cmdlets will write output in the PowerShell window unless piped to the **Set-Content** cmdlet to create a file.

The **Invoke-Item** cmdlet provides a way to run an executable script or open a file using the default app associated with a particular file type – the Microsoft Edge web browser in this case.

The **ConvertTo-Html** cmdlet creates a vertical table by default, or a horizontal table if an **-As List** parameter is specified.

24 Update and maintain

Although you need to regularly update Windows 10 and the apps on your PC to ensure the system keeps working securely and effectively, Windows Update automates this process.

Windows Update

The Windows operating system requires frequent updates to keep it secure and fully operational. Updates are provided on a regular basis for Windows 10 and should be applied when available. To see what the update situation is for your computer:

1. Go to Start, Settings, then click **Update & security**

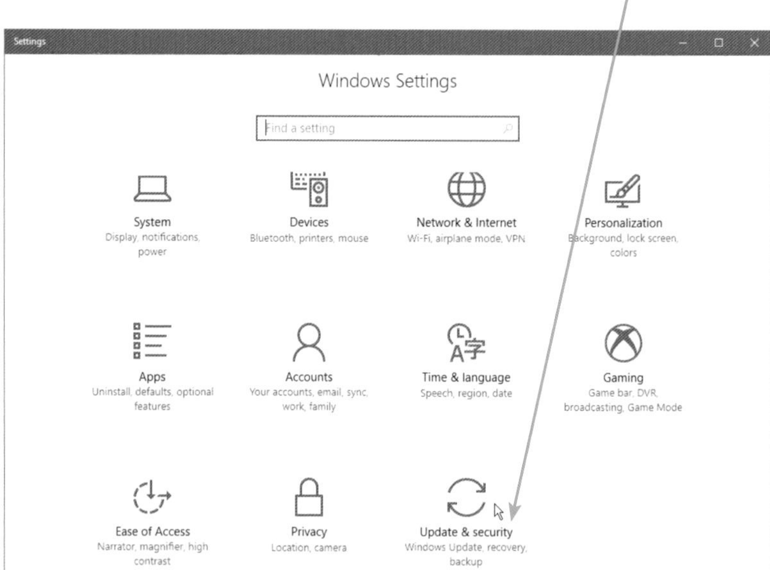

Alternatively, you can type "settings" into the Taskbar Search box, or say "Hey Cortana, start settings", to open the **Settings** window.

2. Next, in the left-hand panel, click **Windows Update**

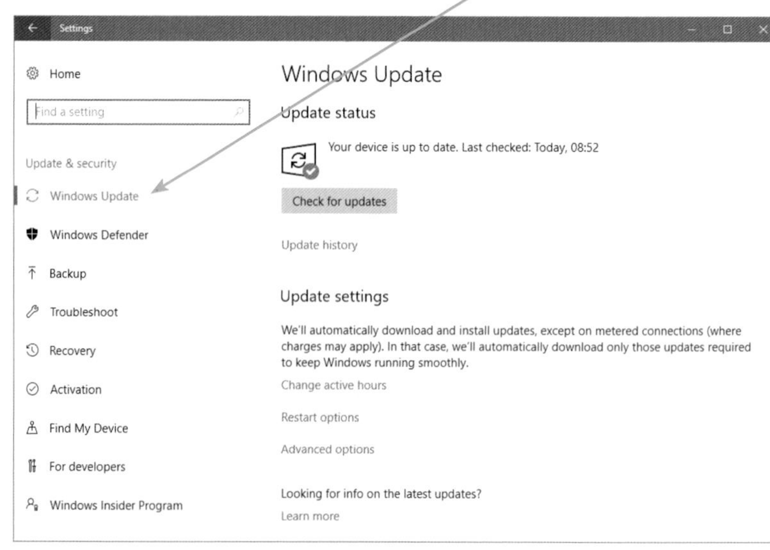

Unlike previous versions of Windows, whose updates only provided periodical security patches and bug fixes, the Update model in Windows 10 provides continuous security and feature improvements.

3 Now, click the **Check for updates** button

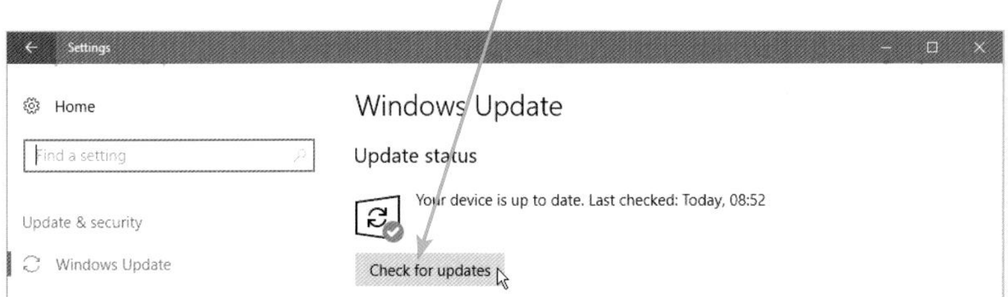

Wait to see if any updates are available

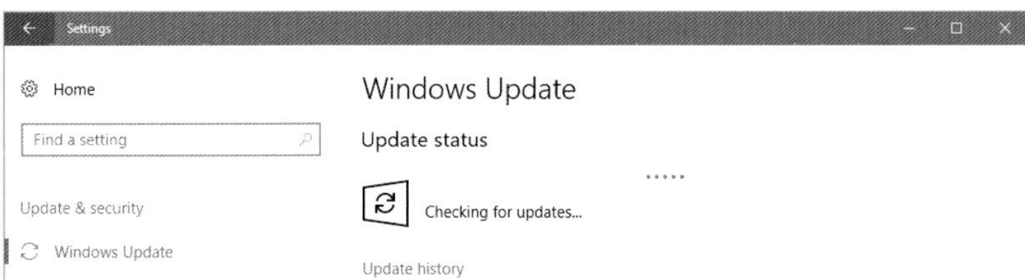

5 Any available updates will be downloaded and installed

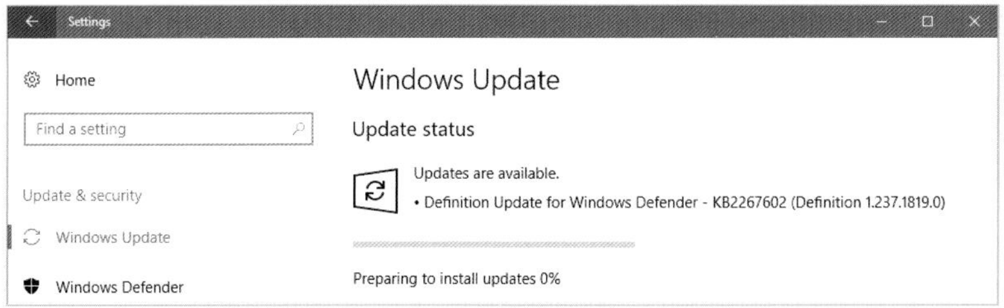

6 When installation completes, you may be asked to restart the system so that appropriate files can be updated

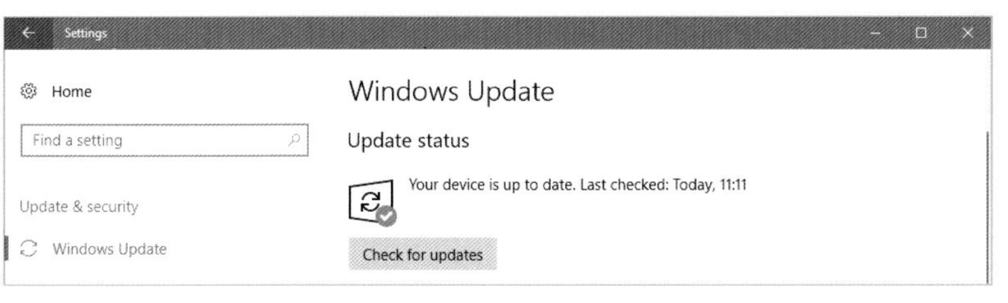

If Automatic Updating has been set, the indication of updates waiting appears immediately when you open Windows Update.

You can selectively apply updates in this manner, but it is much easier to let Windows Update do the job automatically.

Update settings

1. Open Settings, **Update & security**, Windows Update, and select **Change active hours** under "Update settings"

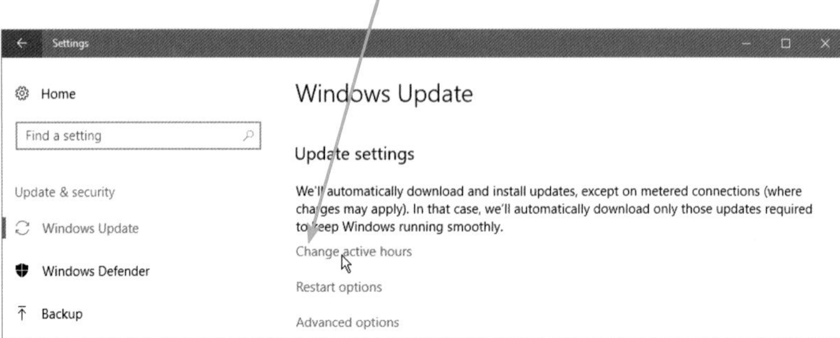
Settings
Home
Find a setting
Update & security
Windows Update
Windows Defender
Backup
Windows Update
Update settings
We'll automatically download and install updates, except on metered connections (where charges may apply). In that case, we'll automatically download only those updates required to keep Windows running smoothly.
Change active hours
Restart options
Advanced options

2. Select the Start time and End time of the period during which you typically use your PC each day

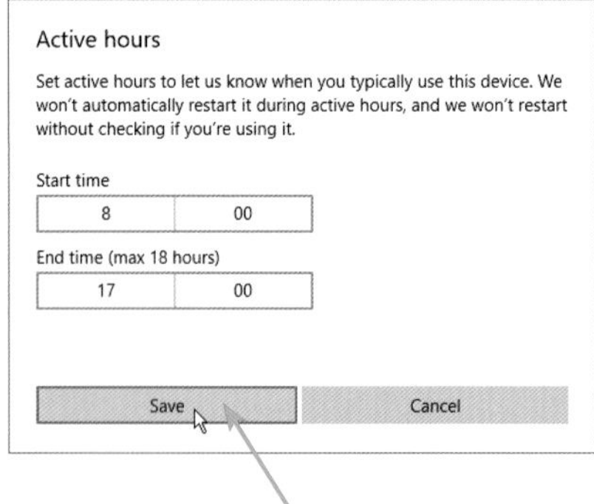
Active hours
Set active hours to let us know when you typically use this device. We won't automatically restart it during active hours, and we won't restart without checking if you're using it.
Start time
8
00
End time (max 18 hours)
17
00
Save
Cancel

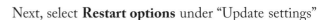

3. Now, click the **Save** button to prevent Windows automatically restarting during the specified period

4. Next, select **Restart options** under "Update settings"

5. Slide the toggle button to the On position

6. If you wish to delay the installation of updates until later, select a convenient time and date for the installation of awaiting updates

NEW

The Active hours feature was improved in the Windows 10 Creators Update to allow you to specify the PC as active up to 18 hours of the day; up from the previous 12-hour maximum.

Beware

The option to schedule update delays for up to 35 days is available in Windows Professional, Enterprise, and Education editions only.

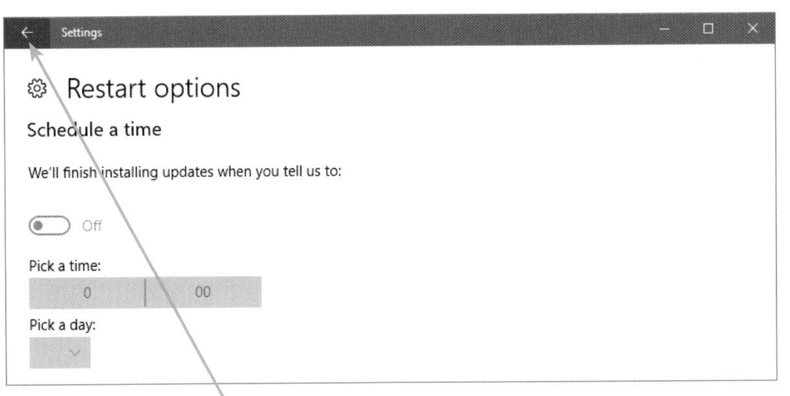

7. Click the **Back** button to return to the Windows Update screen, and select Advanced options under "Update settings"

8. To enable the Microsoft Update feature, check the **Give me updates for other Microsoft products when I update Windows** box

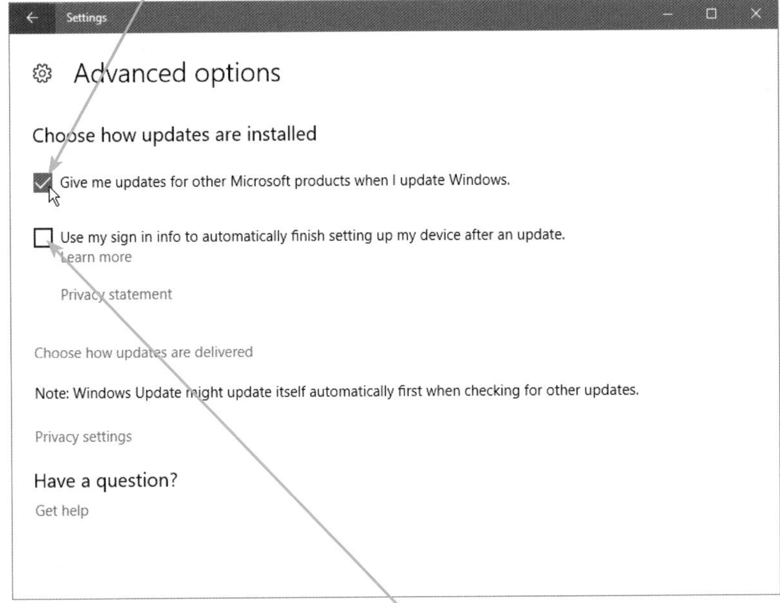

9. Optionally, also check the **Use my sign in info...** box for installations that require your sign-in info

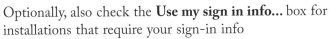

The option to schedule update delays and exclude driver updates was introduced in the Windows 10 Creators Update for Windows Professional, Enterprise, and Education editions.

Microsoft Update will provide updates for Office, MSN, Windows Defender, and various Windows Server-related products.

It is recommended that you use BitLocker if you select the **Use my sign in info...** option.

Update sources

A new Unified Update Platform (UUP) was introduced in the Windows 10 Creators Update to allow much faster downloads and reduced data usage.

1. Open Settings, Update & security, Windows Update, and select Advanced options under "Update settings"

2. Next, click the **Choose how updates are delivered** link

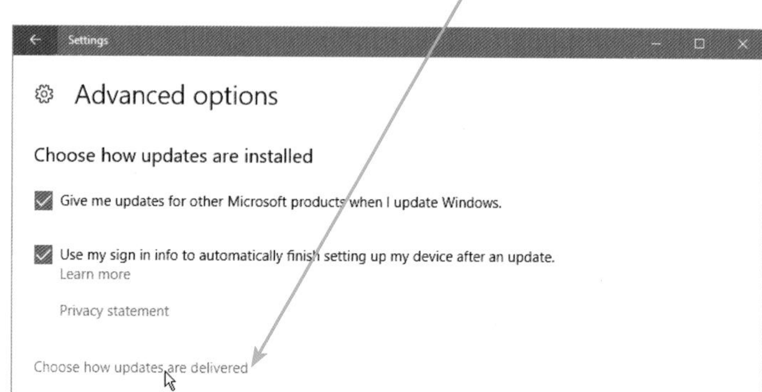

3. If you would like to allow updates from multiple sources, slide the toggle button to the **On** position

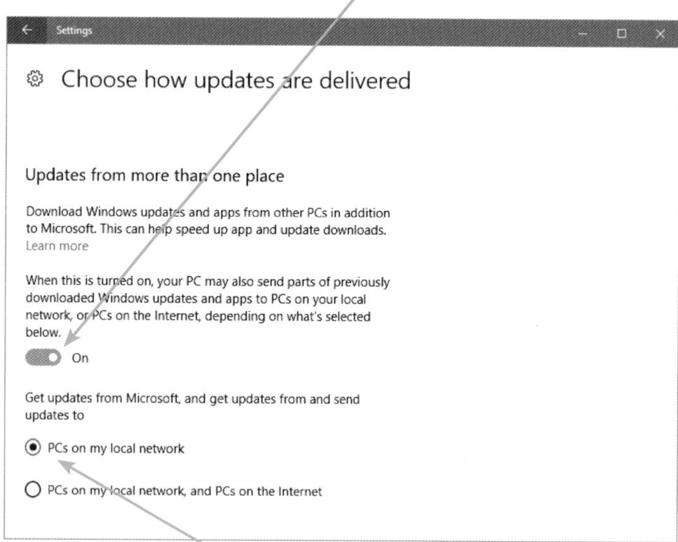

Settings
Choose how updates are delivered
Updates from more than one place
Download Windows updates and apps from other PCs in addition to Microsoft. This can help speed up app and update downloads.
Learn more
When this is turned on, your PC may also send parts of previously downloaded Windows updates and apps to PCs on your local network, or PCs on the Internet, depending on what's selected below.
On
Get updates from Microsoft, and get updates from and send updates to
PCs on my local network
PCs on my local network, and PCs on the Internet

Allow updates from PCs on your local network and from the internet to be downloaded the most quickly.

4. Choose whether or not to allow only update sources on your local network, or also allow internet sources

Update history

Updates may be applied automatically, in the background, but you can review the activities:

1. Open Settings, Update & security, Windows Update, and select the **Update history** link

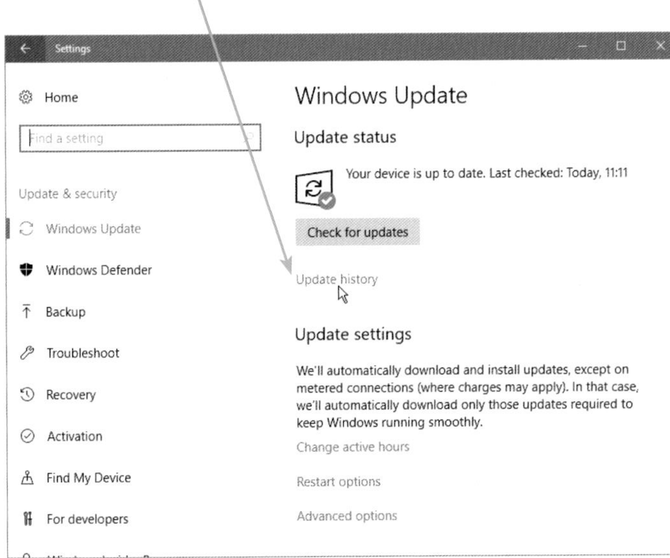

2. The updates are displayed, latest first

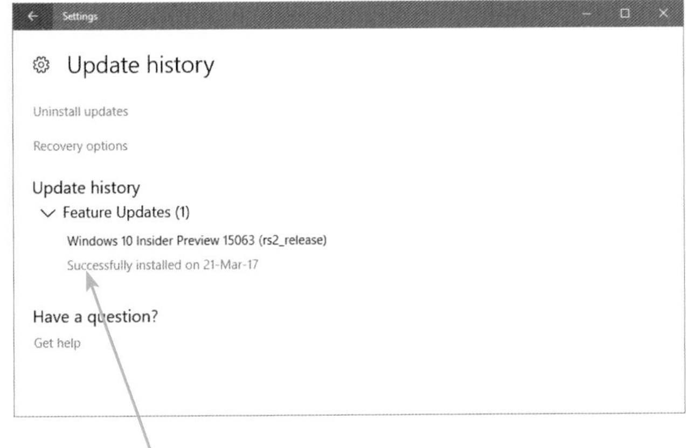

3. Click the link at the bottom of any update item to see more information about that update

The Windows 10 Creators Update added the ability to specify connections as metered, to limit unnecessary downloads – go to Settings, Network & Internet, Status, Change connection properties, and turn On the **Set as metered connection** toggle button.

There's an entry for every attempt to apply an update, and results are marked as **Successfully installed** or **Failed to install**.

Identify important updates that have failed, and check to ensure that a subsequent update attempt succeeded.

...cont'd

You can review the Windows and other updates that have been installed on your computer, and remove any that may be causing problems.

There are some updates that cannot be removed this way. If that is the case, there will be no **Uninstall** button shown when you select the update.

1. On the "Update history" screen, select the **Uninstall updates** link

2. Select an update and click **Uninstall** on the toolbar to remove that update

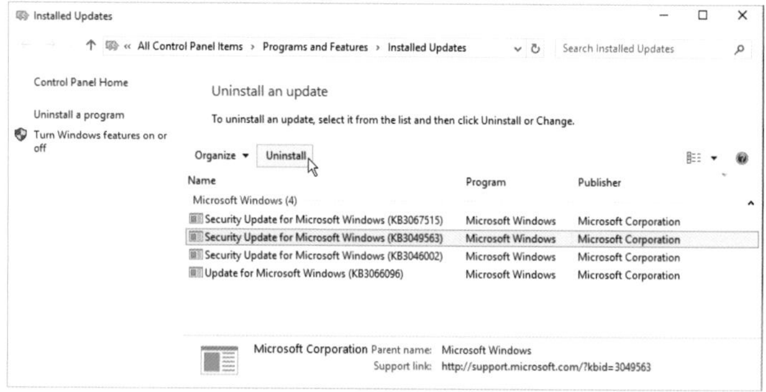

You can switch back and forth between the Updates and the Programs list, using the **Uninstall a program** or **View installed updates** links in the left-hand pane.

3. You can also change the appearance of the update items using the **More options** button on the toolbar – for example, from the Details view above, to Tiles view below

More options button

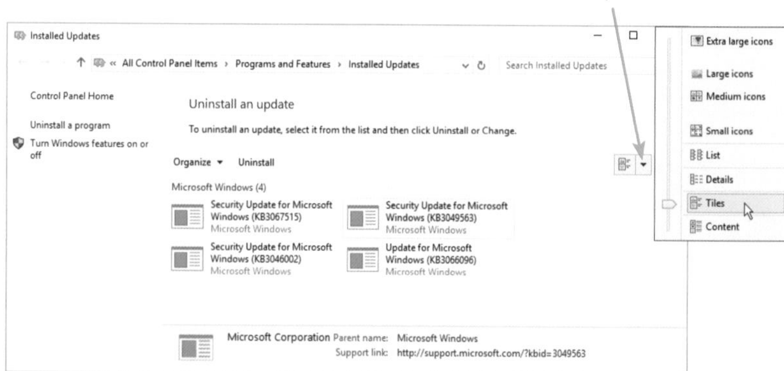

Installed updates

Installed updates can also be managed via the Control Panel:

1. Go to Start, Windows System, Control Panel, Programs, then select Programs and Features

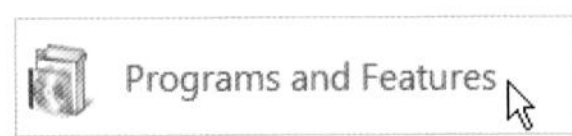

2. In the left-hand pane, click View installed updates

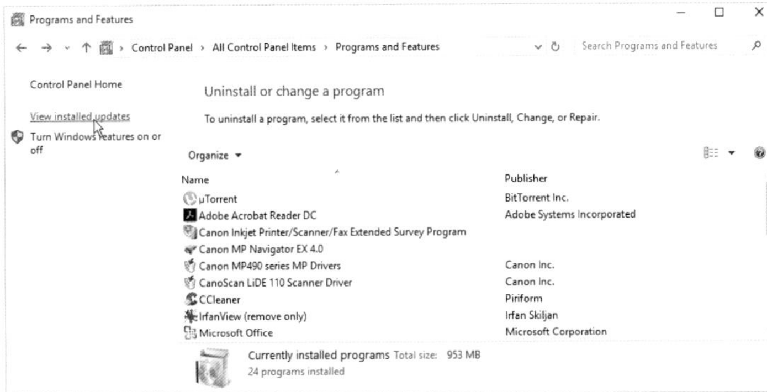

3. Click the arrow buttons to the right of each category heading to expand or collapse the list of updates for each category, and to view details

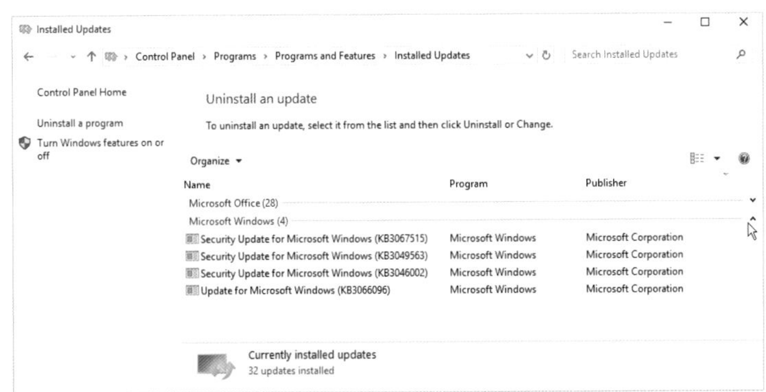

4. Select an update and click Uninstall on the toolbar to remove that update

Click the **Uninstall a program** link in the left-hand pane to manage installed programs.

Upgrading Windows

Sometimes, adding updates isn't enough – you need to upgrade your edition of Windows to an edition that has the extra functions that you need. Alternatively, you may want to upgrade from 32-bit Windows to 64-bit Windows, so your computer can take advantage of the larger amounts of memory that 64-bit systems can utilize.

You can see a comparison of features in each edition of Windows 10 on pages 16-17.

32-bit to 64-bit

This isn't an upgrade in the usual sense – you cannot install the new operating system and retain existing folders and data files. Instead, you create a completely new system, replacing the existing setup, then install your applications and apply Windows updates. You can back up your data files and folders before you make the change and afterwards restore the backup to your revised system. However, you will have to re-install all of your apps, and may need to install 64-bit versions of drivers for devices unless Windows has them.

Upgrading editions

Changing editions can be carried out as a true upgrade. You update the operating system files, but leave your data files and folders unaffected. The application programs that you have installed will continue to operate.

Upgrade paths

With Windows 7 there were a number of upgrade paths possible between the various versions. Windows 10, however, provides only one – if you currently have the entry version, Windows 10 Home, you can upgrade it to Windows 10 Pro. To implement this upgrade you will need to buy the Windows 10 Pro Pack from the Windows Store – open Settings, **Update & security**, Activation, then press the **Go to Store** button:

Go to Store

You can install any edition of 64-bit Windows on your computer, if it is 64-bit capable and has enough memory to make the transition worthwhile – ideally 4GB of memory.

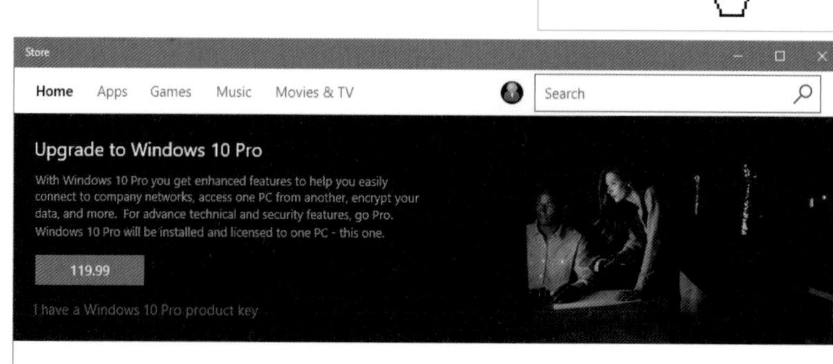

Resetting your PC

If you want to return your system to its initial state, if for example you are disposing of a PC, Windows 10 provides an easy way to reset the system. This procedure provides three options of how thoroughly the reset should clean the system:

- **Reset Windows only** – this restores the Windows system files and keeps your personal files and apps intact.
- **Reset Windows to new** – this restores the Windows system files and deletes your personal files and apps.
- **Reset Windows and clean** – this restores the Windows system files and completely removes your personal files and apps from the hard disk drive.

Beware

Resetting Windows 10 is like re-installing the operating system, so it does take some time.

You may just want to reset Windows 10 to its original pristine state if you have, over time, installed many apps or if you feel the system has become sluggish. OneDrive proves invaluable for this, as you can simply access your personal files there.

1. Open Settings, Update & security, then select the Recovery option on the left-hand pane

2. Under "Reset this PC", click the Get started button

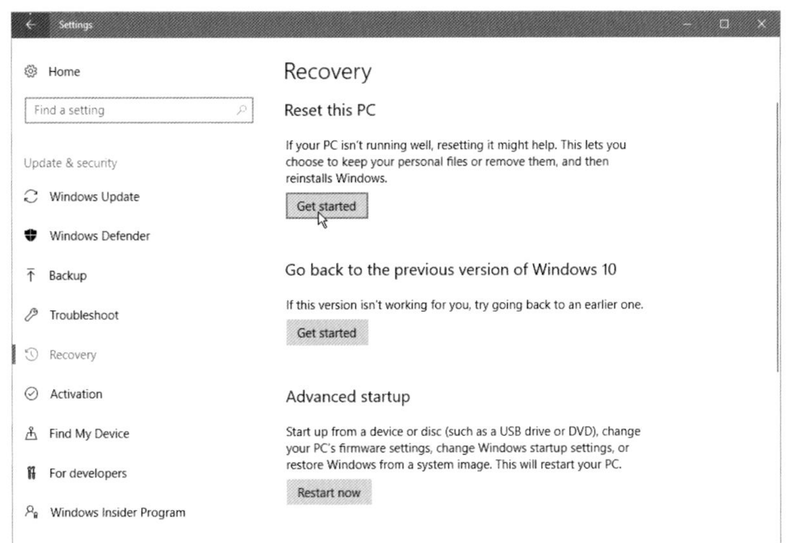
Settings
Home
Find a setting
Update & security
Windows Update
Windows Defender
Backup
Troubleshoot
Recovery
Activation
Find My Device
For developers
Windows Insider Program
Recovery
Reset this PC
If your PC isn't running well, resetting it might help. This lets you choose to keep your personal files or remove them, and then reinstalls Windows.
Get started
Go back to the previous version of Windows 10
If this version isn't working for you, try going back to an earlier one.
Get started
Advanced startup
Start up from a device or disc (such as a USB drive or DVD), change your PC's firmware settings, change Windows startup settings, or restore Windows from a system image. This will restart your PC.
Restart now

Hot tip

Notice that you also have an option here to revert to the previously-installed version of Windows if you recently upgraded the PC to Windows 10.

...cont'd

3. Choose whether to remove or keep your personal files and apps – e.g. click Remove everything

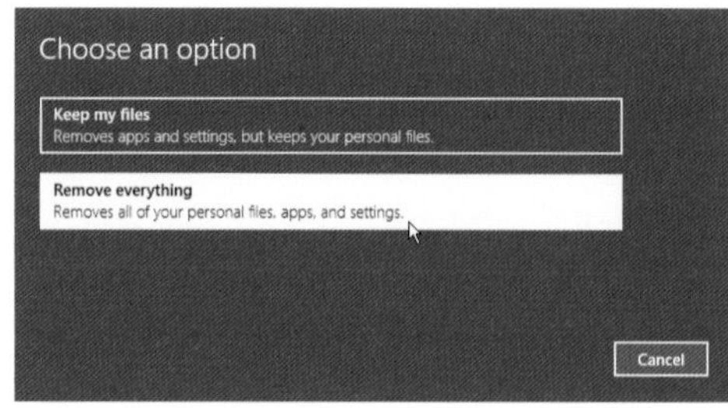

If you are selling the PC you should choose the **Remove files and clean the drive option**.

4. Next, choose whether to remove files from one or more drives – e.g. click All drives

5. Now, choose whether you would also like to clean the drives – e.g. click Remove files and clean the drive

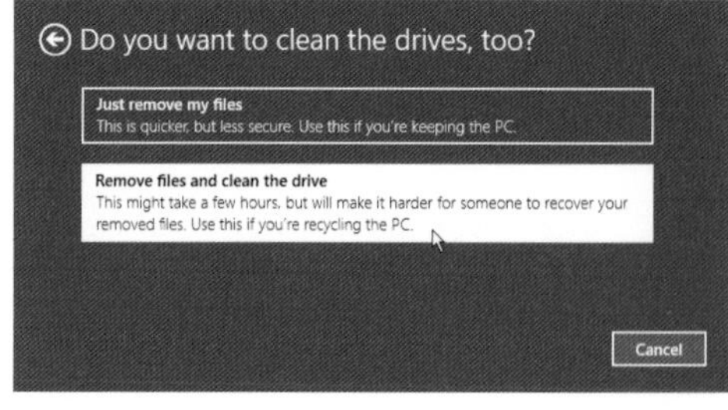

The reset process will require you to enter certain information, such as your location and your Wi-Fi key – just like installing Windows 10 for the very first time.

6. Carefully review the actions to be performed by the reset and, if you are happy with these, click the Reset button

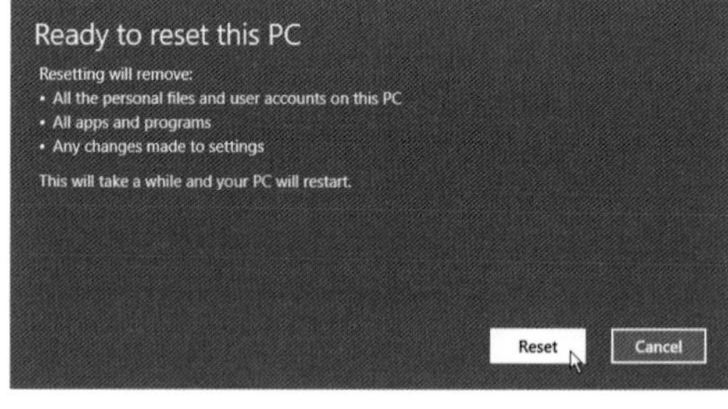

After Windows 10 is re-installed you can sign in with your Microsoft account to sync your files from OneDrive.

Disk Cleanup

For everyday tasks, you can use the tools found in drive Properties.

1. Press **WinKey** + **X**, select File Explorer, This PC, then expand Devices and drives in the right-hand pane

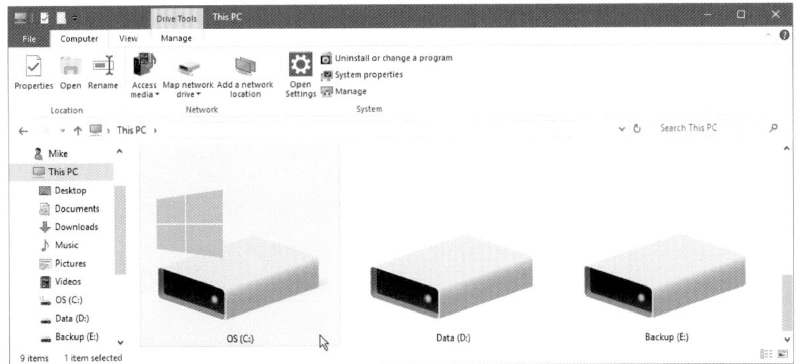

2. Next, right-click on a drive and click Properties from the context menu – to open the drive's Properties dialog box

3. In the Properties dialog box, select the General tab

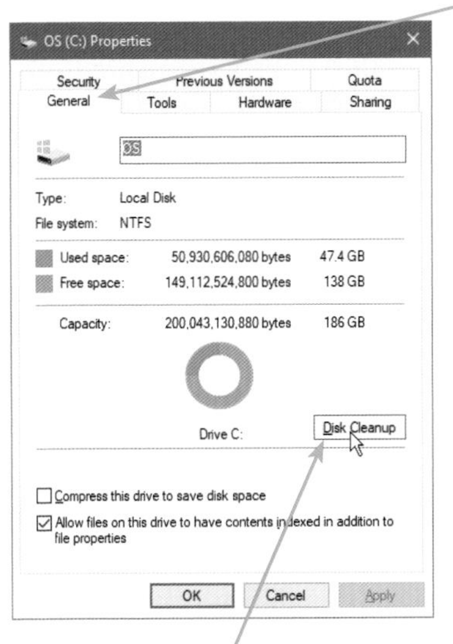

4. Next, click the **Disk Cleanup** button to calculate the disk space that can be released

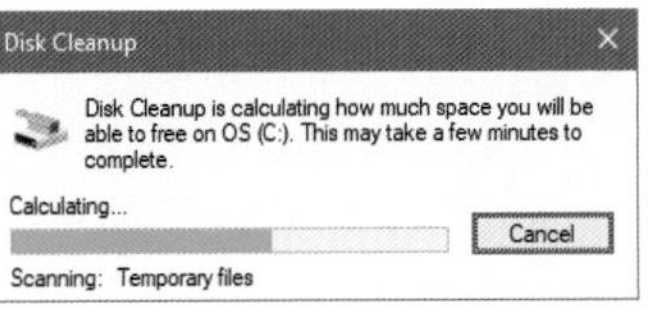

You could also select Disk Cleanup from the list of **Administrative Tools** via Control Panel, or search for it in the Taskbar Search box.

...cont'd

Hot tip

Some categories of file are suggested, but you can select others, e.g. **Recycle Bin** or **Temporary Files**, to increase the amount of space that will be made available.

5. Select or clear file categories and click the **View Files** button to see what will be deleted for each category

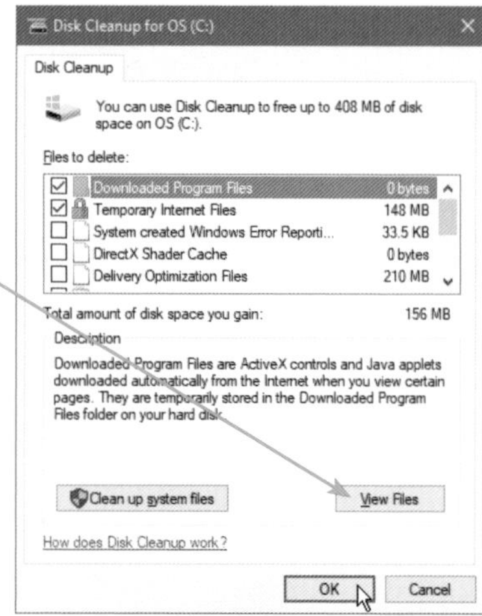

6. When you are happy with your selection, click OK to proceed with Disk Cleanup

Don't forget

Click **Cancel** if you change your mind and want to look again at the categories and files selected.

7. Click **Delete Files** to confirm that you want to permanently delete the selected files

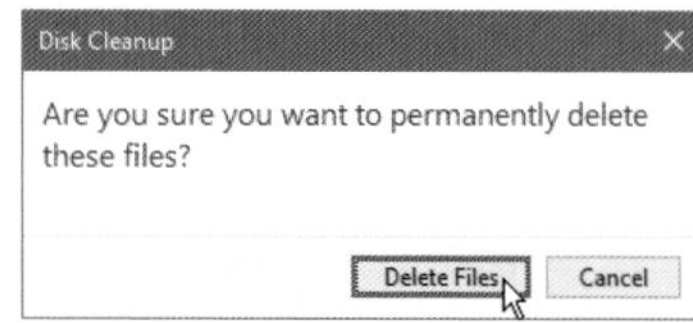

8. Disk Cleanup now proceeds to free the space used by those files on the selected drive

Note that you may be prompted for administrator permission to remove certain types of file. If so, you'll see a box that lets you extend the permission to all the files of that type. Make sure this box is checked, and then click **Continue**.

Clean up system files

If you need more free space, there will almost certainly be some system files that are not really necessary and can be removed safely. Old system restore files are a typical example (these can occupy gigabytes of disk space).

Hot tip

When you choose **Clean up system files** you'll get the More Options tab where you can, additionally, remove programs that you do not use, or remove older restore points, shadow copies and backups.

1. Open the Disk Cleanup dialog, then click the **Clean up system files** button to calculate the disk space that can be released by removing old system files

2. Temporary files can also use a lot of disk space. System error memory dump files are also good candidates for deletion

Defragmentation

Defragmentation optimizes your file system for faster performance by rearranging files stored on a disk to occupy contiguous storage.

1. For any drive, from the Properties dialog, Tools tab, click the **Optimize** button

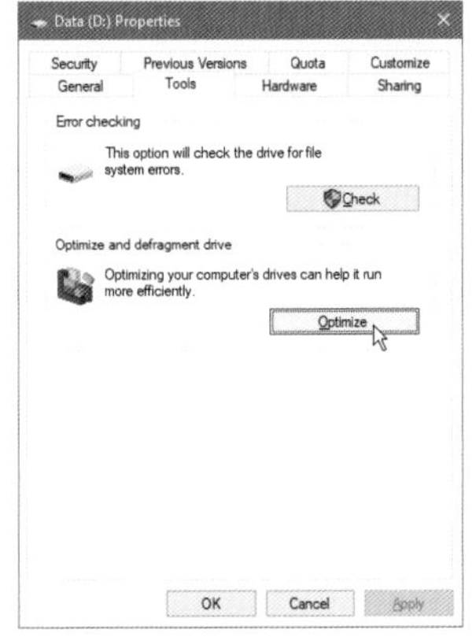

2. All drives that can be defragmented are listed, with the latest information about their fragmentation status

The larger the drive, the longer the optimization process takes.

3. Select a drive and click the **Analyze** button to see the current state of the drive

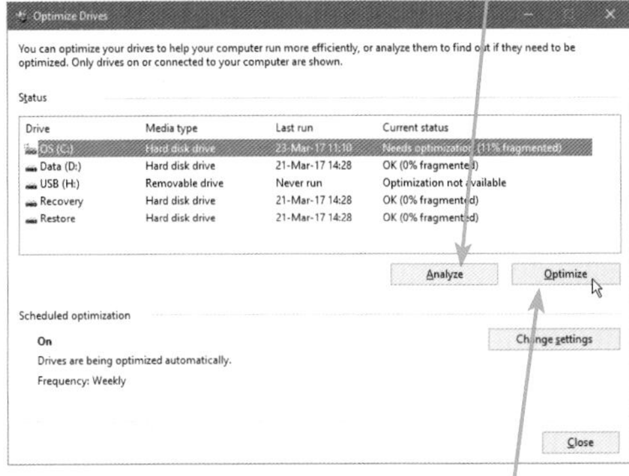

4. Select the drive and click the **Optimize** button to analyze then defragment the drive by relocating files

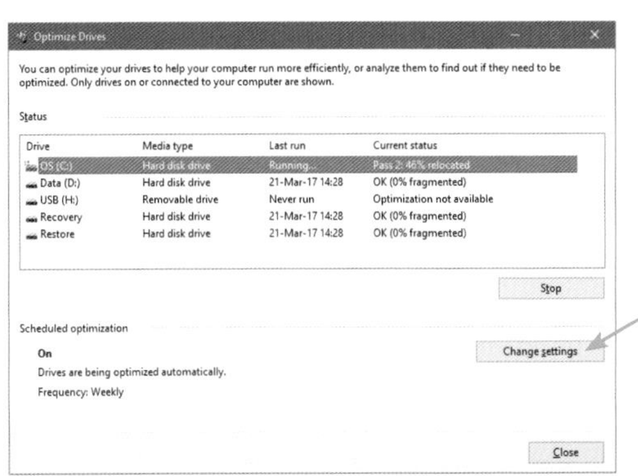

With the schedule turned on, you can still run an immediate defragment. Click **Change settings** to change the frequency or to turn off scheduled optimization entirely.

...cont'd

Windows automates the defragmentation process so that it happens in the background on a regular basis. However, you may wish to change the default settings:

1. If it is not already done, click the **Turn on** button

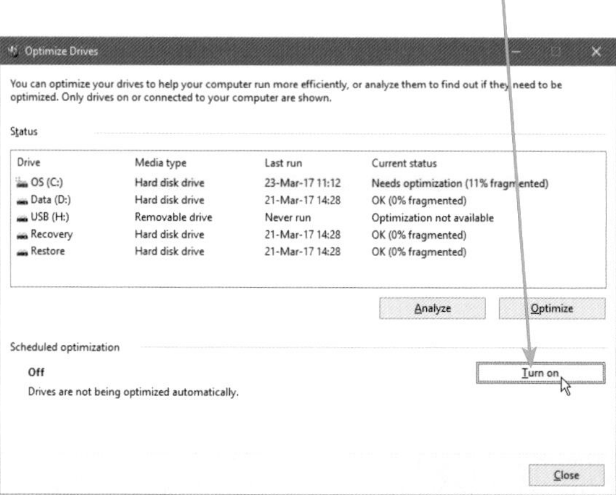

You could also select **Defragment and Optimize Drives** from the Administrative Tools via the Control Panel.

2. Check Run on a schedule. Then, set the desired schedule from the drop-down boxes

3. Click the **Choose** button and select the drives to be optimized

4. Click OK. Your drives will now be defragmented according to the settings specified. Click the **Close** button

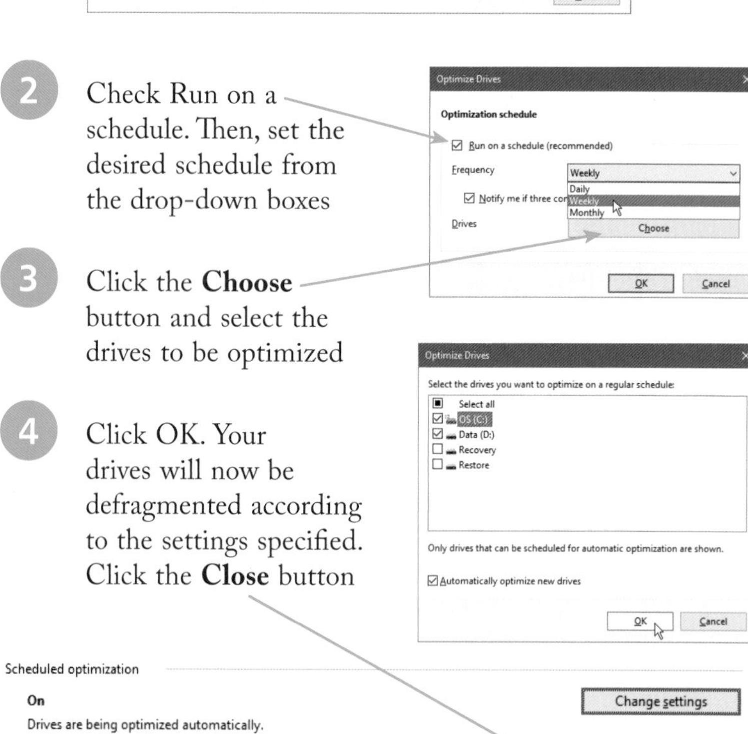

You can choose any drive to defragment, even if you start from Properties for a different drive.

25 Windows performance

Windows 10 provides tools that measure the performance of your PC and identify issues affecting its performance. You can use monitoring tools, and review detailed information about the PC. Windows will even help you speed up the system by using USB flash drives to act as a cache for system files.

System Properties

System Properties is an important location for reviewing and adjusting the performance of your computer, so Windows provides a number of ways for displaying this panel so that it is accessible from various areas within the system.

In Control Panel, System and Security, you'll also display System Properties if you click either **View amount of RAM and processor speed**, or **See the name of this computer** under the System section.

To display System Properties, use any of the following options:

- Go to Start, Settings, System, **About**.

- Open the Power User Menu by pressing **WinKey** + **X** and selecting **System**.

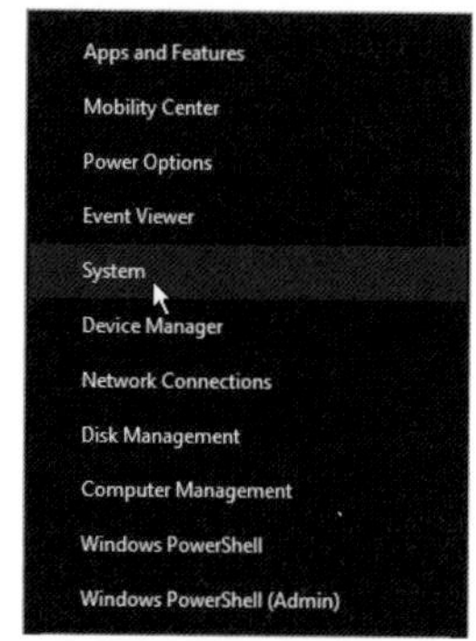

- Press **WinKey** + **X** and select **File Explorer, This PC**. On the ribbon toolbar, click **System properties**.

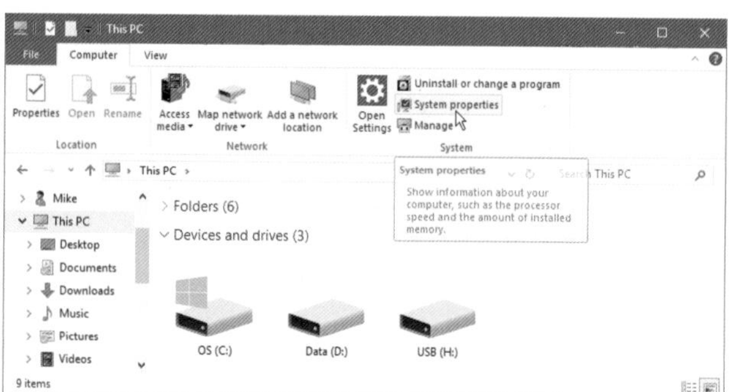

Type "about system" in the Taskbar Search box to display System Properties.

- Go to Start, Windows System, Control Panel, (View by: Category), **System and Security**, and click on the **System** icon link.

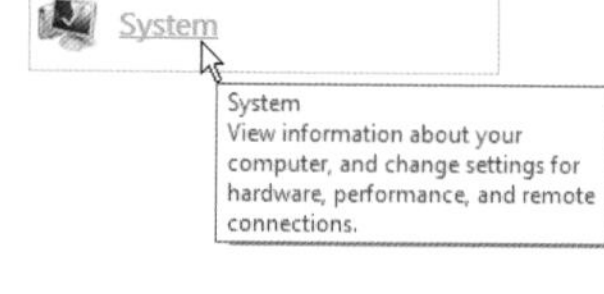

- Press the **WinKey** + **Pause/Break** keys.

Whichever method you use, **System Properties** and **System** display basic information about your computer:

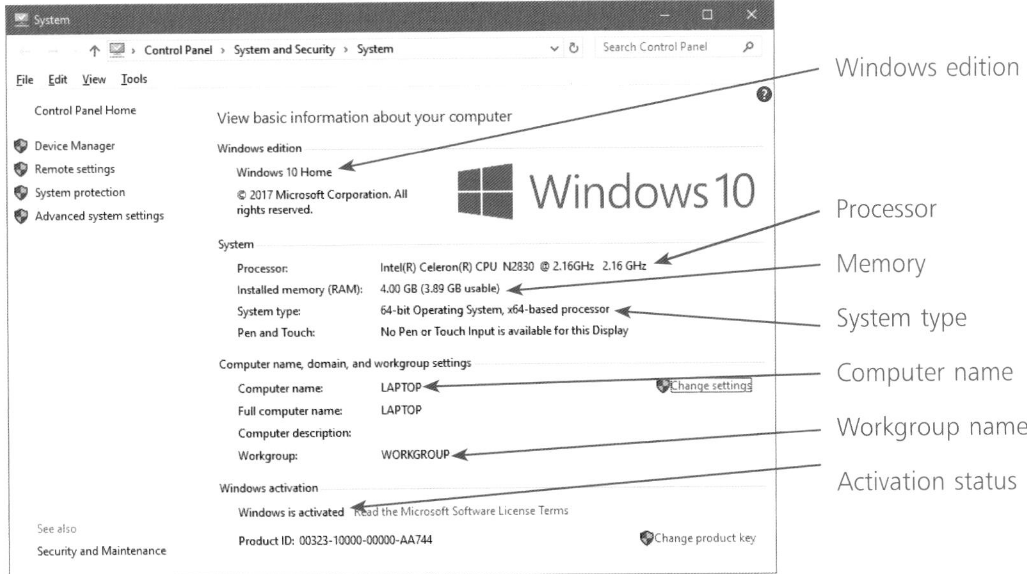

The pane on the left provides various links, including:

- Device Manager
- Remote settings
- System protection
- Advanced system settings

On the right, you'll find details of the operating system. This tells you the edition of Windows installed on the PC.

Next are some basic details about the hardware in the PC. Here, you'll see the processor manufacturer, the model number and the speed of the device. Also listed is the amount of memory.

Device Manager provides details of the system components. **Advanced system settings** provides the full System Properties.

Device Manager

As we saw on page 423, System Properties provides a link to the Device Manager, and you can also access Device Manager from the Power User Menu and from the Control Panel.

The Device Manager displays a list of your hardware, sorted by category. You can expand these categories to view which hardware you have installed in your computer.

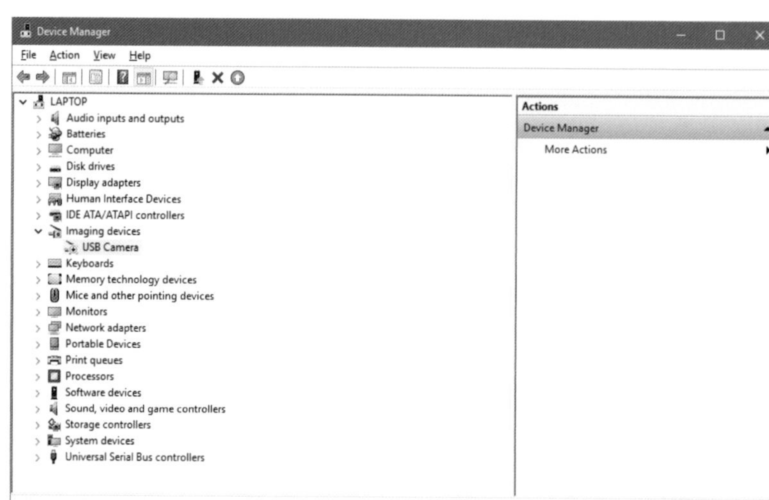

So what is it, and what does it do? Essentially, the Device Manager is an extension of the Microsoft Management Console that provides a central and organized view of all the hardware installed in the computer.

Its purpose is to provide a means of managing this hardware. For example: hard drives, keyboards, sound cards, USB devices, etc.

Click the arrow to the left of the device categories to see what devices are in the category.

Some of the things you can do with the Device Manager include:

- Change hardware configuration
- Manage hardware drivers
- Enable and disable hardware
- Identify and resolve conflicts between hardware devices
- View a device's status
- View a device's technical properties

We'll take a look at how you can troubleshoot malfunctioning devices with the Device Manager on the next page.

Troubleshooting with the Device Manager

When a device in your computer has a problem, it is flagged as such in the Device Manager. Different symbols indicate specific types of problem. For example:

- A black exclamation point (!) on a yellow field indicates the device has a problem – although it may still be functioning.

When you open the Device Manager, take note of any symbols you see. These indicate issues that will need to be resolved.

To see what the issue is, right-click on the device icon and select **Properties**. On the **General** tab under Device Status you may see a message that says "The drivers for this device are not installed". Note that this can also indicate that the driver is present but has been corrupted. To resolve the issue, click the **Update driver** button, or right-click the device icon and choose **Update driver**. Windows will now try to locate the correct driver for the device, and download and install it.

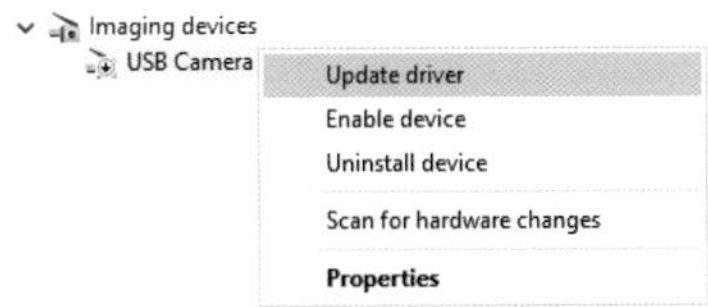

Other symbols indicate other issues that may require attention. For example:

- A down-arrow indicates a disabled device. Note that while the device may be disabled, it is still consuming system resources and is thus reducing the performance of the system.

Right-click on the device icon and select **Properties**. On the **General** tab under Device status you may see a message that says "The device is disabled". To resolve the issue, click the **Enable Device** button, or right-click the device icon and choose **Enable**. Windows will now enable the device ready for use. Click Finish to exit the process.

The Driver tab in a device's Properties offers options to roll back to a previous driver (i.e. one that works properly), to disable the device and to uninstall the device.

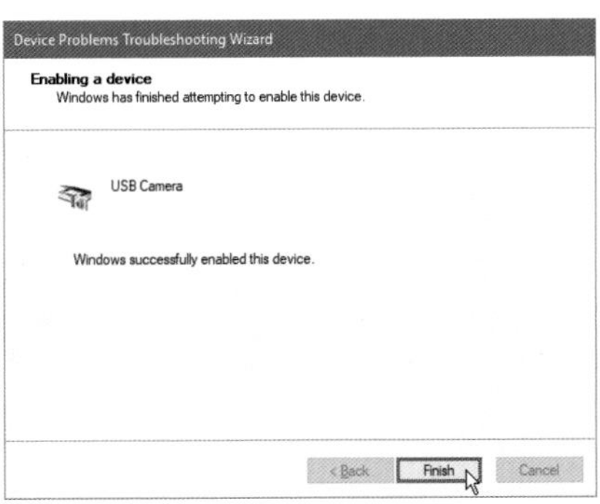

Improving performance

1. Go to Windows System, Control Panel, (View by: Category), **System and Security**, System. Click **Advanced system settings**, and then **Settings...** under "Performance"

2. The default **Let Windows choose what's best for my computer** will have most of the effects selected

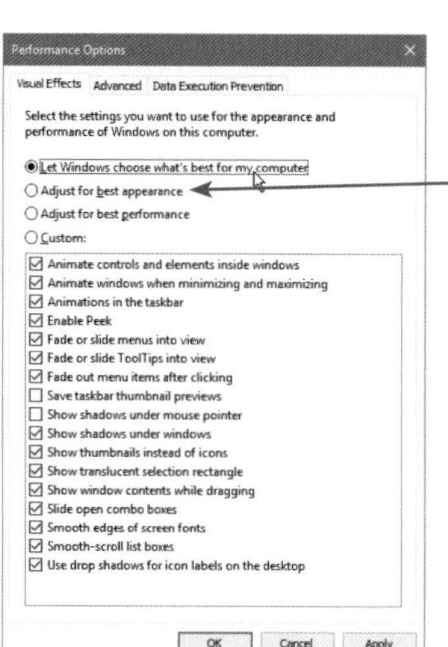

3. Choosing **Adjust for best appearance** means all of the effects will be selected

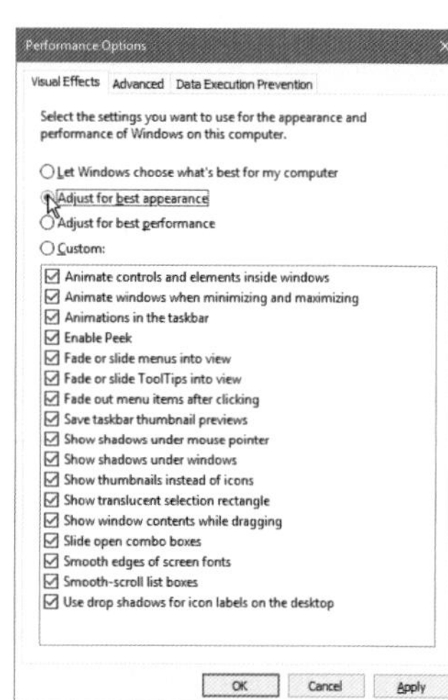

4. You get no effects if you choose **Adjust for best performance**

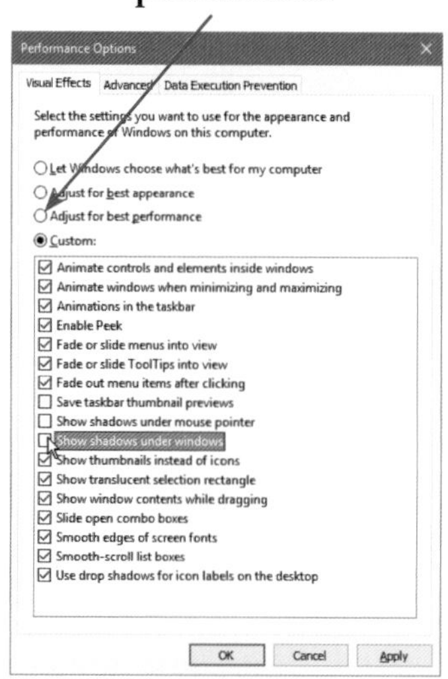

5. The best balance is to select **Let Windows choose what's best for my computer**, click **Apply**, then deselect effects you can manage without

6. Click **OK**, then **Apply**, and your choices of effects become the Custom setting

Don't forget

You don't need to change hardware; you can use **Performance Options** to make changes to the settings to get more efficient operation.

Processor scheduling

1. Click the **Advanced** tab, and you can choose to prioritize **Programs** or **Background services**

The usual choice is Programs, but you might choose Background services for a computer that acts as a print server or provides backups.

You should only consider changing the processor scheduling on computers that are mainly used for background tasks.

Virtual memory

Windows creates a Paging file to supplement system memory. To review or change the settings:

1. From the Advanced tab, click the Virtual memory **Change...** button

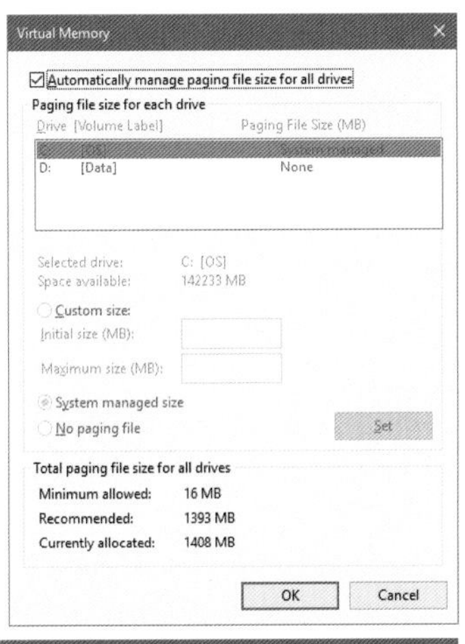

By default, Windows will automatically manage the paging file for your drive or drives. To choose the values yourself:

1. Uncheck **Automatically manage paging file size for all drives**

2. Click **Custom size** and choose sizes, then click the **Set** button to apply

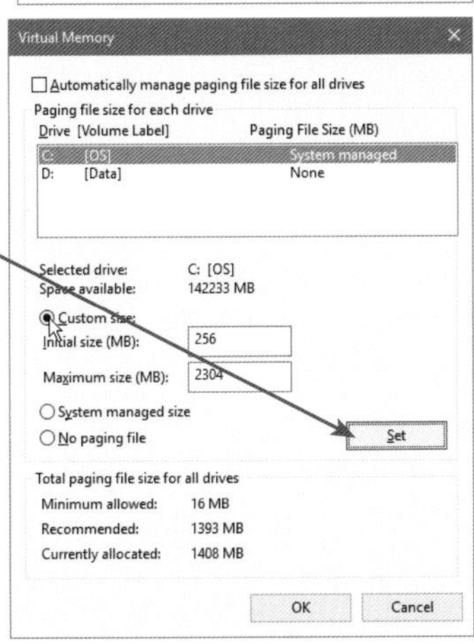

Setting the initial size the same as the maximum will avoid the need for Windows to adjust the size of the paging file, though this may not necessarily improve performance.

With multiple drives, choose the one with most space available.

Make sure you always have at least one drive with a paging file, even on a large-memory PC, since some programs rely on the paging file.

Data Execution Prevention

The third tab in the Performance Options is for Data Execution Prevention or DEP. This is a security feature intended to prevent damage to your computer from viruses and other security threats, by monitoring programs to make sure they use system memory safely. If a program tries executing code from memory in an incorrect way, DEP closes the program.

Don't forget

If you add a program to the exception list, but decide that you do want it to be monitored by DEP, you can clear the box next to the program.

1. By default, Windows will turn on DEP for essential programs and services only

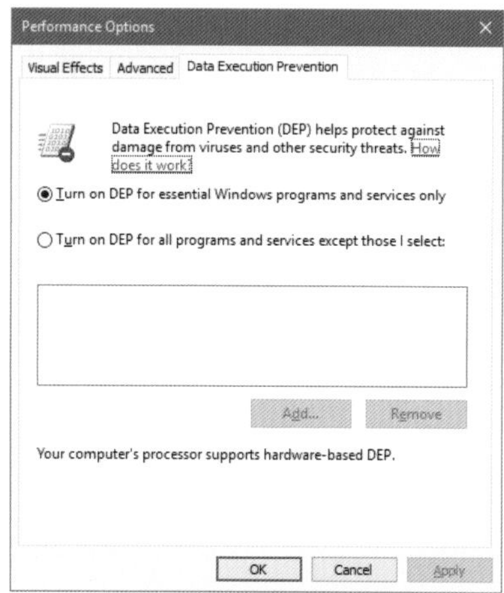

2. You can choose to **Turn on DEP for all programs and services except those I select**

3. Click **Add...** to select programs for which you want to turn DEP off

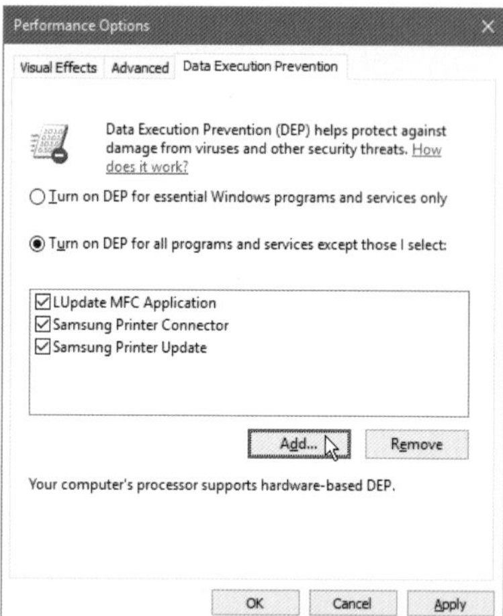

If DEP keeps closing a particular program that you trust, and your antivirus software does not detect a threat, the program might not run correctly when DEP is turned on. You should check for a DEP-compatible version of the program, or an update from the software publisher, before you choose to turn off DEP for that program.

If DEP closes a program that is part of Windows, the cause could be a program you have recently installed that operates inside Windows. Check for a DEP-compatible version.

Hardware-based DEP

Some processors use hardware technology to prevent programs from running code in protected memory locations. In this case, you will be told that your processor supports hardware-based DEP. If your processor does not support hardware-based DEP, your computer will still be protected because Windows will use software-based DEP.

Advanced system settings

Windows provides another way to display the Performance Options:

1. Open System Properties, **Advanced system settings**

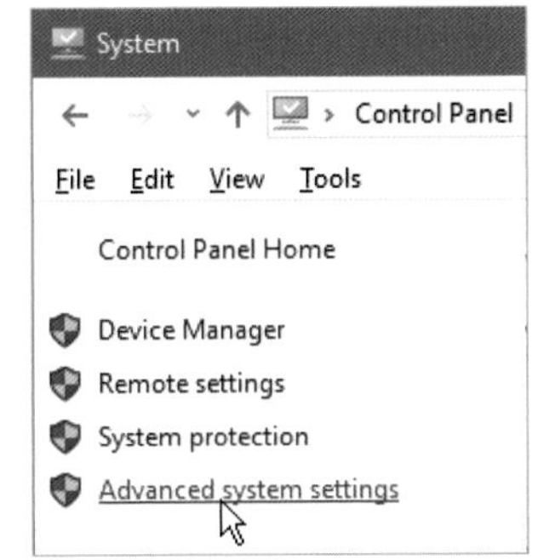

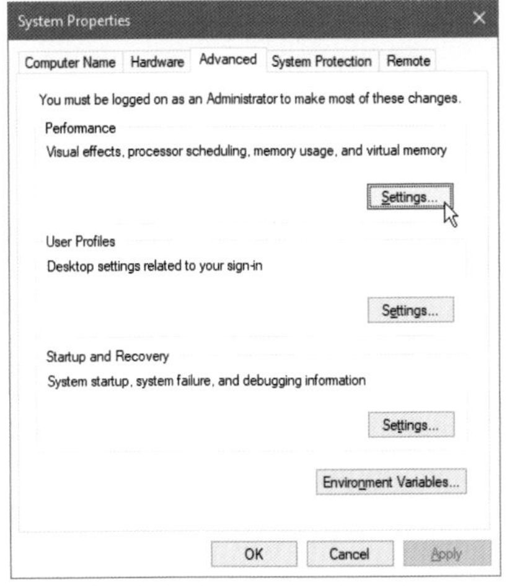

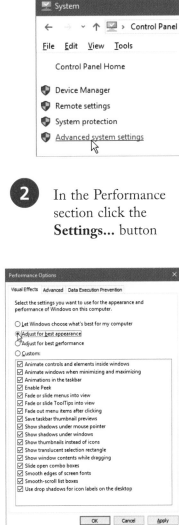

2. In the Performance section click the **Settings...** button

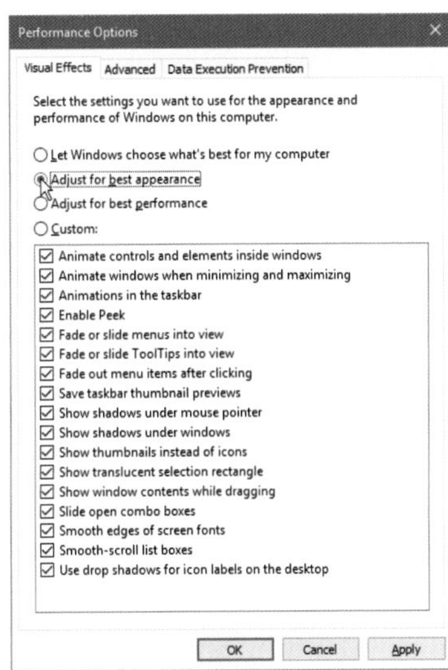

3. Performance Options is displayed, with **Visual Effects** selected

4. Select a tab and adjust settings to your liking

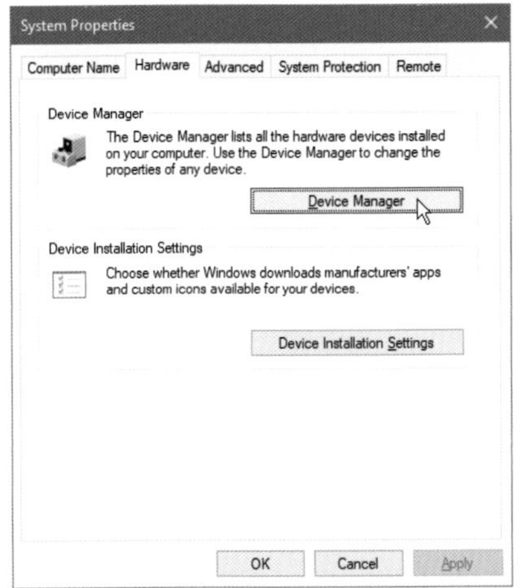

System Properties also gives access to the Device Manager:

1. Click the **Hardware** tab, then click the **Device Manager** button (or click the **Device Manager** link in the System panel)

The Device Manager lists all the hardware devices installed on your computer, and allows you to change their properties.

Task Manager

Windows Task Manager is a very useful utility that is still available in Windows 10. To access the Task Manager, right-click on the Taskbar and select **Task Manager**. Another way is to press **Ctrl** + **Alt** + **Delete** on the keyboard, then select the **Task Manager** option. When the Task Manager opens, click **More details** at the bottom for an extended view.

Hot tip

Your hardware is just one part of your PC that can be monitored with the Task Manager. You can also keep a close eye on your software in the **Processes, App history** and **Startup** tabs.

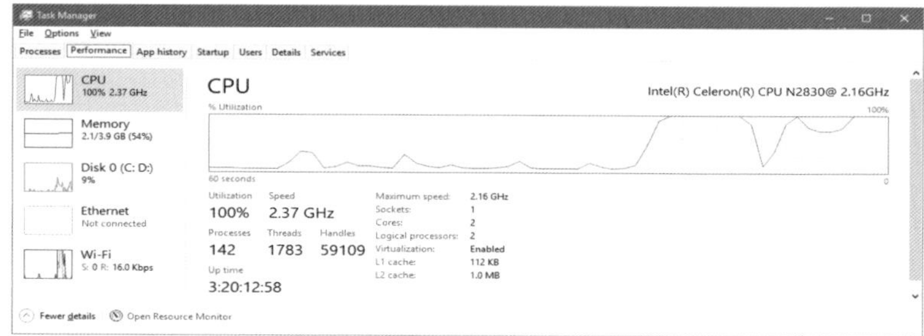

The Task Manager allows you to do a number of things. These include viewing each of the tasks currently running on the computer, each of the **Processes**, your **App history**, **Services** and **Startup** programs. It also allows you to monitor the performance of the PC's hardware. Click the **Performance** tab, and on the left you will see entries for the major hardware in the system – CPU, Memory, Disk (hard drive), Ethernet, and Wi-Fi. These let you see how these devices are functioning and show any problems as they arise. For example, click **Disk** and on the right you'll see two graphs showing disk activity over the past 60-second period. The top graph shows the level of disk access, and the lower graph shows the speed of transfer to the disk in kilobytes per second:

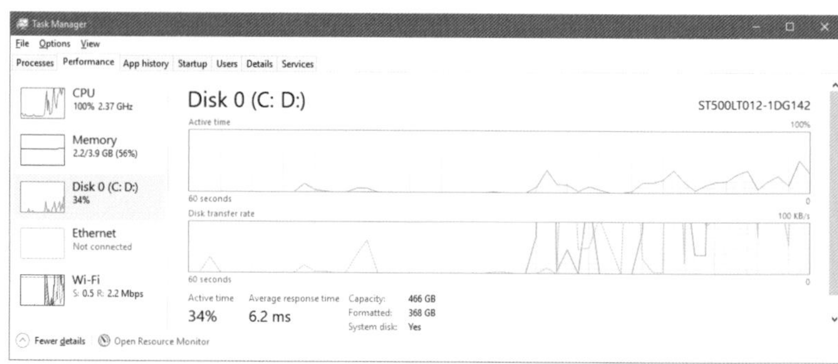

Event Viewer

Another useful tool provided by Windows with which to monitor your system in regard to performance and troubleshooting is the Event Viewer.

1. Go to Windows System, Control Panel, (View by: Category), **System and Security**, then click the **Administrative Tools** icon link

2. Now, click **Event Viewer** then expand **Windows Logs**

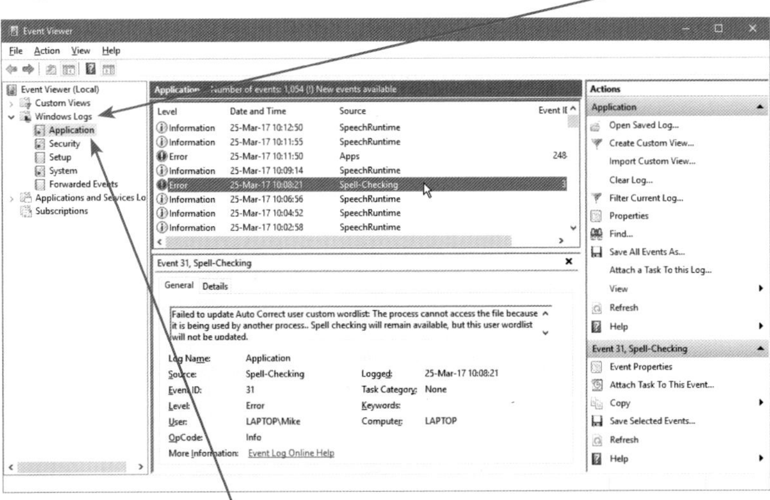

Advanced users might find the information helpful when troubleshooting problems with Windows or other programs. For most users, the Event Viewer will only be used when directed by technical support staff.

3. Select **Application**, and Windows identifies significant app events on your computer. For example: when a program encounters an error or a user logs on. The details are recorded in event logs that you can read using the Event Viewer. Windows keeps the following useful Logs:

System Log – this Log records events logged by Windows' system components. For example, the failure of a driver or other system component to load during startup is recorded in the System Log.

Application Log – the Application Log records events logged by programs. For example, a database program might record a file error in the Application Log.

Security Log – the Security Log records security events, such as valid and invalid logon attempts, and events related to resource use, such as creating, opening, or deleting files or other objects. The Security Log helps track and identify possible breaches to security.

Windows monitors

Open the Performance Monitor by going to Windows System, Control Panel, (View by: Category), **System and Security**, **Administrative Tools**, **Performance Monitor**.

The program starts with an overview and a system summary. There's also a link to open the **Resource Monitor** program.

Use the **Performance Monitor** and **Resource Monitor** to view performance data either in real time or from a Log file.

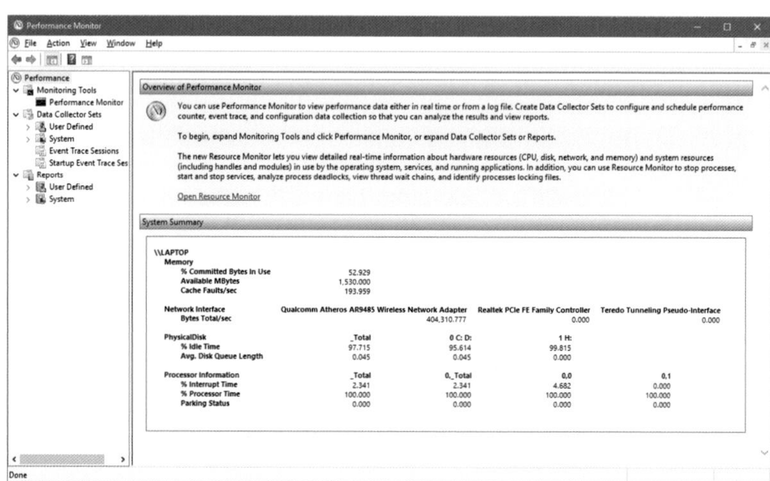

1. Expand **Data Collector Sets** or **Reports** to see Log details
2. Expand **Monitoring Tools** and click **Performance Monitor** to display the graph of processor activity

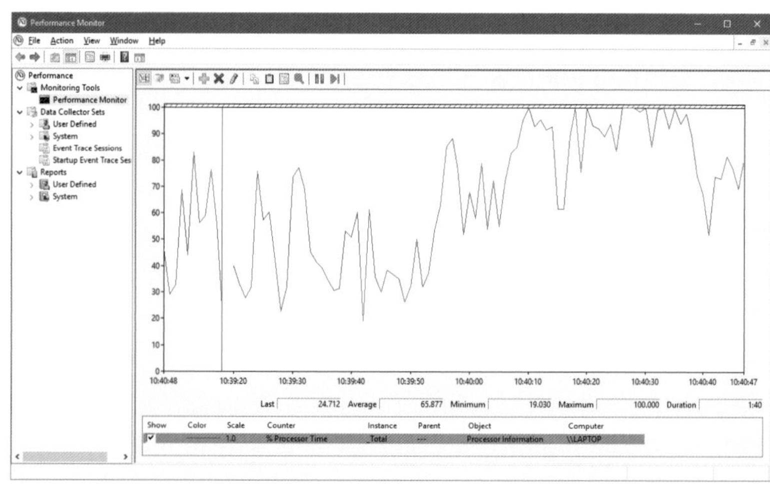

3. Back in **Administrative Tools**, open the **Resource Monitor**

Tabs in the Resource Monitor let you view systems resource usage in real time, and manage the active applications and services:

4. Click **Overview** for a summary of computer activity

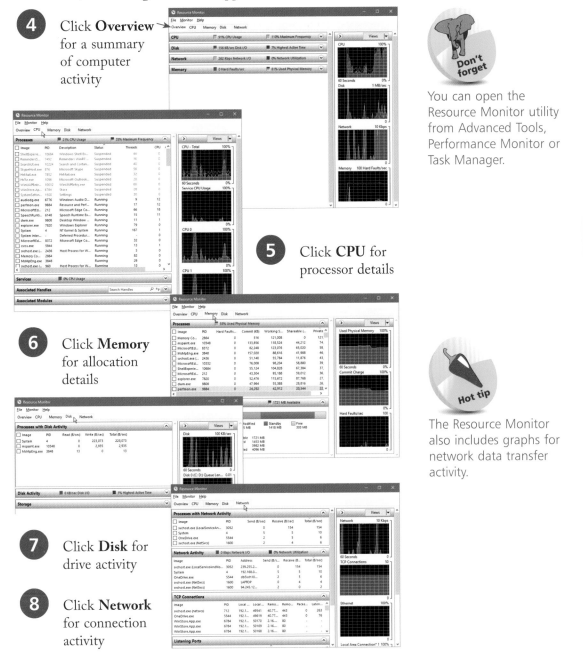

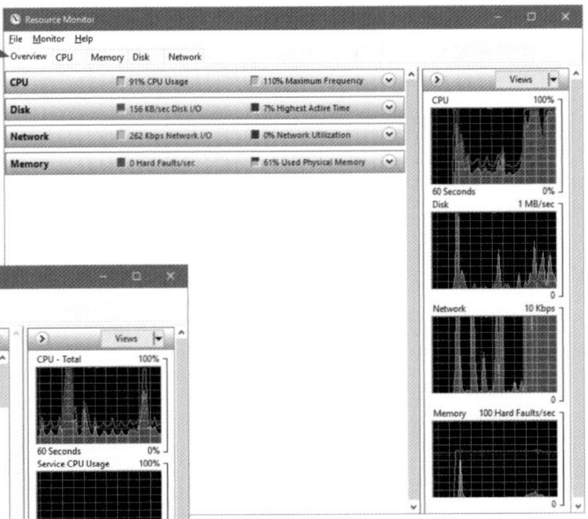

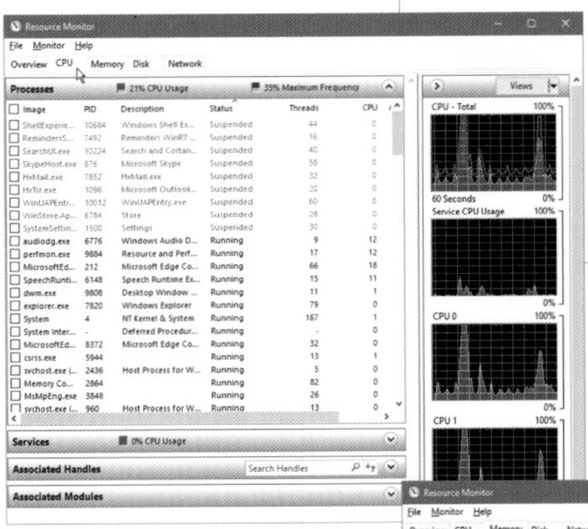

5. Click **CPU** for processor details

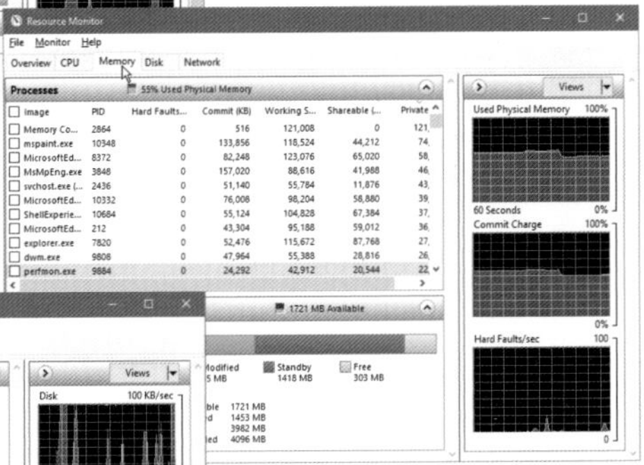

6. Click **Memory** for allocation details

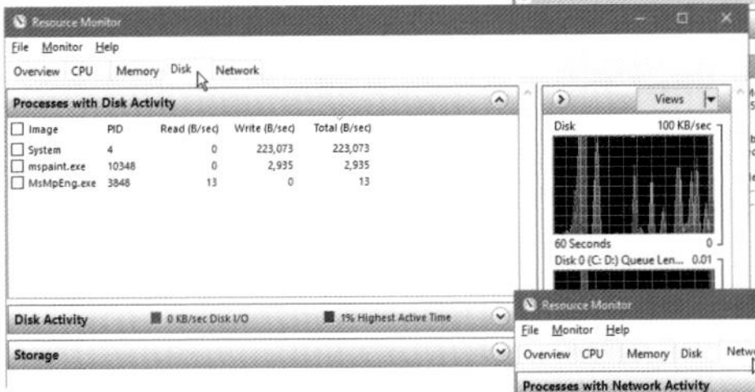

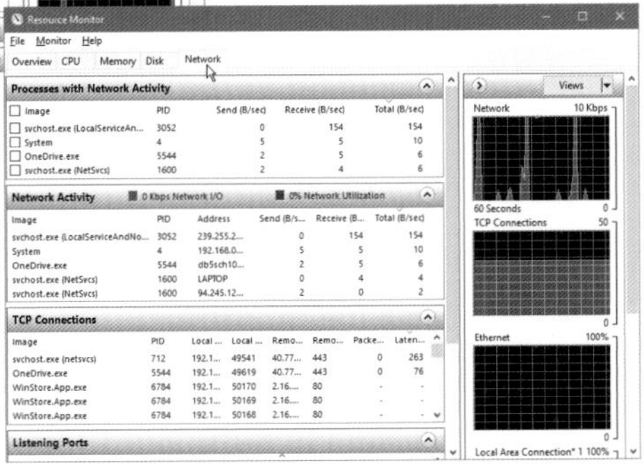

7. Click **Disk** for drive activity

8. Click **Network** for connection activity

You can open the Resource Monitor utility from Advanced Tools, Performance Monitor or Task Manager.

The Resource Monitor also includes graphs for network data transfer activity.

Information on the system

1. Open the **Task Manager** to get information about the programs and processes now running on the computer

2. Click **Processes** for a list of all open applications and background processes for the current user

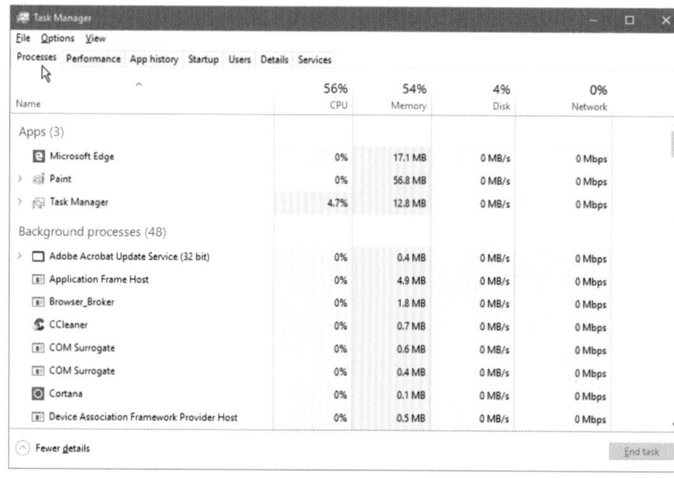

3. Click **Performance** for graphs of the CPU, memory, disk and network usage

4. Click **App history** to see how each of your apps has used the CPU and the network

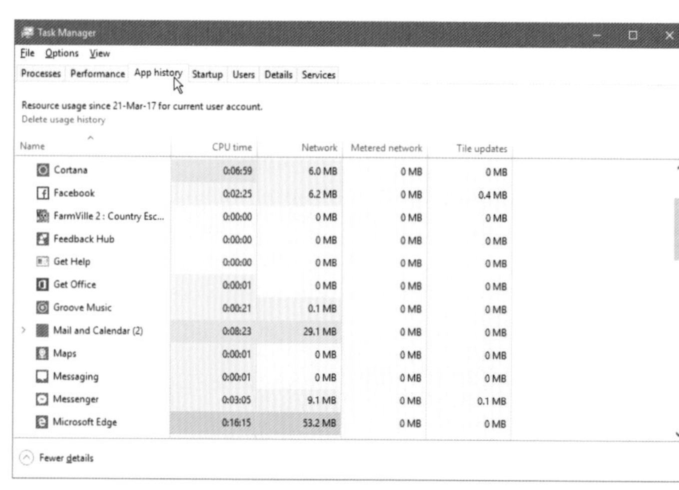

Task Manager
File Options View
Processes Performance App history Startup Users Details Services
Resource usage since 21-Mar-17 for current user account.
Delete usage history
Name CPU time Network Metered network Tile updates
Cortana 0:06:59 6.0 MB 0 MB 0 MB
Facebook 0:02:25 6.2 MB 0 MB 0.4 MB
FarmVille 2 : Country Esc... 0:00:00 0 MB 0 MB 0 MB
Feedback Hub 0:00:00 0 MB 0 MB 0 MB
Get Help 0:00:00 0 MB 0 MB 0 MB
Get Office 0:00:01 0 MB 0 MB 0 MB
Groove Music 0:00:21 0.1 MB 0 MB 0 MB
Mail and Calendar (2) 0:08:23 29.1 MB 0 MB 0 MB
Maps 0:00:01 0 MB 0 MB 0 MB
Messaging 0:00:01 0 MB 0 MB 0 MB
Messenger 0:03:05 9.1 MB 0 MB 0.1 MB
Microsoft Edge 0:16:15 53.2 MB 0 MB 0 MB
Fewer details

You can also open the Task Manager by pressing the keyboard shortcut **Ctrl** + **Shift** + **Esc**, or by right-clicking an empty area on the Taskbar and then selecting Task Manager.

Note that the Task Manager provides a link to open the Resource Monitor (on the Performance tab).

5. Press **WinKey** + **R**, then type "msinfo32" in the Run box to launch the System Information window

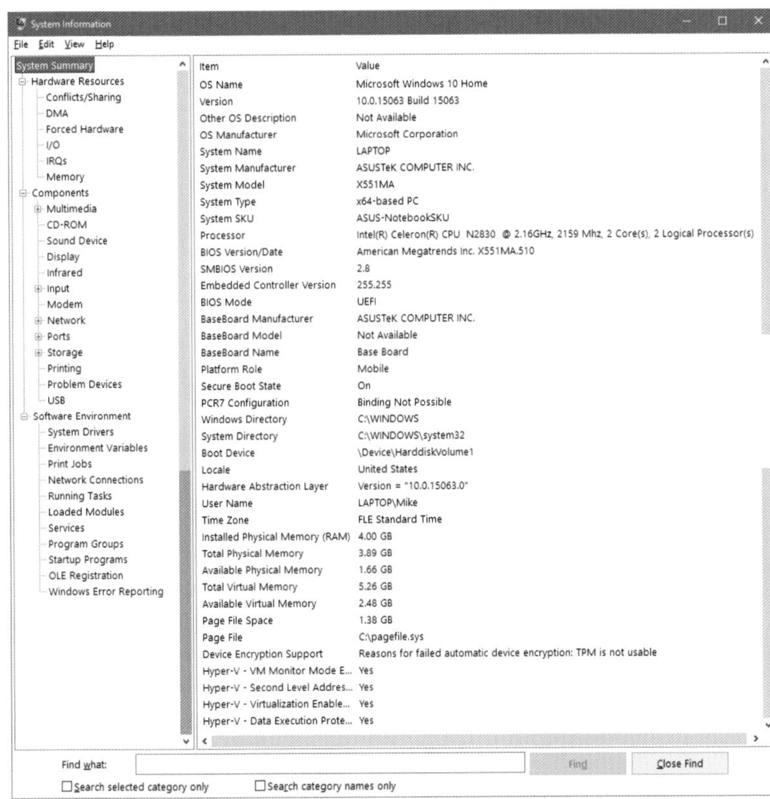

You could also enter "msinfo32" in the Taskbar Search box to open System Information.

System Information opens, listing details of computer hardware configuration, components, software and drivers in four categories:

- **System Summary** – operating system, computer name, type of BIOS, boot device, username, amount of memory, etc.
- **Hardware Resources** – technical details of the computer's hardware, intended for IT professionals.
- **Components** – details of disk drives, sound devices, modems and other devices.
- **Software Environment** – shows information about drivers, network connections, and other program-related details.

To find a specific detail, type keywords in the **Find what:** box, choose **Search selected category only** (if appropriate), then click the **Find** button.

Reliability Monitor

Security and Maintenance provides links to several useful Windows tools.

1. Go to Windows System, Control Panel (View by: Large icons), **Security and Maintenance**, then expand the **Maintenance** section

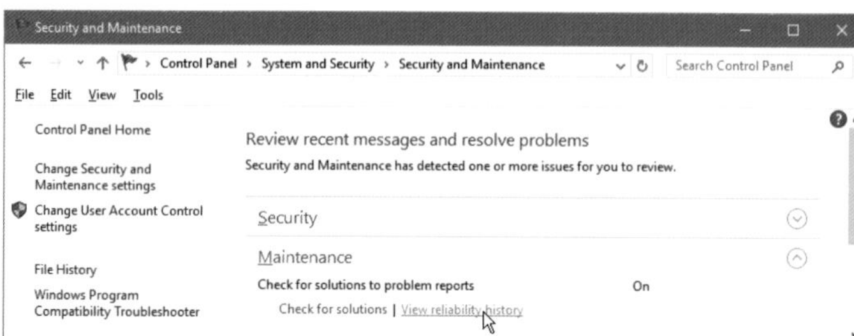

2. Next, click the **View reliability history** link to launch the Reliability Monitor that records system problems

Click the **Check for solutions to all problems** link for help with any problem.

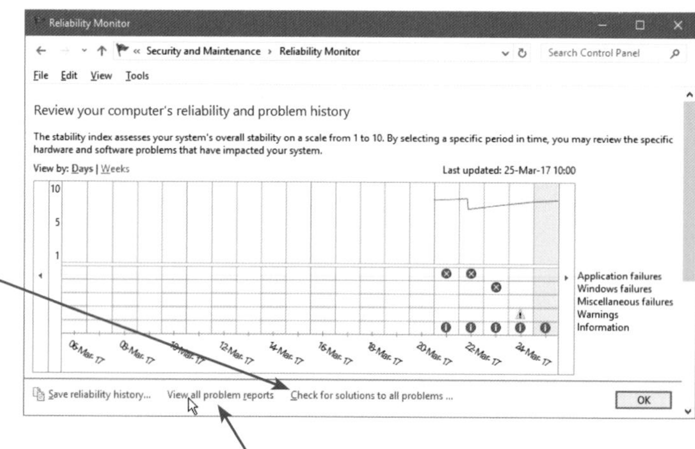

3. Now, click the **View all problem reports** link to see details of each problem encountered

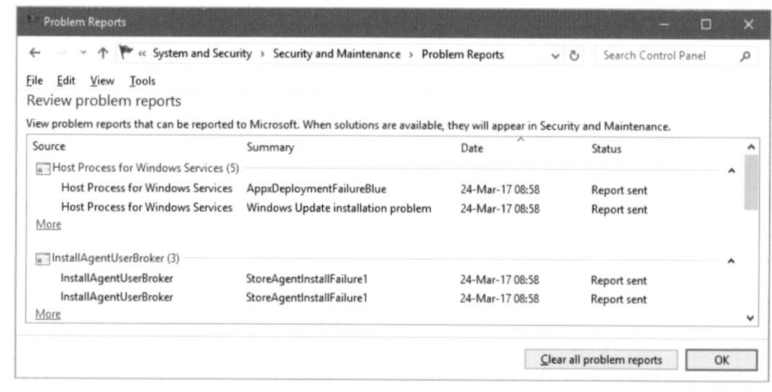

Boosting performance

There's another way to boost the performance of your computer, without having to make major upgrades to the hardware. You can add USB components such as an external drive or a flash drive.

1. Connect a second hard drive. For example, the external hard disk drive (HDD) shown here:

2. The first time you do this, Windows installs the device driver software automatically

3. Windows assigns a drive letter to the drive

The HDD drive is listed under **This PC** in the **Devices and drives** category.

Connect the drive to the mains supply via its power adapter (if required), then connect the USB cable to one of the USB ports on the computer.

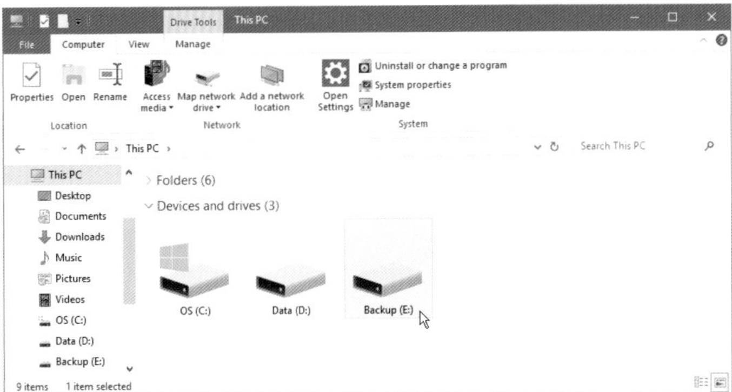

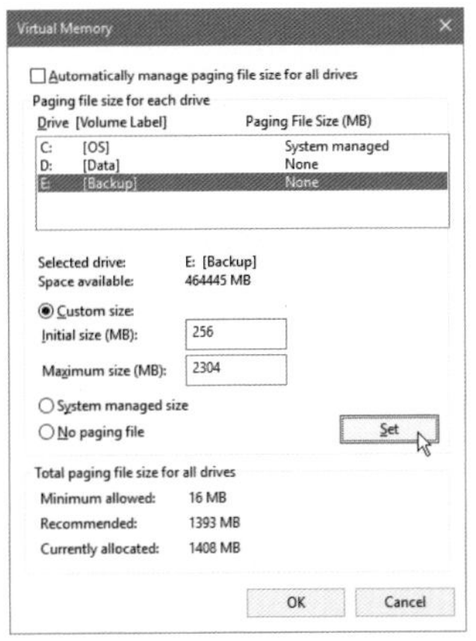

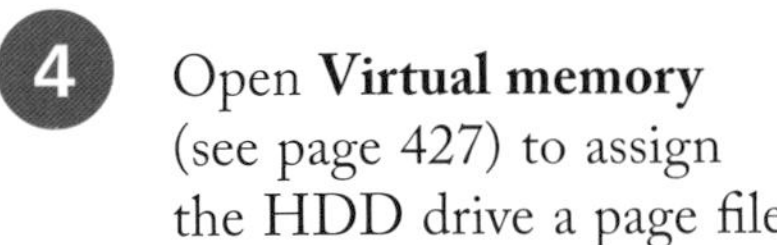

4. Open **Virtual memory** (see page 427) to assign the HDD drive a page file

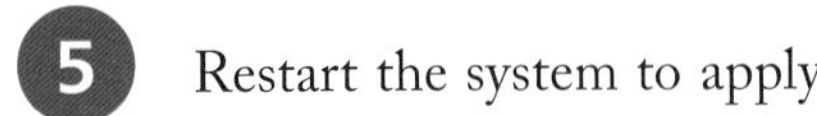

5. Restart the system to apply

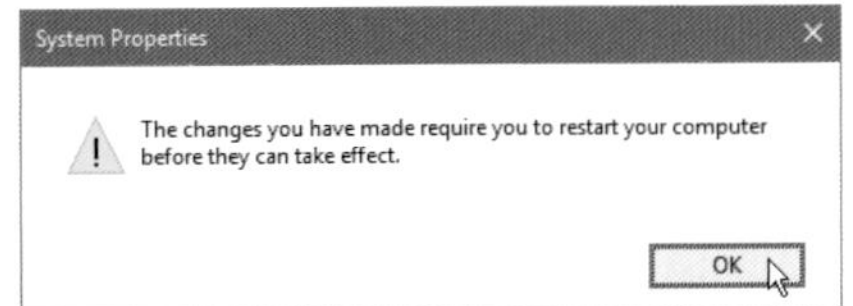

Avoid removing the drive while the system is active, if you have created a page file on it.

...cont'd

If you add a USB flash drive to your computer, you may be able to use ReadyBoost to improve the overall performance.

1. Connect the USB drive, then right-click its icon in File Explorer and select **Properties** from the context menu

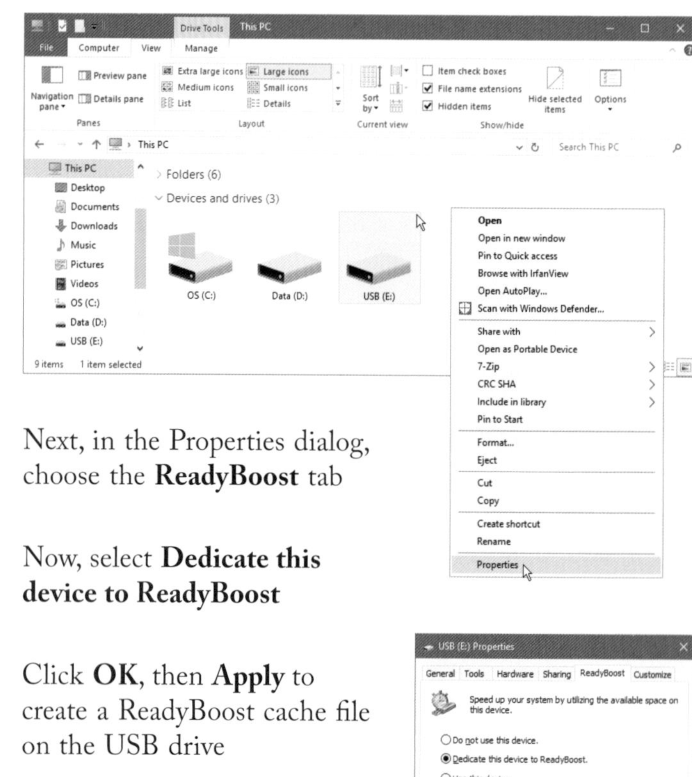

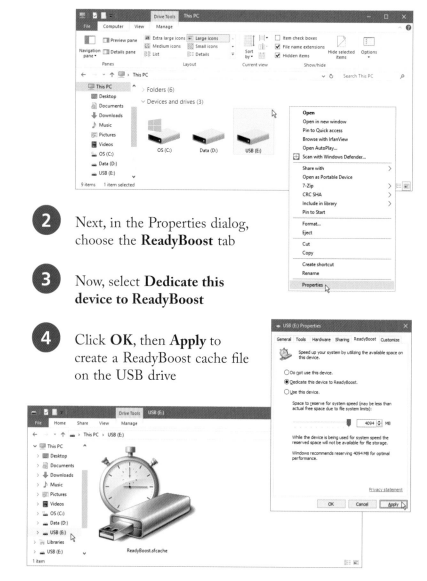

2. Next, in the Properties dialog, choose the **ReadyBoost** tab

3. Now, select **Dedicate this device to ReadyBoost**

4. Click **OK**, then **Apply** to create a ReadyBoost cache file on the USB drive

ReadyBoost will complete successfully, unless it reports the USB drive is unsuitable if the drive has insufficient space or is too slow.

Don't forget

ReadyBoost is disk caching that uses flash memory to boost your system performance. It can use any form of flash memory such as a USB flash drive, SD card, or CompactFlash.

ReadyBoost will not work with just any flash drive – it must be a good-quality model.

Users with a small amount of memory (RAM) will benefit most from using ReadyBoost.

32-bit versus 64-bit

Windows 10 editions are available as either 32-bit or 64-bit. This refers to the addressing structure used by the processor. Desktop computers generally have a 64-bit processor that can run either version of Windows. Some laptop and netbook computers have 32-bit processors, and so can only run the 32-bit Windows. To check the processor level and the current operating system, open System Information (**WinKey** + **R** and type "msinfo32").

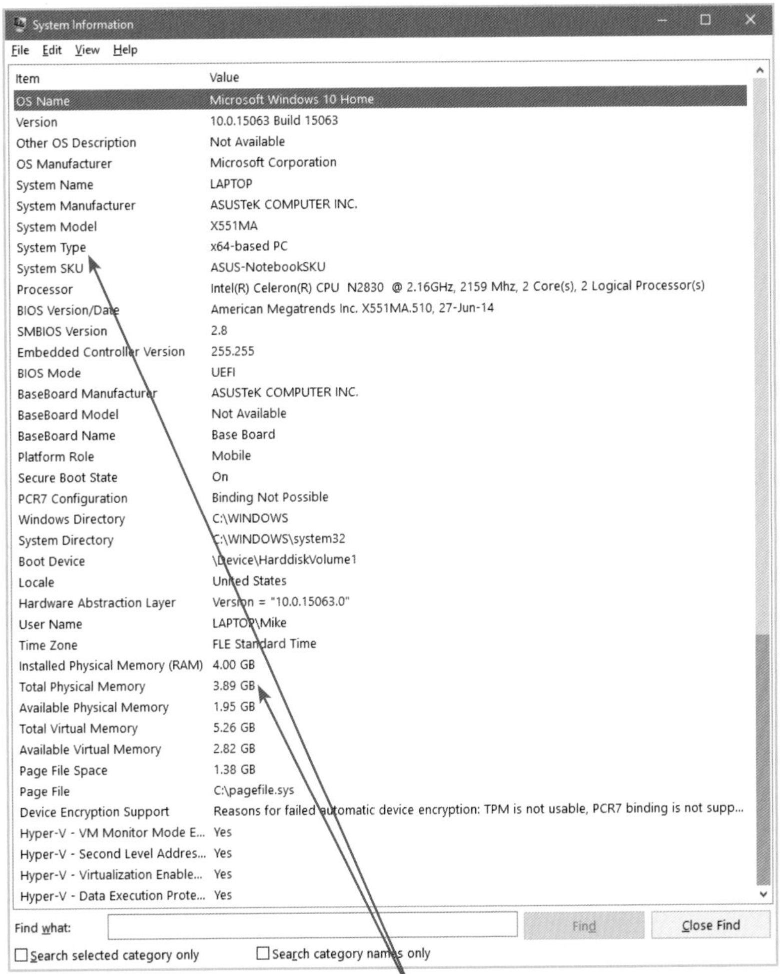

System Information

File Edit View Help

Item	Value
OS Name	Microsoft Windows 10 Home
Version	10.0.15063 Build 15063
Other OS Description	Not Available
OS Manufacturer	Microsoft Corporation
System Name	LAPTOP
System Manufacturer	ASUSTeK COMPUTER INC.
System Model	X551MA
System Type	x64-based PC
System SKU	ASUS-NotebookSKU
Processor	Intel(R) Celeron(R) CPU N2830 @ 2.16GHz, 2159 Mhz, 2 Core(s), 2 Logical Processor(s)
BIOS Version/Date	American Megatrends Inc. X551MA.510, 27-Jun-14
SMBIOS Version	2.8
Embedded Controller Version	255.255
BIOS Mode	UEFI
BaseBoard Manufacturer	ASUSTeK COMPUTER INC.
BaseBoard Model	Not Available
BaseBoard Name	Base Board
Platform Role	Mobile
Secure Boot State	On
PCR7 Configuration	Binding Not Possible
Windows Directory	C:\WINDOWS
System Directory	C:\WINDOWS\system32
Boot Device	\Device\HarddiskVolume1
Locale	United States
Hardware Abstraction Layer	Version = "10.0.15063.0"
User Name	LAPTOP\Mike
Time Zone	FLE Standard Time
Installed Physical Memory (RAM)	4.00 GB
Total Physical Memory	3.89 GB
Available Physical Memory	1.95 GB
Total Virtual Memory	5.26 GB
Available Virtual Memory	2.82 GB
Page File Space	1.38 GB
Page File	C:\pagefile.sys
Device Encryption Support	Reasons for failed automatic device encryption: TPM is not usable, PCR7 binding is not supp...
Hyper-V - VM Monitor Mode E...	Yes
Hyper-V - Second Level Addres...	Yes
Hyper-V - Virtualization Enable...	Yes
Hyper-V - Data Execution Prote...	Yes

Find what: [Find] [Close Find]

☐ Search selected category only ☐ Search category names only

Here, the System Type is a x64-based PC, which means it has a 64-bit processor and can run both 32-bit and 64-bit editions of Windows, and has Total Physical Memory of 3.98GB.

You should note the amount of memory as well as 64-bit capability. You need at least 2GB memory to benefit from the 64-bit version of Windows 10.

If the System Type is an x84-based PC it is a 32-bit system that cannot run 64-bit Windows 10.

...cont'd

It may improve the performance of your 64-bit-capable computer if you install the 64-bit operating system, but only if there is sufficient memory to make this worthwhile. You'll need at least 2GB – and more if possible.

There's no information report to tell you how much memory you can add to your computer, but you can find free memory scanner tools online to check your system.

You can't upgrade from 32-bit to 64-bit – you must install a fresh system, completely replacing the existing system. So make sure you back up your data first. You also need 64-bit versions of drivers for all of your devices.

1. Go to **memory-up.com** and click **Memory Scanner (Begin Auto Check)**, Download Scanner, then **Run** to view results

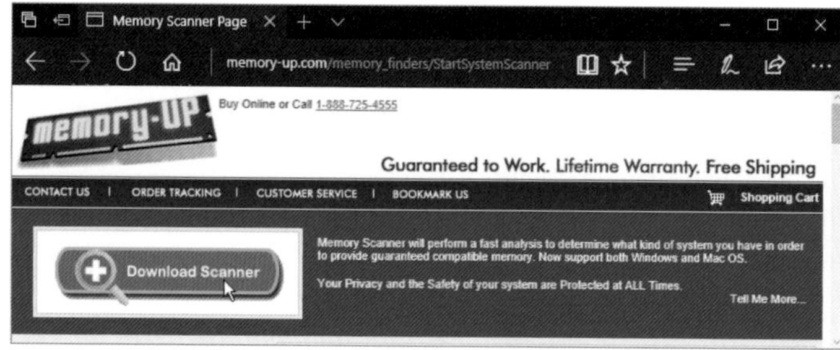

2. When prompted, choose to **Run the scanner** and it will check your system

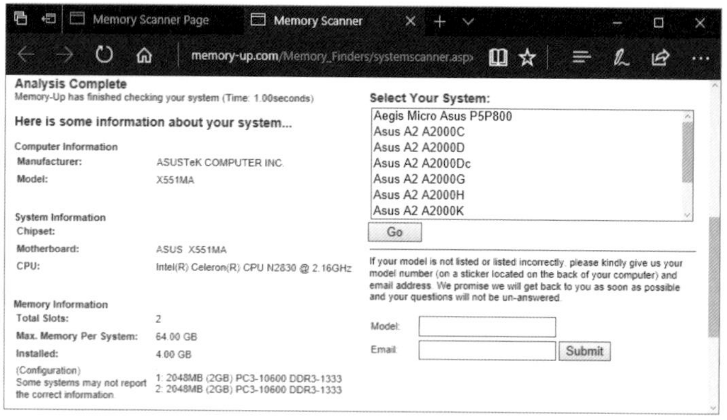

With 64-bit Windows installed, you will find two Program File folders – one for 32-bit (often called x86) and one for 64-bit applications.

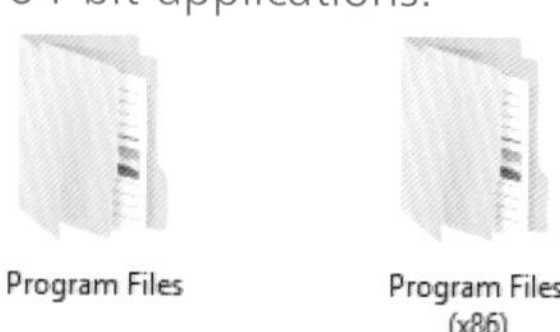

Here, the current installed memory is 4GB, and maximum possible memory is 64GB. Switching to 64-bit Windows is possible, but will only be of marginal benefit. 32-bit Windows can use a maximum of 4GB memory, whereas 64-bit Windows can use up to 192GB memory.

26 Windows Registry

At the heart of the Windows operating system is the Windows Registry. Windows 10 provides a Registry Editor for working with the Registry, and this may let you carry out tasks that are not otherwise supported. However, do be aware that errors in making such changes could leave your system unusable.

The Windows Registry

The Windows Registry was introduced in the early versions of Windows as a way of organizing and centralizing information that was originally stored in separate INI (initialization) files.

From time to time you will encounter Windows tips that are designed to make your system better, faster or easier to use, and such tips often rely on making changes to the Registry.

Change the Registry with care. Only use trusted sources when you do make changes. And make sure you have a Registry backup before you make any changes.

Arguably the most important component in the Windows system, since it records everything about your hardware and software, the Windows Registry is something that in normal circumstances you never need to deal with directly.

The Registry is a structured database that stores the configuration settings and options for applications, device drivers, user interface, services, and all kinds of operating system components. It also stores all the counters that are used to provide the performance reports and charts.

Installation programs, applications and device software all deal directly with the Registry, so all the updates happen in the background. However, the Registry stores user-based settings in a user-specific location, thus allowing multiple users to share the same machine, yet have their own personal details and preferences. The Registry also makes it possible to establish levels of privilege, to control what actions a particular user is permitted to carry out.

Changes to the Registry Editor

When you make changes to the setup for your user account, Windows writes the necessary updates to the Registry for you. Similarly, when you install new programs or hardware devices, many Registry modifications will be applied. Normally, you won't need to know the details.

Registry Editor

There will be times, however, when the developers have failed to provide a necessary change, and the only way (or the quickest way) to make the adjustment is by working directly with the Registry. Windows includes a Registry Editor that you can use, with caution since the Registry is a crucial part of your system, to browse and edit the Registry.

The Registry is made of a number of separate files, but you never need to be concerned with the physical structure since the Registry Editor gives you access to the full Registry, displaying the logical structure and taking care of the specifics of updates.

Before you browse or edit the Registry, you should have an understanding of the structure and how changes get applied, and especially how the original values can be saved – just in case changes get applied that have unwelcome effects.

The structure of the Registry

The data in the Windows Registry is organized in a hierarchical, or tree, format. The nodes in the tree are called keys. Each key can contain subkeys and entries. An entry consists of a name, a data type and a value, and it is referenced by the sequence of subkeys that lead to that particular entry.

There are five top level keys:

- **HKEY_CLASSES_ROOT** **HKCR**
  Information about file types, shortcuts and interface items (alias for parts of **HKLM** and **HKCU**).
- **HKEY_CURRENT_USER** **HKCU**
  Contains the user profile for the currently logged on user, with Desktop, network, printers, and program preferences (alias for part of **HKU**).
- **HKEY_LOCAL_MACHINE** **HKLM**
  Information about the computer system, including hardware and operating system data such as bus type, system memory, device drivers, and startup control data.
- **HKEY_USERS** **HKU**
  Contains information about actively loaded user profiles and the default profile.
- **HKEY_CURRENT_CONFIG** **HKCC**
  The hardware profile used at startup; for example to configure device drivers and display resolution (alias for part of **HKLM**).

Sections of the Registry are stored in the System32 and User folders, each subtree having a single file plus a Log file; for example Sam and **Sam.log**, or System and **System.log**. Subtrees associated with files are known as Registry hives. They include:

HKEY_LOCAL_MACHINE\SAM	Sam
HKEY_LOCAL_MACHINE\SECURITY	Security
HKEY_LOCAL_MACHINE\SOFTWARE	Software
HKEY_LOCAL_MACHINE\SYSTEM	System
HKEY_CURRENT_CONFIG	System
HKEY_CURRENT_USER	System
HKEY_USERS\.DEFAULT	Default

Some products available on the internet suggest the Registry needs regular maintenance or cleaning. Although problems can arise, in general the Registry is self-sufficient and such products are not necessary.

Applications read the Registry to check that a specific key exists, or to open a key and select entry values that are included.

The tree, subtree, alias, hive, and file structure can be very complex, but the view taken via the Registry Editor is fortunately more straightforward.

Registry backup

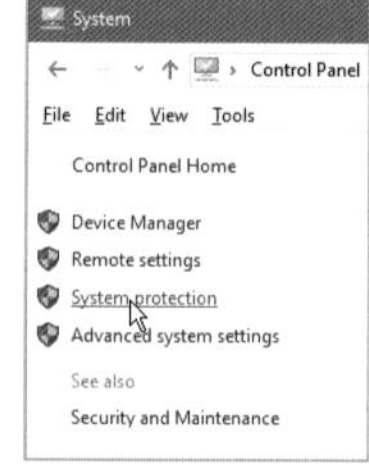

Before using the Registry Editor, you should create a restore point using System Restore. The restore point will contain information about the Registry, and you can use it to undo changes to your system.

To create a manual restore point:

1. Go to Start, Windows System, Control Panel, (View by: Large icons), System, and click the **System protection** link

You can also back up individual parts of the Registry, just before you make changes to them (see page 449).

2. Select the **System Protection** tab and click **Create...** to create a restore point immediately

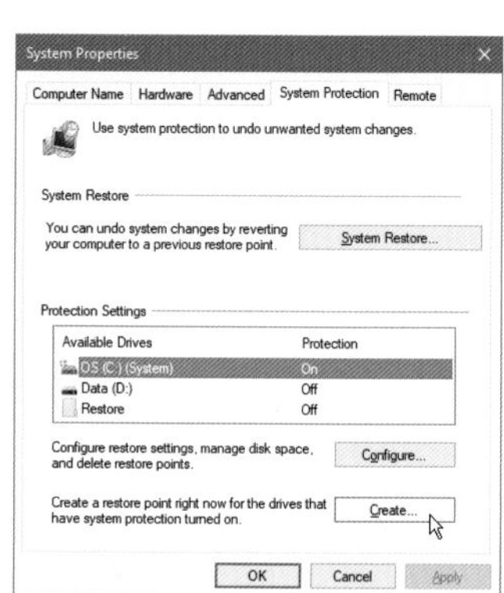

3. Type a description of your new restore point

4. When the restore point completes, click **Close**

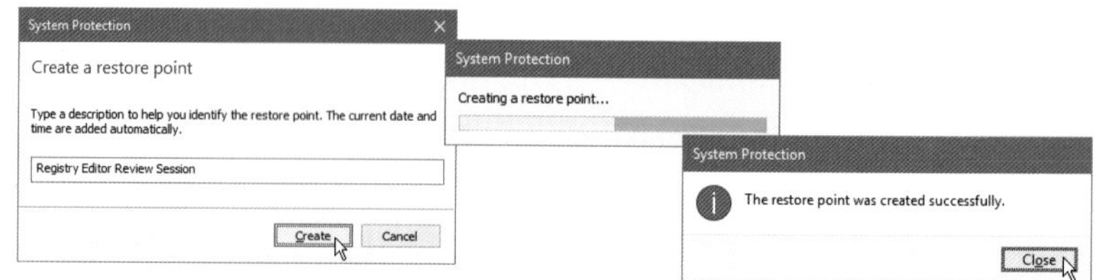

This shows that System Restore had made its daily restore point, so this could be used instead of a manual restore point, unless you've already made some changes during the current session.

5. On the **System Protection** tab, click the **System Restore** button, then click **Next** – to see your new restore point

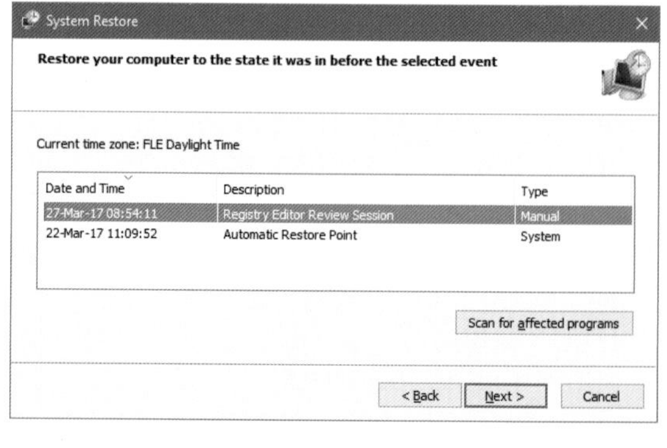

Open Registry Editor

The Registry Editor is not accessible via the Control Panel, Administrative Tools or through any shortcuts. You must run the program **regedit.exe** by name.

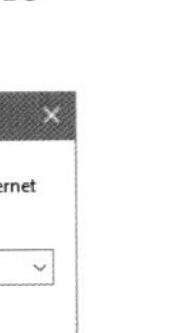

This is an advanced program, which will usually be run via an administrator account, though it can be run using a standard account.

1. Press **WinKey** + **R** to open the Run box. Enter "regedit", and click **OK**

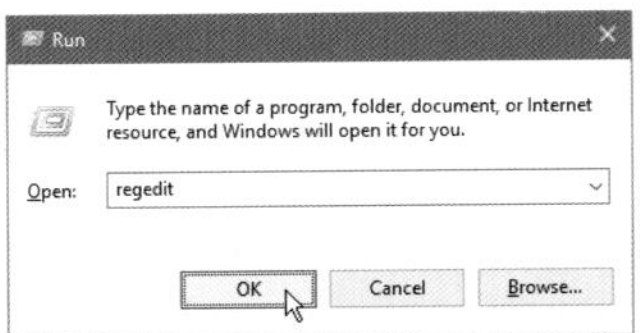

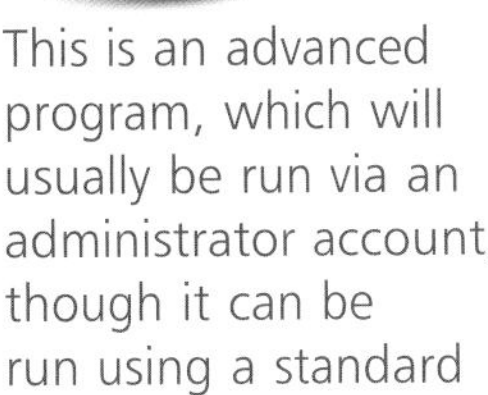

2. Assuming you have an administrator account, click **Yes** to start the Registry Editor with full administrator privileges

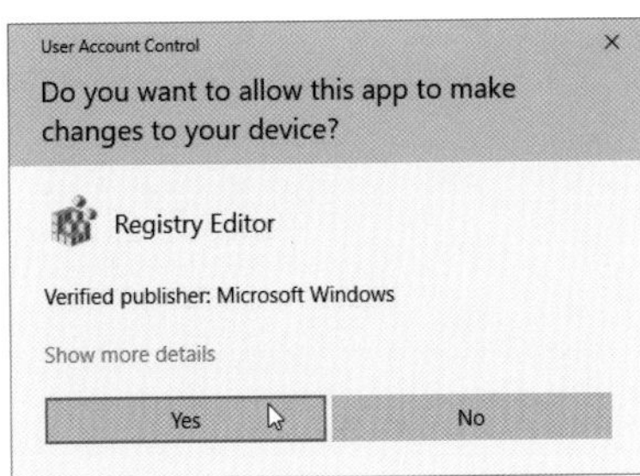

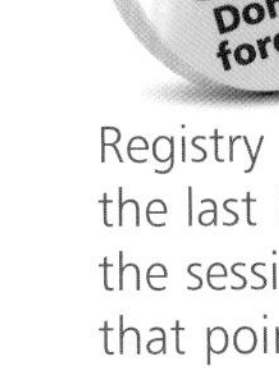

Registry Editor will save the last key referenced in the session, and open at that point the next time you run the program.

3. The Registry Editor starts, and the first time it runs you'll see the five main subtrees, with all their branches collapsed

4. Select a key, e.g. **HKEY_LOCAL_MACHINE** (**HKLM**), and double-click to expand to the next level

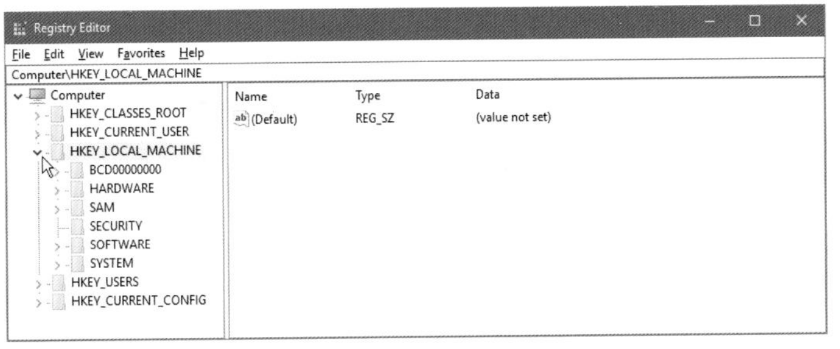

The right-hand pane displays the entries and data values for the selected key. You can also click the arrow buttons to extend or collapse the branches of the subtrees.

Example Registry change

Before exploring the Registry further, it will be useful to look at a typical Registry update, used to make changes for which Windows has no formal method included.

One such requirement is to change the registered organization and registered owner for the computer. These names will have been set up when Windows was installed. The names chosen may no longer be appropriate, perhaps because you've changed companies, or because the computer was passed on or purchased from another user.

To see the registration details:

1. Press **WinKey** + **R** and type "winver"

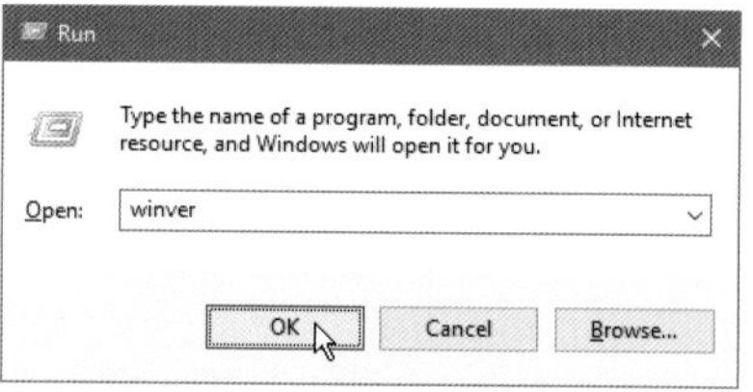

2. The details of the installed version of Windows are shown, along with the registered owner and organization

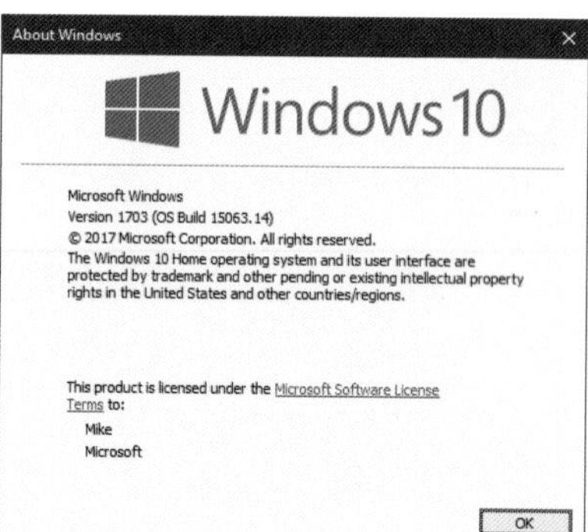

3. Assume that these details need to be revised to "Joanne" and "In Easy Steps"

You will find that this particular change is included in a number of Windows hints and tips lists. You'll even find a solution at the Microsoft website **microsoft.com**

All the suggestions follow a similar pattern. They advise you to run **regedit.exe** and find the Registry key named **HKEY_LOCAL_MACHINE\SOFTWARE\Microsoft\Windows NT\CurrentVersion**, where you can change the owner and organization. Some of the websites also discuss the need for administrator authority, and they usually warn about taking backups before making changes.

Don't forget

You'll find many such suggested changes on the internet, usually in lists of Windows hints and tips, and often referred to as Registry "hacks".

Do make sure that the sites you use as sources for Registry changes are reliable, and check the details carefully to ensure the change does exactly what it claims.

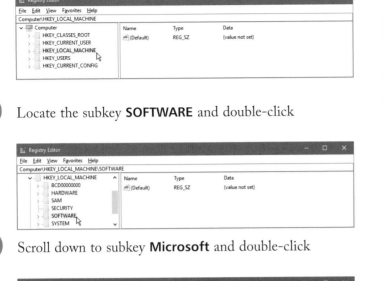

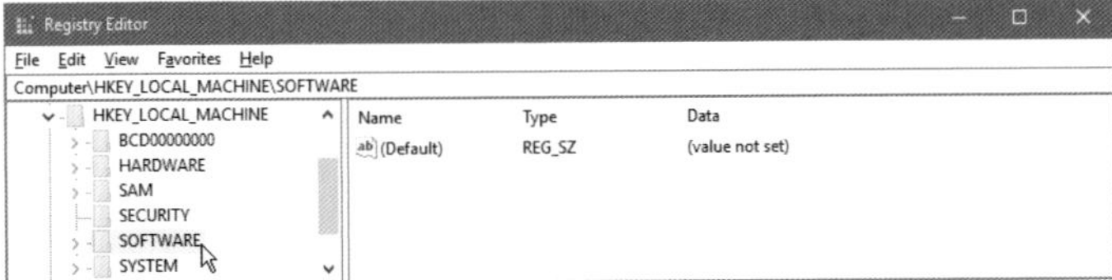

1 Locate the subkey **SOFTWARE** and double-click

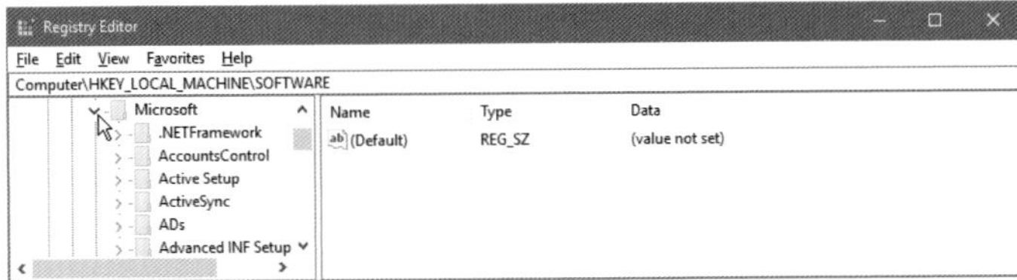

2 Scroll down to subkey **Microsoft** and double-click

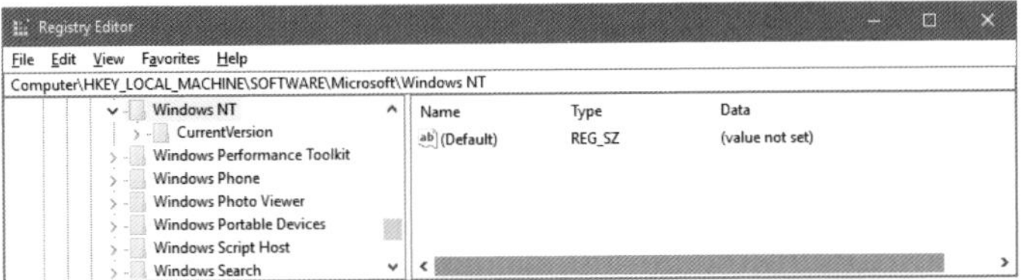

3 Scroll down to subkey **Windows NT** and double-click

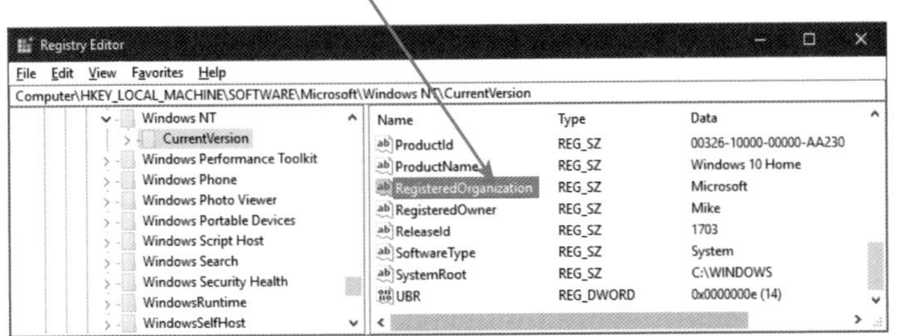

4 Select subkey **CurrentVersion** and scroll through the list of entries to select **RegisteredOrganization**

To locate the key you can step through the path, subkey by subkey, double-clicking each one in turn.

Although the subkeys are shown in capitals or mixed case, as displayed in the Registry, they are in fact not case-sensitive.

If the **RegisteredOrganization** and **RegisteredOwner** keys are absent, you can create them. Right-click on CurrentVersion, then choose New, String Value to create a new key. Right-click the key and choose Modify, then enter Name and Data values and click OK.

Finding a key

Rather than stepping through the path, you could use the **Find** command in Regedit.

Pressing **F3** carries out the **Find Next** operation, to locate the next match.

You'll soon discover that subkey names are not unique, and also the same text could appear in the data content of other Registry entries.

Find is more effective if you restrict the search – for example, putting a **Value** entry name, and clearing the Key and Data boxes. You could also search for known text in the data content.

1. Select the highest level key **Computer**, then click **Edit**, **Find...** (or press **Ctrl** + **F**)

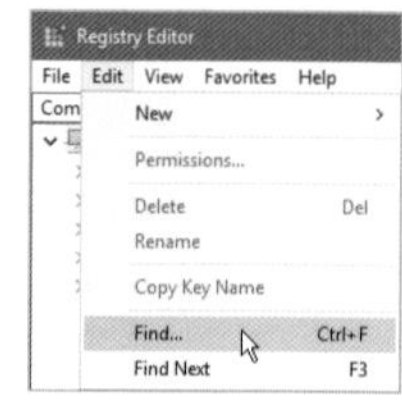

2. Type the required subkey "CurrentVersion" and click **Find Next**

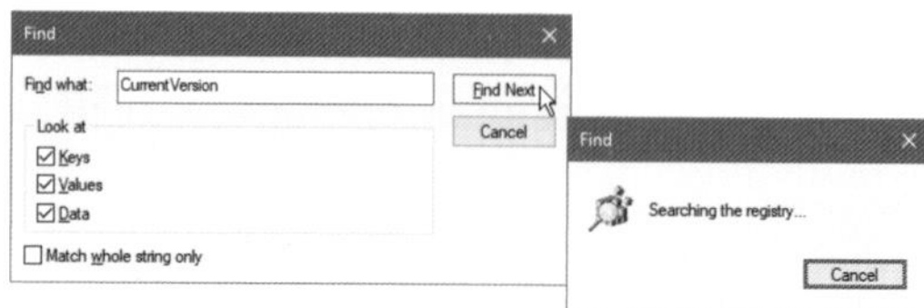

3. The search finds an entry in **HKEY_CLASSES_ROOT**, but this is not the required key – press **F3** to continue searching

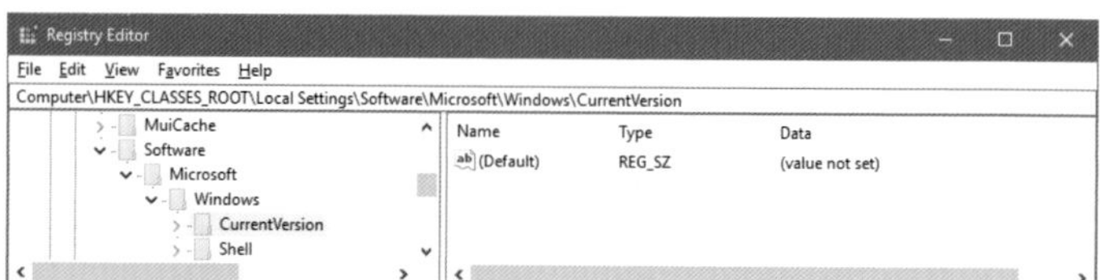

4. The search finds another entry in **HKEY_CLASSES_ROOT**, but this is still not the required key – let's try a different approach

5. Search instead for the **Value** entry name "RegisteredOrganization"

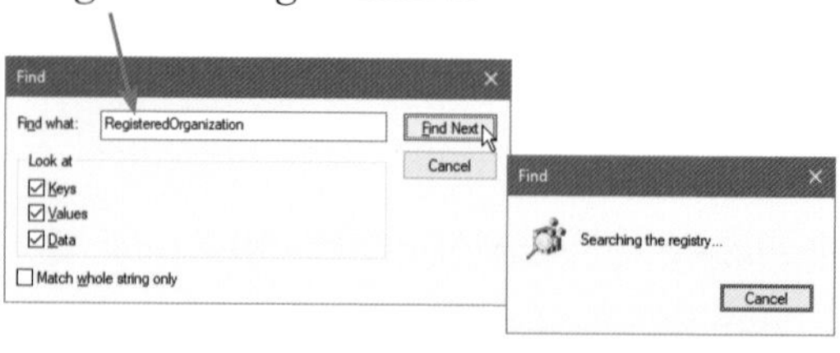

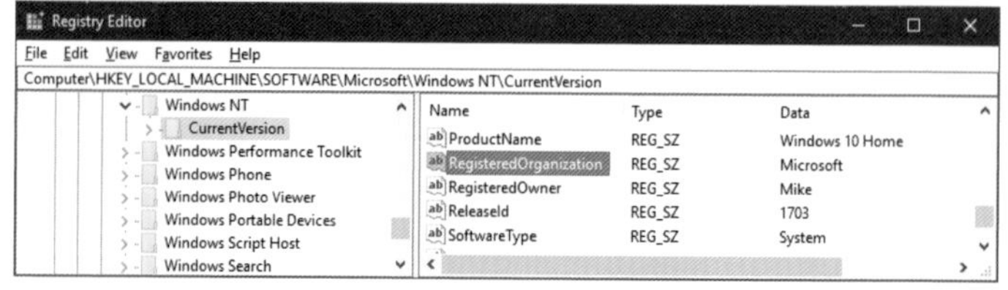

Back up before changes

1. Select the subkey, or a value entry within the subkey, and then click **File**, **Export...**

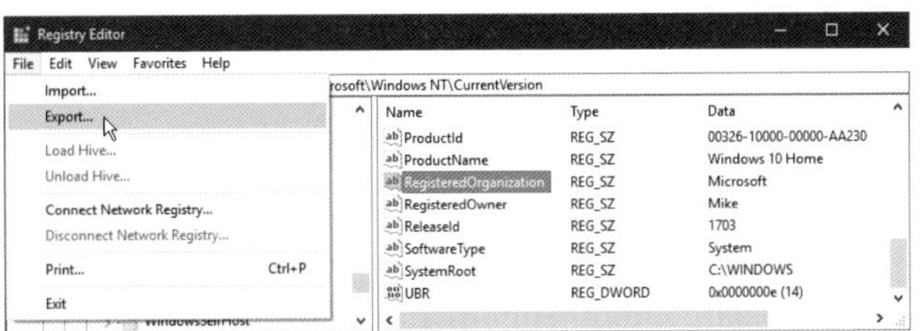

You should make a backup of the branch at the subkey within which changes are required.

2. Your Documents folder will be selected by default, but you can choose a different folder if desired

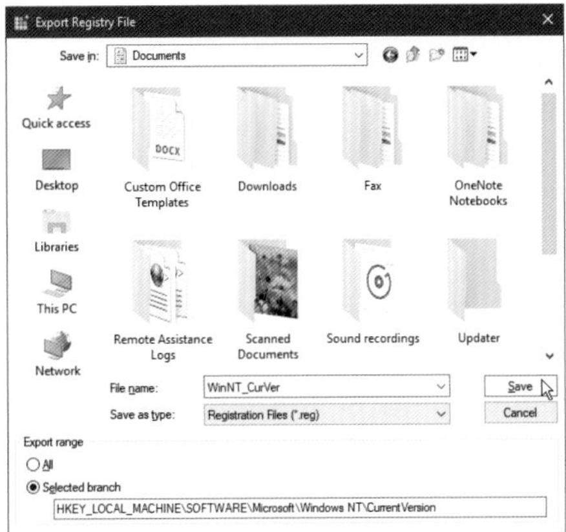

You can create a backup of the whole Registry, but it is sufficient to back up just the branches being changed.

3. Provide a file name for the Registration File (**.reg**) that is being created, and choose **Selected branch**

4. The Registration file is written to the selected folder

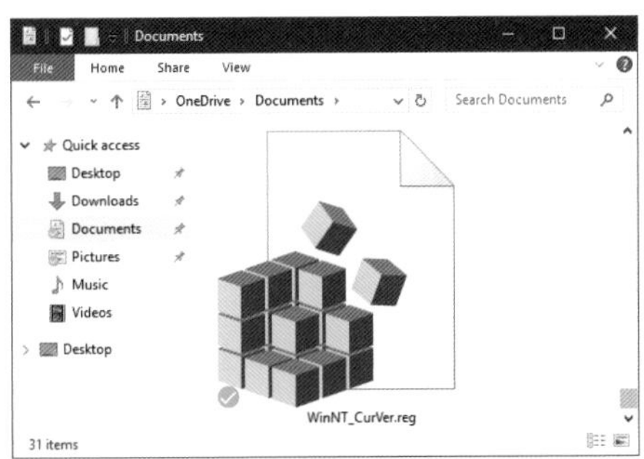

The **.reg** file will have all the subkeys, value entries and data contents for everything within the subkey selected for Export.

Change a Value entry

1. Select the **Value** entry to be changed, and double-click

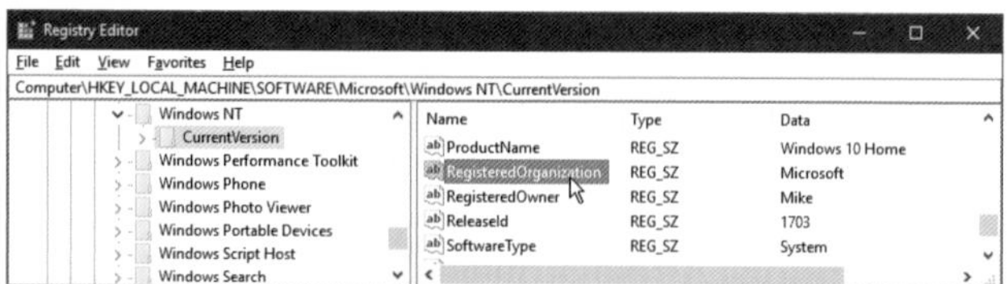

This entry has text data. The value data for other entries could be binary or numbers. You must replace existing contents with the same type of data values.

2. The Value entry is opened with Value data displayed, ready for editing

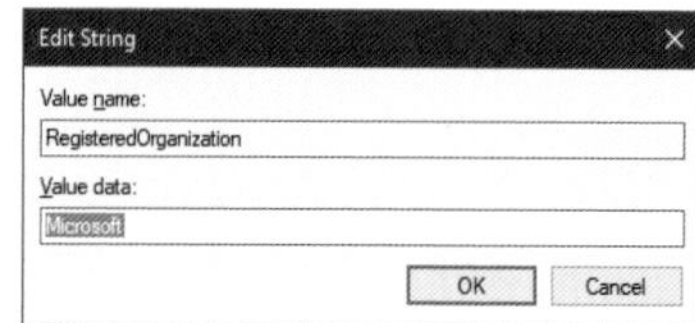

3. Replace the existing contents with the required information

4. Click **OK** to apply and save the change. It is immediately in effect

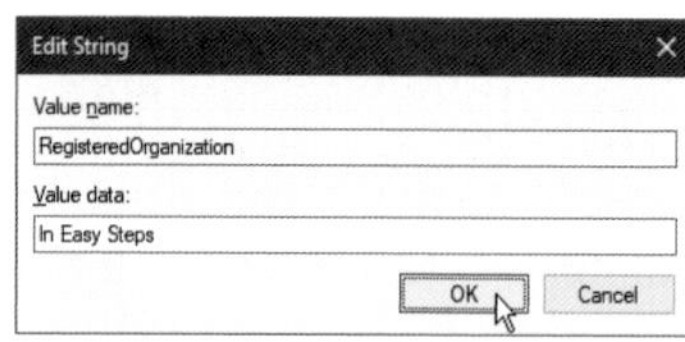

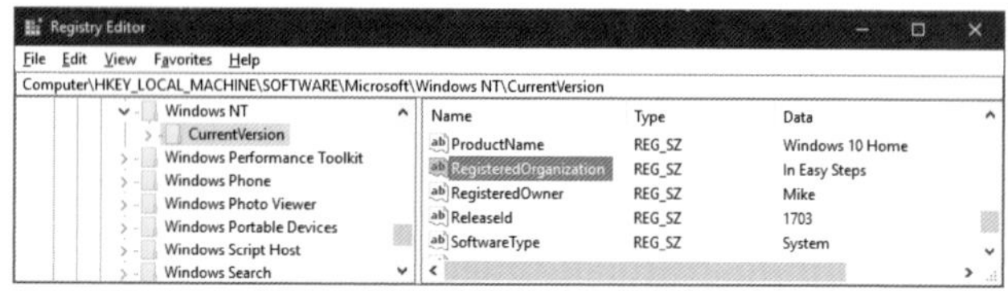

If you change your mind part way through, you cannot just close Registry Editor – you must restore the original values using the branch backup, or else reverse the changes individually.

5. Repeat for any other values to be changed. For example, add a surname for the "Registered Owner"

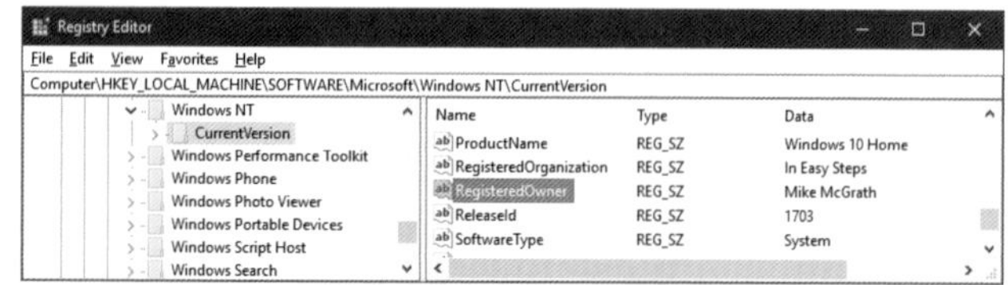

6. Close the Registry Editor when you have finished – no Save is required, since changes are dynamically applied

Using a standard account

Log off and switch to a standard user account (with no Administrator privileges), making sure no other accounts are active.

1. Press **WinKey** + **R** to open the Run box. Enter "regedit" and click **OK**

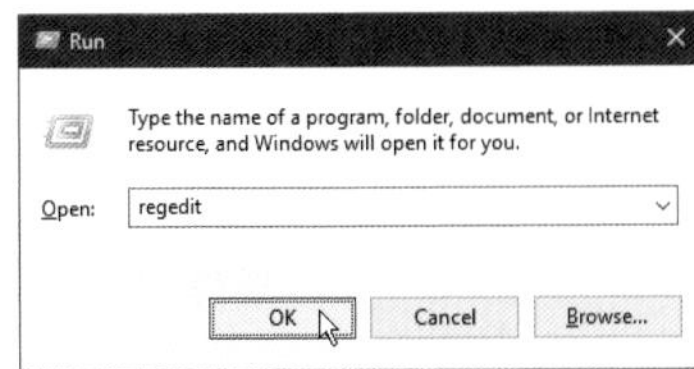

2. There's no UAC interception; Registry Editor starts up at **Computer** (or at the last key referenced by this account)

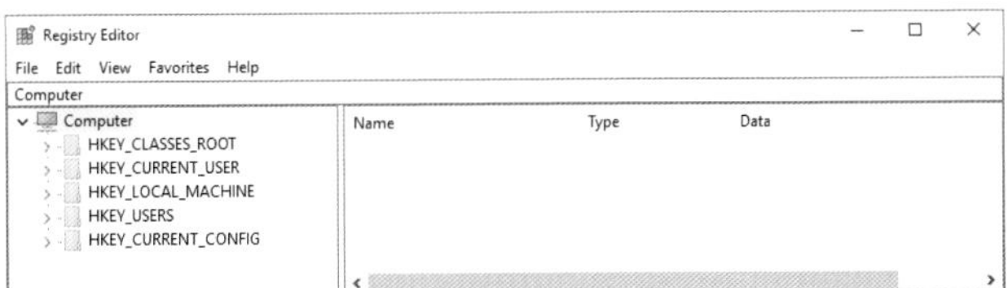

When you run Regedit from a standard user account, it operates at a lower privilege level.

3. Locate the Value entry **RegisteredOrganization** in the **Windows NT** subkey, and double-click the name

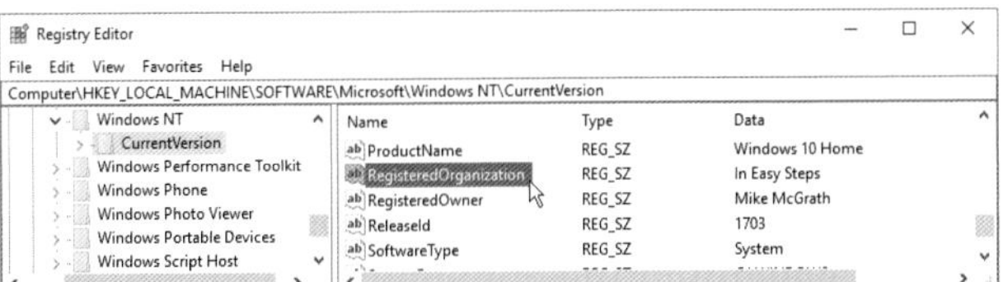

4. The current value is shown

Edit String
Value name:
RegisteredOrganization
Value data:
In Easy Steps
OK Cancel

5. Change the value to the required text and click **OK**

Edit String
Value name:
RegisteredOrganization
Value data:
Acme Corporation
OK Cancel

6. Registry Editor displays an error message to say it is unable to edit the entry

Error Editing Value
Cannot edit RegisteredOrganization: Error writing the value's new contents.
OK

The standard account can edit and create Registry keys under HKEY_CURRENT_USER, but not entries under HKEY_LOCAL_MACHINE. Some Registry entries are even blocked for reading.

...cont'd

Don't forget

If there are several administrator accounts, they'll be listed, and you can choose the appropriate account.

There's no obvious visual difference between the full Regedit session and the previous limited session, but you can now make the changes.

The Windows PowerShell is flagged as Administrator, and running **regedit.exe** from here starts the full session without further UAC prompts.

If you are signed in with a standard user account but you need full Registry Editor access, you must run Regedit as an administrator.

1. Type "regedit" in the Taskbar Search box and press **Enter**

2. Right-click the Regedit search result and select **Run as administrator**

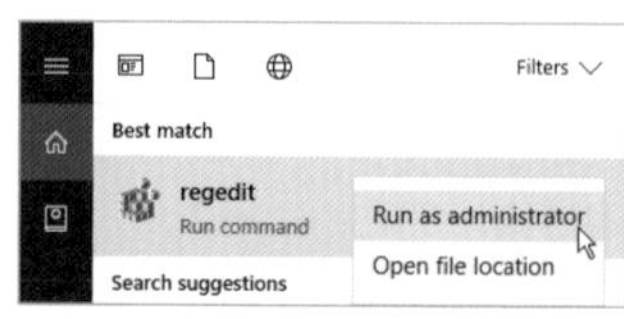

3. Provide the password or PIN for the administrator account displayed, to allow the Registry Editor to start with full administrator privileges

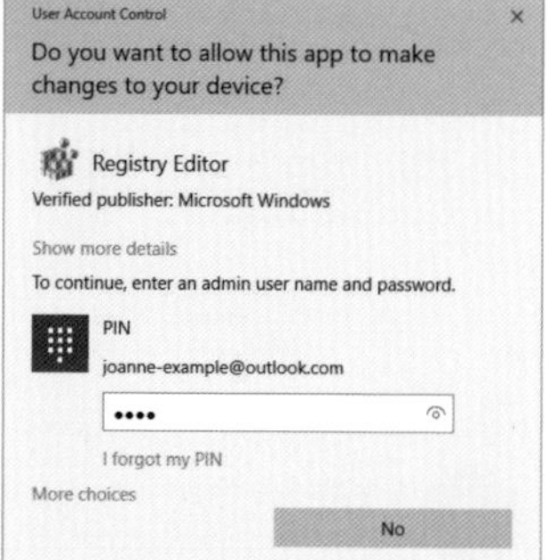

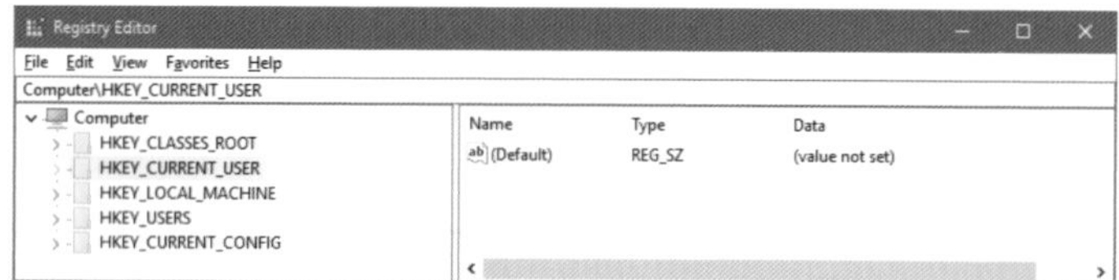

As an alternative, you can open the Windows PowerShell as an administrator, and start **regedit.exe** from there.

1. Press **WinKey** + **X** and click **Windows PowerShell (Admin)**

2. Respond to the UAC prompt, then type "regedit.exe" and press **Enter**. The full Registry Editor will start

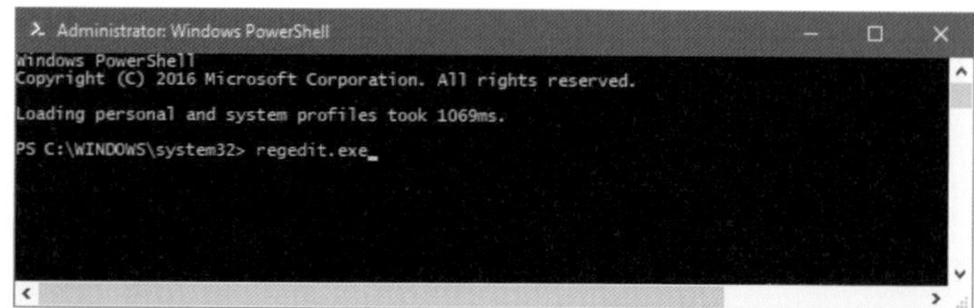

Scripted updates

You'll find that some websites offer scripted versions of Registry updates that you can download and run. These are similar to the Registration files that you create when you back up a branch of the Registry. To illustrate this method, you can create your own script to update the RegisteredOwner details.

1. Open **Notepad** and type the Registry Editor header, the subkey path and the Value entries required

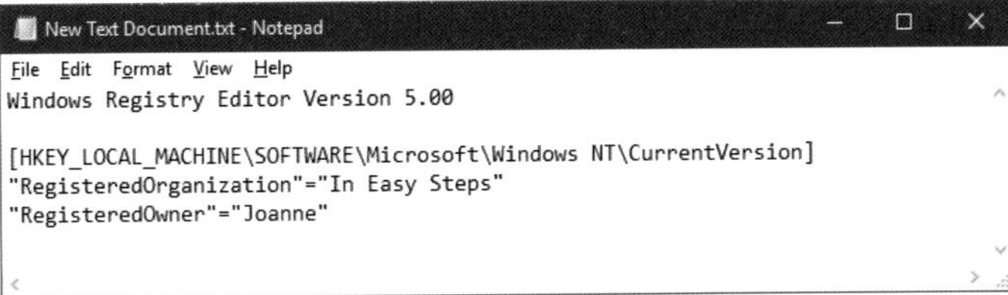

2. Select **File**, **Save** and choose a folder if required, or accept the default – normally this will be the Documents folder

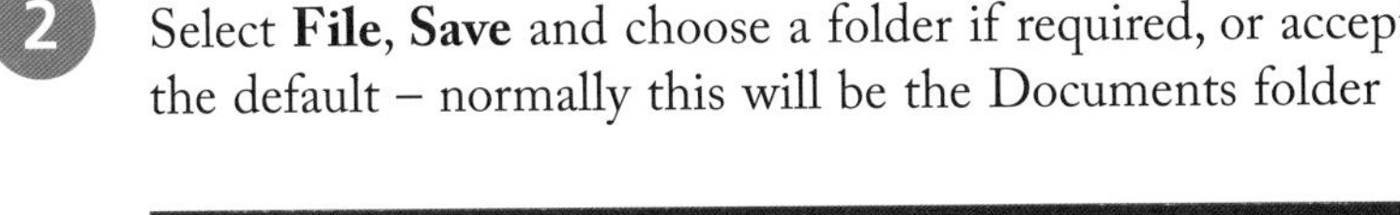

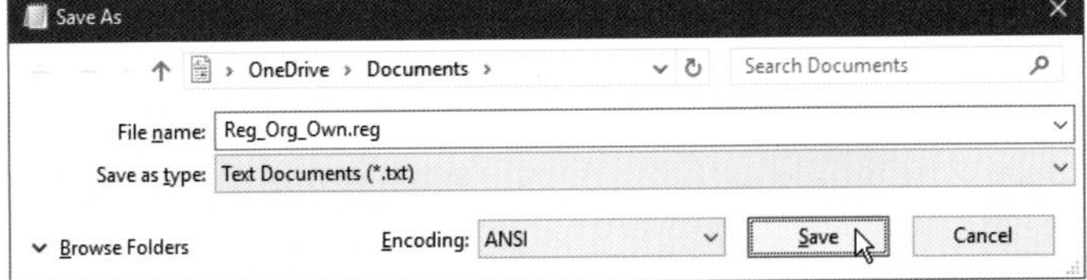

3. Type the file name and file type, e.g. **Reg_Org_Own.reg**

4. Click **Save**, and the Registration file will be added to the specified folder

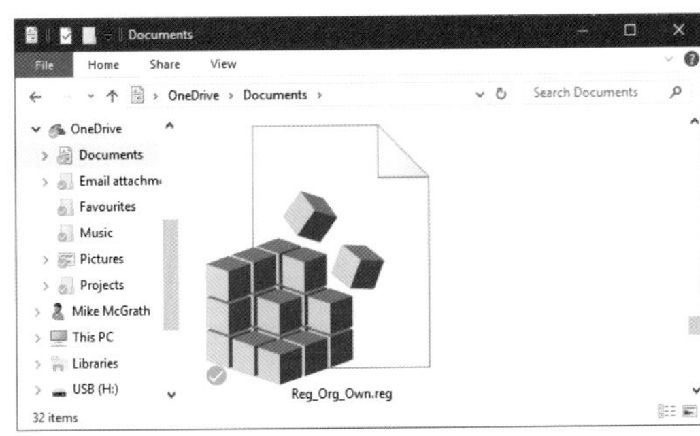

Using scripts that are provided can make it easier to apply updates, as long as you trust the source websites.

This **.reg** file automates the process followed to find the subkey and amend the Value entries for Organization and Owner.

Applying an update

Don't forget

You use this same process to apply the backup Registration file, if you decide to reverse the changes you have made.

1. To apply an update, double-click the Registration file

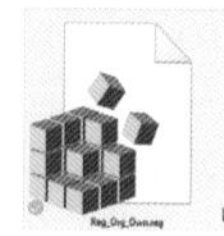

2. There will be a UAC prompt, and then you will be warned of the potential dangers of updates

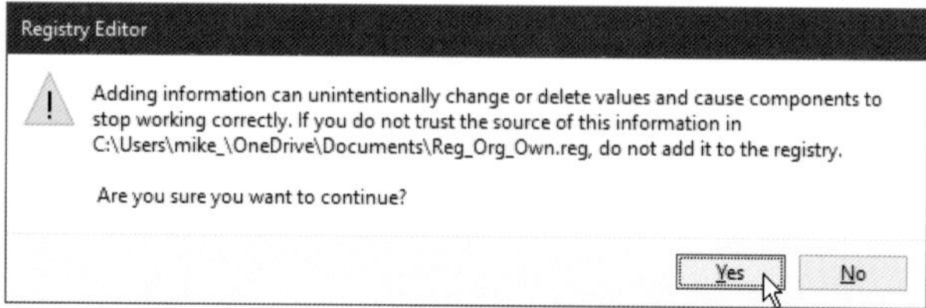

3. If you are happy with the update, click **Yes** then click **OK** to continue

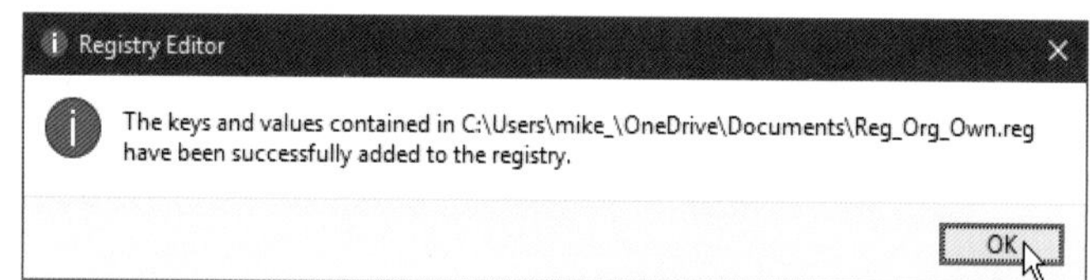

Hot tip

The update is applied without any requirement to run Regedit or open the Registry.

4. The keys and values included are added to the Registry

5. Confirm the update by running **Winver**

6. You can also open the Registry and check the subkey and its Value entries

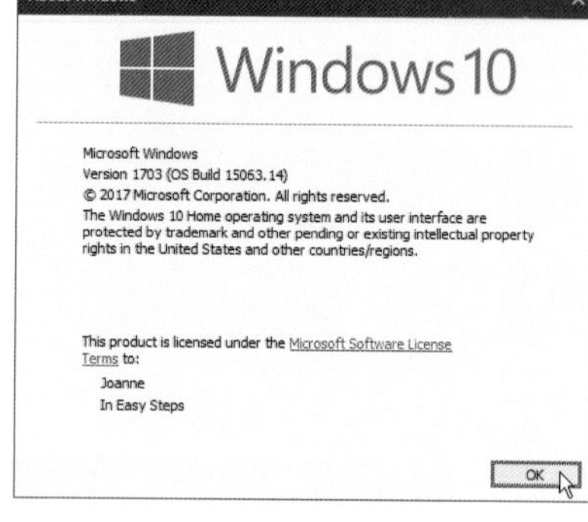

Beware

It is well worth repeating that you must change the Registry with care. Only use trusted sources when you do make changes. And make sure you have a Registry backup before you make any change.

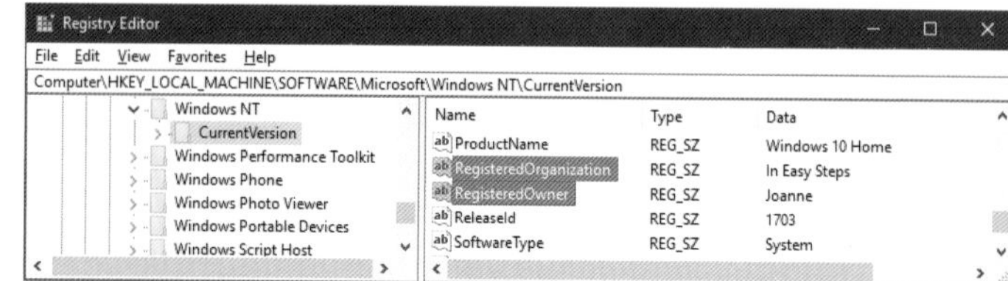

Resize Taskbar thumbnails

When you move the mouse cursor over a Windows 10 Taskbar button, you'll see a small version of the application window.

To make this larger in size:

1. Open Regedit.exe, and locate the subkey **HKEY_CURRENT_USER\Software\Microsoft\Windows\CurrentVersion\Explorer\Taskband**

2. Right-click the right-hand pane and select **New**, **DWORD (32-bit) Value**, then name the value "MinThumbSizePx"

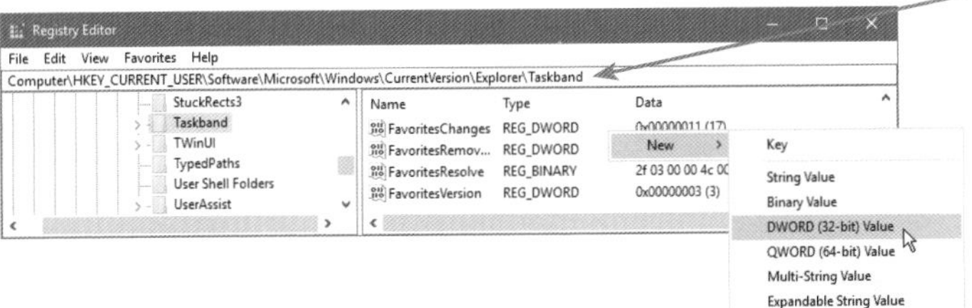

3. Double-click the value, then set the **Decimal** value to "350"

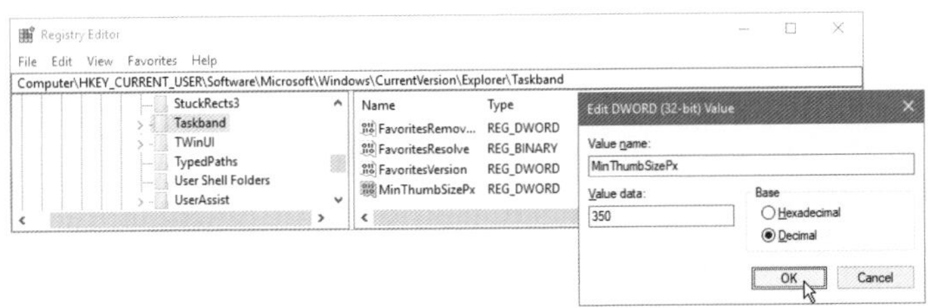

4. Log off and log on again to put the change into effect

5. View a Taskbar thumbnail to see the enlarged thumbnail results

NEW

An address bar was added to the Registry Editor in the Windows 10 Creators update, so you can now search by typing or pasting a registry path – character case is not sensitive.

Registry updates require you to change hexadecimal or decimal number values, or create keys or text values.

Adjust the value again to fine-tune the results, or delete the value entry to return to the default thumbnail.

Remove shortcut suffix

When you create a shortcut on the Desktop, Windows insists on adding the word "Shortcut" to the name. For example:

1. Locate the Notepad.exe program file, which is usually found in **C:\Windows\System32**

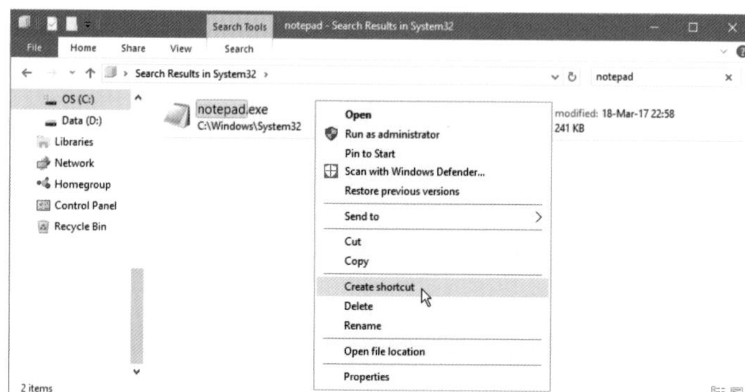

2. Right-click the program icon and select **Create shortcut**

3. The shortcut cannot be added to the program folder, so click **Yes** to place it on the Desktop

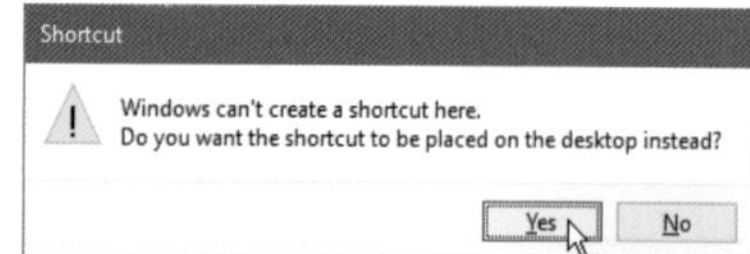

Shortcut
Windows can't create a shortcut here.
Do you want the shortcut to be placed on the desktop instead?
Yes
No

4. The shortcut is created and given the program name followed by **– Shortcut**

If you often find yourself editing the name to remove this addition, you might like to edit the Registry to avoid the suffix for all future shortcuts you create (this change won't affect existing shortcuts).

1. Run **regedit.exe** and find the key **HKEY_CURRENT_USER\Software\Microsoft\Windows\CurrentVersion\Explorer**

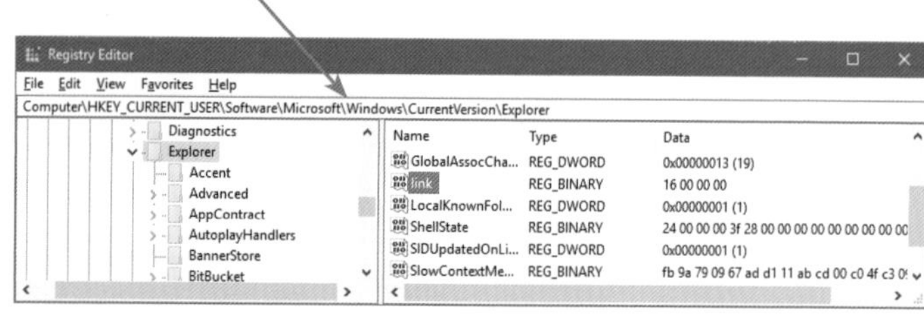

The shortcut suffix and arrow icon help identify links that can safely be deleted. Removing the suffix and arrow icon allows shortcuts to look just like the file to which they point – those that you probably do not want to delete.

2. Right-click the "link" entry, then select **Modify...** from the context menu

3. Change the first part of the number (16) to 00 to give a value of **00 00 00 00**

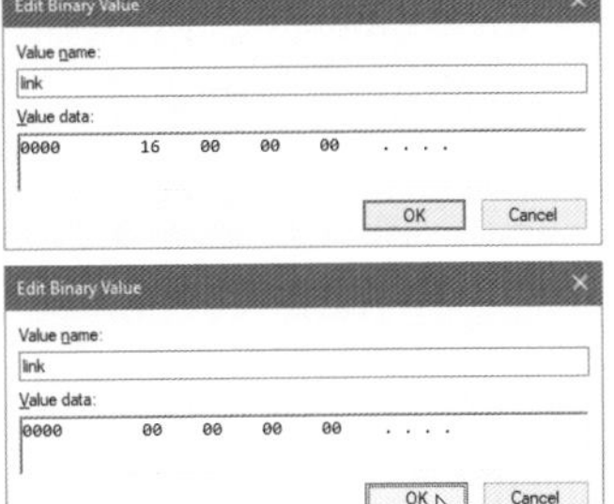

4. Click **OK** to update the value, then close **regedit.exe**

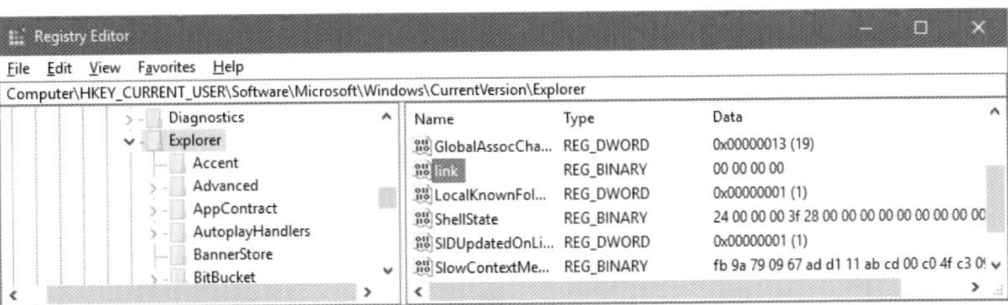

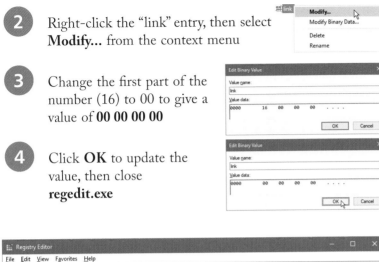

You must log off and log on again for the change to take effect. Now, when you create a shortcut, it will just display the program name with no suffix.

Remove shortcut arrows

You can also use Registry updates to change the shortcut icons, avoiding the shortcut arrow overlay, or using a different, perhaps smaller arrow to overlay the shortcut icons.

There are a number of different methods suggested for this. They involve adding a reference to an alternative icon file in a value entry in the key **HKEY_LOCAL_MACHINE\SOFTWARE\Microsoft\Windows\CurrentVersion\Explorer\Shell Icons**.

You can search the internet for relevant articles using a search term such as "Windows remove shortcut arrow" and choose your preferred website. Note that the instructions provided may differ for Windows 32-bit versus Windows 64-bit systems.

As with all Registry updates, make sure that you back up first, before making any changes.

Sometimes changes such as these have unexpected side effects, so a backup or restore point will be particularly important.

Adjust Desktop Peek

You can change the time delay before Desktop Peek reduces the screen to the Desktop.

1. Run **regedit.exe** and find the key **HKEY_CURRENT_USER\Software\Microsoft\Windows\CurrentVersion\Explorer\Advanced**

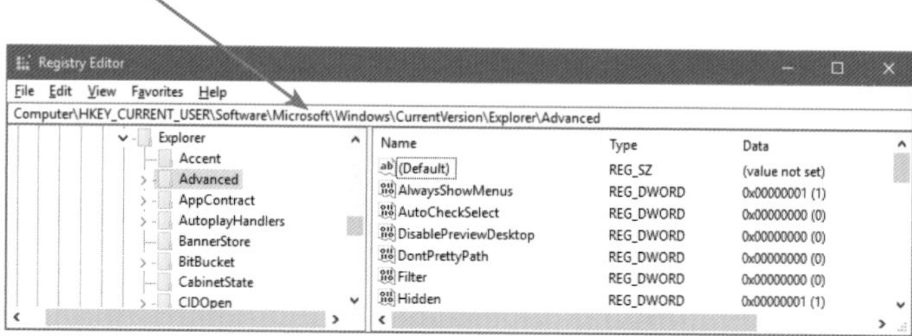

2. Right-click the right-hand pane and select **New**, **DWORD (32-bit) Value** (see page 455) and name the value "DesktopLivePreviewHoverTime"

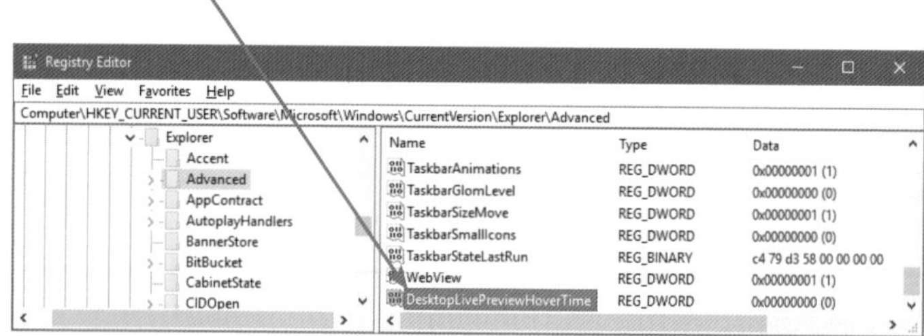

3. Double-click to edit, select **Decimal** and enter a value in milliseconds, for example "2000" (two seconds), then click **OK** to apply the new value

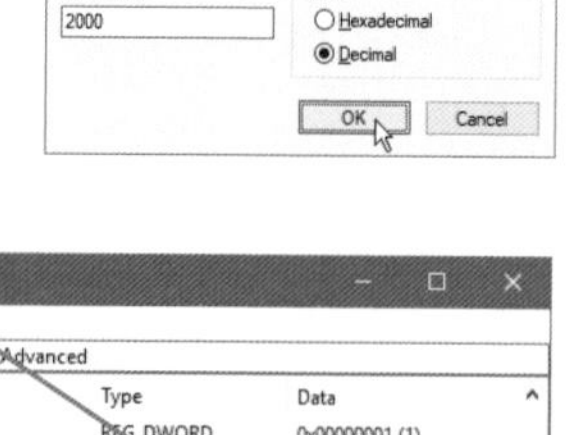

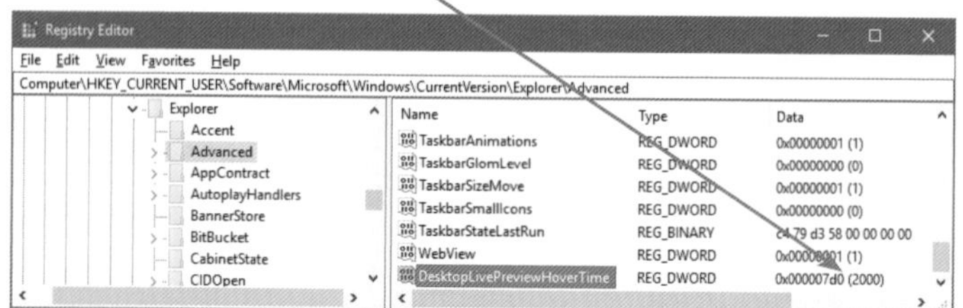

4. Now, log off, then log on again to put this Registry update into effect and try the change to Desktop Peek

When the mouse moves over the Peek button at the bottom-right of the screen, all open windows are replaced by empty frames. This can be distracting when you are just moving the mouse to a corner to help locate the pointer.

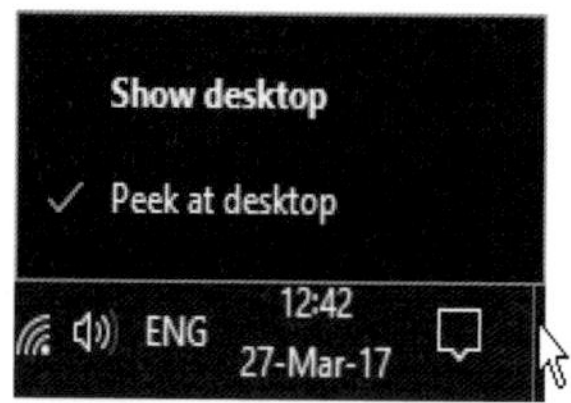

The default is 500 (half a second), 1000 is one second, and 0 is instant. To return to the default, set the value to 500 or delete the Value entry.

27 Extending Windows

Windows 10 provides great extensibility for remote connection, portability, virtual system hosting, and connection to other devices.

Remote Desktop connection

Remote Desktop is used to access one computer from another remotely, e.g. connecting to your work computer from home. You will have access to all of your programs, files, and network resources, as if you were sitting in front of your computer at work.

Hot tip

The difference between Remote Desktop and Remote Assistance is that with the latter, both users can control the mouse. With the former, the remote PC is not physically accessible.

On the Remote Computer

Before Remote Desktop can be used, the computer to be remotely accessed needs to be configured.

1. Go to Start, Windows System, Control Panel, System, and click the **Advanced system settings** link – to open the **System Properties** dialog box
2. In the System Properties dialog, select the **Remote** tab
3. Select **Allow remote connections to this computer**
4. Click OK, then Apply, then go back to **System** and make a note of the computer's name – it's simply named "PC" in the example below

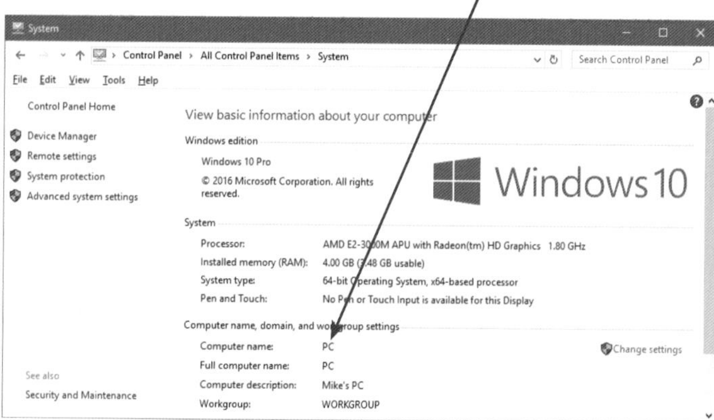

Hot tip

For a secure connection, make sure **Allow connections only from computers running Remote Desktop with Network Level Authentication (recommended)** is checked.

On the Accessing Computer

You now have to open the Remote Desktop Connection:

1. Type "Remote Desktop" in the Taskbar Search box, then click the **Remote Desktop Connection** result

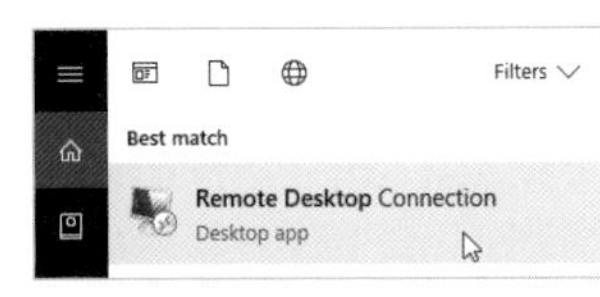

Click **Show Options** to reveal a range of settings with which to enhance the remote connection.

2. Enter the name of the remote computer (type "PC" in our example), then click the **Connect** button

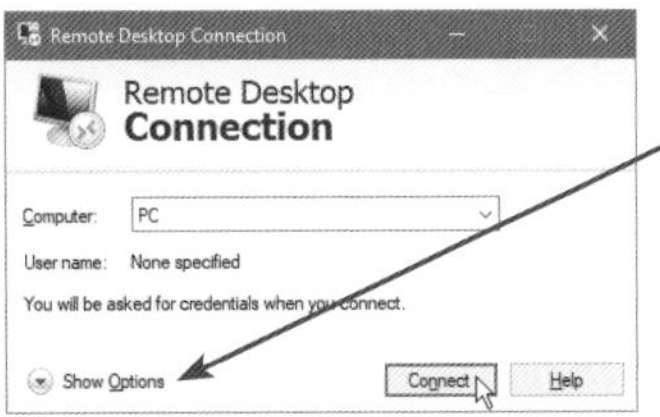

3. Next, enter the user name and password for the account you wish to log in to on the remote computer

4. Now, click the **OK** button to load the remote computer's Desktop onto the accessing computer's screen

This accessing computer user is authorized to access the remote computer, as they belong to the same HomeGroup.

Once the connection is made and authenticated, everything on the remote PC is open to, and can be controlled by, the accessing computer.

Windows To Go

Windows To Go is a feature found in Windows 10 Enterprise that enables a fully-functional copy of Windows 10 to be created on a USB drive. The procedure makes the drive bootable in the same way that Windows installation disks are.

Windows To Go is only available on Windows 10 Enterprise and Windows 10 Education editions.

Not just any USB drive can be used with Windows To Go. Microsoft has specified certain requirements that manufacturers must meet in order for their USB drives to qualify as a supported Windows To Go device. One such USB drive is the Kingston DataTraveler shown below:

External USB drives can be used, as well as flash drives.

The minimum storage space required by Windows To Go is 32GB. This is enough for Windows 10 itself, but if you also need to transport applications such as Microsoft Office, plus files, a larger USB drive will be required. Currently, flash drives up to 512GB are readily available.

A Windows To Go drive can be plugged into a USB socket on any computer and, because it is bootable, a Windows 10 session can be loaded on that computer. Once booted, it functions and is controlled by standard enterprise management tools such as System Center Configuration Manager (SCCM) and Active Directory group policies.

Windows To Go will only work on USB drives built specifically for it.

Windows To Go provides an ideal solution for anyone who needs mobile computer access. For example, business representatives out in the field will be able to work from any computer. Also, it's more cost-effective for IT departments to replace a faulty USB drive than it is to deal with the downtime and expense of returning a laptop to the office, repairing it, and returning it to the field.

Windows To Go is also ideal for trying out Windows 10 (or other software) on a machine, without affecting that machine.

Virtual machine

A virtual computer is one that is created by and run within a computer virtualization program. It is a fully-functional replica of a physical computer and can run programs, access the internet, etc.

Popular programs of this type include VMware and VirtualBox – the latter being a free download from **www.virtualbox.org** However, with some versions of Windows 10 there is no need for third-party virtualization software – one, called Hyper-V, is supplied with Windows 10 Pro edition. It does need to be installed first though, as explained below:

Client Hyper-V has very stringent hardware requirements. Not every PC will be able to run it.

1. Type "Windows features" into the Taskbar Search box, then click the **Turn Windows features on or off** result to open the Windows Features dialog box

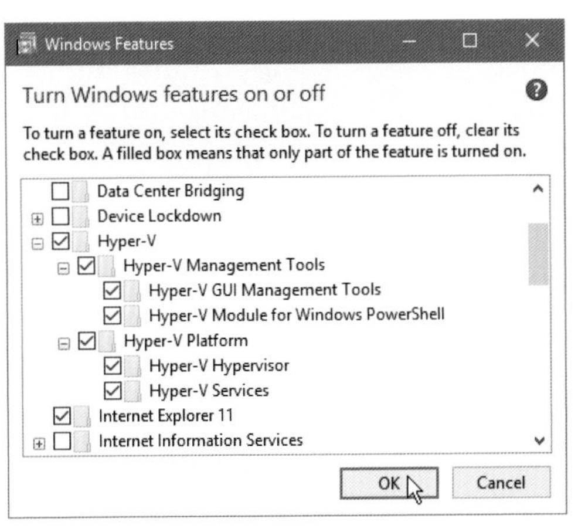

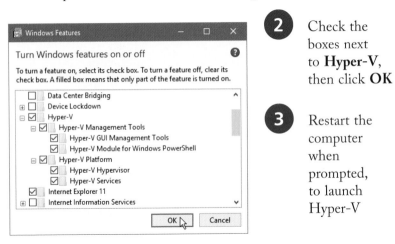

2. Check the boxes next to **Hyper-V**, then click **OK**

3. Restart the computer when prompted, to launch Hyper-V

4. Now, in the Taskbar Search box, type "hyper" and press **Enter**. The Hyper-V Manager opens, as shown below

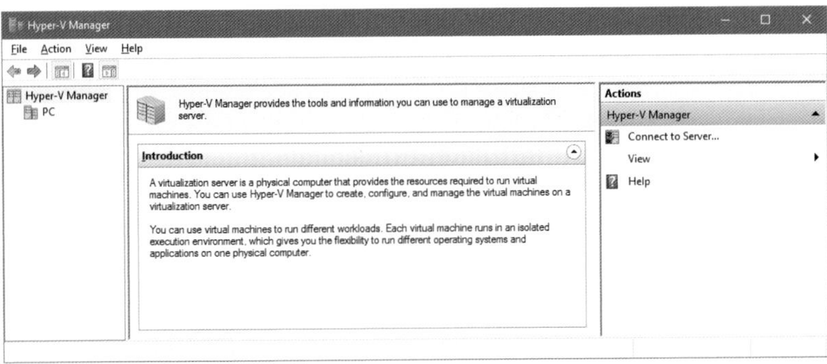

Install guest system

To demonstrate Hyper-V, let's create a Windows 7 virtual PC:

Here, we show you how to create a Windows 7 guest system. However, you can create guest systems for other operating systems.

1. At the top-left of the Hyper-V Manager, select the computer name, then click **Action**, **New**, **Virtual Machine** – to open the New Virtual Machine Wizard

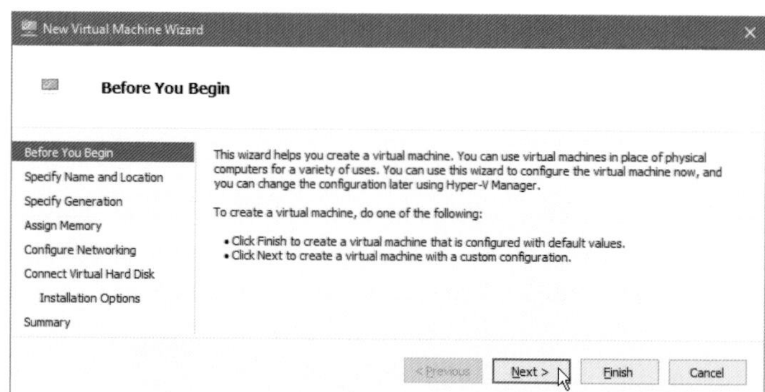

New Virtual Machine Wizard
Before You Begin
Before You Begin
Specify Name and Location
Specify Generation
Assign Memory
Configure Networking
Connect Virtual Hard Disk
Installation Options
Summary
This wizard helps you create a virtual machine. You can use virtual machines in place of physical computers for a variety of uses. You can use this wizard to configure the virtual machine now, and you can change the configuration later using Hyper-V Manager.
To create a virtual machine, do one of the following:
• Click Finish to create a virtual machine that is configured with default values.
• Click Next to create a virtual machine with a custom configuration.
< Previous
Next >
Finish
Cancel

2. Click the **Next** button, then name the new virtual machine "Windows 7" and click **Next** again

3. Choose **Generation 1**, click **Next** and assign a valid startup memory allocation, then click **Finish**

Hyper-V's Hardware options provide a range of settings for all the hardware components found in a computer.

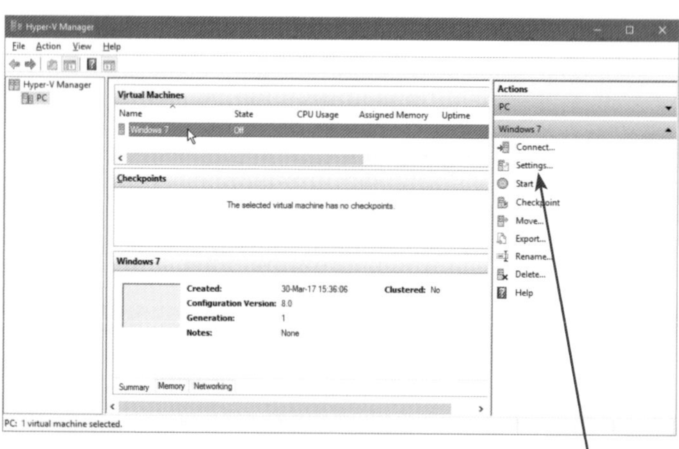

4. Expand "Windows 7" in the Actions pane, then click **Settings...**

5. Next, select **Legacy Network Adapter**, then click **Add**

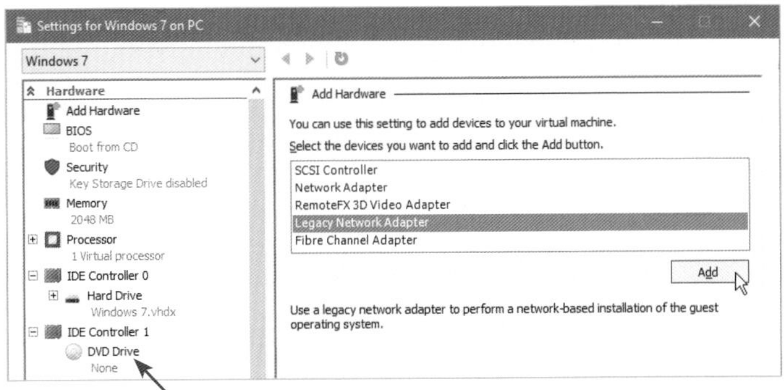

6. Select **DVD Drive** under "IDE Controller 1". Here, you can specify an image file (ISO) or optical drive for installation of the operating system. To use an installation disk, select **Physical CD/DVD drive**, then click **Apply**

7. Insert the Windows 7 installation disk in the DVD drive, then return to the Actions pane and click **Connect...**

Potential uses for virtual PCs include sandboxed software evaluation, other operating systems, and safe web browsing.

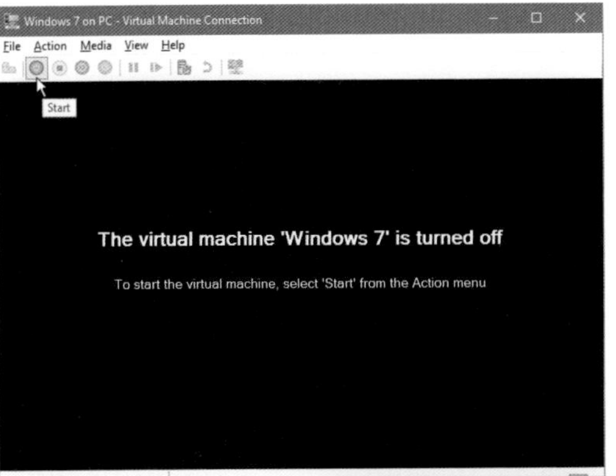

8. Now, click **Start** to begin building the Virtual Machine within Hyper-V

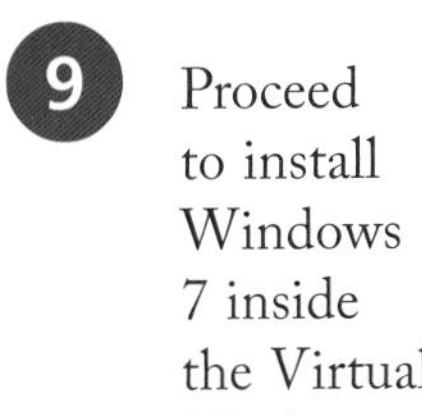

9. Proceed to install Windows 7 inside the Virtual Machine

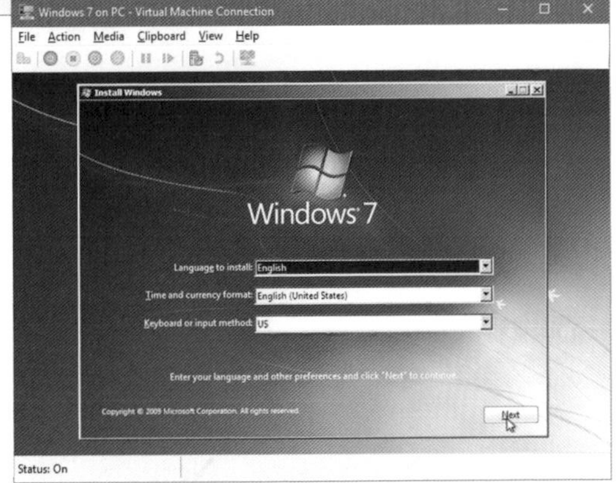

Hyper-V has a feature called Snapshots. These let you save the state of a virtual PC, so you can revert back in much the same way as a system backup lets you roll back to the point when the backup was made.

Windows devices

Windows phones hold only a tiny and diminishing share of the smartphone market, but Microsoft has repeatedly stated its commitment to deliver Windows 10 on mobile devices.

Windows 10 is a unified operating system that will run on desktop PCs, laptops, tablets, and smartphones. The same great features are available across all these devices, with only minor modifications tailored to better suit screen sizes below 8”.

Windows 10 supports direct access to a connected Windows device via File Explorer. This lets you drag and drop content to and from your connected device – just as you can with any USB hard disk drive or flash drive:

1. Connect a Windows device to your Windows 10 computer via a USB cable connection – for instance, let’s connect a phone running Windows 10 Mobile

2. Next, launch File Explorer on your computer and expand the **This PC** item in the Navigation pane to see the connected phone device icon appear under the “Devices and Drives” category

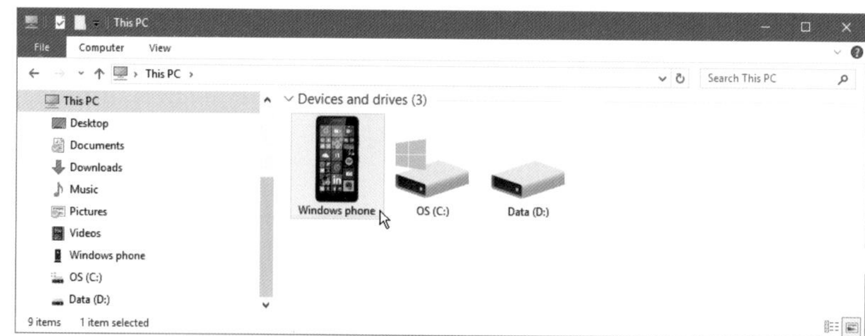

3. You can click the device icon and use File Explorer to navigate through the phone’s file system – just like navigating through your computer’s file system

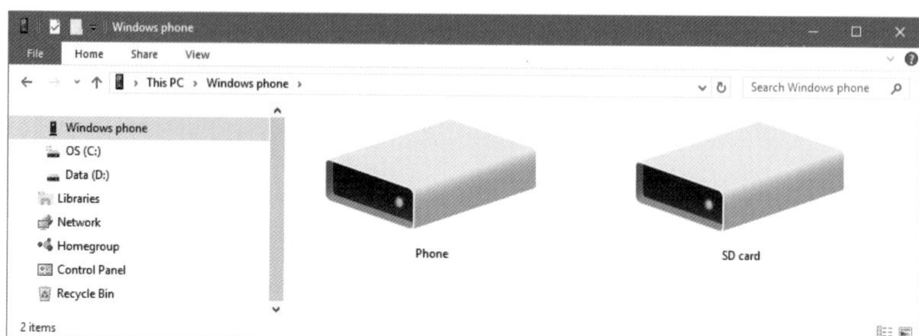

First, connect the cable to your device, then connect to a USB socket on your computer.

4. Right-click a file icon within your computer's file system and choose **Send to**, then select the connected device

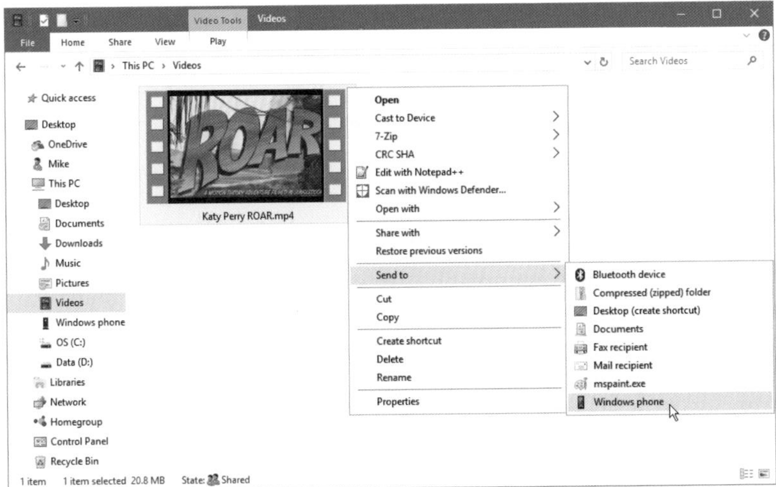

The selected file here is a video that will be copied onto the phone's SD card by default.

5. The file now gets copied to the connected device

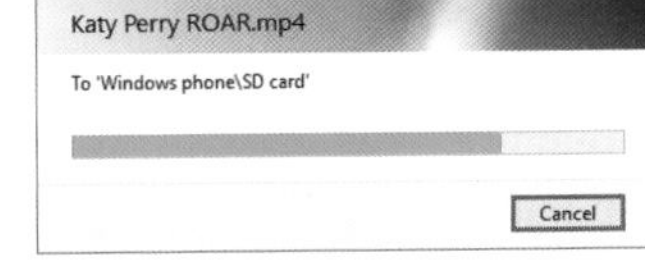

6. Use the File Explorer app on your computer or the app on the connected device to see the file has been copied

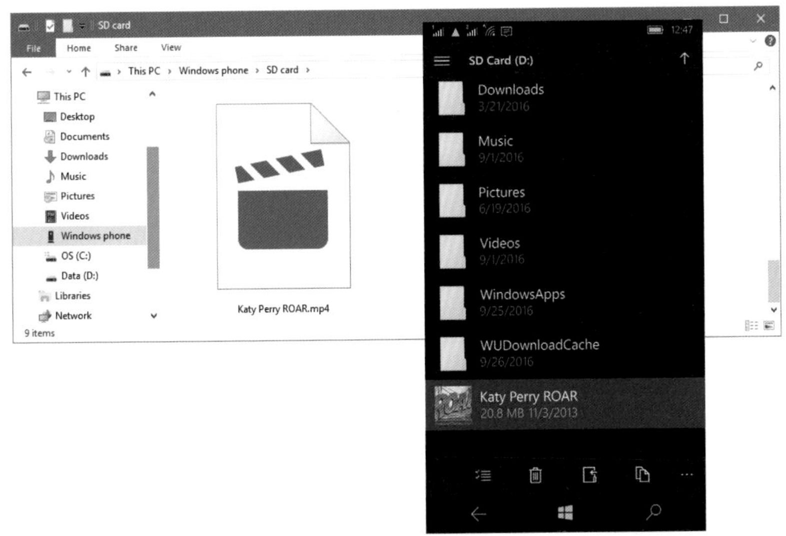

Always use the **Safely Remove Hardware** feature to disconnect USB devices from your computer.

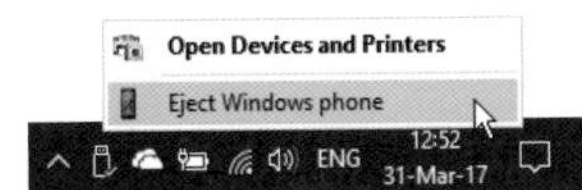

Phone Companion app

The Phone Companion app that is available on Windows 10 lets you easily copy music, photos, videos, and documents between your computer and ANY smartphone or tablet device.

1. Connect a device to your Windows 10 computer via a USB cable connection – for instance, let's connect a tablet running the Android operating system

2. A notification invites you to choose what happens with this device – click on the notification

3. From the pop-up menu that appears, choose the option to "Get your stuff on your PC, tablet, and phone" – to launch the **Phone Companion** app

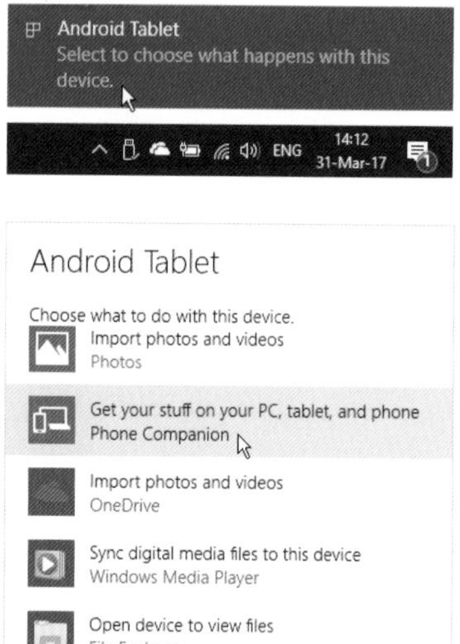

The Phone Companion is new in Windows 10. This Universal Windows App works with Windows, Android, and iOS devices.

Explore the demonstrations available on this screen to see what you can do with different apps.

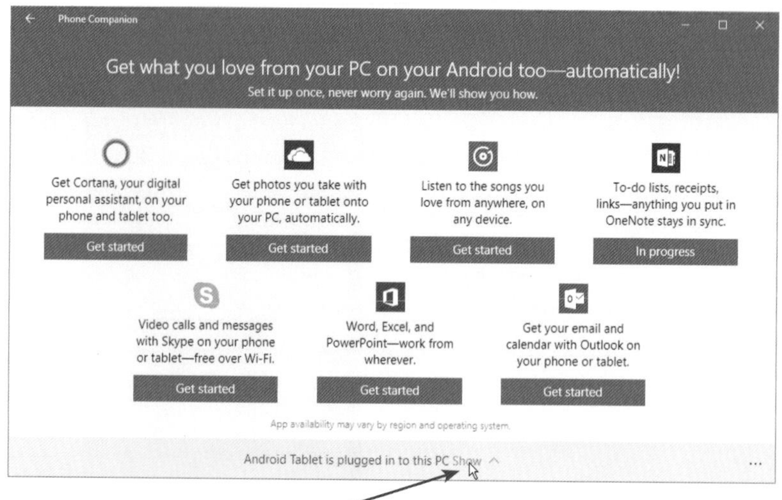

4. Click the **Show** link at the bottom-center of the screen to see information about the connected device

5. To copy media files from the device into the Photos app on your PC, click the **Import photos and videos into the Photos app** link

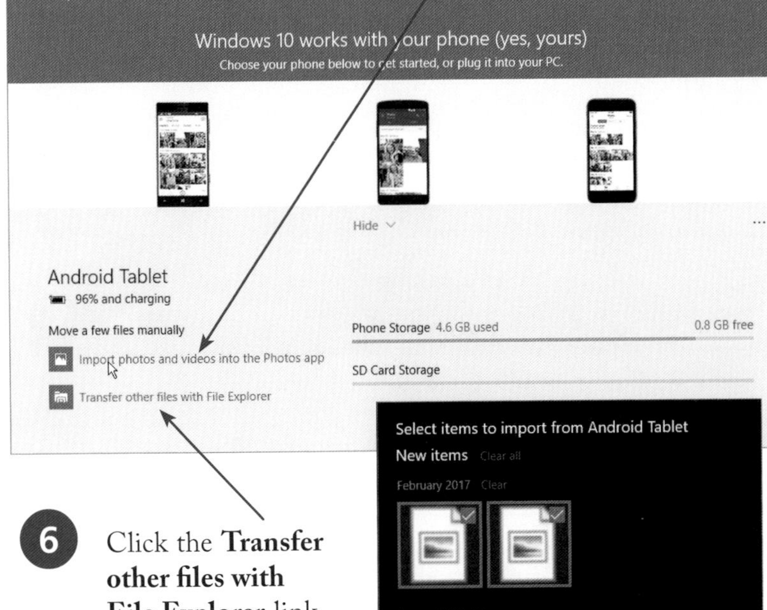

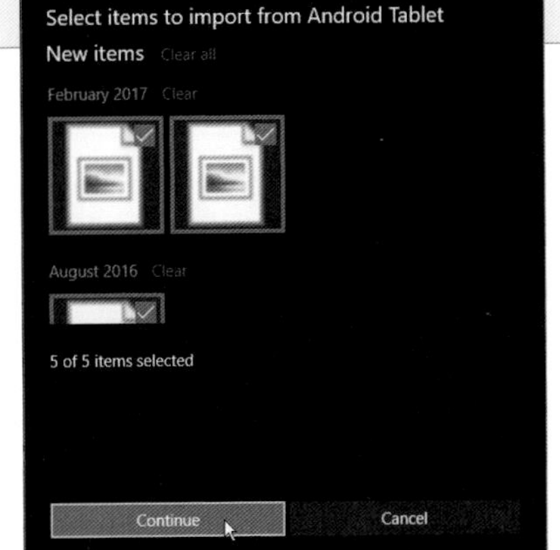

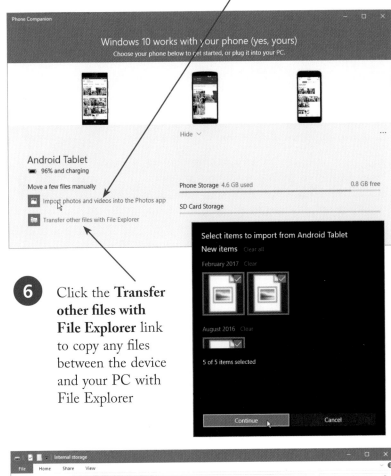

6. Click the **Transfer other files with File Explorer** link to copy any files between the device and your PC with File Explorer

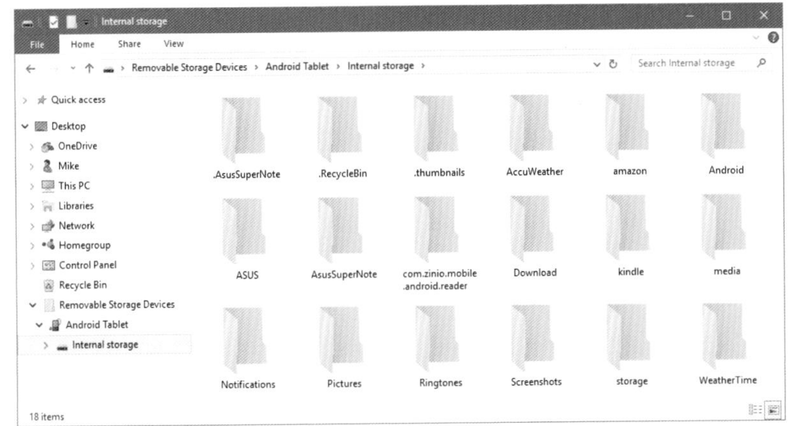

Don't forget

The links in the Phone Companion app let you quickly launch the Photos app Import feature or File Explorer in your device's drive.

Hot tip

You can also launch the Phone Companion app at any time from the Start menu.

Don't forget

Always use the **Safely Remove Hardware** feature to disconnect USB devices from your computer.

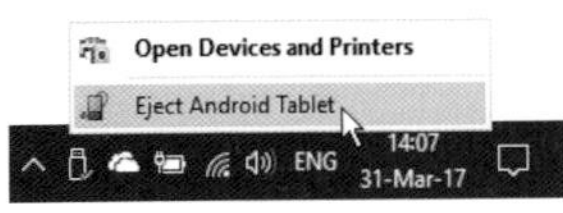

Windows news

Microsoft intends to introduce new features into Windows 10 as it evolves. You can follow development of the latest features by regularly visiting the Windows blog at **blogs.windows.com**

You can join the **Windows Insider Program** to receive new feature updates before they are made available for general release.

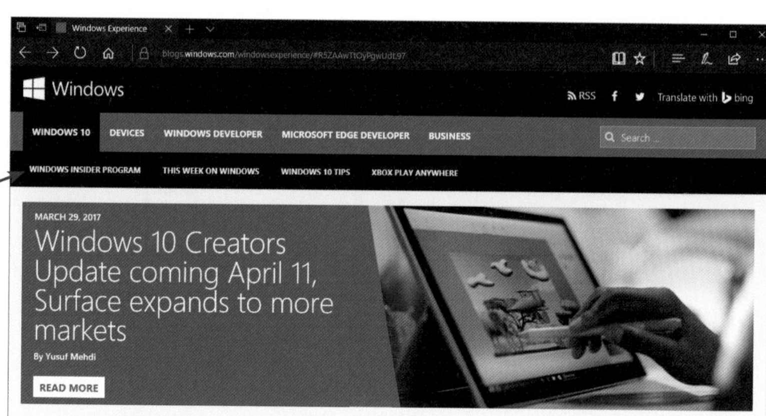

Sometimes you can learn of new features for Windows 10 before their official announcement, from websites that claim to have inside knowledge. There are several of these, such as the "SuperSite for Windows" at **winsupersite.com**

You may also be interested in the "Windows Central" website at windowscentral.com

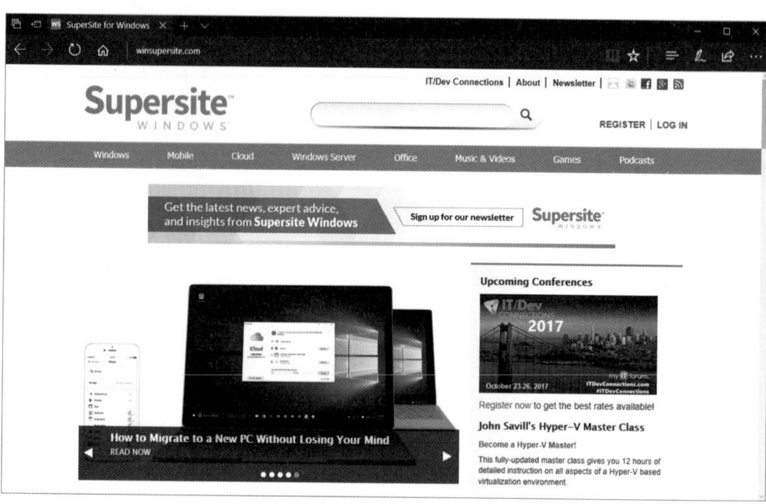

Windows 10 revolves around its convergence for all devices, from phones to PCs, in Microsoft's battle against Android and Apple. Only time will tell if this will be enough.

Symbols

A

B

C

D

E

F

G

N

Q

R

S

T

U